Reviews of *Systematic Trading* by Robert Carver

A remarkable look inside systematic trading never seen before, spanning the range from small to institutional traders. Reading this will benefit all traders.

— Perry Kaufman, legendary trader and author

Being a hedge fund manager myself and having personally read almost all major investment and trading books, this is by far one of the best books I have read in over 15 years on a tough subject for most.

— Josh Hawes, hedge fund manager

Robert has had very valuable experience working for many years in a large quant hedge fund, which makes the book doubly worth reading… Well worth a read for anyone who trades, in particular for systematic traders (whether you're a novice or more experienced)!

*— Saeed Amen, trader and author of *Trading Thalesians**

Reviews of *Smart Portfolios* by Robert Carver

In finance (like many other subjects) there is a large amount of research that is smart but impractical and an equally large amount of popular literature that is practical but dumb. This book is in that rare category of smart and practical – it is also an entertaining read in its own right.

— Francis Breedon, Professor of Finance Queen Mary, University of London and former global head of currency research at Lehman Brothers

The book is a solid piece of work so check it out… It's about the process and there are some really practical ways, mathematical ways, to put a good process in motion for your life.

*— Michael Covel, author of several books on trading including the best selling *Trend Following**

Reviews of *Leveraged Trading* by Robert Carver

Like Robert's other books, *Leveraged Trading* is an excellent guide for traders. Robert does an excellent job of progressing from basic to complicated information, without losing the reader. This book will be one I refer to over and over again. Highly recommended.

— **Kevin Davey, champion full-time trader, author of numerous trading books**

(Rob's) latest book is not just the best coverage of the topic of leveraged trading of small portfolios I've read, it's actually the only good one I've come across… This is a great book. Go buy it.

— **Andreas Clenow, hedge fund manager and author**

I wish I had read a book like this when I was starting my trading. It would have saved me a lot of time and money. Highly recommended!

— **Helder Palaro, hedge fund manager**

Think big. Think positive. Never show any sign of weakness. Always go for the throat. Buy low. Sell high. Fear? That's the other guy's problem.

Nothing you have ever experienced can prepare you for the unbridled carnage you are about to witness. The Super Bowl, the World Series? They don't know what pressure is.

In this building it's either kill or be killed. You make no friends in the pits and you take no prisoners. One minute you're up half a million in Soybeans and the next boom! Your kids don't go to college and they've repossessed your Bentley.

Are you with me?

— **Louis Winthorpe III (Dan Aykroyd) giving strategic advice to Billy Ray Valentine (Eddie Murphy) as they prepare to short orange juice futures in the film *Trading Places***

Every owner of a physical copy of this edition of

ADVANCED
FUTURES
TRADING
STRATEGIES

can download the eBook for free direct from us at
Harriman House, in a DRM-free format that can be read
on any eReader, tablet or smartphone.

Simply head to:

**ebooks.harriman-house.com/
advancedfuturestradingstrat**

to get your copy now.

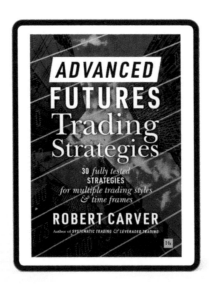

ADVANCED
FUTURES
TRADING
STRATEGIES

HARRIMAN HOUSE LTD
3 Viceroy Court
Bedford Road
Petersfield
Hampshire
GU32 3LJ
GREAT BRITAIN
Tel: +44 (0)1730 233870

Email: enquiries@harriman-house.com
Website: harriman.house

First published in 2023.
Copyright © Robert Carver

The right of Robert Carver to be identified as the Author has been asserted in accordance with the Copyright, Design and Patents Act 1988.

Hardback ISBN: 978-0-85719-968-3
eBook ISBN: 978-0-85719-969-0

British Library Cataloguing in Publication Data
A CIP catalogue record for this book can be obtained from the British Library.

Whilst every effort has been made to ensure that information in this book is accurate, no liability can be accepted for any loss incurred in any way whatsoever by any person relying solely on the information contained herein.

No responsibility for loss occasioned to any person or corporate body acting or refraining to act as a result of reading material in this book can be accepted by the Publisher, by the Author, or by the employers of the Author.

ADVANCED FUTURES TRADING STRATEGIES

30 fully tested strategies for multiple trading styles and time frames

Robert Carver

Harriman House

About the author

Robert Carver is an independent trader, investor and writer. He spent over a decade working in the City of London before retiring from the industry in 2013. Robert initially traded exotic derivative products for Barclays Investment Bank and then worked as a portfolio manager for AHL – one of the world's largest hedge funds – before, during and after the global financial meltdown of 2008. He was responsible for the creation of AHL's fundamental macro trading strategy business, and subsequently managed the fund's multi-billion-dollar fixed income portfolio.

Robert has a Bachelor's degree and a Master's degree in Economics, and is currently a visiting lecturer at Queen Mary, University of London. He is the author of three previous books: *Systematic Trading: A unique new method for designing trading and investing systems* (Harriman House, 2015), *Smart Portfolios: A practical guide to building and maintaining intelligent investment portfolios* (Harriman House, 2017) and *Leveraged Trading: A professional approach to trading FX, stocks on margin, CFDs, spread bets* (Harriman House, 2019).

Robert trades his own portfolio using the methods you can find in his books.

Contents

Introduction

I traded my first futures contract on instinct.

It was September 2002, and I had just stepped onto a trading floor for the first time. The floor was in Canary Wharf, one of London's two key financial districts, and belonged to Barclays Capital. 'Barcap', as I had learned to call it, ran a programme for fresh graduates on which I had recently started as one of just two newly recruited traders. We spent our first day in a classroom learning tedious theory that was mostly unrelated to our future jobs. At 4pm we were told to go and find our future teammates, who we'd be joining properly in a couple of months after the gruelling course had finished.

With some trepidation I glanced at the map of the floor I had been given, and tried to locate the area where I would ultimately be working. Fortunately it didn't take long to find my allocated desk where I also found Richard – the managing director of the team – who had interviewed me earlier in the year.

After a few introductions and some chitchat, Richard asked me if I'd like to do a trade. I nervously said I would. Although I'd done some share trading on my personal account, this would be my first time trading with someone else's money.

He showed me the dealing screen, and asked me to trade a single contract of the December 'Bund', which I had recently learned was the future for 10-year German government bonds[1] (one of the few useful pieces of information we'd been given in the classroom). I froze. Should I buy or sell? How could I possibly know what the right decision was? I'd read somewhere that the ability to make quick decisions was prized amongst traders, and I certainly didn't want Richard to think I was too slow-witted for the job. Not wanting to hesitate any longer, I decided to buy and clicked the button on the screen to lift the offer.

That was my first foray into the futures market, and it certainly wouldn't be my last, although I only lasted 18 months on that particular trading floor. After leaving

---

1 The desk actually traded exotic interest rate options, not futures, but we used bond and interest rate futures to hedge our exposure. Bund is apparently short for *Bundesanleihe*.

1

Barcap I spent a couple of years working in economic research before joining a hedge fund, AHL.

AHL was, and is, one of the largest futures traders in the world. My job was to develop and manage systematic futures trading strategies. Beginning with a relatively small portfolio, I was eventually promoted to manage the fixed income team, responsible for several billion dollars of client funds. The strategies we managed were a significant part of the global futures markets, holding tens of thousands of contracts on any given day, and trading hundreds of thousands of contracts every year.

I decided to leave AHL in 2013, but my trading didn't stop there. After opening a trading account with a futures broker, I spent a few months building my own automated trading strategies which I have run ever since.

It's now over 20 years since I traded that first contract, and a very long time since I last traded on instinct. Nowadays I trade deliberately, using carefully honed trading strategies. Every single one of the trades I do today is backed up by years of experience and detailed analysis. And in this book, I will share that knowledge with you.

30 strategies
Over 50 years of data
100+ instruments

This book contains the details of 30 strategies, specifically designed for trading futures. I explain how and why each strategy works. The rules for each strategy are described in detail, and I analyse the performance of the strategy over historical data, so that you can better understand its strengths and weaknesses, and likely behaviour in the future.

Diversification is the most powerful weapon in the armoury of the financial trader. After reading this book you will have access to a large and diversified set of trading strategies. But, as I will explain in some detail, diversifying across different futures markets is an even more potent route to extra profits. Fortunately, there are hundreds of futures traded all around the world, covering every possible kind of tradeable instrument: US interest rate futures, the cryptocurrency Bitcoin, Japanese iron ore, Russian stocks, and milk – to name just a few.

Each market is different. Equities are driven by emotion: greed, fear and the current mood of a million meme stock buyers. Bonds march to a mathematical drum; although rates and credit spreads are driven by market forces, their relationship to bond prices can be calculated using precise formulae. Currency markets move wildly with every interest rate change and macroeconomic announcement. The commodities space is packed with hedge funds and giant multinational commodity traders. But there are also farmers, hedging their Wheat exposure on their laptops whilst their boots are still covered with the dust of the fields.

As a result, opinion amongst traders is divided: should each market be traded differently, or should we use common strategies that work equally well irrespective of the underlying asset? There are certainly benefits to using common strategies. If we can test strategies across a range of markets then that gives us more confidence that they will work in the future.

I use data from over 100 different instruments to test the strategies in this book, some of which have over 50 years of data. So you can be confident they are not one-trick ponies that work on one or two markets, or only in benign market environments. But it's also important to make sure that a given strategy is suitable for a specific instrument, and if necessary to adapt it: I will explain how. I will discuss how you can select the best set of markets to trade, given the capital you have available to trade with, and how to allocate risk across your portfolio.

This book will also cover diversification across different trading strategies and time scales. I also explain how you can evaluate the performance of a strategy, how to ensure you are using the correct degree of leverage, how you can predict and manage your risk, and how you can measure and reduce your trading costs.

Of course futures trading isn't just about the exciting job of predicting the direction of the market. It's also about relatively dull stuff: deciding which contract to trade, executing your trades, managing your risk, and making the most efficient use of your cash. I will be discussing these potentially boring, but very important, subjects in the final part of the book.

Can you read this book? Should you read this book?

You need significant capital to trade futures. Although some instruments can be accessed with a few thousand dollars, most require much more. As a rule of thumb, you will find this book most useful if you have at least $100,000 in your trading account[2] (or the equivalent in another currency). With that sort of capital many of you will be managing institutional money, perhaps as part of a hedge fund or commodity advisor. But this book will also be useful if, like me, you are trading your own money with a decent-sized account, and are serious about futures trading.

---

2   If you do not have the equivalent of $100,000 to hand, and you are based outside the USA, then you could potentially use dated Contracts for Difference (CFDs) or spread bets as an alternative to futures. Although these are more expensive to trade, they have significantly lower funding requirements. I explain how you can trade CFDs and spread bets in one of my earlier books, *Leveraged Trading*.

This is not a book for beginners. You will notice that I've already used some financial jargon, as I'm expecting you to have at least a rudimentary understanding of the futures market, and trading generally. If you need a primer on futures trading,[3] then I can recommend my previous book *Leveraged Trading*.

I will be using US dollars throughout the book for simplicity, but this book is not just for traders living in the Land of Liberty. There are futures exchanges in many different countries, and thanks to the internet you can trade them from wherever you live (except where regulatory restrictions apply). As long as you can legally trade futures, you will find this book useful regardless of where you are domiciled. Later in the book I'll discuss the issues created by cross-border trading, and how you can address them.

If you've read any of my previous books, you will probably know that I'm a strong advocate of using *systematic* trading strategies. These strategies allow no room for discretionary judgement, and traders are expected to follow their instructions without deviation. Naturally, fully systematic traders will be able to use this book without any difficulties, since all the strategies in this book are fully described using clear rules. So I won't be showing you a series of charts and expecting you to identify a 'head and shoulders', 'broadening top', or 'abandoned baby bottom' pattern.

But not everyone is comfortable with the idea of trading without human input. Unlike me, you may possess a genuine ability to use your intuition and experience to identify profitable trades that exceeds what a simple rule based system can do. If so, then it would make sense to use the strategies in this book as part of a discretionary trading setup, combining them with your own judgement[4] to decide which trades to take.

You don't need to be able to code to use the vast majority of strategies in this book. Almost everything here can be implemented in a spreadsheet. On the website for this book[5] are links to spreadsheets that you can copy and adapt as you require. Having said that, there are also web links to snippets of Python code for those who are comfortable with programming.

Finally, there are many equations in this book, but almost all[6] are at the level of high school math.[7] You don't need a PhD to read this book. I didn't need one to write it!

---

3 There is a list of suggested reading in Appendix A.
4 I wouldn't even be offended if you use the strategies in this book as 'counter-strategies', deliberately doing the opposite trade to what is indicated, as long as you've paid for the book. Of course I wouldn't recommend that, either.
5 See Appendix A for the link.
6 A few chapters contain slightly more advanced material which is necessary for certain strategies, but you can skip them if you wish.
7 That's secondary school *maths* for my UK readers.

My other books

If you already have the requisite basic knowledge of futures trading, you do not need to read anything else before you read *Advanced Futures Trading Strategies (AFTS)*. Should you feel the need to improve your basic knowledge of the futures market then I would recommend another of my books, *Leveraged Trading (LT)*. This covers the mechanics of trading leveraged instruments, such as futures, without assuming any prior knowledge. Reading *LT* will also give you a head start in understanding some of the concepts I introduce in Part One of this book.

Another book I've written, *Systematic Trading (ST)*, also includes some material on futures trading and briefly covers a couple of trading strategies that I also write about in detail here in *AFTS*. But *ST* is primarily about the general design of trading strategies and is not written primarily for futures traders. In contrast, *AFTS* describes many strategies in detail, which are specifically for the futures markets. If you want to develop and test your own futures strategies then it's worth reading both *ST* and *AFTS*. If you haven't read either, then I'd recommend reading *AFTS* first. All this implies that if you're completely new to futures trading, and want to design your own strategies, then a suitable reading order would be: *LT* first, then *AFTS*, and finally *ST*.

I have written a further book, *Smart Portfolios*, but that relates to investment and not trading. But if you also want to buy a copy of *Smart Portfolios*, I won't stop you!

Scope

Here is a list of what this book does *not* cover:

- Subjective decision making. All the strategies in this book are objective: given some data, they will always recommend the same action. This makes them suitable for a purely systematic trader like myself. But you can also use these strategies as part of a discretionary trading methodology: signals from various strategies can be used to inform your trading decisions, but you then make the final call based on your judgement.

- Fundamental data. I only use price data. So there is no strategy that uses CPI releases, nonfarm payrolls, equity earnings information, commitment of traders figures, or Baker-Hughes rig count. This significantly reduces the number of possible strategies to a manageable figure. It's also easier to construct objective trading strategies if you're using only price data.[8] Having said that, in Part Three I

---

8 In particular, I don't use volume data even though this is a very popular source of information for many traders. Volume data for futures is tricky to analyse systematically, since it is affected by rolling from one contract expiry to the next.

explain how to construct a trading strategy given some arbitrary data input, which could certainly be fundamental data as long as it is quantifiable.

- Candlesticks. I only use closing prices for each relevant time period. I don't use 'OHLC' (open, high, low, close) prices from which 'candlestick' charts can be constructed. This makes the strategies in this book easier to explain, and simpler to trade. Also, after thorough testing I'm not convinced that the market patterns which only candlesticks can allegedly reveal make for profitable objective trading strategies. No doubt there are traders that can make good subjective decisions by staring at such charts, but I am not one of them.

- High frequency and other fast trading. The smallest time interval I collect prices for is hourly. This rules out any strategy with a holding period of less than a few hours, since we could not accurately test it. In any case, I believe it's impossible for most traders to compete with specialised high frequency trading firms, and they should not try.

- Options. Whilst it would be possible to use options on futures to trade the strategies in this book, for example by buying calls when the market is expected to rally, this is emphatically not a book about options trading.

- Stocks. Many of the strategies in this book could certainly be applied to shares, but I have not checked if they are suitable or done any kind of analysis with individual equity data. However, I have tested many strategies using equity index futures, such as the S&P 500 index.

- Other asset classes. This is not a book about trading crypto currencies, FX, or bonds. But this is no significant impediment, since we can usually trade futures which are based on crypto, FX, bonds, and many other different assets.

- Tax. The taxation of futures trading is very complex, varies across countries, depends on the legal status of the account owner, and is constantly changing. It would be complete madness to try and cover this in a single book. I am fairly sane, so I won't attempt this particular challenge here. As a result, none of the strategies in this book take taxation into consideration, and there are no tax optimisation or tax-loss harvesting strategies to be found here.

- This book does not cover every single future in the world. But I did test the strategies in this book using data for over 100 different futures, which meet my requirements[9] for liquidity and costs. However, there are many

---

9   These requirements are outlined in some detail in strategy three. I have also tested the strategies on another 50 or so instruments which are too expensive or illiquid to trade, and the results were not significantly different.

others[10] where finding the data was too difficult or expensive. But I'm confident that the strategies in this book can be easily adapted to trade almost any type of future (and of course I'll explain how).

How should you read this book?

Like a good novel, you should ideally read this book in order, from cover to cover. In particular, you must read **Part One: Basic Directional Strategies** before anything else. A *directional* strategy bets on the overall direction of the market rather than the relative performance of two or more instruments. The first four Parts of this book are exclusively about directional strategies.

It probably seems strange that the first part of a book on *advanced* trading strategies is entitled *basic* strategies… If you're a relatively experienced trader, or if you've read my other books, you might be tempted to skip Part One. Do not do this!

Let me explain: I decided not to write a book where the first few chapters are full of tedious theory that you need to know before getting to the juicy bits that provide practical value. Every single chapter of this book includes one or more strategies that you can actually trade. But during Part One I also gradually introduce a number of concepts that you will need throughout the book. Hence, it's vital that you read this Part first.

The other Parts of the book are designed to stand alone, since they cover different types of trading strategy. **Part Two: Advanced Trend Following and Carry Strategies** explores two of the key strategies in futures trading: trend following (where we try to identify trends which we assume will continue) and carry (where we use futures prices for different expiry dates to try and predict the future). These two strategies are introduced towards the end of Part One, but in Part Two I extend them and explore alternative ways to capture these important market effects. Next there is **Part Three: Advanced Directional Strategies**. Trend following and carry are directional strategies, but in Part Three I'll explore other kinds of directional strategy that exploit other sources of returns.

All the strategies in Parts One, Two and Three can be combined together in a mix and match fashion. This is possible because they are all built using a consistent position management methodology. Also, they are all designed to trade once a day, using daily data to calculate required trades. This is not true of the strategies in Parts Four and

---

10   For example, rather ironically given I am based in the UK, due to prohibitive data acquisition costs I am unable to trade, and hence was unable to test, futures listed on the UK-based Intercontinental Exchange (ICE), including short sterling interest rate futures, UK gilts (bonds) and FTSE 100 equity index futures.

Five. **Part Four: Fast Directional Strategies** explains a couple of strategies which trade more frequently than daily. Although this is not a book about high frequency trading, there are a couple of strategies included here whose holding period can be measured in hours and days, rather than weeks.

I then pivot from directional strategies to **Part Five: Relative Value Strategies**. As you might expect, these strategies try to predict the *relative* movement of futures prices, whilst hopefully hedging against overall market movements. In Part Five I will explain both *calendar* strategies – that trade different delivery months of the same future against each other – and *cross instrument* strategies, which trade the relative value of different futures.

Finally, we have **Part Six: Tactics**. These are not chapters about trying to predict the absolute or relative movement of prices. Instead they seek to improve the less glamorous but still important aspects of futures trading: contract selection, risk control, execution, and cash management.

Please note that the word *chapter* may refer to either a strategy in Parts One to Five, or a tactic in Part Six.

At the end of the book there are **Appendices**: Appendix A has further resources, including lists of books and websites that you may find useful. Appendix B contains details of key calculations used throughout the book. Appendix C has a full list of the futures contracts used in this book.

There are also many useful resources on the website for this book, the link to which you can find in Appendix A, including code and spreadsheets.

PART ONE

Basic Directional Strategies

You must read all of Part One before reading the rest of the book.

You must read the chapters in Part One in order: each depends on the previous chapters.

Strategy one introduces the simplest possible strategy. **Strategies two to eight** gradually improve upon previous strategies, introducing several important components that any trading strategy should have.

Strategies nine, ten and eleven are fully featured trading strategies which can be used as a basis for other strategies in Parts Two and Three:

- **Strategy nine** implements a specific kind of trading signal, trend following, which is traded across multiple time frames.

- **Strategy ten** introduces an additional trading signal, carry.

- **Strategy eleven** combines both trend following and carry.

Buy and hold, single contract

What have I told you since the first day you stepped into my office? There are three ways to make a living in this business. Be first. Be smarter. Or cheat. Now, I don't cheat.

— John Tuld, the fictional bank CEO played by Jeremy Irons in the film *Margin Call*

Like John Tuld, I don't cheat. And I believe that consistently being first is not a viable option for futures traders, except for those in the highly specialised industry of high frequency trading. That just leaves being *smart*.

How can we be smart? First, we need to **avoid doing anything stupid**. Examples of rank stupidity include: (a) trading too quickly – slowly draining your account through excess commissions and spreads; (b) using too much leverage – quickly blowing up your account; and (c) designing a set of trading rules that assume the future will be almost exactly[11] like the past (also known as *over fitting* or *curve fitting*). During the rest of this book I'll be explaining how to avoid these pitfalls by using properly designed trading strategies.

Avoiding stupid mistakes is a necessary but not sufficient condition for profitable trading. We also need to create strategies that are expected to earn positive returns. There are a couple of possible methods we could consider to achieve this.

The first way, which is very difficult, is to find some **secret** unique pattern in prices or other data, which other traders have been unable to discover, and which will predict

---

11 I do test strategies based on historic data, which is an implicit assumption that the future will look somewhat like the past. But as I shall explain in some detail it is important not to extrapolate the results of these tests blindly into the future.

the future with unerring accuracy. If you're looking for secret hidden formulae you're reading the wrong book. Of course, if I did know of any secret formula I'd be crazy to publish it; better to keep it under my hat and keep making millions in easy profits. Sadly, highly profitable strategies tend not to stay secret for very long, because of the substantial rewards for discovering them.

Alternatively, to earn positive returns we can **take a risk** that most other people are unwilling, or unable, to take. Usually if you are willing to take more risk, then you will earn higher returns. This might not seem especially smart, but the clever part is understanding and quantifying the risks, and ensuring you don't take too much risk, or take risks for which the rewards are insufficient. Blindly taking risks isn't smart: it's terminally stupid. The trading strategies in this book aren't secret, so to be profitable they must involve taking some risks that most people in the market aren't comfortable with.

The advantage of a risk taking strategy is that human beings' risk preferences haven't changed much over time. We can check these strategies have worked for long historical periods, and then be pretty confident that they will continue to work in the future. They tend not to be as profitable as secret strategies, but this is also an advantage because the fact of their already being known about, and existing for a long period of time already, means they are unlikely to be competed away in the future when other traders discover them.

What sort of risks do we get paid for? The list is almost endless, but for starters the most well-known risk in financial markets is equity market risk, which is informally known in the financial markets as *beta (β)*. Equities are almost always riskier than bonds, and certainly riskier than bank deposits, and thus we would expect them to earn a higher return.

Economists usually assume we can buy the entire stock market, with portfolios weighted by the market capitalisation of every company. In most countries it's not realistic to buy every listed stock, but you don't have to, because the largest firms make up the vast majority of the market. If you want to earn US stock market beta, then you could just buy all the stocks in the S&P 500 index of the largest firms in the US, spending more of your money on shiny gadget maker Apple (at the time of writing, the largest stock in the S&P 500 with around 6.4% of the index weighting) and only a tiny fraction on preppy clothing outlet Gap (just 0.013% of the weighting).

However, buying 500 stocks is going to be an expensive and time-consuming exercise. You will also have to spend more time and money adjusting your exposure whenever stocks are added to and removed from the index.[12] There is a much simpler way, and that's to buy a futures contract that will provide exposure to all the stocks in the S&P 500.

---

12   There are quantitative techniques to make this cheaper and easier, but they are out of scope for this book.

This is our first trading strategy, and it's the simplest possible:

Strategy one: Buy and hold a single futures contract.

Initially we'll focus on the S&P 500 future as a way to get exposure to – and be rewarded for – equity market risk. Later in the chapter I'll explain how and why we'd want to buy and hold other kinds of future from different asset classes. We'll also learn about some important concepts in futures trading:

- Futures multipliers, tick size and tick value.

- Expiry dates and rolling.

- Back-adjusting futures prices.

- Trading costs.

- Calculating profits.

- Required capital.

- Assessing performance.

Multipliers, tick size and tick value

As you might expect, given the S&P 500 is a US index, the primary exchange where you can trade S&P 500 futures is also in the US: the Chicago Mercantile Exchange (CME). Perusing the CME website, we can see that there are two sizes of S&P 500 future, defined as follows:[13]

- The *e-mini* future (symbol ES), with a 'contract unit' of $50, and a 'minimum price fluctuation' of 0.25 index points = $12.50

- The *micro e-mini* (symbol MES), with a 'contract unit' of $5, and a 'minimum price fluctuation' of 0.25 index points = $1.25

The 'contract unit' defines the relationship between the price and value of different futures contracts. Let's imagine that the S&P 500 is currently at a level of 4,500 and we decided to buy a single contract – the smallest possible position. The price rises by 45 to 4,545. What is our profit? A buy of the e-mini would have resulted in a profit of 45 × $50 = $2,250. Whereas if we had bought the micro contract there would be an extra 45 × $5 = $225 in our account.

---

13   There used to be three. As I started writing this book in September 2021, the CME delisted the original S&P 500 'big contract', which had a multiplier of $250.

To calculate our profit we *multiply* each \$1 rise in price[14] by the 'contract unit'. Hence, rather than contract unit, I prefer to use the term futures **multiplier**.[15] Another way of thinking about this is as follows: Buying one contract is equivalent to buying stocks equal in value to the price (4,500) multiplied by the contract unit. For example, if we were using the e-mini we'd have exposure to 4,500 × \$50 = \$225,000 worth of S&P 500. You can easily check this assertion: a 45 point change in the price is equal to 45 ÷ 4500 = 1%, and 1% of the notional value (\$225,000) is \$2,250, which is the profit for holding the e-mini that we've already calculated. I call this quantity the **notional exposure per contract**:

$$\text{Notional exposure per contract (\$)} = \text{Multiplier (\$)} \times \text{Price}$$

Here the notional exposure and multiplier are in US dollars, but in principle we could convert a notional exposure into any currency. I define the **base currency** as the currency my account is denominated in. Then:

$$\text{Notional exposure per contract (Base currency)}$$
$$= \text{Multiplier} \times \text{Price} \times \text{FX rate}$$

The FX rate is the relevant exchange rate between the two currencies. We'll need this formula if our trading account base currency is different from the instrument currency. As an example, if I'm a UK trader trading the S&P 500 e-mini then the relevant FX rate would be USD/GBP. At the time of writing the FX rate is 0.75, hence my notional exposure is:

$$\text{Notional exposure per contract (£)}$$
$$= \text{Multiplier (\$)} \times \text{Price} \times \text{FX rate (£/\$)}$$
$$= \$50 \times 4500 \times 0.75 = £168{,}750$$

Now, what about the 'minimum price fluctuation'? Simply, the futures price cannot be quoted or traded in smaller units than this minimum. Hence a quote of 4500.25 would be okay for the e-mini and micro contracts with a minimum fluctuation of 0.25, but a price of 4500.10 would be forbidden.

As minimum price fluctuation is a bit of a mouthful, I will instead use the alternative

---

14 There are a small number of futures which have variable futures multipliers such as the Australian bond and interest rate futures, and UK Natural Gas.
15 Readers of *Leveraged Trading* should recognise this term. In my earlier book *Systematic Trading* I use the term **block value**.

term **tick size**. Multiplying the minimum fluctuation by the futures multiplier gives us the **tick value**.

$$\text{Tick value} = \text{Multiplier} \times \text{Tick size}$$

In the case of the e-mini contract this is 0.25 × $50 = $12.50.

The decision as to which of the two S&P 500 futures we should trade is not entirely straightforward, and I will answer it in a subsequent chapter. For now we'll focus on the smallest micro future, with a futures multiplier of $5, a tick size of 0.25, and a tick value of 0.25 × $5 = $1.25.

Futures expiries and rolling

Having decided to trade the micro future, we can check out the order book to see what there is available to buy. An order book[16] is shown in table 1, with some other useful statistics.

TABLE 1: ORDER BOOK (I) FOR S&P 500 E-MINI MICRO FUTURES, PLUS VOLUME AND OPEN INTEREST

	Bid	Offer	Mid	Volume	Open interest
Sep 2021	4503.25	4503.50	4503.375	119,744	123,856
Dec 2021	4494.00	4494.25	4494.125	6,432	6,073
Mar 2022	4483.25	4483.75	4483.500	12	227
Jun 2022	4485.25	4486.25	4485.750	0	4

Order book as of 9th September 2021. Mid is average of bid and offer.

S&P 500 micro futures expire on a quarterly cycle in March, June, September and December. The current **front month**, September 2021, is the most liquid. It has the highest *volume* traded today (just under 120,000 contracts), and also the largest number of open positions (*open interest* of over 120,000 contracts). But this future will expire on 17th September, in just eight days. It hardly seems worth bothering with the September

---

16   An order book shows all the prices at which people are willing to buy (bid) and sell (offer) the relevant future, and the quantities in which they will trade. What I've shown here is the *top* of the order book, which just shows the best prices: the highest bid and the lowest offer. I've also excluded the available quantities, since I assume we are only trading a single contract and can definitely get filled at these prices.

contract: instead we will purchase the next future, December 2021, which is already reasonably liquid. With a market order we will buy at the offer, paying 4494.25.

Trading costs

Sadly brokers and exchanges don't work for free: it costs money to buy or sell futures contracts. I split trading costs into two categories: **commissions** and **spread costs**. Commissions should be familiar to all traders, although many equity brokers now offer zero commission trading. For futures, we normally pay a fixed commission per contract. For example, I pay $0.25 per contract to trade micro S&P 500 futures and $2 for each e-mini. These are pretty good rates for retail traders, but large institutional traders can negotiate even lower commissions.

Additionally we need to pay a spread cost, which is the value you are giving up to the market when you buy or sell. I define this as the difference between the price you pay (or receive if selling) and the mid-price that you'd pay or receive in the absence of any spread between bid and offer prices. Later in the book I'll discuss how to avoid or reduce your spread costs, but for now I assume we have to pay up every time.

In table 1 we can't get the December future for the mid-price (4494.125). Instead we lift the offer at 4494.25, for an effective spread cost of 4494.25 − 4494.125 = 0.125. If we were selling instead and hit the bid we would receive 4494.00, again for a spread cost of 0.125. The spread cost is the same, regardless of whether we are buying or selling. It has a value of 0.125 × $5 = $0.625 for the single contract we trade.

Another way of describing this is as follows: **if the bid/offer is one tick wide,**[17] the spread cost is half of this, and thus **the value of the spread cost is half the tick value** (half of $1.25, or $0.625). The total cost here is $0.25 commission, plus $0.625 in spread cost, for a total of $0.875. Of course, if the bid/offer was two ticks wide, then the spread cost would be one unit of tick value, and so on.

This is applicable for orders which are small enough to be filled at the top of the order book in a liquid market where spreads are at their normal level. Large institutional traders will usually pay higher spread costs and will need to consider their market impact.

---

17 Notice that the bid-offer can only ever be expressed as integer units of tick size: 0 ticks (this is a rarely seen *choice* price, where the bid and offer are identical), 1 tick (which is what we normally see in a tight liquid market, as for the first two contract months), or multiples of a tick (the less liquid back months of March and June).

Now, we can hold December 2021 for somewhat longer than September, until 17th December to be exact. However, this is supposed to be a buy and hold strategy: equities are expected to go up, but only in the long run. If we want to continue being exposed to the S&P 500 then we're going to have to *roll* our December 2021 contract into March 2022, at some point before 17th December.

We roll by selling our December contract, and simultaneously buying the March 2022 contract. Subsequently, we're going to have to roll again in March 2022, to buy the June contract. And so on, until we get bored of this particular strategy.

This question of which contract to hold, and when to roll it, is actually pretty complex. For now, so we don't get bogged down in the detail, I will be establishing some simple rules of thumb. In Part Six of this book I'll explain in more detail where these rules come from, and how you can determine for yourself what your rolling strategy should be. For the S&P 500 the specific rule we will adopt is to **roll five days before the expiry of the front month**. At that point both the front and the second month are both reasonably liquid.

How will this roll happen in practice? Well, let's suppose that we bought December 2021, which expires on 17th December. Five days before the expiry – 12th December – is a Sunday, so we roll the next day, 13th December 2021. The order book on 13th December is shown in table 2.

TABLE 2: ORDER BOOK (II) FOR S&P 500 E-MINI MICRO FUTURES, PLUS VOLUME AND OPEN INTEREST

	Bid	Offer	Mid	Volume	Open interest
Dec 2021	4706.25	4706.50	4706.375	119,744	123,856
Mar 2022	4698.00	4698.25	4698.125	64,432	35,212
Jun 2022	4690.50	4691.00	4690.750	12	227

Order book as of 13th December 2021. Mid is average of bid and offer.

We need to close our December 2021 position, which we can do by hitting the bid at 4706.25. So that we aren't exposed to price changes during the roll, we want to simultaneously buy one contract of March 2022, lifting the offer at 4698.25. On each of these trades we'd also be paying $0.25 commission, and also paying the same $0.625 spread that we had on our initial entry trade.

Alternatively, we could do the trade as a **calendar spread**, so called because we're trading the spread between two contracts of the same future but with different expiries. Here we do the buy and the sell as a single trade, most probably with someone who is also rolling but has the opposite position. With luck we can do a spread trade for a lower spread cost[18] and it would also be lower risk since we aren't exposed to movements in the underlying price. For now I'll conservatively assume we submit two separate orders, but I will discuss using calendar spreads for rolling in Part Six.

Time for some tedious, but important, calculations. The profits and losses so far from the buy and hold trading strategy can be broken down into a number of different components:

- The commission on our initial trade, $0.25.

- The profit from holding December 2021 from a buy price of 4494.25 to a sell of 4706.25: 4706.25 − 4494.25 = 212, which in cash terms is worth 212 × $5 = $1,060.

- The commission on the part of the roll trade we do to close our position in mid-December, $0.25.

Subtracting the two commission payments from the profit we get $1,059.50 in net profits. If we continue to implement the buy and hold strategy, we'd then have:

- The commission on the opening part of our roll trade in mid-December, $0.25.

- Any profit or loss from holding March 2022 from a purchase price of 4698.25 (which is not yet known).

- The commission on both parts of our next roll trade, rolling from March to June.

- Any profit or loss from holding June 2022 from its purchase price, whatever it turns out to be.

- The commission on the next roll trade.

- And so on.

We can break these profits and costs down a little differently as:

- The spread cost ($0.625) and commission ($0.25) on the initial trade: $0.875.

- The profit from holding December 2021 until we close it, as it goes from a mid of 4494.125 to a mid of 4706.375 (we can use mid prices here, since the spread cost is being accounted for separately): $1,061.25.

- The spread cost and commission on the closing part of the mid-December roll trade: $0.875.

Notice that if I subtract the commissions from the gross profit I get the same figure as before: $1,059.50. If we continue with the strategy we'd earn:

---

18 Calendar spreads in micro S&P 500 futures trade with a tick size of 0.05 index points. If the calendar spread was trading at 1 tick wide, we could end up paying only 0.0025 index points for the trade, worth just $0.0125 per contract.

- The spread cost and commission on the opening part of the mid-December roll trade.

- The profit from holding March 2022 until we close it, as it goes from a mid of 4698.125 to wherever it ends up.

- The spread cost and commission on the subsequent roll trade.

- And so on.

The terms in this second breakdown can be summed so that the profits (or losses) from *any* futures trade can be expressed as:

- The costs (commission and spread) on the initial trade, and any other trades which aren't related to rolling (there are none for this simple buy and hold strategy, but this won't usually be the case).

- The costs (commission and spread) on all our rolling trades.

- The profit or loss from holding the different contracts between rolls: calculated using *mid* prices.

This seemingly pedantic decomposition of returns is *extremely* important. As I will demonstrate in a moment, it is absolutely key to dealing with the problem of running and testing trading strategies on futures contracts that, annoyingly, keep expiring whilst we're trying to hold on to them.

Back-adjusting futures price

Suppose we now want to test the S&P 500 buy and hold futures trading strategy. We go to our friendly futures data provider,[19] and download a series of daily closing prices[20] for each contract expiry date. Later in the book I'll look at faster trading strategies that require more frequent data but initially I test all strategies on daily data.

We're now ready for the process of *back-adjustment*. Back-adjustment seeks to create a price series that reflects the true profit and loss from **constantly holding and rolling a single futures contract, but which ignores any trading costs**. We'll consider the effects of these costs separately.

Why should we use a back-adjusted series? What is wrong with simply stitching

---

19   Some suggested data providers appear in Appendix A.
20   Unfortunately, the micro e-mini contract was only introduced in May 2019. As I'll discuss later in the book, we need as much data as possible to test any trading strategy, and a few years isn't really enough. However, we do have data for the e-mini, and also the delisted S&P 500 'big contract' which goes back much further. Since any difference in the prices of the different futures could easily be arbitraged out, it's safe to assume that we can use S&P 500 big contract prices to backfill the prices we have for S&P 500 micro futures.

together the prices from different expiry dates? Indeed, many respectable providers of financial data do exactly that. Are they all wrong?

In fact, doing this would produce incorrect results. Consider the switch from the December to the March contract shown above. When the switch happens on 13th December the relevant mid prices are 4706.375 and 4698.125 (remember, we use mid prices, as costs are accounted for elsewhere). If we used the March price after the roll date, and the December price before it, there would be a fall of 8.25 in the price on the roll date. This would create an apparent loss on a long position.

But rolling doesn't actually create any real profit or loss, if we ignore costs and assume we can trade at the mid price. Just before the roll we own a December contract whose price and value is 4706.375. We assume we can sell it at the mid-market price. This sale does not create any profit or loss, since we are trading at market value. Similarly, when we buy a March contract, we are paying the mid-market price. Although the notional value of our position has changed, as the prices are different, no profits or losses occur as a result of rolling.

All this means that, in the absence of any actual price changes, the **back-adjusted price should remain constant over the roll**. To achieve this we'd first compare the December and March price differential on the roll date: \$8.25. We now subtract this differential from all the December contract prices.

The effect of this is that the December prices will all be consistent with the March prices; in particular on the roll date both prices will be the same. We can join together the adjusted December and actual March prices, knowing there will be no artificial jump caused by rolling. Our adjusted price series will use adjusted December prices prior to (and on) the roll date, and actual March prices afterwards.

We could then go back in time and repeat this exercise, ensuring that the September 2021 prices are consistent with December 2021, and so on. Eventually we'd have a complete series of adjusted prices covering the entire history of our data. Once we include costs this series will give a realistic idea of what could be earned from constantly holding and rolling a single S&P 500 futures contract.[21]

You can do this back-adjustment yourself, and I describe how in more detail in Appendix B, but it's also possible to purchase back-adjusted data. Be careful if you use third party data. Make sure you understand the precise methodology that's been used, and avoid series of data that have just been stitched together without any adjustment.

---

21   This is the simplest method for back-adjustment, which is known as the *Panama* method (since prices rise and fall when adjusted like ships passing through the locks in the Panama canal). There are more complex methods, but in practice they do not improve trading strategy performance, so they are not worth the effort.

Using pre-adjusted data also means that you lose the flexibility to test different rolling strategies, something I'll explore in Part Six.

Figure 1 shows the original raw futures contract prices (to be pedantic, a number of raw futures prices for different expires plotted on the same graph) for the S&P 500 with the back-adjusted price in grey.

FIGURE 1: BACK-ADJUSTED AND ORIGINAL PRICES FOR S&P 500 MICRO FUTURE

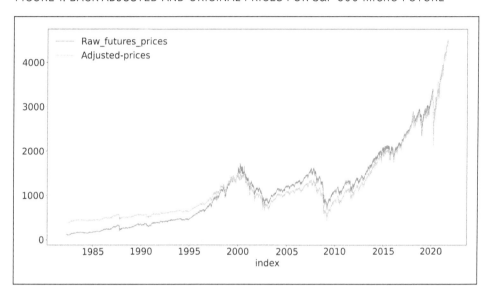

Notice that the original prices and the back-adjusted price are not identical, although the lines precisely overlap at the end. This will always happen: by construction,[22] the adjusted price will be identical to the final set of original futures prices. Initially, the back-adjusted price is lagging below until around 2008, and then it begins to outpace the original prices. This effect is even clearer if we plot the difference between the two series, in figure 2.

---

22 This is a nice property of back-adjustment. An alternative method is *forward-adjustment*, where the initial adjusted price is equal to the price of the earliest contract in the data. This has the advantage of requiring less work, since we do not need to repeatedly rewrite previous data, but results in final adjusted prices that can be substantially different from the current futures price. For the strategies in this book you can use either method, and you will get the same results.

FIGURE 2: DIFFERENCE BETWEEN BACK-ADJUSTED AND ORIGINAL FUTURES PRICE
FOR S&P 500

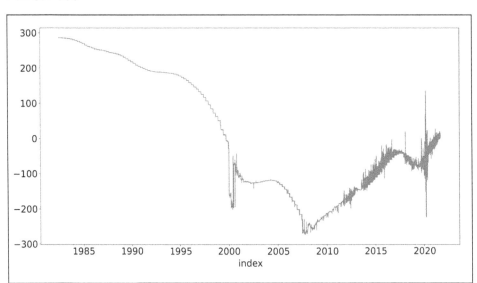

Ignoring the weird noise in the plot (which is due to differences in roll timing and data frequency), there is a clear pattern. Before 2008 we mostly lost money from rolling the contract, as the adjusted price went up more slowly than the original raw prices. After 2008, we usually earned money.

Let's think a little more deeply about what the different price series are showing. An S&P 500 index value just includes the price. This series doesn't include dividends.[23] If we include dividends, we get a **total return** series:

$$\text{Total return} = \text{Spot return} + \text{Dividends}$$

Now for the futures. Through a no-arbitrage[24] argument, we know that the futures

---

23 Some equity indices include dividends, in particular the German DAX equity index future.

24 It's not necessary to understand no-arbitrage futures pricing theory in any detail, and I won't be covering a spot versus futures arbitrage strategy in this book. Here's the elevator pitch version: suppose the futures price was higher than the cash price plus expected dividends minus the margin interest rate (the excess return on the stock). You could borrow money using a margin loan, buy a basket of S&P 500 stocks, and short the future. At expiry, any gains or losses in the stock and future would be perfectly hedged, and after paying off the margin loan and receiving the dividends you would be left with a clear risk-free profit. A similar argument explains why the futures price can't be lower than the cash price plus the expected value of dividends minus interest. You can find more detailed discussion of no-arbitrage pricing in books such as John Hull's classic work (see Appendix A).

price at any one time is equal to the spot price of the index, plus any expected dividends we will get before the future expires, minus the interest we would pay to borrow money for buying stocks. This is known as the **excess return**:

$$\text{Excess return} = \text{Total return} - \text{Interest}$$
$$= \text{Spot return} + \text{Dividends} - \text{Interest}$$

This extra component of excess return over and above the spot return is also known as **carry**:

$$\text{Excess return} = \text{Spot return} + \text{Carry}$$
$$= \text{Spot return} + \text{Dividends} - \text{Interest}$$

For the S&P 500 the carry was negative until 2008, because dividends were lower than interest rates. Hence the adjusted price was underperforming the raw futures price, as shown in the downward slope in figure 2. Subsequent to that, on the back of the 2008 crash and recession there was a massive reduction in interest rates. Dividends were also reduced, but they did not fall by as much.

With dividends above interest rates after 2008, carry went positive. As a result the line begins to slope upwards in figure 2, as the adjusted price returns were higher than the spot price. This upward trend was briefly interrupted from 2016 to 2019 when the Fed raised interest rates, but then resumed with a vengeance during the COVID-19 pandemic when rates were hurriedly slashed. Later in the book I'll discuss how we can construct a trading strategy using carry. For now, the important point to remember is that **an adjusted futures price includes returns from both spot and carry.**

Note that the adjusted futures price is *not* a total return series. The adjusted price is the cumulated *excess* return, which has interest costs deducted. When we buy futures, we are able to earn additional profits from interest paid on any cash we were holding in our trading account (to cover initial margin payments[25] and potential losses).

Because the amount of cash in any given trading account can vary dramatically, depending on the leverage you want to operate at, it's difficult to calculate exactly what we could expect in additional profits from interest on cash held. So I won't be including interest on cash in any calculations. Hence **all profits shown in this book will be for excess returns only.**

---

25   Margins are cash deposited in a futures trading account to cover potential losses. An *initial margin* is required when a trade is opened, and if losses are subsequently made you will require additional *variation margin*. If you are unfamiliar with margin trading, I suggest you read my previous book, *Leveraged Trading*.

Measuring the profits from a trading strategy

We're now in a position to calculate exactly what profits we could have made from the buy and hold strategy.

Given a series of positions in contracts, N_t (where a positive number means we are long, and a negative is short), and a series of back-adjusted prices, P_t, the return in *price points* for time period t is:

$$\text{Return (in price points), } R^{points}_t = N_{t-1} \times (P_t - P_{t-1})$$

For the simple buy and hold strategy where our position N is always one (a single contract), our cumulative return in price points will be equal to the change in price over the full period that we are trading (from $t = 0$ to $t = T$):

$$\text{Cumulated return (in price points)}_{t=0,T} = (P_T - P_0)$$

To work out our returns in dollars, or whatever currency the relevant future is priced in (the *instrument currency*), we'd multiply by the futures multiplier:

$$\text{Return (in currency of future), } R^{instr.}_t = R^{points}_t \times \text{Multiplier}$$

Once again, for the simple buy and hold strategy, our cumulative return in currency terms will be equal to the change in price over the full period that we are trading, multiplied by the futures multiplier. Finally, to convert this into the currency our account is denominated in (the *base currency*), we'd multiply by the relevant exchange rate:

$$\text{Return (base currency), } R^{base}_t = R^{instr}_t \times \text{FX rate}$$

As an example, suppose we're UK traders investing in the S&P 500 micro future, we have a long position on ($N_t = 1$, for all t), and the price goes up from 4,500 to 4,545 over a single day. With the multiplier of $5, and assuming an FX rate of $1 = £0.75:

$$R^{points}_t = N_{t-1} \times (P_t - P_{t-1}) = 1 \times (4545 - 4500) = 45$$

$$R^{instr.}_t = R^{points}_t \times \text{Multiplier} = 45 * \$5 = \$225$$

$$R^{base}_t = R^{instr}_t \times \text{FX rate} = \$225 * £0.75 = £168.75$$

Summing up the values of $R^{base}{}_t$ over time will give us our cumulative profits from holding a single futures contract, or indeed for any trading strategy for which we've been able to calculate a series of historic positions. The cumulative return series for a US dollar trader holding the S&P 500 micro future is shown in figure 3. Incidentally, these cumulative return series are also known as **account curves**.

This is our first **backtest**: a test of a trading strategy using historic data.

FIGURE 3: ACCOUNT CURVE (CUMULATIVE RETURN IN US$) FROM HOLDING A CONSTANT LONG POSITION IN A SINGLE MICRO S&P 500 CONTRACT

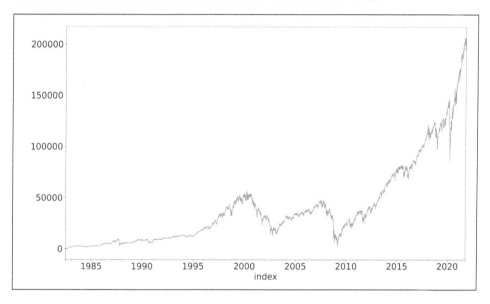

This plot is identical to the back-adjusted price series in figure 2, but the *y*-axis shows different values as we have effectively multiplied the price by the futures multiplier, and started at a base of zero. We end up earning a total profit of over $200,000.

Bear in mind that these profits do not allow for the costs of *rolling* our position. We can easily get a rough idea of the likely costs. The backtest is around 40 years in length, rolling four times a year, with a total cost calculated above of $0.875 × 2 = $1.75 on each roll. This gives a grand total of 4 × 40 × $1.75 = $280. That doesn't make much of a dent in our total profit. Feel free to deduct another two chunks of $0.875 for the initial purchase and final closing trade if you're feeling pedantic! But you could well ask if it was really realistic to assume that we would have paid precisely $1.75 every single time we rolled, even way back in 1982? This is a question I will address in a later chapter.

Remember, these are *excess* returns. We would have made additional returns from earning interest on the cash in our account, especially earlier in the testing period when interest rates were usually at least 5%, and sometimes occasionally over 10%. But receiving interest on deposits isn't part of our trading strategy, and the amount earned will depend on our leverage. We should ignore any interest payments to get a purer measure of performance.

Backtesting

It's fairly easy to define a backtest: it's a test of a trading strategy using historical data. But that still leaves some important questions unanswered. Firstly, **what exactly is the point of doing a backtest?**

We run backtests for a couple of different reasons. The first, which is what most people think about, is to make decisions about how we should trade in the future. Decisions such as: which trading strategy should we use? Which instrument(s) should we trade? How should we allocate our risk across strategies and instruments? More often than not, those decisions are made by looking just at outright or risk adjusted performance: which of these alternatives is more profitable?

The second reason for backtesting, which is often overlooked, is to get an idea of the *behaviour* of a given trading strategy. How often does it trade? How expensive are its trading costs? How much leverage does it use?

How should we backtest?

Backtests have a dual nature. They run over historical data, so they show us what would have happened in the *past*. But we then use their results to make decisions about what to do in the *future*. There is an inherent contradiction here. Should we make our backtests as realistic as possible, reflecting what we could have actually achieved in the past. Or should we create something that would be a better guide to how we will trade in the future?

For example, suppose that you run a backtest to decide whether to use strategy A or strategy B, and you have data back to 1970. With the benefit of hindsight strategy B is much better than A, but at the start of the backtest you have no information about whether strategy A or B was superior. To make it a realistic simulation of the past, you would have to include both strategies in the backtest until you had evidence, based only on backward looking information, that strategy B was better.

This means your backtest will begin as a blend of A and B, and gradually morph into containing only strategy B. The returns from that hybrid strategy would be a realistic indication of what someone starting in 1970, with no forward-looking information, would have been able to achieve.

But this weird concoction of strategies is not what you are going to trade now! Instead, you will be trading strategy B without a hint of A to be seen. If you want to understand or calibrate the likely behaviour of your trading strategy, then you would be better off just backtesting strategy B, once you had determined it was the better option.

This is a common approach, but it is fraught with danger. The backtested returns from just strategy B will, by definition, be higher than the more realistic figures you would have got from a purer backtest blending A and B with no forward-looking information. Testing only strategy B is pejoratively known as *in sample*. We have made decisions with the full knowledge of what occurs in the future, such as selecting B over A. These decisions are known as *fitting*, hence what we have done here is *in sample fitting*.

To an extent this is unavoidable; if we want to understand whether we should trade A or B then we need to test both. If we subsequently want to understand the behaviour of the strategy we have selected, then we will need to examine the returns and trading patterns of the chosen strategy, which will be 100% invested in strategy B. As long as we bear in mind that the returns achieved are almost certainly unrealistically high, then not too much harm has been done.

However, there is another trap for users of in sample backtests, and that is the curse of *over fitting*. It is fine to choose B over A, but only if there is sufficient evidence that this is the correct decision. In practice it's unlikely that our hypothetical strategy B is so much better than strategy A that we would be justified in dropping A entirely. This is because financial data is noisy, and almost never has sufficiently clear patterns that we can be significantly confident about such decisions.

To take an extreme example, suppose your backtest suggested that the day of the year with the highest returns was 26th January. Would it make sense to sit on your hands for the rest of the year, and only trade on that single day? Of course not, that would be absurd. But plenty of traders are prepared to, for example, only trade the EUR/USD future purely because it has the highest returns in their backtest.

(A more subtle problem with backtests is that there are some aspects of the past that we know for sure will not be repeated. As an example, the US Fed fund interest rate has fallen from over 10% in 1980 to 0.25% as I'm writing this paragraph. This significantly flattered bond performance, but it would clearly be a serious mistake to allocate our money only to strategies which had a bias to being long US bond futures. In later strategies I'll explore how we can try and avoid this problem by extracting the effect of these trends from performance statistics, but for now it's a serious concern.)

By only trading strategy B there is a serious danger that we have extrapolated the past blindly into the future, putting all our eggs into a single basket that is balanced dangerously on the edge of a cliff. Just because B has done a little better in the past, does not give us any guarantee that B will outperform A over some period in the future. Even if B is a fundamentally better strategy, the laws of chance mean that it could very well underperform A in the next few years.

With an understanding of statistical significance, a properly designed backtest would begin with a blend of A and B, and then gradually reallocate capital to the better strategy as more information about their relative performance was discovered over time. The most likely outcome would be that there would still be allocations to both A and B, but with more in B.

Going forward, you would want to trade both A and B in the final proportions you obtained in the backtest. And to test and understand how this mixture of A and B behaved, you would probably run a second test with those proportions fixed. But again, the returns from this backtest would be overstated, although not by as much as a backtest only of strategy B. Still, by continuing to trade both A and B you have limited the dangers of in sample fitting to a minimum: hedging your bet on B with an allocation to A. This approach is more *robust* than the alternative of just trading B.

How should we use backtest results?

Good traders will use backtest results when their results are significant, but also consider other information. For example, it makes sense for a long position in volatility futures to return a negative return over time, for reasons I will discuss later in this chapter. We can trust this result in a backtest, and expect it to be repeated in the future. In contrast, where backtest results can't be logically explained, there is a good chance it is *data-mining*: pure luck, and not to be trusted regardless of the statistical significance.

In this book I'll show you the results of my backtests, but I will also suggest what would be a robust course of action to take, given the statistical significance of my analysis. Of course you are free to ignore my suggestions, for example by taking decisions that assume the backtested results are a perfect guide to the future. Just be aware that there are potential dangers in taking this approach.

Please also bear in mind that the results of *any* backtest will be potentially overstated, if they include decisions made with information that could not have been known in the past. Where possible my backtest results include decisions made without the benefit of hindsight by using automated fitting techniques that are only allowed to see past data, but you should always assume that backtested results overstate what we could really achieve in the future, no matter how carefully they have been constructed.

Capital

Quoting profits in US dollars is generally frowned upon in finance, as they are meaningless without any context, although this message hasn't got through to the leagues of Instagram trading influencers who hook you in with inflated claims of making a guaranteed income of $500 per day. Making $24,000 in just over 40 years, as we do in figure 3, is fantastic if you start with just $100. It's less impressive if you started with $1 million. The *y*-axis in figure 3 starts at zero dollars, but we couldn't actually have run this trading strategy with no money.

How much trading capital would we actually have needed to make these profits?

If we weren't trading futures, and had no access to leverage, the answer seems straightforward. The S&P index at the start of the testing period was around 109. To get the equivalent exposure that we had with micro futures, we'd need to have bought 109 × $5 = $545 worth of the underlying stocks. Nowadays, with the index at around 4,500, we'd need $22,500.

However, one of the more useful attributes of futures markets is that we don't need to put the entire exposure value up in cash – only what is required for initial margin. Right now, to buy one micro future only requires $1,150 initial margin. Given the current notional value of a single contract (around $22,500), this works out to a potential leverage ratio of almost 20:1.

But it would be pretty crazy to buy a single micro contract with just $1,150. Things would be fine if the price went up in a straight line, without ever moving against you, but of course this will never happen. We also require additional *variation* margin to cover potential losses. Since the multiplier here is $5, for every point the index price moves against us, we'd be required to put up an additional $5.

If that cash wasn't already in our account, then there's a good chance the broker would liquidate our position unless we moved quickly to top up our trading account. How much additional cash do we need? If we were ultra cautious, then for a long position you would want to put up enough cash to cover yourself against the price going to zero. This would be equivalent to the entire notional value[26] of the futures exposure. That is extremely conservative! There are some circumstances when that might make sense, but generally you would hope that you could close your long position long before the price hit zero. But for now I am going to assume that we put up the entire current notional exposure value as capital; effectively trading without any leverage.

This will allow us to get an understanding of the performance characteristics of each

---

26 For a short position you'd technically need infinite quantities of cash available to cover all eventualities.

individual asset. When we get to strategy two, I'll discuss how we can adjust the capital required to reflect the *risk* of a given asset.

Figure 4 again shows the cumulated profits graph, this time overlaid with the required capital. It isn't a surprise that they follow each other closely; the grey capital line is the current futures price multiplied by the futures multiplier, whilst the darker profits line is the sum of differences in the adjusted price also multiplied by the multiplier.

FIGURE 4: ACCOUNT CURVE ($) AND REQUIRED CAPITAL ($) FOR S&P 500 MICRO FUTURES

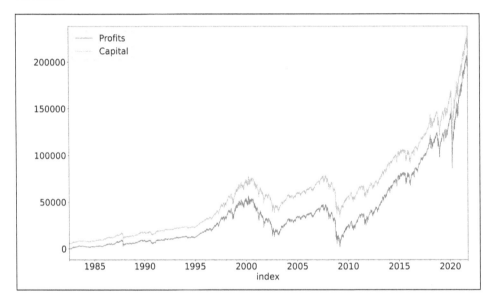

If we divide the profits made each day by the capital required on the previous day, then we can calculate percentage returns:

$$R\%_t = 100 \times R^{base}_t \div Capital_{t-1}$$

Then we get the percentage returns shown in figure 5.

FIGURE 5: PERCENTAGE RETURNS FROM BUY & HOLD SINGLE CONTRACT STRATEGY IN S&P 500

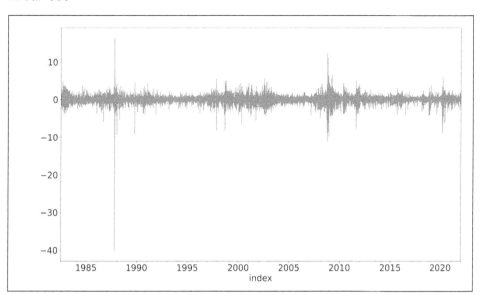

The scary days of 1987, 2008, and to a lesser extent 2020 are fairly clear; and should also be familiar, since this is how stock returns are normally shown. Another way to visualise our performance would be to cumulate up[27] these daily percentage returns, adding each return to the previous day's return.

Figure 6 gives quite a different picture from figure 3. When looking at dollar returns, movements in earlier years appear much smaller in figure 3. But in summed percentage terms they are quite significant. My preference is to use graphs[28] like figure 6, since it's easier to see the full range of returns throughout the history of data.

---

27   The normal way to cumulate up percentage returns is to take the product of $(1 + r_t)$, where r_t is the percentage return expressed as a decimal (e.g. 1% = 0.01). But charting this cumulated product would again result in a graph where the early returns were small and difficult to distinguish.
28   Incidentally, if we were to plot figure 3 with a logarithmic scale, it would look pretty similar to figure 6 but on a different scale.

FIGURE 6: ACCOUNT CURVE (CUMULATED SUM OF PERCENTAGE RETURNS) FROM BUY AND HOLD S&P 500 STRATEGY

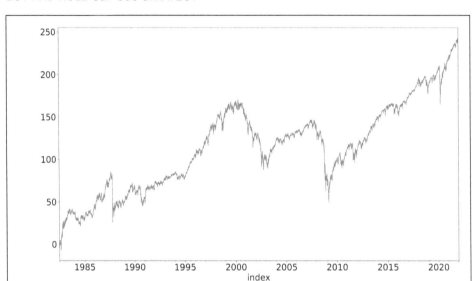

Assessing performance characteristics

Annual returns

Quoting performance figures as percentage returns is only the first step to properly evaluating the returns of our strategy. The total return in figure 6 is nearly 250%. That would be incredible over a single year, but we took over 40 years to earn that lucrative sum. We need to calculate an *average* annual return.

We could do this by measuring the return in each year, and taking an average. Alternatively we could measure the daily returns, take an average of those, and then *annualise* them. Assuming we're using the mean as our average, we'll get the same result.

To annualise daily returns, we need to multiply by the number of days in a year.[29] This is not the usual 365, the less common 366, or the approximate 365.25 (or an extremely pedantic 365.2422), since we only have returns for business days when the market is

---

29 If you're familiar with financial mathematics, this will seem wrong. We really ought to calculate the CAGR: the compounded annual growth rate (also known as the geometric mean), which assumes that returns are compounded on a daily basis. However, we're not dealing with compounded returns in this book. I'll explain why in strategy two, but for now please bear with me.

open. The number of business days per year varies depending on the year and the market you are trading but – for reasons that will become apparent below – I prefer to assume there are exactly 256 business days in a year.[30]

The average daily return for the S&P 500 strategy is 0.0235%, which if I multiply by 256 equals 6.02% per year. We could also measure the average weekly, monthly or quarterly return. But I prefer to focus only on daily returns (since we're using daily data to calculate our series of profits) and annual returns (as I find them more intuitive).

Risk and standard deviation

Futures are leveraged instruments which often have very low margin requirements. With Eurodollar interest rate futures anything up to nearly 500:1 is theoretically possible (although not sensible!). As a result we have a degree of latitude in deciding how much leverage to use. If we double our leverage, then we double our returns, but we also double our risk. So it's meaningless to talk about outright returns, rather we should discuss *risk adjusted* returns.

But it's extremely difficult to define what is meant by risk. For starters, should we use a *symmetric* or *asymmetric* measure of risk? A symmetric measure of risk treats all returns as equally risky, whether they are positive or negative. An asymmetric measure is only concerned with negative returns.

What possible logic could there be for using a symmetric measure of risk? Surely, we only worry about unexpected losses, whilst an unexpected gain is a joyous event to be celebrated? There are however a few reasons why symmetric risk makes some sense. Firstly, to get technical, if we measure our risk using all the available returns, then our risk statistic will be a more robust measure and less susceptible to occasional outliers.

Secondly, once we are using daily returns it becomes likely that we'll see both negative and positive returns: for the S&P 500, 54% of the daily returns are positive and 46% negative. If we are currently taking a lot of risk, then we're only ever a coin flip away from a pleasingly large positive return turning into a depressingly large negative return. Hence, it makes sense to treat positive and negative returns as equally risky.

Finally, when trading futures we can be both long and short, even if for now we're limiting ourselves to long positions. If we used an asymmetric measure of risk, we'd have a different measure of price risk depending on our position. That would rather overcomplicate our lives!

---

30 It's not a bad approximation: equal to 365 minus 104 Saturdays and Sundays, and a few extra public holidays.

With that in mind, my preferred measure for a symmetric measure of risk is the **standard deviation** of returns.

Why not use drawdowns?

A very popular measure of risk is the **maximum drawdown**. This is the maximum cumulative loss experienced at any point during the backtest of a trading strategy. It's an asymmetric measure of risk, which seems to make more intuitive sense. Similarly, you could use the average return divided by the maximum drawdown as a measure of risk adjusted returns. And in fact this is a very popular measure amongst many traders: it even has a name – the 'Calmar Ratio'.

But there are a few reasons why I'm not especially enamoured of the maximum drawdown as a risk measure. There is only one maximum drawdown in a data set, so our statistics are dependent on a small subset of the data.[31] Secondly, the size of the maximum drawdown depends on the length of your data set; the largest drawdown seen over a 30 year backtest will usually be much larger than the same statistic for a single year.

Finally, using our maximum drawdown as the risk measure may give us a false sense of security, and fool us into thinking that this figure is the most we can lose. This is unlikely to be the case.[32]

We could make the measure a little more robust by using the *average* drawdown and I will also calculate this figure as it does give some insight into the returns of a strategy (to estimate this we measure the current drawdown on all the days in our data set, and then calculate the mean of those daily drawdown figures).

But for my primary risk measure I still prefer to use the standard deviation.

---

31 To get technical for a moment, the sampling distribution of the maximum drawdown statistic shows very high variability, as it can be heavily influenced by the inclusion or exclusion of just a few days of returns.

32 There are a couple of reasons for this. One is that our data may not go back far enough. For example, we don't have equity futures data going back to the 1929 crash, and if we hadn't backfilled the S&P 500 micro data with the big contract, we wouldn't have data back to 1987 or even 2008. Secondly, it's especially dangerous to think that the worst events in the past really reflect what could possibly go wrong in the future. Someone trading S&P 500 futures in late September 1987, using data from 1975 to 1987, would have thought it was utterly impossible to lose over 20% in a single day. But then just a few weeks later the impossible happened.

To calculate the standard deviation of a series of returns $r_1 \dots r_T$ we'd first find the mean r^*:

$$r^* = [1 \div T]r_t + [1 \div T]r_{t-1} + [1 \div T]r_{t-2} \dots + [1 \div T]r_1$$

We can then calculate a standard deviation:

$$\sigma = \surd\{[1 \div T](r_T - r^*)^2 + [1 \div T](r_{T-1} - r^*)^2$$
$$+ [1 \div T](r_{T-2} - r^*)^2 + \dots [1 \div T](r_1 - r^*)^2\}$$

We can calculate this on an annual or daily basis, or for any other frequency. We can also *annualise* the daily standard deviation of returns, as we did for average returns. This means we can use more data (over 10,000 daily returns rather than just 40 annual returns), but end up with a more intuitive annual figure.

Under certain assumptions, which I'll come to in a second, we can do this by multiplying the daily standard deviation by the square root of the number of business days in a year. If, like me, you assume there are always 256 business days in a year then we can annualise a daily standard deviation by multiplying it by the square root of $\surd 256 = 16$. This nice round number is my reason for assuming there are precisely 256 business days in every year.

If we measure the daily standard deviation of returns in figure 5 we get 1.2%, which when annualised is 19.2% per year. But if we directly measure annual standard deviation we get 17.2%. These figures are different, and not just because the actual number of business days is not precisely 256 days in every year. They are different because the 'certain assumptions' that I made are not true in practice.

The first assumption I made when annualising was that there was zero *auto-correlation:* yesterday's return has no influence on tomorrow's return. This is unlikely to be the case in practice. In financial data we often get positive auto-correlation, which is the phenomenon by which up days tend to be followed by up days, and vice versa; or negative auto-correlation when up days are usually followed by down days, with the reverse being true.

Consider an extreme situation in which we made $1 one day, and then lost $1 on the subsequent day, then made $1, lost $1, and so on; an example of perfectly negative auto-correlation. Every year we would make $0 or $1, and our standard deviation measured using annual returns would be around $1. But our daily standard deviation would be $1, or $16 once annualised. Negative auto-correlation of daily returns results in annualised standard deviation being too high.

The second assumption was that daily returns have a symmetric, *well-behaved* distribution. For example, suppose we earn $1 every day, and then on the final day of the year we either lose $364 or gain $364. Trivially, the annual standard deviation will be $364, since in half the years we break even and in the other half we make $728. However the daily standard deviation is $19.05, which when annualised comes to just $304.

These are contrived examples designed to give extreme results, and generally the annualised figure is pretty close to the value calculated by using actual annual returns, as we can see for S&P 500. It's usually better to use the annualised figure calculated with daily returns since it uses more data points for its estimation, and thus is more robust. But you should be aware that it may sometimes give misleading results.

Risk adjusted returns: Sharpe ratio

Now we have a measure of risk, we can use it to calculate risk adjusted returns. The **Sharpe ratio (SR)** is the average excess return (mean return less risk-free interest rate), divided by the standard deviation of returns:

Sharpe ratio (SR)
= (Mean return − Risk-free rate) ÷ Standard deviation

In this book we exclusively use excess returns, so we do not need the risk-free rate:

SR for futures = Mean excess return ÷ Standard deviation

Note that both the mean and the standard deviation need to be estimated with the same frequency. So we can divide the average daily return by the standard deviation of returns, which for the S&P 500 strategy gives a daily SR of 0.023% ÷ 1.2% = 0.0196. Or we could divide the average annual return by the standard deviation of annual returns to calculate an annual SR.

Once again, as it's better to use more data, we'd rather calculate a daily SR and annualise it. We already know we can annualise daily means by multiplying by the number of days in a year, whilst annualising standard deviations involves multiplying by the square root of the number of days. Using trivial mathematics, we can show that annualising daily SR also requires multiplying by the square root of the number of days in a year (which I assume is 256). The annualised SR for the S&P 500 is:

$$0.0196 \times \sqrt{256} = 0.0196 \times 16 = 0.31$$

For the rest of this book, unless I specify otherwise, **all Sharpe ratios I quote will be annualised**.

Since we know that annualising standard deviations is fraught with potential danger, the same must be true[33] of annualising SR. But because standard deviations aren't usually too badly affected, the effect on SRs is also pretty minimal.

Measuring asymmetry: Skew

Many people are critical of the assumption of symmetric returns that underpins standard deviation, which makes the Sharpe ratio guilty by association. They prefer the **Sortino ratio** which is similar, but instead of standard deviation (the average deviation of both positive and negative returns) uses the deviation of only negative returns.

This has some value when deciding which of several trading strategies to implement, but it does not help when trying to understand the behaviour of a given strategy. If a strategy or asset has a high Sortino ratio, is it because it has a high Sharpe, or because it has a low Sharpe but has fewer negative returns?

For this reason, I prefer to use the SR,[34] but then to measure the symmetry of returns separately. There are a few different ways to do this. The classical method for measuring symmetry is with **skew**. The returns from a *positively* skewed asset will contain more losing days than for those that are negatively skewed. But the losing days will be relatively small in magnitude. A *negatively* skewed asset will have fewer down days, but the losses on those days will be larger.

Buying insurance on your house or car is a positive skew strategy. You will experience frequent small losses (paying monthly or annual premiums) with occasional large gains (receiving payouts when you crash your car or get burgled). The insurance companies you are paying premium to will see frequent small gains on your account (receiving premiums) and occasional large losses (making payouts) – negative skew.

Right at the start of the chapter I said it was smart to take a risk that most other people are unwilling, or unable, to take. Most people strongly dislike negative skew, so taking on this risk should result in higher profits. Running an insurance firm is usually profitable, hence we'd expect negative skew to be associated with higher returns.[35] It's important to be aware of the degree of skew in a given asset. If an asset has strongly

---

33   See Lo, Andrew, 'The Statistics of Sharpe Ratios', *Financial Analysts Journal* 58 (2003).

34   There are also some technical benefits from using the Sharpe ratio (SR) and standard deviation that will become evident later.

35   Later in the book I show how to use the current level of estimated skew as the basis for a trading strategy.

negative skew, then we know our assumptions about symmetrical returns will be way off the mark, and its price is likely to be highly unstable.

Skew can also be measured for different time periods. It doesn't matter so much right now, but we'll see later in the book that you can get very different skew figures when using daily, monthly or annual returns. Again, this is down to auto-correlation. For example, suppose we had a strategy with positive auto-correlation that consistently made money in the first three weeks of each month, but then lost most of it in the fourth week. The weekly returns would have serious negative skew, but the monthly returns would be just fine.

I'm mostly going to use monthly skew, since daily and weekly skew can be seriously affected by a couple of extreme daily returns, and annual skew does not give us enough data points for a reliable estimate. The skew of S&P 500 monthly percentage returns come in at −1.37. Negative skew of this magnitude is fairly typical of assets seen as risky, like equities.

Measuring fat tails

As well as negative skew, equities also famously have *fat tails*. A fat-tailed distribution is one where extreme returns are more likely than in the standard normal Gaussian distribution. If equity returns were Gaussian, then a six standard deviation move would occur every 2.7 million years or so. With a typical daily standard deviation for S&P 500 of 1.2%, a six standard deviation move is around 7.2%. Theoretically, we would have been *very* unlucky to see a single daily return of 7.2% or more in the last 100 years. In fact there have been around *40* such days!

How can we measure these fat tails? We could continue down the route of classical statistics, by using **kurtosis**: the counterpart of skew that measures fat tails. However, I am not keen on this for a few reasons.

Firstly, I find it quite difficult to interpret figures like 6.65 (which, as you may have guessed, is the monthly kurtosis of S&P 500 futures). Also, a single figure for kurtosis does not tell you whether you have unwanted fat left tails (unusually sizeable negative returns), or extremely pleasant fat right tails (unexpectedly large positive returns). Finally, kurtosis is not a robust statistical measure, and it will swing wildly if one or two extreme days are removed or added to a data series.

Instead I'm going to use an alternative measure of fat tails. This statistic directly measures just how extreme our large returns are compared to a normal Gaussian distribution.

The first step is to *demean* the return series, by subtracting the daily mean return from every data point. Next, we measure the *percentile* of the demeaned returns at various points. Firstly, the 1st percentile: the point at which 1% of the returns in the distribution are lower, which comes in at –3.25% for the S&P 500. Then we measure the 30th percentile (–0.28%), 70th percentile (+0.42%), and 99th percentile (+3.04%).

I've chosen the 30% and 70% percentile as they're roughly equivalent to a minus one and plus one standard deviation move. The 1% and 99% points reflect the extremities of the distribution. If you wish you could use 0.1% and 99.9% to get more extreme estimates, but then you would have fewer data points contributing to your estimate, making it less reliable. This isn't so much of a problem with the 40 years of S&P 500 data, but we might only have a few years of data for some other instruments.

The next step is to divide the first two percentiles to get a **lower percentile ratio**:[36]

$$\text{Lower percentile ratio} = \text{1st percentile} \div \text{30th percentile}$$
$$= -3.25\% \div -0.28\% = 11.6$$

Similarly we can calculate an **upper percentile ratio**:

$$\text{Upper percentile ratio} = \text{99th percentile} \div \text{70th percentile}$$
$$= 3.04\% \div 0.42\% = 7.2$$

For a Gaussian normal distribution, both of these ratios will be equal to 4.43, as it's a symmetric distribution. To get an idea of how the S&P 500 compares to a normal distribution, we divide each of the ratios by 4.43 to get a *relative* ratio:

$$\text{Relative lower fat tail ratio}$$
$$= \text{Lower percentile ratio} \div 4.43 = 11.6 \div 4.43 = 2.16$$

$$\text{Relative upper fat tail ratio}$$
$$= \text{Upper percentile ratio} \div 4.43 = 7.2 \div 4.43 = 1.60$$

These are rather unwieldy phrases, so for the remainder of the book I will use these abbreviated terms: **lower tail** and **upper tail**. Each of these gives us an indication of how extreme the lowest and highest returns are. **Any value higher than 1 indicates our extreme returns are more fat tailed than a normal Gaussian distribution.** To put it another way, 1% of the time with a Gaussian distribution we'd get a loss that's

---

36 Notice that if we didn't demean then there is a possibility that the 1% and 30% percentiles would have different signs, resulting in a negative figure here.

about 4.43 times larger than our average loss. But for the S&P 500, 1% of the time we get a loss that's more than double that, 2.16 times bigger to be precise.

Summary statistics for S&P 500

I could continue discussing performance statistics for many more pages, and for several additional chapters, but I feel the statistics we have so far are sufficient to judge the performance and risk of any given trading strategy. Here's a summary of the statistics I've calculated for the S&P 500:

Strategy: Buy and hold, single contract	S&P 500 micro future
Years of data	41
Mean annual return	6.0%
Average drawdown	−23.2%
Annualised standard deviation	19.2%
Sharpe ratio	0.31
Skew	−1.37
Lower tail	2.16
Upper tail	1.60

Buy and hold with US 10-year bond futures

We originally decided to buy and hold the S&P 500 micro future to benefit from the equity risk premium. We can earn another well-known financial risk premium from taking interest rate risk (also known as *duration* risk). We can realise this through holding bond futures, of which the US 10-year government bond is one of the most liquid.

The relevant information about the contract is shown below:

Instrument	US 10-year bond future ('T-note')
Symbol and Exchange	TN, CBOT
Futures multiplier	$1,000
Tick size	0.015625 (1/64)
Commission	$0.85
Current cost of trading, per contract	$8.6625
Delivery	Physical
Expiry months	Quarterly: March, June, September, December
Roll pattern	Hold first contract until around 25 days before expiry

The raw futures contract prices, and back-adjusted prices, are shown in figure 7.

FIGURE 7: RAW AND BACK-ADJUSTED PRICE SERIES FOR US 10-YEAR BOND FUTURES

You may find this plot quite startling; the adjusted price series significantly outperforms the raw futures price, and has done so consistently over time. Almost all of this is due to significantly higher levels of carry.

One consequence of this high carry, and the length of time we have data for, is that the back-adjusted price is actually negative for the first few years. This is nothing to worry about, as long as we ensure our strategies aren't sensitive to negative prices. In fact, the current price of crude oil futures did actually go negative in March 2020, in response to the COVID-19 pandemic. Fortunately my trading system code had been written to be robust in the presence of negative numbers and this did not cause any computer glitches!

Magic numbers and round numbers

An unwanted side effect of using adjusted prices is that we can't incorporate 'magic' or 'round' numbers into our strategies, because market participants wouldn't be using adjusted prices for their trading decisions but the actual futures prices that prevailed in the market at that time. Here's an example of one magic number strategy, based on the Fibonacci series:

> *Suppose the price of a stock rises $10 and then drops $2.36. In that case, it has retraced 23.6%, which is a Fibonacci number. Fibonacci numbers are found throughout nature. Therefore, many traders believe that these numbers also have relevance in financial markets.*
>
> **Source: investopedia.com**

I am not one of these many traders. Personally, I think Fibonacci numbers are complete hokum.

Round number strategies are marginally more plausible. Most people who are putting in stops (orders to close or open positions if some price level is achieved) will choose round numbers for their stop levels (e.g. $10 rather than $10.02). So we might expect unusual patterns of price movements nearer to round numbers (and if you are using stops, you might want to avoid round numbers!).

If you really wanted to use such strategies then you could use the current futures price rather than the adjusted price as an input into your model. But, if you do this your strategy would have a different opinion just after a roll has taken place, as the current futures price will change without anything meaningful happening in the market.

In any case, there is also debate as to whether we should use spot or futures prices with magic or round number strategies. People may think that 4,000 is an important technical level on the S&P 500, but that could equate to a less meaningful 4,013 on the future. If you're going to use magic numbers you need to decide whether the spot or futures traders are the primary driver of the market.

I prefer to use the adjusted price as it means my strategy will consistently keep its positions through a roll, and because I'm not a disciple of either magic or round number strategies.

Following the same procedure as for S&P 500 micro futures, I calculated the US$ profits from holding a single US 10-year bond future, and assumed that I had to use sufficient capital to cover my entire current notional exposure. Then I divided US$ profits into capital to get percentage returns, which are shown in figure 8.

FIGURE 8: BUY & HOLD PERCENTAGE RETURNS FROM A SINGLE US 10-YEAR BOND FUTURE

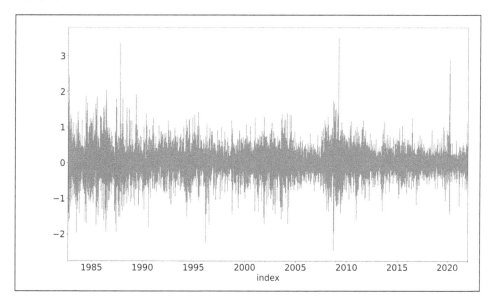

Compare and contrast with figure 5: this is clearly much better behaved than the S&P 500! I then cumulated up the percentage returns, which you can see in figure 9.

FIGURE 9: BUY & HOLD ACCOUNT CURVE FOR A SINGLE US 10-YEAR BOND FUTURE

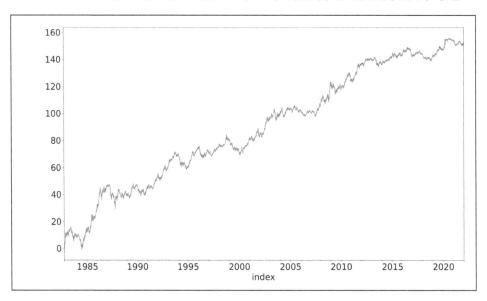

Strategy: Buy and hold, single contract	US 10-year bond future
Years of data	41
Mean annual return	3.75%
Average drawdown	−3.90%
Annualised standard deviation	6.39%
Sharpe ratio	0.59
Skew	0.15
Lower tail	1.49
Upper tail	1.36

Being long US bonds has been an extraordinarily profitable and yet relatively safe trade over the last four decades. Of course much of that profit is down to a secular fall in US interest rates, but US bond futures have continued to earn carry even in periods when rates were flat or even rising.

We can also see that the small positive skew and relatively low percentile ratios imply that 10-year US bond returns have been reasonably close to a normal distribution.

Buy and hold with crude oil futures

I won't bore you with details of every single futures contract, but it's worth looking at a couple more instruments before I start summarising the results of the buy and hold strategy. Firstly, let's consider WTI (West Texas Intermediate) crude oil futures.

Instrument	WTI Crude Oil futures (full size)
Symbol and Exchange	CL, NYMEX
Futures multiplier	$1,000
Tick size	0.01
Commission	$0.85
Current cost of trading, per contract	$10.425
Delivery	Physical
Expiry months	Monthly
Roll pattern	Hold next December contract until 40 days before expiry

That should all be unsurprising, with the possible exception of the roll pattern. Why do I hold the December contract? Why do I roll it 40 days before expiry?

Well, commodity prices are affected by the weather, something that is not a serious issue for the S&P or US bond futures. There is a seasonal component[37] in crude oil prices, and this is true to an extent in most other commodities.

It will usually suit us to remove this seasonal component and focus on the 'true' movement in the price. So when we can, we should stick to trading a specific month in the year. I've chosen December, since it is one of the more liquid months. Unfortunately this isn't possible for every commodity future as it requires at least the next year or so of contracts to be liquid.[38] So it's not a viable option for the mini version of the WTI Crude contract, nor for natural gas futures.

As for the question of rolling so long before expiry: this is to suit a particular trading strategy that is based on the expected *carry*, and I'll discuss it in chapter ten.

---

37 Actually the seasonality of crude oil isn't too much of an issue because it's relatively cheap to store. Seasonality is much more of a problem for natural gas, which is expensive to store, and agricultural commodities with limited shelf life.

38 This will also depend on your account size. A smaller trader might be able to trade months that aren't liquid enough for a large fund.

Strategy: Buy and hold, single contract	WTI Crude Oil futures
Years of data	33
Mean annual return	4.03%
Average drawdown	−66.9%
Annualised standard deviation	27.7%
Sharpe ratio	0.15
Monthly skew	−0.49
Lower tail	1.81
Upper tail	1.33

Crude oil is risky, with a high standard deviation, and also subject to downward shocks (negative skew, high relative lower tail ratio). But like many commodities it will tend to perform well when macroeconomic conditions are running hot and inflation is rising. Bonds do famously badly when inflation is high, and with stocks the picture is mixed, so it seems that WTI Crude can provide us with an additional source of risk premium: an inflation hedge.[39]

Buy and hold with VIX futures

The final future I'm going to look at in some detail is the VIX future. The underlying index is effectively an aggregation of the expected volatility of all the stocks in the S&P 500, calculated using option prices. The VIX will rise when US equities are perceived to be riskier, and fall when investors feel more relaxed.

Instrument	Volatility index futures (VIX)
Symbol and Exchange	VX, CBOE
Futures multiplier	$1,000
Tick size	0.05
Commission	$0.85
Current cost of trading, per contract	$25.85
Delivery	Cash
Expiry months	Weekly and then monthly
Roll pattern	Hold second monthly contract

---

39   Also, oil often performs well during times of conflict, such as the 2022 Russian invasion of Ukraine.

I focus on holding the second monthly contract for VIX. So, for example, if it was 1st March 2022, I would be holding April 2022 VIX. I will roll into May 2022 sometime in mid-March, before the March contract expires and April becomes the first contract (and May will be the second). The reasons for this are explained in Part Six, when I discuss contract selection in more detail.

Figure 10 is not a picture of a particularly dangerous roller-coaster or ski slope, as you may have initially thought, but is the cumulated percentage return series for a single VIX contract buy and hold strategy. The strategy does well in times of market crisis, most obviously in 2008 and 2020. But the rest of the time it drifts downwards, consistently losing money. In fact if we were stupid enough to hang on to this position, and keep topping up our trading account, we'd eventually lose over six times our starting capital.

FIGURE 10: ACCOUNT CURVE FOR BUY & HOLD STRATEGY ON SINGLE VIX CONTRACT

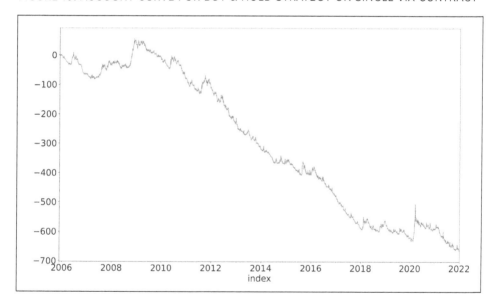

Strategy: Buy and hold, single contract	Volatility index futures (VIX)
Years of data	17
Mean annual return	−40.6%
Average drawdown	More than 100%
Annualised standard deviation	45.9%
Sharpe ratio	−0.88
Monthly skew	0.96
Lower tail	1.34
Upper tail	1.96

Unlike the other instruments in this chapter, we're not earning a risk premium here, but paying one out. Constantly buying[40] VIX is a bet that volatility will rise. We're effectively purchasing an insurance policy: we pay a small premium every day (the negative return), and occasionally get a big payout (as in 2008 and 2020). This is a strategy with substantial positive skew and those payouts create a nice fat upper tail. But the payouts are insufficient to overcome the drag of the premiums. In the long run, properly managed insurance companies always make money!

It could make sense to run this strategy to provide insurance for a portfolio of long equities, but not on an outright basis. Remember my guiding principle from earlier in the chapter: "It is smart to take a risk that most other people are unwilling, or unable, to take. Usually if you are willing to take more risk, then you will earn higher returns." We ought to be willing to take the risk, and *sell* rather than buy the VIX. As you might expect, the more sophisticated strategies in this book will generally have a bias towards being short VIX futures.

---

40 If you're familiar with options, buying the VIX is effectively like buying a delta hedged straddle, or going long on a variance swap.

Summary statistics for buy and hold futures trading

This book is already too long, so I won't bore you with a detailed look at the other 99 futures in my data set. Instead let's look at some summary statistics[41] for instruments in different asset classes.[42] These are in tables 3 and 4. I will use similar tables throughout the book. Table 3 shows the financial assets: equities, volatility, FX and bonds. Table 4 has the commodities: energies, metals and agricultural (Ags) markets, plus the median across all instruments, irrespective of asset class.

TABLE 3: INDIVIDUAL PERFORMANCE FOR BUY AND HOLD ACROSS FINANCIAL ASSET CLASSES

	Equity	Vol	FX	Bond
Mean annual return	7.6%	−51.6%	−0.39%	3.2%
Standard deviation	28.9%	64.6%	15.0%	6.3%
Sharpe ratio	0.30	−0.80	−0.03	0.57
Skew	−0.78	0.73	−0.18	0.11
Lower tail	1.98	1.29	1.65	1.62
Upper tail	1.39	1.92	1.42	1.47

---

41   I calculated these figures by running backtests for every instrument in my data set, and calculating all the required statistics: mean return, standard deviation, SR, and so on. For each asset class I took the median value of the relevant statistic. So, for example, the SR shown for FX is the median value out of all the SRs for instruments in the FX asset class. Finally, in the final column of table 4, I took the median across all instruments, regardless of asset class. I use the median as it is more robust than the mean, which can be influenced by one or two extreme outliers.

42   Instruments include those with at least one year of data, and which meet my requirements for liquidity and cost, discussed later in the book. Examples of **Ags** (Agricultural) markets are Corn, Wheat and Soybeans. **Bonds** include government bond futures, like the US 10-year, short-term interest rate futures (STIR) such as Eurodollar, and interest rate swaps. **Equity** consists of equity indices like the S&P 500, but also sector indices in Europe and the USA, e.g. European technology. I do not trade individual equity futures. **FX** includes rates versus the dollar for G10 countries like GBP/USD, for emerging markets such as CNH/USD, and cross rates like GBP/EUR. **Metals** encompass precious metals such as Gold, industrial metals like Copper, but also Crypto: Bitcoin and Ethereum. **Energy** markets include Crude Oil and Natural Gas, but also products such as Ethanol. Finally there are the **Vol** (Volatility) markets: VIX, and the European equivalent VSTOXX. A full list of instruments is given in Appendix C.

TABLE 4: INDIVIDUAL PERFORMANCE FOR BUY AND HOLD ACROSS COMMODITY ASSET CLASSES

	Metals	Energy	Ags	Median
Mean annual return	−0.94%	0.17%	−1.5%	1.35%
Standard deviation	38.3%	43.1%	28.8%	23.2%
Sharpe ratio	−0.03	0.00	−0.04	0.13
Skew	−0.50	−0.38	0.21	−0.38
Lower tail	1.86	1.72	1.54	1.74
Upper tail	1.41	1.32	1.45	1.40

We get positive adjusted returns in only two asset classes: bonds and equities. Elsewhere there are mostly small losses, except for volatility (Vol) where performance is terrible.

Now let's consider the annualised standard deviation. There is a lot of variation across asset classes. Bonds are safest, as you might expect, with average annualised risk of around 6%. FX markets are also reasonably safe. The commodity and equity markets are all pretty risky. Finally, vol is also very – and I wish I could think of a more original way of saying this – volatile.

Vol also has strong positive skew, but most other assets have negative skew. Bonds and agricultural (Ags) markets are the exception with small positive skew, whilst equities are especially nasty examples of negative skew. Equities also have distinctly fat lower tails. Most other assets aren't as bad, although none are perfectly Gaussian. Finally, bear in mind that there is considerable variation across instruments within a given asset class which these tables do not show.

Conclusion

Strategy one is the simplest possible futures trading strategy. But it still involves trading, as we have to roll our exposure. You can't just buy a futures contract, and put it under a metaphorical mattress, as you could if you bought equities. Is something so simple worth implementing?

Trading a single contract with a buy and hold strategy can be lucrative if you can somehow pick the right instrument. But that could be tricky without the benefit of the foresight we have here, and the risks are often considerable. High standard deviations, negative skew, and fat tails all lurk in the return series of most of the instruments we've considered. Although some have decent risk adjusted returns – bonds and equities in particular – it would be foolhardy to assume these will be as superb in the future.

Even if you do not trade this strategy, it's been useful to understand the performance of the underlying instruments we're going to trade. These are the raw materials we have to construct our strategies out of. We'll spend much of this book trying to improve on the statistics above: increasing return, reducing or at least stabilizing risk, nudging skew in a positive direction, and turning account killing drawdowns into survivable hiccups.

Strategy one: Trading plan

Strategy	Buy and hold single contract
Instrument	Any that provide expected positive risk premium (go short instruments like vol with negative risk premium)
Position sizing	Single contract
Capital required	Equal to current notional exposure per contract:
	Multiplier × Price × FX rate
Trading frequency	Opening trade only, plus rollovers

Buy and hold with risk scaling

Let's review what we did in strategy one. We assumed that we had a fixed position: one contract. We then calculated a measure of how much cash – *capital* – we'd need to hold that position. This capital amount was conservatively set as equal to the notional value of the future: our position was fully funded.

But that is not how the world works! When I was working for AHL, a large hedge fund that traded futures, we didn't first decide what markets we wanted to trade, calculate the required capital for the size of positions that we wanted to have, and then go to our investors and ask them to write an appropriately sized cheque. Instead, our investors decided how much capital they were going to provide. Then it was up to us to calculate an appropriate position size.

That is the correct order: given (a) the amount of capital, decide on (b) position size. But what sort of elements would go into a calculation of appropriate position size? In this chapter I will show that the most important input into this process is the *risk* of the relevant instrument. Instruments that are riskier will usually have higher initial margin requirements, so we'd need more cash to start trading them. They also have the potential for larger losses once we're holding them, requiring more cash to cover these losses in the form of variation margin.

We saw in strategy one (in tables 3 and 4) that there is a lot of difference in risk between different futures. If an instrument has higher risk, then we'd want to hold a smaller position for a given amount of capital. In this strategy I will explain precisely how to calculate the right position for a buy and hold strategy, taking risk into account:

> **Strategy two:** Buy and hold, with positions scaled for risk.

As well as explaining the strategy in some detail, I'll also cover the following topics in this chapter:

- Measuring risk.

- Position scaling.

- Determining the correct risk to target.

- Compounding of returns for performance evaluation.

- Calculating the minimum capital required to trade a particular future.

This is a pretty heavy chapter, with a fair number of equations. But it's vital to understand the material here before proceeding, so make sure you're happy before moving on.

Measuring the risk of a single contract

Step one in calculating position size will be to measure **how risky a single contract of a given instrument is**. Let's return to our old favourite, the S&P 500 micro future.

We need to know how risky it is to hold one contract of S&P 500. This will depend on how volatile the price of the S&P 500 future is. We'll measure this riskiness as an *annualised standard deviation of returns*. To make the maths simpler, let's assume for now that the daily standard deviation of the S&P 500 is approximately 1%, which if I annualise using the method outlined in strategy one is 0.01 ×16 = 16%.

The next step is to translate this risk into dollar terms. Here are the values we already used for strategy one:

Instrument	S&P 500 micro future
Futures multiplier	$5
Current price	4500
Current notional value	4500 × $5 = $22,500

We can use these figures to calculate our risk in currency terms, rather than percentage terms:

Current annualised standard deviation($)

= Notional value × % standard deviation

= 22500 × 16% = $3,600

So owning a single futures contract exposes us to $3,600 of risk, measured as an expected standard deviation per year. Not everyone finds the standard deviation measure to be an intuitive measure of risk, so it is worth thinking about what a standard deviation of $3,600 a year implies.

To do this we have to assume that returns are well behaved, symmetric, and drawn from a normal Gaussian distribution. None of this is true in practice, which means the figures I'm about to calculate should be taken with a large bucketful of salt. In reality you should expect the downside to be significantly bigger.

With that caveat in mind, if we assume that the Sharpe ratio (SR) of S&P 500 futures is 0.3055 (roughly what it has been historically), then the average annual excess return will be:

$$\text{SR} = \text{Mean} \div \text{Standard deviation}$$

$$\text{Mean} = \text{SR} \times \text{Standard deviation} = 0.3055 \times 3600 = \$1,100$$

The region of the normal distribution between the mean and one standard deviation above the mean covers around 34% of the entire distribution. As the normal distribution is symmetric the region between plus and minus one standard deviation around the mean encompasses 68% of the distribution.

So 68% of the time, our annual return will be between 1100 − 3600 = −$2,500 (loss) and 1100 + 3600 = $4,700 (profit). Alternatively, this means that we will lose more than $2,500 in any given year at least 16% of the time,[43] or roughly one in every six years.

We could also translate these figures into expectations for daily losses. But any caveats about non-Gaussian distributions are even more important for daily frequencies, and we have the usual problem that converting annual to daily standard deviations relies on some additional assumptions.

Basic position scaling

My method for calculating position size using risk is best illustrated with an example. Let's begin by making a few highly unrealistic assumptions. First suppose we have exactly $22,500 in capital. Next suppose that we're comfortable with risk on that capital of exactly 16% per year, measured in annualised standard deviation terms (I'll discuss how you'd come up with that figure in a couple of pages' time). I call this

---

43 If we spend 68% of our time in the range, we must be outside of the range 32% of the time. Half of that time we will be above the range, and half the time (16%) below it. So 16% of the time we'll lose at least $2,500.

figure the **target risk**. Given those parameters, how many S&P 500 contracts would we want to own?

The answer is **exactly one contract**. We want 16% of risk on capital of $22,500, which works out to 22500 × 16% = $3,600 per year. We also know, from above, that each S&P 500 contract has risk of $3,600 per year. What an astonishing coincidence (not really)!

What if we had twice as much capital ($45,000)? Then we'd require twice as much risk (45000 × 16% = $7,200). So we'd need to buy two contracts instead of one, giving us risk of 2 × 3600 = $7,200.

Now suppose that the S&P 500 was twice as risky. With annualised risk of 32% a year, that would be equivalent to a risk on each contract of 22500 × 32% = $7,200. We'd need half as many contracts. So for capital of $45,000 and a risk target of 16% a year on that capital, equivalent to $7,200, we'd once again only need to buy a single contract.

I can formalise these results into a single equation that accounts for the possibility of different currencies. From strategy one, the notional exposure value of a single contract is:

$$\text{Notional exposure (Base currency)}$$
$$= \text{Multiplier} \times \text{Price} \times \text{FX rate}$$

The price should be for the expiry date we currently hold (*not* the back-adjusted price), and the FX rate translates between the two currencies. The risk of a single contract position measured as an annualised standard deviation (σ) is:

$$\sigma(\text{Contract, Base currency})$$
$$= \text{Notional exposure(Base currency)} \times \sigma_\%$$

Where $\sigma_\%$ is the annualised standard deviation of percentage returns for the relevant instrument in the instrument currency.[44] For a given number of contracts, N, the risk of our entire position will be:

$$\sigma(\text{Position, Base currency}) = \sigma(\text{Contract, Base currency}) \times N$$

Next we need to specify how much capital we have, and a predetermined *target risk* (I'll explain where this comes from later), τ which we also specify as an annualised percentage standard deviation. Given that, we can calculate what our risk target is in currency terms:

---

44 Notice that the standard deviation is unaffected by the volatility of the FX rate.

$$\sigma(\text{Target, Base currency}) = \text{Capital(Base currency)} \times \tau$$

We now set our required position risk to be equal to the risk target in currency terms:

$$\sigma(\text{Target, Base currency}) = \sigma(\text{Position, Base currency})$$

Substituting and rearranging, we get the required position in contracts N to achieve a given target risk:

$$N = \text{Capital} \times \tau \div (\text{Multiplier} \times \text{Price} \times \text{FX rate} \times \sigma_\%)$$

Notice that the following will all result in a larger position:

- Lower instrument risk, $\sigma_\%$
- A higher percentage risk target, τ
- More capital
- A lower futures multiplier
- A lower price
- A different FX rate, where the instrument currency has depreciated relative to the account currency

Let's check that this works for the surprisingly coincidental example from above:

$$N = (\text{Capital} \times \tau) \div (\text{Multiplier} \times \text{Price} \times \text{FX rate} \times \sigma_\%)$$
$$= 22500 \times 0.16 \div (5 \times 4500 \times 1.0 \times 0.16) = 1.0$$

There is an alternative formulation which I will use later in the book, which involves measuring our risk in *daily price points* rather than in *annualised percentage points*. The daily risk in price points (σ_P) is just equal to the current price multiplied by the annual percentage risk, divided by 16:

$$\sigma_P = (\text{Price} \times \sigma_\%) \div 16$$

We can also calculate σ_P directly by taking the standard deviation of a series of differences in daily back-adjusted prices:

$$\sigma_P = \text{Standard deviation}(P_t - P_{t-1}, P_{t-1} - P_{t-2}, ...)$$

This has the advantage that it works even if the current futures price is negative, and gives us the following marginally simpler formula:

$$N = (Capital \times \tau) \div (Multiplier \times FX \times \sigma_P \times 16)$$

Some useful ratios

It can sometimes be helpful to use the following intuitive ratios:

$$Contract\ leverage\ ratio$$
$$= Notional\ exposure\ per\ contract \div Capital$$

$$Volatility\ ratio = \tau \div \sigma_{\%}$$

The *contract leverage ratio* is the ratio of the notional exposure per contract to our trading capital. The smaller this number is, the more contracts we need to hold for a given amount of capital. The *volatility ratio* is the ratio of our target risk to the instrument risk. So if we require double the risk versus what is offered by the instrument, we'd need to hold twice as many contracts. Rearranging the original formula we get an interesting and intuitive result:

$$N = (Capital \times \tau) \div (Multiplier \times Price \times FX \times \sigma_{\%})$$

$$N = [Capital \div (Multiplier \times Price \times FX)] \times (\tau \div \sigma_{\%})$$

$$N = (\tau \div \sigma_{\%}) \times (Capital \div Notional\ exposure\ per\ contract)$$

$$N = Volatility\ ratio \div Contract\ leverage\ ratio$$

Another figure that we'll sometimes need is the *leverage ratio*. The leverage ratio is just the total notional exposure of our position, divided by our capital:

$$Leverage\ ratio = Total\ notional\ exposure \div Capital$$

If we substitute we get the following identity:

$$Leverage\ ratio = N \times Notional\ exposure\ per\ contract \div Capital$$

$$\text{Leverage ratio} = N \times \text{Contract leverage ratio}$$

$$\text{Leverage ratio} = \text{Volatility ratio}$$

So the **required amount of leverage will be equal to the volatility ratio**: our target volatility divided by the price volatility of the instrument we're trading. Note that this is only true if we are trading a single instrument, but this is the case for the first three strategies in this book.

Setting target risk

We've got all the inputs for the formula above, with one glaring exception: the target risk (τ). How should we determine what our target risk should be? There are a number of different factors we need to consider. Our target risk should be the most conservative (i.e. lowest value) from the following:

- Risk possible given margin levels. This is set by the exchange, and/or the broker.

- Risk possible given prudent leverage. This depends on your ability to cope with extreme losses.

- Personal risk appetite. This is determined by your own feelings, or those of your clients if you are trading external funds.

- Optimal risk given expected performance. This depends on the return profile of your trading strategy.

Let's discuss these in turn.

Risk possible given initial margin levels

You can't just buy as many contracts as you'd like, since ultimately you will be constrained by having to put up sufficient margin. Each S&P 500 micro contract currently requires $1,150 initial margin. It would be completely insane, but if we were to use our entire capital for initial margin payments we'd be able to buy the following number of contracts:

$$\text{Maximum N} = \text{Capital} \div (\text{Margin per contract} \times \text{FX})$$

If we substitute for N in the formula, we can work out the implied maximum possible risk target given some margin level:

$$\text{Maximum } \tau = (\text{Multiplier} \times \text{Price} \times \sigma_\%) \div (\text{Margin per contract})$$

Let's take an example. Suppose that we are trading the S&P 500 with risk of 16% a year, current price of 4500, multiplier of $5 and margin per contract of $1,150.

$$\text{Maximum } \tau = (5 \times 4500 \times 0.16) \div (1150) = 313\%$$

That's a lot of risk! You can achieve extremely high risk targets if you use the full amount of available leverage. **For most sensible futures traders, the initial margin required is unlikely to be a constraint on their leverage.**

Risk possible given potentially large losses

Given that it's a little crazy to use the maximum possible leverage, what is a prudent level of leverage to use? We could be fairly conservative, as in strategy one, and use no leverage at all – fully fund the strategy and set our notional exposure equal to our capital. Then we could never lose all of our money, unless the futures price went to zero or below.[45] To achieve that we'd always set our target risk to be equal to our instrument risk.

Alternatively, we could take the view that we'd be prepared to lose a certain amount in a serious market crash. Let's suppose that a 1987 sized crash is possible, resulting in a one-day loss of 30%. Assume that we'd be relatively relaxed about losing half of our capital in such a situation. A one day 30% loss would lose us half of our capital if our leverage ratio was $50\% \div 30\% = 1.667$. From before we know that with the optimal position:

$$\text{Leverage ratio} = \text{Volatility ratio} = \tau \div \sigma_\%$$

So we can calculate the maximum risk target as:

$$\text{Maximum } \tau = \sigma_\% \times \text{Maximum leverage ratio}$$

$$= \sigma_\% \times (\text{Maximum capital loss} \div \text{Worst return})$$

And for our specific example of a 1987 crash:

$$\text{Maximum } \tau = 0.16 \times (0.50 \div 0.30) = 26.7\%$$

———————————

45   As happened in Crude Oil in the early part of 2020.

Whilst it's easy to do this calculation, assuming you can calibrate your ability to withstand large losses, it's more difficult to work out what the expected worst return should be. Using the worst possible daily return in our historical data is a good starting point, but we'll often need some imagination to consider possible worst-case scenarios.

For example, prior to 2015 the Swiss franc:euro (CHF/EUR) FX future rarely moved more than 0.005 price units each day; about 0.5% of the price. Indeed, from late 2011 to January 2015 it hardly budged at all, reflecting the Swiss central bank's policy to stop the rate moving below a pegged level of 1.20. At this point most traders would have thought that 5% was a fairly pessimistic maximum loss; a little worse than CHF/EUR experienced in the 2008 financial crisis.

They were wrong. In January 2015 the central bank dropped the currency peg, and the exchange rate plummeted below 1.0; a move of over 0.20 price units in a matter of seconds, and about 16% of the closing price the previous day.

In retrospect it would have been sensible to look beyond the CHF/EUR market, and consider what happened in other countries when central banks dropped currency pegs. A prudent FX trader would have remembered Black Wednesday in 1992, when the British pound dropped out of the European Exchange Rate mechanism which pegged it to the deutschmark and other currencies. On Black Wednesday and the day after the pound depreciated by around 14%; showing that double digit losses are possible even in normally safe G10 currencies like the pound and the Swiss franc.

Personal risk appetite

It doesn't make sense to take more risk than you are comfortable with. Taking on too much risk can lead to suboptimal behaviour, such as closing positions too early because you can't take the pain of the losses you have suffered. This is especially true if you are managing money for other people; you should only take risk that your clients can stomach. Institutional traders whose risk levels are too high will probably suffer heavy withdrawals by clients when their funds go into deficit territory.

In practice it's quite difficult to calibrate someone's risk appetite,[46] and even harder to do so in the somewhat abstract units of annualised percentage standard deviation. Of course, we could infer what a given risk target implies for the chance of a given daily or annual loss, but that requires making some unrealistic assumptions about the distribution of returns.

---

46 Many wealth management firms and financial advisers have developed questionnaires that try to quantify risk appetite, but this sort of exercise is a long way from being a precise scientific measurement.

One possible solution is to present a selection of typical portfolios, and see which one best represents the trader or institutional client's appetite for risk. For example:

- For a diversified portfolio of bonds the annualised standard deviation will usually be between 2% and 8%, depending on the maturity and credit rating.

- A typical investment portfolio with a mixture of stocks and bonds will have risk of around 12%.

- A diversified portfolio of global stocks will probably have an annualised standard deviation of 15% a year.

- Blue chip individual stocks in developed markets typically have volatility of 20% to 40%.

- An especially volatile individual stock or a cryptocurrency could easily have an annualised standard deviation of over 100%.

Optimal risk given expected performance

Futures traders tend to have a higher tolerance for risk than most people, and the leverage on offer is very generous. So if you are comfortable with the possibility of large losses in a severe market crash, then risk targets of over 50% are not unachievable.

It feels like it would be highly imprudent to trade with that risk target, but would it also be unprofitable? Figure 11 shows the expected final account value for a long-only investor in the S&P 500 future, running with various risk targets. The figure assumes we begin with capital of one unit, and shows the final capital valuation at the end of a 40 year back test using compounded returns.

FIGURE 11: FINAL ACCOUNT VALUE GIVEN RISK TARGET FOR S&P 500 BUY AND HOLD STRATEGY

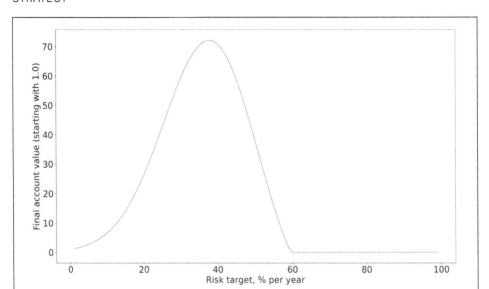

It's clear from this plot that increasing the risk target gradually increases the final account value return we expect, until the target reaches around 40% a year. Thereafter the final account value falls sharply, and goes to zero once the risk target approaches 60% a year.

What is happening here? As our leverage and risk increases, our worst days are getting larger in magnitude. It then takes us longer to recover from those especially bad days. For modest increases in risk target this isn't a problem, since we get a larger offsetting benefit from improving our good days. But once our risk gets too high, those bad days really hurt.

Why do we end up losing all our money once the risk target is too high? Well, the worst day for this buy and hold S&P 500 strategy is a loss of 27% (in October 1987). The volatility of the S&P 500 is around 16%, so a risk target of 60% corresponds to a leverage factor of 3.75. If we leverage a 27% loss 3.75 times, then we'll lose over 100%. Of course, it's impossible to come back from a 100% loss.

The optimal level for our risk target is known as the **Kelly optimal risk**. From the graph above the Kelly optimal for this strategy is a risk target of around 38%. It can be shown that this level is theoretically equal to the SR for the underlying strategy, if the returns are Gaussian normal.[47] In this case the SR is 0.47,[48] which would normally equate to a Kelly optimum risk target[49] of 47%. The actual optimum is lower on this occasion, because S&P 500 returns are certainly not Gaussian normal. Assets with negative skew and fat tails require Kelly optimal risk targets that are lower than implied by their SRs.

Because returns are rarely Gaussian, and because Sharpe ratios are difficult to forecast, it's generally accepted that a more conservative risk target of **half Kelly** should be used. In this case we'd use half the full Kelly value of 47%, for a risk target of 23.5%.

In summary: to calculate the optimal risk target given an expected SR, we halve the expected SR and use the resulting figure as an annualised percentage standard deviation risk target. This will usually give a more conservative value for target risk than the other calculations in this section.

Summary: Target risk

To summarise then our target risk, measured as an annualised percentage standard deviation, should be the lowest value of the following:

- Risk possible given margin levels. This is set by the exchange, and/or the broker. As an example, for the S&P 500 micro future the maximum risk is around **313%**.

- Risk possible given potentially large losses. This depends on your ability to cope with extreme losses, e.g. for S&P 500, assuming we wish to survive a 1987-size crash with half our capital intact: **27%**.

- Personal risk appetite. This is determined by your own feelings, or those of your clients if you are trading external funds. This varies according to the trader, but

---

47 This can be derived from the more commonly known optimum Kelly leverage, which is $f = \mu \div \sigma^2$ where μ is the average excess return, and σ is the standard deviation of the unleveraged portfolio. The optimal target risk with this leverage factor is $f\sigma = \mu \div \sigma$, which is equal to the SR. The Kelly optimum, or Kelly criterion, was developed by John L. Kelly at Bell Labs in 1956 and popularised by Ed Thorp, who started as a card counter before becoming one of the most successful hedge fund managers in history. See the bibliography in Appendix A.

48 There is an apparent chicken and egg problem here. To calculate the optimal risk target you need the expected SR, for which you probably need to run a backtest, which requires knowing what risk target to use! In practice, since the SR is a risk adjusted measure, you can just run an initial backtest at some nominal risk target, then calculate the SR, and then decide what your final risk target should be. Finally, run a backtest with the appropriate risk target to understand the system's likely behaviour. Or don't run a backtest, and just use the recommended risk target of 20% a year.

49 In practice I'd probably be quite sceptical about expecting an SR of 0.47 for a buy and hold strategy on the S&P 500 for reasons I'll explain later, but at this stage it's more important to understand the calculations.

is most likely to be in the range **10% to 100%**, typically with lower values for institutional traders.

- Optimal risk given expected performance. This depends on the return profile of your trading strategy. For S&P 500 using the backtested value for strategy one this is around **23%**.

The most conservative of these values is the final one: **23%**, derived from the half Kelly calculation assuming a SR of 0.46 (which is probably optimistic, but I'll let that slide for now). For simplicity I'm going to use a relatively conservative risk target of **20%** for the rest of this book, which is roughly in line with the target used by many institutional futures traders.

Risk scaling the S&P 500 micro future

Let's see how the buy and hold risk targeted strategy works in practice. We'll use the risk target of 20% per year we derived above, and an arbitrary capital of $100,000. Assuming the standard deviation of the S&P 500 is 16%, we get:

$$N = (Capital \times \tau) \div (Multiplier \times Price \times FX \times \sigma_\%)$$

$$N = 100000 \times 0.20 \div (5 \times Price \times 1 \times 0.16) = 25000 \div Price$$

We'd have to recalculate the required optimal position every day, according to the current futures price and FX rate,[50] by taking the rounded value of N. Every time N changed we would have to buy or sell to ensure our current position was in line with what is required to hit our target risk. This would result in a number of trades, so this strategy will have higher trading costs than strategy one, where we only have to pay for rolling from one contract to the next. I'll discuss in more detail how I calculate trading costs in strategy three, but for now it's worth noting that these extra costs only reduce our returns for the S&P 500 by 0.17% a year.

In the backtest I don't use $\sigma_\% = 16\%$, but instead measure the average standard deviation over the entire time period[51] for which we have data. This comes in a fraction higher at 16.1%.

---

50 For now we don't recalculate our estimate of $\sigma_\%$; I will do this in strategy three.
51 Strictly speaking, this is a forward looking in-sample estimate and hence cheating, since we wouldn't have known that figure when we started our hypothetical trading in the early 1980s. I'll address this point in the next chapter.

Discrete versus continuous trading

As you are no doubt realising, I trade futures a little differently to most people. The way I trade is common amongst quantitative hedge funds, but almost unknown for retail traders. You won't see any discussion in this book about 'opening a position', 'entry filters', 'closing out', or 'stop losses'. Those are all the hallmarks of *discrete* trading. I prefer to trade *continuously*.

What exactly do I mean by discrete trading? It's how most people trade. You decide to open a position. You buy a few contracts. Then at some point in the future you decide to close it. You can point to the chart and say, "This is where I opened my trade," and then point to another point and say, "Here is where I closed my trade." You can calculate your profits (or losses) on each individual trade. You will have an interesting story you can tell about every trade, which is nice, especially if you want to become one of those YouTube or Instagram trading gurus.

I don't get to tell interesting stories (as is becoming clear as you read this book!), because that is not what I do. Instead I *continuously* calculate an **optimal position** (although in practice for most of this book, continuously means once a day). That's the position I would like to have on right now. I then round it, since we can't hold fractional positions. Then I look and see what position I actually have on. If the two are different, then I trade so that my optimal and actual positions are equal.

This means I don't have discrete 'trades', in the sense of positions that were opened and then closed. If I turn on a strategy and it wants to be long three contracts, then I will immediately buy three contracts. If the next day it only wants to be long two contracts, then I will sell one. Maybe I will buy it back the next day. Depending on the strategy I am running, I will probably close the position at some point, and then go short. Where are the discrete trades? There aren't any. Just a series of buys and sells to ensure I always have the optimal position.

Of course, you can still use many of the strategies in this book as a discrete trader, and I will explain how later in the book. But, as I demonstrated in my previous book *Leveraged Trading*, continuous trading is more profitable and, as I will explain later in this book, makes it easier to trade multiple strategies.

Figure 12 shows the number of contracts held over time in the backtest for S&P 500 micro futures. We begin with nearly 250 contracts, since the initial price is just over $100, but by the end of the testing period we have just under six (as the price is over $4,000).

FIGURE 12: POSITION IN CONTRACTS OVER TIME GIVEN RISK SCALING OF S&P 500

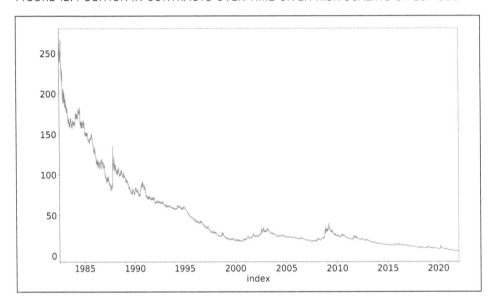

Let us now turn to performance. We can use the same formula outlined back on page 24 to calculate the profit and loss in dollar terms, but with two important differences. Firstly, we have a varying number of contracts over time rather than just a single contract position. Secondly, when working out percentage returns we'll now use the fixed notional capital figure of $100,000 rather than the varying capital figure from strategy one.

One consequence of using fixed capital is that we don't need to plot cumulated account curves in both currency and percentage terms, since the graphs will be identical except for the y-axis. Personally I prefer to plot account curves in percentage terms, since the capital used is to an extent an arbitrary figure.

With that in mind, figures 13 and 14 show the daily percentage returns, and the cumulative sum of percentage returns respectively.

FIGURE 13: DAILY PERCENTAGE RETURNS FOR S&P 500 BUY AND HOLD WITH FIXED RISK TARGET

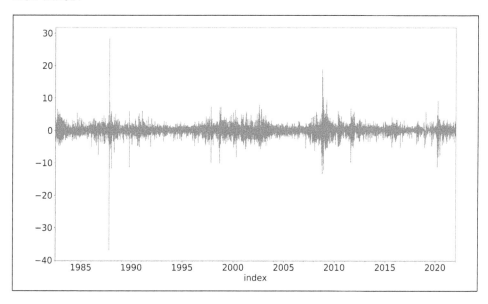

FIGURE 14: ACCOUNT CURVE FOR S&P 500 BUY AND HOLD WITH FIXED RISK TARGET

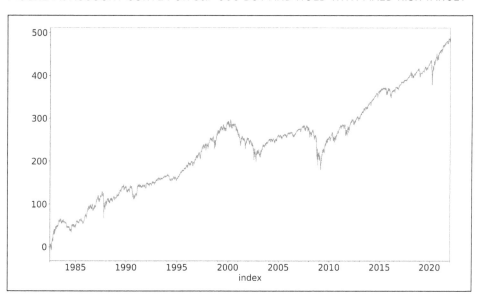

Compounding

Compounding of returns is a very important concept in finance, even if it's probably not "The strongest force in the universe," as Albert Einstein allegedly once said. Earning 10% a year for ten years will double your money with simple interest, but with compounding you can double your money in just over seven years and end up with 160% of your initial investment after ten.

However, with the futures trading strategies which I describe in this book, **we don't compound our returns when backtesting**. After a year of trading the S&P 500 with $100,000 where we've made a hypothetical 10%, we don't increase our capital to $110,000: instead it remains at $100,000. If we did compound, then we'd end up buying more contracts, and then making a greater dollar profit in any subsequent years. Since the number of contracts we hold isn't affected by any profits that we've made to date, we don't compound our returns.

(Strategy one is an exception to this rule. Because it uses the current price to decide how much capital to hold, it implicitly compounds its returns.)

I do this because cumulated account curves for compounded returns are hard to interpret. Assuming you have a profitable strategy, they will show exponential growth, with small variations early on, getting larger and larger over time. For example, figure 4 shows a compounded account curve for strategy one. You can barely see the crash of 1987 without a magnifying glass.

Instead, so that it's easier to see what's happening for the early years of a strategy, I cumulate percentage returns by summing them up over time (I use percentage returns as they can be easily compared, without considering the actual amount of capital traded). In my cumulated percentage plots 100 is equal to 100%, hence if you wanted to know how much profit you would have made trading a particular strategy with a given amount of fixed capital, you can infer this from the cumulated percentage plots.

From this point onwards, all the strategies in this book will show performance statistics and graphs for *non-compounded percentage returns*. Incidentally, this is why I was able to take an arithmetic mean of daily percentage returns when measuring the performance of strategy one, something that would be inappropriate for compounded returns (with compounded returns, to get an average we should really use the compound annual growth rate, CAGR, which is the annualised geometric mean of daily returns).

VERY IMPORTANT WARNING: it would be extremely dangerous to actually run your strategy with real money and fixed capital! An important consequence of Kelly (or half Kelly) risk targeting is that you should reduce your position size when you lose money. A simple way to achieve this is to **use the current value of your trading account as the notional capital** when calculating your required position. Then any losses you make will result in your positions being automatically reduced, and vice versa for profits.

How often should you update the figure for the value of your account that is used for position calculation? I update it daily, but then my system is fully automated. With a risk target of 20%, it's probably safe enough to update it weekly except when the market is under stress, in which case more frequent updates would be prudent. Institutional traders will have to consider the liquidity and rules of their fund, and will usually update their notional AUM on a weekly or monthly basis.

In the final part of this book I'll discuss in more detail other methods you can use to manage the compounding of your account.

Let's look at some performance characteristics:

Strategy: Buy and hold, single contract	S&P 500 micro future
Years of data	41
Mean annual return	12.1%
Average drawdown	−16.9%
Annualised standard deviation	25.0%
Annualised Sharpe ratio	0.48
Skew	−0.47
Left tail	2.21
Right tail	1.79

Overall these figures are better than for strategy one, although it's quite difficult to compare given the very different way that they handle capital. More interestingly, the annualised standard deviation comes in at 25.0%. This is pretty good, although it has overshot our target of 20% because of a few extreme days (if I used monthly rather than daily returns, I get a better annualised figure: 19.8%). Of course, we know from figure 13 that the risk is actually sometimes a lot higher, and sometimes a lot lower, than 20%. I'll address this problem in strategy three.

Minimum capital

In the example above I used \$100,000 for the notional capital. But not everyone has \$100,000 spare. What if you only had \$5,000? How many micro contracts would you buy now, given the current S&P 500 price of 4500?

$$N = (Capital \times \tau) \div (Multiplier \times Price \times FX \times \sigma_\%)$$

$$N = 5000 \times 0.20 \div (5 \times 4500 \times 1 \times 0.16) = 0.278$$

Futures contracts have one substantial disadvantage – they are indivisible. You can't buy or sell[52] 0.278 of a futures contract. This means we can't actually trade the S&P 500 micro future if we only had \$5,000. What then is the minimum amount of capital that we need to trade the S&P 500 micro future? Let's rearrange the standard formula for position sizing:

$$Capital = (N \times Futures\ multiplier \times Price \times FX \times \sigma_\%) \div \tau$$

The smallest number of contracts we can hold, N, is one, which implies:

$$Minimum\ capital\ for\ 1\ contract$$
$$= (Multiplier \times Price \times FX \times \sigma_\%) \div \tau$$

For example, with the S&P micro future we get the following minimum capital with the current price of 4500, an estimated standard deviation of 16% a year, and a risk target of 20% per year:

$$Minimum\ capital\ for\ 1\ contract$$
$$= (\$5 \times 4500 \times 1.0 \times 0.16) \div 0.2 = \$18,000$$

That makes intuitive sense, as in figure 12 we have just over five contracts at the end of the data, using capital of \$100,000.

However even \$18,000 isn't likely to be enough. Suppose we started trading the S&P micro future with \$18,000. On day one of trading we have a single contract. Then a couple of years later the price of the future has doubled (a nice problem to have!).

---

52   Some brokers offer other products such as spread bets and contracts for difference which are sized so they are fractions of a futures contract, but these are not actually futures. See *Leveraged Trading* for more information.

Now the optimal number of contracts to hold is just 0.5. But we can't hold half a contract. We have the choice of either closing our position completely, in which case our expected risk will drop to 0%, or continuing to hold on to our single contract implying our expected risk will be twice its target: 40%.[53]

Neither option is ideal. To avoid this dilemma, it would be nice if we could start off with more than one contract. That way we'll have the option to adjust our position as prices and risk change (and as the FX rate changes, where relevant). As a rule of thumb I advise setting your minimum capital **so that you own at least four contracts when you begin trading**. Four contracts gives us enough wiggle room to keep our position risk at approximately the right level.

How much capital do we need if we want to own at least four contracts?

$$\text{Minimum capital 4 contracts}$$
$$= (4 \times \text{Multiplier} \times \text{Price} \times \text{FX} \times \sigma_\%) \div \tau$$

That would give us \$72,000 for the S&P 500 micro future. Expressing the formula in terms of notional exposure per contract:

$$\text{Notional exposure per contract}$$
$$= \text{Multiplier} \times \text{Price} \times \text{FX}$$

$$\text{Minimum capital 4 contracts}$$
$$= 4 \times \text{Notional exposure per contract} \times (\sigma_\% \div \tau)$$

$$\text{Minimum capital 4 contracts}$$
$$= 4 \times \text{Notional exposure per contract} \div \text{Volatility ratio}$$

Note that minimum capital will be higher if:

- The futures multiplier is higher. Thus, if you have limited capital, it makes sense to use mini and micro futures if they are available: the full-size contracts will have higher minimum capital.

- The price and/or the exchange rate is higher. We would have required less capital in the past, when the S&P 500 future was much cheaper.

---

53 We would have the same problem if the risk ($\sigma_\%$) halved. It's also possible, but probably unlikely, that the FX rate could halve.

- Taken together, the above two points imply that minimum capital will be higher if *notional exposure per contract* is larger.

- Minimum capital will also be larger if the standard deviation of the instrument is higher. With limited capital you will find it difficult to trade especially risky instruments.

- You will require a higher minimum capital when your risk target is lower. This is potentially dangerous, since an apparently easy way to make the most of limited capital is to take more risk with it. Do not be tempted to do this!

Rather than murder several trees with a list of minimum capital for every instrument in my data set, I've put the relevant statistics on the website for this book. Still, it is interesting to look at some of the highlights, shown in table 5.

TABLE 5: VERY LARGE AND VERY SMALL MINIMUM CAPITAL REQUIREMENTS

	Minimum capital		Minimum capital
Schatz (Bond)	$7,600	Palladium (Metal)	$1,880,000
US 2-year (Bond)	$15,600	S&P 400 (Equity)	$860,000
BTP 3-year (Bond)	$19,600	Gas – Last (Energy)	$844,000
Korean 3-year (Bond)	$24,400	US 30-year (Bond)	$552,000
VSTOXX (Volatility)	$26,400	Copper (Metal)	$548,000
Eurodollar (Interest rate)	$29,200	AEX (Equity)	$533,000
MXPUSD (FX rate)	$34,000	NOKUSD (FX rate)	$520,000
US 3-year (Bond)	$40,000	Gasoline (Energy)	$468,000

Current capital required to hold a single contract using a 20% annualised risk target.

Most of the smallest minimum capital instruments are bonds with short duration: the 2-year German (Schatz) and US bonds, and the 3-year Italian (BTP), Korean, and US bonds; plus the Eurodollar short-term interest rate futures. Bonds usually have lower volatility than other assets, with short duration bonds the safest of all.

The European volatility index (VSTOXX), and the MXPUSD FX future are also in this group. VSTOXX has a very low price – it was around 22.9 when I did this calculation (implying the expected standard deviation of the European Eurostoxx 50 index was 22.9% a year). It also has a low multiplier of just 100, in contrast to the US VIX which is also priced in volatility units but has a multiplier of 1000, and hence a minimum capital almost ten times larger ($250,000).

Similarly, the notional exposure per contract for MXPUSD is just $24,000; so even though it's relatively risky for a currency (standard deviation of 8.3% a year), the minimum capital is relatively modest.

At the other end of the spectrum, Palladium has a price of nearly $1,900 a contract, which combined with a multiplier of 100 gives it a notional exposure per contract of $189,500. But it's also insanely risky, with an annualised standard deviation of nearly 50%, resulting in a near two million dollar minimum capital requirement to hold four contracts.

How well does risk targeting work over different instruments?

Tables 6 and 7 show the average performance across different asset classes for strategy two. They are directly comparable with tables 3 and 4.

TABLE 6: PERFORMANCE FOR FIXED RISK TARGETING ACROSS FINANCIAL ASSET CLASSES

	Equity	Vol	FX	Bond
Mean annual return	11.5%	−8.3%	1.5%	12.3%
Average drawdown	−8.7%	−76.9%	−29.2%	−12.5%
Annualised standard deviation	22.2%	21.8%	21.2%	21.4%
Sharpe ratio	0.48	−0.39	0.07	0.60
Skew	−0.40	2.27	−0.24	0.15
Lower tail	1.98	1.30	1.74	1.81
Upper tail	1.54	2.68	1.65	1.53

TABLE 7: PERFORMANCE FOR FIXED RISK TARGETING ACROSS COMMODITY ASSET CLASSES

	Metals	Energy	Ags	Median
Mean annual return	6.7%	6.5%	4.5%	6.3%
Average drawdown	−38.3%	−33.4%	−45.5%	−15.0%
Annualised standard deviation	21.9%	22.5%	21.4%	21.5%
Sharpe ratio	0.31	0.29	0.20	0.34
Skew	−0.13	−0.20	0.45	−0.17
Lower tail	1.80	1.65	1.64	1.82
Upper tail	1.64	1.58	1.71	1.62

The relative picture is similar to strategy one. Equities have unpleasant skew and ugly tails but a decent SR. Bonds are better behaved, and have the highest SR of all. Volatility still has a negative SR, compensated for by positive skew and a fat right tail. The other assets sit somewhere between these extremes. Finally, as we would hope given we are explicitly targeting it, the standard deviation averaged across each asset class[54] isn't far off the target of 20%.

It is interesting to compare strategies one and two. The SR is better in strategy two for every asset class, with the median instrument improving from 0.13 to 0.34. That is nearly a threefold increase! Skew is also more positive across the board, with the negative skew of –0.38 for strategy one more than halved. These are spectacular improvements.

Conclusion

For strategy two I introduced the idea that we should calculate position size according to available capital, and we also saw that position sizing using a risk target resulted in a substantial improvement in performance compared to strategy one. Many people say that diversification is the only free lunch in finance. I would add that **risk targeting is the second free lunch** (or perhaps as I'm English, the free afternoon tea).

Although this strategy is more logical than the single contract version of strategy one, it is clearly still flawed. Even for instruments which do a better job of hitting the 20% risk target, such as the S&P 500, there is still substantially different risk over time. Skew and fat tails remain an issue. Strategy two is far from perfect: we can do better.

---

54   Rebalancing purely because of price changes – as we do in strategy two – could mean we are affected by a phenomenon known as the *leverage effect* in equity futures. In this theoretical setup firms which hold debt will get riskier when prices fall, so we end up with more risk from buying more stock. Hence we'd expect higher risk, and poorer risk targeting, for equities. In practice I don't find significantly different results here across different asset classes.

Strategy two: Trading plan

Strategy	Buy and hold with variable position calculated using fixed risk estimate.
Instrument	Any that provide expected positive risk premium. Consider going short instruments like VIX with negative risk premium.
Position sizing	Long N contracts, where N is the current rounded value of: $$N = (\text{Capital} \times \tau) \div (\text{Multiplier} \times \text{Price} \times \text{FX} \times \sigma_\%)$$
Annualised standard deviation of percentage returns for instrument ($s_\%$)	Take average over backtested data series, or use risk level when the strategy begins trading. See Appendix B for calculation details.
Risk target, annualised standard deviation of percentage returns ($s_{\%T}$)	Set at the minimum of: • Risk possible given margin levels: $$(\text{Multiplier} \times \text{Price} \times \sigma_\%) \div (\text{Margin per contract})$$ • Risk possible given prudent leverage: $$(\sigma_\% \times \text{Maximum capital loss})$$ $$\div \text{Expected worst return})$$ • Optimal risk given expected performance (Half Kelly): $$0.5 \times \text{Expected SR}$$ • Personal risk appetite Or use the recommended value of **20%**.
Capital	Use the current value of your trading account as the notional capital when calculating your required position. Minimum capital required for a four-contract position: $$(4 \times \text{Multiplier} \times \text{Price} \times \text{FX} \times \sigma_\%) \div \tau$$
Trading decision	Calculate optimal position N each day, and round to nearest whole contract. If this differs from your current position, buy or sell contracts as required.
Trading frequency	Daily, although in principle could be done at different frequencies. Trades will not be required every day, but depend on the size of changes in capital, price and FX rates. There will be additional rollover trades.

STRATEGY THREE

Buy and hold with variable risk scaling

Sailing is my favourite sport. Indeed in my early 20s I seriously considered turning professional – but I wasn't good enough. I still sail occasionally now, but I spend more time teaching others.

One of the first lessons we teach novices is the vital importance of adjusting their sails according to the strength and direction of the wind. If you keep the sails pulled in when a gust hits, you're going to end up swimming. Conversely, if you don't trim your sail correctly when the wind lightens, you will lose speed and end up falling behind the rest of the fleet.

This is directly relevant to strategy two. Figure 15 shows a rolling estimate of standard deviation for strategy two: buy and hold with risk scaling, for the S&P 500 micro future. It shows the average risk experienced over the last two months at any given point in time. We already know that the strategy does a decent job of targeting risk on average, since the standard deviation of the strategy returns came out at around 25%, not much over our risk target of 20%. This isn't the Olympic level sailing that hitting the 20% risk target precisely would imply, but it's not a bad effort.

FIGURE 15: ROLLING TWO-MONTH ANNUALISED STANDARD DEVIATION OF RETURNS FOR STRATEGY TWO WITH S&P 500 MICRO FUTURES

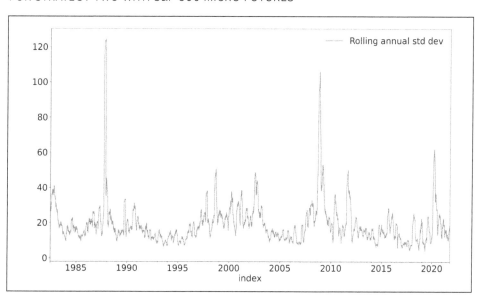

But that's *on average*. It's all very well hitting 25% risk on average, but that includes calm periods like 2017 when the S&P 500 marched upwards without a losing month and the realised standard deviation was under 8%. It also includes extremely stormy periods when our standard deviation went over 50% such as 2020, 2008 and the financial hurricane[55] of 1987.

If only we could know in advance when risk was going to change. Then if we knew a storm was coming we could reef down our sails, batten down the hatches and reduce our positions. Conversely, if the market was due to be calm we could put up more sail: equivalent to taking larger positions.

Experienced sailors can forecast changes in the wind by looking at clouds and wave patterns. Similarly, it is actually relatively easy to forecast risk in financial markets, most of the time, just **by using the most recent risk estimate that we've seen over the last month or so**. If we scale our positions according to a recent estimate of volatility, we can make significant improvements to strategy two.

---

55   Coincidentally, there was an actual storm in the UK in 1987 a couple of days before the stock market crash of Black Monday, with record-setting hurricane strength winds (records that weren't broken until Storm Eunice hit in February 2022). One possible aggravating factor in the 1987 crash was that many traders couldn't get to their London desks because of severe disruption to roads and railways. Without the modern day option of working from home, this resulted in significantly reduced liquidity in the markets.

Strategy three: Buy and hold, with
positions scaled for variable risk.

I will be covering the following topics in this strategy:

- Forecasting future risk.

- Position sizing with variable risk forecasts.

- Measuring risk adjusted costs.

- Which instrument should we trade?

Forecasting future volatility

It's very hard to forecast returns, or all traders would be billionaires. But it's relatively easy to forecast risk. That's because volatility tends to *cluster*; periods of low volatility tend to follow periods of low volatility, and vice versa. It turns out that **using an estimate of standard deviation derived from the last month or so of returns does an excellent job**[56] **of forecasting what standard deviation will be in the near term**: over the next few days or few weeks.

To calculate a standard deviation on recent returns we first need to calculate a moving average of returns. If we have a *window size* of N returns:

$$r^*_t = [1 \div N]r_t + [1 \div N]r_{t-1} + [1 \div N]r_{t-2} \ldots + [1 \div N]r_{t-N+1}$$

We can then calculate a standard deviation:

$$\sigma(N)_t = \sqrt{\{[1 \div N](r_t - r^*_t)^2 + [1 \div N](r_{t-1} - r^*_t)^2}$$
$$+ [1 \div N](r_{t-2} - r^*_t)^2 + \ldots [1 \div N](r_{t-N+1} - r^*_t)^2\}$$

If we are calculating $\sigma_\%$, the annualised percentage risk, then we'd use percentage returns for r_t and multiply our estimate of σ by 16. However, if we are working out σ_p, the daily risk of price changes, then we'd use changes in price for r_t and not multiply our estimate by anything. To look at the last month of returns we would use something like N = 22 (given that we exclude weekends and holidays from our data series, there are around 22 business days in each month).

---

56 It's possible to further improve upon this estimate in various ways (and with a lot of extra work), for example by using higher frequency data, more complex volatility models, or implied volatility from options data.

However, there is a problem with this approach. Firstly, if we use the last month of returns, then we will get a noisy estimate. As returns are all equally weighted in our estimate, if we had a large daily return just under a month ago, then our standard deviation estimate would change significantly the following day when that large return dropped out of our estimation window.

As we're going to use our standard deviation estimate as a forecast of future risk, and to decide what our positions will be, a noisy estimate will require a lot of trading as our risk forecast changes. How could we solve this? We could use a more sluggish estimate which looked further into the past and used several months of returns, but that will reduce our ability[57] to forecast future risk.

A better way is to use an **exponentially weighted** standard deviation. This is a smoother estimate which reduces the costs of trading without impairing our ability to forecast future standard deviation. Given a series of daily returns $r_0 \ldots r_t$ the mean will be an **exponentially weighted moving average (EWMA)**:

$$r^*(\lambda)_t = \lambda r_t + \lambda(1 - \lambda)r_{t-1} + \lambda(1 - \lambda)^2 r_{t-2} + \ldots)$$

And the corresponding exponentially weighted standard deviation will be equal to:

$$\sigma_{exp}(\lambda)_t = \sqrt{[\lambda(r_t - r^*_t)^2 + \lambda(1 - \lambda)(r_{t-1} - r^*_t)^2 + \lambda(1 - \lambda)^2(r_{t-2} - r^*_t)^2 + \ldots]}$$

Notice that the fixed weights on each return in the moving average, or squared return in the standard deviation, have been replaced with λ terms that get smaller the further into the past we go. A higher λ parameter on an EWMA is equivalent to a shorter window for a simple moving average (SMA); it will result in more recent prices being given a higher weight.

We can directly compare simple and exponential moving averages by looking at their **half life**. The half life is the number of data points in the past when exactly half of the moving average weight has been used up. For an SMA the half life is exactly half the window length, whilst calculating the half life for an EWMA is a little more involved. Because the calculations to convert between half life and λ are complex, it's more intuitive to define our EWMA in terms of their **span** in data points.[58] For a given span in days N, we can calculate the λ as:

---

57 For example, using the last three months rather than one month of past returns reduces the predictability of our estimate by about 40% (as measured by the R^2 of a regression of realised standard deviation over the next 40 days on the forecasted estimate).

58 The term *span* comes from the Python coding language's Pandas library implementation of exponential weighting.

$$\lambda = 2 \div (N + 1)$$

It turns out that an EWMA with a span of 32 days has almost exactly the same half life as an SMA with a 22-day window: 11 days. So if we want an EWMA that is equivalent to an SMA covering the last month of returns – about 22 days – then the appropriate span is 32 days, which corresponds to $\lambda = 0.06061$. Research by myself and others[59] confirms that an EWMA with a λ of around 0.06 is the optimal λ for forecasting future volatility

Sadly, this does not solve our next problem: although standard deviation tends to cluster in the short run, **it also mean reverts in the long run**. For example, for several weeks during the March 2020 COVID-19 market selloff standard deviations in equity markets were very high. As they were high they were likely to stay high in the short term. However, standard deviations do not stay high forever, and they were always likely to return to less elevated levels. By the summer they were back at pre-crisis lows.

This effect is especially problematic when standard deviation estimates are currently relatively low. As you will see later in the chapter we will increase our positions when our risk estimate is falling. This means we'll tend to have very large positions in the quiet periods just before market crises occur. Not a good idea.

Hence, it makes sense to use an estimate that blends together a long run and short run estimate of volatility.[60] This improves our forecasting power and makes it less likely we'll have huge positions on just before a crisis. It has the added bonus that it reduces trading costs further: because the long run estimate changes very slowly, it dampens changes in the blended estimate.

Given some current estimate of σ_t the blended estimate[61] I use is:

$$\sigma_{blend,t} = 0.3(\text{Ten year average of } \sigma_t) + 0.7\sigma_t$$

From here on when I refer to an estimate of standard deviation of returns, I will be using this method: a blend of long (weight 0.3) and short run (weight 0.7) estimates

---

59   For example, a λ of 0.06 is used by the RiskMetrics methodology developed by JPMorgan. Performance of trading strategies using this volatility estimation will not be substantially different if you used a different span, as long as it is roughly correct. Much shorter spans produce higher trading costs, whilst forecasting ability loses its efficacy if the span is much longer.

60   This is also the motivation behind more complex ways of forecasting volatility, such as the well-known GARCH model.

61   The weight of 0.3 on historical risk and 0.7 on current risk came from a regression of future standard deviation on the two estimates of historical standard deviation. My estimates of these values are stable over time and across instruments, suggesting that the estimates are robust. Retesting various trading strategies using a purely backward looking estimate of these weights did not damage performance, so there is unlikely to be any in sample fitting effect here.

of volatility, calculated using an exponential weighting with λ = 0.06061 (a span of 32 days, with a half life of around 11 days).

Position sizing with variable risk

Recall the formula for positions sizing in strategy two:

$$N_t = (Capital_t × τ) ÷ (Multiplier × Price_t × FX_t × σ_\%)$$

We use this same formula, but whereas before we used a *fixed* value for the instrument risk ($σ_\%$), we replace this with a *variable* estimate of standard deviation as discussed above. So for example, for the S&P 500 micro future with a 20% risk target, we'd have:

$$N = (100000 × 0.20) ÷ (5 × Price × 1 × σ_\%) = 25000 ÷ (Price × σ_\%)$$

You should contrast figure 16 (which shows the position calculation for S&P 500 with variable risk) with the earlier figure 12 (strategy two, page 66), which is the same plot for fixed risk. Figure 12 shows a fairly steady downward trend: as the S&P 500 contract gets more expensive we can afford fewer contracts given our fixed capital. When there is a crash, as in 1987, our position increased as the price fell.

FIGURE 16: NUMBER OF CONTRACTS OF S&P 500 HELD WITH VARIABLE RISK ESTIMATE

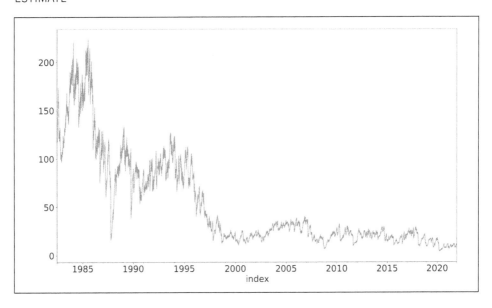

Figure 16 has roughly the same pattern as figure 12, but is also driven by recent volatility. We have smaller positions when our standard deviation estimate rises and crank up our leverage when things calm down. In 1987 when the market crashed, the volatility of the index skyrocketed, resulting in our position being cut sharply, despite the fall in price.

Risk adjusted costs

Adjusting our positions daily as both volatility and price change is likely to lead to a fair number of trades, even if we use a blended estimate of volatility. So it's important that we get a handle on how to accurately measure trading costs.

In strategy one I said we could measure costs per contract traded in currency terms by adding up the commission and the spread cost. I also noted that we'd do a certain number of trades per year because we have to regularly roll our positions, but that we also trade for other reasons. For strategy one there were no other reasons, since we only ever held a single contract. Strategy two results in some extra trading: as the price of the future changes we'd adjust our optimal position. Strategy three has even more trading, as we take account of changes in volatility as well as price.

I also noted that it was a big assumption to measure costs by multiplying the number of contracts traded by a dollar fixed cost per trade. We don't know for sure that costs in currency terms would have been the same 30 years ago as they are now: it seems unlikely!

Fortunately there is an easier way and that's to use *risk adjusted* costs. Effectively we calculate our costs based on today's trading environment, risk adjust them and assume those can be used to estimate trading costs in a historical backtest. Of course that's also unrealistic, but remember that one key purpose of backtesting is to see how feasible it is to trade something with real money in the current trading environment. So using today's trading costs as our starting point isn't an unreasonable thing to do.[62]

Because everything is done in risk adjusted terms, we don't have to worry about exactly how many contracts are traded, and our results can be used for any account size.[63] Using this method also makes it easier to compare costs across instruments, and

---

62   However, it does mean we should be suspicious of trading strategies which trade frequently but were apparently profitable in a backtest until a few years ago. It's likely that past trading costs were higher than the risk adjustment suggests, and the strategies wouldn't actually have made money in earlier years. I return to this issue in strategy nine.

63   That isn't strictly true for very large account sizes: large institutional traders will have to estimate their likely market impact rather than measuring the spread using the top of the order book.

later in the book I will also use these costs to derive some useful rules of thumb about which instruments and trading rules you should use.

Calculations

A risk adjusted cost can be defined as **the reduction in your expected return due to costs, divided by an estimate of risk**. As usual, I measure risk as an annualised standard deviation of returns. A risk adjusted cost is effectively a Sharpe ratio (SR) but with costs instead of excess returns. Hence we can express risk adjusted costs in SR units:

SR = Annual mean excess return ÷ Annualised standard deviation

Costs in SR terms = Annual cost ÷ Annualised standard deviation

If, for example, your expected excess return is 10% a year with a 20% standard deviation, but you are paying 1% in costs then:

Pre-cost SR = 10% ÷ 20% = 0.50

Post-cost SR = 9% ÷ 20% = 0.45

Costs in SR terms = 1% ÷ 20% = 0.05

Or:

Costs in SR terms

= Pre-cost SR – Post-cost SR = 0.50 – 0.45 = 0.05

We already know that there are two sources of trading costs, rolling costs from just **holding** our positions, and costs from **other trading**. To calculate both we're going to need to know our likely **risk adjusted cost per trade**.

First of all, let's remind ourselves of the calculations from earlier in the book:

Spread cost, price points = (Bid – Offer) ÷ 2

That will be valid for smaller traders whose trades can be filled at the top of the order book; large institutions will need to work out their likely market impact. Next we can work out the value of this spread cost, in the currency the contract is denominated in:

Spread cost, currency = Multiplier × Spread cost price points

Some traders prefer to measure the spread in ticks, which gives us this alternative calculation:

Spread cost, currency = Tick value × (Spread in ticks) ÷ 2

Finally we can add on the commission:

Total cost per trade, currency
= Spread cost currency + Commission per contract

In the earlier example for S&P 500 micro futures the bid in table 1 (page 15) was 4503.25 and the offer was 4503.30. This gives us a spread cost of 0.125 in points, or \$0.625 in currency. With \$0.25 in commissions, the total cost of trading one contract was \$0.875.

Since we're measuring risk in percentage terms, it makes sense to calculate costs in the same way. We divide by the current notional exposure of the contract in instrument currency, equal to the current futures price multiplied by the futures multiplier:

Total cost per trade, %
= Total cost per trade currency ÷ (Price × Multiplier)

Finally we can risk normalise the cost per trade by dividing by our current estimate of risk as an annual standard deviation of instrument returns, $\sigma_\%$:

Risk adjusted cost per trade = Total cost per trade % ÷ $\sigma_\%$

For the S&P 500 micro future the current price is 4500, the multiplier is 5 and the standard deviation around 16%. This gives us the following:

Total cost per trade, % = 0.875 ÷ (5 × 4500) = 0.0039%

Risk adjusted cost per trade = 0.0039% ÷ 16% = 0.000243

That seems like a small number and indeed, as we'll see in a moment, S&P 500 futures are amongst the cheapest instruments you can trade. Let's continue with our calculations. Our **holding** costs will depend on how many rolls we do each year:

Risk adjusted holding cost
= Risk adjusted cost per trade × Rolls per year × 2

This assumes – conservatively – that we have to pay two lots of costs each time we roll, as discussed back on page 18. For other trading costs, which I label **transaction costs**, we need to know how many other trades we do annually – the *turnover* of our trading strategy:

Risk adjusted transaction cost
= Risk adjusted cost per trade × Turnover

Then it's trivial to work out the total risk adjusted costs we'd pay over a year. We use a year, because we want the result in annual SR units to be consistent with our other statistics, and we have an annualised standard deviation for risk adjustment.

Annual risk adjusted cost
= Risk adjusted holding cost + Risk adjusted holding cost

Let's return to the example of the S&P 500 micro future. We roll this future quarterly, so:

Risk adjusted holding cost = 0.000243 × 4 × 2 = 0.00194

If other trades are six times a year (I'll explain where this figure comes from below):

Risk adjusted transaction cost = 0.000243 × 6 = 0.00145

Annual risk adjusted cost = 0.00194 + 0.00145 = 0.0034

That would mean for example that if our pre-cost SR was 0.5034, then deducting costs would reduce it to 0.5000 exactly.[64]

---

64   These calculations only make sense if we always have a position on, and if we have a well-defined average position. Later in the book, in strategy five, I explain a more complex calculation for backtested costs which works regardless of the pattern of positions produced by a given strategy.

Annual turnover

What does a turnover of six imply in the above calculation? Does that mean we're trading six contracts a year? Clearly that wouldn't make any sense, as the number of contracts traded would depend on our capital, and this measure of risk adjusted costs is supposed to be the same regardless of our account size.

The turnover above is defined as the **number of times we turnover our average position**. For example, in the backtest during 2021 for the S&P 500 micro future with capital of $100,000 and a risk target of 20% we trade 60 contracts. Over the same period our average position is 9.3 contracts. Hence we trade our average position 60 ÷ 9.3 = 6.5 times. Of course we'd actually want to estimate turnover over our entire backtest to get a more accurate figure,[65] and if I do this I get a figure of 5.1. I rounded this up to 6.0 for the purposes of the calculations in the previous section.

To be clear, what we're doing is calculating our expected costs, assuming that (a) the turnover we saw in our backtest will continue in the future, and (b) our estimate of risk adjusted costs per trade accurately reflects what we'd pay today. I'd argue that (a) should be true, as long as our trading strategies are properly designed, and (b) is a fairly safe bet, as long as we regularly recalculate our costs.

Figure 17 shows the average turnover for S&P 500 with variable risk, estimated on a rolling basis using trades over the previous six months. This excludes rolling costs (which would be another four trades per year). Turnover is fairly constant over time, running at between four and six times a year, with no clear trend over time. Hence it is reasonable to use the average estimate of 5.1 times a year when estimating future trading costs for this strategy. In fact, because this measure of turnover is comparable across all the instruments we trade, we can work out a more accurate likely turnover by taking an average from the results we get from backtesting all the instruments in our data set.

---

65   The precise calculation is explained in Appendix B.

FIGURE 17: ROLLING AVERAGE TURNOVER OVER LAST 6 MONTHS FOR S&P 500 MICRO FUTURES WITH VARIABLE RISK TARGET

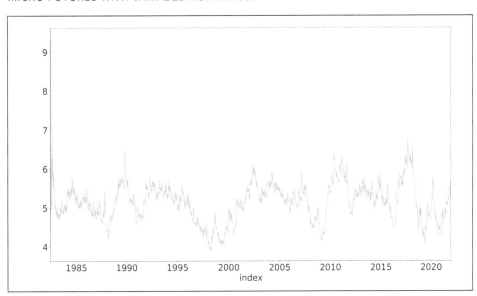

Because I will provide an estimate of the expected turnover for every strategy, you will be able to calculate your expected trading costs for any instrument, even if the risk adjusted trading costs for a given market have changed since the book was published (which they will!).

Estimated costs by instrument

As I've already noted a significant advantage of using risk adjusted costs is that we can compare costs on a like for like basis across different instruments. This is useful: we probably want to avoid trading very expensive instruments entirely. Or we could continue to trade them, but more slowly.[66] So, which futures have bargain basement costs and are the equivalent of Costco (in the UK, Lidl)? Which are pricey and expensive like Whole Foods, or Waitrose? Table 8 has the answer.

---

66   I'll discuss methods for calibrating trading strategies according to costs later in the book.

TABLE 8: VERY EXPENSIVE AND VERY CHEAP INSTRUMENTS

	Cost, SR units		Cost, SR units
Milk (Commodity)	0.083	S&P 500 micro/mini (Equity)	0.00024
Cheese (Commodity)	0.028	NASDAQ micro/mini (Equity)	0.00038
US 2-year (Bond)	0.024	Dow Jones (Equity)	0.00045
German 2-year (Bond)	0.023	Russell 2000 (Equity)	0.00078
Rice (Commodity)	0.022	Gas-Last (Energy)	0.00081
VSTOXX (Volatility)	0.020	Henry Hub Gas (Energy)	0.00081
Iron (Metal)	0.019	Gold micro (Metal)	0.00083
Italian 3-year (Bond)	0.015	Nikkei (Equity)	0.00092

Costs per trade in SR units based on prices, spreads and standard deviation estimates at the time of writing.

Notice that the micro and mini futures for both NASDAQ and S&P 500 have identical costs. This is not a surprise. In the absence of commissions, applying a different futures multiplier would have exactly no effect on risk adjusted trading costs, and commissions are roughly scaled according to the multiplier. Also notice a pattern; thrillingly risky equities tend to be cheap, whilst dull as ditchwater short duration government bonds tend to be expensive.

A comprehensive list of instrument trading cost estimates can be found on the website for this book. Remember, costs will change over time. You should always check any cost calculations before you trade, using your broker's commission figures and current market spreads.

Performance for S&P 500: fixed versus variable risk estimate

We're now in a position to do some detailed risk analysis for the S&P 500 micro futures strategy with variable risk targeting. First of all, let's check to see how well we target risk compared to strategy two: fixed risk targeting.

Figure 18 shows an estimate for annualised standard deviation of returns over rolling two-month periods for strategy two (the darker dotted line, which we've already seen in figure 15) and strategy three (the solid lighter line), both trading the S&P 500. Using a variable estimate of risk (strategy three) results in much more accurate risk targeting, with the standard deviation of returns mostly between 15% and 25%.

FIGURE 18: TWO-MONTH ROLLING ANNUALISED STANDARD DEVIATION OF PERCENTAGE RETURNS FIXED (STRATEGY TWO) AND VARIABLE (STRATEGY THREE) RISK TARGETS

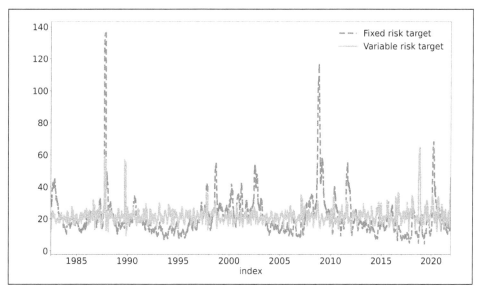

Of course we don't hit our 20% target exactly every day, because we can't forecast future risk perfectly. That's especially true when the market goes completely haywire without warning, like in 1987 when we hit annualised risk of 60%, more than three times our target. But that's a huge improvement on strategy two, whose risk is briefly *six* times the target.

Conversely, when increases in volatility happen more gradually we can reduce our positions and stick closely to our risk target. In late 2008 strategy two goes to over 100% standard deviation; at the same moment strategy three has just 22% risk. The relevant figures during the early 2020 COVID-19 selloff are 62% and 28% respectively.

Overall, the average risk is slightly above target (22.8% for strategy three, a little better than the 25% for strategy two – refer to table 9). This is seriously impressive since the risk estimate used in strategy two was based on the entire backtest and hence was fitted in sample. Strategy three uses a regularly updated backward looking estimate, and so is not cheating.

The daily returns in figure 19 are certainly more stable than those in figure 13, the equivalent for strategy two with a fixed risk estimate. Variable risk scaling has the effect of pulling in outliers[67] and generally making the distribution closer to the classic bell curve shape of a Gaussian distribution. The outliers are removed because periods of high volatility are rescaled back to look like more typical days, as long as the volatility is not a complete shock and has been present for long enough to affect our estimate of standard deviation.

FIGURE 19: DAILY PERCENTAGE RETURNS FOR S&P 500 MICRO FUTURE WITH VARIABLE RISK TARGET

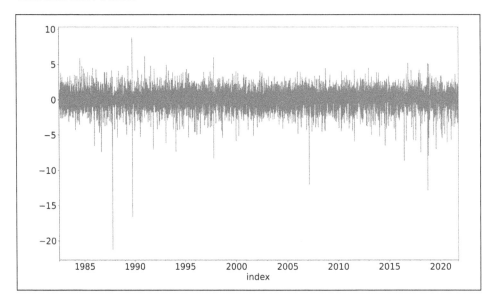

So the risk properties appear to be improved, but what about other measures of performance?

---

67 This is because it corrects for 'volatility of volatility', a phenomenon that produces kurtosis and fat tails. An extreme example of this would be a market with two volatility regimes: high and low, producing a bimodal distribution of returns. If we use a position calculated on a single estimate of standard deviation measured across the entire history of the market, then we'll always have risk that is either too low or too high, resulting in a fat tailed distribution. If we use a variable estimate, then we will have positions on that are correct, except for the short periods when there is a transition between regimes, and our risk estimate and hence position size are temporarily wrong. Although the fat tails won't be completely removed, due to the transition periods, they will be much smaller.

TABLE 9: PERFORMANCE FOR S&P 500 MICRO FUTURES

	Strategy two Fixed risk estimate	Strategy three Variable risk estimate
Mean annual return	12.1%	12.2%
Annual costs	−0.04%	−0.06%
Average drawdown	−16.9%	−18.8%
Standard deviation	25.0%	22.8%
Sharpe ratio	0.48	0.54
Skew	−0.47	−0.68
Lower tail	2.21	1.76
Upper tail	1.79	1.21

It isn't quite a slam dunk for the variable risk estimate. We do have slightly higher returns and slightly lower risk, resulting in a boost to the SR. Costs have increased, as we might expect given we have more position adjustments, but they are still extremely low. Both average drawdown and skew are actually slightly worse for the variable risk estimate. Looking at figure 19, we don't have as many bad days for strategy three, but those we have are comparatively worse than the more numerous large negative returns of strategy two; even though they are actually better in absolute terms. It's this effect that produces a worse skew estimate.

But the more robust percentile measures show a clear reduction in fat tails at both ends of the distribution.

Summary of performance for strategy three

We can't draw too many conclusions from a single instrument, so let's analyse the results across the entire set of 102 different instruments that I have data for, and which meet my requirements for liquidity (refer to tables 10 and 11). These should be compared to tables 6 and 7 for strategy two.

TABLE 10: MEDIAN PERFORMANCE FOR VARIABLE RISK TARGETING ACROSS FINANCIAL ASSET CLASSES

	Equity	Vol	FX	Bond
Mean annual return	9.6%	−8.7%	1.7%	12.1%
Costs	−0.2%	−1.1%	−0.3%	−0.3%
Turnover	3.3	3.4	2.4	2.9
Average drawdown	−12.9%	−87.5%	−41.2%	−14.5%
Standard deviation	21.1%	21.9%	20.5%	20.7%
Sharpe ratio	0.46	−0.40	0.09	0.59
Skew	−0.33	1.43	−0.10	−0.08
Lower tail	1.76	1.20	1.55	1.52
Upper tail	1.17	2.58	1.38	1.27

TABLE 11: MEDIAN PERFORMANCE FOR VARIABLE RISK TARGETING ACROSS COMMODITY ASSET CLASSES

	Metals	Energy	Ags	Median
Mean annual return	6.9%	5.9%	1.3%	6.9%
Costs	−0.3%	−0.3%	−0.3%	−0.3%
Turnover	2.6	2.3	2.1	2.7
Average drawdown	−52.0%	−36.7%	−52.7%	−18.7%
Standard deviation	22.1%	21.7%	20.7%	20.9%
Sharpe ratio	0.32	0.27	0.07	0.32
Skew	0.46	0.07	0.43	−0.09
Lower tail	1.66	1.42	1.36	1.56
Upper tail	1.55	1.29	1.46	1.29

Generally, moving from strategy two to strategy three results in:

- A small reduction in annualised standard deviation[68] and a slight rise in mean annual return.

- The SR is mostly unchanged, except in Agricultural markets where it is a little lower.

- A rise in annual turnover, resulting in higher costs.

- A substantial reduction in the lower tail ratio (which means the left side of the return distribution has a smaller fat tail: we have fewer large losses).

- A similar fall in the upper tail.

- Skew becomes less negative, although there is a large drop in the positive skew of volatility futures.

Risk targeting and expected performance

In strategy two I noted that the ideal target risk (τ) will usually be determined by the expected profitability of the system, using the half Kelly rule of thumb which implies that τ should be set equal to half the expected SR. I used an arbitrary risk target of 20%, which would be fine as long as the expected SR is 0.40 or greater.

But the average SRs in tables 10 and 11 are lower than 0.40 for all asset classes apart from two: equities and bonds. And these are both assets that have seen huge repricing due to secular trends in inflation, interest rates and equity valuations. These trends are unlikely to be repeated in the future.

Even if we used the median SR across all instruments of 0.32, we'd still have too much risk. Like many of the earlier strategies in this book I don't expect many people will trade strategy three, which is here mainly as an educational tool. But if you do, I strongly suggest that you use a lower risk target than the 20% which I've used for my calculations.

Later in the book we will see strategies that can produce higher SRs, which will justify using a risk target of 20%.

---

68   As I noted in an earlier footnote, rebalancing purely because of price changes – as we do in strategy two – could mean we are affected by a phenomenon known as the *leverage effect*. In this theoretical setup firms which hold debt will get riskier when prices fall, so we end up with more risk from buying more stock. Hence we'd expect higher risk and poorer risk targeting for equities in strategy two. Using a variable measure of risk – as we do for strategy three – should improve the risk targeting of equities. Comparing the two strategies there is indeed an improvement for equity risk targeting, but it is very small.

Which instruments to trade

Minimum capital, performance and costs

There is one question we need to answer for strategy three: which instrument to trade it with. Firstly, we need to think about minimum capital, a concept I introduced in strategy two. This is even more important for strategy three, since we'll want to adjust our position as risk ($\sigma_\%$) changes. Risk can easily double overnight, requiring us to halve our position. We'll use the same formula, which assumes we want to start trading with four contracts, giving us room for future adjustment:

$$\text{Minimum capital 4 contracts}$$
$$= (4 \times \text{Multiplier} \times \text{Price} \times \text{FX} \times \sigma_\%) \div \tau$$

Next let's assume that we want to trade the best instrument, which I define as **the instrument with the highest SR after costs**. That means we want to:

- Maximise the pre-cost SR.

- Minimise costs.

First consider the pre-cost SR. The solid lines in figure 20 show the backtested SR for each instrument running strategy three, with the lowest SR on the left and the highest on the right. Only a few instruments are labelled on the x-axis, or it would be extremely crowded. The thin bars are error bars; they show the range of values in which we can be 95% confident of the historical SR estimate, accounting for sampling uncertainty.[69] Instruments with wider error bars have less data, just a year or so in some cases.

For us to be sure that one strategy performed significantly better in the past we'd need to see non-overlapping error bars, indicating that one SR was superior to another, even once statistical uncertainty is taken into account. But almost all the error bars

---

69 Sampling uncertainty occurs because we are unable to measure any variable precisely, as we only ever have a sample of the available data. In trading backtests, we never really know what the SR would be with certainty, since we only have a limited sample: a certain number of years of backtested performance. The shorter the data history, the less certainty we have and the wider the sampling uncertainty. The instruments with the widest sampling uncertainty (longest grey bars) in figure 20 will generally be those with the most limited availability of data. For example, I have just one year of data for Ethereum, so its strong performance shouldn't be trusted. The standard deviation of an SR estimate is the square root of $(1 + 0.5SR^2) \div N$, where N is the number of data points. The thin bars are two standard deviations either side of the mean estimate of SR, covering approximately 95% of the distribution of the SR estimate.

overlap.[70] Although there are fairly large differences between Sharpe ratios in backtests, these aren't actually statistically significant.

FIGURE 20: SHARPE RATIO WITH ERROR BARS ACROSS INSTRUMENTS FOR STRATEGY THREE

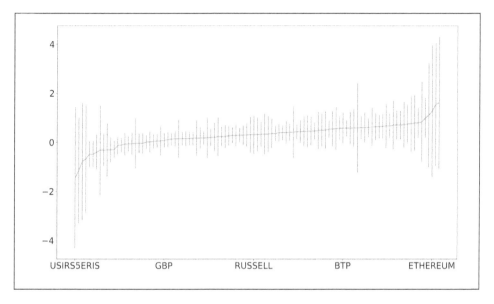

Even if they were significant, there is no guarantee that these patterns will be repeated in future. For example, the excellent historical performance of bonds was driven by a secular downward trend in interest rates, which is unlikely to be repeated.

If we can't use pre-cost returns to make decisions, then we are left with minimising costs, or at least excluding instruments for which the costs are excessive. A useful rule of thumb I use is this: **we don't want to spend more than a third of our likely pre-cost SR on costs.** I call this the trading *speed limit*. If an instrument is trading at or below the speed limit, then we are keeping at least two-thirds of the expected returns after paying trading costs.

What pre-cost SR should we expect to earn trading strategy three? From table 11 if we chose an instrument at random then its backtested SR would be around 0.30. This implies that the speed limit would be a third of this, 0.10 SR units. Let's rewrite the cost formula from earlier in the chapter:

---

70   We would expect a few non-overlapping error bars just by luck, given the large number of instruments we have, even if there were no statistically significant differences in performance.

Annual risk adjusted cost = Transaction costs + Holding cost

= (Rolls per year × 2 + Turnover) × Risk adjusted cost per trade

This needs to be less than 0.10 SR units. Most instruments roll at least quarterly (rolls per year = 4), and the average turnover for strategy three is around three times a year.

(Rolls per year × 2 + Turnover) × Risk adjusted cost per trade < 0.10

(4 × 2 + 3) × Risk adjusted cost per trade < 0.10

Risk adjusted cost per trade < 0.0091

If we round this up slightly, then this implies that we shouldn't trade anything with a risk adjusted cost per trade of greater than 0.01 SR units per trade, since anything more expensive will result in an annual cost of greater than 0.10 SR.[71] A look back at table 8 (page 88) reveals that there are many futures that are too expensive to trade.

Now compare table 8, which shows unusually cheap or expensive instruments, with the previous table 5 (page 72) that lists instruments with especially large or small minimum capital. Notice that the short duration bonds are both expensive to trade but also have the lowest minimum capital.

Generally speaking, instruments with very low minimum capital are also too expensive to trade. When instruments are riskier minimum capital will be lower (since we multiply by $\sigma_\%$ in the minimum capital formula), but risk adjusted costs will be higher (since we divide by $\sigma_\%$ to risk adjust costs). Of course that relationship won't be precisely true, as these calculations also depend on spreads, commissions, futures multipliers and prices. But it's true to say that traders with smaller accounts will have a more limited choice of cheap instruments than those who can deploy more generous portions of capital.

Liquidity

Our cost calculations assume we are able to execute our trades at a loss of half the bid-ask spread. That's a pretty safe assumption for a one contract trade in the S&P

---

71   Subsequent strategies will generally have higher turnover than strategy three, and instruments that roll monthly will have a higher number of annual rolls and hence a lower maximum risk adjusted cost. As a result there will be some instruments which have risk adjusted costs below 0.01 SR which we can't trade with certain strategies.

500 micro future, with a volume of over half a million contracts a day. But what about the non-fat dry milk future, which in its most active expiry month is currently trading less than 50 contracts a day? Can we really safely trade such a thin contract, with the obvious risk that the market will evaporate[72] just when we need to quickly exit a position?

Personally, I'd be unhappy trading **any market with a volume**[73] **of less than 100 contracts a day**. Otherwise, even if I traded a single contract I'd still be more than 1% of the average daily volume. An institutional investor would probably want an even higher minimum volume threshold. However, this rule alone doesn't guarantee that a market is liquid enough to trade. If the futures multiplier is small, or the market has very low risk, then we'd need to take large positions on to achieve a given amount of risk. So I also use another measure of liquidity[74] that accounts for contract risk:

$$\text{Average daily volume in USD risk}$$
$$= \text{FX rate} \times \text{Average daily volume} \times \sigma_{\%} \times \text{Price} \times \text{Multiplier}$$

For the S&P 500 micro future, using the figures we've calculated before for risk and price, we get:

$$\text{Average daily volume in USD risk}$$
$$= 1.0 \times 588000 \times 16\% \times 4500 \times \$5 = \$2.1 \text{ billion}$$

What is a reasonable minimum threshold for daily volume in risk terms? Well it depends on your typical trade size, and how much of the daily volume you are prepared to use up. For my own trading I set a minimum of $1.25 million per day. Clearly this would not cause problems with the S&P 500 micro future! But there are other contracts, including many that easily exceed 100 contracts a day in volume, which do not meet this requirement. Again, institutional traders will probably want to set an even higher minimum before considering a particular instrument.

---

72   If you came here for jokes about liquidity evaporating in dry milk futures, you are reading the wrong book.

73   This measurement should be done by measuring the average volume on the most actively traded expiry date. Don't add up volumes across different months, as you will usually only be trading a single expiry. I use volume averaged over the last 20 business days.

74   There are other sensible minimum liquidity requirements. You might for example want to impose a minimum threshold for open interest, either in outright contracts or risk terms.

Which S&P 500 contract

Many pages ago (page 15 in fact) I promised that I'd explain how to select the appropriate S&P 500 contract to trade. We have a choice of:

- The *e-mini* future, with a futures multiplier of $50.

- The *micro e-mini*, with a futures multiplier of $5.

To decide we need to consider liquidity, costs, and minimum capital. Liquidity is not an issue, with volumes in excess of 500,000 contracts a day for both contracts. Costs come in at almost exactly 0.00024 SR units for both the micro and the e-mini. Finally, the minimum capital required will obviously be smaller for the micro future, than for the e-mini. So I'd strongly advise selecting the micro future, which will allow you to take more granular positions for a given account size due to its smaller minimum capital requirement.

There are many other instruments that have contracts of different sizes, or where the same instrument is traded in multiple venues, so this decision is not an uncommon one to have to make. For the S&P 500 the choice is easy, however this isn't always the case. Mini or micro futures may not meet liquidity thresholds, or be too expensive, leaving you forced to use the bigger contracts: assuming you have sufficient capital. The web page for this book includes a list of suggested markets to use where multiple options are available.

Conclusion

Moving from a fixed to a variable risk estimate does not produce the outstanding performance boost we get from introducing risk targeting strategy two, but it does produce a strategy whose returns are more stable, without the evil fat tails of the underlying assets.

Perhaps the hardest decision to make when trading strategy three is deciding which instrument to trade. Even if we assume that there is nothing to choose between different markets when it comes to outright performance, there is still a difficult balance to strike between minimum capital and costs. There is also the very real possibility that you happen to choose an instrument whose performance ends up being sub-par, regardless of how well it has done historically.

Fortunately, you aren't necessarily limited to trading a single future. There is an alternative option available: trading *multiple* instruments (if you have sufficient capital). I'll look at this in strategy four.

Strategy three: Trading plan

All other elements are identical to strategy two.

Strategy	Buy and hold with position calculated using variable risk estimate
Instrument	Any that provide expected positive risk premium, but which also meet minimum capital, liquidity, and cost thresholds.
Position sizing	Long N contracts, where N is the current rounded value of: $$N_t = Capital \times \tau \div (Multiplier \times Price_t \times FX_t \times \sigma_{\%t})$$
Annualised standard deviation of percentage returns for instrument ($s_\%$)	We initially estimate $\sigma_{\%,t}$ using an exponentially weighted standard deviation with a span of 32 business days (see Appendix B). We then combine this with a slow moving average of $\sigma_\%$, $$\sigma_{\%t} = 0.3(\text{Ten year average of } \sigma_{\%t}) + 0.7\sigma_{\%t}$$

STRATEGY FOUR

Buy and hold portfolio with variable risk position sizing

So far in this book I've covered strategies for trading a single instrument. But there are hundreds of different contracts trading in futures markets across the world. It makes no sense to limit ourselves to a single lonely and isolated instrument. Remember that we're trying to put together strategies that earn *risk premia*. Different instruments offer various kinds of premia; thus a diversified portfolio of instruments should give us access to a diversified set of risk premia. Diversification across multiple instruments also makes it less likely that we'll pick an instrument that doesn't perform once we start trading.

Fortunately, there is a straightforward way to achieve diversification across instruments. All we have to do is split our trading capital into chunks. Each chunk can then be used to trade a *sub-strategy*. Each sub-strategy will be a version of strategy three, each trading a different instrument. Because of the way that strategy three works, we know that we will get approximately the same risk within each sub-strategy. This means that our capital allocation will also be our *risk allocation*: the proportion of our portfolio risk that is expected from a single instrument.

> **Strategy four:** Buy and hold a portfolio of instruments, each with positions scaled for a variable risk estimate.

I will be covering the following topics in this chapter:

- Two specific variations of strategy four: **risk parity** and **all-weather**.

- A **generic** version of strategy four which works for any number of instruments.

- The **Jumbo portfolio**: a set of over 100 instruments we will use to test many other strategies in this book.

- Risk scaling a portfolio of multiple instruments.

- Minimum capital requirements when trading with multiple instruments.

- Selecting instruments and allocating capital.

Strategy variation: risk parity

Why earn just the equity risk premium (beta) or bond risk premium (duration), when we can earn both? Traditional long only investment portfolios consist of a chunk of stocks, and a dollop of bonds. A popular allocation is 60% in stocks and 40% in bonds. With $1,000,000 in cash, you would buy $600,000 worth of equities and $400,000 of bonds.

However, as we know from strategy one, the risk of a typical equity market (like the S&P 500) is considerably higher than for bonds (e.g. the US 10-year bond). With annualised standard deviation in returns of 16% and 8% respectively, the proportion of portfolio risk coming from equities will be much higher than what is implied by their 60% cash allocation: around 75%.

If we adjust our cash allocations so that they reflect the different risk levels, we'd have just 42% of our cash invested in equities, with the remainder in bonds. This would be fine, except that the higher bond allocation implies this portfolio is likely to have significantly lower expected returns than the original 60:40 portfolio, albeit accompanied by lower risk and with a higher Sharpe Ratio (SR).

That lower return is acceptable for investors with limited risk tolerances, but for most this is not a trade-off worth making. Happily this isn't a problem with futures, since we can use leverage to adjust any portfolio to achieve almost any desired target level of risk and expected return. The method we used in strategy three provides us with a neat way to construct a risk parity portfolio which can then be leveraged to hit any required risk target or return expectation.

Let's begin with the basic formula for position sizing:

$$N_t = \text{Capital} \times \tau \div (\text{Multiplier} \times \text{Price}_t \times \text{FX rate}_t \times \sigma_{\%t})$$

Remember for strategy three, we use a variable estimate of the current risk of each instrument, $\sigma_{\%}$. We can now generalise the position sizing formula as follows. The optimal number of contracts for instrument i, given the proportion of capital (weight) allocated to it, is:

$$N_{i,t} = \text{Capital} \times \text{Weight}_i \times \tau \div (\text{Multiplier}_i \times \text{Price}_{i,t} \times \text{FX rate}_{i,t} \times \sigma_{\%i,t})$$

Up until now, our capital has consisted of the entire value of our trading account. For a risk parity strategy, we're going to split our capital into two. Half will be allocated to the S&P 500 micro future, whilst the rest will be placed into the US 10-year bond future. Given a total capital of $1,000,000 with a risk target of 20%, we would calculate our current required positions in each instrument as follows, where both have *weight* = 0.50 (50% for each instrument):

$$\text{N (S\&P 500)} = 1000000 \times 0.50 \times 0.20 \div (5 \times 4500 \times 1 \times 0.16)$$
$$= 27.8 = 28 \text{ contracts (rounded)}$$

$$\text{N (US10)} = 1000000 \times 0.50 \times 0.20 \div (1000 \times 130 \times 1 \times 0.08)$$
$$= 9.62 = 10 \text{ contracts (rounded)}$$

Backtesting the risk parity portfolio

Let's have a look at the performance of the risk parity portfolio. Table 12 shows the individual performance of each instrument in the portfolio, plus the aggregated performance.

TABLE 12: INDIVIDUAL AND AGGREGATE PERFORMANCE IN RISK PARITY PORTFOLIO

	S&P 500	US 10-year	Aggregated
Mean annual return	6.2%	5.6%	11.8%
Mean annual costs	−0.03%	−0.17%	−0.20%
Average drawdown	−9.4%	−7.5%	−6.9%
Standard deviation	11.5%	10.0%	15.1%
Sharpe ratio	0.54	0.56	0.79
Turnover	2.3	5.0	5.1
Skew	−0.68	−0.07	−0.20
Lower tail	1.76	1.28	1.60
Upper tail	1.21	1.19	1.31

There are some very interesting figures in this table. Firstly, the annualised standard deviation is roughly the same on each instrument, indicating we have done a pretty good job of achieving an ex-post equal risk allocation across equities and bonds. But risk is roughly half the expected target (20%) on each individual instrument. That shouldn't be surprising, since each has exactly half the total capital allocated to it and the denominator for calculating percentage returns is the entire capital allocated to the strategy.

Similarly, the average returns are also half what we'd expect to see given the figures for strategy three.[75] Of course, halving both excess returns and standard deviations does not affect SRs and these are the same as they were for strategy three trading just S&P 500 or 10-year bonds.

When we turn to the aggregate figures in the final column we see that the mean return is equal to the sum of the returns on each instrument, as we would expect. But the annualised standard deviation at just 15.1% a year is well below the target level of 20%. What is going on here?

What we are seeing is an example of **portfolio diversification**. If the two instruments had perfectly correlated returns, then the standard deviation would be equal to the sum of the standard deviation on each instrument, 21.5%: very close to the target. But they are not perfectly correlated. The correlation of the two sets of trading sub-strategy returns[76] is effectively zero: −0.004.

As they are uncorrelated, we end up with lower risk than we were expecting. Also, as the mean return is roughly double that for each instrument, and the increase in standard deviation has not doubled, it should be no surprise to see that the SR for the aggregate portfolio is higher than for the individual instruments.

Incidentally, the skew and lower tail measures for the aggregate portfolio are roughly an average of what we get for each instrument, without much diversification benefit (although, for what it's worth, the upper tail has improved). This suggests there is a tendency for both strategies to do badly in certain market environments. The lesson here is that correlation is an imperfect measure of how asset returns co-move. Just like the use of standard deviations as a risk measure, assuming linear correlations is a useful approximation, but we should never forget it does not reflect reality.

---

75   They aren't exactly half as there are rounding effects, which also affect the other statistics in the table.

76   Note this correlation is *not quite* the same as the correlation between the returns of the S&P 500 and US 10-year bond; it's the correlation between the returns of a *trading sub-strategy* for the S&P 500, and another sub-strategy run on the US 10-year. The strategy here is quite simple – variable risk targeting of a long only position – and so the two correlations will be pretty similar, but as we produce more complex strategies which can go both long and short the difference between underlying instrument correlation and strategy correlations will increase. As a rule, correlations are lower between trading strategies than between the underlying instrument returns.

Correcting for diversification

At this point we have two options. We can enjoy the reduced risk, whilst getting roughly the same average return as we would for each individual instrument trading in its strategy three guise. However, we spent a great deal of time carefully calibrating our risk target back in strategy two, so it seems a shame to allow some pesky diversification to spoil all our good work. There is an alternative: we can apply more leverage to the aggregated portfolio until it reaches the required risk target. This will convert the lower risk into a higher return.

Let's modify the position sizing formula above to include a new variable, the **instrument diversification multiplier (IDM)**. The IDM is a number greater than 1 which is calculated so that we hit our expected risk target. We can get a rough figure for the IDM[77] by dividing the target risk (20%) by the realised aggregate risk in table 12 (15.1%): 1.32.

We then multiply all our positions by the IDM:

$$N_i = \text{Capital} \times \text{IDM} \times \text{Weight}_i \times \tau$$
$$\div (\text{Futures multiplier}_i \times \text{Price}_i \times \text{FX rate}_i \times \sigma_{\%,i})$$

If we repeat the risk parity backtest with all positions multiplied by 1.32, then we get the results in table 13.

TABLE 13: INDIVIDUAL AND AGGREGATE PERFORMANCE IN RISK PARITY PORTFOLIO AFTER APPLYING IDM OF 1.32

	S&P 500	US 10-year	Aggregated
Mean annual return	8.3%	7.5%	15.7%
Costs	−0.04%	−0.23%	−0.26%
Average drawdown	−12.4%	−9.7%	−9.0%
Standard deviation	15.2%	13.2%	19.9%
Sharpe ratio	0.54	0.57	0.79
Turnover	5.1	5.0	6.8

Let's compare the two tables, table 12 without the IDM, and table 13 with the IDM applied. The IDM has increased the standard deviation and the mean return, as

---

77   A longer explanation of how to calculate the IDM is given in Appendix B. There are also some approximations you can use for IDM later in this chapter.

expected. The average drawdown scales linearly with leverage, and so this has also increased. Because we're effectively trading positions that are 31% larger with the same capital, portfolio turnover and hence costs have also increased. SRs are risk adjusted and hence unaffected by leverage. The remaining statistics, which I've excluded from table 13 to save space, are also risk adjusted and thus unchanged (ignoring small differences due to rounding).

Figure 21 shows the backtested account curves for strategy three on each of the two instruments, and the curve for the aggregated risk parity strategy. You can see why risk parity has been such a popular choice in recent years.

FIGURE 21: RISK PARITY: ACCOUNT CURVES FOR INDIVIDUAL INSTRUMENTS RUNNING STRATEGY THREE, AND AGGREGATE STRATEGY FOUR PORTFOLIO

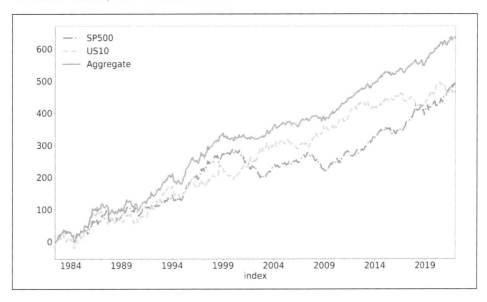

It would be very difficult to trade this strategy without futures. The leverage required varies between 1.5 and 6.0. To obtain that leverage elsewhere would be challenging. For example, it is difficult to find Exchange Traded Funds (ETFs) with more than 2× leverage, and using such funds is particularly dangerous.

Strategy variation: All Weather

The stellar performance of risk parity has two principal causes. Firstly, both bonds and equities have benefited from related repricing effects: lower interest rates and higher price-earnings ratios. The second cause is the very low correlation between US bonds and equities. This results in low aggregate risk and allows significant additional gearing to be applied. What explains this low correlation? Well, since the turn of the century we have had a low inflation environment, and these two assets have been driven mainly by risk appetite. When people are hungry for risk they have bought equities, and when they are feeling nervous they have loaded up on bonds.

However, as I write this chapter in early 2022, there are fears of a return to a higher inflation environment with rising interest rates. Such a period would be unequivocally bad for bonds. Unfortunately, equities could also do badly as a hedge against high and uncertain inflation. After all, they did pretty badly in the 1970s, which was the last significant inflationary decade for most developed economies. It's also the case that correlations tend to be higher between equities and bonds when levels of inflation are elevated.

One solution is to bring in more instruments[78] to pick up additional risk premia which could hedge against inflation. A popular extension of the standard 60:40 equity bond model is the 'All Weather' portfolio, popularised by Ray Dalio, founder of the giant Bridgewater fund. Various versions of this concept have been published over the years, but here is a typical recipe. These are the notional *cash* weights that you can use to build a typical 'All Weather' portfolio:

- 30% US stocks

- 40% long-term Treasuries

- 15% intermediate Treasuries

- 7.5% commodities, diversified

- 7.5% Gold

The *risk allocations* – the expected proportion of our risk coming from each asset – would be quite different; in particular the risk allocation of bonds would be lower than the 55% total cash allocation. Unlike the classic 60:40 portfolio, which has a high risk allocation to equities, there is some attempt here to get an equal amount of risk from each type of asset. There is a lower relative cash allocation to the riskier instruments: stocks, commodities and gold.

Here is a set of instrument weights for my own take on the 'All Weather' portfolio. As these are instrument weights, they reflect risk allocations not cash weightings. Because we scale positions according to expected standard deviation, these instrument weights don't require any adjustment to reflect different levels of risk across instruments.

---

78   This brings us closer to the mythical 'market portfolio' of the Capital Asset Pricing Model, which in theory would contain every investable asset in the world.

- 25% US stocks: S&P 500 micro futures
- 25% bonds, made up of:
  - 12.5% long-term Treasuries: US 10-year bond futures
  - 12.5% intermediate Treasuries: US 5-year bond futures
- 25% diversified commodities, made up of:
  - 12.5% WTI Crude Oil mini futures
  - 12.5% Corn futures
- 25% Gold: Gold micro futures

I constructed these weights by first splitting my capital into four equal buckets, one for each asset class: stocks, bonds, commodities and gold. Then for bonds and commodities where I have multiple instruments, I split the capital again.

We can use the same position sizing formula as we did for risk parity, replacing the instrument weights and various instrument specific parameters as appropriate. I calculated the IDM for this portfolio as 1.81. This is higher than the IDM for the risk parity strategy, as we have more instruments providing additional diversification.

The results[79] for the All Weather strategy are shown in tables 14 and 15.

TABLE 14: INDIVIDUAL PERFORMANCE IN ALL WEATHER STRATEGY, FINAL IDM 1.81

	S&P 500	US 10-year	US 5-year
Mean annual net return	5.2%	2.8%	2.8%
Mean annual costs	−0.03%	−0.09%	−0.07%
Average drawdown	−9.2%	−3.2%	−3.3%
Standard deviation	10.1%	4.6%	4.6%
Sharpe ratio	0.52	0.60	0.61
Turnover	5.2	5.1	5.1
Skew	−0.48	−0.04	−0.01
Lower tail	1.83	1.39	1.42
Upper tail	1.21	1.27	1.34

---

79   The individual results for S&P 500 and US 10-year are slightly different from what we've seen before, as I've had to push forward the starting date of this backtest by a few years as there is less data history available for the US 5-year bond and Crude Oil futures.

TABLE 15: INDIVIDUAL AND AGGREGATE PERFORMANCE IN ALL WEATHER STRATEGY, FINAL IDM 1.81

	Crude oil	Corn	Gold	Aggregate
Mean annual net return	1.8%	0.0%	2.00%	14.7%
Mean annual costs	−0.09%	−0.03%	−0.04%	−0.34%
Average drawdown	−7.2%	−14.3%	−23.8%	−10.2%
Standard deviation	5.0%	4.8%	10.1%	19.1%
Sharpe ratio	0.36	0.00	0.19	0.77
Turnover	5.1	5.0	5.3	9.3
Skew	−0.22	0.11	0.47	−0.26
Lower tail	1.57	1.40	1.72	1.50
Upper tail	1.28	1.55	1.52	1.21

Let's focus on the standard deviation figures. We can see that these are roughly similar for the instruments with ⅛ weights (crude, corn and the two bond futures); and about twice that for the two instruments with ¼ weights (S&P 500 and gold). The overall portfolio risk is 19.1%, fairly close to our expected target of 20%, so the IDM is doing its job.

The portfolio SR is higher than for any individual instrument, but you might be disappointed to see a slightly lower SR and annualised return than we had for risk parity in table 13, with a worse drawdown. Although we've added more diversification, some of the additional instruments have significantly lower SR than the original S&P 500 and US 10-year bond. Crude oil, gold and especially corn drag down the overall SR, detracting from the benefits we'd expect from adding uncorrelated instruments to the strategy.

Proponents of the All Weather portfolio would no doubt argue that we have to be wary of trusting backtest results. There are good reasons to expect lower returns for equities and bonds in the future, which would severely affect the risk parity portfolio. The All Weather portfolio will also benefit if inflation drives up commodity and gold prices.

Strategy variation: generalised risk premia portfolio

Now let's turn to a generic strategy consisting of any given number of instruments. We need to consider how to choose the relevant instruments to include and what instrument weights to allocate to them.

Which instruments to trade

We can use the same criteria as we did for strategy three when selecting instruments:

- Risk adjusted cost below 0.01 SR units.

- Average daily volume of at least 100 contracts, and annualised standard deviation in dollar terms of greater than $1.5 million.

- Minimum position of at least four contracts given our available capital.

We need to modify our minimum capital formula to reflect the fact we have multiple instruments in our strategy. The required minimum capital to hold four contracts in a given instrument i will be:

Minimum capital 4 contracts

$$= (4 \times \text{Multiplier}_i \times \text{Price}_{i,t} \times \text{FX rate}_{i,t} \times \sigma_{\%i,t}) \div (\text{IDM} \times \text{Weight}_{i,t} \times \tau)$$

Clearly this means that the minimum capital will be higher to hold a given instrument in strategy four, versus strategy three. For example, suppose we need $50,000 to get a four contract position in one particular instrument traded with strategy three. Then if we trade it in strategy four with one other instrument, each with equal weights, we would need twice as much – $100,000 – to maintain a four contract position. That assumes an IDM of 1; a more realistic IDM of say 1.3 would reduce the required total minimum capital to $83,333, but this is still considerably more than $50,000.

How to set instrument weights

Deciding which weights to allocate to a given instrument is equivalent to the well-known problem in finance of portfolio optimisation: deciding how much cash to allocate to a given asset within a portfolio. However, instead of assets, we have *sub-strategies*, each one trading a different instrument. And instead of cash, we are allocating *risk capital* by setting instrument weights.

There are other important differences between the usual portfolio optimisation process and constructing portfolios of trading sub-strategies. Each sub-strategy is effectively a mini strategy three, set up so that it will have the same expected risk. Hence our instrument weights are agnostic as to whether we are allocating to a high risk equity, or to a low risk bond. We don't have to estimate a *covariance matrix*, which embodies both the standard deviation and correlation of our assets; instead we just need the *correlation matrix*: a set of estimates for all pairwise correlations[80] between sub-strategy returns.

Also, we don't need to worry about the 'efficient frontier' – the set of optimal portfolios that achieve different levels of risk in the standard optimisation method. Assuming a sensible risk target we'll always have access to enough leverage such that we can choose the instrument weights we want, and then calculate the required IDM to achieve our risk target.

Futures and the efficient frontier

The efficient frontier is a core component in portfolio optimisation theory. It shows the best possible portfolios that can be achieved by an investor who does not have access to leverage. Since different investors have different preferences for risk, there is more than one such portfolio. For example, an investor with a high tolerance for risk will choose a portfolio containing significantly more equities than bonds, since they can cope with the higher risk and desire the higher return.

Conversely, an investor who dislikes risk would have more bonds in their portfolio, accepting the lower return that is offered. If we join together all possible sets of weights that are optimal for a given risk tolerance, we get a curved line: the efficient frontier. Unless you are an investor with very low tolerance for risk, it's impossible to do better than this line without using leverage, so we must choose the point on the line which corresponds to our preferred risk appetite.

None of this applies to futures traders. They can achieve any level of risk they require, within reason. If the optimal combination of instrument weights happens to produce a portfolio with a 10% annualised standard deviation, and their risk target is 20%, then they just need to double the size of their positions by applying an IDM of 2. As long as the trader does not run into any issues with margin, they will be fine. And margin issues are unlikely to be a problem as long as their risk target is not excessively high.

---

80   As I mentioned in an earlier footnote, the correlations for trading sub-strategies will generally be closer to zero than for instrument returns. If you're familiar with the maths behind portfolio optimisation, you will know that this makes the optimisation more robust, since performing optimisation with highly correlated assets tends to result in extreme portfolio weights.

Finally, we will not wish to trade sub-strategies that are expected to lose money.[81] This means that negative instrument weights are not permitted: they must be zero or positive. With all that in mind, what will determine the correct instrument weights? The potential factors are:

- The expected pre-cost SR: better performing instruments should get a higher weight.

- The costs of trading a given instrument: cheaper instruments will get a higher weight, since their after costs SR will be higher.

- The correlation between instruments: we want a higher weight to instruments that are more diversifying.

We already know from our analysis for strategy three that we can dismiss the first of these points. There is insufficient statistical evidence to suggest that any one instrument is likely to outperform another on a pre-cost basis, with the possible exception of the poorly performing volatility instruments (VIX and VSTOXX).

In contrast, there is very clear evidence that different instruments have different trading costs. But we already avoid trading anything which is too expensive by enforcing a maximum risk adjusted cost of SR of 0.01 units. As a result costs will not significantly impact optimal instrument weights,[82] and in the interests of simplicity can safely be ignored.

We might also be tempted to allocate more to instruments so that we can meet minimum capital requirements. For example, suppose that we have two instruments A and B with minimum capital of \$40,000 (A) and \$60,000 (B) respectively, so a total account size of \$100,000, and for simplicity assume an IDM of 1. In the absence of any useful information about post cost SRs we'd allocate 50% to each instrument. But this means we wouldn't hit the minimum capital required on instrument B.

It would be tempting to tweak our instrument weights to 40% (A) and 60% (B) to get round this problem. However, this means you are making an implicit bet that the sub-strategy on instrument B is expected to outperform instrument A, without

---

81 If a sub-strategy is expected to lose money, either its costs are too high (which is something we can avoid by excluding expensive instruments which exceed the speed limit for a given strategy), or its pre-cost SR is strongly negative (for example, a buy and hold VIX strategy). There is potential for over fitting when excluding money losing strategies on the basis of their pre-cost SR, without a good reason. I discuss this more in my first book, *Systematic Trading*.

82 Let me prove why this is so. Consider an imaginary portfolio with two instruments, both with the same expected SR of 0.3, whose returns are uncorrelated with a 20% standard deviation target. One has zero costs, the other is the most expensive instrument I would consider trading with costs per trade of 0.01 SR units. The theoretically optimal instrument weights would be approximately 55% (for the zero cost instrument) and 45% respectively. But ignoring costs and using weights of 50/50 would reduce our expected portfolio returns by only 0.06% per year. This is an extreme example, and in reality the benefits of optimising with costs in mind are usually negligible.

any evidence to support it. A modest reweighting of this size is acceptable, but if the required weights to achieve minimum capital levels were 1% and 99% that would be a very different matter. If we had three or more instruments then applying this kind of jiggery pokery would also get rather complicated.

Naturally you should check that each instrument meets its minimum capital requirement for a given instrument weight, but minimum capital levels should not influence how you actually set instrument weights.

An algorithm for allocating instrument weights

At this point if you have a favourite method for portfolio optimisation and the necessary data to estimate correlations, then you can go away and come up with your own instrument weights. If you don't, then don't panic. Firstly, be assured that having exactly the right set of instrument weights is relatively unimportant. It's impossible to know which trading sub-strategies will perform best ahead of time, and any sensible approach will have expected returns that are almost indistinguishable from those with weights derived with the most sophisticated optimisation technology.

Secondly, it's actually quite easy to sensibly allocate instrument weights without requiring any software.[83] The secret is to use a *top down* method, which I've named **handcrafting** (since the weights can be created 'by hand', with only a pencil and paper, and perhaps a calculator – although it's much easier with a spreadsheet). The method assumes that grouping instruments by asset classes is the optimal approach, so I'm effectively assuming that correlations within asset classes are higher than those across asset classes.[84]

In fact, we've already seen this method in action, as I used it for the All Weather strategy:

- Firstly, I split the available capital into four equal buckets, one for each *asset class*: equities, bonds, commodities and Gold.

- Then for bonds and commodities I further split them into two, as there were two instruments in each of those buckets.

We can generalise this approach for any number of instruments:

---

[83] The approach here is also described in my first book, *Systematic Trading*, where I also discuss the general problem of portfolio optimisation in more detail. More details, and an implementation in the Python language, are available on the website for this book. That is a slightly different method from the method presented here, since for automated implementation we need to use a systematic method of clustering instruments by correlation.

[84] If I test this assumption by grouping instruments using only correlations, then I get very similar results, although such groupings do change over time.

- Divide the available instruments into asset classes. Allocate each asset class an equal fraction of the 100% in instrument weighting that is available.

- Within each asset class, divide the available instruments into similar groups. Allocate each group within an asset class an equal fraction of the instrument weight share for that asset class.

- Within each group, allocate to each instrument within the group an equal fraction of the instrument weight share for that group.

Of course it's possible to add additional intermediate layers, and we can have different numbers of layers for each asset class. The question of how the various instruments should be grouped together has some subjectivity, but here is a suggested grouping:

Agricultural	Grain: e.g. Corn, Wheat, Soy
	Index: e.g. GICS
	Meats: e.g. Feeder cattle, Lean hogs
	Softs: e.g. Coffee, Milk, Sugar
Bonds and interest rates	Government bonds: e.g. US 10-year, German Bund
	Short term interest rates: e.g. Eurodollar
	Swaps: e.g. US 5-year swaps
Equity	US: e.g. S&P 500, NASDAQ, US tech sector
	European: e.g. EUROSTOXX, DAX, European utilities sector
	Asian: e.g. NIKKEI, TOPIX
FX	Developed: e.g. JPYUSD, EURUSD
	Emerging: e.g. MXPUSD, KRWUSD
	Cross: e.g. YENEUR
Metals	Crypto: e.g. Bitcoin, Ethereum
	Industrial: e.g. Copper, Aluminium
	Precious: e.g. Gold, Silver
Energies	Gas: e.g. Henry Hub Natural Gas
	Crude Oil: e.g. WTI Crude, Brent Crude
	Products: e.g. Heating Oil, Ethanol
Volatility	US: VIX
	European: VSTOXX
	Asian: Nikkei 225 Volatility Index

You could argue that crypto should have its own sector or be part of the FX complex, or that bonds should be split by geography like equities, or that volatility should be included with equities. The advantage of this approach is that you can easily modify it for yourself if you disagree with my classification.

Let's look at a concrete example. Suppose we have the following arbitrary set of instruments: Soybean, Coffee, Orange Juice, Italian 10-year bonds, German 10-year bonds, US 10-year bonds, Eurodollar, CAC40 French equity, DAX30 German equity, NASDAQ equity, NOKUSD FX, Gold, Silver, Copper, Ethanol and VIX.

Let's first allocate to each asset class. There are seven asset classes, so each gets 1/7 of 100%, or 14.3% of the total.

- Agricultural (14.3%): Soybean, Coffee, Orange Juice

- Bonds and rates (14.3%): Italian 10-year bonds, German 10-year bonds, US 10-year bonds, Eurodollar

- Equity (14.3%): CAC40, DAX30, NASDAQ

- FX (14.3%): NOKUSD

- Metals (14.3%): Gold, Silver, Copper

- Energies (14.3%): Ethanol

- Volatility (14.3%): VIX

Now we allocate to groups within each asset class:

- Agricultural:

    - Grains (7.14%): Soybean

    - Softs (7.14%): Coffee, Orange Juice

- Bonds and rates:

    - Government bonds (7.14%): Italian 10-year bonds, German 10-year bonds, US 10-year bonds

    - Interest rates (7.14%): Eurodollar

- Equity:

    - American (7.14%): NASDAQ

    - European (7.14%): CAC40 French equity, DAX30 German equity

- FX:

    - NOKUSD (14.3%)

- Metals:

    - Precious (7.14%): Gold, Silver,

- - Industrial (7.14%): Copper
- Energies:
  - Ethanol (14.3%)
- Volatility:
  - VIX (14.3%)

Notice that in asset classes with only one instrument, no further decomposition is required. Now for the final step: allocating to instruments within each group:

- Agricultural:
  - Grains:
    - Soybean (7.14%)
  - Softs:
    - Coffee (3.57%), Orange Juice (3.57%)
- Bonds and rates:
  - Government bonds:
    - Italian 10-year bonds (2.38%), German 10-year bonds (2.38%), US 10-year bonds (2.38%)
  - Interest rates:
    - Eurodollar (7.14%)
- Equity:
  - American
    - NASDAQ (7.14%)
  - European:
    - CAC40 (3.57%), DAX30 (3.57%)
- FX:
  - NOKUSD (14.3%)
- Metals:
  - Precious:
    - Gold (3.57%), Silver (3.57%)
  - Industrial:
    - Copper (7.14%)

- Energies:

  - Ethanol (14.3%)

- Volatility:

  - VIX (14.3%)

An approximation for IDM

One of my goals in this book is to provide you with trading strategies that are complete, 'out of the box', and where you don't need to run backtesting software to estimate any further parameters. However, to properly calculate the instrument diversification multiplier (IDM), you would in theory need to run a backtest.[85] To save you the trouble, table 16 shows some approximate values of IDM you can use, given a certain number of instruments in your portfolio.

TABLE 16: INSTRUMENT DIVERSIFICATION MULTIPLIER (IDM) TO USE FOR A GIVEN NUMBER OF INSTRUMENTS

	IDM
One instrument	1.00
Two instruments	1.20
Three instruments	1.48
Four instrument	1.56
Five instruments	1.70
Six instruments	1.90
Seven instruments	2.10
8 to 14 instruments	2.20
15 to 24 instruments	2.30
25 to 29 instruments	2.40
30+ instruments	2.50

Note: table 16 assumes that your instrument set is relatively diversified. It won't be valid if you have 30 instruments, all of which are equity futures markets.

---

85 Since the IDM depends on the correlation between sub-strategies, it will be time varying as correlations change. Also, we usually add instruments to a backtest over time as data becomes available. The correct IDM will usually increase as more instruments are added to a backtest. Hence, calculating a single IDM based on the entire backtest is a weak form of in sample fitting, and will also result in an IDM that is too high in earlier periods and too low later in the backtest. Strictly speaking then, we should recalculate the IDM throughout the backtest using only backward looking information. In all the backtest results I present in the rest of the book I use rolling backward looking IDM estimates.

An algorithm for automatically selecting instruments

Even after we've applied the requirements for cost and liquidity, there are still over 100 futures in my data set that we could potentially trade. Most people will be unwilling or unable to trade them all. This is especially true for retail traders like me, who need to make the best use of our relatively small accounts. Trading over 100 futures whilst avoiding issues with minimum capital thresholds would require many tens of millions of dollars in capital.

Let's say we had much less than $10 million in capital. How many instruments could we trade with? Which instruments should we choose? I faced this problem myself when I downsized from a multi-billion dollar institutional portfolio to a much smaller retail account. After considerable thought, I came up with the following procedure for selecting an appropriate set of instruments, given a particular level of capital. The portfolio of instruments it selects will reflect the best trade-off between diversification and costs, and ensures we have the minimum capital required for all the instruments chosen.

Here are the steps you should follow:

1. Decide on a set of possible instruments.

2. Choose the first instrument for the portfolio.

3. This forms the initial *current portfolio*. Measure the expected SR for this portfolio, using the instrument cost.

4. Iterate over all instruments not in the current portfolio, considering each in turn as a potential new instrument:

    i. Construct a *trial portfolio* consisting of the current portfolio and the potential new instrument.

    ii. Allocate instrument weights for the trial portfolio. Calculate an IDM.

    iii. Check the minimum capital requirement for all instruments. If not met, skip this instrument.

    iv. Measure the expected SR for this trial portfolio using the instrument weights, correlation matrix and instrument cost.

5. Choose the instrument which produces the highest trial portfolio SR from step 4. Replace the current portfolio with the trial portfolio. The new current portfolio will consist of the old current portfolio plus this new instrument.

If the expected SR for the new current portfolio is 10% lower than the highest current portfolio SR seen so far, stop. Otherwise continue again from step 2.

Unlike the handcrafting algorithm above, this is not really suitable for running by hand: you will need to be able to write code to implement a version of this.[86] However, you can find my recommended list of futures for a given level of capital on the web page for this book.

Now let's dive into the details of each step.

1: Decide on a possible set of instruments

We need to discard all the instruments which we can't trade for legal reasons, or which do not meet our costs and liquidity thresholds. Note that we don't need to worry about minimum capital; that will be taken care of by the algorithm.

2: Choose the first instrument

To choose the first instrument we need to make some assumptions about what roughly the final portfolio will look like. So, for example, we might expect that we'll end up with about ten instruments. With ten instruments equally weighted, we would have an instrument weight of 10%, and from table 16 the appropriate IDM would be 2.2. It isn't critical to get these initial guesses exactly right, but they are necessary to ensure we don't select a first instrument with a very high minimum capital, and then find we can't add any more as we've run out of money.

Next, we cycle through all available instruments and calculate the minimum capital required for each using our assumed instrument weight and IDM:

Minimum capital 4 contracts

$$= (4 \times \text{Multiplier}_i \times \text{Price}_{i,t} \times \text{FX rate}_{i,t} \times \sigma_{\%i,t}) \div (\text{IDM} \times \text{Weight}_i \times \tau)$$

We discard any instruments for which this is greater than the available capital. Of the remaining instruments, we choose the one which has the **lowest risk adjusted cost**, as calculated using the equations in strategy three.

3: Measure the expected Sharpe ratio of the current portfolio

In theory this would require a full blown backtest, but instead we're going to make some simplifying assumptions. I'm going to assume that all instruments have the same pre-cost SR so that their post-cost SR depends only on costs.

---

86 You don't need full blown backtesting software to do this. Python code that implements this method can be found on the website for this book.

If each instrument sub-system has the same[87] notional pre-cost annual SR^*, and if the estimated turnover for each instrument is equal to T, then the net SR will be equal to the pre-cost SR less the costs: turnover multiplied by the risk adjusted cost for the instrument, c_i:

$$\text{Instrument annual SR}_i = SR^* - (T \times c_i)$$

As an example, for strategy three a reasonable pre-cost SR is 0.3, and T is around 7.0 (turnover around three times a year with quarterly rolls). Now, if we have an SR, then we can easily calculate the expected mean by multiplying it by the annual risk target, τ:

$$\text{Instrument annual mean}_i = \tau \times [SR^* - T \times c_i]$$

So far I have assumed we are only trading a single instrument, but in subsequent stages we need to account for the fact the instrument is part of a portfolio by including the instrument weight and IDM:

$$\text{Instrument annual mean in portfolio}_i$$
$$= \text{Weight}_i \times IDM \times \tau \times [SR^* - (T \times c_i)]$$

The expected annual mean return for the portfolio is just the sum of these terms across all instruments:

$$\text{Portfolio mean}$$
$$= \text{Sum}_i (\text{Weight}_i \times IDM \times \tau \times [SR^* - (T \times c_i)])$$

We can now calculate the portfolio standard deviation. For this I can use a simplified version of the standard formula, because all the trading sub-strategies for each instrument will all target the same risk τ:

$$\text{Portfolio } \sigma = IDM \times \tau \times \sqrt{(w \, \Sigma \, w')}$$

Here w is the vector of instrument weights, Σ is the correlation matrix of sub-strategy returns, and we are performing matrix multiplication inside the brackets.

We can now divide the portfolio mean by the standard deviation to get the expected

---

87   I'd strongly advise against using the actual backtested SR for a given instrument for the reasons I've already explained. Take a long look at figure 20 if you are tempted to ignore me.

SR (note that τ and IDM will cancel, as we would expect since by design SRs are invariant to leverage and risk):

$$\text{Portfolio SR} = \text{Sum}_{i=0...N}(\text{Weight}_i \times [\text{SR}^* - (T \times c_i)]) \div \text{sqrt}(w \, \Sigma \, w')$$

This will be higher when instruments are more diversified or cheaper to trade. Note that for our initial portfolio of a single instrument this simplifies to the original equation:

$$\text{Portfolio SR} = \text{SR}^* - T \times c_i$$

4. Iterate over all instruments not in the current portfolio

Construct a trial portfolio	This will consist of the instruments in the current portfolio and the potential new instrument.
Allocate instrument weights for the trial portfolio	Ideally you should use an automated method of the handcrafting method described above. However, you can get good results from just using equal instrument weights as an approximation.
	You will also need to estimate the instrument diversification multiplier; see Appendix B or use table 16.
Check the minimum capital requirement for all instruments	Given the instrument weights and IDM, you can check to see that all instruments in the proposed portfolio meet their minimum capital threshold using the usual formula.
	If any instruments fail the minimum capital requirement, then this proposed new instrument is not suitable and we try adding the next on our list. This will most likely be because the instrument we are considering has a large minimum capital.
Measure the expected Sharpe ratio for the trial portfolio	Given the instrument weights, costs and IDM, use the formula described above which was used for stage three.

5: Choose the instrument with the highest expected SR for its trial portfolio

Normally at this stage we will now have one extra instrument in the portfolio, which will reflect the best trade-off between diversification and costs, and which does not cause any minimum capital issues anywhere in the trial portfolio. If no instruments are suitable for adding because they would all cause the minimum capital requirements to fail, then we would stop and keep the current portfolio.

6: Check to see if expected SR for the current portfolio has fallen by more than 10%

Clearly if the expected SR has fallen, then adding the additional instrument will not make sense, and we should stick to the portfolio that we had in the previous iteration. Why do we allow a modest reduction in SR before terminating our search? Well, because it's possible that the SR can fluctuate over the course of several iterations, going slightly lower before rising again.

However, once the SR has fallen sufficiently, we know that we probably can't do any better by adding yet more instruments.

An example

In the introduction I suggested that the minimum account size that was practical for this book was $100,000. To give you some idea of how this methodology works in practice, here are the 16 instruments the algorithm selected for a $100,000 trading account, using figures for costs and correlations that were correct at the time of writing.

• Equities: Korean KOSPI, NASDAQ micro

• Metals: Gold micro

• Bonds: Eurodollar, Korean 3-year and 10-year, US 2-year, German 2-year Schatz, Italian 10-year BTP

• Agricultural markets: Lean hogs

• FX: JPY/USD, MXP/USD, GBP/USD, NZD/USD

• Energies: Henry Hub Natural Gas mini, WTI Crude mini

With $500,000 it selects 27 instruments, and for $1 million the algorithm chooses 36 markets. You can find the selected list of instruments for other sizes of account on the website for this book.

Testing a generalised risk premia strategy with a Jumbo portfolio

Let's see what a very large risk premia earning strategy would look like. I took all the instruments which met my liquidity and cost thresholds, and for which I have at least one year of data: 102 in all.[88] Then I assumed that I had a very large amount of capital

---

88   The breakdown by asset class of the Jumbo portfolio is as follows: Agricultural 13, Bonds and Rates 21, Equity 34, FX 17, Metals and Crypto 9, Energies 6, Volatility 2. Of the 102 instruments, 18 have 40 or more years of data, 28 have more than 30 years, 40 have more than 20 years, 65 have more than 10 years, and 87 have more than 5 years.

($50 million) so that minimum capital does not cause any problems. I named this combination of a huge capital allocation and vast number of instruments the '**Jumbo**' portfolio,[89] and I'll be using it to assess strategy performance throughout the book.

The instrument weights were constructed using the handcrafting method, and the IDM comes out at 2.47.[90]

The first column in table 17 shows the averages across every instrument running in strategy four as if they had all the available capital: effectively these are the same as the median results for strategy three. In the second column we have the *aggregate* performance for strategy four across all available instruments.[91]

The difference between these two columns reflects the improvements we can get from diversification. Diversification increases the SR and therefore returns, improves skew and reduces the size of the tails of the distribution. On the downside we have a significantly higher average drawdown. This reflects the fact that correlation is a linear measure of co-movement that doesn't account for extremes. If many instruments have a tendency to perform badly at the same time, then drawdowns will be worse on an aggregate portfolio even though standard deviation – a measure of *average* risk – remains stable.

---

89   All the instruments in this 'Jumbo' portfolio currently meet my requirements for liquidity and minimum costs. That does not mean they would have met those requirements in the past, as I am excluding instruments which met those requirements historically but no longer do. I have tested all the strategies in this book on a wider set of instruments including illiquid and expensive markets, and the results are not significantly different. On a different note, my backtests do not include delisted instruments like the iconic pork belly futures which were removed in 2011. As a result, you could argue that all my statistics are subject to what is known in the jargon as *survivorship bias* – testing only on instruments that have survived (and are currently liquid and not too expensive to trade). This is a serious problem when testing trading strategies on individual equities, particularly with small cap firms, but is not such a significant issue with futures trading. It's comparatively unusual for futures to be delisted by exchanges, and when it happens the relevant future is often one which was never liquid enough to trade.

90   Actually the method I used is slightly different from what I presented earlier in the chapter, and uses sub-strategy return correlations to group similar instruments together, rather than doing this manually. This makes it suitable for use in backtesting where it can be applied on a rolling basis, using only backward looking data and accounting for additional instruments as they appear in the data set. The IDM was also calculated on a rolling basis, using only historic information; 2.47 is the final value of the IDM.

91   These results would be slightly different if I had allowed the strategy to go short, rather than long, the volatility ('vol') indices (VIX, and VSTOXX). The SR would be slightly higher, whilst the skew and lower percentile ratio would be a little worse. However, the total instrument weight allocated to volatility is just 5.4%, so this wouldn't make a substantial difference to the aggregate performance. Similarly, the two vol markets would barely affect the median results for a single instrument.

Costs are also higher due to the additional leverage that is required, evidenced by an IDM over 2.0. The turnover is much higher, but this is mainly because we have many more instruments and so need to do more trades, and doesn't translate to a proportionate increase in costs.

TABLE 17: AVERAGE FOR INDIVIDUAL INSTRUMENT AND AGGREGATE PERFORMANCE IN JUMBO PORTFOLIO RISK PREMIA STRATEGY

	Strategy four: Median instrument	Strategy four: Aggregated
Mean annual return	6.9%	15.4%
Mean annual costs	−0.3%	−0.8%
Average drawdown	−18.7%	−24.7%
Standard deviation	20.9%	18.2%
Sharpe ratio	0.32	0.85
Turnover	2.7	20.7
Skew	−0.09	−0.04
Lower tail	1.56	1.44
Upper tail	1.29	1.24

As figure 22 shows, the performance of this strategy performs well apart from the large drawdown in the early 1980s. Digging into the backtest, there are only 22 instruments with data at that point, and there is a preponderance of agricultural, currency and metals, all of which did badly in the monetary tightening that followed their excellent performance in the inflationary 1970s.

FIGURE 22: ACCOUNT CURVE FOR STRATEGY FOUR WITH JUMBO PORTFOLIO

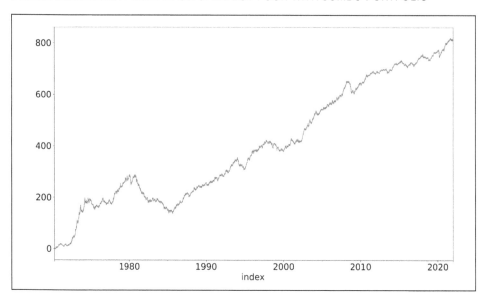

For much of the rest of the book I'll use this approach of presenting results for both (a) the average instrument, and (b) aggregate results for the Jumbo portfolio of instruments. The former gives an indication of what can be expected from trading any single arbitrary instrument,[92] whilst the latter is a reflection of what is achievable for an institutional trader trading a given strategy with a fund of at least $50 million.

In reality most retail traders won't be able to trade a portfolio with well over 100 instruments, so for a realistic set of five, ten or perhaps 20 instruments you will get performance that lies somewhere between these two extremes.

Risk targeting and portfolio size

Remember that the primary driver when deciding the level of our risk target (τ) was to take half the expected SR of our trading strategy: half the leverage required by the theoretical Kelly criteria result. In this book I have decided to use an annual standard deviation target of 20%, which will only be prudent if the SR is expected to be 0.40 or higher.

From table 17 the SR for an individual instrument taken at random will be just

---

92 With the caveat for strategy four that different instruments do have their own return characteristics, as we saw in strategy one, and volatility targeting doesn't completely erase these, as I explained in strategy three.

0.32. As I noted in strategy three, this is too low to support a risk target of 20%, and you should use a lower risk target if you are only trading one instrument: I suggested 10%. However, the SR of the Jumbo portfolio is much higher at 0.85.

You may well ask if an SR of 0.85 implies that we can use a risk target of half that, 42.5%. This will become a more significant issue later in the book, as we'll see strategies with even higher SRs. Strategy four is long only and has an upward biased SR from historical trends that are unlikely to be repeated, but I'd be reasonably confident of achieving an SR of 1.0 in the Jumbo portfolio with many of the strategies in this book which aren't as badly affected by these issues. Does this mean it is safe to increase our risk target from 20%, potentially up to 50%, or even higher?

Personally, I would be very wary of doing this. My own risk target is around 25%, despite a backtested SR which is well above 1.0.

I would advise the following approach:

- For any strategy trading a single instrument use a risk target of 10%.

- If you have between two and six instruments, you should interpolate your risk target between 10% and 20%.

- You should only use a risk target of 20% if you have at least one instrument from each of the seven asset classes I use in your strategy.

If you have at least two instruments from each asset class in your strategy, you can go up to 25%. Do not go higher than 25%

Conclusion

Strategy four is what we'd trade if we didn't think we could forecast asset returns – we just throw up our hands in disgust and go long everything we can get our hands on, allowing for liquidity, costs and minimum capital constraints. Since most of the assets in my data set have gone up in price over the last 50 years, this proves to be a fairly successful strategy. The more instruments we can select, the more diversification we can benefit from: going from 1 to 100 instruments almost triples our expected SR.

This is a nice strategy to use if you are an investor who wants a cheap and easy way to trade a diversified portfolio, using leverage so you don't have to compromise on your performance goals just because you want to include low volatility assets like bonds. But it still looks and feels like an *investment* strategy, and not really 'proper trading'. Beginning in the next chapter we will shift from investing to trading, as I discuss methods to forecast returns so that we won't always be long every instrument in our portfolio.

Strategy four: Trading plan

All other elements are identical to strategy three.

Strategy	Buy and hold multiple instruments with variable risk estimate
Instrument(s)	Any that meet minimum capital, liquidity and cost thresholds. Minimum capital required to hold four contracts:
	$$(4 \times \text{Multiplier}_i \times \text{Price}_{i,t} \times \text{FX rate}_{i,t} \times \sigma_{\%i,t})$$ $$\div (\text{IDM} \times \text{Weight}_i \times \tau)$$
	Use the instrument selection algorithm to select instruments.
Position sizing	Long N contracts, where N is the current rounded value of:
	$$N_i = \text{Capital} \times \text{IDM} \times \text{Weight}_i \times \tau$$ $$\div (\text{Multiplier}_i \times \text{Price}_{i,t} \times \text{FX}_{i,t} \times \sigma_{\%i,t})$$
Instrument weight	Use handcrafted algorithm to calculate instrument weights.
Instrument diversification multiplier (IDM)	Use table 16 or see calculation in Appendix B.

Slow trend following, long only

I don't know about you, but I certainly couldn't trade strategy four in its Jumbo variation with over 100 instruments, even if I had the necessary capital. Nearly a quarter of the instruments we are trading lose money! Imagine sitting there month after month, year after year, whilst the likes of VIX and Rice futures gradually bleed your account dry.

If only there was a way we could drop the instruments which are temporarily, or permanently, going down in price. Then we'd start to feel like real traders and hopefully make some more money. Fortunately, it's very straightforward to come up with simple systematic ways to identify the direction of the current price trend. In this chapter I'll describe such a method, which we can then use to decide when to close our long only positions. Assuming those trends continue, we can avoid holding instruments which are likely to lose us money.

> **Strategy five:** Buy and hold a portfolio of one or more instruments when they have been in a long uptrend, each with positions scaled for a variable risk estimate.

I will be covering the following topics in this chapter:

- A simple way to see if a market is an uptrend.

- How to manage positions depending on trend direction.

- Calculating costs when we do not always hold a position.

- Assessing the performance of the trend filter.

Testing for a market uptrend

There are hundreds of technical indicators that you can use to see if a market is trending, but we're going to focus on a relatively simple method: the **moving average**. Firstly, we take a moving average of the back-adjusted[93] futures price p_t over the last 12 months, which is approximately 256 business days:

$$\text{Moving average (256)}_t = \text{sum}(p_{t-255} + p_{t-254} + \dots p_{t-1} + p_t) \div 256$$

We now compare this to the current price (p_t). If the current price is higher than the moving average, then we are in an uptrend.

Figure 23 shows the 12-month moving average for the S&P 500 micro future, overlaid on the price, for the last 20 years or so. The dark line is the price, whilst the smoother grey line is the trend line. You can see that it is mostly in an uptrend, with the exception of the early 2000s and 2008–9, with several short-lived bear markets in between, most recently in March 2020.

FIGURE 23: 12-MONTH MOVING AVERAGE ON S&P 500 PRICE

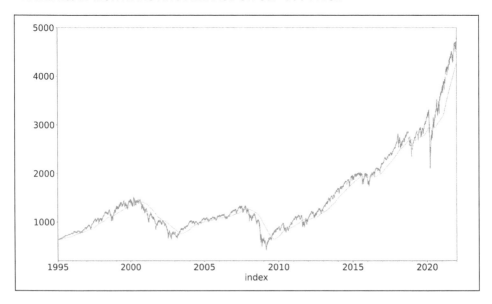

---

93   We use the back-adjusted futures price as it will be smooth, without disjointed sections when we have a futures roll. This is not so important for a 12-month moving average, but will be important once we're considering shorter trends. A consequence of this is that we'll be more likely to see an uptrend in an instrument with positive carry. I'll discuss the ramifications of this later in the book.

During these short-lived periods the indicator turns on and off many times; far too many for what is supposed to be a slow-moving indication of long-term trends. For example, between October 2018 and March 2019, we change our mind about being long on a total of 14 occasions!

Fortunately, there is an easy way to make this indicator smoother without destroying its ability to tell us what the long-term trend is. We do this by calculating a second moving average, this time for a shorter period:[94]

$$\text{Moving average } (64)_t = \text{sum}(p_{t-63} + p_{t-62} + \dots p_{t-1} + p_t) \div 64$$

We now compare the two moving averages to get a moving average *crossover*.

Go (or stay) long if: moving average (64)$_t$ > moving average (256)$_t$

Figure 24 shows two moving averages for the S&P 500 (I've removed the raw price to make the plot clearer). As an example of how this works, you can see that in late 2000 the light grey faster moving average moves below the slower dark grey line, so we'd close our position, not reopening it until the lines cross again in mid-2003.

---

94   It doesn't matter exactly what length the shorter moving average is. However, if it's too short then we'll still see frequent changes in opinion, whereas if the average is too long then we will be slow reacting to changes in market direction. My own research indicates that any ratio between the two moving average lengths of between two and six gives statistically indistinguishable results with both real and artificial data (the latter was used to avoid potential in sample fitting). Using a shorter length that is one quarter the longer length is also mathematically satisfying, especially since $2^8 = 256$, which means we can create a neat series of moving average crossovers of different speeds: 64&256, 32&128, 16&64, 8&32 and so on; I'll use this series later in the book.

FIGURE 24: TWO MOVING AVERAGES ON S&P 500

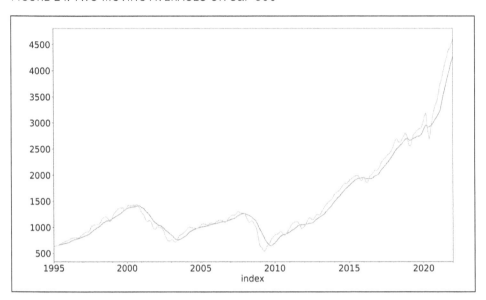

Severe bear markets are now clearly identified, although there are also still a few short-lived periods when we're not sure what's happening. But we change our position less than once per year, so this is a lot smoother than the single moving average. This **moving average crossover (MAC)** is perfectly adequate for identifying slow-moving trends. However, it's less satisfying when identifying faster *trends*, as it still tends to produce too many short-lived reversals.

What causes this? In a simple moving average (SMA), all the points in the moving average window are equally weighted. That makes the moving average quite noisy. When large returns in the past drop out of the window the average will change dramatically. This is more of a problem with shorter windows where each individual day has quite a high weight.

The secret is to use **exponentially weighted moving averages (EWMA)**. In an EWMA, we weight more recent values more highly than those further in the past. This results in much smoother transitions since the impact of a large price change will get gradually reduced over time, rather than falling out in a single day.

In general terms, an EWMA is defined as follows:

$$\text{EWMA}(\lambda)_t = \lambda p_t + \lambda(1 - \lambda)p_{t-1} + \lambda(1 - \lambda)^2 p_{t-2} + \ldots$$

A higher λ parameter is like a shorter window on an SMA; it will result in more recent prices being given a higher weight. It's more intuitive to define our EWMA in terms of their *span*.[95] For a given span in days N, we can calculate the λ as:

$$\lambda = 2 \div (N + 1)$$

So instead of an SMA with a 64-day *window*, we have an EWMA with a 64-day *span*. Similarly, we can replace the 256-day SMA with a 256-day EWMA.[96] The λ for these two EWMA are approximately 0.031 and 0.0078 respectively.

Hence we can define an EWMA version of our trend filter – an **exponentially weighted moving average crossover (EWMAC)** with the following rule:

$$\text{EWMA } (N = 64, \lambda = 0.031)_t$$
$$= 0.031p_t + 0.031(1 - 0.031)p_{t-1} + 0.031(1 - 0.031)^2 p_{t-2} + \ldots$$

$$\text{EWMA } (N = 256, \lambda = 0.0078)_t$$
$$= 0.0078p_t + 0.0078(1 - 0.0078)p_{t-1} + 0.0078(1 - 0.0078)^2 p_{t-2} + \ldots$$

$$\text{EWMAC}(64,256)$$
$$= \text{EWMA}(N = 64)_t - \text{EWMA}(N = 256)_t$$

$$\text{Go long if EWMAC > 0 else remain flat.}$$

In my analysis, the performance of a given EWMAC is superior to the corresponding MAC, with the difference most pronounced for faster trend filters.[97]

Managing positions with a trend filter

We can easily manage our positions with this trend filter by treating it like strategy four with an additional on/off switch. Every day we'd calculate our optional position, using the standard strategy four position sizing equations, accounting for current levels of

---

95 The term span comes from the Python coding languages Pandas library implementation of exponential weighting.
96 These are not exactly equivalent. In fact an EWMA with a span of 92 days has almost exactly the same half life as an SMA with a 64-day window. However, it's convenient to stick to a series of parameter values that are powers of two, and a strategy run with a 64-day span will be highly correlated to the 92-day version, with very similar performance.
97 So for example for strategy eight, which is a fast trend filter that can go both long and short, using a MAC and EWMAC with matched half lives, the SR doubles when using exponential weighting with a one-third reduction in both costs and turnover.

volatility, price and exchange rates. However, if the trend was showing a downward movement, then we'd set our optimal position to zero.

What this means in practice is we would open positions once an upward trend was established, buying the current sized optimal position according to the position sizing formula used in strategy four:

$$N_i = Capital \times IDM \times Weight_{i,t} \times \tau \div (Multiplier_i \times Price_{i,t} \times FX_{i,t} \times \sigma_{\%i,t})$$

Then whilst the trend was still upward, we'd adjust those positions from day to day as the optimum position changed (principally due to changes in the instrument risk σ% but also due to changes in price, FX rates and capital). Finally, when the trend reversed, we would close our position completely and wait until the trend line has turned upwards again.

Trend filter on S&P 500 micro futures

To understand the trend filter a little better, let's consider the impact it has on the S&P 500 micro future. Figure 25 shows the position series for the S&P 500 with $100,000 in capital and a 20% annualised risk target. You can compare this directly with figure 16 (back on page 81), which shows the position we'd have without a trend filter. The positions in figure 25 closely track the positions we'd have without any filter, except when a downward trend temporarily closes the trade.

FIGURE 25: POSITIONS HELD IN S&P 500 BY STRATEGY FIVE

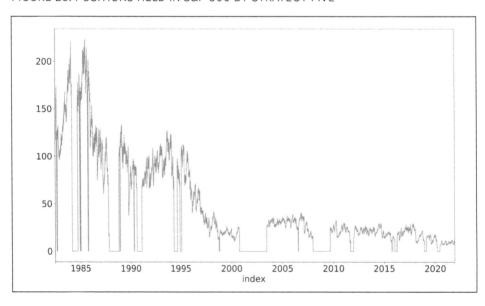

Table 18 summarises the performance of strategy four[98] without the trend filter, against strategy five (with the filter). Applying the trend filter makes the dynamic strategy safer with slightly lower risk and better average drawdown, but at a cost of lower returns. Unsurprisingly, the turnover is higher due to the average position size being reduced and the additional opening and closing trades introduced by the trend filter. But average annual costs are unchanged as there are periods when we do no trading at all.

TABLE 18: PERFORMANCE FOR S&P 500 MICRO FUTURES WITH AND WITHOUT TREND FILTER

	Strategy four (No trend filter)	Strategy five (trend filter)
Mean annual return	12.1%	9.6%
Costs	−0.06%	−0.06%
Average drawdown	−18.8%	−12.8%
Standard deviation	22.8%	19.5%
Sharpe ratio	0.54	0.49
Turnover	2.34	6.4
Skew	−0.68	−0.57
Lower tail	1.76	1.85
Upper tail	1.21	1.18

The main conclusion is that it's difficult to compare strategies that do very different things: one always has a position on (strategy four), the other (strategy five) does not. These differences result in a considerably different profile of returns so it's difficult to use simple summary statistics like means and Sharpe ratios (SRs) to determine which is superior. Ultimately, it comes down to your preferences.

Risk adjusting costs in backtests

Back in strategy three (on page 83) I explained how to calculate risk adjusted costs, as an easy way of working out the likely after cost performance of a particular instrument trading a particular strategy. We can then use these costs to make decisions about whether we can trade a given instrument, or if it's too expensive.

For the first four strategies in this book, this is also a good enough approximation to use when calculating the costs to apply in a historical backtest of a trading

---

98 Remember strategy four is just a portfolio of sub-strategies, each trading strategy three for a different instrument. So this is effectively strategy three as well as four.

strategy. The relevant calculation involved estimating the total turnover of an average position, adding on the number of roll trades, and multiplying by the risk adjusted cost per trade.

However, strategy five is different. Partly this is because we don't always have a position on, and also because the pattern of trades is unusual: a few large trades when the trend filter switches on or off, and then a large number of small position adjustments.

It makes no sense to use the original risk adjusted cost calculation to calculate the costs for a historical backtest. Instead, every time a trade occurs in the backtest, I deduct a cost in my account currency for each contract traded. This cost is based on the current cost of trading a single contract, adjusted for the difference in volatility between now and the relevant historical period. The volatility I use for this period is not the annualised percentage standard deviation, $\sigma_\%$ calculated using percentage returns, but instead the daily σ_p calculated using *price* differences. I estimate this with the usual exponentially weighted standard deviation estimate that I've used since strategy three:

Historical trading cost

= Current cost × (Historical σ_p ÷ Current σ_p)

Let's take an example. Earlier on page 16, I estimated the current trading cost of the S&P 500 micro future as $0.875 per contract, including both commissions and spread cost.

Suppose the current price of the S&P 500 is 4500 with an estimated annualised standard deviation of 16%, which equates to a daily standard deviation in price units of 4500 × 16% ÷ 16 = 45. Back in early October 1990, the price of the S&P 500 future was around 500 with an estimated annualised standard deviation of roughly 10%, giving a daily standard deviation in price units of 500 × 10% ÷ 16 = 3.125. This implies that we should adjust the trading cost for trades done in October 1990 as follows:

Historic trading cost = $0.875 × (3.125 ÷ 45)

= $0.061 per contract

Notice that if the annualised percentage standard deviation is unchanged, then the cost of trading as a percentage of the notional contract value will remain constant, which seems reasonable. Otherwise the cost will change as the standard deviation changes, which is in line with my earlier assumption that risk adjusted costs are constant.

(A common alternative is to ignore the risk adjustment and instead normalise costs by the change in price. Effectively this assumes that costs are always a fixed percentage of the notional value of the contract. This is probably alright for commissions, but not for spreads which tend to widen when markets get more volatile.)

Of course these are all approximations; in fact it's likely that trading costs were higher in the past especially for retail traders. I don't remember any newspaper adverts for brokers charging 6 cents a contract to trade S&P 500 futures back in 1990! But in the absence of any accurate historical data on trading costs, I think this is a reasonable method to use, and importantly it will allow us to make decisions about whether to implement particular trading strategies given today's current cost levels.

Nevertheless, you should always be very distrustful of historical trading costs calculated in a backtest. Keep this in mind when assessing whether to trade a strategy with especially high turnover.

Evaluating the performance of strategy five

It's premature to draw any definitive conclusions about performance without looking at more than one instrument. Let's examine the average performance across all the instruments in my data set. Table 19 shows the performance of the average (median) instrument for strategy four (no trend filter), and for strategy five with the trend filter applied.

TABLE 19: PERFORMANCE OF AVERAGE (MEDIAN) INSTRUMENT WITH AND WITHOUT TREND FILTER

	Strategy four (No trend filter)	Strategy five (Trend filter)
Mean annual return	6.9%	5.6%
Costs	−0.3%	−0.23%
Average drawdown	−18.7%	−20.2%
Standard deviation	20.9%	17.2%
Sharpe ratio	0.32	0.32
Turnover	2.7	5.8
Skew	−0.09	−0.07
Lower tail	1.56	1.60
Upper tail	1.29	1.26

Averaging across multiple instruments the results aren't quite as dramatic as they were for the S&P 500 alone. Dynamic position sizing with the trend filter delivers identical risk adjusted performance to strategy three without any filter, but as we only have positions on some of the time both returns and risk are a little lower.

Table 20 shows the *aggregated* backtest statistics for the Jumbo portfolio of 102 instruments, trading $50 million of notional capital to ensure there are no issues with minimum capital on any instrument. Perhaps surprisingly given the results for the average instrument, there is a significant improvement in both risk and return when we add the trend filter to strategy four and obtain strategy five. Admittedly the tails look a little worse, but the average drawdown is slashed by two-thirds.

TABLE 20: PERFORMANCE OF AGGREGATE JUMBO PORTFOLIO WITH AND WITHOUT TREND FILTER

	Strategy four (No trend filter	Strategy five (Trend filter)
Mean annual return	15.4%	16.4%
Costs	−0.8%	−0.7%
Average drawdown	−24.7%	−10.4%
Standard deviation	18.2%	14.8%
Sharpe ratio	0.85	1.11
Turnover	20.7	24.1
Skew	−0.04	0.22
Lower tail	1.44	1.64
Upper tail	1.24	1.39

Figure 26 clearly illustrates how the trend filter manages to avoid most of the deep drawdown in the early 1980s by reducing positions in markets that fell in price.

FIGURE 26: CUMULATIVE PERFORMANCE OF JUMBO PORTFOLIO WITH AND WITHOUT TREND FILTER

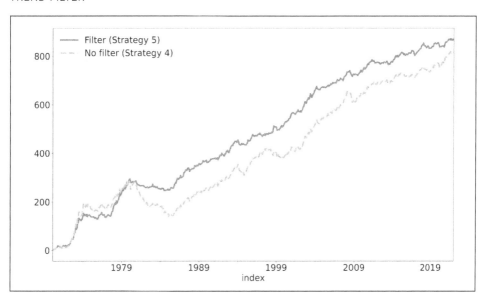

Of course strategy five would look even better here if it were leveraged up to hit the expected risk target of 20%, which it substantially undershoots due to spending considerable time with no positions on.

An alternative method to managing positions

By now you should have got used to my relatively unusual method of trading, where positions are continuously managed after opening to ensure their risk is correct. But there is an alternative which is simpler to manage and closer in spirit to how most people trade. Here we do not adjust our position once it has been established during an uptrend. I call this the **static** method for position management,[99] as opposed to the **dynamic** variant presented above.

For strategy five, once a position has been opened on an uptrend, we would keep the same number of futures contracts open, rolling as required, until the trend has turned downwards.[100] Then we close our position, and once an uptrend is re-established

---

99   Readers of my previous book *Leveraged Trading* will recognise the static variation as the 'Starter System'. The dynamic variation is similar to the more complex system introduced later in that book.
100   A third variation is to resize positions whenever a roll occurs. Its performance will be somewhere between that of the static and dynamic strategies.

we reopen it, but now with a newly calculated position that reflects current levels of volatility.

Deciding whether to use static or dynamic methods is partly down to individual choice – I've had many debates over the years with other traders[101] about whether it is better to adjust open positions for risk (dynamic) or leave them fixed (static). But it is worth reviewing the available evidence, especially as it is such a common trading approach, rather than dismissing it out of hand. I have not included detailed figures for static strategy performance, but a summary of my findings is below.

Turnover and costs	Obviously the static method results in lower turnover and costs, since we don't trade once a position is established. But the improvements in average returns from using dynamic position sizing are usually many multiples what we pay in extra costs.
Average return **Standard deviation** **Sharpe ratio**	Looking at the results for both average instruments, and aggregated Jumbo portfolios, the dynamic versions are almost always clear winners in all of these metrics. Indeed, at times the standard deviation in particular is much higher for the static variation.[102]
Leverage required	Because the dynamic variants often have lower realised standard deviation, it's sometimes argued that they will require higher leverage to hit the same risk targets. By doing so we could convert the higher SR of the dynamic strategies into higher returns.
	But it's worth bearing in mind that at the inception of each static trade (when the trend filter changes sign) the leverage on both variations will be identical, since the positions are equally sized. Subsequently, the dynamic strategies actually end up using *less* leverage on average, since they reduce their positions in the face of increased risk.
	Of course we *could* apply more leverage to the dynamic strategies if we really wanted to match the higher risk of the static alternatives. But I wouldn't advocate this, as I think it's better to use the dynamic strategy without any further leverage. This does a great job of hitting the required risk target.
Average drawdown **Lower tail**	My analysis suggests these are nearly always better for the dynamic version of each strategy.

---

101   Yes Jerry Parker, I'm talking about you.

102   For example, there is a massive one-off spike in returns for the static strategy which is caused by the infamous attempt by the Hunt brothers to corner the silver market in 1980 (which affected the entire metals complex, and hence severely distorts the risk profile of the aggregated strategy).

Upper tail **Skew**	These are the only risk measures where static strategies sometimes show an improvement. This is a consistent result: a 'fat right tail' of returns will usually be associated with a trading strategy that has relatively more positive skew.
	A fat right tail is more likely with a static strategy. This is because if a winning position spikes sharply up or down, then we'll capture more of that spike if we don't reduce our position in response to the increase in volatility – which is what a dynamic strategy would do. But this also makes unwanted fat left tails more likely with static strategies!
	These improvements aren't universal; they appear more often in the aggregated Jumbo portfolio statistics, but not when considering the average instrument. Neither are they significant improvements.[103] For me at least these aren't compelling enough improvements to justify using the static variation.

For me personally the decision is clear: I use a dynamic sizing method in this book and in my own trading system.

Conclusion

Trend following is one of the most popular trading strategies available. Using it to temporarily close long positions is a favoured tool for many investors. But these investors often can't go short; in a falling market they can at best avoid losses. They will never get the full benefit of trend following, because they can't go short.

As futures traders we aren't limited in this respect: going short is as easy as going long. As you will see in the next chapter, going both long and short adds an additional boost to strategy performance.

---

103   The improvement in skew for static strategies is slightly more pronounced if we measure skew on individual trades, rather than across daily returns. I discuss this in more detail in a blog post, which you can find a link to on the website for this book.

Strategy five: Trading plan

All other elements are identical to strategy four.

Strategy	Buy and hold one or more instruments with variable risk estimate and slow trend filter.
Trend filter	Calculate the 64 business day span price exponentially weighted moving average using the back-adjusted price: $$\text{EWMA } (N = 64, \lambda = 0.031)_t$$ $$= 0.031p_t + 0.031(1 - 0.031)p_{t-1}$$ $$+ 0.031(1 - 0.031)^2 p_{t-2} + \ldots$$ Also calculate the $N = 256$, $\lambda = 0.0078$ span EWMA. If EWMA(64) is higher than EWMA(256), we are in an uptrend. Otherwise, we are in a downtrend.
Position sizing	Long N contracts, where N is the current rounded value of: $$N_i = \text{Capital} \times \text{IDM} \times \text{Weight}_i \times \tau$$ $$\div (\text{Futures Multiplier}_i \times \text{Price}_{i,t} \times \text{FX}_{i,t} \times \sigma_{\%,i,t})$$
Trading decision	If an uptrend is present in a given instrument, calculate the optimal position as above, updating values of capital, price, FX and standard deviation estimate ($\sigma\%$). Trade as required to achieve this optimal position, rolling as required.
	If a downtrend is present, close any existing position and do not open a new position until an uptrend is re-established.

Slow trend following, long and short

Do you have any idea what you just did? You just bet against the America economy.

Ben Rickert, played by Brad Pitt, in the film *Big Short*

In most financial markets it's quite tricky to bet on falling prices. In stocks, for example, you have to borrow some shares from someone, pay borrowing fees, arrange for dividends to be rerouted and then return the shares when you close the trade. A similar process is required in bonds. My mind boggles if I think about how I could possibly short a physical barrel of Oil, or bushel of Wheat. The protagonists in the film *Big Short*, which is based on a true story, have to construct all kinds of esoteric derivative bets to implement a trading idea which reflects their expectations for US house prices and mortgage bonds. Perhaps only foreign exchange offers the simplicity of going both long and short with relative ease.

In contrast, it's as easy to bet on the price of a future going down as it is to bet on them going up. And yet, so far in this book I've ignored the possibility of going short. This meant that we avoided the pain of being consistently long the perpetually poorly performing volatility futures by closing our positions in downtrends, we were unable to benefit by going short. It may also have been profitable to short certain other instruments that were in a temporary bear market.

Back in chapter one I said I would explain strategies that took advantage of the various types of risk premia that could be earned in the market. Right up to strategy four I focused on the risk premia that can be collected just by being long certain instruments. But we're beyond simple long only risk premia now, because the returns available from trend following are generally considered to be a risk premium in their own right.

Let's adapt the trend filter from strategy five to allow for the possibility of going short when the market has been trending downward for some time.

> **Strategy six:** Trade a portfolio of one or more instruments, each with positions scaled for a variable risk estimate. Hold a long position when they have been in a long uptrend, and a short position in a downtrend.

I will be covering the following topics in this chapter:

- Applying a trend filter to trade both long and short positions.

- Comparing the strategy to more traditional trading techniques, such as using stop losses.

- Why it's better to run long/short strategies on a diversified portfolio of instruments.

- Measuring relative performance for a long/short strategy.

Adapting the trend filter to go both long and short

You should remember the following calculations from strategy five:

$$EWMA(N = 64, \lambda = 0.031)_t$$
$$= 0.031p_t + 0.031(1 - 0.031)p_{t-1} + 0.031(1 - 0.031)^2 p_{t-2} + ...$$

$$EWMA(N = 256, \lambda = 0.0078)_t$$
$$= 0.0078p_t + 0.0078(1 - 0.0078)p_{t-1} + 0.0078(1 - 0.0078)^2 p_{t-2} + ...$$

$$EWMAC(64,256) = EWMA(N = 64)_t - EWMA(N = 256)_t$$

Let's adapt the rule[104] in strategy five as follows:

$$\text{Go long if: } EWMAC(64,256) > 0$$

$$\text{Go short if: } EWMAC(64,256) < 0$$

––––––––––

104   In the unlikely event of both moving averages being equal, we'd hold no position.

We now adjust our positions from day to day so they are always at the optimal level, using the standard position sizing formula but with an additional element to reflect the trend filter:

$$N_{i,t} = (Sign(trend)_t \times Capital \times IDM \times Weight_i \times \tau)$$
$$\div (Multiplier_i \times Price_{i,t} \times FX_{i,t} \times \sigma_{\%,i,t})$$

Here, if N > 0 we go long (in an uptrend), otherwise with N < 0 we would be short (in a downtrend). We would keep our position open, making small adjustments each day as price, FX and risk changed, until the trend filter reversed direction. At this point we'd close our position and put on a new trade in the opposite direction for a number of contracts reflecting the current optimal value of N.

Long and short trend following on the S&P 500

Let's look at how the position sizing works on the S&P 500 micro futures. The time series of positions in my backtest is shown in figure 27. The absolute size of the position is effectively identical to the volatility targeted position for strategy three (refer to figure 16 on page 81) with the crucial difference that we have a long position when the trend filter is bullish and a short position when bearish.

FIGURE 27: POSITION SIZING FOR S&P 500 WITH LONG/SHORT TREND FILTER

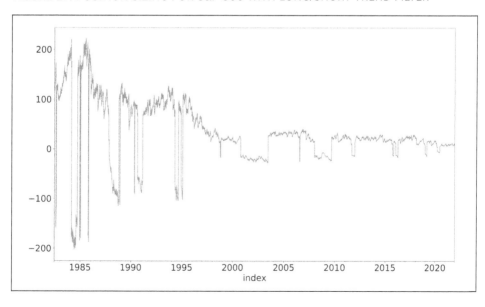

In the interests of space I won't bore you with the details of how the S&P 500 instrument performed for this particular strategy. Instead we'll move straight on to consider the average performance across all the instruments in my data set.

Isn't this the same as using a stop loss?

The series in figure 27 looks superficially similar to what you might expect from a more traditional trading strategy, where we open our positions based on some technical indicator, and then close them using a *stop loss*. A stop loss is triggered when a price retraces by some amount from its high (if we're long) or low (when short). A properly configured stop loss will close positions in a similar way to the trend filter, since if we're long in an uptrend (or short in a downtrend) we will want to close our position once the trend has reversed, which will also be when our position has incurred a certain degree of loss.

However, in this book, I prefer to use the same trading rule to both open and close positions. This is simpler than using a separate stop loss, and as we'll see later allows us to automatically adjust our positions as trends weaken or strengthen. In my previous book *Leveraged Trading* I demonstrated that replacing the stop loss with a single opening and closing rule results in slightly better backtested trading performance.

Still, if you are wedded to the idea of a stop loss, then you can modify strategy six (and most of the other strategies in this book) accordingly. When you begin trading, open a position in a direction dictated by the sign of the trend filter. Close the position when you hit your stop loss. Open a new position once the trend filter has reversed direction, which may be immediately or after a few days or weeks.

Your stop loss should be calibrated so that you will generally be closing positions at the same time as the trend filter would have done so. If your stop loss is too tight, then you will prematurely close positions before the trend is exhausted. If too loose, then you will hold positions long after the trend has reversed. Stop losses should also be scaled so they are proportional to the current volatility in the relevant instrument. I explain how to calibrate a stop loss so that it matches a particular trend length in two of my earlier books: *Systematic Trading* and *Leveraged Trading*, and also on my blog in an article linked to the web page for this book.

Results

Table 21 shows the performance of the average instrument for strategy six, compared to the long only benchmarks of strategies four and five. Bear in mind the different profile of the various strategies: strategy three (or four) always has a long position on, strategy six is always long or short, whilst strategy five may be long or have no position on at all. This makes it difficult to interpret raw statistics like average return and standard deviation. It actually makes more sense to compare strategies four and six, both of which always have positions on.

Allowing the strategy to go short seems to mostly harm the average return. This is perhaps logical, since we know from the earlier chapters that most of the instruments in our data set have gone up over time. Looking into the future, when the direction of asset returns is quite uncertain, we might expect better relative performance from strategy six than we see in a historical backtest.

There is no benefit in reduced risks, since we always have a position on the standard deviation that is almost identical to strategy four, whilst drawdowns are worse. One tiny crumb of comfort: in the tails strategy six does a little better than the long only benchmarks.

TABLE 21: PERFORMANCE OF AVERAGE INSTRUMENT: LONG ONLY AND WITH DIFFERENT TREND FILTERS

	Strategy four (No trend filter: Long only)	Strategy five (Trend filter: Long only)	Strategy six (Trend filter: Long short)
Mean annual return	6.9%	5.6%	4.8%
Costs	−0.3%	−0.23%	−0.34%
Average drawdown	−18.7%	−20.2%	−25.4%
Standard deviation	20.9%	17.2%	20.9%
Sharpe ratio	0.32	0.32	0.21
Turnover	2.7	5.8	7.0
Skew	−0.09	−0.07	−0.01
Lower tail	1.56	1.60	1.53
Upper tail	1.29	1.26	1.31

We haven't looked at the average performance within each asset class for a while. The relevant statistics are in tables 22 and 23. These can be compared directly with tables 10 and 11, for strategy three. Since both strategies are using dynamic risk targeting and always have a position on, the only difference is the application of the slow trend filter.

TABLE 22: MEDIAN PERFORMANCE FOR SLOW TREND FILTER ACROSS FINANCIAL ASSET CLASSES

	Equity	Vol	FX	Bond
Mean annual return	3.0%	−0.5%	3.4%	5.6%
Costs	−0.3%	−1.3%	−0.4%	−0.4%
Average drawdown	−20.1%	−31.7%	−37.9%	−20.5%
Standard deviation	21.1%	21.8%	20.5%	20.7%
Sharpe ratio	0.15	−0.02	0.17	0.27
Turnover	7.2	6.5	6.7	6.9
Skew	−0.19	−2.15	−0.15	−0.01
Lower tail	1.65	2.07	1.54	1.51
Upper tail	1.21	1.37	1.37	1.30

TABLE 23: MEDIAN PERFORMANCE FOR SLOW TREND FILTER ACROSS COMMODITY ASSET CLASSES

	Metals	Energy	Ags
Mean annual return	12.3%	5.1%	4.3%
Costs	−0.4%	−0.4%	−0.3%
Average drawdown	−20.8%	−37.5%	−38.1%
Standard deviation	22.1%	21.7%	20.7%
Sharpe ratio	0.53	0.26	0.21
Turnover	6.8	6.9	7.1
Skew	0.28	0.10	0.12
Lower tail	1.67	1.43	1.40
Upper tail	1.56	1.31	1.38

That is a lot of numbers! Let me try to summarise them:

- Standard deviations and turnovers are effectively identical across asset classes. We've done a great job of risk targeting and designing a trading strategy with a consistent turnover profile.

- Costs vary slightly, because the cost per trade is different across instruments.

- Average drawdowns have partly converged across asset classes, compared to strategy three. They are worse in assets that had smaller drawdowns in strategy four (like bonds) and better in assets that had high strategy three drawdowns (like volatility).

- Sharpe ratios (SRs) have also improved, except in equities and bonds where they were originally very good. Just being long these two assets was an excellent trade in the past; we give up some of those returns when we go long and short – which is probably a better bet for the future.

- The improvement in the volatility ('vol') assets is particularly striking, and this is because we've gone from being consistently long vol to being mostly short. Indeed, where it not for the 2020 COVID-19 selloff, where we were caught with a short position when levels of vol spiked, we'd have made good profits in both vol markets.

- Skew is slightly better on average except in the two vol instruments. This is because we have replaced a long position in a positive skew asset, with a varying long and short position that has a short bias, producing negative skew.

- Lower tails are better in most asset classes, again vol being the clear exception.

Table 24 shows the backtest statistics for the *aggregate* Jumbo portfolio[105] for strategies four through six. Average return is higher than for both strategies four and five. Risk and costs are also higher than strategy five, since we always have a position on. Costs and turnover are also larger for the dynamic long/short strategy six relative to strategy four, since we have the additional large trades done each time the risk filter changes direction, as well as the smaller daily adjustments to positions when prices or standard deviation estimates change.

Overall the SR is improved versus strategy four, although it is not as good as for strategy five whose risk is reduced by having periods with no positions on for a given instrument. Skew and tail ratios also look better for the dynamic strategy six.

---

105   As before this consists of 102 instruments, trading $50 million of notional capital to ensure there are no issues with minimum capital on any instrument.

TABLE 24: PERFORMANCE OF AGGREGATE JUMBO PORTFOLIO LONG ONLY AND WITH DIFFERENT TREND FILTERS

	Strategy four (No trend filter)	Strategy five (Trend filter: Long only)	Strategy six (Trend filter: Long short)
Mean annual return	15.4%	16.4%	18.5%
Costs	−0.8%	−0.7%	−1.1%
Average drawdown	−24.7%	−10.4%	−10.7%
Standard deviation	18.2%	14.8%	18.4%
Sharpe ratio	0.85	1.11	1.01
Turnover	20.7	24.1	31.6
Skew	−0.04	0.22	0.16
Lower tail	1.44	1.64	1.48
Upper tail	1.24	1.39	1.30

The magical trend following diversification machine

Look again at tables 21 and 24. If we compare each of the performance statistics in turn, comparing strategy six to strategy four, then we see this striking pattern:

- Average return: Strategy six is worse on average (table 21), but better in aggregate (table 24).

- Average drawdown: Worse on average, better in aggregate.

- SR: Worse on average, better in aggregate.

(I'm ignoring the standard deviation and other risk measures, where the differences are relatively small and not significant. We also know that – for obvious reasons – the turnover and costs will be higher for strategy six in both cases.)

Remember these strategies are identical – except one is long only, and the other is long/short with a trend filter. How can it be possible that the trend filter makes individual average instruments do worse – presumably because in the past most instruments have mostly gone up in price – but results in a better performance for an aggregate portfolio?

One possible explanation is related to the different lengths of data history that we have. The average median performance weights all instruments equally, whilst the aggregate performance across instruments effectively assigns a higher weight to instruments with more data.

Imagine that we have two instruments, one which does a little better with a trend filter (like a commodity market) and the other that does worse (such as an equity instrument). Taking an average across these two instruments will make the trend filter look bad. But if the first instrument has more history, then once we look at the aggregated return the trend filter will show an improvement, since for most of the aggregate history we only have the better instrument in our data.

Although I remove instruments with less than one year of data from my analysis, this could still potentially affect our results. However, upon investigation, this effect only explains a very small part of the difference.

In fact, the primary reason for the difference between individual and aggregate performance is that instruments trading in the long/short portfolio are more diversified than those in the long only portfolio.

To see why, consider two instruments whose returns are highly correlated (such as two US equity markets like the NASDAQ and S&P 500). There will still be times when they have different trend signals and hence positions with opposing signs. A recent example would be the 2020 COVID-19 crisis when the S&P 500 trend filter went negative, whilst NASDAQ tech stocks – more resilient in a stay-at-home lockdown economy – remained in an uptrend. After the crash the S&P 500 rebounded and rallied, but for many weeks we were still short S&P 500 and long NASDAQ. During this period the correlation of the trading sub-systems was negative, bringing down the average correlation over time.

We can quantify this diversification benefit using the IDM. The IDM is calculated from the sub-strategy correlations and hence is a measure of diversification. The more diversification, the lower the average correlation, the higher the IDM will be. The sub-strategies for each instrument in strategy six (which can go both long and short) have a lower correlation than those in the long only strategy four. As a result, the final IDM for the Jumbo portfolio in strategy four is 2.46, whereas for the dynamic strategy six it comes out at 2.89.

However, the improvement in performance from the trend filter cannot be explained entirely by this difference in IDM values, suggesting that a linear estimate such as correlation is an imperfect measure of the true diversification benefits that can be gained when using trend filters or other trading rules.

Whilst only institutional traders or very wealthy individuals can trade the full Jumbo portfolio, you should be able to benefit from most of the diversification available if you can hold a portfolio with a reasonably diversified set of instruments.

Figure 28 shows the cumulated percentage returns for strategy six, plus the strategy four benchmark. You will recall that strategy five mostly managed to avoid the horrific drawdown that occurred for strategy four in the early 1980s, as it was not holding the commodity and FX markets that formed the bulk of the portfolio back then, and which were all in free-fall. But strategy six actually thrives during this period, since it can go short falling instruments.

FIGURE 28: CUMULATED RETURNS FOR STRATEGY SIX AND STRATEGY FOUR, JUMBO PORTFOLIO

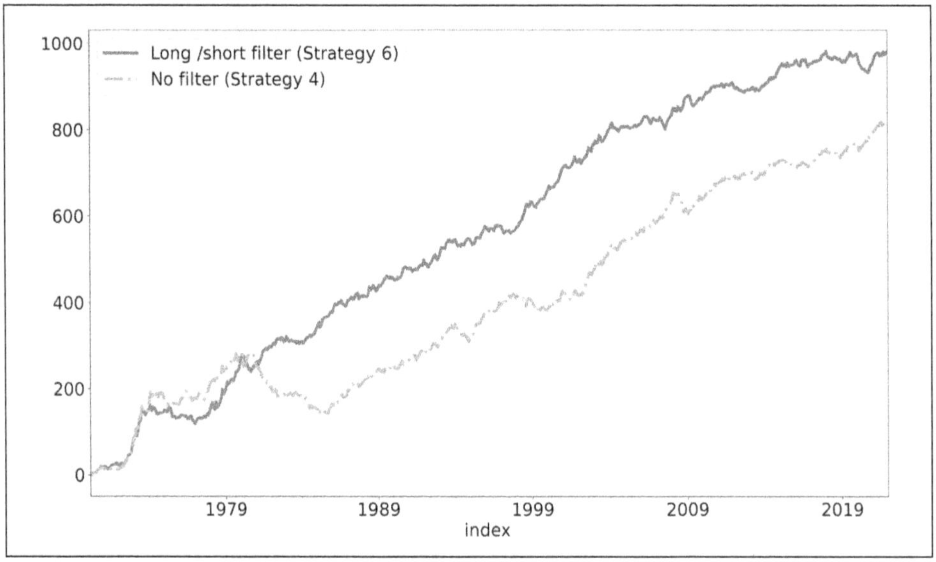

Formally assessing relative performance

Notwithstanding the fact that the aggregate performance of the trend filter on the Jumbo portfolio in table 24 is excellent, it's still rather unsatisfactory that the average performance for a single instrument in table 21 is inferior to a long only strategy. Not everyone can trade the Jumbo portfolio: should ordinary mortals bother with a long and short trend following if they can only hold one or two instruments in their portfolio? Bear in mind that the long only backtest performance of strategy four has been flattered by some unusually good performance in certain asset classes, principally equities and bonds since the late 1970s.

It seems unlikely that these exceptional performances will be repeated in the near future, relying as they did on secular downward trends in inflation and interest rates. These were accompanied by, and partially caused, a significant repricing of equity risk. For example, the price-earnings ratio on US equities has nearly quadrupled from around 10 in the mid-1970s when my backtest data begins, to nearly 40 as I write this chapter.

We need a fairer way of measuring performance against our benchmark long only strategy which accounts for the fact that certain strategies will receive a relative benefit from secular trends in underlying asset prices. Fortunately there are well-established techniques for dealing with this problem and we will use one of them: a linear regression on monthly returns.[106]

I regressed the monthly aggregate returns of the Jumbo portfolio trading strategy six (y) on the benchmark strategy four (x), using the standard linear regression formula which is common in financial economics:

$$y_t = \alpha + \beta x_t + \varepsilon_t$$

If we minimise the sum of squared errors (ε_t) we can estimate coefficients of α (alpha) and β (beta). But do not worry too much about these technical details. The important point is that the beta tells us how the two strategy returns co-move, with a positive number indicating that the strategy returns are positively correlated. The beta for this regression comes in as positive (+0.34), which is to be expected given that the average instrument is an uptrend most of the time during the backtest period. More interestingly, the alpha is 1.13% per month and is highly statistically significant.[107] This implies that the dynamic version of strategy six is generating over 13% a year in additional returns over and above what can be explained by the benchmark, strategy four.

This result should give you more confidence that a long/short trend following strategy can add significant value, especially if long only returns in the future are less impressive.

Conclusion

Going long and short according to a trend following filter is fantastically helpful – it means we can make profits in a falling market. Although this hasn't been an unqualified success in our historical backtest, that is mainly because there has been a paucity of falling markets due to the significant macro trends we've seen since the early 1980s. If we correct for that effect using a linear regression, then we see substantial benefits.

---

106   Daily and weekly returns given a poorer regression fit, but the estimated alpha added by the trend filter is even higher.

107   The 't-statistic' is 9.6, which in plain English means that – in theory – there is less than a one in a zillion chance of the estimated alpha really being negative. A t-statistic of around 2 is normally considered sufficient for statistical significance.

In the next strategy I will introduce the notion of *forecasting*: creating quantified estimates of future risk adjusted returns, and using these to determine the size of our positions. The use of forecasts is extremely powerful. It will allow us to combine disparate sets of trading strategies together. All the remaining strategies in this book use forecasts. This allows them to be combined together in a mix and match fashion.

Strategy six: Trading plan

All other elements are identical to strategy four.

Strategy	Go long or short one or more instruments with variable risk estimate and slow trend filter.
Trend filter	Calculate the 64 business day span price exponentially weighted moving average using the back-adjusted price: $$EWMA(N = 64, \lambda = 0.031)_t$$ $$= 0.031p_t + 0.031(1 - 0.031)p_{t-1}$$ $$+ 0.031(1 - 0.031)^2 p_{t-2} + ...$$ Also calculate the N = 256, α = 0.0078 span EWMA. If EWMA(64) is higher than EWMA(256), we are in an uptrend. Otherwise, we are in a downtrend.
Position sizing	If in an uptrend, long N contracts, where N is the current rounded value of: $$N_{i,t} = Capital \times IDM \times Weight_i \times \tau$$ $$\div (Multiplier_i \times Price_{i,t} \times FX_{i,t} \times \sigma_{\%i,t})$$ If in a downtrend, short N contracts.
Trading decision	Calculate the optimal position as above, updating values of capital, price, FX and standard deviation estimate ($\sigma_\%$). If in an uptrend the position will be long; in a downtrend it will be short. Trade as required to achieve this optimal position, rolling as required.

Slow trend following with trend strength

Have a look at the plot in figure 29. It shows the price for the S&P 500 micro future, and also the fast (64-day) and slow (256-day) EWMA we used in the previous chapter. The time period shown is rather interesting: it's the 2020 COVID-19 market crash.

FIGURE 29: FAST AND SLOW EWMA FOR S&P 500 LEADING UP TO COVID-19 CRASH

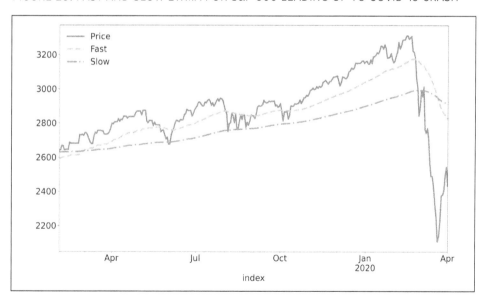

For most of the time period covered by figure 29 we are long (fast moving average above slow), and our positions would have the same expected risk. Hence we are equally long (in terms of risk exposure) on all three of these days:

- On 1st April 2019 when the price has recently been moving sideways and an upward trend is about to begin.

- On 25th January 2020 when there has been a solid upward trend for several months.

- On 19th March 2020 when there has already been a 1,000 point drop in the index (including the second worst day in history, after Black Monday), after the WHO declared COVID-19 a pandemic, there are several thousand COVID-19 cases in the US alone, and President Trump has declared a national emergency. We don't actually close our long until the following day.

Now of course we could have gone short earlier than 20th March by just increasing the speed of our EWMA crossover, and I'll discuss that possibility in the next chapter. But there is a more subtle point here. There is clearly a difference between a clear trend that has been consistently in place for several months (January 2020), one that has just started (April 2019), and a trend that has clearly ended (March 2020). And yet, we have the same sized position on – adjusted for risk – in all three cases.

How can we distinguish between these different periods? The answer is to use a *forecast* – a quantified indication of how strong the trend is, which we can use to size our position differently.

> **Strategy seven:** Trade a portfolio of one or more instruments, each with positions scaled for a variable risk estimate. Hold a long position when they are in an uptrend, and hold a short position in a downtrend. Scale the size of the position according to the strength of the trend.

I will be covering the following topics in this chapter:

- The concept of a forecast.
- Position scaling with forecasts.
- Capping forecasts.

From trend strength to forecast

Let's plot the value of the *crossover* for the EWMAC(64,256) trend filter we introduced in the previous chapter. The crossover is the faster EWMA minus the slower:

$$EWMAC(64,256) = EWMAC(64) - EWMAC(256)$$

As you can see from figure 30 the crossover is quite variable over different periods. There are a couple of reasons for this. Firstly, the price of the S&P 500 has increased, so a 10 point crossover difference back in 1985 (when the price was around 400) is equivalent to a 100 point difference now (when the price is over 4,000). Secondly, the volatility of the S&P 500 varies over time. A 100 point difference, as we see in early 2020, may seem like a lot until we bear in mind that the index was moving more than 100 points per day.

FIGURE 30: EWMA64 MINUS EWMA256 FOR S&P 500

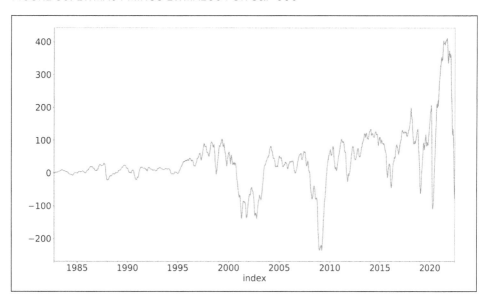

To get a meaningful value for the crossover that we can use to measure trend strength throughout the backtested history, we need to use – you guessed it – *risk adjustment.* This has another advantage, which is that we can compare forecast values for different instruments. That brings huge benefits in terms of calibrating and fitting our trading strategies, since we can use pooled results for many different instruments.

I formally define a **forecast** as a **value that is proportional to an expected risk adjusted return**. Note this means that forecasts are proportional to expected Sharpe ratios (SRs),[108] since these are also risk adjusted returns.

I also define anything that produces a forecast as a **trading rule**. Specifically for our current trading rule – the trend filter – to calculate a forecast we divide the crossover

---

108   Technical note: If the forecast was exactly equal to the expected SR, and we were using full Kelly scaling with a single instrument, we'd set our leverage ratio equal to the forecast divided by the standard deviation of the relevant instrument.

by the standard deviation of returns, but using σ_p the risk calculated in units of daily price, rather than annualised percentage points.[109] The risk in daily price points[110] is just equal to the price multiplied by the annualised percentage risk, divided by 16. Hence the raw forecast for any trend filter using EWMA is:

$$\text{Raw forecast} = (\text{Fast EWMA} - \text{Slow EWMA}) \div \sigma_p$$

$$\sigma_p = \text{Price} \times \sigma_\% \div 16$$

Clearly the sign of the forecast indicates whether we should be long (positive) or short (negative). With a forecast that is above average, we'd have a position that is larger than usual; if the forecast was smaller than average, then our position would be more modest in size.

How do we know if a forecast is equal to its average value? There is usually no easier way[111] than running a backtest, plotting the forecast value over time and measuring the average. To get a more accurate estimate for the average value, we can measure it across many different instruments and take an average of those estimates. Of course, it's only possible to do this because the risk adjustment ensures that forecasts are directly comparable for different instruments.

Because it makes the forecasts easier to read and understand, I prefer to scale my forecasts so that they have an average absolute value[112] of 10. So, once I have estimated the average value of the forecast:

---

109   It's important that this standard deviation is in price and not percentage points, since the crossover is in price points. It's less important that we use daily rather than annualised standard deviations here, since that is just a scaling factor. I've used daily for consistency with my own trading system and my previous books.

110   You can calculate this directly, or derive it from the percentage standard deviation $\sigma_\%$ estimated in earlier chapters with the formula provided here. See Appendix B for more details.

111   For some trading strategies, including this one, we could derive the expected average mathematically, given some assumptions about the distribution of returns. Since these assumptions are usually unrealistic, it's better to do the estimation using a backtest.

112   Technical note: I use the *average absolute value* rather than the *standard deviation*, which might seem the logical way to calibrate forecast scaling. There are two key differences between these two measures. The first difference, which is unimportant, is that the standard deviation is the square root of the average squared value, whilst the average absolute value is just an average of absolute values. The other difference, which is more significant, is that the standard deviation is calculated by subtracting the mean from each value before squaring. This means that the standard deviation will be smaller in value relative to the average absolute value, if a forecast has a bias to being long or short. Trend filters usually have a long bias, since many instruments have gone up in price over time.

Scaled forecast

= Raw forecast × 10 ÷ (Average absolute value of raw forecast)

We can replace the latter part of this equation with the *forecast scalar*:

Forecast scalar = 10 ÷ (Average absolute value of raw forecast)

Scaled forecast = Raw forecast × Forecast scalar

It is considerable work to get robust estimates of the forecast scalar, but for all the strategies in this book I will provide you with my own figures. For the EWMAC(16,64) trading rule, I estimated the forecast scalar to be approximately 1.9.

Important note: Strictly speaking, to avoid in sample cheating, we should use a purely backward looking rolling estimate of the forecast scalar when backtesting. All my backtested results use backward looking estimates, but as these scalars are relatively stable over time there is no harm in using the fixed values I will provide for each strategy.

Hence to calculate the scaled forecast for this trading rule:

Scaled forecast = [(EWMA(64) − EWMA(16)) ÷ σ$_p$] × 1.9

The scaled forecast for S&P 500 is shown in figure 31. As you can see the average absolute value is around 10; to be precise it's a little higher: 10.5. There is no guarantee it would be exactly 10, since I estimated the scaling factor across many different instruments, but for a trading strategy like this I'd expect the realised average on an instrument with plenty of historical data to be very close to our target.[113]

---

113   There are circumstances where that wouldn't be the case. For example, a trend filter that had only seen a bull market for a particular instrument would have a biased average forecast. You would get different problems wiith a market like VIX, where the forecast distribution will have high kurtosis. This is one of the reasons why I use results from multiple instruments to estimate my forecast scalars.

FIGURE 31: SCALED FORECAST FOR EWMA(64,256) TREND FILTER, S&P 500

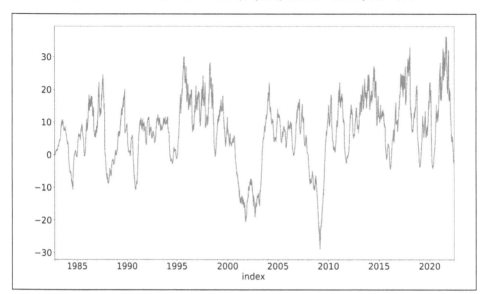

Let's return to the three days I highlighted at the start of the chapter:

- On 1st April 2019 when the price is moving sideways and the trend is just beginning, the forecast is less than five, so we'd have less than half our average position on.

- On 28th January 2020 when there has been a solid upward trend for several months, the forecast is around 20. This translates to a position that is double our average.

- On 19th March 2020 when all hell has broken loose the forecast is less than one. We'd have a tenth of our normal position on. Unless we had a large amount of capital allocated to this instrument, we'd most likely have a position of zero and would have closed our trade a few days beforehand.

Position scaling with forecasts

There is another benefit to having a risk adjusted forecast with a common interpretation across different instruments and different time periods: **we can use the same equation to determine our optimal position – regardless of precisely what strategy or instrument we're trading:**

$$N_i = \text{Scaled forecast}_{i,t} \times \text{Capital} \times \text{IDM} \times \text{Weight}_i \times \tau$$
$$\div (10 \times \text{Multiplier}_i \times \text{Price}_{i,t} \times \text{Fx}_{i,t} \times \sigma_{\%i,t})$$

There are two new elements we haven't seen before: the scaled forecast[114] and the fixed constant, 10. The effect of these is twofold. Firstly, if the scaled forecast is positive we'd go long, whereas if it's negative we'd want to be short. Secondly, the size of our position will depend on the absolute value of the scaled forecast. If it's equal to 10, we'll have on an average sized position (exactly as we had for strategies three to six). Otherwise, our position in contracts will be smaller or larger.

Let's examine the positions for S&P 500 from late 2019 to early 2020. These are shown in figure 32.

FIGURE 32: SCALED FORECAST AND POSITION IN CONTRACTS FOR S&P 500

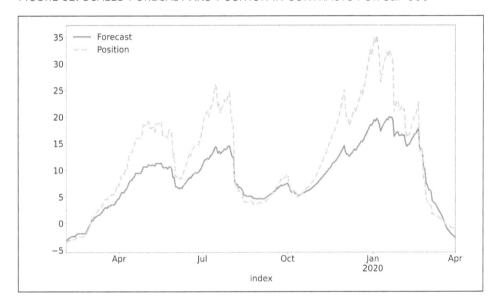

I've plotted the scaled forecast as well, since by chance[115] with $100,000 in capital the position in contracts during this period is on a similar scale. You can see that in early April our position is very small, reflecting the very weak forecast. By late January we have a much larger trade on. Then, as the market gets riskier, we have smaller positions for a given forecast level. During the next couple of weeks our position is cut savagely, partly because risk levels are elevated, but also because our forecast is falling rapidly. As a result we are less exposed to the ensuing selloff.

An important difference here is that we don't do a single huge trade on one day when

---

114 Very technical note: If you substitute in the scaled forecast calculation above, you will notice that our position is proportional to $1 \div \sigma_{\%i}^2$. This will be a familiar result to students of financial economics who have studied mean variance optimisation.

115 Not really.

the trend filter reverses in late March, as we did for strategies five and six. Instead the trade is closed gradually as the forecast reduces in the weeks beforehand. Our backtested costs will increase slightly when we introduce forecasting, since we have additional trades caused by forecast adjustment. However, for institutional traders,[116] it's plausible that this smoother trading profile will lead to lower costs, since they will pay dearly if they actually try to close their entire position on a single day rather than gradually over a period of weeks.

A maximum forecast value

As figure 31 showed it's possible for a scaled forecast to reach two or even three times its average value of ten. This means that at times we'll be running positions that are over three times what we'd be running in our earlier strategies. This isn't a very good idea, since it concentrates our risk into instruments which have high forecasts.[117] Plus there are other trading rules for which even more extreme forecast values are possible.

There are other good reasons for limiting the forecast value, and I will explain those in Part Two. For now just take it as read that the **maximum absolute forecast value you should use is 20**. This means we'd never have more than twice our average position in play. You should use the following modified position scaling formula:

$$\text{Capped forecast}_{i,t} = \text{Max}(\text{Min}(\text{Scaled forecast}_{i,t}, +20), -20)$$

$$N_{i,t} = \text{Capped forecast}_{i,t} \times \text{Capital} \times \text{IDM} \times \text{Weight}_i \times \tau$$
$$\div (10 \times \text{Multiplier}_i \times \text{Price}_{i,t} \times \text{FX}_{i,t} \times \sigma_{\%i,t})$$

Evaluating the performance of strategy seven

Let's now turn to our usual evaluation. First of all we'll check the performance of the median instrument in our data set. This is shown in table 25.

---

116 If costs were linear, then costs would probably be unchanged. But institutional traders face non-linear costs, because their costs increase dramatically when they start to severely impact the market through their trading.

117 In hindsight it was a very bad idea indeed to have a large long position in S&P 500 futures going into January 2020.

TABLE 25: PERFORMANCE OF AVERAGE INSTRUMENT, LONG ONLY, TREND FILTER AND WITH FORECASTS

	Strategy four Long only	Strategy six Slow trend filter long/short	Strategy seven Slow trend filter with forecasts
Mean annual return	6.9%	4.8%	4.1%
Costs	−0.3%	−0.3%	−0.3%
Average drawdown	−18.7%	−25.4%	−31.2%
Standard deviation	20.9%	20.9%	22.9%
Sharpe ratio	0.32	0.21	0.18
Turnover	2.7	7.0	8.9
Skew	−0.09	−0.01	0.18
Lower tail	1.56	1.53	3.80
Upper tail	1.29	1.31	3.09

The results are slightly disappointing. We'd expect a modest rise in turnover, because we have more adjustment trades, although the closing trades we do when the trend filter reverses are much smaller, so we see no significant change in costs. But the other statistics also look worse, with the exception of skew. Let's turn to the aggregate performance of the Jumbo portfolio, since we know that diversification effects can often change the picture.

Table 26 shows the aggregate figures. These are better; returns have improved, although the SR is down very slightly. The risk statistics are still a little uglier.

TABLE 26: PERFORMANCE OF AVERAGE INSTRUMENT, LONG ONLY, TREND FILTER, AND WITH FORECASTS

	Strategy four Long only	Strategy six Slow trend filter long/short	Strategy seven Slow trend filter with forecasts
Mean annual return	15.4%	18.5%	21.6%
Costs	−0.8%	−1.1%	−1.2%
Average drawdown	−24.7%	−10.7%	−15.9%
Standard deviation	18.2%	18.4%	22.5%
Sharpe ratio	0.85	1.01	0.96
Turnover	20.7	31.6	40.1
Skew	−0.04	0.16	−0.33
Lower tail	1.44	1.48	1.90
Upper tail	1.24	1.30	1.62

However, as I've pointed out before – and will do so again – we need to be wary of backtest results since they will favour strategies with a long position bias in a historical period when many instruments went up in price. To correct for this I will use the same method that I implemented for strategy six. I regressed the monthly aggregate returns of the Jumbo portfolio trading strategy seven (y) on the benchmark strategy four (x), using a linear regression formula, and I got the following results:

$$y_t = 1.17\% + 0.51x_t + \varepsilon_t$$

This is actually a small improvement on strategy six, where the alpha is 1.13% per month versus the 1.17% we see here. Once we've corrected for the different exposure to a long only benchmark, forecast scaling looks pretty good. Still this isn't a slam dunk for the idea of using forecasts to modify position sizes. However, there are some good reasons for sticking with it:

- It turns out that forecasting works better for faster trend filters and for other kinds of strategy. I will introduce this evidence later in the book.

- Using forecast strength makes it easier to combine different trading strategies together, as I will explain in strategy nine.

- As I've noted already, for institutional traders using forecast scaling it is likely to reduce costs considerably even though retail traders may see a modest rise (there is a way to reduce those extra costs, and I will explain it in the next strategy).

Conclusion

You can think of a forecast as measuring the level of conviction we have in our trades. Trends that have been around for longer, with lower volatility, look more convincing than weak choppy trends that have just been established. It makes intuitive sense that we should have larger positions on when we are more convinced about the direction of the market. There is also convincing empirical research that this is the case, but you will have to wait for strategy twelve in Part Two to see that.

Although its benefits currently appear to be somewhat marginal, the use of forecasting as a tool to combine different trading strategies together will mean we can easily trade multiple types of strategy, realising the substantial benefits of holding a diversified set of strategies rather than having to choose a single one. These benefits will become clearer from strategy nine onwards. If diversification is the best free lunch in finance, and risk targeting is the second, then perhaps forecasting can claim to be at least a decent afternoon snack.

However, before then we will widen our choice of strategies further by adding a faster trend following filter.

Strategy seven: Trading plan

All other elements are identical to strategy six.

Strategy	Go long or short one or more instruments with variable risk estimate and variable forecast based on strength of a trend filter.
EWMA calculations	See strategy six.
Trading rule: EWMAC(64,256)	$$\text{Raw forecast}_{i,t}$$ $$= (\text{EWMA(64)}_{i,t} - \text{EWMA(256)}_{i,t}) \div \sigma_p$$
Scaled forecast	$$\text{Scaled forecast}_{i,t} = \text{Raw forecast}_{i,t} \times 1.9$$
Capped forecast	$$\text{Capped forecast}_{i,t}$$ $$= \text{Max(Min(Scaled forecast}_{i,t}, +20), -20)$$
Position sizing	Long or short N contracts, where N is the current rounded value of: $$N_{i,t} = \text{Capped forecast}_{i,t} \times \text{Capital}$$ $$\times \text{IDM} \times \text{Weight}_i \times \tau \div (10 \times \text{Multiplier}_i$$ $$\times \text{Price}_{i,t} \times \text{FX}_{i,t} \times \sigma_{\%i,t})$$
Trading decision	Calculate the optimal position as above, updating values of forecasts, capital, price, FX and standard deviation estimate ($\sigma_\%$). If in an uptrend the position will be long, in a downtrend it will be short. Trade as required to achieve this optimal position, rolling as required.

Fast trend following, long and short with trend strength

As equity investors know to their cost, markets don't go up in a straight line; there are bull and bear markets that often last for several years. These big secular trends are what we're trying to capture with the slow trend filter developed in strategy five, and further refined in strategies six and seven. But even within a bull market there are reversals which will be far too brief for our filter to notice.

Fortunately there is more to trend following than just the relatively slow variant that we used to filter our positions in the last few chapters. Academic researchers have found evidence of trends at shorter time horizons as well. In this chapter we'll focus on a relatively quick trend filter.

> **Strategy eight:** Trade a portfolio of one or more instruments, each with positions scaled for a variable risk estimate. Hold a long position when they are in a recent uptrend, and hold a short position in a recent downtrend. Scale the size of the position according to the strength of the trend.

I will be covering the following topics in this chapter:

- Constructing a faster measure of our trend filter.

- Using buffering to reduce trading costs.

Constructing a faster trend filter

Our original trend filter took the form EWMA(64) – EWMA(256). I choose 256 days as it is approximately the number of business days in a year. But why did I choose 64 days as the faster moving average, exactly a quarter of 256?

If you are the type of person who reads and remembers footnotes, then you will know that any ratio between the two moving average lengths of two and six gives statistically indistinguishable results with both real and artificial data (the latter was used to avoid potential in sample fitting). Using a shorter length that is one quarter the longer length is mathematically neat, especially since $2^2 = 4$ and $2^8 = 256$, which means we can create a neat series of moving average crossovers of different speeds: 64&256, 32&128, 16&64, 8&32 and so on.

With that in mind, let's modify our calculations from strategies six and seven to construct a more nimble version of the trend filter with spans of 16 and 64 days:[118]

$$EWMA(N = 16, \lambda = 0.118)_t$$
$$= 0.118p_t + 0.118(1 - 0.118)p_{t-1} + 0.118(1 - 0.118)^2 p_{t-2} +...$$

$$EWMA(N = 64, \lambda = 0.031)_t$$
$$= 0.031p_t + 0.031(1 - 0.031)p_{t-1} + 0.031(1 - 0.031)^2 p_{t-2} +...$$

Here are the general formulae from the previous chapter:

$$\text{Raw forecast} = (\text{Fast EWMA} - \text{Slow EWMA}) \div \sigma_p$$

$$\text{Scaled forecast} = \text{Raw forecast} \times \text{Forecast scalar}$$

My estimate for the forecast scalar is 4.1 for this faster crossover, hence we have:

$$\text{Raw forecast} = (EWMA_{16} - EWMA_{64}) \div \sigma_p$$

$$\text{Scaled forecast} = \text{Raw forecast} \times 4.1$$

---

118 Readers of my earlier book, *Leveraged Trading*, will recognise this as the trend speed used for the 'Starter System' in the first part of the book.

Finally we use the capping[119] and position sizing formula:

$$\text{Capped forecast} = \text{Max}(\text{Min}(\text{Scaled forecast}, +20), -20)$$

$$N_{i,t} = \text{Capped forecast}_{i,t} \times \text{Capital} \times \text{IDM} \times \text{Weight}_i \times \tau$$
$$\div\ (10 \times \text{Multiplier}_i \times \text{Price}_{i,t} \times \text{Fx}_{i,t} \times \sigma_{\%i,t})$$

What we have done here is construct a new *trading rule variation*. The generic *trading rule* is the EWMAC trend rule, and we now have two possible variations of that rule: the original EWMAC(64,256), and the new EWMAC(16,64).

Buffering to reduce trading costs

Let's return to one of my favourite obsessions: trading costs. These are clearly going to be higher for a faster trend filter. This isn't a major problem for the S&P 500, which is a very cheap future to trade, but it will be problematic for more expensive instruments.

There are a couple of different ways we can address this problem,[120] which we can use for any trading rule. One is to smooth the forecast in some way, by using a moving average or an exponentially weighted moving average. This doesn't apply here since the trend filters we're using are already constructed of moving averages. Further smoothing would reduce their efficacy in picking uptrends. But we will use this technique with other strategies later in the book.

The second method we can use is *buffering*.[121] Here we don't smooth the forecast, but instead ignore small changes in the forecast that aren't important and are causing unnecessary trading. We only trade when our current position is significantly different from the optimal position.

We start by setting a **trading buffer**. The buffer is a region around our optimal position

---

119   It turns out that capping is much more important for faster trend filters, since it's more likely they will reach extreme values. I'll discuss this more in Part Two.
120   Actually there are some other things we can do. We can avoid trading expensive instruments with faster trading rule variations, and I discuss that option in strategy nine. We can also try to reduce the average cost for each trade; that will be covered in Part Six.
121   This is a slightly more complicated version of the 'position inertia' method I introduced in chapter twelve of *Systematic Trading*. But it is identical to the position management rule in chapter ten of *Leveraged Trading*. Buffering is the optimal method for traders who experience transaction costs that are a fixed percentage irrespective of trade size. This is approximately true for futures traders who pay fixed per contract commissions, and who are not so large that their trades begin to impact the market. See *Efficiently Inefficient* by Lasse Pedersen for more details (full reference details in Appendix A).

where we don't trade. The buffer B is set as a fraction, F, of the average long position (i.e. the position we'd take for strategy four, or equivalently the position we'd have for strategy eight with a forecast of +10):

$$B_{i,t} = F \times Capital \times IDM \times Weight_i \times \tau$$
$$\div (Multiplier_i \times Price_{i,t} \times FX_{i,t} \times \sigma_{\%i,t})$$

Theoretically the correct value of F depends on several factors, including the speed and profitability of the relevant trading rule, and the costs we have to pay, but it's most convenient to set it at a fairly conservative value of 0.10.

We now set a lower and upper buffer limit around the unrounded optimal number of contracts, N (which we calculate in the usual way and which could be positive or negative):

$$Lower\ buffer,\ B^L_{i,t} = round(N_{i,t} - B_{i,t})$$

$$Upper\ buffer,\ B^U_{i,t} = round(N_{i,t} + B_{i,t})$$

We now use the following rule. Given a current position in round contracts of C:

$$B^U_{i,t} \leq C_{i,t} \leq B^L_{i,t} : \text{No trading required}$$

$$C_{i,t} < B^L_{i,t} : \text{Buy } (B^L_{i,t} - C_{i,t}) \text{ contracts}$$

$$C_{i,t} > B^U_{i,t} : \text{Sell } (C_{i,t} - B^U_{i,t}) \text{ contracts}$$

Let's look at a specific day to get a feel for the calculations, and then consider the general behaviour we get from buffering. On 22nd July 2021 the optimal value of N was long 13.2 contracts, for capital of $100,000 with a strategy just trading the S&P 500 micro futures. I calculated this value of N using the current forecast value, price, FX and standard deviation. On the same day the average long position was 8.8 contracts. With $F = 0.1$ that gives us a value for B of 0.88:

$$Lower\ buffer,\ B^L = round(13.2 - 0.88)$$
$$= round(12.3) = 12 \text{ contracts}$$

$$Upper\ buffer,\ B^U = round(13.2 + 0.88)$$
$$= round(14.1) = 14 \text{ contracts}$$

The current position in round contracts C_i is 12 contracts (and has been since 20th July). Since 12 falls between B^L and B^U, no trading is required.

Figure 33 shows the effect of applying buffering on the S&P 500 in early 2021.

FIGURE 33: EFFECT OF BUFFERING ON THE S&P 500 IN EARLY 2021

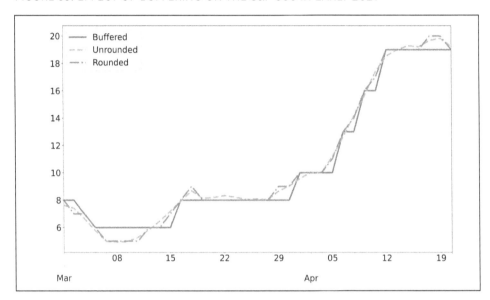

The light grey dashed line ('unrounded') shows the position we'd take if we could trade fractional contracts. If we just rounded this optimal position, as we have done in earlier strategies, we'd get the darker dashed line ('rounded'). The buffered position is the solid dark line. Notice how this trades significantly less than the rounded position, especially in the period from 7th April to 30th April. With simple rounding we trade a total of seven contracts during this time interval, whilst with buffering we only do a single trade on 16th April, for two contracts.

Buffering reduces the turnover[122] of our trading substantially without damaging performance.[123]

---

122   It *usually* reduces the turnover; of course if the position is going up in a straight line then turnover will be unchanged when buffering is applied.

123   Technical note: To be pedantic, buffering reduces linear costs (of the type experienced by retail investors), but not the non-linear costs experienced by large funds. I discuss ways to reduce non-linear trading costs in Part Six.

Detailed results

In the following tables, I've included three different strategies:

- The original strategy four, which is a long only strategy with no trend filter, but with dynamic position sizing according to risk.

- A version of strategy seven using a slow trend filter EWMAC(64,256) with forecasting. For consistency with strategy eight, I have modified this strategy so it also uses buffering. Of course, as this strategy trades quite slowly, buffering doesn't really affect it that much.

- Strategy eight using a fast trend filter: EWMAC(16,64), with forecasting and buffering.

As usual, let's first look at the average (median) performance across all the instruments in my data set. The results are in table 27.

TABLE 27: MEDIAN PERFORMANCE ACROSS INSTRUMENTS: LONG ONLY, FAST AND SLOW TREND FILTERS

	Strategy four Long only	Strategy seven (with buffering) Slow trend long/short	Strategy eight (with buffering) Fast trend long/short
Mean annual return	6.9%	4.0%	6.5%
Costs	−0.3%	−0.3%	−0.5%
Average drawdown	−18.7%	−30.1%	−28.8%
Standard deviation	20.9%	22.6%	23.6%
Sharpe ratio	0.32	0.19	0.27
Turnover	2.7	8.9	16.7
Skew	−0.09	0.14	1.00
Lower tail	1.56	3.29	3.35
Upper tail	1.29	2.63	2.99

On average, the faster trend does seem to be more profitable than the slower trend. This is true on every measure except of course turnover and costs, where we have to pay out more to capture the faster trends. It also has much better skew, albeit with slightly fatter tails. In fact one of the desirable properties of trend following is that it is expected to provide us with positive skew, and faster trend filters tend to provide better skew. I'll explore this effect more in strategy nine.

Table 28 shows the aggregated backtest statistics for the Jumbo portfolio, across the same three strategies.

TABLE 28: PERFORMANCE OF AGGREGATE JUMBO PORTFOLIO: LONG ONLY, FAST AND SLOW TREND FILTERS

	Strategy four Long only	Strategy seven (with buffering) Slow trend long/ short	Strategy eight (with buffering) Fast trend long/ short
Mean annual return	15.4%	21.5%	24.1%
Costs	−0.8%	−1.0%	−1.7%
Average drawdown	−24.7%	−16.0%	−11.4%
Standard deviation	18.2%	22.3%	22.7%
Sharpe ratio	0.85	0.96	1.06
Turnover	20.7	27.5	60.5
Skew	−0.04	0.61	0.81
Lower tail	1.44	1.90	1.97
Upper tail	1.24	1.63	1.81

The pattern of outperformance continues for the aggregated Jumbo portfolio. On almost every measure the faster trend following matches or outperforms the slower, with the obvious exception of costs and turnover. Once again, the skew is noticeably better.

Figure 34 clearly shows the very different character of the three strategies. For example, in late 2008 the slow trend filter remained long most equity markets as they crashed, and hence did about as badly as the long only strategy four. In contrast the fast trend filter was able to pick up this downtrend and had its best performing year.

FIGURE 34: ACCOUNT CURVE FOR LONG ONLY STRATEGY FOUR, PLUS FAST AND SLOW TREND FOLLOWING STRATEGIES

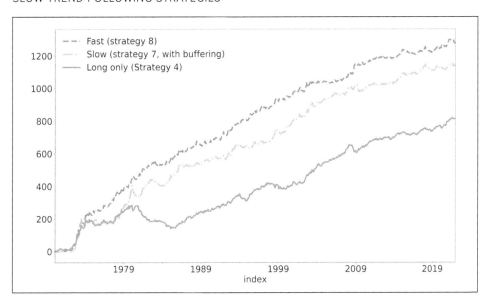

Now let's do a regression to see if (a) the trend filter returns are due to an exposure to the long only strategy four, or (b) we are adding 'alpha': uncorrelated additional returns. I used monthly returns to do the following regressions (again using buffering on both strategies seven and eight for consistency):

$$\text{Regressing strategy eight (fast): } y_t$$
$$= \alpha + \beta x_t + \varepsilon_t = 1.55\% + 0.38x_t + \varepsilon_t$$

$$\text{Regressing strategy seven (slow): } yt$$
$$= \alpha + \beta x_t + \varepsilon_t = 1.13\% + 0.53x_t + \varepsilon_t$$

The beta is much lower for the fast trend filter than for the slow.[124] This is easily explained by the fact that in our backtest most instruments have gone up most of the time, so our slow trend filter spends more time being long than short. With a faster trend filter we are more likely to have a balanced set of longs and shorts, and hence be more dissimilar to a long only strategy.

---

124 Technical note: Beta is a *covariance*: the product of the relative standard deviation and correlation of the returns in each strategy. Because the standard deviations for all three strategies are roughly the same, the beta estimates are almost identical to the correlations.

The alpha for the fast trend filter is also significantly higher at an extra 0.17% a month or around 2% a year.

Conclusion

Strategy eight is undoubtedly the star of the book so far. Its performance exceeds that of the long only benchmark (strategy four), and its slower cousin (strategy seven), on almost every possible benchmark. Does that mean we should drop the slow trend filter entirely? No. As I explain in the next chapter we can do even better than strategy eight, by combining it with strategy seven and with other variations of the EWMAC trading rule.

This combination is possible because of the magic of **forecasting**. Because forecasts are all in a consistent scale, we can take averages across forecasts from different trading rules, and variations of the same rule. This allows us to continue using exactly the same position sizing equations, replacing the forecast from a single rule with a combined forecast.

Strategy eight: Trading plan

All other elements are identical to strategy seven.

Strategy	Go long and short one or more instruments with variable risk estimate and variable forecast based on the strength of a fast trend filter and using a buffer to reduce trading costs.
EWMA calculations	Calculate the 64 business day span price exponentially weighted moving average using the back-adjusted price: $$\text{EWMA}(N = 64, \alpha = 0.031)t =$$ $$0.031pt + 0.031(1 - 0.031)pt{-}1$$ $$+ 0.031(1 - 0.031)^2pt{-}2 + ...$$ Also calculate the $N = 16$, $\alpha = 0.118$ span EWMA.
Trading rule: EWMAC Variation: EWMAC(16,64)	Raw forecast$_{i,t}$ $$= (\text{EWMA}(16)_{i,t} - \text{EWMA}(64)_{i,t}) \div \sigma_{p,i,t}$$
Scaled forecast	Scaled forecast $_{i,t}$ = Raw forecast $_{i,t}$ × 4.1

Capped forecast	**Capped forecast$_{i,t}$**
	= Max(Min(Scaled forecast$_{i,t}$, +20), −20)
Optimal position sizing	Buy or sell N contracts, where N is the current *unrounded* value of:
	N_i = Capped forecast$_{i,t}$ × Capital × IDM × Weight$_i$
	× τ ÷ (10 × Multiplier$_i$ × Price$_{i,t}$ × FX$_{i,t}$ × σ$_{\%i,t}$)
Buffer width	**$B_{i,t}$ = 0.1 × Capital × IDM × Weight$_i$ × τ**
	÷ (Multiplier$_i$ × Price$_{i,t}$ × FX$_{i,t}$ × σ$_{\%i,t}$)
Buffer zone	**Lower buffer, $B^L_{i,t}$ = round($N_{i,t}$ − $B_{i,t}$)**
	Upper buffer, $B^U_{i,t}$ = round($N_{i,t}$ + $B_{i,t}$)
Trading decision	Calculate the optimal position as above, updating values of forecasts, capital, price, FX and standard deviation estimate. Calculate the buffer zone around the optimal position. Then given a current position in round contracts of C_j:
	$B^U_{i,t} \leq C_{i,t} \leq B^L_{i,t}$: No trading required
	$C_{i,t} < B^L_{i,t}$: Buy ($B^U_{i,t}$ − $C_{i,t}$) contracts
	$C_{i,t} > B^U_{i,t}$: Sell ($C_{i,t}$− $B^U_{i,t}$) contracts

Note: We can also trade a buffered version of strategy seven, which is identical to the above trading plan except for the use of an EWMAC(64,256) trend filter.

Multiple trend following rules

The faster trend filter of strategy eight is better than the slower filter we were originally using. But does that mean we should exclusively use strategy eight as our trend following system? Is there any benefit to trading both?

Back in strategy four I said we wanted to trade as many instruments as possible, as they give us access to many different kinds of risk premia. That neat theory is confirmed by clear evidence: the returns from trading these many instruments are relatively uncorrelated,[125] and adding together multiple uncorrelated return streams consistently improves almost all our available measures of performance. To see this effect for yourself, just compare the superior returns of any Jumbo portfolio to the matching figures for median statistics across individual instruments.

But diversifying across instruments isn't the only game in town. We can also diversify across uncorrelated *trading strategies*. We don't have to pick a single one. Now, the correlation between the two trend filters we have developed so far (strategies seven and eight) is fairly high: 0.70. This is not surprising. Both filters are constructed using the same method, with only the spans being different. To put it another way, a strategy in a slow uptrend is also likely to be in a fast uptrend. But the correlation isn't a perfect 1.0, so there ought to be some benefits from trading both trend speeds.

Just as we were able to benefit from diversifying over different instruments, we can benefit from using two or more different strategies that target different lengths of trend. This means that we'd benefit from using both strategy seven (for slow trends) and strategy eight (for fast trends), and indeed any other speed of trend filter. This will

---

125 At this point I will wearily mention the usual caveat that correlations are purely a linear measure of co-movement. However, if anything, the diversification benefits from trading multiple instruments is even higher than we'd expect given our estimates of their correlations, especially for trend following like rules.

give us a combined strategy that is superior to any individual speed of filter: including that of strategy eight.

Strategy nine: Trade a portfolio of one or more instruments, each with positions scaled for a variable risk estimate. Calculate a number of forecasts for different speeds of trend filter. Place a position based on the combined forecast.

I will be covering the following topics in this chapter:

- Selecting a series of trend filters.

- How different trend filters behave over time: costs, performance over time and risk.

- Combining a number of different forecasts.

- Optimizing forecast weights.

- Accounting for forecast diversification.

- Position scaling with different forecasts.

Selecting a series of trend following filters

The two trend filters we've used so far are EWMA(64) – EWMA(256), and EWMA(16) – EWMA(64). As I've noted before, using a shorter length that is one quarter the longer length is rather neat and means we can create a neat series of moving average crossovers of different speeds; different **variations** of the generic **trading rule**: EWMAC:

- EWMAC(64,256): EWMA(64) – EWMA(256). This was strategy seven.

- EWMAC(32,128)

- EWMAC(16,64): This was strategy eight.

- EWMAC(8,32)

- EWMAC(4,16)

- EWMAC(2,8)

We could also include EWMAC(1,4) but as we'll see later even EWMAC(2,8) is too expensive for almost all futures instruments.[126] At the other end of the spectrum anything slower than EWMAC(64,256) becomes too correlated with a long only strategy and we get fewer trades, which makes it difficult to evaluate whether we're

---

126   Also EWMA(1) is just equal to the last price and no longer qualifies as an average.

adding any value. At some point, we'd be trading so slowly this book would have to be renamed 'Advanced Futures *Investing* Strategies'.

As we will see in a few pages time, we don't need to look at intermediate filters like EWMAC(12,48), since the pairings above are already highly correlated, hence there is no benefit from using a more granular set of pairs.

Similarly, the choice of ratio between fast and slow EWMA spans, for which I'm using the fixed value of four, won't affect our results very much. Any ratio between two and six does equally well. We could consider trading both EWMAC(16,64) (a ratio of four) and EWMAC(16,32) (a ratio of two), and perhaps EWMAC(16,92) as well (a ratio of six), but once again they'd be very highly correlated. Using a fixed ratio also means that I can save space by referring to EWMACn as a shorthand for EWMAC($n,4n$). Hence, EWMAC16 is equivalent to EWMAC(16,64).

For all of these variations we can use exactly the same position sizing and management rules as we used in strategy eight:

- Calculate the raw crossover value for each trading rule variation.

- Divide by the standard deviation to find the risk normalized forecast.

- Scale the forecast so it has an expected absolute average value of 10.

- Cap the forecast.

- Calculate an optimal risk adjusted unrounded position, N contracts, using the capped forecast, risk target, current risk of the instrument, current price, FX rate, plus the capital, instrument weights and instrument diversification multiplier (IDM).

- Calculate a buffer zone around the optimal position.

- Compare the current position to the buffer zone to decide whether to trade.

We just need the forecast scalars,[127] which you can find estimates for in table 29.

---

127   Notice the ratio of the forecast scalars for consecutive trend filters (where each time we double the span) is around 1.414: the square root of 2. This shouldn't be a surprise to fans of financial mathematics.

TABLE 29: FORECAST SCALARS FOR DIFFERENT SPEEDS OF TREND FILTER

	Forecast scalars
EWMAC2	12.1
EWMAC4	8.53
EWMAC8	5.95
EWMAC16	4.10
EWMAC32	2.79
EWMAC64	1.91

Should we use a different measure of volatility for different trend speeds?

In the calculations above we use the same estimate of standard deviation that we've used since strategy three: an exponentially weighted standard deviation with a span of 35 days (plus a weighting of the current estimate and a very long moving average). Does that make sense? If we're using EWMAC2, then we expect to be holding positions for a few days. But with EWMAC64 our trades are in place for months at a time. We are trying to predict future volatility at very different time horizons, depending on the speed of trend filter.

Intuitively, you might expect that using a shorter span for our volatility estimate would result in a more accurate forecast for strategies that trade more quickly. Conversely, if we expect to hold our position for many weeks, then a longer span would be in order.

In fact the optimum span for estimating the standard deviation is not affected by the period of time for which we're trying to forecast future volatility. Spans of between 10 and 50 days do reasonably well at forecasting future volatility, regardless of time period, and the optimum is somewhere around 30 to 35 days.

We are not as good at forecasting risk for holding periods typical of very fast (EWMAC2) or very slow (EWMA64) trading rules. For short holding periods of a few days the standard deviation can vary wildly, and it is very difficult to forecast anything several months ahead. But that doesn't change the key finding: the optimal look back is around 30 days, with other look backs doing a relatively poor job of forecasting future risk, regardless of the time horizon involved.

All this means that we can stick to using a single estimate of standard deviation, irrespective of which trading rule we are using.

The performance of different trend filters

Let's take a closer look at the performance of different trend filters, which are shown in tables 30 and 31. I'm showing the aggregate Jumbo portfolio statistics; the averages across individual markets would produce a similar result, at least on a relative basis (although the absolute Sharpe ratios (SRs), for example, would obviously be lower).

TABLE 30: PERFORMANCE FOR DIFFERENT SPEEDS OF TREND FILTER (FAST FILTERS)

	EWMAC2	EWMAC4	EWMAC8
Mean annual return (gross)	13.0%	19.6%	24.1%
Mean annual return (net)	3.5%	14.8%	21.5%
Costs	−9.3%	−4.7%	−2.5%
Average drawdown	−161.7%	−23.1%	−13.0%
Standard deviation	22.9%	23.1%	23.3%
Sharpe ratio	0.15	0.64	0.92
Turnover	381	195	97.9
Skew	1.32	0.75	1.48
Lower tail	1.94	1.98	1.84
Upper tail	2.28	2.15	2.11
Annualised alpha (gross)	10.2%	15.9%	19.4%
Annualised alpha (net)	0.9%	11.2%	16.9%
Beta	0.17	0.25	0.32

Aggregated Jumbo portfolio results with buffering and forecast scaling.

TABLE 31: PERFORMANCE FOR DIFFERENT SPEEDS OF TREND FILTER (SLOW FILTERS)

	EWMAC16 (Strategy 8)	EWMAC32	EWMAC64 (Strategy 7)
Mean annual return (gross)	25.8%	24.4%	22.5%
Mean annual return (net)	24.1%	23.2%	21.5%
Costs	−1.7%	−1.2%	−1.0%
Average drawdown	−11.4%	−13.4%	−16.0%
Standard deviation	22.7%	22.7%	22.3%
Sharpe ratio	1.06	1.02	0.96
Turnover	60.5	35.3	27.5
Skew	0.81	0.75	0.61
Lower tail	1.97	1.98	1.90
Upper tail	1.81	1.72	1.63
Annualised alpha (gross)	19.3%	17.3%	14.6%
Annualised alpha (net)	17.6%	16.2%	13.6%
Beta	0.38	0.48	0.53

Aggregated Jumbo portfolio results with buffering and forecast scaling.

Firstly, let's deal with the obvious stuff. Turnover and costs are insanely high for the fastest trend filter, and then get more reasonable as we slow down. There isn't much to choose between the pre-cost (gross) annual means, although EWMAC2 looks a little worse, but once we account for costs (net) the faster two filters definitely underperform the others.

EWMAC2 in particular appears to be a sure fire money loser. Should we exclude it from further consideration? Perhaps not. I'm using every single instrument in my data set here, to ensure I am calculating statistically significant figures for pre-cost returns. It could be that some instruments are cheap enough to profitably trade the fastest filters. I'll explore this possibility later in the chapter.

I've also included figures for regressions in tables 30 and 31. Each regression has been done on the returns of the standard strategy four, long only, benchmark. Firstly, let's focus on the betas. The slower we trade, the more likely we are to be persistently long instruments that have generally gone up in price, such as the bond futures. Hence the betas are higher for slower trend filters: more of their returns can be explained by their exposure to the benchmark long only portfolio.

There are also figures for alphas calculated both with and without costs. Ignoring costs, the faster filters look better on gross alpha than they do on outright returns, because of those lower betas. Once we apply costs the net alphas on the very fastest trends aren't as impressive.

The monthly skew shows an interesting pattern. With the exception of the very fastest filter, the skew reduces as we slow down. This is a well-known effect with trend following. Because we ride winners and cut losses, each trade we do when trend following has positive skew. But this skew is most prominent when observed at a frequency that is commensurate with the holding period of the strategy.[128]

When we look at the pattern of skew calculated using daily, weekly, monthly and annual returns, we can see this effect playing out. Table 32 has the relevant figures. The slower the filter is, the more infrequently we need to measure skew to see the expected positive skew of trend following. Apart from the very fastest filters, each trade lasts for several weeks or months, so we end up with daily and weekly skew that is more like the skew of the underlying instruments.

The upper tail shows a similar pattern to skew as we'd probably expect, although it's not as dramatic. Interestingly, the lower tail also gets smaller as we slow down our filter.

TABLE 32: SKEW MEASURED OVER DIFFERENT TIME PERIODS

	Daily skew	Weekly skew	Monthly skew	Annual skew
EWMAC2	0.37	0.94	1.32	1.09
EWMAC4	0.46	0.75	1.53	1.27
EWMAC8	0.26	0.60	1.48	1.10
EWMAC16	−0.08	0.02	0.92	1.44
EWMAC32	−0.22	−0.13	0.75	0.94
EWMAC64	−0.34	−0.18	0.61	0.66

Aggregated Jumbo portfolio results with buffering and forecast scaling.

The most profitable filter historically on both outright returns and alpha has been EWMAC(16,64) (strategy eight). If I had to pick just one filter to trade this would be it. But we don't have to: we can trade more than one, as I shall now demonstrate.

---

128   For an explanation, read this paper by an ex-colleague, which you can find on researchgate.net: Martin, Richard. (2021) 'Design and analysis of momentum trading strategies'.

Combining different forecasts

Now we have a menu of six different speeds of trend filter available, how do we combine them? I can think of several options, each at a different stage of the trade generation process:

1. Averaging the raw forecasts before any capping takes place.

2. Averaging capped forecasts.

3. Averaging calculated positions, either before or after buffering.

4. Trading each trend filter as a completely different system, netting off the trades generated.

5. Completely separate systems, with no netting.

Trading each filter separately without netting is clearly a non-starter as it will result in higher trading costs, as we don't get the benefits of netting. In my opinion, it's better to do the averaging as early as possible as it results in a simpler trading strategy with fewer calculations.[129] However, it's best to do the averaging on capped rather than uncapped forecasts. Applying a cap before averaging ensures we won't end up with a combined forecast that is temporarily dominated by a single trend filter, just because it happens to have a very large forecast on a given day.

Hence, my preferred method is to **take a weighted average**[130] **of capped forecasts from different trading rules** (option 2). The weights used when calculating this average are **forecast weights**. Just like instrument weights, the forecast weights will sum to 1 and none will be negative.[131] Since all the forecasts are consistently scaled to achieve an average absolute forecast value of 10, we can do this averaging very easily.

For this strategy, each trading rule will represent a different speed of trend filter: a variation of the generic EWMAC trading rule. But as we shall see in subsequent

---

129   Perhaps the only benefit of averaging later, for example after required positions have been calculated, is that it makes it easier to precisely decompose the live performance of different trading rule variations. To get round this, you could paper trade a separate version of each strategy, or just use updated backtests to give an indication of the contribution of each speed of trend filter.

130   There are other methods we could use, but this is the simplest that will produce a combined scaled forecast. I discuss alternatives in *Systematic Trading*.

131   A negative weight would only make sense if a given trend filter was expected to lose money, and we could profitably short the rule (e.g. its losses weren't due to excessive trading costs). In this case it would make more sense to reframe the rule so it works in the opposite direction to what was originally intended, so that a positive forecast weight would be appropriate. Arguably there is an element of potential over fitting in following this path, as I discuss in my first book, *Systematic Trading*.

chapters, trading rules can take any form, as long as they produce **a forecast value that is consistently scaled**.

Let's now define precisely how we would scale our positions given multiple forecasts. For each trend filter j we are trading, we calculate a capped forecast at time t using the equations below on a given instrument i that we are trading:

$$\text{Raw forecast}_{i,j,t} = (\text{Fast EWMA}_{i,j,t} - \text{Slow EWMA}_{i,j,t}) \div \sigma_{p,i,t}$$

We then apply a filter specific forecast scalar (which is the same for all instruments), and a cap of 20 on the absolute value of the scaled forecast:

$$\text{Scaled forecast}_{i,j,t} = \text{Raw forecast}_{i,j,t} \times \text{Forecast scalar}_j$$

$$\text{Capped forecast, } f_{i,j,t} = \text{Max}(\text{Min}(\text{Scaled forecast}_{i,j,t} +20), -20)$$

We now take a **weighted average** of these capped forecasts, using forecast weights $w_{i,j}$ summing to 1 that are specific to a given instrument:

$$\text{Raw combined forecast}_{i,t} = w_{i,1}f_{i,1,t} + w_{i,2}f_{i,2,t} + w_{i,3}f_{i,3,t} +...$$

Factors to consider when choosing forecast weights

As with instrument weights, estimating the best forecast weights for a given instrument is a portfolio optimisation problem. One important difference is that there is only one set of instrument weights, whereas there could potentially be different forecast weights for every instrument we trade.

Recall the potential factors determining instrument weights outlined in strategy four:

- The expected pre-cost SR: better performing instruments should get a higher weight (in theory, but I found no significant differences between instrument sub-strategy SR).

- The costs of trading a given instrument: cheaper instruments will get a higher weight, since their post-cost SR will be higher (in theory, but once we've excluded expensive instruments costs had almost no effect on weights).

- The correlation between instruments: we want a higher weight to instruments that are more diversifying.

These factors are the same for forecast weights:

- The expected pre-cost SR: better performing trading rules should get a higher weight. Potentially, certain rules will perform differently for different instruments.

- The costs of trading a given filter: cheaper and slower trading rules will get a higher weight, since their post-cost SR will be higher. These costs will be different for each instrument.

- The correlation between forecasts: we want a higher weight to rules that are more diversifying. Correlations for trading rule variations should be similar, regardless of the instrument they are measured on.

Let's consider in more detail what the evidence is on each of these points.

Costs

Firstly, let us consider costs, as this is the most straightforward factor. Since the speed of trading each filter measured by annual turnover is roughly the same across instruments, these costs will be different depending on the cost per trade for each instrument. Costs for the fastest EWMAC2 rule come in at a reasonable 0.73% a year for the very cheap S&P 500 micro future, whilst for the US 2-year bond future they are a heart stopping 6.3% annually. We'd certainly want to allocate less to faster filters when instruments have a higher cost per trade.

Correlation and diversification

Next, we have the question of diversification. Diversification patterns for trend filters don't vary much for different instruments, so we can use aggregated results. Consider[132] the correlation matrix[133] of aggregate returns for each trend filter, in table 33.

---

132   These are empirical correlations. I leave the calculation of theoretical correlations as an exercise for the reader. Hint: use a series expansion.

133   This is the correlation of the aggregate returns for each filter, using the Jumbo portfolio set of instruments. Strictly speaking, we should use the correlation of filter returns for a given instrument. However, these will be very similar, and using aggregate returns gives us more robust results.

TABLE 33: CORRELATION MATRIX OF RETURNS FOR DIFFERENT TREND FILTERS, PLUS AVERAGE CORRELATIONS

	EWMAC2	EWMAC4	EWMAC8	EWMAC16	EWMAC32	EWMAC64
EWMAC2	1	0.88	0.64	0.40	0.23	0.12
EWMAC4		1	0.88	0.62	0.40	0.24
EWMAC8			1	0.85	0.64	0.42
EWMAC16				1	0.86	0.65
EWMAC32					1	0.89
EWMAC64						1
Average versus other filters	0.45	0.60	0.69	0.68	0.60	0.46

There is a clear pattern here:

- Adjacent filters, such as EWMAC2 and EWMAC4, have a correlation of around 0.87. Incidentally, this is why we don't need to include additional filters that lie between the six I have selected – they would have correlations over 0.90 with the existing set and would not be adding sufficient diversification.

- Correlations for filters that are two steps apart, e.g. EWMAC2 and EWMAC8, are around 0.64.

- Correlations continue to get lower for filters that are further apart.

The average correlations for a given filter against the other filters are lowest for the slowest and fastest trend filters, and higher for those in the middle. This means that the optimal forecast weights for a set of trend filters, *accounting only for diversification*, would have a 'U' shape: **higher weights on the more diversifying very fast and very slow filters, and lower weights in the middle**.

Pre-cost performance

Earlier in strategy three I found substantial differences between the performance of different instruments, but I pointed out that the differences were not statistically significant.[134] Is this also true for the performance of different trend filters?

---

134 Although I haven't explicitly said it, this is not just the case for strategy three. In general, we can't distinguish statistically between the performance of different instruments regardless of the strategy used to trade them. So you should continue to use the method described in strategy four to allocate instrument weights.

We know from tables 30 and 31 that there are some noticeable differences in the aggregate performance of different speeds of trend filter. Of course, these figures will also vary considerably if we look at the performance of these filters for different instruments. However, these differences across instruments are *not* statistically significant. Hence, I will use **the aggregate results for performance by trading rule across instruments**, rather than trying to vary forecast weights by instrument depending on the differing pre-cost performance of trading rule variations for each instrument.

Using those aggregate results, it's true to say that the two fastest filters are particularly unimpressive. Your first instinct should be to ask if this result is statistically significant, or just noise. In fact, since our results in tables 30 and 31 are derived from the backtested statistics of over 100 different instruments, we can say with some certainty that there is definitely a significant underperformance by EWMAC2 and EWMAC4, compared to the slower variations of the EWMAC trading rule.

It's worth spending a few moments exploring this underperformance in more detail, to see if we can explain it. Consider first the changing performance of different speeds of filter over time. In figure 35 up until around 1990 all the filters do equally well. Subsequently the slower filters (all shown as grey lines, since we don't need to distinguish them) continue to perform well. But the two fastest filters see their returns flat-line; and the quickest – EWMAC(2,8) – actually loses money.

FIGURE 35: CUMULATIVE PERFORMANCE OF DIFFERENT SPEEDS OF TREND FILTER (NUMBER IS SPAN OF FASTER EWMA)

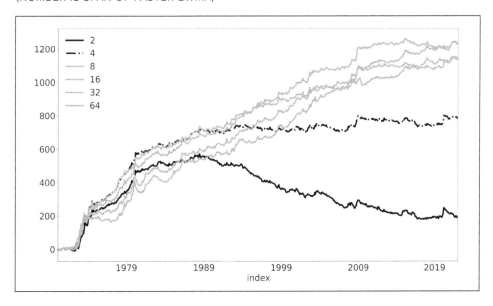

Figure 36 shows the gross and net after cost performance of the fastest EWMAC2 filter. We can see that, ignoring costs, performance was strong up to 1990, and since then it has remained flat (with the notable exception of the COVID-19 market crash). Costs are the difference between the two lines; these were very small initially, but have since widened. So two things changed after 1990: gross performance went to zero, and costs increased.

FIGURE 36: GROSS AND NET PERFORMANCE OF AGGREGATE JUMBO PORTFOLIO FOR EWMA(2,8) FILTER

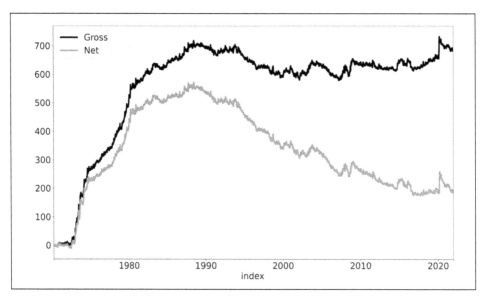

There are a number of possible explanations for this effect:

1. The simplest is that fast trend following is something that used to work for most instruments, and doesn't any longer.

2. It might be that fast trend following never really worked, it's just that our technique for adjusting historical costs isn't accurate. If costs were higher than we thought prior to 1990, then we wouldn't actually have realised the apparent net profit that was available.

3. Another possibility is that fast trend following only works in certain asset classes, and as we've added more instruments into our data set we've included more and more markets where the faster trend filters aren't working.

4. A subtle twist on the previous theory is that fast trend following works well everywhere pre-cost, but only in instruments that have high costs. Hence in practice we can't realise the potential pre-cost returns.

Some digging reveals there is some truth in most of these explanations. If we just look at a single instrument that was around for the entire time period, we do indeed see a clear degradation of performance after 1990 (supporting theory #1). It seems highly plausible that costs were actually much higher in the past than I've assumed: per contract dollar commissions in particular were certainly higher even if our slippage assumptions are correct (theory #2). It's also the case that many of the instruments added after 1990 have higher costs (theory #3). But there is no evidence that fast momentum might have better gross returns for instruments with higher costs (theory #4).

Bearing all that in mind, should we allocate less of our trading capital to the two fastest filters? Remember that allocating weights using pre-cost performance statistics is arguably a form of in sample fitting (since we're using the entire backtested history to estimate the pre-cost SRs). This is not true of trading costs and correlations.[135]

This isn't going to have an impact on the weights we use for live trading, as long as we are careful not to over fit. For example, if we were to use *only* the best performing filter, EWMAC16, that would certainly be a case of over fitting. Dropping the fastest couple of filters feels more defensible; we'd still be left with a robust trading strategy. But it will mean the backtested SR of any strategy that uses forecast weights derived using the entire history of data will be potentially overstated.[136]

For the purposes of my analysis in this chapter I will *not* be removing the two fastest filters, to ensure that my backtested performance statistics are as realistic as possible. However, it would not be stupid to remove the fastest EWMAC2 filter in a live trading strategy, although I'd personally prefer to keep EWMAC4.

Putting it together: a method for allocating forecast weights

Let's consider some useful principles for allocating forecast weights, based on the evidence above:

- Forecast weights should be the same across instruments, except where trading costs dictate otherwise.

---

135   Because of the way the strategy is designed with risk standardisation, it's possible to infer accurate figures for turnover and correlations from only a small section of data, whilst costs per trade are calculated without using any backtested data at all. That means in principle we could derive those figures on a rolling basis throughout the backtest using only backward looking data, or even from entirely artificial data or from theoretical calculations. In my own backtesting I use a backward looking estimate of these statistics.

136   You may want to refer back to the discussion on backtesting in strategy one.

- Forecast weights should be lower on rules that trade faster where instruments have a higher cost per trade.

- We should avoid over fitting forecast weights: placing too much weight on a single trading rule variation.

- Forecast weights should ideally be higher on more diversifying rule variations: the slowest and the fastest.

Bearing all of that in mind, I use the following procedure for allocating forecast weights. Firstly, on an instrument by instrument basis, I remove **trading rules that are too expensive**. Secondly, I allocate forecast weights using a **top down** methodology. For strategy nine, this implies that **all remaining trend filters get the same forecast weight**.[137]

Removing expensive trading rules

In strategy three I explained how to exclude instruments that were too expensive to trade. I introduced the concept of the trading **speed limit**. Effectively, we do not want to trade any instrument which uses up more than a third of our expected pre-cost return in costs. Costs can be calculated on a risk adjusted basis, in SR terms, and I set the notional speed limit for trading a particular instrument at a maximum of 0.10 SR units. How do we use this concept when considering which trading rules to select?

Back in strategy three I separated costs into transaction and holding costs:

Annual risk adjusted costs
= Transaction cost + Holding costs

We can break these down further:

Risk adjusted transaction costs
= Risk adjusted cost per trade × Annual turnover

Risk adjusted holding costs
= Risk adjusted cost per trade × Rolls per year × 2

---

137   My choice of EWMAC filters has a curious property. If you have equal weighting to a series of filters: EWMAX – EWMA4X, EWMA2X – EWMA8X, EWMA4X – EWMA16X, EWMA8X – EWMA32X, and if they have equal forecast weights, then this simplifies to EWMAX + EWMA2X – EWMA16X – EWMA32X (all of these terms are also divided by σ_p).

As usual this makes the somewhat conservative assumption that we will have to do two separate trades to roll our position, and pay two lots of trading costs for each roll.

A limit of 0.10 SR units is appropriate for instruments, but for trading rules we can have a higher maximum for a couple of reasons. Firstly, if our most expensive trading rule incurs exactly 0.10 SR units in costs for a given instrument, then on average we'll have a combined forecast which always comes in well under 0.10 SR units. Secondly, the effect of buffering our positions will slow down our trading and allow us to trade a set of forecasts that is a little quicker. Because of these two effects, I use a higher limit of 0.15 SR units for selecting trading rules.

Okay, so for a given instrument if we set a maximum of 0.15 SR units in costs, then we can derive the maximum allowable turnover for a given trading rule variation:

$$\text{Annual risk adjusted costs} < 0.15$$

$$(\text{Cost per trade} \times \text{Turnover})$$
$$+ (\text{Cost per trade} \times \text{Rolls per year} \times 2) < 0.15$$

$$\text{Turnover} < [0.15 - (\text{Cost per trade} \times \text{Rolls per year} \times 2)]$$
$$\div \text{Cost per trade}$$

Table 34 shows how many instruments can currently be traded in the Jumbo portfolio for a trading rule with a given turnover. A trading rule with a turnover of 50 can trade less than half the Jumbo portfolio.

TABLE 34: NUMBER OF INSTRUMENTS IN JUMBO PORTFOLIO THAT CAN BE TRADED FOR A GIVEN TURNOVER

	Number of instruments
Turnover, 1 per year	All: 101
10	96
25	67
50	42
75	22
100	11
150	4
300	1

Remember from strategy three that the turnover figure shown here is actually the turnover of our *average* position. These turnovers can be calculated through backtesting and will be very similar across different instruments, and we can use the same turnover figure regardless of the instrument. My turnover estimates are shown in table 35.

TABLE 35: TURNOVER PER YEAR FOR EACH TREND FILTER, AVERAGED ACROSS INSTRUMENTS

	Turnover
EWMAC2	98.5
EWMAC4	50.2
EWMAC8	25.4
EWMAC16	13.2
EWMAC32	7.6
EWMAC64	5.2

Let's look at an example. For this I will use a rather expensive instrument: Eurodollar interest rate futures. These roll four times per year and currently have a cost per trade of 0.0088 SR units. If we plug these numbers into this formula:

Maximum turnover

= [0.15 − (Cost per trade × Rolls per year)] ÷ Cost per trade

Then we get:

Maximum turnover = [0.15 − (0.0088 × 4)] ÷ 0.0088

Maximum turnover = 13.0

On this basis, looking at table 34, we'd only trade the two slowest trend filters with Eurodollar: EWMAC32 and EWMAC64. The next fastest, EWMAC16, has a turnover of 13.2, which is just above our limit.

At the other extreme, if I plug in the cost per trade for the quarterly rolling S&P 500 micro future, then I get a maximum turnover of well over 100. For this instrument we'd be able to allocate to all six of the available filters. Notice that it's possible that we can't allocate to *any* of the available variations for a given instrument. In that case we wouldn't be able to trade it in this particular strategy.[138]

Top down method for choosing forecast weights

We now have a set of trading rules, which for a given instrument will not be too expensive to trade. How do we choose forecast weights for these? Remember, back in strategy four, I introduced a top-down method for selecting instrument weights called **handcrafting**. We can use a similar method here, with the following steps:

- Split the list of trading rules by **style**. Allocate between styles according to your preferences.

- Within a given style, allocate equally across **trading rules**.

- Within a given trading rule, allocate equally across **variations** of each given trading rule.

What do I mean by trading *style*? I use a common system for categorizing trading strategies, as either **divergent** or **convergent**.[139] Divergent strategies make money when markets diverge away from equilibrium: trend following is a classic divergent strategy. Convergent strategies make money when markets move towards their equilibrium. We will see an example of a convergent strategy, called carry, in the next chapter.

This method will make more sense in later chapters, when we have multiple trading rules. For our current strategy, applying it is very easy:

- We only have one style: divergent. Allocate 100% of our forecast weights to that style.

- We only have one trading rule: trend following with EWMAC. Allocate 100% of our forecast weights to that rule.

- We have between one and six variations of our trading rule, depending on the instrument we're trading. Equally divide 100% of our forecast weight between these rules.

As an example, suppose that for a given instrument we drop the fastest variation of the EWMAC rule: 2,8. We then allocate a 20% forecast weight in each of the five slowest variations. For Eurodollar, where only two variations can be traded, we'd have a 50%

---

138 Out of 102 instruments in the Jumbo portfolio set: 5 cannot trade any of the filters, 1 instrument can only trade 1 filter, 11 can trade 2, 24 can use 3, 21 can allocate to 4, 29 utilise 5 filters, and 11 have all 6.

139 I believe this categorisation was first used by Mark Rzepczynski in 'Market Vision and Investment Styles', *The Journal of Alternative Investments*, 1999.

forecast weight in each of EWMAC64 and EWMAC32. Whereas, for S&P 500, where we keep all six filters, we'd have 100% ÷ 6 = 16.667% in each variation.

Are these equal weights really the best we could have? Perhaps we should have more in each of the slower variations, firstly, because they will have lower trading costs, and, secondly, the very slowest variation EWMAC64 will be more diversifying than the medium speed variations, because of the 'U-shaped' effect I discussed earlier. (Our quicker variations are also more diversifying, but there is evidence from figure 35 that the two fastest variations have been unprofitable for some time.) On the other hand, medium speed variations have higher alpha against a long only benchmark, so perhaps we should be allocating more to those?

On balance, I feel it's better to keep things simple and avoid potential over fitting by just allocating equally to rule variations which are cheap enough to trade.

Accounting for forecast diversification

If I take an equally weighted average of the forecasts produced by all six trend filters for the S&P 500 micro future, then I get the result shown in figure 37.

FIGURE 37: AVERAGE FORECAST FOR S&P 500 MICRO FUTURE

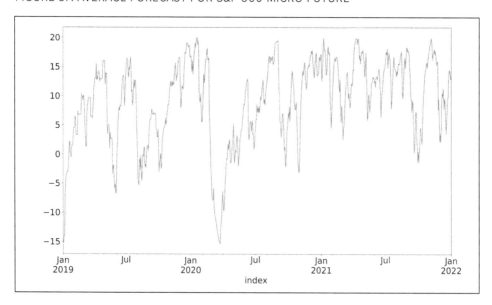

Remember that each individual forecast is calibrated to achieve an average absolute value of 10, with a maximum absolute value of 20. The combined forecast rarely takes extreme values; only briefly do we hit a situation where all six forecasts are capped at a long forecast of +20, resulting in an average of +20. Overall, the average absolute value of this combined forecast is just 7.5, well below the individual average of 10.

We've seen this effect before, when calculating instrument weights, when we noticed that the realised standard deviation of the risk parity version of strategy four was lower than the target we'd set for each individual instrument. The cause of that effect was that returns from trading each strategy were not perfectly correlated, so we received a diversification benefit. The solution was to apply an **instrument diversification multiplier** to our positions, which corrected for the diversification effect.

We have an analogous issue here. The problem now is that the forecasts from each trading rule variation are not perfectly correlated. The solution is to apply a **forecast diversification multiplier (FDM)** to our combined forecast. Calculation details are in appendix B.

Because the correlation of trading rules is fairly similar for different instruments, we can estimate this figure by pooling correlation information from multiple instruments.[140] Table 36 shows the appropriate FDM and forecast weights for a given set of trend filters. You should select the appropriate row for a given instrument, given the set of trading rule variations that you have identified as cheap enough to trade.

TABLE 36: FORECAST WEIGHTS AND FDM FOR A GIVEN SET OF TREND FILTERS

	Forecast weight for each rule variation	FDM
EWMAC2, 4, 8, 16, 32 and 64	0.167	1.26
EWMAC4, 8, 16, 32 and 64	0.2	1.19
EWMAC8, 16, 32 and 64	0.25	1.13
EWMAC16, 32 and 64	0.333	1.08
EWMAC32 and 64	0.50	1.03
EWMAC64	1.0	1.0

Notice that none of these FDM is especially high: the trend filters are all fairly correlated so there isn't much diversification available.[141]

With an FDM applied it's now possible for the combined forecast to exceed an absolute

---

140 They can also be estimated theoretically if certain assumptions are made. This approach produces very similar results and has the advantage of requiring no in-sample fitting.

141 If our trading rules were 100% correlated, then the FDM would always be 1. If we had N trading rules with zero correlation, then the FDM would be equal to the square root of N. If the six variations had a correlation of zero, then their FDM would be the square root of six: 2.45. It's much lower than this, 1.26 to be precise, because the correlations are considerably higher than zero.

value of 20. I'm not comfortable with that due to the likely risk, so I would also apply a cap if the combined forecast were less than –20 or greater than +20.

Time for a quick recap. We calculate a weighted average of capped forecasts for various trading rule variations, using forecast weights w summing to 1 that are specific to a given instrument, and which depend on the trading costs and turnover:

$$\text{Raw combined forecast}_{i,t}$$
$$= W_{i,1}F_{i,1,t} + W_{i,2}F_{i,2,t} + W_{i,3}F_{i,3,t} + ...$$

To account for diversification we now apply a forecast diversification multiplier for the given instrument FDM_i:

$$\text{Scaled combined forecast}_{i,t}$$
$$= \text{Raw combined forecast}_{i,t} \times FDM_j$$

As we did for individual filters, to avoid a situation when we have too much risk in a given instrument, we cap the combined forecast:

$$\text{Capped combined forecast}_{i,t}$$
$$= \text{Max(Min(Scaled combined forecast}_{i,t}, +20), -20)$$

Finally, we can plug the capped combined forecast into the now familiar position sizing equation, after which we would apply buffers and decide whether any trading was required:

$$N_{i,t} = \text{Capped combined forecast}_{i,t} \times \text{Capital} \times \text{IDM} \times \text{Weight}_i$$
$$\times \tau \div (10 \times \text{Multiplier}_i \times \text{Price}_{i,t} \times \text{FX}_{i,t} \times \sigma_{\%i,t})$$

Performance evaluation

As usual I'm going to evaluate the performance of this multiple momentum strategy based on both the *average* performance across instruments, and the *aggregate* results for the Jumbo portfolio. First let's consider the average performance, broken down by asset classes.

TABLE 37: MEDIAN INSTRUMENT PERFORMANCE FOR MULTIPLE MOMENTUM ACROSS FINANCIAL ASSET CLASSES

	Equity	Vol	FX	Bond
Mean annual return	0.7	13.3	5.2	9.5
Costs	−0.4%	−1.1%	−0.5%	−0.6%
Average drawdown	−29.5%	−25.2%	−39.4%	−20.3%
Standard deviation	22.1%	25.9%	22.8%	23.1%
Sharpe ratio	0.03	0.51	0.19	0.43
Turnover	15.3	11.5	15.0	13.2
Skew	0.62	0.20	0.95	0.79
Lower tail	3.60	3.16	3.59	2.86
Upper tail	2.57	2.43	3.08	2.81

TABLE 38: MEDIAN INSTRUMENT PERFORMANCE FOR MULTIPLE MOMENTUM ACROSS COMMODITY ASSET CLASSES

	Metals	Energy	Ags	Median
Mean annual return	8.9	8.9	5.4	5.2%
Costs	−0.5%	−0.5%	−0.4%	−0.5%
Average drawdown	−28.5%	−30.2%	−36.0%	−30.0%
Standard deviation	24.3%	25.5%	22.8%	23.0%
Sharpe ratio	0.37	0.39	0.24	0.23
Turnover	18.9	16.9	14.6	15.2
Skew	2.0	0.87	1.49	0.84
Lower tail	3.82	3.56	3.12	3.47
Upper tail	4.00	3.11	3.25	2.88

The tables show that, generally, multiple momentum is pretty good for both risk and performance measures. The left tail is a little fat, but skew is mostly very positive. The transformation of the volatility asset class is particularly notable. Originally, when traded on a long only basis our volatility instruments had strongly positive skew, but at the cost of seriously negative performance. Now we've still got some positive skew, but with an SR that is over 0.5: the best of any asset class! Admittedly there are only two instruments in this group, so we can argue about the significance of this result, but even so it's still an indication of how trading strategies can radically transform the underlying properties of a given instrument.

There is one fly in this particular ointment, which is the relatively poor performance of the equities strategy. We saw back in strategy six, when we last analysed asset class performance back in table 22 (page 146), that equities were not doing that well when we were just trading a single slow trend filter. The bad news is that they do even worse when trading quicker filters.

This could justify a change to forecast weights (a lower allocation to trend following within equities, once of course we have other trading rules to allocate to), or a change to instrument weights (a lower allocation to equities within a pure trend following strategy). Personally, I think that would potentially be over fitting, but I discuss these options more in Part Two.

Now let us turn to the aggregate results for the Jumbo portfolio, shown in table 39. You can clearly see that the effort from trading multiple momentum is rewarded, with an improvement in almost every statistic. Even though the EWMAC16 variation used in strategy eight is the most profitable individual trend filter, we can do even better by adding five other filters.

TABLE 39: PERFORMANCE OF AGGREGATE JUMBO PORTFOLIO: LONG ONLY, SLOW AND FAST TRENDS, MULTIPLE TRENDS

	Strategy four Long only	Strategy seven Slow trend long/short	Strategy eight Fast trend long/short	Strategy nine Multiple trend
Mean annual return	15.4%	21.5%	24.1%	25.2%
Costs	−0.8%	−1.0%	−1.7%	−1.2%
Average drawdown	−24.7%	−16.0%	−11.4%	−11.2%
Standard deviation	18.2%	22.3%	22.7%	22.2%
Sharpe ratio	0.85	0.96	1.06	1.14
Turnover	20.7	27.5	60.5	62.9
Skew	−0.04	0.61	0.81	0.98
Lower tail	1.44	1.90	1.97	1.99
Upper tail	1.24	1.63	1.81	1.81
Alpha	0	13.6%	17.6%	18.8%
Beta	1.0	0.53	0.38	0.43

All strategies have buffering and forecast sizing applied.

The results from regressing each strategy on the benchmark strategy four are particularly interesting. We already know that slower EWMAC variations will have a higher beta than faster filters, so it's no surprise that the beta for the multiple momentum strategy comes in somewhere between the betas for strategies seven and eight. However, the excess performance measured by alpha is still better than for any individual filter.

Figure 38 also illustrates the power of diversifying across different speeds of trend filters. Consider the period since 2014. The faster strategy eight, which until then had matched the performance of multiple momentum, started to underperform. Meanwhile the slower strategy seven, which had lagged, improved significantly. Because strategy nine has an allocation to both strategies, and also to other speeds of trend filter, it continues to do well.

FIGURE 38: CUMULATIVE PERFORMANCE FOR MULTIPLE TREND VERSUS EARLIER TREND STRATEGIES AND BENCHMARK

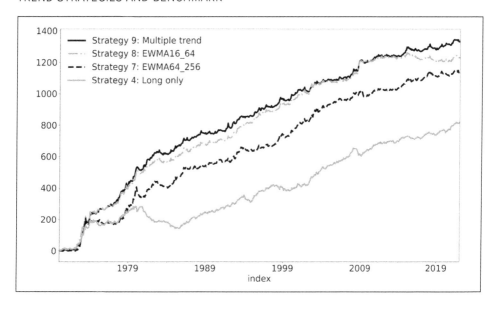

Is trend following dead?

The financial press are very fond of publishing articles with the title 'Is X dead', where X is some kind of trading strategy that has underperformed recently. Certainly there have been many recent opportunities to declare the premature death of trend following. Strategy nine lost money in 2018, 2016, 2015 and 2009.

But losing years are common with any trading strategy, unless it is exceptionally profitable. And because trend following is a positive skewed strategy, the losses in negative years are much smaller in magnitude than the winners. We lost almost 9% in 2009, but that was sandwiched by gains of over 30% in 2008 and 2010. The total loss in 2015 and 2016 was around 6%; but we made 35% in 2014 and 30% in 2017. Even our relatively high loss of 12% in 2018 – the worst in the backtest – was quickly obscured by three straight years of positive performance averaging 14% annually.

Having said that, it does look like the returns from strategy nine are falling over time. The inflationary 1970s were particularly strong, with a total non-compounded return of over 500% over the decade (if we had been compounding, our returns would have been even more spectacular). We then made over 200% in each of the next three decades. But since 2010 our average return has roughly halved.

Still, it is way too soon to say whether trend following is 'dead'. It still seems to be producing positive returns, and although these are at a lower level than seen before, they are not out of line with what we'd expect given the historical distribution of returns from the strategy. There are other factors which should give us some comfort. For example, several researchers have done tests of trend following going back many centuries. In these very long backtests, decades of relative underperformance are not uncommon.

It also seems unlikely that the psychological biases which seem to underpin trend following are going away any time soon, unless human traders are completely replaced by computers (something that has happened at the high frequency end of the trading spectrum, but certainly not for the typical holding periods we are using in this book). Finally, it seems likely that coming trends like higher inflation will probably produce stronger trends in the near future, particularly in commodity futures prices.[142]

Nevertheless, it makes sense to diversify our portfolio beyond trend following, as I will start doing in the next strategy.

Conclusion

Trend following is an extremely popular trading strategy which forms the bedrock of systems used by commodity trading advisors (CTAs) like AHL, my former employer. It has some very attractive properties: it is profitable, has positive skew making it easier to risk manage, and often performs well in periods when markets generally are doing badly (including 2008, and early 2022 as I write this chapter).

---

142   Indeed, as I am finishing this book in late 2022, inflation appears to be making a comeback and trend following has had a stellar year of performance.

However, this is not a book just about trend following: there are plenty of good books on that subject (some of which I mention in Appendix A). We can improve our returns further by adding additional trading strategies to our metaphorical shopping basket. The next strategy introduces the first of these new strategies: carry.

Strategy nine: Trading plan

All other elements are identical to strategy eight.

Strategy	Go long or short one or more instruments with variable risk estimate and a combined forecast from multiple momentum filters.
Instrument(s)	Any that meet minimum capital, liquidity and cost thresholds.
Choose trading rules for each instrument	Only choose trading rule variations where: $$\text{Turnover} < [0.15 - (\text{Cost per trade} \times \text{Rolls per year})] \div \text{Cost per trade}$$ Turnover figures are in table 35.
Trading rule variations	Construct one or more trend filters of the form EWMAC(N,4N) where N is one of 2,4,8,16,32,64.
EWMAC calculations	To calculate the N business day span price exponentially weighted moving average using the back-adjusted price: $$\lambda = 2 \div (N + 1)$$ $$\text{EWMA(N)}_{i,t}$$ $$= \lambda p_{i,t} + \lambda(1 - \lambda)p_{i,t-1} + \lambda(1 - \lambda)^2 p_{i,t-2} + ...$$
Raw forecast for a given EWMAC(N)	$$\text{Raw forecast}_{N,i,t}$$ $$= [\text{EWMA(N)}_{i,t} - \text{EWMA(4N)}_{i,t}] \div \sigma_p$$
Scaled forecast for a given EWMAC	$$\text{Scaled forecast}_{N,i,t}$$ $$= \text{Raw forecast}_{N,i,t} \times \text{forecast scalar}_N$$ Forecast scalars can be found in table 29.
Capped forecast for a given EWMAC	$$\text{Capped forecast}_{N,i,t}$$ $$= \text{Max(Min(Scaled forecast}_{N,i,t}, +20), -20)$$
Allocating forecast weights	See page 187 and table 36.

Forecast combination	Given a set of forecasts $f_{i,j,t}$ for instrument i, trading rule variation j with forecast weights $w_{i,j}$:

Raw combined forecast$_i$

$$= w_{i,1}f_{i,1,t} + w_{i,2}f_{i,2,t} + w_{i,3}f_{i,3,t} + ...$$

Forecast diversification	See table 36 for FDM values

Scaled combined forecast$_{i,t}$

$= $ Raw combined forecast$_{i,t}$ $\times$ FDM$_i$

Capped combined forecast	

Capped combined forecast, $f_{i,t}$

$= $ Max(Min(Scaled combined forecast$_{i,t}$, +20), −20)

Optimal position sizing	Buy or sell N contracts, where N is the current *unrounded* value of:

N$_{i,t}$ = Capped combined forecast

$\times$ Capital $\times$ IDM $\times$ Weight$_i$ $\times$ τ

$\div$ (10 $\times$ Multiplier$_i$ $\times$ Price$_{i,t}$ $\times$ FX$_{i,t}$ $\times$ $\sigma_{\%i,t}$)

Buffer width	

B$_{i,t}$ = 0.1 $\times$ Capital $\times$ IDM $\times$ Weight$_i$ $\times$ τ

$\div$ (Multiplier$_i$ $\times$ Price$_{i,t}$ $\times$ FX$_{i,t}$ $\times$ $\sigma_{\%i,t}$)

Buffer zone	

Lower buffer, B$^L_{i,t}$ = round(N$_i$ − B$_{i,t}$)

Upper buffer, B$^U_{i,t}$ = round(N$_i$ + B$_{i,t}$)

Trading decision	Calculate the optimal position as above, updating values of forecasts, capital, price, FX and standard deviation estimate. Calculate the buffer zone around the optimal position. Then given a current position in round contracts of C:

B$^U_{i,t}$ $\leq$ C$_{i,t}$ $\leq$ B$^L_{i,t}$: No trading required

C$_{i,t}$ < B$^L_{i,t}$: Buy (B$^U_{i,t}$ − C$_{i,t}$) contracts

C$_{i,t}$ > B$^U_{i,t}$: Sell (C$_{i,t}$− B$^U_{i,t}$) contracts

STRATEGY TEN

Basic carry

I recently re-read a book with the catchy title:[143]

The Rise of Carry: The Dangerous Consequences of Volatility Suppression and the New Financial Order of Decaying Growth and Recurring Crisis

What is 'carry', and why is it so dangerous? Well, we've already come across carry way back in strategy one. You may remember this equation, which decomposes the excess return for the S&P 500 future:

$$\text{Excess return} = \text{Spot return} + \text{Carry}$$

Hence, even if the price of the underlying S&P 500 index doesn't change, we can still make profits from the carry. For the S&P 500, carry is equal to the dividends we'd earn, less the interest required to fund a loan used for buying all the stocks in the S&P 500 index. In fact, **all futures have carry**, although the source of this return differs depending on the asset class.

Up until now we've been trying to predict the total excess return, using a series of trend filters which use the back-adjusted price as an input. The back-adjusted price is effectively the cumulated history of past excess returns, so it incorporates the effects of both spot returns and carry. But it turns out that **the carry component can be predicted independently**, and very successfully.

Remember from strategy one that we are trying to capture diversified sets of risk premia in our trading strategies. Carry is a well-known risk premium that is quite different from the trend premium. However, as the authors of the book above point out, it's also potentially hazardous without the nice positive skew we've grown accustomed to

---

143   Written by Tim Lee, Jamie Lee and Kevin Coldiron, and published in 2019 by McGraw Hill.

seeing from momentum. For this reason you should use it with care, or better still combine it with trend following: I will explain how to do that in strategy eleven.

> **Strategy ten:** Trade a portfolio of one or more instruments, each with positions scaled for a variable risk estimate. Scale positions according to the strength of their forecasted carry.

I will be covering the following topics in this chapter:

- Decomposing the causes of carry for different asset classes.

- Measuring expected carry.

- Incorporating carry as a trading strategy.

- Trading carry without excessive costs.

- The properties of carry for different asset classes.

- Skew and carry.

The causes of carry

Before we think about estimating and forecasting carry returns, we need to understand where it comes from. To reiterate, **carry is the component of excess returns for a future over and above what we earn from the spot price changing:**

$$\text{Excess return = Spot return + Carry}$$

These carry returns come from different sources, depending on the asset class of the instrument you are trading. We can decompose these returns by thinking about an arbitrage trade that will replicate a long position in the future. I already identified the source of carry for equity indices, such as the S&P 500, back in strategy one. The arbitrage trade is to borrow funds to buy the shares that make up the index, giving us this excess return:

$$\text{Excess return (equities) = Spot return + Dividends − Interest}$$

$$\text{Carry (equities) = Dividends − Interest}$$

Hence, as we saw back in strategy one, carry in equities can be positive or negative depending on the relative size of dividend yields and interest rates.

Let us now turn to other asset classes. Firstly, let's consider the bond market:[144]

Excess return (bonds) = Spot return + Yield – Repo rate

Carry (bonds) = Yield – Repo rate

This is analogous to the equity market, except instead of dividends we earn a bond yield, and the funding of the trade is done at a specific short-term interest rate known as the 'repo' rate. As interest rates are normally higher in the future, reflecting lenders' preferences, the yield on bonds (which will usually have a maturity of at least a year) is usually higher than the short-term repo rate. Hence, carry in bonds is normally positive. The exception is when a central bank has set short-term interest rates at a high level, and they are expected to fall in the future, resulting in an inverted yield curve.

In foreign exchange (FX) markets we have two different interest rates:

Excess return (FX) = Spot return + Deposit rate – Borrowing rate

Carry (FX) = Deposit rate – Borrowing rate

Consider for example a long GBPUSD trade, which is equivalent to borrowing dollars, converting them into pounds, and then depositing the pounds.[145] Here the deposit rate would be the appropriate interest rate in the UK, and the borrowing rate would be the US interest rate. Carry in G10 FX markets like GBPUSD is usually fairly small as interest rates are often quite similar, but emerging market currencies normally have significant positive carry against the dollar.

The final two types of financial asset are the volatility indices (VIX and the European VSTOXX), and the short-term interest rate (STIR) futures markets. Describing exactly where the carry comes from here is a bit tricky, as it would require introducing a great deal of superfluous financial mathematics. However there is an alternative method for thinking about carry, which relates to the *futures curve*: the prices of contracts with different expiry dates. This concept will also be very helpful when we think about forecasting carry for all futures markets.

---

144   This is a simplification, since the spot return will also include returns from 'roll down': the effect of the underlying bond becoming shorter in maturity. If the yield curve is upward sloping then this will result in the spot price increasing even if interest rates are unchanged. Most bond traders consider roll down to be part of the carry from owning bonds. However, as we're not concerned with cash futures arbitrage in this book, we will ignore it.

145   Again, I am ignoring many details here related to forward interest rates amongst other things.

Suppose that we're trading Eurodollar interest rate futures, and the next contract is just about to expire. Subsequent contracts expire in three, six, nine, 12 months and so on. To make the maths simpler I will make the unlikely assumption that each three-month period is exactly the same number of days in length. Even more unrealistically, suppose that the prices for these futures are exactly $99 for the contract that is expiring, $98 for the front contract (expiring in three months), $97 for the next expiry (six months away), $96, $95… and so on. Eurodollar prices are calculated as (100 – interest rate), so a price of $99 implies an interest rate[146] of 1%, $98 is 2% and so on. As the current future is expiring at a price of $99, the current spot interest rate must be 1%.

We decide to buy the next contract at a price of $98 and hold it for three months when it will expire. How do we calculate the carry we expect to earn? Easy: it will be the difference in the price of the contract at expiry versus the purchase price. But what will the price be of the contract we've bought at expiry?

To work this out we assume nothing happens to interest rates, which are the spot price of the underlying 'asset' which Eurodollar futures are priced on. If the spot interest rate is still 1% in three months' time, then as the contract we bought is now expiring it should also reflect a current interest rate of 1%, and at expiry it will be priced at 100 – 1 = $99. We buy at $98 and sell for $99, making a $1 profit; and since spot prices (interest rates) haven't changed, this is entirely down to carry.

A similar argument can be made with volatility futures, except that instead of current interest rates, the futures price at expiry is based on the implied volatility of equity options. Hence we can write:

$$\text{Excess return (STIR, Vol)}$$
$$= \text{Spot return} + \text{Current spot price} - \text{Futures price}$$

$$\text{Carry (STIR, Vol)} = \text{Current spot price} - \text{Futures price}$$

Both STIR and volatility assets normally have downward sloping futures price curves as in the example I have described, and hence normally earn positive carry.

Now let's deal with the more complex world of commodity futures. We'll begin with the metals complex, since these are most like financial assets: it turns out we can borrow Gold and other metals relatively easily, at some rate of interest. But unlike equities and bonds, Gold doesn't earn any yield. In fact it costs money to hold physical

---

146   Whilst I write this chapter Eurodollar futures still reference the infamous LIBOR benchmark which was traditionally calculated by surveying a panel of banks. However, this benchmark was felt to be prone to market manipulation, a crime which some of my former Barclays colleagues were convicted of (unfairly, in my opinion). From July 2023 the futures will switch to using SOFR, which is based on actual transaction data.

Gold, since you need to find somewhere very safe to store it, with impressive security and a fully comprehensive insurance policy (or more likely, pay someone to store it on your behalf). Hence for metals:

Excess return (Metals)

= Spot return – Borrowing cost – Storage costs

Carry (Metals) = – (Borrowing cost + Storage costs)

Unless interest rates are negative and exceed the storage costs, carry on metals will normally be negative.

We are now left with the other commodities: energy markets like Oil and Natural Gas, and agricultural markets such as Wheat and Soybeans. There is an important difference between these markets and other futures. Having physical Gold now is as good as having it in a few months' time. But there is a big difference between having Gas now – I'm writing this sentence during a very cold January – and having it in a few months' time (when it's hopefully going to be much warmer). Hence we have another term in our equation:

Excess return (Energy, Agricultural)

= Spot return – Borrowing cost – Storage costs

+ Convenience yield

Carry (Energy, Agricultural)

= – Borrowing cost – Storage costs + Convenience yield

The *convenience yield*[147] reflects the markets' current expectations about future supply and demand for the commodity. This could be positive – reflecting a lot of short-term demand pressure – or negative. To take an extreme example of a negative convenience yield, on 20th April 2020 the price of WTI Crude Oil futures,[148] which were due to expire in the near future, actually went below zero. There was a massive glut of oil due to the COVID-19 crisis shutting down the economy, and hence people were willing to pay others to take oil off their hands.

---

147   It's plausible that convenience yield could also apply to Metals; for example if there was a shortage of available Gold in storage and high demand. But there is normally sufficient inventory for that not to be a problem. Generally speaking, the more expensive and difficult it is to store a product, the more important convenience yield will be.

148   This was only an issue because WTI futures are physically and not cash settled.

On average, commodities will have negative carry, which implies an upward sloping futures price curve. However, it's possible for commodity futures to have positive carry for long periods of time.[149]

Carry: What can go wrong

Carry seems like free money. But there are no free lunches in finance, apart from perhaps diversification.[150] If we buy some future for $98, when the current spot price is $99, then we'd expect to earn $1 of carry if nothing happens to the spot price. However, we face the risk that the spot price will move against us. If it drops by $1, then our carry gain will be negated, and we'll have zero return: the infamous 'spot drag' (if the price drops by more than $1 then our carry profits will become losses, whilst a price rise will add to our carry gains). This is the outcome you would expect if you believed in the strictest form of the efficient markets hypothesis, which basically says it's impossible to make money from trading.

As it turns out, we do normally earn that $1 in carry: as you will see later, we actually make $1.15 on average for each $1 in expected carry in my backtest. However, it isn't an easy ride. Assets which offer positive carry are only doing so because there are risks from holding them. They normally have negative skew, for example. A classic example of this would be a carry trade in an emerging market FX rate versus the dollar. These are positive carry because it's very risky to hold emerging market currencies, which tend to suffer from rather sudden and especially savage depreciation events. We earn carry because we're effectively providing insurance against these events and being paid for it.

But that is fine: remember we are in the business of being paid for risk premia. If the market is willing to pay us for holding assets with positive carry, then we should gladly take it. In fact, because the source of carry is different depending on the asset class, the characteristics of owning positive carry assets (or shorting negative carry assets) can be quite different depending on what you are trading, as we shall see later in the chapter.

Measuring expected carry

In the previous section I described a method for explaining carry in volatility and interest rate futures, by looking at the difference between spot and futures prices. We

---

149 Many futures traders use the term **backwardation** to refer to a downward sloping futures curve (resulting in positive carry), and **contango** when futures curves slope upwards (negative carry). I don't use these terms, in fact I just had to check to make sure I got them the right way round. But you may hear them used elsewhere, so it's useful to be aware of them.

150 And risk normalisation, and possibly forecasting.

can use this method to measure expected carry for any future. Our expected carry can be measured by comparing the current price of the future and the spot. For example, if we buy some future for $98, when the current spot price is $99, then we'd expect to earn $1 of carry if nothing happens to the spot price before the expiry of the future.

In practice this is tricky. It's difficult to get spot prices for many assets – especially commodities. Also, spot and futures prices need to be synchronized in time to get an accurate estimate, which isn't always easy. Even if we do have spot prices, it's a hassle and potentially expensive to add another source of data to our strategies workload.

However, this isn't a problem if we're holding a future that is further out on the curve. Remember the hypothetical Eurodollar futures curve example above? There the prices were $99 for the spot price, $98 for the next expiry in three months, $97 for the following expiry and so on. If we buy the six-month expiry future at $97, then using the same argument as before in three months' time we'd expect it to have the same price as the three-month expiry future: $98. We will earn carry of $1 if the spot price doesn't change. Hence, we can calculate the carry by comparing the two futures prices:

Raw carry = Price of nearer futures contract
– price of currently held contract

Another advantage of this approach is that both contracts are trading on the same exchange, so if we use daily closing prices to calculate the carry we know that they will be synchronized.

None of this is much help for most financial futures, where we are typically limited to holding the front contract and there isn't a nearer contract we can use for comparison. We can get around this limitation: if we assume that the gradient of the futures curve is constant, then the expected carry on the contract we are holding will be equal to the difference between the price of a further out contract and the current contract:

Raw carry = Price of currently held contract
– price of further out contract

This assumes we can get a price for a further out contract. Even if the second contract isn't liquid enough to be actively traded, as is the case for many bond futures, there is normally a quoted price available for it. This price reflects the market's expectations about the various sources of carry. At the very least, there will be a price available for the further out contract shortly before the current contract is due to roll – or it would be impossible to roll into the new contract! The worst case scenario is that we will have an accurate reading for carry a few times a year, when each roll happens. As we shall see, this is normally sufficient.

Let's look at a couple of examples. In November 2021, I was trading the S&P 500 micro December 2021 contract. This was the front contract, so I didn't have the option of calculating carry using a nearer delivery month, and I didn't collect spot S&P 500 index prices. Instead I had to go to the further out March 2022 contract. The prices were 4578.50 (December) and 4572.00 (March). So the raw carry was:

Raw carry = Price of currently held contract

– price of further out contract

= 4578.50 – 4572.00 = 6.50

Now consider the WTI Crude Oil future. As I mentioned in strategy one, for reasons that will be explained later in this chapter, I only trade the December delivery. At this point I'd already begun holding the December 2022 contract, which was priced at 62.09. Obviously this isn't the front month – far from it – so I can use a nearer month in my calculation.[151] Crude has monthly deliveries so the previous contract is November 2022, trading at 62.61:

Raw carry = Price of nearer futures contract

– price of currently held contract

= 62.61 – 62.09 = 0.52

Annualisation

We now have a price difference between two contracts, which will reflect the carry in price units that we expect to earn over the time between their expiries. But some contracts trade quarterly, whilst others trade monthly; and there are even instruments where the rolls are usually two but sometimes three months apart. To get a consistent estimate of carry we need to annualise the raw carry. First we calculate the time between expiries as a fraction of a year. Although in theory we could use the exact number of days, it's acceptable to approximate this using the difference in months:

Expiry difference in years

= abs(Months between contracts) ÷ 12

---

151 For Crude, and any contract where we hold a position far in the future, this is a simplifying approximation. I will discuss this more in Part Two.

We now annualise the raw carry:

$$\text{Annualised raw carry}$$
$$= \text{Raw carry} \div \text{Expiry difference in years}$$

Let's return to our examples. For WTI Crude the expiry difference between November and December is $1 \div 12 = 0.08333$ years. For S&P 500 it is three months: $1 \div 12 = 0.25$ years. We can now calculate the annualised carry using the raw carry figures from above:

$$\text{Annualised raw carry S\&P 500} = 6.50 \div 0.25 = 26.0$$

$$\text{Annualised raw carry WTI Crude} = 0.52 \div 0.083333 = 6.24$$

Risk adjustment

What has the better carry, the S&P 500 or Crude Oil? We expect to earn 26 price units of carry in the S&P 500 every year on a long position, and 6.24 in Crude Oil. So what? These numbers are meaningless by themselves. We could convert them into percentages of price, but to compare them directly it is better to *risk adjust* them. Since annualised carry is in units of price, it makes sense to divide it by the annualised standard deviation of returns for the relevant instrument, also in price units.

From strategy nine we already have an estimate for the daily standard deviation of price differences, σ_p, which was used to risk adjust trend following strategies, so the calculation is easy:

$$\text{Carry} = \text{Annualised raw carry} \div (\sigma_p \times 16)$$

Alternatively, if you prefer to use the estimated annual standard deviation of returns in percentage terms, $\sigma_\%$, then you can use this equivalent formula:[152]

$$\text{Carry} = \text{Annualised raw carry} \div (\sigma_\% \times \text{Current contract price})$$

In our examples, using current prices and assuming 16% annual standard deviation for S&P 500 with 28% for Crude Oil:

---

152   As when we've done this conversion before, remember that in a backtest you should use the contract price that was being traded at the time, *not* the back-adjusted price.

$$\text{Carry (S\&P 500)} = 26 \div (0.16 \times 4578) = 0.035$$

$$\text{Carry (Crude Oil)} = 6.24 \div (0.28 \times 62.09) = 0.358$$

The risk adjusted carry for Crude Oil is actually more than ten times higher than for the S&P 500.

Carry as a trading strategy

Now we have a risk adjusted measure of carry for any given instrument, how do we actually implement it as a trading strategy? This is where the magic of the *forecast* comes in. Back in strategy seven I formally defined a forecast as a **value that is proportional to an expected risk adjusted return**. I also noted that this implies forecasts are proportional to expected Sharpe ratios (SRs).

Since carry is defined as an expected annual return divided by an annualised standard deviation, both in the same price units, **expected carry is equal to expected SR.** Hence, the carry calculation above naturally produces a forecast:

$$\text{Carry forecast} = \text{Annualised raw carry} \div (\sigma_p \times 16)$$

Let's have a look at the carry forecast for the S&P 500 micro future, as shown in figure 39.

FIGURE 39: CARRY FORECAST FOR S&P 500

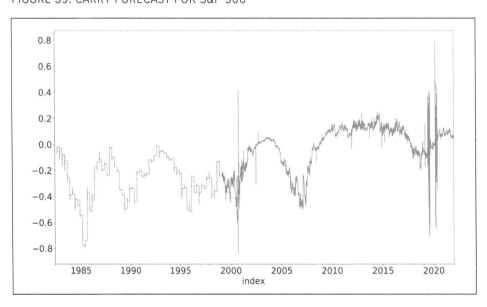

Firstly, you can see that prior to 2000 we have a rather 'blocky' forecast. This is because I have sparse historical data for the second contract, and I am only able to calculate carry on roll days. This is no longer a problem for the S&P 500, but is still a present day issue for many bond futures.

After 2000 the carry estimate is very noisy and jumpy. Some of the worst noise – such as in 2019 – is due to a poor data feed and could possibly be removed by data cleaning. But I believe a robust trading system is one that can cope with a certain amount of bad data.[153] Much of the noise is real, but even this real noise isn't adding any useful information. We basically want to be short S&P carry until about 2009, to varying degrees: there is clearly a cycle in carry driven by the interaction of interest rates and dividend yields. Then we want to be long thereafter, with the exception of the 2018 and 2019 where we go short.

Now let's examine our other example, WTI Crude Oil futures, in figure 40. We have slightly better data here, but there is still evidence of noise. The Gulf War in 1990 was a particularly chaotic period.

FIGURE 40: CARRY FORECAST FOR WTI CRUDE OIL

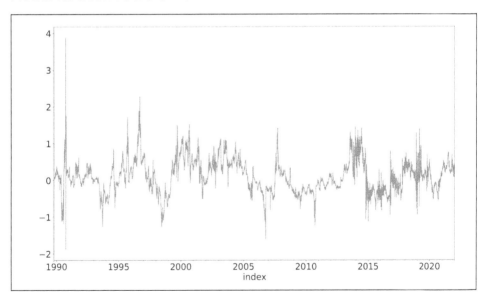

Next, let's consider another energy market, Henry Hub Natural Gas. An important difference between Crude and Gas is that I always trade the December contract for Crude Oil, but this isn't possible for Gas because there are no liquid expiries that far

---

153   Perry Kaufman has a memorable phrase for this preference: "Loose pants fit everyone."

in the future. Instead I trade a couple of months ahead, thus allowing me to use the more accurate *near-current* version of the carry calculation, whilst still holding a liquid expiry. For example if it's currently January 2022, I would hold March 2022, and calculate carry by comparing February and March.

The carry for Gas is shown in figure 41, and we can immediately see something odd: a very persistent seasonal pattern. Carry is significantly negative in May and October, whilst in January and July it is usually around zero or even slightly positive. This makes sense – Gas is a commodity which is subject to seasonal changes in supply and demand, and these will also change the relative pricing of adjacent expiries throughout the year. It's also very difficult and expensive to store, which magnifies these seasonal effects.

We don't see this for Crude, another product that has some seasonality,[154] because we only ever trade December.[155] This is one of the reasons why I prefer to trade a fixed month for seasonal commodities, when it's possible to do so.

FIGURE 41: CARRY FORECAST FOR NATURAL GAS

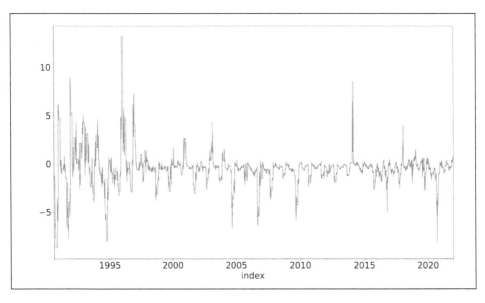

Now let's look at the first future I ever traded: the 10-year German bond ('Bund'). Like most bond futures it's only possible to trade the front month as subsequent deliveries usually aren't especially liquid. This means that we have to use the second expiry to

---

154   Seasonality is more of a problem for Natural Gas than for other energy futures, because it is much more difficult to store and transport.
155   I discuss the possibility of choosing which expiry to trade for a given instrument based on carry available in each contract in Part Six.

calculate the carry. For example, right now in late January 2022 I'm trading March 2022, and working out carry by taking the difference between March and June 2022. The carry is shown in figure 42.

FIGURE 42: CARRY FORECAST FOR GERMAN 10-YEAR BUND FUTURES

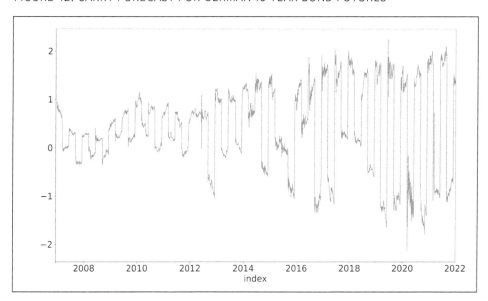

No, I haven't accidentally plotted the futures price for a seasonal commodity, typing bratwurst rather than Bund into my data search. The carry for Bund futures is extremely seasonal, with the sign of the carry forecast switching every quarter when we roll to a new contract. The September and March contracts have strong positive estimated carry, whilst the June and December contracts have strong negative carry. But because we're using an imprecise method of comparing carry for the first two contracts, the real carry for the June and December contracts is actually positive, and vice versa! Our carry estimate will always have the wrong sign.[156] There are similar patterns in 5-year German bonds (Bobls) and Spanish 10-year bonds (Bonos).

Finally, let's look at another financial market: the Eurostoxx 50 equity index. Like Bunds we hold the first contract, and hence have to calculate carry by comparing the prices of the first and second contracts. Once again in figure 43, there is a unexpected seasonal pattern.

---

156 Footnote for bond nerds: What is going on here? Do people like to buy bunds as presents for their relatives at Christmas and for German unity day (on 3rd October, in case you wondered)? The real explanation is that every six months the German government issues a new batch of bunds, which then become the 'cheapest to deliver' (CTD) (as yields are very low the new bonds with the longest maturity become the new CTD). I'd like to thank an ex-colleague, Yoav Git, for clarifying this for me.

FIGURE 43: CARRY FORECAST FOR EUROSTOXX

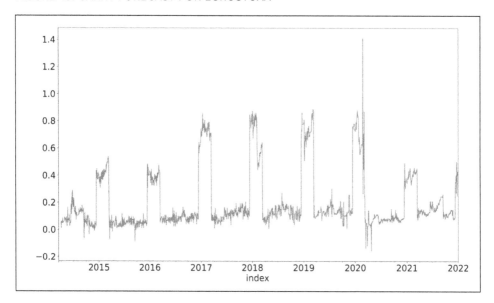

When we are holding the March contract, in the first quarter of each year, carry is unusually positive. The price of June Eurostoxx is usually lower than that of March. There is a simple explanation for this – most firms in the Eurostoxx pay their largest dividend in April. Once again, our carry forecast will be systematically wrong. When holding March it will be biased upwards and for June it will be far too low.

In theory this problem affects all equity futures, except for the German DAX30, which is a total return index. However, it is more noticeable outside of the USA where dividends tend to be paid annually or semi-annually, rather than quarterly as in the USA. Historically, dividends in the USA have also been lower than in Europe, dampening the effect further.

Reducing costs when carry trading

From the above it's clear we have (a) a general problem and (b) some instrument specific problems.

The *general* problem is that carry estimates are unusually noisy, as the price difference between adjacent futures contracts can move around from day to day.

We then have *specific* problems with seasonal instruments where carry varies persistently depending on which month we are currently trading. These fall into two categories. Firstly, those where we are accurately estimating the seasonality because we trade the second contract, such as Natural Gas. Secondly, instruments where we are getting it wrong because we can only trade the front contract, but are imprecisely measuring carry using the difference between the first and second contracts. This includes a few bond markets, and most non-US equity markets.

Let's first consider the problem of noise. Noise will lead to unnecessary trading, and thus increase trading costs without realising additional profits. Back in strategy eight, I said there were a couple of different ways to address this problem. One method was to use *buffering*, which I described in detail. The other is to *smooth* the forecast in some way, by using a moving average, or better still an exponentially weighted moving average.

Smoothing isn't appropriate for trend filters, since they are already constructed of moving averages. But it can be used for carry:

Smoothed carry forecast(Span) = EWMA$_{span}$(carry forecast)

What should the smoothing span be? A longer span will make the forecast smoother but make it less reactive to changes. Different length spans may be appropriate for different instruments. Natural Gas, and other instruments with correctly estimated seasonality, would require quite a short span. This is necessary so our carry estimate can quickly adjust to changes after each roll. A longer span would probably make sense for most other instruments.

What about instruments with the wrong carry entirely: equities and some bonds? We could of course use some instrument specific methods to deal with this problem, and get a more accurate forecast estimate.[157] However for this strategy I want to keep things simple. So I will also use smoothing to deal with the instrument specific problem: if we take the average carry over a long enough period, it will smooth out any seasonal effects.

I decided to use four different spans as my carry *trading rule variations*:

- 5 business days (about a week).

- 20 business days (about a month).

- 60 business days (about three months).

- 120 business days (about six months).

---

[157] For example, we could estimate the seasonal component and adjust the carry accordingly. I will explore this further later in the book. There are also asset class specific methods, such as using the underlying yield curve to estimate bond futures carry, but these require significantly more data and complexity and are out of scope for this book. Finally, we could just avoid trading carry on these assets.

Using intermediate spans, such as 40 business days, results in very high correlations between adjacent variations. Longer smooths do not result in any meaningful reduction in costs or improvement in performance. We can now wheel out the same formula that we've used in the last three chapters:

Scaled carry forecast(Span)

= Smoothed carry forecast(Span) × Forecast scalar

What value should we use for the forecast scalar? Remember, our scaling is set so that the scaled forecast has an average absolute value of 10. The carry forecast is in SR units, and if I measure the average absolute value across all of our different futures instruments with all available data history, it comes in at around 0.33. This implies an appropriate scalar would be 30. Since smoothing doesn't affect average values, except for instruments with very short data history, we can use this scalar for all four variations of carry.

(You could argue that it is not appropriate to use the same scalar for all assets, since different assets typically have different average levels of carry.[158] I will explore this question in a few pages' time.)

Finally we cap our forecast, for the reasons I've discussed before:

Capped carry forecast(Span)

= Max(Min(Scaled forecast(Span), +20), −20)

If we were only trading one speed of carry, then we'd calculate these forecasts every day, using closing prices. We'd then recalculate the optimal position using the standard position scaling equations that we used in strategy nine, and in previous strategies. However it's better to trade multiple carry trading rule variations to get some diversification benefit, and I will explain how to do this in the next section.

Trading multiple carry trading rules

The problem of how to trade multiple carry spans is one we've already solved: it's identical to the problem of having multiple speeds of trend filter. Let's quickly review the procedure we followed and see how it applies to carry trading.

---

158   The average of absolute values for unscaled forecasts varies considerably across different asset classes: agricultural markets 0.82, bonds 0.73, equity 0.17, FX 0.44, metals 0.24, energies 0.72, and volatility 1.46.

Firstly, for a given instrument, we need to select the set of **trading rule variations** which are cheap enough to trade. We do this with the following formula, comparing the turnover per year for each carry span to see if it meets the appropriate test:[159]

Maximum turnover

= [0.15 − (Cost per trade × Rolls per year)] ÷ Cost per trade

Next we select a set of forecast weights. The forecast weight determines how the forecasts from each carry variation are averaged into a combined forecast. I devoted a lot of thought to this when creating the multiple trend strategy, considering the performance before costs of each trend filter and their likely costs. I also calculated figures for correlations, because we should allocate more to trading rules that provide more diversification.

But after all that effort I decided to keep things simple and equally weighted all the trend filters that met the maximum turnover threshold (refer to table 40).

TABLE 40: TURNOVER PER YEAR FOR EACH CARRY SPAN, AVERAGED ACROSS INSTRUMENTS

	Turnover
Carry5	5.75
Carry20	3.12
Carry60	1.82
Carry120	1.22

I'm inclined to use the same method for carry, but first let's check that this wouldn't be completely crazy. Consider the performance for each span in table 41. As I did with trend following, I'm using the aggregated Jumbo portfolio results here. The relative results for individual instruments won't be very different, although of course we're seeing diversification benefits here, so the individual instrument averages won't be as good.

---

159   Most instruments can trade all four carry spans: 96 out of my sample of 102. Three instruments can only trade the three slowest spans, and four can't trade any of them as their cost budget is eaten up entirely by rolling costs.

TABLE 41: PERFORMANCE FOR DIFFERENT CARRY SPAN LENGTHS

	Carry5	Carry20	Carry60	Carry120
Mean annual return	18.9%	18.3%	18.5%	17.7%
Costs	−1.0%	−0.9%	−0.8%	−0.7%
Average drawdown	−18.9%	−21.8%	−19.3%	−20.3%
Standard deviation	21.7%	21.1%	20.8%	20.4%
Sharpe ratio	0.87	0.87	0.89	0.87
Turnover	28.5	20.7	16.2	13.2
Left tail	1.59	1.61	1.59	1.60
Right tail	1.51	1.48	1.45	1.51
Alpha	19.4%	18.4%	17.4%	15.7%
Beta	−0.01	0.01	0.09	0.15

Aggregated Jumbo portfolio results with buffering and forecast scaling.

The carry spans are all extremely similar, as you might expect given they use the same underlying rule with just a change in the smoothing parameter. Naturally, the larger spans trade more slowly and have slightly lower costs. There is nothing else of interest except that, when regressing against our benchmark strategy four, the beta seems to be a little higher for slower spans and alpha a little lower.

I also considered skew over different time periods when I looked at trend following. Table 42 has the figures for carry, which you can compare with the values for trend in table 32 (page 180). Carry has a reputation for being a negative skew strategy, but mostly the skew is only a little below zero. When measured at a monthly frequency it comes in modestly positive for most span lengths. I will discuss this surprising finding in more detail later in the chapter.

TABLE 42: SKEW MEASURED OVER DIFFERENT TIME PERIODS FOR DIFFERENT CARRY SPAN

	Daily skew	Weekly skew	Monthly skew	Annual skew
Carry5	0.02	0.04	0.57	−0.01
Carry20	−0.03	−0.03	0.35	−0.15
Carry60	−0.12	−0.11	0.08	−0.08
Carry120	−0.07	0.02	0.24	0.04

Aggregated Jumbo portfolio results with buffering and forecast scaling.

So far we have seen nothing suggesting that any span of carry is fundamentally different from another, but we need to zoom in a little more to see if the smoothing process has dealt with the seasonality problems I highlighted earlier. Table 43 shows the median SR for different carry spans, averaged across different groups of instruments. The figures here are lower than in the previous table as they are medians per instrument, rather than for an aggregated portfolio.

TABLE 43: MEDIAN SHARPE RATIO BY CARRY SPAN FOR DIFFERENT SETS OF INSTRUMENTS, AFTER COSTS

	Carry5	Carry20	Carry60	Carry120
All instruments	0.27	0.28	0.27	0.27
All FX	0.31	0.29	0.28	0.26
All Vol	0.64	0.61	0.48	0.46
All Metals	0.26	0.25	0.26	0.21
All Bonds	0.40	0.46	0.45	0.52
Bund, Bobl, Bono	0.62	0.77	0.74	0.74
All equities	0.22	0.34	0.30	0.29
Non-US equities	0.22	0.34	0.31	0.31
All energies	0.18	0.22	0.24	0.22
WTI Crude (December only)	0.53	0.47	0.36	0.28
All agricultural	0.16	0.17	0.10	0.00
Wheat, Corn (December only)	0.03	0.02	−0.03	−0.08

The first few rows show asset classes where I have no particular concern about seasonality. Even so there are a couple of brief observations worth making. Firstly, carry returns are fairly consistent across different asset classes. Secondly, it looks like in volatility ('vol') instruments specifically, there might be an argument for trading a little faster. But this is a very small asset class with only two instruments, so we can't be certain if these figures are meaningful.

The more interesting part of the table begins with bonds. Bonds generally have no seasonality issues and have above average returns from carry. The next row shows the bonds with inaccurate carry due to seasonality issues: Bunds, Bobls and Bonos. We would expect carry to improve as we apply a longer smooth, which should iron out the seasonality problems. It does, but not significantly.

Even with shorter spans these three bonds do exceptionally well, despite the fact that with the shortest smooth we are changing the sign of our position every three months due to seasonal effects! But you should not read too much into these results. The outright performance of going long Bunds and Bobls, and to a lesser extent Bonos, has been very strong, and even a strategy that consistently gets the carry wrong can be profitable.

Now consider equities. I noted earlier that non-US equities are likely to have inaccurate seasonal carry. Still, there is no difference for the SR in equities generally, and non-US equities specifically.

Most of the energy markets in my data set will have seasonal carry, albeit measured accurately since I am calculating the carry by comparing a nearer contract with the current contract. The exception is WTI Crude,[160] where I only hold the December contract. We would expect that a longer span would be needed for the other energy markets to correct for this seasonality. Sure enough, Crude does better than the other energy markets with shorter smooths. But as this is just one instrument, it's hard to know if this is really a meaningful effect.

There is a similar situation in agricultural markets, where I usually have seasonal carry problems. Wheat and Corn are the exception: here I stick to holding the December contract. Interestingly the 'cleaner' carry of Wheat and Corn makes less money than the seasonal carry of the rest of the complex. Again, we may be data mining here given the small number of instruments involved.

There might be a case for not trading carry at all in some of these instruments, where carry is measured inaccurately, but there is no compelling evidence suggesting that we should deviate from equal forecast weights.

Table 44 shows the correlation matrix for the different carry spans.[161] As with momentum, we get a pattern where adjacent spans are more correlated, suggesting that it might make more sense to increase forecast weights on the shorter and longer carry spans. However, the correlations here are extremely high, unsurprising given these are all based on the same underlying raw carry estimates. There will be little benefit from moving the forecast weights away from equal weighting.

---

160   This is true of the full size WTI contract. The mini contract isn't liquid enough, and I have to roll this monthly.

161   Correlations between adjacent carry smoothing spans are very high, and much higher than for the adjacent EWMAC filters seen in strategy nine. You could argue that four variations of carry is excessive, and two or three would be sufficient. My use of four carry variations in my own trading strategy is mainly for sentimental reasons. For instruments that are cheap enough, we have six trend rule variations and four carry. As you will see in the next chapter, my preferred weights to trend and carry are 60% and 40% respectively. There is something neat about having exactly 10% in each rule variation.

TABLE 44: CORRELATION MATRIX OF RETURNS FOR DIFFERENT CARRY SPANS, PLUS AVERAGE CORRELATIONS

	Carry5	Carry20	Carry60	Carry120
Carry5	1	0.96	0.89	0.84
Carry20		1	0.94	0.89
Carry60			1	0.96
Carry120				1
Average versus other spans	0.90	0.93	0.93	0.90

In conclusion then, I will stick to my preferred method: use equal forecast weights across the carry variations that are cheap enough for a given instrument to trade.

From strategy nine, the next step is this: given a set of capped forecasts $f_{i,j,t}$ for instrument i, trading rule variation j with forecast weights $w_{i,j}$:

$$\text{Raw combined forecast}_i = w_{i,1}f_{i,1,t} + w_{i,2}f_{i,2,t} + w_{i,3}f_{i,3,t} + ...$$

As with multiple trend filters, we need to account for diversification by applying the FDM:

$$\text{Scaled combined forecast}_{i,t} = \text{Raw combined forecast}_{i,t} \times \text{FDM}_i$$

Appropriate FDM are given in table 45.

TABLE 45: FDM AND SUGGESTED FORECAST WEIGHTS FOR CARRY

	Forecast weight	FDM
Carry5, 20, 60, 120	0.25	1.04
Carry20, 60, 120	0.333	1.03
Carry60, 120	0.5	1.02
Carry120	1.0	1.0

The FDM are all very low, reflecting the very high correlations between carry spans, and thus a lack of diversification. We can now plug the combined forecast into the familiar position sizing and buffering equations that we've been using for a while now.

Reviewing carry performance

Now we have constructed a carry strategy, let's evaluate its performance. Will carry turn out to be dangerous, but rewarding, as we would expect from the introduction to this chapter? Or is it a paper tiger whose roar is worse than its bite? As usual, I will begin by evaluating the average performance of individual instruments, taken across asset classes. The results are in tables 46 and 47, and I have removed statistics that are very similar and uninteresting, as well as adding some carry specific values.

TABLE 46: MEDIAN INSTRUMENT PERFORMANCE FOR COMBINED CARRY STRATEGY ACROSS FINANCIAL ASSET CLASSES

	Equity	Vol	FX	Bond
Mean annual return	3.1%	21.4%	5.1%	13.3%
Standard deviation	9.9%	36.0%	18.3%	27.5%
Sharpe ratio	0.40	0.59	0.30	0.48
Median absolute carry (MAC)	0.12	0.67	0.21	0.41
Mean return ÷ 20% (AMR)	0.15	1.07	0.25	0.67
% Carry realised = AMR ÷ MAC	170%	160%	109%	142%
Percentage long	86%	12%	60%	81%
Skew	−0.01	−0.64	−0.38	−0.11
Lower tail	2.86	2.69	3.56	2.22
Upper tail	2.36	1.67	2.70	2.09

TABLE 47: MEDIAN INSTRUMENT PERFORMANCE FOR COMBINED CARRY STRATEGY ACROSS COMMODITY ASSET CLASSES

	Metals	Energy	Ags	Median
Mean annual return	3.5%	5.0%	3.5%	4.4%
Standard deviation	16.7%	28.2%	29.3%	19.8%
Sharpe ratio	0.25	0.20	0.14	0.28
Median absolute carry (MAC)	0.15	0.42	0.45	0.24
AMR = Mean return ÷ 20%	0.18	0.25	0.17	0.22
% Carry realised = AMR ÷ MAC	115%	77%	46%	115%
Percentage long	18%	47%	40%	66%
Skew	−0.36	−0.05	0.07	−0.17
Lower tail	3.36	2.41	2.12	2.62
Upper tail	3.73	1.95	1.98	2.14

Notice that the annualised standard deviation is *not* the same across asset classes. Has something gone wrong with my much vaunted risk targeting method? In fact this is to be expected. The beauty of using positions scaled by forecasts is that we will take less risk when forecasts are weaker, and vice versa. This hasn't been noticeable when trading trends, but the strength of carry does vary considerably across asset classes. It's clearly lower in equities and higher in volatility. Using a common forecast scalar value of 30 for all instruments results in different risk levels depending on the average value of carry within a given asset class.

The new rows I have added to these tables help explain what is going on. *Median absolute carry* (MAC) is the median expected SR of carry. We derive it by dividing the average scaled forecast by the forecast scalar (30), thus reversing the normal process to get a scaled forecast, and taking the median absolute value. MAC will be larger for asset classes with instruments that have stronger carry forecasts on average: long or short. We can see that where the MAC is higher, the annualised standard deviation is also higher.

The difference in standard deviation also implies that SRs may not be the most sensible metric to evaluate performance across different asset classes. An alternative measure is included here: *adjusted mean return* (AMR). This is also a Sharpe ratio (SR), but it's the annual return divided by the risk target of 20%, *not* the realised standard deviation we use for a standard SR calculation. Unlike the actual SR it will be smaller when carry forecasts are lower, and vice versa.

We can directly compare the AMR to the MAC, since both are Sharpe ratios.[162] You can think of MAC as the 'Sharpe ratio *promised* by carry', and AMR as the 'Sharpe ratio *delivered* by carry'. The final new row, *% carry realised*, is equal to the AMR divided by the MAC. If this is greater than 100%, then carry has delivered more than it promised. When below 100%, carry is under delivering.

On average, based on the median instrument, carry delivers 115% of what it promises. At the start of the chapter I said that carry looked like free money, but that we faced the risk that the spot price will move against us: $1 of promised carry could be lost if the spot price moved against us by $1 or more. But in fact for every $1 of potential carry gain, we stand to gain another $0.15 in *favourable* price movements! Carry under promises and over delivers in all but two asset classes: agricultural and energy

---

162   We can't do this for trend following, or most other trading strategies, since they don't produce forecasts that are equal to expected SRs, only forecasts that are *proportional* to expected SRs.

markets. Perhaps not coincidentally, these are also where we have many seasonal instruments.[163]

Skew is mostly negative, and worst of all in the volatility instruments. That isn't surprising when we look at another new row: *percentage long*. This shows the proportion of the time that we have a long carry position, averaged across instruments in each asset class. For volatility we are mostly short; and since we know from earlier strategies that long volatility is a positive skewed asset, it's unsurprising that we end up with heavy negative skew.

We only have two instruments in the volatility asset class, and skew is not a very robust statistic, so it's also worth considering the tail ratios. The lower tail ratios are all fairly high, and mostly worse than the upper tail, which is a strong suggestion of negative skew. But it's FX and metals that have the fattest tails using this more robust measure.

The pattern of percentage longs is also interesting in its own right. In trend following any long or short biases were due to historical trends in asset prices that may not continue. But for carry different assets generally have consistent carry positions with persistent causes. Bonds, for example, usually have long carry as the yield curve is normally upward sloping. Dividends normally exceed funding costs in equities, so we are usually long here as well. Conversely, in metals, we are usually short carry, for reasons I noted at the beginning of the chapter.

At this point it's worth asking whether we would be justified in using different instrument weights for carry strategies. With trend following there were differences between asset classes, but we could mostly put those down to random noise or secular trends in historical prices that seem unlikely to be repeated. But with carry there seem to be genuine reasons why different instruments outperform others. Indeed, there are some instruments where our measurement of carry is just plain wrong.

Personally, I don't take this approach, and I continue to use the method of setting instrument weights with an assumption that we can't distinguish between the performance of different instruments trading a given strategy.

With that in mind let's turn to the aggregate Jumbo portfolio, the results of which are shown in table 48.

---

163   If we had used a different estimate of the forecast scalar for each asset class, then this linkage between promised and realised carry would be broken. We would have a larger forecast scalar, and hence a higher standard deviation, in asset classes where carry was systematically low such as equities. We would be taking on more risk with very poor rewards for our efforts.

TABLE 48: JUMBO PORTFOLIO PERFORMANCE FOR BENCHMARK, MULTIPLE TREND AND MULTIPLE CARRY

	Strategy four Long only	Strategy nine Multiple trend	Strategy ten Carry
Mean annual return	15.4%	25.2%	19.7%
Costs	−0.8%	−1.2%	−0.8%
Average drawdown	−24.7%	−11.2%	−18.6%
Standard deviation	18.2%	22.2%	20.8%
Sharpe ratio	0.85	1.14	0.94
Turnover	20.7	62.9	19.2
Skew	−0.04	0.98	0.41
Lower tail	1.44	1.99	1.57
Upper tail	1.24	1.81	1.49
Alpha	0	18.8%	19.1%
Beta	1.0	0.43	0.06

First of all notice that we have some positive skew[164] for the aggregate Jumbo portfolio. In contrast, table 47 shows that the median individual instrument has negative skew on average. This reflects dramatic episodes in individual instruments such as FX depreciation, spikes in volatility, flights from risk, or weather events in commodities. But for the most part these dramatic episodes are not correlated with each other, and they don't affect our aggregate returns.

As is standard practice in this book, the reported skew in these tables is monthly. Skew figures for different frequencies are as follows: daily[165] skew is –0.01, weekly –0.01, monthly 0.41 and annual 0.16. To explain the fall in carry skew from 0.41 (monthly) to 0.16 (annual), we can look at years like 2007 and 2008 when there were a number of episodes that were bad for carry positions; however, these were not concentrated in a particular month. For example, the VIX volatility future lost money in summer 2007 but nothing thereafter; Gold was hurt in the third and fourth quarter of 2007, whilst Crude Oil and EM FX carry suffered in summer 2008. These losses were more than offset elsewhere in the portfolio, and the carry strategy lost just –8.5% in 2007 before making 17.9% in 2008.

---

164 The results here are broadly in agreement with those in the seminal academic work on this subject: Koijen, Ralph S. J., Moskowitz, Tobias J., Pedersen, Lasse H. and Vrugt, Evert B., 'Carry' (August 2013). *NBER Working Paper*. There are some differences, which are to be expected given the different data sets, definition of carry and time periods used. But they also find that aggregate skew is much better than it is for individual asset classes.

165 For the multiple trend strategy the relevant figures are daily –0.11, weekly 0.05, monthly 0.98 and annual 1.28.

Skew for carry is certainly not as good as for trend following, and for most frequencies the skew is effectively zero, but the bogeyman of significant negative skew isn't present at the aggregate portfolio level. It also has nicer tails than trend; again the aggregate lower tail is significantly better than the median figure across instruments. It looks like diversification is not just reducing the 'vanilla' risk measure of standard deviation but also the more exotic skew and tail risk estimates.

Carry is cheaper to trade than trend; indeed it costs about the same as a long only strategy.[166] But its SR isn't as good. However, it does have a significantly lower beta, as unlike trend it usually has a more mixed set of longs and shorts. This results in a higher alpha. Of course we know that the beta will depend on the asset class; in metals and vol where we are usually short the beta will certainly be quite negative, whilst in bonds and equities it will be significantly positive.

Let's close out this chapter with figure 44. This shows the cumulated Jumbo portfolio performance of our long only benchmark, the multiple trend of strategy nine and the multiple carry strategy we've built in this chapter.

FIGURE 44: CUMULATED PERFORMANCE OF JUMBO BENCHMARK, CARRY AND MOMENTUM STRATEGIES

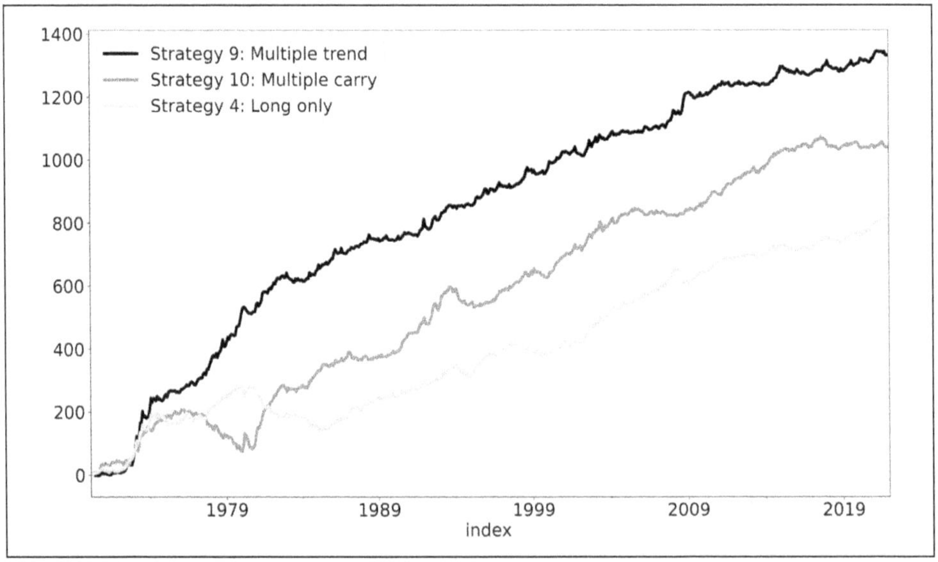

Just as we did for trend following we could argue that 'carry is dead': we've made no money since late 2017. But this is by no means an exceptionally long or deep

---

166 This might seem unlikely, bar some weird offsetting interaction between volatility changes and carry forecasts, but don't forget that the positions in the carry strategy are buffered before trading. Without buffering the turnover of carry would be higher than the long only strategy.

drawdown. Remember: one of the advantages of using a backtest is that we can determine whether a period of poor returns is unusual, or to be expected.

Conclusion

Carry isn't quite as terrifying as you might have expected. It doesn't have the nice positive skew of momentum, but the skew isn't horrifically negative either with the possible exception of volatility. With enough diversification, as we get in the Jumbo portfolio, the skew is effectively zero at most time frequencies.

The outright performance of carry isn't as good as trend following, but you can clearly see that (a) it's less correlated with an outright long only portfolio as we'd expect from the low beta estimate in table 48, and (b) it's not especially correlated with trend. In fact the correlation between strategies nine and ten – trend and carry – is just 0.36. This suggests we can get some significant diversification benefit from combining them, and I'll do this in the next strategy.

Strategy ten: Trading plan

All other elements are identical to strategy nine. We construct an optimal position and then trade as required every day.

Strategy	Go long or short one or more instruments with variable risk estimate and a combined forecast from multiple smoothed carry forecasts.
Instrument(s)	Any that meet minimum capital, liquidity and cost thresholds.
Choose trading rules for each instrument	Only choose trading rule variations where: $$\text{Turnover} < [0.15 - (\text{Cost per trade} \times \text{Rolls per year})] \div \text{Cost per trade}$$ Turnover figures are in table 40.
Trading rule variations	Construct one or more smoothed carry forecasts with span N, where N is one of 5,20,60,120.
Raw carry	Preferred: $$\text{Raw carry} = \text{Price of nearer futures contract} - \text{price of currently held contract}$$ Alternative (if trading first contract): $$\text{Raw carry} = \text{Price of currently held contract} - \text{price of further out contract}$$

Expiry difference	**Expiry difference in years**
	= abs(months between contracts) ÷ 12
Annualise	**Annualised raw carry**
	= Raw carry ÷ Expiry difference in years
Risk adjustment	**Carry$_{i,t}$ = Annualised raw carry$_{i,t}$ ÷ ($\sigma_{p,i,t}$ × 16)**
Smoothing	**Smoothed carry forecast (Span)$_{i,t}$**
	= EWMA$_{span}$ (Carry forecast)$_{i,t}$
Scaling	**Scaled forecast (Span)$_{i,t}$**
	= Smoothed carry forecast(Span)$_{i,t}$ × 30.0
Capping	**Capped forecast(Span)$_{i,t}$**
	= Max(Min(Scaled forecast(Span)$_{i,t}$, +20), −20)
Allocating forecast weights	See page 216 and table 45.
Forecast combination	Given a set of forecasts $f_{i,j,t}$ for instrument i, trading rule variation j with forecast weights $w_{i,j}$:
	Raw combined forecast$_i$
	= $w_{i,1}f_{i,1,t} + w_{i,2}f_{i,2,t} + w_{i,3}f_{i,3,t}$ + ...
Forecast diversification	See table 45 for FDM values.
	Scaled combined forecast$_{i,t}$
	= Raw combined forecast$_{i,t}$ × FDM$_i$
Capped combined forecast	**Capped combined forecast, f$_{i,t}$**
	= Max(Min(Scaled combined forecast$_{i,t}$, +20), −20)

STRATEGY ELEVEN

Combined carry and trend

Time for a quick recap: we began in strategy one with the simplest possible approach – owning a single contract. Then I introduced the idea of scaling our positions by risk. We went from owning a single instrument, to being able to trade a portfolio of 100 or more. I then introduced the concept of a trading rule to change our position: a *trend* rule.

Subsequently, I showed you how to vary positions according to the strength of a *forecast*: a risk adjusted measure of expected future returns. Because forecasts are calibrated to a consistent scale we can combine them together to produce a more diversified trading strategy. Initially I demonstrated this with different speeds of trend filter. Then in strategy ten I followed the same approach, but this time with different speeds of carry.

Now, in this final chapter of Part One I will show you how to combine trend and carry together. We can do this easily, as **all the carry and trend rule forecasts are calibrated so they have a common scale**.

> **Strategy eleven:** Trade a portfolio of one or more instruments, each with positions scaled for a variable risk estimate. Scale positions according to the strength of a combined forecast which is a weighted average of carry and trend forecasts.

I will also be covering the following topic in this chapter:

- Choosing the appropriate mixture of carry and trend.

Building blocks

The approach of building a trading strategy from individual trading rules, each producing their own scaled forecast, is like building something out of Lego™ blocks. We can use almost any kind of block with any other, as they are all designed to fit neatly together. This is also true of trading rules, thanks to the scaling properties of trading rule forecasts. This allows us to trade a wide variety of different trading rules in a single strategy, and I will continue to use the approach in this chapter for much of the rest of this book: the whole of Part Two, and Part Three.

What building blocks are we going to use in strategy eleven?

- Trend (from strategy nine) – EWMAC rule:

  - EWMAC2

  - EWMAC4

  - EWMAC8

  - EWMAC16

  - EWMAC32

  - EWMAC64

- Carry (from strategy ten): Smoothed carry rule, with an N day EWMA smooth:

  - Carry5

  - Carry20

  - Carry60

  - Carry120

For each of these we will calculate a raw forecast, then scale it so it has an absolute average value of 10, and finally apply a cap so it does not exceed an absolute value of 20.

Forecast weights for a combined strategy

The next stage is to combine these disparate forecasts together. Again, we'll use the same method as in strategies nine and ten. Firstly, for any given instrument we will select the subset of forecasting rules which don't exceed my *speed limit* of 0.15 Sharpe Ratio (SR) units in costs, using the turnover figures in tables 35 and 40, and the risk adjusted cost per trade for the relevant instrument.

The next step is to calculate the forecast weights. Here's a reminder of the 'top down' method I introduced in strategy nine:

- Split the list of trading rules by **style**. Allocate between styles according to your preferences.

- Within a given style, allocate equally across **trading rules**.

- Within a given trading rule, allocate equally across **variations** of each given trading rule.

Let's apply this method here:

- Our two styles are **convergent** and **divergent**. We've already established that trend is a divergent strategy. Carry, since it assumes that spot prices remain stable, is very much of the convergent family.

- We only have one trading rule within each style: EWMAC trend in the divergent group, and carry in the convergent category.

- We have up to six variations of the EWMAC rule, and up to four variations of carry.

How then do we decide how much to put into carry and trend? Tables 49 and 50 show some performance statistics for Jumbo portfolios with different proportions of carry and trend.

TABLE 49: CHARACTERISTICS OF MIXED TREND AND CARRY STRATEGY, 50–100% IN TREND

	100%	90%	80%	70%	60%	50%
Sharpe ratio	1.14	1.19	1.24	1.26	1.27	1.27
Average drawdown	−11.2%	−10.1%	−9.6%	−9.2%	−8.9%	−9.3%
Weekly skew	0.05	0.08	0.12	0.16	0.18	0.20
Monthly skew	0.98	0.94	0.88	0.83	0.76	0.72
Annual skew	1.28	1.27	1.26	1.25	1.22	1.16
Lower tail	1.99	1.95	1.91	1.88	1.86	1.78
Upper tail	1.81	1.79	1.76	1.76	1.75	1.76
Alpha	18.8%	19.1%	20.4%	21.5%	22.3%	22.9%
Beta	0.43	0.40	0.39	0.37	0.30	0.30

Percentage shown is proportion allocated to trend.

TABLE 50: CHARACTERISTICS OF MIXED TREND AND CARRY STRATEGY, 0–50% IN TREND

	50%	40%	30%	20%	10%	0%
Sharpe ratio	1.27	1.25	1.20	1.12	1.03	0.94
Average drawdown	−9.3%	−9.8%	−11.1%	−13.2%	−16.0%	−18.6%
Weekly skew	0.20	0.19	0.16	0.12	0.08	−0.01
Monthly skew	0.72	0.68	0.63	0.57	0.50	0.41
Annual skew	1.16	1.04	0.85	0.62	0.38	0.16
Lower tail	1.78	1.74	1.67	1.62	1.60	1.57
Upper tail	1.76	1.67	1.59	1.55	1.54	1.49
Alpha	22.9%	22.87%	22.4%	21.6%	20.5%	19.1%
Beta	0.30	0.25	0.20	0.15	0.10	0.06

Percentage shown is proportion allocated to trend.

Which option you choose will depend on your preferences. I will use a split of 60/40 in this chapter, as this proportion[167] is what I use in my own trading system. It maximizes the SR, minimizes drawdown and has a pretty decent alpha. I'd get better skew and right tails if I had more trend, but a nicer left tail with added carry. Feel free to choose a different combination if you prefer.

With that in mind, let's look at an example of how we'd fit the forecast weights for an arbitrary instrument: Eurodollar futures. These currently have a risk adjusted cost per trade of 0.0088 SR units. Back in strategy nine I used that figure to derive a maximum turnover of 13 trades annually. Tables 35 and 40 imply we can allocate to the two slowest EWMAC variations, and to all four carry variations. Let's follow the top down allocation process:

- Our two styles are convergent (40%) and divergent (60%), reflecting carry and trend respectively.

- We only have one trading rule within each style.

- We have two variations of the EWMAC rule. Each gets half of 60%, which is 30%.

- We have four variations of carry. Each gets a quarter of 40%, which is 10%.

---

167   It also echoes the classic 60:40 long only portfolio, with cash weights of 60% in equities and 40% in bonds.

So our forecast weights are as follows:

- Divergent:
    - EWMAC trend:
        - EWMAC(32,128): 30%
        - EWMAC(64,256): 30%
- Convergent:
    - Smoothed carry:
        - Carry5: 10%
        - Carry20: 10%
        - Carry60: 10%
        - Carry120: 10%

Table 51 shows the appropriate forecast weights for a given set of trading rules.

TABLE 51: FORECAST WEIGHTS FOR A GIVEN SET OF EWMAC AND CARRY TRADING RULE VARIATIONS

	Forecast weight each EWMAC	Forecast weight each carry
EWMAC2, 4, 8, 16, 32, 64 Carry5, 20, 60, 120	0.10	0.10
EWMAC4, 8, 16, 32, 64 Carry5, 20, 60, 120	0.12	0.10
EWMAC8, 16, 32, 64 Carry5, 20, 60, 120	0.15	0.10
EWMAC16, 32, 64 Carry5, 20, 60, 120	0.20	0.10
EWMAC32, 64 Carry5, 20, 60, 120	0.30	0.10
EWMAC32,64 Carry20, 60, 120	0.30	0.13333
EWMA64 Carry20, 60, 120	0.6	0.13333
Carry20, 60, 120	0	0.3333
Carry60, 120	0	0.5
Carry120	0	1.0

Eagle eyed readers will spot that I've missed a crucial step, which is the application of an FDM. Table 52 shows the appropriate forecast weights and FDM for a given set of trading rules. This table can be used for any arbitrary strategy, and I will continue to use it in Parts Two and Three. You can interpolate intermediate values if necessary.

TABLE 52: APPROXIMATE FORECAST DIVERSIFICATION MULTIPLIER FOR ANY STRATEGY, GIVEN AN INSTRUMENT HAS A GIVEN NUMBER OF TRADING RULES

Number of trading rules	FDM	Number of trading rules	FDM
13	1.39	40 or more	2.00
12	1.38	35	1.93
11	1.36	30	1.81
10	1.35	25	1.69
9	1.34	22	1.55
8	1.32	21	1.54
7	1.29	20	1.53
6	1.27	19	1.50
5	1.25	18	1.48
4	1.23	17	1.46
3	1.03	16	1.44
2	1.02	15	1.42
1	1.0	14	1.41

Evaluating trend and carry

Now we have a combined forecast with the correct scale, it's just a matter of applying the usual procedure for capping, position sizing calculation and buffering. Then we can wheel out the standard diagnostic tables to examine the performance of the strategy, firstly by considering the returns of each instrument averaged across asset classes. The now familiar figures are in tables 53 and 54. They are worth comparing with the same figures for trend (tables 37 and 38), and carry (tables 46 and 47).

TABLE 53: MEDIAN INSTRUMENT PERFORMANCE FOR COMBINED TREND AND CARRY WITHIN FINANCIAL ASSET CLASSES

	Equity	Vol	FX	Bond
Mean annual return	2.4%	18.5%	6.8%	13.3%
Costs	−0.3%	−1.3%	−0.4%	−0.4%
Average drawdown	−21.9%	−30.7%	−40.2%	−20.2%
Standard deviation	18.6%	32.2%	21.6%	23.3%
Sharpe ratio	0.13	0.58	0.30	0.54
Turnover	12.1	11.4	11.8	11.5
Skew	0.51	−0.50	0.53	0.64
Left tail	3.56	2.98	3.42	2.52
Right tail	2.46	1.79	2.96	2.52

TABLE 54: MEDIAN INSTRUMENT PERFORMANCE FOR COMBINED TREND AND CARRY WITHIN COMMODITY ASSET CLASSES

	Metals	Energy	Ags	Median
Mean annual return	6.8%	10.2%	5.4%	5.7%
Costs	−0.3%	−0.5%	−0.4%	−0.4%
Average drawdown	−29.7%	−34.8%	−40.0%	−24.9%
Standard deviation	19.6%	25.6%	23.8%	21.7%
Sharpe ratio	0.36	0.41	0.23	0.27
Turnover	13.4	12.4	11.4	11.8
Skew	2.2	0.66	0.70	0.63
Left tail	3.27	2.85	2.74	3.11
Right tail	4.07	2.44	2.56	2.67

Most asset classes perform similarly across carry and trend, and their combined performance reflects this. The main exception is equities, where our trend returns are especially poor, but carry is better. This doesn't improve the combined performance as much as you might expect; remember from table 46 that the annualised standard deviation of equities is only half the target in the carry strategy, so the contribution of carry isn't 40% of equity return risk, but more like 20%.

Now we turn to the aggregated results across a 'Jumbo' portfolio of over 100 instruments. Table 55 has the low down. I have already demonstrated that the 60:40 combined portfolio represents a good compromise that improves on every performance statistic of the pure trend strategy, apart from skew. The cumulated account curve in figure 45 shows that the carry plus trend portfolio has performed consistently well over time.

TABLE 55: PERFORMANCE OF AGGREGATE JUMBO PORTFOLIO: BENCHMARK, TREND, CARRY AND COMBINED

	Strategy four Long only	Strategy nine Multiple trend	Strategy ten Carry	Strategy eleven Carry and trend
Mean annual return	15.4%	25.2%	19.7%	26.5%
Costs	−0.8%	−1.2%	−0.8%	−1.1%
Average drawdown	−24.7%	−11.2%	−18.6%	−8.9%
Standard deviation	18.2%	22.2%	20.8%	20.9%
Sharpe ratio	0.85	1.14	0.94	1.27
Turnover	20.7	62.9	19.2	46.5
Skew	−0.04	0.98	0.41	0.76
Lower tail	1.44	1.99	1.57	1.86
Upper tail	1.24	1.81	1.49	1.75
Alpha	0	18.8%	19.1%	22.3%
Beta	1.0	0.43	0.06	0.30

FIGURE 45: CUMULATIVE PERFORMANCE FOR AGGREGATE JUMBO PORTFOLIO: LONG ONLY BENCHMARK, TREND, CARRY AND COMBINED

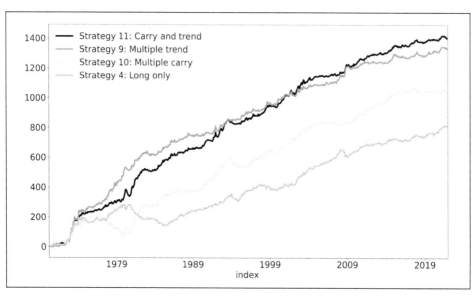

The magical diversification machine: Part two

Consider table 56. The first row is the median SR, averaged across all instruments in my data set, for each of the strategies shown. The second row is the aggregate SR for the Jumbo portfolio.

TABLE 56: SHARPE RATIO, SKEW AND TAIL RATIOS IMPROVE WITH DIVERSIFICATION, BUT DIFFERENTLY DEPENDING ON THE TYPE OF STRATEGY

	Strategy four Long only	Strategy nine Multiple trend	Strategy ten Carry	Strategy eleven Carry and trend
A: Median Sharpe ratio across instruments	0.32	0.23	0.28	0.27
B: Aggregate Sharpe ratio for Jumbo portfolio	0.85	1.14	0.94	1.27
SRR B ÷ A	**2.66**	**4.96**	**4.1**	**4.70**
C: Median skew across instruments	−0.09	0.84	−0.17	0.63
D: Aggregate skew for Jumbo portfolio	−0.04	0.98	0.41	0.76
Skew Improvement D − C	**0.05**	**0.14**	**0.58**	**0.13**
E: Median lower tail ratio across instruments	1.56	3.47	2.62	3.11
F: Aggregate median lower tail ratio for Jumbo portfolio	1.44	1.99	1.57	1.86
Tail improvement E − F	**0.12**	**1.48**	**1.05**	**1.25**

I noted earlier, in strategy six, that it is a little weird that the SR for an individual instrument is lower for trend than for a long only benchmark, yet the aggregate SR is much higher. Another way of looking at this is to consider the ratio between these two SRs – individual and aggregate – a 'Sharpe ratio ratio' (SRR). This is shown in the third row.

The SRR reflects the *realised* diversification benefits in risk adjusted returns from diversifying across multiple instruments. The SRR on a long only portfolio is pretty good at over 2.5, but for trend it's nearly twice as much.

Now let's bring in carry. On an instrument only basis, carry is better than trend, but we already know that its aggregated SR is worse. So it's no surprise to see a lower SRR: the realised diversification benefits for carry are a little lower than those for trend. We can speculate what the possible reasons are. One might be that positions in carry are stickier; we're more likely to be long or short a given instrument over long periods of time. Another is that we get an outsized benefit from outlier markets in trend, something we don't enjoy in carry.

The combined strategy sits somewhere between these two extremes, with a median SR a fraction below carry, but an aggregate SR that is better than trend, resulting in a very respectable SRR of 4.7.

Next consider skew. Again, if we examine the skew for the median instrument, and compare it to the aggregate instrument, we get some interesting results. There is a small improvement in skew for the long only strategy, and a slightly bigger one for trend, but for carry the skew improves significantly. The figures shown here are for monthly skew, but the pattern is similar for other time periods. The nasty skew that carry exhibits for individual instruments is diversified away, because bad skew events are mostly uncorrelated across assets.

(Interestingly the more robust lower tail ratio risk measure shows the largest improvement for momentum, but the tails are generally better for carry than momentum for both individual median and aggregate results.)

Aside from intellectual interest, what use is this information? It shows that the optimal mixture of carry and trend might be different, depending on the size of your portfolio, and your preferences for outright performance (SR) or positive skewness. If you were trading a single instrument, then you face a stark choice between a better SR (carry) or nicer skew (trend). But if you had enough capital to trade the Jumbo portfolio, trend is the better option on both metrics.

For all sizes of traders a combined strategy is likely to be better than pure trend or carry, assuming you are happy to trade off a small amount of skew or SR for a larger improvement in the other metric.

Conclusion

That is the end of Part One. We have built a number of useful trading strategies, most of which perform well in their own right, culminating in a strategy which combines both carry and trend with excellent results. But, more importantly, we have learned how to use a number of useful tools and techniques.

The remaining Parts of the book can be read independently. The tools you have learned in Part One are sufficient to read ahead to any of the following Parts of the book.

However, the strategies in Parts Two and Three will probably be of particular interest. Because of the building block nature of trading strategies using forecasts, you can easily combine these with the forecast based strategies I have developed in Part One: in particular strategies nine, ten and eleven.[168] The strategies described in Part Two are a further development of the carry and trend strategies, whilst in Part Three I consider other types of trading strategy.

But feel free to skip ahead to Parts Four or Five where I discuss other types of strategy that do not fit into the forecasting framework I've presented here; or to Part Six where I explain tactics to help manage your trading strategies better.

Strategy eleven: Trading plan

All other elements are identical to strategies nine and ten.

Strategy	Go long or short one or more instruments with variable risk estimate and a combined forecast from multiple smoothed carry forecasts, and multiple exponentially weighted moving average crossover (EWMAC) forecasts.
Instrument(s)	Any that meet minimum capital, liquidity and cost thresholds.
Choose trading rules for each instrument	Turnover figures are in tables 35 (trend) and 40 (carry).
Trading rule variations	See strategies nine (trend) and ten (carry).
Allocating forecast weights	See table 51.
Forecast diversification multiplier	See table 52 .

---

168   I'm ignoring strategies seven and eight here since they are part of strategy nine. Strategies one to six do not use forecasting.

PART TWO

Advanced Trend Following and Carry Strategies

You must read all of Part One before reading Part Two.

All the strategies in Part Two are standalone: you can use them in any combination with strategies nine, ten or eleven, or with each other. Strategies twelve to sixteen *modify* the carry or trend strategies from Part One. Strategies seventeen to twenty are *new* standalone strategies.

The following strategies *modify* the multiple trend strategy (strategy nine):

- **Strategy twelve:** Adjusted trend.
- **Strategy thirteen:** Trend and carry in different risk regimes.
- **Strategy fourteen:** Spot trend.
- **Strategy sixteen:** Trend and carry allocation.

The following strategies *modify* the carry strategy (strategy ten):

- **Strategy thirteen:** Trend and carry in different risk regimes.
- **Strategy fifteen:** Accurate carry.
- **Strategy sixteen:** Trend and carry allocation.

The following standalone strategies can be used *in addition* to carry and trend:

- **Strategy seventeen:** Normalised trend.
- **Strategy eighteen:** Trend over asset classes.
- **Strategy nineteen:** Cross-sectional momentum.
- **Strategy twenty:** Cross-sectional carry.

Adjusted trend

The trend is your friend – until it stabs you in the back with a chopstick.

Original source unclear, but widely attributed to @StockCats on Twitter

Trend following is a great strategy when things are going well. You ride the trend serenely upwards, whilst the bears sit on the sidelines since "it's obviously a bubble". On a downtrend you hold a consistent short position whilst the bulls claim that the market is desperately undervalued, their trading accounts gradually bleeding to death from repeatedly trying to 'catch the falling knife' and buy in at a bottom which never arrives.

But then the chopstick appears, and you get stabbed in the back. The market viciously turns against you. What's more, it often seems to do so at the worst possible time. Using the method for scaling positions I introduced in Part One, a calm market, with a strong uptrend, means you will have especially large position when the metaphorical chopstick goes into your allegorical spine.

In this chapter I will introduce a variation on the basic trend strategy, which adjusts the size of the forecast to reflect the likely probability of a sudden reversal.

Strategy twelve: A variation on any strategy that uses EWMAC trend filters. Adjust the trend forecast according to the probability of a reversal.

Forecasted and actual risk adjusted returns

Remember from Part One that a forecast is an *expected risk adjusted return*. We know that these forecasts are broadly correct when generated using exponentially weighted moving average crossovers (EWMAC), since the resulting trading strategies are profitable.

But there is still a great deal we don't know. For example, should we adjust positions according to the strength of a trend, using a *forecast*? Or just go long or short with a fixed amount of risk? Back in strategy seven, when I introduced this innovation, I noted that the evidence in favour of using trend strength in a forecast to size positions was weak, at least for the relatively slow EWMAC64 filter I was using at that point. I also introduced the idea of forecast *capping* as a fait accompli, without much justification.

Taken together, forecasting and capping imply that there is a linear relationship between trend strength and expected risk adjusted return, but only up to the point when the forecast cap bites. In the units of forecast I use in this book, that implies we would scale our position linearly with forecast value until it reaches a value of −20 or +20. Is this really the best we can do?

To try to answer these questions, I did some research. Firstly, I plotted a scatter graph, with forecasts on the *x*-axis and realised risk adjusted returns on the *y*-axis. Forecasts are proportional to risk adjusted return, so we'd expect a linear relationship if forecast strength actually predicts returns. Initially I used forecasts before any capping has taken place, but after forecast scaling. As risk adjusted returns can be compared directly across instruments, I pooled the results from all 102 instruments in the Jumbo portfolio data set.

Note that I used a different time period for measuring realised risk adjusted returns, depending on the trading rule. It makes no sense to measure returns over the following year for the EWMAC2 crossover, which only holds positions for a matter of days. Equally, it would be daft to use a one-day return to evaluate EWMAC64 which only trades a few times a year.

To find the correct time period I took the turnover for each EWMAC pair (table 35, page 190), and calculated the appropriate holding period in business days, assuming 256 days in a year. For example, for EWMAC2 with a turnover of 98.5 times a year the holding period is $256 \div 98.5 = 2.6$. I rounded this up and calculated the risk adjusted return for the following three days, as I'm using daily data. For EWMAC64 whose turnover is just 5.2 times a year, I used $256 \div 5.2 = 49.2$, rounded up to 50 days.

Let's first consider the fastest trading rule, EWMAC2, whose scatter plot is shown in figure 46. The uncapped forecast is on the *x*-axis, and the risk adjusted return over the following three days is on the *y*-axis.[169]

FIGURE 46: SCATTER PLOT OF RISK ADJUSTED RETURN AGAINST UNCAPPED FORECAST FOR EWMA2, POOLED ACROSS ALL INSTRUMENTS

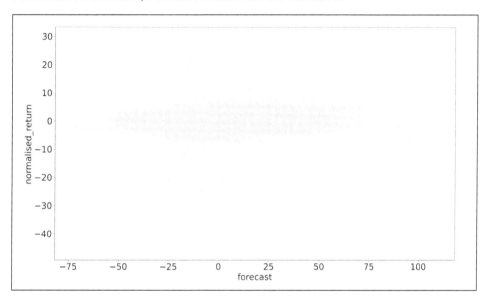

It looks like a photograph of a very distant galaxy. There probably isn't very much we can usefully conclude from this picture, so instead I'll be using plots like figure 47.

---

169   The risk I use to normalise the return is the estimated risk at the moment the forecast was made. This is because we adjust our position size based on this risk estimate. If we used the actual risk over the forecasting horizon, then increases in volatility would be downplayed. We don't want this, as we want large surprises to be reflected in the graphs. Also for EWMAC2 in particular, calculating a standard deviation based on just three daily data points would result in an extremely noisy estimate.

FIGURE 47: SCATTER PLOT WITH 30 BINS OF RISK ADJUSTED RETURN AGAINST
UNCAPPED FORECAST FOR EWMA2, POOLED ACROSS ALL INSTRUMENTS

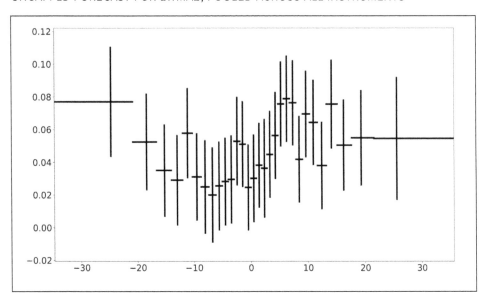

Figure 47 also shows the relationship between the forecast value (on the *x*-axis), and
the risk adjusted return over the three days after the forecast was made (*y*-axis), but
I've removed the cloud of points and replaced them with lines that show the pattern
of the data more clearly. The centre of each cross shows the average expected return for
a typical range of forecasts. The arms of the cross show the range of forecasts and the
uncertainty of the median of actual risk adjusted return.[170] Because most assets have
gone up in price over the data history I'm using, all the medians of actual risk adjusted
returns are positive.

For example, look at the cross on the extreme left of the plot, which represents
the lowest 3.33% of forecast values. Because extreme forecasts are rare, the forecast
range covered by this cross is wide: from around –71 (truncated in this plot) up to
approximately –21. So the full horizontal line of this cross goes from –71 to –21. For
forecasts between –71 and –21, the median risk adjusted return for the following four
days – the centre of the cross – was around 0.077. The range for that median estimate
– vertical lines of the cross – was between 0.044 and 0.11.

---

170   Each cross shows the results for one of 30 bins: each covering 3.33% of the distribution of
forecasts. The length of the horizontal lines in each cross show the range of forecasts covered by a
specific bin. The vertical line crosses the horizontal at the median forecast value for a given bin. The
horizontal line crosses the horizontal at the median risk adjusted return within a given bin. The
length of the vertical lines in each cross is +/– 2 *omega* around the median adjusted return, where
omega is the sampling error of the risk adjusted return for a specific bin.

Note that the next cross along, covering forecasts in the range −21 to −19, has a lower median for actual risk adjusted returns of around 0.05, with a similar sized range of estimates for risk adjusted returns.

This is one reason why I chose to cap extreme forecasts. If I didn't, then a forecast of −30 would have a position 50% bigger than a forecast of −20: we'd be far more bearish. But as the figure shows, we should actually be more bullish! The median risk adjusted return for a forecast of −30 (0.077) is higher than that for a forecast of −20 (0.05). At the other end of the forecasting spectrum, an extremely bullish forecast of +30 doesn't seem to have a higher median risk adjusted return than a forecast of +20.

Since there is so much noise and uncertainty around these extremely bearish and bullish forecasts, evidenced by the large overlaps between the vertical lines, it seems safest to cap them. In any case, only about 6% of EWMAC(2,8) forecasts have an absolute value greater than 20.

Figure 48 shows another version of the plot, but this time I've reduced the number of crosses plotted to make things clearer, as we don't need to focus on the extremes. In this, and in subsequent plots, the forecasts I've used are capped at −20 and +20.

FIGURE 48: SCATTER PLOT FOR REALISED RISK ADJUSTED RETURN AGAINST FORECAST FOR EWMA2 WITH CAPPING, POOLED ACROSS ALL INSTRUMENTS

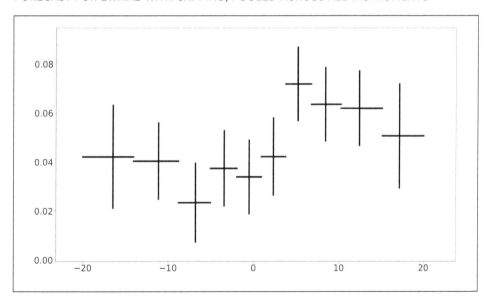

You can see that there is indeed a positive correlation between forecast and risk adjusted returns, but only for forecasts between around −5 and +5. Outside of that range the relationship isn't as clear.

The next few plots in figures 49 to 52 show the same results, but for the other EWMAC rules that I introduced in strategy nine. I haven't included EWMAC(16,64) since it is indistinguishable from EWMAC(8,32).

FIGURE 49: SCATTER PLOT FOR REALISED RISK ADJUSTED RETURN AGAINST FORECAST FOR EWMA4 WITH CAPPING, POOLED ACROSS ALL INSTRUMENTS

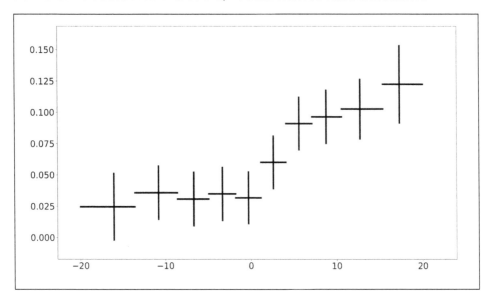

FIGURE 50: SCATTER PLOT FOR REALISED RISK ADJUSTED RETURN AGAINST FORECAST FOR EWMA8 WITH CAPPING, POOLED ACROSS ALL INSTRUMENTS

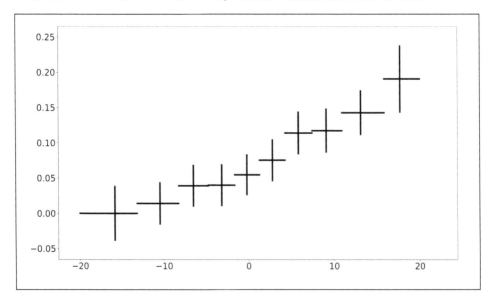

FIGURE 51: SCATTER PLOT FOR REALISED RISK ADJUSTED RETURN AGAINST
FORECAST FOR EWMA32 WITH CAPPING, POOLED ACROSS ALL INSTRUMENTS

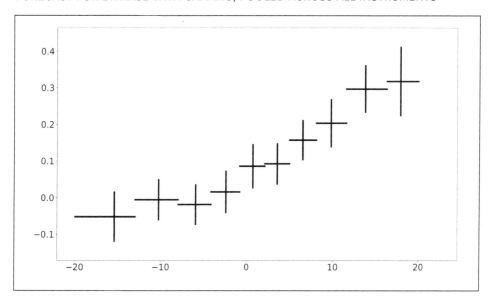

FIGURE 52: SCATTER PLOT FOR REALISED RISK ADJUSTED RETURN AGAINST
FORECAST FOR EWMA64 WITH CAPPING, POOLED ACROSS ALL INSTRUMENTS

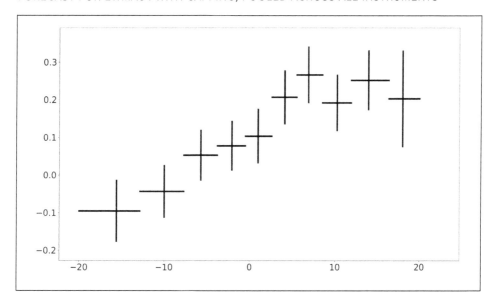

Examining these plots produces some interesting findings:

- For the fastest trend speed EWMAC2 trend seems to stop working outside of a fairly narrow range of forecasts. Instead we get a mean reversion effect.

- As we move into slower trend speeds the mean reversion effect disappears, and there is a clearer linear response to the forecast.

- The clear linear response is less apparent for the very slowest speed, EWMAC64. Here trend works well, up to a point. But for forecasts above +10 the response becomes somewhat muddied. However, there isn't a similar effect for negative forecasts.

These findings are consistent with the individual performance of each trend filter, the figures for which were in strategy nine (tables 30 and 31, pages 178 and 179). Variations with the clearest linear response, like EWMAC16, have the best return statistics. EWMAC2 gets its forecast very wrong most of the time, and is also the rule variation with the worst performance, even before costs.

The results are also consistent with market folklore. Take the mean reversion in EWMAC2. After a strong down move, producing a negative forecast, the market is actually more likely to go up. This could be the amusingly named 'dead cat bounce',[171] which is well known in equity markets: if a stock moves sharply down, then we usually see a rebound on the following day. We could also tell a nice story about the modest mean reversion in EWMAC64 when forecasts are strongly positive. It looks like the market becomes 'exhausted' after a clear uptrend and is less likely to rally further.

Of course these stories don't explain everything. What is causing the mean reversion for EWMAC2 for strong *positive* forecasts? Is it a levitating cat hitting the ceiling? Perhaps it is because these plots aren't just for equities: there are many other types of instrument in the underlying data. Clearly 'uptrend' and 'downtrend' have very different connotations for different asset classes. Some kind of sudden market crisis will cause equities to fall, but usually results in precious metals, bonds and volatility markets rising.

Let us dig a little deeper and examine the results specifically for equities, which are in figure 53. To save space, I've squashed all six EWMAC speeds into a single plot. Because we have fewer data points it isn't sensible to split the data into ten different buckets; instead I have used just four.

---

171   According to Investopedia: "A dead cat bounce is a temporary, short-lived recovery of asset prices from a prolonged decline or a bear market that is followed by the continuation of the downtrend. The name 'dead cat bounce' is based on the notion that even a dead cat will bounce if it falls far enough and fast enough." I have been unable to verify this result experimentally.

FIGURE 53: FORECAST AND REALISED RISK ADJUSTED RETURNS ACROSS DIFFERENT SPEEDS OF EWMAC POOLED ACROSS EQUITY INSTRUMENTS

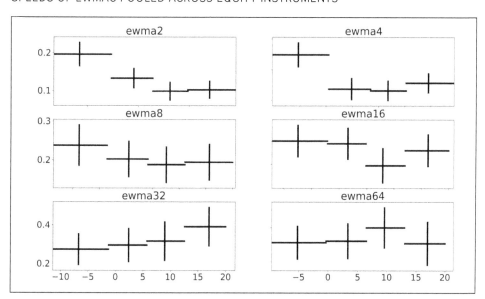

Lo and behold, for the fastest two EWMAC rules we see a strong bounce back after a strong negative trend, *without* a similar effect for strong positive trends. There is clearly a bouncing cat here! For what it's worth, the opposite effect can be seen in volatility markets like the VIX: after a strong positive trend in VIX, which would be associated with falling equity prices, vol tends to *fall* sharply.

Importantly, the results here are much less significant than those for the entire data set. I have divided the data into just four buckets in figure 53, to try to compensate for the fact that equities form only a part of the larger data set. Even so, the vertical lines mostly overlap, indicating there is no statistical difference between the risk adjusted return for each range of forecasts. The implication of this is that **I wouldn't advise trying to use asset class specific effects** like these in adjusting your trend forecasts: there is just too much noise once we get down to the granular level of a single type of asset. It goes without saying that trying to fit these effects for a single instrument would be completely futile.

The role of volatility

We have an issue with particularly large forecasts: they're generally less effective at predicting than small forecasts. Instead of increasing linearly the forecast response, measured by risk adjusted returns, becomes weaker than you would expect when forecasts get too large.

Sometimes this effect is very strong: in figure 53 for a fast equity filter a strong negative forecast implies the market will rally strongly in the next few days (it's especially strong for forecasts larger than 20, but we cap those rare events so we can ignore those). Often it is modest: for EWMAC32 (figure 51); a large negative forecast is still correct, but the expected price response is identical to that for a more modest negative forecast. The effect can be symmetric – applying to both negative and positive forecasts, as for the faster EWMAC filters. Or it can be asymmetric, as for the slower filters.

Let's take a step back and think about what could be causing this. Why would a forecast be especially large? Remember: a trend forecast is (a) the difference between two smoothed prices, divided by (b) the standard deviation of price changes. So there are two possible causes for an outsized forecast. Firstly, it could be because prices have changed a lot: a strong trend. Secondly, it might be that recent volatility has been especially low.

The interplay of these effects will depend on the market involved. The results are especially strong in equities (when they get riskier, they tend to fall in price) and volatility markets (which rise automatically when equity risk goes up).

In equities large downtrends are usually associated with increased risk. We would not expect to see large negative forecasts in equities, since any large trend difference will probably be wiped out by the increased risk. Conversely, large positive forecasts are generated frequently when in a smoothly rising bull market.

As expected, figure 53 shows a bias towards positive forecasts, even for the shorter trend filters which are unaffected by the secular uptrend in equity prices over the backtest. Conversely, in the volatility markets we would expect to see very few large positive forecasts and plenty of significantly negative forecasts, and this is exactly what the data shows.

Similarly, the strong 'dead cat bounce' we see in equities for rules EWMA2 and EWMA4 in figure 53 – a tendency for the market to rally after an extreme loss – is reversed for the volatility markets such as the VIX. A strong short-term rally in the VIX due to increased levels of equity risk, resulting in a positive forecast, is generally followed by a fall in the VIX.

Patterns across other asset classes aren't as clear, but we can often see appropriate responses for individual instruments. For example in FX we have traditional 'risk off' safe haven markets like CHFUSD (which behave like the volatility indices) and 'risk on' emerging market currencies such as MXPUSD (which is more like an equity index).

There are two conclusions we can draw from this analysis. Firstly, it probably explains why we see strong mean reversion in *both* directions for faster trend filters, when pooling results across different asset classes. The pooled results are effectively the sum of two diametrically opposed effects in risk-on and risk-off markets, plus a bunch of instruments without any clear pattern.

Secondly, since we've ruled out asset class specific fitting due to a lack of statistically significant results, the results above suggest that we should try to avoid implementing any kind of adjustment that is asymmetric, since it's most likely that it will be fine for some assets classes but plain wrong for others.

Incidentally, you might also be tempted to make *separate* adjustments to your trading strategy, depending on each of volatility and trend strength, rather than adjusting according to forecast strength which is affected by the joint interaction of the two types of estimate. However, it's easier to directly control for the effect of volatility levels on trading rule profitability, and I will do this in strategy thirteen.

Adjusting trend forecasts for trend strength

How do we adjust our forecasts for trend following filters, given the above results? Remember, as a general principle we don't want to make the adjustment too complex, or we risk over fitting our trading strategies. We also don't want to use asset class specific effects, as there isn't enough statistical significance to get robust estimates for the required adjustments. Finally, because different instruments have different behaviour in selloffs and rallies, any adjustment that is applied globally to all instruments ought to be symmetrical.

I suggest the following approach:

- For EWMAC2 use a 'double V' forecast mapping.

- For EWMAC4 'scale and cap' the forecast at +15 instead of +20.

- For EWMAC64 'scale and cap' the forecast at +15 instead of +20.

- For all other filters keep the forecast unchanged.

The 'double V' mapping works as follows, and replaces the normal forecast capping stage. Taking the original scaled forecast for the EWMAC2 trend filter, F:

F < −20: Capped forecast = 0

−20 < F < −10: Capped forecast = −40 − (2 × F)

−10 < F < +10: Capped forecast = 2 × F

+10 < F < +20: Capped forecast = +40 − (2 × F)

F > +20: Capped forecast = 0

We behave normally when forecasts are modest, but then reduce forecasts when they reach extreme values. 'Normally' isn't quite correct: we have forecasts that are double what they would otherwise be for absolute forecasts less than 10. If we didn't introduce this change then the resulting forecast would have the wrong scaling, and the average absolute forecast value would be lower than our target. The downside of doubling these modest forecasts is that it increases trading costs.

The 'scale and cap' mapping also replaces the normal forecast capping stage and prevents us from increasing our forecast once it reaches an absolute value of +15, rather than the usual limit of +20. Once again, we apply a multiplier to the forecast and the cap to ensure that our forecasts still have the correct scaling. The correct multiplier this time is 1.25. Taking the original scaled forecast for the EWMAC4 or EWMAC64 trend filter, F:

F < −15: Capped forecast = −15 × 1.25 = −18.75

−15 < F < +15: Capped forecast = F × 1.25

F > +15: Capped forecast = +18.75

Evaluating the adjusted forecasts

The results of applying the modified forecast capping can be found in tables 57 and 58. For consistency with the results in strategy nine, I've run each trend filter as a separate system with the Jumbo portfolio of over 100 instruments. This assumes that we trade the relevant trading rules on every single instrument, which in practice we would not, as EWMAC2 in particular is far too expensive for most markets.

TABLE 57: EFFECT OF APPLYING 'DOUBLE V' FORECAST ADJUSTMENT TO EWMAC2, AGGREGATE JUMBO PORTFOLIO

	EWMAC2 Unadjusted	EWMAC2 Adjusted
Mean annual return (gross)	13.0%	12.6%
Mean annual return (net)	3.5%	−4.5%
Costs	−9.3%	−16.7%
Average drawdown	−161.7%	−171.4%
Standard deviation	22.9%	20.5%
Sharpe ratio	0.15	−0.22
Turnover	381	704
Skew	1.32	0.07
Lower tail	1.94	1.43
Upper tail	2.28	1.61
Annualised alpha (gross)	10.2%	10.9%
Annualised alpha (net)	0.9%	−5.8%
Beta	0.17	0.08

TABLE 58: EFFECT OF APPLYING 'SCALE AND CAP' FORECAST ADJUSTMENT TO EWMAC4 AND EMWAC64, AGGREGATE JUMBO PORTFOLIO

	EWMAC4 Unadjusted	EWMAC4 Adjusted	EWMAC64 Unadjusted	EWMAC64 Adjusted
Mean annual return (gross)	19.6%	21.5%	22.5%	25.3%
Mean annual return (net)	14.8%	16.2%	21.5%	24.2%
Costs	−4.7%	−5.3%	−1.0%	−1.1%
Average drawdown	−23.1%	−23.7%	−16.0%	−17.2%
Standard deviation	23.1%	24.9%	22.3%	24.4%
Sharpe ratio	0.64	0.65	0.96	0.95
Turnover	195	220	27.5	28.5
Skew	0.75	1.38	0.61	0.47
Lower tail	1.98	1.85	1.90	1.77
Upper tail	2.15	1.99	1.63	1.63
Annualised alpha (gross)	15.9%	17.5%	14.6%	15.9%
Annualised alpha (net)	11.2%	12.3%	13.6%	14.8%
Beta	0.25	0.27	0.53	0.56

Let's begin with EWMAC2. It isn't great! Pre-cost returns fall and costs absolutely explode. The results for EWMAC4 are a little better, but not dramatically so. Still, we are tinkering with the extremes here, so the behaviour of the rule is unlikely to change very much. EWMAC64 shows a small decrease in risk adjusted performance, although the alpha is improved.

This is already dispiriting, but to get a more realistic picture we turn to a modified version of strategy eleven. You will remember that strategy eleven includes both carry and trend, with each instrument allocated to the set of trading rules that it can trade without incurring excessive trading costs. What happens to the aggregate Jumbo portfolio for strategy eleven when we apply adjustments to the three EWMA rules above?

The second column of table 59 shows the effect of applying just the 'double V' adjustment on EWMAC2. EWMAC2 is cheap enough to trade for a small number of instruments in the Jumbo portfolio (11 to be exact[172]), and it only has a 10% forecast weight in those instruments, so there is zero effect on the strategy overall.

TABLE 59: JUMBO PORTFOLIO RESULTS WHEN ADJUSTING EWMAC FORECASTS IN STRATEGY ELEVEN

	Strategy eleven Carry and trend Unadjusted	Strategy twelve Adjust: EWMAC2	Strategy twelve Adjust: EWMAC4, EWMAC64	Strategy twelve Adjust: EWMAC2, EWMAC4, EWMAC64
Mean annual return	26.5%	26.5%	27.1%	27.3%
Costs	−1.1%	−1.1%	−1.1%	−1.1%
Average drawdown	−8.9%	−8.9%	−9.0%	−9.1%
Standard deviation	20.9%	20.9%	21.2%	21.2%
Sharpe ratio	1.27	1.27	1.27	1.29
Turnover	46.5	46.5	47.3	45.6
Skew	0.76	0.76	0.70	0.70
Lower tail	1.86	1.86	1.82	1.84
Upper tail	1.75	1.75	1.71	1.70
Alpha	22.3%	22.3%	22.5%	22.6%
Beta	0.30	0.30	0.32	0.33

172   For the record, as I'm writing this chapter, the bargain basement futures that can trade EWMAC2 are two long duration bond futures: Buxl (German) and US 30-year, EURUSD FX, Copper, and seven equity markets: CAC 40, Dow Jones, Gold (micro and full), NASDAQ (micro and e-mini), Nikkei, Russell 2000, S&P 500 (micro and e-mini).

If instead we only apply the 'scale and cap' adjustment to EWMAC4 and EWMAC64, we get the results in the third column. The results are not compelling, with a small increase in performance. Neither are the figures in the final column, which show what would happen if we applied adjustments to all three trend filters.

Conclusion

Personally, **I wouldn't trade strategy twelve**. There are small improvements certainly, but there is no way they are justified by the considerable increase in complexity they require. It might seem odd that I've included a strategy[173] that I wouldn't consider trading with my own money. But it's quite common amongst quantitative futures trading hedge funds to implement this kind of strategy, so I thought it worth reviewing the available evidence.

Additionally, the intuition we have gained will be helpful in understanding strategy thirteen which also adjusts forecasts – but based on the current level of volatility.

---

173 There is an alternative way to implement this idea, which is to trade momentum alongside a strategy that only puts positions on when momentum hits extreme values, effectively cancelling out the positions that momentum would have on. But as this trades quite rarely it's difficult to judge its individual performance; in aggregate it looks almost identical to the modification I have presented here.

Strategy twelve: Trading plan

The adjustments in strategy twelve can be applied to any strategy that has one or more trend filters, and is adjusting positions using a capped forecast.

Strategy	Modify any strategy that uses EWMAC trading rules to construct forecasts.
EWMAC(2,8)	Replace the forecast capping stage with the following. Given a scaled forecast *F*:

$$F < -20: \text{Capped forecast} = 0$$

$$-20 < F < -10: \text{Capped forecast} = -40 - (2 \times F)$$

$$-10 < F < +10: \text{Capped forecast} = 2 \times F$$

$$+10 < F < +20: \text{Capped forecast} = +40 - (2 \times F)$$

$$F > +20: \text{Capped forecast} = 0$$

	Forecast combination will work as usual.
EWMAC(4,16) **EWMAC(64,256)**	Replace the forecast capping stage with the following. Given a scaled forecast *F*:

$$F < -15: \text{Capped forecast} = -18.75$$

$$-15 < F < +15: \text{Capped forecast} = F \times 1.25$$

$$F > +15: \text{Capped forecast} = +18.75$$

STRATEGY THIRTEEN

Trend following and carry in different risk regimes

The hedge fund where I used to work had an office in Oxford, which was focused on trying to fuse together academic and industry researchers. They sponsored the occasional academic conference, which I usually tried to attend to see if there was any new research that might be relevant to our business. At one particular event during a coffee break I was chatting to some eminent professor when he asked me how our fund was doing.

> *"Not great," I said, "The current market volatility is proving to be rather painful."*

> *"I thought you guys liked volatility," he said.*

I thought for a moment, then answered:

> *"We do. But this is the wrong kind of volatility."*

Different levels of volatility affect trading strategies in different ways. We try to scale our positions according to our current estimate of risk, which helps somewhat in trying to cope with changes in the prevailing threat level in the financial markets. Beyond that, you would expect that trend following strategies would like markets to move, whilst carry strategies should prefer stability. As I was employed by a trend following fund, my professorial interlocutor expected us to be enjoying the rapidly moving stock market that was hitting the newspaper headlines on a daily basis.

But there is a big difference between a steadily rising market, such as the S&P 500 in 2017, and a market that is veering sharply from one extreme to another. The latter will usually be highly unprofitable for trend style trading, whilst the former is a dream come true.

It turns out that there is a significant variation in the performance of both trend and carry systems in different volatility regimes. What's more, we can actually use this information to improve the profitability of our trading strategies.

Strategy thirteen: A variation on any strategy that trades EWMAC and carry where we adjust the strength of the forecast according to the volatility regime.

Defining the level of volatility

Our first job is to find some way of defining the current level of volatility for a given instrument. It needs to be a backward looking measure, or we won't be able to use it to improve our trading. We need a different measure for each instrument, as crisis events can be idiosyncratic as well as global. Finally, to ensure we can do our analysis across different instruments, it needs to be 'scale free' and consistently defined regardless of what we are trading.

I decided to use this relatively simple measure, which calculates the *relative* volatility of an instrument, compared to its long run average. Let $\sigma_{\%i,t}$ be the current estimated level of percentage standard deviation of returns for a given market i, measured using the method developed in strategy three. Then the *relative* level of volatility $V_{i,t}$ is the current estimate divided by the ten-year rolling average. Assuming 256 business days in a year that would be:

$$V_{it} = \sigma_{\%i,t} \div mean(\sigma_{\%i,t-2560}, \sigma_{\%i,t-2559}, \dots \sigma_{\%i,t})$$

Figure 54 shows the estimate of *V* for the S&P 500 micro future.

FIGURE 54: RELATIVE VOLATILITY OVER TIME FOR S&P 500 MICRO FUTURE

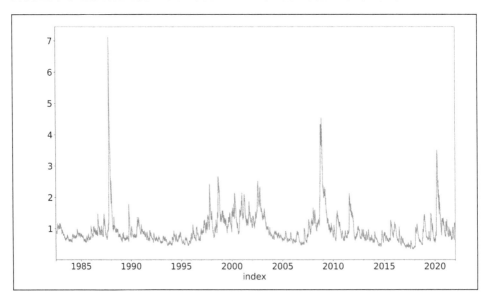

We can clearly see that there are distinct periods of low, normal and high volatility. How can we systematically separate out these regimes? I could pick some arbitrary numbers, e.g. below 0.75 is low, above 2 is high. But we'd need to have a definition of different regimes which works across different instruments. What does the distribution of relative volatility look like, if I glue together the results from the 102 instruments in the Jumbo portfolio?

The distribution pooled across all my instruments[174] is in figure 55.

FIGURE 55: DISTRIBUTION OF RELATIVE VOLATILITY FOR ALL INSTRUMENTS

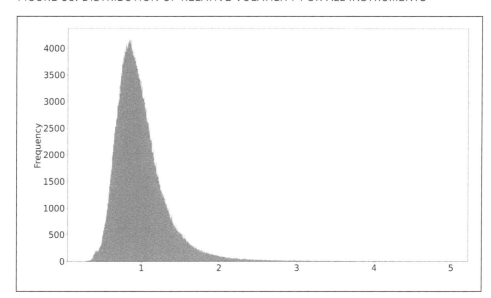

For now, I am going to use some arbitrary points on this distribution to define my low, medium and high volatility ('vol') regimes. If I take the 25% percentile point of the distribution, then anything below that is low vol. Above the 75% percentile I define as high vol. Anything in between is, unsurprisingly, medium vol. In my analysis I calculate these using backward looking estimates of the distribution of vol, to avoid in sample cheating.[175] But for reference, the current values that define each regime are:

- Low vol: V between 0.28 and 0.77.

- Medium vol: V between 0.77 and 1.12.

---

174   Notice the long tail of very high relative volatility. Actually, it's even worse than that, because I've truncated the plot. The maximum figure for V is actually 24.4!

175   In fact because I'm using a backward looking estimate of the distribution of volatility, and because of secular downward trends in vol in many assets, I end up with around half the data classified as a low vol regime, and roughly a quarter in each of the medium and high vol regimes.

- High vol: *V* between 1.12 and 24.4.

Performance in different volatility regimes

Now we have defined our three different volatility regimes, we can see how the performance of trend and carry trading rules varies depending on the level of risk in any given market.

In figure 56 I have plotted the Sharpe Ratio (SR) for a given trading rule, averaged across all the instruments in my data set, conditioned on the current volatility environment for each instrument. The results are striking. Performance is badly degraded as we move from a low to high volatility environment. Things look especially bad for the EWMAC rules, which become sure fire losers when markets get especially risky; in the same high vol regime carry just about manages to break even.

FIGURE 56: SHARPE RATIO OF DIFFERENT TRADING RULES ACROSS VOL REGIMES, AVERAGE ACROSS INSTRUMENTS

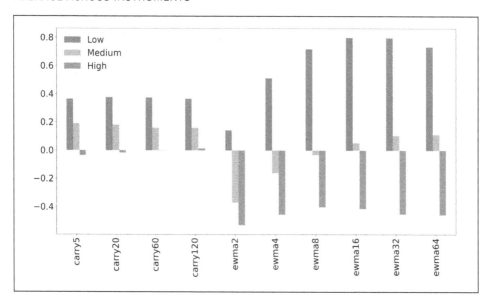

These results would be the same if I showed you the aggregate Jumbo portfolio of each trading rule, and the overall pattern is identical even if I plot the SR on a pre-cost basis, although relatively speaking this makes the faster EWMAC rules look a little better. These figures are highly significant and pass every statistical test I can think of.

Adjusting forecasts for volatility regimes

There are a number of different ways we could act on this information. We could, for example, stop trading entirely when volatility hits the highest regime. But there are some problems with that. For example, we could end up selling everything, then buying it back when risk drops just below the relevant threshold, leading to a substantial rise in trading costs.

Instead, I decided to use a continuous adjustment which gradually scales our position, depending on how high or low volatility currently is versus its historical average. This also has the advantage of not relying on a calibration of the boundaries of the volatility regimes, which could potentially be fitted in sample.

Given the relative level of volatility, V, which we defined earlier we take the quantile point Q based on historical data for a given instrument:

$$Q_{i,t} = \text{Quantile of } V_{i,t} \text{ in distribution}(V_{i,0} \ldots V_{i,t})$$

The quantile point will vary between 0 (if this is the lowest value we've seen so far) and 1 (for the highest). A value of 0.5 would indicate this is the median point in the historical distribution. We then calculate a vol multiplier, M:

$$M_{i,t} = \text{EWMA}_{span=10}(2 - 1.5 \times Q_{i,t})$$

How does this work? If volatility is especially low, with $Q = 0.0$, then we'd multiply our forecast by two, and hence take double the normal position. Conversely, if volatility is at historical highs, with $Q = 1.0$, we would halve our forecast. To reduce trading costs, I also apply an exponentially weighted moving average with a ten-day smooth. This modest smooth removes noise from the multiplier without reducing its efficacy.

We then multiply the raw forecast for a given trading rule by M. For example, for trend:

$$\text{Raw EWMA(N) forecast}_{i,t} = (\text{EWMA\_N}_{i,t} - \text{EWMA\_4N}_{i,t}) \div \sigma_{p,i,t}$$

$$\text{Adjusted raw EWMA(N) forecast}_{i,t} = \text{Raw forecast}_{N,i,t} \times M_{it}$$

Whereas for carry:

$$\text{Smoothed carry (span) forecast}_{i,t} = \text{EWMA}_{span}(\text{Carry forecast}_{i,t})$$

$$\text{Adjusted Smoothed carry (span) forecast}_{i,t}$$
$$= \text{Smoothed carry (span) forecast}_{i,t} \times M_{it}$$

The next step is to apply a forecast scalar. It turns out that we can use the same forecast scalars for EWMAC, but for carry we need to reduce the scalar from 30 to 23. This is because instances of high carry forecasts tend to occur when volatility is low, so applying the multiplier increases the average value of carry forecasts. To correct for this effect, we lower the forecast scalar.

The forecast capping which we subsequently apply to scaled forecasts isn't affected by this change. This implies that if we increase our raw forecast, because we are in an especially low vol regime, it still wouldn't end up being larger than 20 after the capping stage has taken place.

Evaluating the performance of the adjusted system

We can now measure the effect of adjusting our forecasts to account for the level of volatility in each instrument. I am using strategy eleven as my benchmark,[176] which is the 'plain vanilla' version of combined carry and trend. Strategy thirteen is identical to this, except that I will adjust the forecasts of each trading rule according to the level of volatility. To isolate exactly what's happening, I tested three versions of strategy thirteen. In one I adjusted the carry forecasts but not EWMAC, in another I only adjust EWMAC, whilst in the third I adjust both.

Since my analysis above concentrated on individual instruments, I'm only going to show you the aggregated performance of the Jumbo portfolio. However, the relative results for an average across instruments are similar. Table 60 has the figures.

---

176   Each of the strategies in Part Two can be implemented independently, or – where appropriate – in combination. This means I won't be considering the performance of strategy twelve in this chapter, neither will I consider the performance of strategy thirteen in subsequent chapters. Instead I will focus on the improvement, or otherwise, from implementing the appropriate changes versus a common benchmark: strategy eleven.

TABLE 60: AGGREGATE JUMBO PORTFOLIO RESULTS FOR STRATEGY ELEVEN: UNADJUSTED BASELINE, THEN WITH VOLATILITY REGIME ADJUSTMENTS FOR CARRY AND EWMAC TREND

	Strategy eleven EWMAC & carry Unadjusted	Strategy thirteen Adjust carry	Strategy thirteen Adjust EWMAC	Strategy thirteen Adjust both
Mean annual return	26.5%	25.5%	30.0%	28.9%
Costs	−1.1%	−1.1%	−1.2%	−1.2%
Average drawdown	−8.9%	−9.2%	−8.7%	−9.3%
Standard deviation	20.9%	20.5%	21.5%	21.6%
Sharpe ratio	1.27	1.25	1.39	1.34
Turnover	46.5	47.7	53.1	53.8
Skew	0.76	0.74	0.59	0.43
Lower tail	1.86	1.82	1.76	1.73
Upper tail	1.75	1.73	1.66	1.61
Alpha	22.3%	21.1%	24.8%	24.4%
Beta	0.30	0.31	0.36	0.34

Adjusting carry – in the second column – doesn't result in any improvement. Perhaps that isn't a huge surprise: from figure 56 we know that carry still returns a profit in medium volatility regimes, and manages to break even when volatility is relatively high.

In contrast, adjusting the EWMAC forecasts results in a significant performance increase in column three. Only the skew gets a little worse; perhaps we are giving up some of the upside on the rare occasions when volatility is high, but we manage to be on the right side of the trade. Unsurprisingly, making an adjustment to both types of trading rules results in performance that sits somewhere between the second and third columns.

I won't plot the performance of these strategies together as they are too similar to distinguish from each other; instead let's consider the cumulated *difference* in returns.[177] This is shown in figure 57. The outperformance of the EWMAC adjustment is fairly consistent, with the obvious exception of the financial crash in 2008. Obviously this was a period of heightened volatility, but it also happened to be a banner year for trend following, so in retrospect not a good year to dial down our position sizes.

---

177 Strictly speaking we should probably adjust the strategies so they have the same standard deviation before comparing them in this way, but they are very similar, so this will not affect the results very much.

FIGURE 57: RELATIVE PERFORMANCE OF VARIOUS STRATEGY THIRTEEN VOLATILITY REGIME ADJUSTMENTS AGAINST STRATEGY ELEVEN BENCHMARK

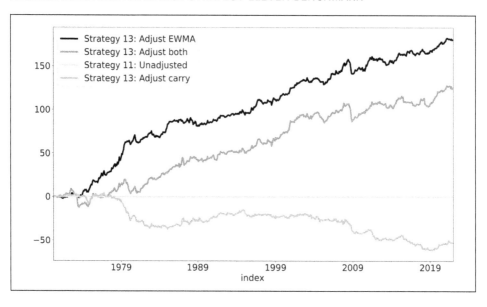

Strategy thirteen: Trading plan

The adjustments in strategy thirteen can be applied to any strategy that has one or more EWMAC or carry trading rules.

Strategy	Modify any strategy that uses EWMAC or carry trading rules to construct forecasts.
Relative volatility	If $\sigma_{\%i,t}$ is the current estimated level of percentage standard deviation of returns for a given market i: $$V_{i,t} = \sigma_{\%i,t} \div mean(\sigma_{i,t-2560}, \sigma_{i,t-2559}, \dots \sigma_{i,t})$$
Quantile of relative volatility	$$Q_{i,t} = \text{Quantile of } V_{i,t} \text{ in distribution}(V_{i,0} \dots V_{i,t})$$
Vol multiplier	$$M_{i,t} = EWMA_{span=10}(2 - 1.5 \times Q_{i,t})$$
Forecast adjustment	Multiply the raw forecast for a given trading rule variation by M. Then apply forecast scaling and capping as normal. Reduce the forecast scalar for carry to 23. Forecast combination is unaffected.

Spot trend

Way back in strategy one I pointed out that a back-adjusted price includes the return from both carry and changes in spot prices. So if there has been a rally, it could be because there has been positive carry, or because the spot price has risen, or both.

Our EWMAC trend strategies use trend filters to determine whether the adjusted price has been going up, or going down. But there are two possible causes for recent price changes: spot and carry. Is one cause more predictable than the other? In strategy eleven, which trades both carry and trend, isn't it double counting if we end up going long in both our carry and trend trading rules on the back of a rally caused by positive carry?

Would it be better to separate out the returns from carry and those from spot, and run our trend following filters just on the spot return alone? Perhaps we will get a cleaner trend following signal. The resulting forecasts should be less correlated with carry, potentially improving the performance of our combined strategy.

In this chapter I describe how to trend follow using a *synthetic spot* price: a futures price which has the returns from carry extracted, and reflects the returns purely from spot price changes. Arguably, this is a purer measure of trend in prices than using the back-adjusted price – which is contaminated with carry.

> **Strategy fourteen:** A variation on any strategy that trades EWMAC where we use a synthetic spot price as the input for our forecasts.

Constructing a synthetic spot price

Before I explain how to calculate a synthetic spot price, it's worth asking why we don't use the *actual* spot price. As I noted back in strategy ten, we can't always get spot prices, especially for non-financial assets. Even when it's possible to get them, it's often a hassle to collect, clean and store yet more data. **A synthetic spot price can be derived purely from futures prices** and doesn't require an additional data feed.

How do we do this? Remember that the adjusted price series is a total return series. From Part One, we know that total return is equal to the return from spot changes, plus the carry return. If we deduct carry returns from the adjusted price, then we are left with the returns from spot movements.

To do this calculation we need the annualised raw carry calculated back in strategy ten, the number of price points of carry that we expect to get in a year. Then, for a given instrument, if the adjusted price is P_t, the synthetic spot price S_t can be derived as follows:

$$\text{Adjusted price change}_{t,t-1}$$
$$= \text{Spot price change}_{t,t-1} + \text{Carry accrued}_{t,t-1}$$

$$\text{Carry accrued}_{t,t-1} = [\text{Annualised raw carry} \times \text{Year fraction}(t, t-1)]$$

$$\text{Adjusted price change } P_t - P_{t-1} = S_t - S_{t-1} + \text{Carry accrued}_{t,t-1}$$

$$\text{Synthetic spot } S_t = S_{t-1} + P_t - P_{t-1} - \text{Carry accrued}_{t,t-1}$$

Where *year fraction* is the fraction of a year that has elapsed between $t-1$ and t. For daily data indexed to business days this will be approximately 0.00391.

For convenience, I set the initial synthetic spot price S_0 to be equal to the initial back-adjusted price, A_0. This is an arbitrary decision and will not affect the forecasts or performance of any trading rule that uses the synthetic spot price. You could fix the final spot price to be identical to the final adjusted price, or set the initial or final prices to any arbitrary figure like your PIN number (but don't use your PIN number, unless you have excellent computer security).

In figure 58 we can see the adjusted price series and the cumulative returns from carry[178] for the US 10-year bond future. The synthetic spot price, which is also plotted, is the difference between these.

---

178   The unusual upward tick in carry returns in late 1999 is due to the change in the coupon rate for the reference bond.

FIGURE 58: CUMULATIVE RETURNS FROM CARRY, ADJUSTED PRICE AND SYNTHETIC
SPOT FOR US 10-YEAR BOND FUTURE

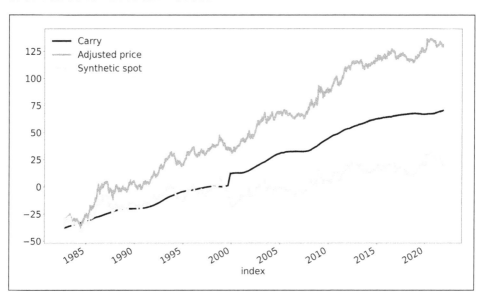

You can see that about half of the returns from this bond future have been due to
carry. Without carry the synthetic spot series has less of a clear trend. It's likely that
a trend strategy would have had smaller positions on had it been using the synthetic
spot price and not the back-adjusted price. It's also likely that the EWMAC strategy
would have been less profitable, since there were fewer clear trends for it to pick up on.

This would justify a higher weight to the carry strategy than the 40% I allocated to it
in strategy eleven. But since trend following the adjusted price is also trend following
the carry, the true implicit allocation to carry is actually higher in strategy eleven than
you might think. To properly evaluate the performance of this strategy we're going
to have to consider how it interacts with carry, but initially let's see how it performs
in isolation.

Evaluating the performance of spot trend

Which type of trend filter will be most affected by this change of input? You might
expect that the very fastest trend rules will barely notice it, whilst the slowest are piggy
backing off slow trend components that are largely caused by carry, especially in asset
classes like bonds and volatility with a lot of carry.

Figure 59 confirms this. It shows the Sharpe Ratio (SR) for strategies using different
speeds of trend, with adjusted and synthetic spot prices as their input. As we move

from left to right on the *x*-axis we slow down from EWMAC2 through to EWMAC64. You can see that the performance is always worse when using synthetic spot, but the gap gets bigger as we shift to trading with a slower filter. We lose about a third of our SR when shifting to synthetic spot for the EWMAC64 strategy.

A similar pattern can be seen with the beta versus our long only benchmark, strategy four. Beta is always lower when using synthetic spot, but the difference increases as we slow down. For EWMAC64 the beta when deriving our forecast from spot prices is 0.46, versus the 0.53 with adjusted prices.

FIGURE 59: SHARPE RATIO (*Y*-AXIS) FOR COMBINED TREND STRATEGY USING ADJUSTED VERSUS SYNTHETIC PRICES, OVER DIFFERENT SPEED TREND FILTERS (*X*-AXIS)

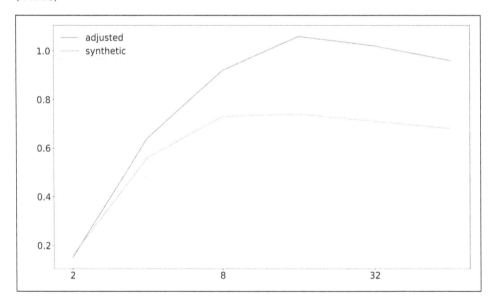

Next, I'm going to analyse the average results for individual instruments within asset classes. Since the degree to which carry affects prices is very different across different types of asset, we might also expect to see varying performance when switching to a price measure that excludes carry. Tables 61 and 62 have a selection of performance statistics. The first two rows have a couple of different measures of carry, which we've seen before in strategy ten.

The next few rows in each table show the performance when trend following with back-adjusted prices: effectively these are the figures we've already seen for strategy nine – multiple trend. Each of these figures reflects the average performance across instruments, with a subset of trading rules selected from the possible options (EWMAC2 to EWMAC64) according to the cost of each instrument. I then replaced the back-adjusted price input so that we are trend following synthetic spot, and these results are in the three final rows of each table.

TABLE 61: CARRY CHARACTERISTICS AND PERFORMANCE FOR MEDIAN INSTRUMENT WITHIN FINANCIAL ASSET CLASSES, PLUS MULTIPLE TREND PERFORMANCE USING BACK-ADJUSTED AND SYNTHETIC SPOT

	Equity	Vol	FX	Bond
Median absolute carry	0.12	0.67	0.21	0.41
Sharpe ratio of carry	0.40	0.59	0.30	0.48
Back-adjusted trend:				
Mean annual return	0.7%	13.3%	5.2%	9.5%
Standard deviation	22.1%	25.9%	22.8%	23.1%
Sharpe ratio	0.03	0.51	0.19	0.43
Synthetic spot trend:				
Mean annual return	1.1%	2.4%	0.0%	5.4%
Standard deviation	15.8%	15.7%	17.6%	19.5%
Sharpe ratio	0.07	0.15	0.0	0.28

TABLE 62: CARRY CHARACTERISTICS AND PERFORMANCE FOR MEDIAN INSTRUMENT WITHIN COMMODITY ASSET CLASSES, PLUS MULTIPLE TREND PERFORMANCE USING BACK-ADJUSTED AND SYNTHETIC SPOT

	Metals	Energy	Ags	Median
Median absolute carry	0.15	0.42	0.45	0.24
Sharpe ratio of carry	0.25	0.20	0.14	0.28
Back-adjusted trend:				
Mean annual return	8.9%	8.9%	5.4%	5.2%
Standard deviation	24.3%	25.5%	22.8%	23.0%
Sharpe ratio	0.37	0.39	0.24	0.23
Synthetic spot trend:				
Mean annual return	9.8%	6.3%	3.9%	3.0%
Standard deviation	24.7%	23.1%	22.4%	18.9%
Sharpe ratio	0.42	0.25	0.17	0.15

Almost all the asset classes show performance getting worse when adjusted prices are replaced with spot. Two asset classes with high levels of carry, bonds and vol, do especially badly. At the other end of the spectrum, equities and metals – which don't have much carry – actually show a small improvement. This supports my thesis that much of the excellent performance of trend in certain asset classes is actually down to trends created by carry.

You will also notice that the standard deviation is also lower in each case, with the exception of metals. As I pointed out earlier, with the carry trend removed from prices trends will become murkier, and apparent trend strength reduced,[179] resulting in smaller forecasts and lower standard deviation of returns.

Spot trend and carry

You might be thinking that this chapter should have already ended! By itself, 'pure' trend measured with synthetic spot prices is much worse than using 'impure' back-adjusted prices. However, as I've already mentioned, it makes no sense to look at this strategy in isolation. We need to bring in carry. We can do this by retrofitting our reliable workhorse for a blend of carry and trend, strategy eleven, with a different trend component utilising synthetic spot prices.

Originally, I decided that a blend of 60% trend and 40% carry was appropriate for strategy eleven. What mixture would be appropriate given the change in our trend strategy? Tables 63 and 64 show the effect of blending different proportions of carry and trend together.

---

179   It would be possible, though not recommended, to compensate for this by changing the forecast scalars for the EWMA trading rules.

TABLE 63: CHARACTERISTICS OF STRATEGIES THAT ARE A MIX OF TREND AND CARRY, WHERE TREND CAN BE FROM SYNTHETIC SPOT OR BACK-ADJUSTED PRICES, 50–100% IN TREND

	100%	90%	80%	70%	60%	50%
Carry & synthetic spot trend:						
Sharpe ratio	0.76	0.86	0.96	1.04	1.12	1.16
Alpha	10.8	12.8	14.9	17.1	19.0	20.4
Beta	0.36	0.36	0.35	0.34	0.31	0.28
Monthly skew	1.22	1.21	1.19	1.14	1.07	0.99
Carry & back-adjusted trend:						
Sharpe ratio	1.14	1.19	1.24	1.26	1.27	1.27
Alpha	18.8%	19.1%	20.4%	21.5%	22.3%	22.9%
Beta	0.43	0.40	0.39	0.37	0.30	0.30
Monthly skew	0.98	0.94	0.88	0.83	0.76	0.72

Percentage shown is proportion allocated to trend.

TABLE 64: CHARACTERISTICS OF STRATEGIES THAT ARE A MIX OF TREND AND CARRY, WHERE TREND CAN BE FROM SYNTHETIC SPOT OR BACK-ADJUSTED PRICES, 0–50% IN TREND

	50%	40%	30%	20%	10%	0%
Carry & synthetic spot trend:						
Sharpe ratio	1.16	1.16	1.12	1.07	1.00	0.94
Alpha	20.4	21.1%	22.2%	20.8%	20.1%	19.1%
Beta	0.28	0.23	0.18	0.14	0.10	0.06
Monthly skew	0.99	0.88	0.77	0.65	0.53	0.41
Carry & back-adjusted trend:						
Sharpe ratio	1.26	1.25	1.20	1.12	1.03	0.94
Alpha	22.9%	22.87%	22.4%	21.6%	20.5%	19.1%
Beta	0.30	0.25	0.20	0.15	0.10	0.06
Monthly skew	0.72	0.68	0.63	0.57	0.50	0.41

Percentage shown is proportion allocated to trend.

To recap, I originally selected a 60/40 blend when using back-adjusted prices to construct my trend forecasts back in Part One. From my comments earlier in this chapter, we also know that back-adjusted trend is 'double counting' carry, and so the true allocation to carry in strategy eleven is probably higher than 40%. The SR of trend with synthetic spot is lower, and it's also less correlated with the carry trading rules, implying a higher allocation to carry would be justified.

Rather neatly, a mirror image allocation of 40% to synthetic spot trend and 60% to carry produces the highest SR, and one of the highest alphas.

I can now compare strategy eleven directly with its potential replacement, identical apart from two changes. Firstly, I replaced back-adjusted prices with synthetic spot when calculating EWMAC forecasts. Secondly, I reduced the allocation of trend from 60% to 40% and replaced it with carry. The results are shown in table 65. For completeness I've also compared the results from strategy nine (which only trades trend, with adjusted prices) with the spot trend only variant of strategy fourteen, which we already know is inferior to adjusted price trend.

TABLE 65: PERFORMANCE OF AGGREGATE JUMBO PORTFOLIO FOR DIFFERENT TYPES OF TREND, WITH AND WITHOUT CARRY

	Strategy nine Trend (adjusted prices)	Strategy fourteen Trend (spot prices)	Strategy eleven Carry and trend (adjusted) 60:40 blend	Strategy fourteen Carry and trend (spot) 40:60 blend
Mean annual return	25.2%	15.3%	26.5%	24.1%
Costs	−1.2%	−1.3%	−1.1%	−1.0%
Average drawdown	−11.2%	−14.4%	−8.9%	−9.5%
Standard deviation	22.2%	20.0%	20.9%	20.0%
Sharpe ratio	1.14	0.77	1.27	1.20
Turnover	62.9	65.4	46.5	33.7
Skew	0.98	1.21	0.76	0.94
Lower tail	1.99	2.10	1.86	1.78
Upper tail	1.81	2.06	1.75	1.78
Alpha	18.8%	11.5%	22.3%	22.6%
Beta	0.43	0.34	0.30	0.18

Firstly, let's consider the two trend only strategies: the original strategy nine and a synthetic spot replacement. Performance is worse and beta is lower, but these are results we should expect given our analysis so far: removing carry from the price makes trends less trendier, but reduces systematic long only exposure. More intriguingly, the skew is significantly improved when we have a purer price trend. By removing the polluting effect of carry in adjusted prices we are also making our returns more like pure trend following, with higher positive skew.

With carry in the mix, is this a change worth making? Perhaps. There is a modest drop in SR, but alpha, beta, costs and skew are all improved, as are the tails.

Although there is a small increase in complexity, the calculation of synthetic spot is trivial. Further improvements could be possible if different weights were applied to carry and trend depending on the asset class that is being traded, but I am against this kind of strategy as it's usually over fitted.

The biggest arguments for and against this modification are ones of philosophy, rather than statistical evidence. Trend following the adjusted prices means that we have a natural stop loss built into our strategy since the adjusted price accurately reflects our recent profitability. But with trend following applied to the spot price, we get a more honest picture of where our returns are coming from: spot or carry.

Strategy fourteen: Trading plan

The adjustments in strategy thirteen can be applied to any strategy that has one or more EWMAC trading rules.

Strategy	Modify any strategy that uses EWMAC trading rules to use synthetic spot rather than adjusted prices.
Input price	Replace the back-adjusted price as an input into the EWMAC with the synthetic spot price. For a given instrument, if the adjusted price is P_t, then the synthetic spot price change is: $$\textbf{Synthetic spot } S_t = S_{t-1} + P_t - P_{t-1}$$ $$- \textbf{[Annualised raw carry} \times \textbf{Year fraction(t, t–1)]}$$ where *year fraction* is the fraction of a year that has elapsed since t–1 and *annualised raw carry* is the number of price points of carry that we expect to get in a year (see strategy ten).
Forecast weights	If allocating to both carry and trend, reduce the proportion of the strategy in trend from 60% to 40%, and increase the proportion in carry from 40% to 60%.

STRATEGY FIFTEEN

Accurate carry

In the last few strategies we have tried to improve upon the basic trend trading rules introduced in Part One, with mixed success. Now let us turn our attention to carry. Remember from strategy ten that we measure carry for futures instruments in two different ways:

- More accurately: by comparing the prices of the contract we currently hold, with a nearer contract that expires first.

- Less accurately: by comparing the price of the contract we currently hold, with a further out contract that expires next. We use this method when we are trading the nearest contract.

However, this won't always actually reflect the carry we experience, even assuming we take for granted the unspoken assumption about carry that spot prices remain unchanged. We would need the futures curve to have an identical gradient, with no unusual patterns due to seasonal weather, bond auctions, or the timing of dividends payments.

In this chapter I describe some techniques to get a more accurate estimate of carry.

> **Strategy fifteen:** A variation on any strategy that trades carry, where we adjust carry estimates to make them more accurate.

Accurate carry where we hold a contract that is not the nearest

Let's first consider the case where we hold a fixed contract which is *not* the nearest contract. This covers short-term interest rates like Eurodollar, volatility instruments, Natural Gas, and many other commodities such as Butter, Feeder cattle, Heating Oil and Rice.

In this case we measure carry by comparing the current contract with a nearer contract. So for example, if we are currently holding March 2025 Eurodollar, then we'd compare that with December 2024.

This is an accurate measure of expected carry, and there is nothing else required.

Accurate carry where we always hold the nearest contract

Now consider instruments where we hold the nearest contract (also known as the *front month*). Because there is no nearer contract, we need to measure carry using the **difference between the current contract price and the price of the next contract to expire**. But the true carry we will actually experience is **the difference between the current contract price and the spot price**.

As we saw in strategy ten this will lead to problems if the slope of the futures curve is not constant. This can happen for a variety of reasons. For example, in the metals and FX markets, the futures curve normally has a constant slope, but an exception to this rule is when interest rates[180] are expected to change in the near future. Because there is no consistent historical pattern in this effect, it's difficult to do very much about[181] it without using some additional sources of data like interest rates.

However, in many instruments the differences in slope are due to *seasonal* effects. We get seasonal effects where we'd expect them, in commodity markets. But we also see them in equity indices – due to the timing of dividends – and in some bond markets. Since these effects are relatively predictable, we can correct for them and get a more accurate carry signal.

---

180   Carry in metals is driven by storage costs and funding costs; the former is fairly static so interest rates are the key factor. In FX it is relative forward interest rates that determine futures prices, and thus carry.

181   In metals we could extract the expected storage cost given the yield curve, and then use that to imply the correct carry value for the front contract. In FX we could achieve the same exercise using the forward curve. In both cases we need accurate interest rate data that is synchronised with the futures price, and even with that in hand this exercise is not for the faint hearted.

Why not use the spot price?

The best solution to this problem is to use the difference between the current contract price and the spot price for our carry measure. I noted in strategy ten that this wasn't all that straightforward, and would involve collecting additional data which needed to be synchronised with the futures price.

With that in mind, however, how easy is it to obtain the spot price in different markets?

Spot prices are readily available for:

- Equity indices

- Volatility, e.g. VIX

- FX rates

They are usually available for:

- Agricultural commodities

- Energy markets

- Metals and crypto

They are difficult to obtain for:

- Bond markets

For bond markets we need to know the 'cheapest to deliver' bond, get the price of the bond, and also obtain or calculate the conversion factor. All of this is a considerable amount of work. It's also possible to measure the expected bond carry from the yield curve, but that is also a little complicated and requires you to know or estimate the duration of the bond.

Seasonal adjustment for carry

The goal is to correct our carry calculations to reflect the expected seasonality for carry. This requires several years of data, since we have to average seasonal adjustments across years: I suggest a minimum of three years of price history. We do this by deducting the seasonal component of carry we have incorrectly included. This can then be further refined by adding back the seasonal carry we would actually have experienced.

As an example, suppose we are holding a quarterly rolling contract which has strong positive carry in between mid-December and mid-June, and then negative carry for the rest of the year. Now imagine that it is mid-September and we are holding the

December contract. As this is the nearest contract, we calculate our carry by comparing the price of December with the following March contract. This carry forecast would be highly positive, when in reality we'd be earning negative returns from carry.

To correct for this, we begin by *subtracting* the expected seasonal component of carry for December to March. This gives us a carry signal which has its seasonality removed. We then *add* the expected seasonal carry that we normally expect to earn between September and March. Our carry signal would now truly reflect the carry we'd actually expect to make.

Let's dive into the calculations. We begin with our raw carry forecast, before any smoothing takes place, including the volatility normalisation:

$$\textsf{Carry forecast = Annualised raw carry} \div (\sigma_p \times 16)$$

We start with the volatility normalised forecast for a couple of reasons. Firstly, there is a chance that volatility is also seasonal, and this formulation will correct for that. Secondly – and more importantly – by using a volatility normalised forecast we can compare forecasts across time which will make the seasonality adjustment easier.

From this forecast, we subtract a rolling one-year moving average of the carry forecast. This will give us our current estimate of the seasonal component of carry. If the current carry forecast is C_t and there are 256 business days in a year:

$$\textsf{Seasonal carry estimate, } S_t$$
$$= C_t - (C_t + C_{t-1} + C_{t-2} + \dots C_{t-256}) \div 256$$

Next, we label our forecasts by their year and calendar day index, where the index 1 is 1st January, 2 is 2nd January, 3 is 3rd January and so on. To simplify things we ignore 29th February. For an imaginary instrument whose data begins in the year 2000 and ends in 2021 with seasonal carry component S we will have the following values:

$$S_{1,2000}, S_{2,2000}, S_{3,2000} \dots S_{365,2000}, S_{1,2001}, S_{2,2001} \dots S_{365,2021}$$

Now take an average for each day in the year across years.[182] For example:

$$S_{average,1} = (S_{1,2000} + S_{1,2001} + S_{1,2002} + \dots S_{1,2021}) \div 22$$

---

182 You can improve on this methodology by using an exponentially weighted moving average so that recent years are weighted more heavily. I do this using a span of five years. Strictly speaking, when backtesting you should also recalculate these seasonal adjustments on an annual basis using only backward looking information.

We can now adjust our carry forecast to get our estimate of the *net carry forecast* with the seasonal component removed. For example, for our carry forecast on 3rd February 2021 we would subtract $S_{average,34}$ as it is the 34th day of the year.[183]

At this stage we could use the net carry forecast to size our positions, which would make sense if we believed that seasonality in carry should be completely removed. Alternatively, we can continue to adjust the forecast further so that it reflects the correct seasonal patterns.

We already know that our seasonal averages are wrong, as we have calculated them using the current and further out contract, when we actually experience carry between the spot and current contract. To correct for this, we now shift them in time depending on the number of times that we roll per year. So, for example, if we roll four times per year, that is approximately $365 \div 4 = 91$ days, and we would do the following shifts:

- $S_{average,92}$ would be replaced with $S_{average,1}$
- $S_{average,93}$ would be replaced with $S_{average,2}$
- $S_{average,94}$ would be replaced with $S_{average,3}$

. . .

- $S_{average,365}$ would be replaced with $S_{average,274}$
- $S_{average,1}$ would be replaced with $S_{average,275}$
- $S_{average,2}$ would be replaced with $S_{average,276}$

. . .

- $S_{average,91}$ would be replaced with $S_{average,365}$

Next, we add back our shifted seasonal averages to the net carry forecasts. For example, for the net carry forecast on 2nd April 1998 we would add the shifted $S_{average,92}$ as it is the 92nd day of the year.

It feels like it's time for an example, with some graphs. Let's begin with the carry forecast for Eurostoxx, as shown in figure 60.

---

183   For 29th February I would use the average seasonal component for 28th February.

FIGURE 60: ORIGINAL RAW CARRY FOR EUROSTOXX

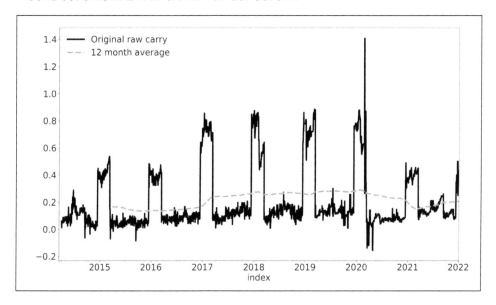

I have also plotted the 12-month rolling average. The difference between these two lines is the seasonal carry estimate. If I plot the seasonal carry estimate for different years so that they share a common *x*-axis (I have used the year 2001, but this is purely arbitrary), I get figure 61.

FIGURE 61: SEASONAL CARRY ESTIMATE ACROSS YEARS FOR EUROSTOXX, PLUS AVERAGE (*X*-AXIS IS FOR AN ARBITRARY YEAR)

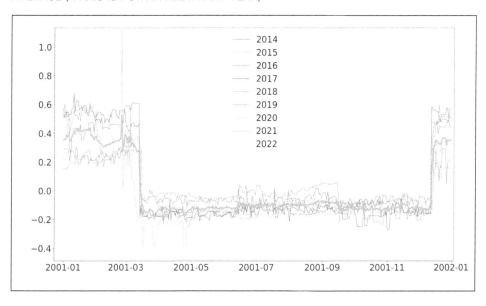

The thick line is the average seasonal component across the year, taken by averaging the estimates for each year represented by the thinner lines. It clearly shows that we had a positive seasonal component whilst holding the March contract (between mid-December and mid-March). However, we know that is incorrect, since we would have been measuring carry by comparing the March and June contracts. Let's see what happens if we shift the seasonal component by three months to give us a more accurate estimate, in figure 62.

FIGURE 62: AVERAGE SEASONAL COMPONENT FOR EUROSTOXX: ORIGINAL AND SHIFTED (*X*-AXIS IS FOR AN ARBITRARY YEAR)

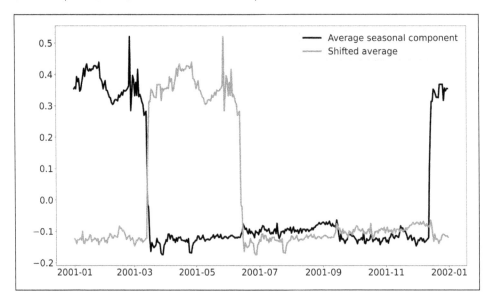

In figure 63 you can see the effect of subtracting the original unshifted seasonal average from raw carry, giving us the *net carry*. At this stage we could stop and use this as our carry forecast.

FIGURE 63: NET CARRY FORECAST WITHOUT SEASONAL COMPONENT FOR EUROSTOXX

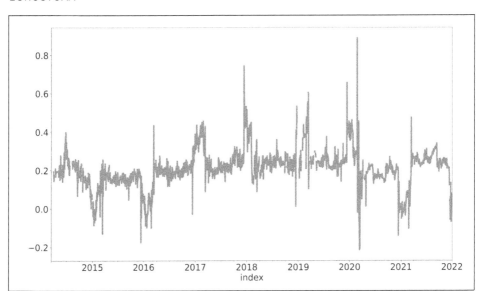

Although there are still some seasonal patterns, these vary from year to year and thus aren't easily predicted. Finally, in figure 64, we *add back* the shifted seasonal component to give a more accurate carry forecast.

FIGURE 64: RAW CARRY FORECAST BEFORE AND AFTER SEASONAL ADJUSTMENT

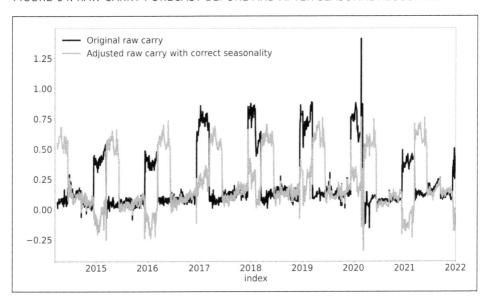

Evaluating performance

To evaluate the performance of accurate carry I used a cut-down version of the Jumbo portfolio, in which I only included instruments which were trading the nearest contract, and from which I excluded the FX and metals markets where there is no predictable seasonality in carry. Finally, I selected instruments with at least three years of data, so I could get a reasonably accurate estimate of seasonality. This left me with a total of 57 instruments: 35 equities, 20 bond markets, and one each from the agricultural and energy markets.

I considered the following three options in table 66:

1. The original raw carry, with incorrect seasonality.

2. The net raw carry, with the seasonal component removed.

3. Raw carry with the shifted seasonal component added back.

TABLE 66: PERFORMANCE OF SUBSET OF JUMBO PORTFOLIO WITH DIFFERENT CARRY CALCULATIONS

	Original raw carry – incorrect seasonality	Net raw carry – no seasonality	Adjusted raw carry – correct seasonality
Mean annual return	11.3%	10.6%	9.9%
Costs	−0.6%	−0.6%	−0.6%
Average drawdown	−18.5%	−18.3%	−19.7%
Standard deviation	19.2%	19.3%	19.4%
Sharpe ratio	0.59	0.55	0.51
Turnover	15.5	15.0	17.1
Skew	0.06	0.02	0.06
Lower tail	1.83	1.80	1.80
Upper tail	1.68	1.67	1.70
Alpha	6.8%	6.5%	5.8%
Beta	0.18	0.17	0.17

The results do not hit the ball out of the park! In fact, we have completely missed the ball and are now walking back to the dugout or pavilion (depending on which sport you thought this metaphor was alluding to). We have gone to a great deal of trouble and all we have to show for it is slightly worse performance. It might be that a more complex method for extracting seasonality would produce better results, but if you are really uncomfortable with incorrect seasonality your best bet is probably to drop the carry trading rule entirely for those instruments or use the spot price if that is available.

Accurate carry for fixed seasonal instruments

The final case we need to consider are instruments where we hold the same contract month each year. This is my preferred strategy for commodities with seasonal patterns, since it removes the seasonality component from the price and makes life much easier, although it's only possible when there is sufficient liquidity far enough out on the futures curve. Instruments in my data set where this happens include the full-sized contracts for Corn, WTI Crude Oil, Soyabeans and Wheat.

For these instruments we measure carry by comparing the current contract with a nearer contract. So, for example, imagine it is currently late December 2022 and we are currently holding December 2023 Wheat, then we'd compare that with September 2023 to calculate our carry forecast. At some point before the expiry of September 2023, we would then roll into the next contract, December 2024. This ensures we can still measure carry by comparing September and December 2024.

On the face of it, this should give us an accurate estimate of carry. But it does not! Consider a scenario where the September 2023 price is lower than December 2023, giving us a negative carry forecast created by an upward sloping futures curve. But also suppose[184] that the spot price, and the March and May expiries, are all higher in price than December 2023. If we make up some arbitrary prices, the futures curve looks like this:

- Spot: $900.

- March 2023: $880 (as it's currently mid-December 2022, this is a three-month contract price).

- May 2023: $860 (a five-month price).

- September 2023: $820 (a nine-month price).

- December 2023: $840 (12 months).

If the shape of the futures curve remained unchanged – the key assumption of carry – then we'd earn:

---

184   Is this really an extreme example? No; in fact this is not that different from the actual shape of the Wheat futures curve when I wrote this chapter, although I have changed and simplified the numbers to increase the magnitude of carry.

- From mid-December to March, as December 2023 aged from being a 12-month to a nine-month contract, the price would go from $840 to $820, and we would earn negative carry. We would also have a negative carry forecast.

- From March to May 2023, as December 2023 aged from a nine-month to a five-month contract, and the price went from $820 to $860, we'd earn positive carry. We would also have a positive carry forecast.

- From May to September 2023, as December 2023 aged from a five-month to a three-month contract, and the price went from $860 to $880, we'd earn positive carry. We would also have a positive carry forecast.

Over the entire year, we would earn positive carry of $40. Now, is our method for forecasting carry correct here? It depends. If we're going to hold the initial position for less than three months and close it by mid-March, then it does make sense, since our carry forecast and the carry we earn are perfectly aligned. But if our holding period was a year or more, then it would probably be sensible to use a carry estimate that gives a positive forecast taking into account the entire year.

The solution here is relatively easy: instead of comparing the currently held contract with the previous contract, **we compare the currently held contract with the current front contract**. This means that:

- From mid-December to March, we would compare the March 2023 and December 2023 contract prices. Our carry forecast would be positive, although we'd be earning negative carry.

- From March to May, we compare May 2023 and December 2023 contract prices. Our carry forecast would be positive and we would be earning positive carry.

- From May to September 2023, we compare September 2023 and December 2023. Our carry forecast would be positive and we would be earning positive carry.

I tested this out using the five instruments for which I use fixed months in the year to hold positions. Did it work? It does not. Just like removing seasonality, measuring long-term carry in this way does not improve performance. Admittedly, we only have five relevant instruments with data, so it is hard to draw any firm conclusions. But since we don't usually hold positions for more than a few months, even with the slowest carry trading rules, it perhaps isn't a surprise that this modification doesn't lead to better performance.

There may be some circumstances in which using a more accurate estimate for carry can give you better results, but personally I do not feel the additional work justifies any marginal gain.

Strategy fifteen: Trading plan

The adjustments in strategy fifteen can be applied to any strategy that has one or more carry trading rules.

Strategy	Modify any strategy that uses carry to get more accurate estimates.
Instruments where we hold a variable contract that is not the nearest	Examples include volatility, short-term interest rates and many commodities. No adjustment is necessary.
Instruments where we hold the nearest contract, but without predictable seasonality	Examples include FX and metals. No adjustment is possible.
Seasonal instruments where we hold the nearest contract, and spot prices are available	Examples include equity indices and some commodities. If the spot price is synchronised with futures, and of good quality, then replace: **Raw carry = Price of current futures contract** **– Price of next contract** With: **Raw carry = Spot price – Price of current contract**
Seasonal instruments where we hold the nearest contract, and spot prices are unavailable	Examples include German and Spanish bond futures, equity indices, and some commodity markets. Either: Remove the seasonal component from raw carry. Or: Add back a shifted seasonal component to get a more accurate estimate of seasonal raw carry.
Seasonal instruments where we hold a fixed contract in each year, e.g. December	Examples include full-sized contracts for Corn, WTI Crude Oil, Soybeans and Wheat. Modify the carry calculation from: **Raw carry = Price of nearer futures contract** **– Price of current futures contract** To: **Raw carry = Price of nearest futures contract** **– Price of current futures contract**

STRATEGY SIXTEEN

Trend and carry allocation

In the last few chapters I've looked at a few different ways we can potentially improve the basic trend and carry strategies that I introduced in Part One. However, there is another area of improvement that we haven't yet addressed, and that is the allocation of our risk between these two sources of return, which we set using *forecast weights*.

In strategy eleven I suggested that a 60% trend, 40% carry combination seemed the best compromise. But perhaps we can do better than that. Perhaps we can tactically vary those weights over time, to improve our performance. And maybe, just maybe, we can use different forecast weights for carry and trend within different instruments.

> **Strategy sixteen:** A variation on any strategy that trades trend and carry where we adjust the relative forecast weights for the two types of trading.

Is strategy performance predictable?

Consider figure 65, which shows the year by year performance for the Jumbo portfolio for strategies nine (multiple trend) and ten (carry) for the last 30 years.

FIGURE 65: ANNUAL PERFORMANCE OF CARRY AND TREND STRATEGIES FOR THE JUMBO PORTFOLIO

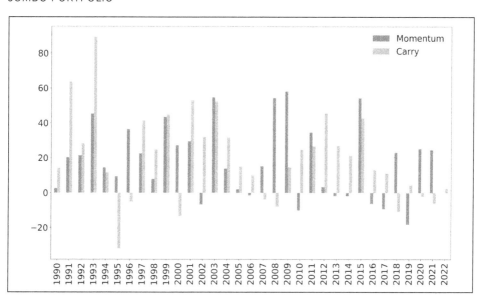

Wouldn't it be nice to have known in advance that 2017 was a bad year for trend, whilst carry would still be profitable? Similarly, it would have been great to have switched into 100% trend for the following year, 2018, when carry was the laggard.

A method for seeing whether the returns of a strategy can give us a clue about future returns is to measure the *auto-correlation* of returns. This is the correlation of each daily return with the return from the day before. We can also measure auto-correlation for other time periods: weekly, monthly and so on. It's effectively the momentum of the account curve.

If a strategy has a *positive* auto-correlation of returns, then it would make sense to increase the allocation to a given strategy if it's just had a good period, and reduce its weighting after poor performance. Conversely, negative auto-correlation implies 'taking profits' after good performance and reducing our allocation, but also 'catching a falling knife' and increasing positions following losses.

There is some research suggesting that the returns of trend following *funds* are weakly negatively auto-correlated.[185] However, it is not clear if this is because the underlying

---

185   For example, Burghardt and Li 'It's the autocorrelation, stupid' 2012 (www.trendfollowing. com/whitepaper/newedge.pdf). The authors find that monthly returns for commodity trading advisers – systematic futures traders who tend to have a bias towards trading trend – have negative auto-correlation. In a research brief by Winton Capital Management from 2015 'Autocorrelation of trend-following returns: illusion and reality' (www.valuewalk.com/2015/09/autocorrelation-of-trend-following-returns-illusion-and-reality/) quarterly returns have weak negative auto-correlation, but there is no effect at monthly or annual frequencies.

trend strategy returns have negative auto-correlation, or if the effect is caused by performance fees.[186] Certainly, hedge funds often encourage investors to buy into strategies when performance has recently been poor. Cynically, this might be more to do with negative performance resulting in lower assets under management, which in turn means lower fees all round!

Figure 66 shows the auto-correlation of returns for carry, trend and a *relative* strategy. The relative strategy is the outperformance of the trend versus the carry strategy. It is logical to consider relative performance if we're planning to change the relative weights of carry and trend. I used non-overlapping time periods to calculate these figures. This makes them more reliable but reduces the number of data points used to calculate each number, so they are less statistically significant.

FIGURE 66: AUTO-CORRELATION OF RETURNS FOR DIFFERENT STRATEGIES AND TIME PERIODS

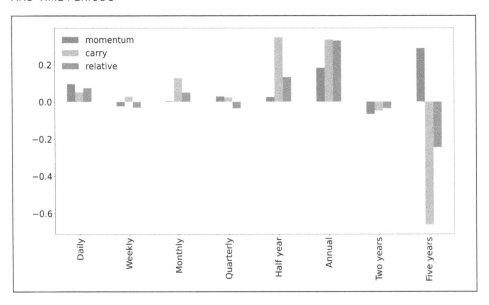

---

186   As noted by Winton (ibid.), some or all of the negative auto-correlation of funds' trading trend could be due to performance fees. Performance fees tend to detract from the performance of positive months, whilst making negative months look relatively better. This is because performance fees are only charged when a fund is making a new high watermark, not when it is in drawdown. If you manage to invest at the bottom of a prolonged drawdown you will enjoy positive returns without paying performance fees until the fund returns to its previous peak. This effect will appear at a frequency commensurate with the typical length of time between performance peaks.

Many of the shorter auto correlations aren't especially significant. They would also be very expensive to trade; switching between carry and trend on a weekly basis would result in a great deal of additional turnover. Things start to get interesting at the six-month frequency, and there are significantly positive auto-correlations for annual returns. The results for five-year auto correlations are mixed, but there are only eight non-overlapping five-year periods in the data set so they are very unlikely to be statistically significant.

Let's focus on the positive one year auto-correlation[187] as it has the largest magnitude, and is a nice balance between shorter time periods (which would probably be too expensive to make the required adjustment trades) and longer frequencies (with mixed empirical results that aren't likely to be statistically significant).

We can exploit this effect in the following way. Firstly, calculate the relative daily performance, R, given the daily performance as a percentage of capital for a spot trend strategy T and carry strategy C:

$$\text{Relative performance } R_t = T_t - C_t$$

Secondly, measure the rolling one-year relative performance, RP. To make it meaningful, this performance is scaled by dividing by the volatility target, τ (which I've set at 20% throughout this book). Assuming there are 256 business days in a year:

$$RP_t = (R_t + R_{t-1} + R_{t-2} + \ldots R_{t-255}) \div \tau$$

To get some intuition, RP is plotted in figure 67.

---

187   Expecting positive performance for a strategy to continue is also known as 'trend following the account curve'. Some people use very complex technical indicators to see whether an account curve is going up or down, and thus requires more or less leverage. I'm not a fan of such indicators for building my trading strategies, so you won't be surprised to hear I'm not a fan of using them in this context.

FIGURE 67: ROLLING RELATIVE PERFORMANCE OF TREND VERSUS CARRY

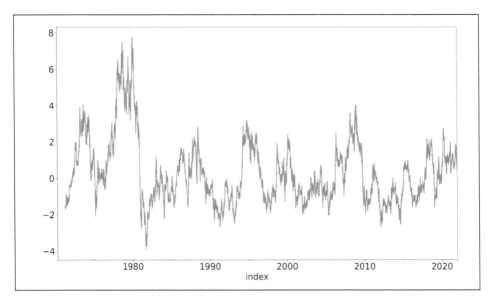

We now calculate a weighting factor which will be higher when trend has recently outperformed: a weight of 1 indicates a 100% allocation to trend, and a weight of 0 would be 100% in carry. There are a number of plausible formulae we could use for this weighting, but I arbitrarily chose the following:

$$W_t = EWMA_{span=30}(min(1, max(0, 0.5 + RP_t \div 2)))$$

For obvious reasons the weighting factor is limited to lie inside the range 0 to 1, and we take an exponentially weighted moving average with a 30-day span to smooth out some of the noise and reduce trading costs. When RP is 0, and trend and carry have performed equally well, the weight W_t will be 0.5: a 50% allocation to trend and the same to carry. If RP is positive and trend has done better than carry, then W_t will get closer to 1, with the converse being true for negative RP. If RP is equal to or higher than 1, then we would be entirely allocated to trend – this would be the case if trend had outperformed carry over the last 12 months by τ; a 20% outperformance with the risk target I've used in this book. Similarly an RP of –1 or lower, reflecting a 20% underperformance by trend, would result in a 100% allocation to carry. My backtested estimate for the weighting factor W_t is in figure 68.

FIGURE 68: WEIGHT TO TREND BASED ON ROLLING 12-MONTH RELATIVE
PERFORMANCE

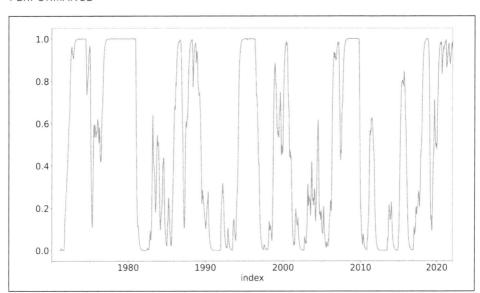

Finally, we trade a strategy with top level forecast weights W_t allocated to divergent
trend forecasts, and $(1 - W_t)$ allocated to convergent carry, rather than our normal
practice of fixing $W_t = 0.60$. These weights will change on a day to day basis, but not
too much because of the smooth and because we're looking back at performance over
a full year. I evaluate the performance of this strategy modification in table 67.

TABLE 67: PERFORMANCE OF AGGREGATE JUMBO PORTFOLIO WITH FIXED AND
VARIABLE ALLOCATIONS TO CARRY AND TREND

	Strategy eleven Carry (40%) and trend (60%)	Strategy sixteen Variable allocation to carry and trend
Mean annual return	26.5%	28.1%
Average drawdown	−8.9%	−10.1%
Standard deviation	20.9%	21.0%
Sharpe ratio	1.27	1.33
Skew	0.76	0.89
Lower tail	1.86	1.84
Upper tail	1.75	1.74
Alpha	22.3%	20.7%
Beta	0.30	0.46

These results are okay: there are small but statistically significant improvements in most metrics, drawdown and alpha excepted. In fact these results are surprisingly good. The average allocation to trend is actually lower than in strategy eleven: just under 50%, versus 60%. Given that a standalone trend strategy is superior to carry for both Sharpe ratio (SR) and skew, we would expect a strategy with a higher average carry exposure to be a little worse. We could probably improve them further by modifying the weighting function so that it matches an average allocation of 60% to trend, but this would arguably be over fitting.

Personally I'd be a little bit scared of completely de-allocating from trend and into carry, or vice versa. It's possible to modify the weighting scheme so that, for example, we never go below 20% or above 80% trend. But this will make strategy sixteen look a lot more like strategy eleven, reducing the benefits we could earn from making this change.

Are there other ways that we could try to time our allocation to carry and trend? Possibly, but I am sceptical. As a general rule it is very hard to time a reallocation from one risk/return factor like trend, and into another like carry. Here is the introduction to a white paper[188] on factor timing by uber-quant and head of giant systematic hedge fund AQR, Cliff Asness:

> *Overall, these results suggest that one should be wary of aggressive factor timing. Instead, investors are better off identifying factors they believe in, and staying diversified across them.*

This is especially true for trading strategies that use *forecasts*, as these will naturally reduce their own implicit portfolio allocation when they have weak forecasts, and increase them when forecasts are strong. Forecasts effectively produce an implicit factor timing effect. Further improvement on this is difficult.

Do different instruments have different relative performance?

Can we improve our performance by allocating more or less to trend and carry for instruments in different asset classes? Consider the numbers in tables 68 and 69, which collect together some performance statistics for carry and trend from previous

---

188　Asness, Cliff S., 'My Factor Philippic' (22 June 2016). Although this is a paper about timing factors in cross-sectional equity strategies, not futures, the principle still stands. Available at *SSRN*: https://ssrn.com/abstract=2799441.

chapters. I've also included the difference between SRs for trend and carry, since it is *relative* performance that is important here.

TABLE 68: MEDIAN INSTRUMENT PERFORMANCE FOR CARRY AND TREND ACROSS FINANCIAL ASSET CLASSES

	Equity	Vol	FX	Bond
Carry (Strategy 10)				
Mean annual return	3.1%	21.4%	5.1%	13.3%
Standard deviation	9.9%	36.0%	18.3%	27.5%
Sharpe ratio	0.40	0.59	0.30	0.48
Trend (Strategy 9)				
Mean annual return	0.7%	13.3%	5.2%	9.5%
Standard deviation	22.1%	25.9%	22.8%	23.1%
Sharpe ratio	0.03	0.51	0.19	0.43
SR trend – SR carry	−0.47	−0.08	−0.11	−0.05

TABLE 69: MEDIAN INSTRUMENT PERFORMANCE FOR CARRY AND TREND ACROSS COMMODITY ASSET CLASSES

	Metals	Energy	Ags	Median
Carry (Strategy 10)				
Mean annual return	3.5%	5.0%	3.5%	4.4%
Standard deviation	16.7%	28.2%	29.3%	19.8%
Sharpe ratio	0.25	0.20	0.14	0.28
Trend (Strategy 9)				
Mean annual return	8.9%	8.9%	5.4%	5.2%
Standard deviation	24.3%	25.5%	22.8%	23.0%
Sharpe ratio	0.37	0.39	0.24	0.23
SR trend – SR carry	0.12	0.19	0.10	−0.05

If we order the relative SRs from best for trend to worst, then we have: energies, metals, agricultural markets, bonds, volatility, FX and equities. Are there any discernible patterns here? One obvious effect is that the traditional commodity markets all have better results for trend than the financial markets of equities, bonds, FX and volatility for which carry is superior. We can probably think of some reasons why this makes sense: perhaps financial markets are more efficient and have fewer commercial traders who are more interested in hedging than making outright profits.

However, this result is a mirage. As the commodity markets have been around longer, they have more data history. A typical commodity instrument has a performance record stretching back to the pre-1990 period when trend was particularly good and carry was less compelling (see figure 45, page 236 for proof). Financial instruments generally have shorter data history, and almost all of their performance is coming from the latter part of the backtest when trend was relatively poorer. If I rerun the backtest for just the period since the mid-1990s to correct for this effect,[189] then the pattern in tables 68 and 69 goes away.

The other obvious outlier, which is unaffected by the length of history used, is the particularly poor performance of equity trend. It is the only relative SR that is significantly different from zero, due to a combination of decent carry performance and an SR for trend that is basically zero.

One possible explanation for this is that the very fastest moving averages do relatively poorly (tables 30 and 31 on pages 178 and 179), but because equity instruments are generally cheaper to trade, they have a higher allocation to these faster trend speeds (remember, we remove trading rules which are too expensive for a given instrument, but many equity markets are able to trade almost everything). However, if I check the performance of equity trend at different speeds it is pretty poor across the board, and worse in equities than for any other asset class, regardless of speed.[190]

In conclusion, then, there does seem to be a case for having less trend and more carry specifically for equities. A reduction in the forecast weight allocation from 60% to 10% only for equities[191] produces the results in table 70.

189　This is almost exactly half the entire backtest period.
190　After cost SRs for trend in equities range from −0.08 for EWMAC2; up to the giddy heights of +0.08 for EWMAC64.
191　I do not go to zero, as it is usually a bad idea to put all your eggs in one basket, even if that basket has a superior backtested SR.

TABLE 70: PERFORMANCE OF AGGREGATE JUMBO PORTFOLIO WITH A LOWER WEIGHT TO TREND IN EQUITIES

	Strategy eleven Carry (40%) and trend (60%)	Strategy sixteen Equities: 10% trend, 90% carry for equities Other: As strategy eleven
Mean annual return	26.5%	26.5%
Costs	−1.1%	−1.0%
Average drawdown	−8.9%	−8.0%
Standard deviation	20.9%	19.9%
Sharpe ratio	1.27	1.33
Turnover	46.5	36.8
Skew	0.76	0.86
Lower tail	1.86	1.83
Upper tail	1.75	1.87
Alpha	22.3%	22.5%
Beta	0.30	0.28

Given we're only modifying a single asset class out of the seven available, we wouldn't expect to see a significant effect for the entire Jumbo portfolio. Sure enough, the improvements are modest, with the exception of turnover, which is significantly improved. This is because we now have a significantly lower allocation at the portfolio level to faster trend, which was mostly only traded by cheap equity instruments.

We could continue down this path and have different allocations for individual instruments within an asset class, but suffice it to say there is insufficient data to draw any meaningful conclusions.

Strategy sixteen: Trading plan

The adjustments in strategy sixteen can be applied to any strategy that has both trend and carry trading rules.

Strategy	Modify any strategy that trades trend and carry so that the top level of forecast weights are not always 60% trend and 40% carry.
Modify allocation between trend and carry according to recent performance	Dynamically modify the top level forecast weight according to recent relative performance of trend and carry.
	Calculate the relative daily performance, R, given the daily performance as a percentage of capital for a spot trend strategy T and carry strategy C:
	$$\text{Relative performance } R_t = T_t - C_t$$
	Next, measure the rolling one-year relative performance, RP:
	$$RP_t = (R_t + R_{t-1} + R_{t-2} + \ldots R_{t-255}) \div \tau$$
	Calculate a weighting factor, which will be higher when trend has recently outperformed. A weight of 1 indicates a 100% allocation to trend, and a weight of 0 would be 100% in carry:
	$$W_t = \text{EWMA}_{\text{span}=30}(\min(1, \max(0, 0.5 + RP_t \div 2)))$$
	We trade a strategy with top level forecast weights W_t allocated to divergent trend forecasts, and $(1 - W_t)$ allocated to convergent carry.
Modify allocation between trend and carry according to asset class	Equities: Reduce top level forecast weight for trend to 10%, and increase for carry to 90%.
	Other asset classes: Maintain 60% trend, 40% carry.

STRATEGY SEVENTEEN

Normalised trend

As is hopefully apparent by now, I'm a big fan of diversification. Diversification across instruments, across styles of trading, and across speeds of trend and carry. But up until now we have only used a single measure of trend, with the catchy name: exponentially weighted moving average crossovers (EWMAC). Is this because it's the best and only way of measuring trend? Not at all. I used EWMAC because it's relatively easy to explain,[192] and has allowed me to introduce some important concepts like smoothing and forecasting.

But there are other ways of measuring trend, which are likely to have relatively similar performance, but which aren't 100% correlated with EWMAC. We would get some benefit from adding them to our suite of trading rules. There will be periods of time when EWMAC isn't performing well, and when other methods can do a better job of detecting and predicting trends. Over the next few chapters I will explore a few different alternatives to EWMAC that we can use to complement it.

In this chapter I introduce the first of these, **normalised trend**. This is identical to the EWMAC rule, but before passing the futures price into the usual equations we standardise it by dividing by a recent estimate of volatility. As well as being a nice trend rule in its own right, this normalisation is also required to construct a couple of other strategies which I explain in the next two chapters.

> **Strategy seventeen:** A trend strategy that uses a normalised futures price as an input into the EWMAC trading rule.

---

192   I'm also sentimentally attached to EWMAC. When I started working in AHL, a futures hedge fund, EWMAC was used as their core trading strategy. It was also the first strategy I implemented when I started trading my own money.

Normalisation of futures prices

Prices in financial markets are messy. Sometimes they go up really quickly, other times they crash suddenly. Then they are relatively calm for days or weeks on end. That is one reason why we apply a *volatility normalisation* to the difference between moving averages. Using this technique means we can compare trends across different time periods and for different instruments. We end up with a forecast that is proportional to the expected risk adjusted return, irrespective of the market environment.

However, there is an alternative. What if we applied a volatility normalisation to the price itself?

We begin with the back-adjusted price, p_t, and the estimate of daily standard deviation of price differences, σ_p, that we've used before. These can be used to construct a normalised price, P_t^N:

$$P_t^N = (100 \times [p_t - p_{t-1}] \div \sigma_{p,t}) + P_{t-1}^N$$

The price is recursively generated, with the price P_1^N set at the point when we can first estimate a standard deviation. I arbitrarily set $P_0^N = 0$, but this does not make any difference as this just applies a level shift to all the values of P^N. The multiplier of 100 is there to put the prices into more familiar orders of magnitude, and again is purely arbitrary.

Let's get a feel for what these normalised prices look like. In figure 69 we have the now familiar back-adjusted price for S&P 500 micro futures, plus the normalised price. For display purposes, I've multiplied the normalised price by 10. With this particular instrument, that handily puts it on the same scale as the price.

FIGURE 69: PRICE AND NORMALISED PRICE FOR S&P 500

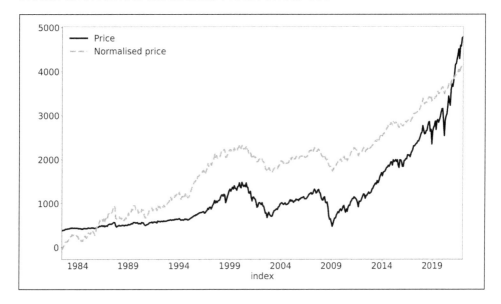

Notice that the normalised price follows roughly the same path as the actual back-adjusted price, but it has a more consistent volatility. In fact, the *expected* volatility is identical for every day, although we don't quite achieve identical realised volatility because we can't perfectly forecast standard deviation. As a result of this standardisation, it is easier to see the changes which occur in the early part of the period, whilst those in later years are not as dramatic.

Everything else is unchanged from previous trend strategies. So we apply the usual process for calculating an EWMAC forecast. We can use the same set of moving average pairs as before: EWMAC(2,8), EWMAC(4,16) ... EWMAC(64,256). Next, as before, we divide by an estimate of the daily standard deviation of price differences, σ_p. But instead of using the back-adjusted price to calculate this, we use the normalised price. This step isn't as important as before, since the prices are already normalised, but it is still worth doing.

We then multiply the forecast by a forecast scalar. Because EWMAC scalars are a property of the trading rule, not the prices that are used for calculations, we can use the same scalars that I calculated in Part One. You can find these in table 29 on page 177. Finally, we apply a cap of 20 to the absolute forecast value.

The performance of different trend filters

Let's pause for a second and consider the individual performance of each speed of normalised trend trading rule.

For consistency with the analysis I did in Part One, these figures are for the Jumbo portfolio trading all instruments, regardless of costs. Performance for an individual instrument will be considerably lower than that shown here, and some instruments won't actually trade the relevant trend filter as it would be too expensive.[193] You can compare the results in tables 71 and 72 directly with tables 30 and 31 on pages 178 and 179, which have the same statistics for 'vanilla' trend following. I've omitted some less interesting statistics to save space.

TABLE 71: PERFORMANCE FOR DIFFERENT SPEEDS OF TREND FILTER USING NORMALISED PRICE: AGGREGATED JUMBO PORTFOLIO RESULTS, FASTER EWMAC

	EWMAC2	EWMAC4	EWMAC8
Mean annual return (gross)	18.9%	24.6%	26.3%
Mean annual return (net)	8.5%	19.1%	23.4%
Costs	−10.2%	−5.4%	−2.9%
Sharpe ratio	0.33	0.75	0.93
Turnover	435	230	119
Skew	1.25	1.58	1.31
Lower tail	1.77	1.81	1.79
Upper tail	2.09	2.03	1.99
Annualised alpha (gross)	15.7%	20.4%	21.0%
Annualised alpha (net)	5.5%	15.0%	18.1%
Beta	0.20	0.29	0.36

---

193   As I've done before, I'm including instruments here that are too expensive for faster filters to get as much data as possible about potential pre-cost returns.

TABLE 72: PERFORMANCE FOR DIFFERENT SPEEDS OF TREND FILTER USING NORMALISED PRICE: AGGREGATED JUMBO PORTFOLIO RESULTS, SLOWER EWMAC

	EWMAC16	EWMAC32	EWMAC64
Mean annual return (gross)	27.4%	27.1%	25.2%
Mean annual return (net)	25.5%	25.7%	23.9%
Costs	−1.9%	−1.4%	−1.2%
Sharpe ratio	1.03	1.04	0.95
Turnover	65.3	42.1	34.2
Skew	0.98	0.88	0.60
Lower tail	1.96	1.87	1.77
Upper tail	1.86	1.68	1.59
Annualised alpha (gross)	20.4%	18.7%	15.0%
Annualised alpha (net)	18.6%	17.4%	13.7%
Beta	0.47	0.56	0.68

Generally we see a similar pattern as we did for the original EWMAC rules. Most rules have similar profitability before costs, apart from the very fastest. Costs and turnover reduce as we slow down, whilst beta increases. Monthly skew reduces as we slow down, although skew over different periods would show more interesting results, similar to those found in table 42 (page 218).

But if we compare these results directly with those in tables 30 and 31, there are some interesting differences:

- The two fastest speeds are a little better for normalised trend than they were originally.

- Costs and turnover are about a quarter higher across the board.

- Skew and lower tail measures are slightly improved.

- Beta is a little higher than before, but so is alpha.

Creating a combined forecast

Let's now modify strategy nine, which consists of half a dozen different trend trading rules, replacing back-adjusted prices with normalised prices. To do this we first need to come up with some *forecast weights*, which will determine how the different forecasts from each trading rule are combined.

For this I'm going to use the same method as in strategy nine. For any given instrument:

- Select a subset of trading rule variations which are cheap enough to trade, given the cost of the instrument, the turnover of the trading rule and my *speed limit*: a cap on trading costs.

- If no trading rules satisfy this test, don't trade the relevant instrument. This affects four instruments in my data set.

For the trading rule variations we have selected, equally weight them.

Here is a reminder of the formula to check if a particular trading rule can be used with a given instrument. The annual turnovers you need are in table 73.

Maximum turnover

= [0.15 − (Cost per trade × Rolls per year)] ÷ Cost per trade

TABLE 73: TURNOVER PER YEAR FOR EACH TREND FILTER USING NORMALISED TREND, AVERAGED ACROSS INSTRUMENTS

	Turnover
EWMAC2	109.9
EWMAC4	56.2
EWMAC8	28.7
EWMAC16	15.2
EWMAC32	9.0
EWMAC64	6.5

Next, because of the diversification across forecasts, we need to apply a forecast diversification multiplier (FDM) to the combined forecast. Because the rules are so similar, we can use the same values that I presented in strategy nine (see table 36, page 193). Finally, we cap the combined forecast at a maximum absolute value of 20.

Standalone performance

Based on what we've seen so far, you might expect that the performance of normalised trend would be very similar to the original strategy nine. And as table 74 shows, you would be right.

TABLE 74: PERFORMANCE OF AGGREGATE JUMBO PORTFOLIO WITH TREND, WITH BACK-ADJUSTED AND NORMALISED PRICES

	Strategy nine Multiple trend (adjusted prices)	Strategy seventeen Multiple trend (normalised prices)
Mean annual return	25.2%	28.2%
Costs	−1.2%	−1.4%
Average drawdown	−11.2%	−12.9%
Standard deviation	22.2%	24.4%
Sharpe ratio	1.14	1.15
Turnover	62.9	72.1
Skew	0.98	0.93
Lower tail	1.99	1.87
Upper tail	1.81	1.80
Alpha	18.8%	20.1%
Beta	0.43	0.55

We already know that turnover, beta, standard deviation and costs are likely to be a little higher. On the upside, the SR is a fraction higher and the alpha is somewhat improved. Skew is slightly worse, but the lower tail is a little more amiable.

In reality though, there is little to choose between these two strategies: the correlation of their returns is a massive 0.97!

Strategy eleven with normalised trend

You might think that the next step would be to rewire strategy eleven – trend and carry – by including normalised trend instead of our original trend rules. But there is another possibility: we could trade *both* normalised and original trend. Given how similar the two types of trend rule are, this could make a lot of sense: personally, I couldn't pick one trend strategy over the other based on the evidence above.

To do this we're again going to require some forecast weights and a forecast diversification multiplier. Let's first consider the case where we replace the original trend rules with normalised trend filters. That is straightforward, because the two kinds of trend are so similar, we can use exactly the same forecast weights and FDM that I calculated for strategy eleven (table 51, page 233).

Now what happens if we trade *both* normalised and original trend? We need to return to the basic principles of top down forecast weight allocation that I outlined in strategy nine:

- Split the list of trading rules by **style**. Allocate between styles according to your preferences.

- Within a given style, allocate equally across **trading rules**.

- Within a given trading rule, allocate equally across **variations** of each given trading rule.

If we maintain a 60% weight to divergent trend strategies and 40% to convergent carry, then we get:

- Allocate 60% to divergent (trend) rules. Allocate 40% to convergent (carry) rules.

- Within trend: Allocate half to original trend and half to normalised trend (30% each).

- Within carry: We only have a single trading rule, which receives 40% of the allocation.

- Within a given trading rule, allocate equally across variations of each given trading rule. This will depend on the number of variations selected for a given instrument.

Let's take an example. The WTI Crude Oil future can trade all four carry rules and the four slowest trend rules (of both flavours):

- Allocate 60% to divergent trend and 40% to convergent carry.

- Within trend: Allocate half to original trend and half to normalised trend (30% each):

  - Within original trend: Allocate 30% ÷ 4 = 7.5% to each of EWMAC8, EWMAC16, EWMAC32 and EWMAC64.

  - Within normalised trend: Allocate 30% ÷ 4 = 7.5% to each of EWMAC8, EWMAC16, EWMAC32 and EWMAC64.

- Within carry: We only have a single trading rule, which receives 40% of the allocation:

  - Allocate 40% ÷ 4 = 10% to each of carry5, carry20, carry60 and carry120.

Forecast diversification multipliers for an appropriate number of trading rule variations can be found in table 52 (page 234).

We can now compare the Jumbo portfolio results for (a) strategy eleven, (b) a version with normalised trend instead of original trend and (c) a version with both kinds of trend. The results are in table 75.

TABLE 75: PERFORMANCE OF AGGREGATE JUMBO PORTFOLIO: A COMBINATION OF CARRY, PLUS DIFFERENT TYPES OF TREND

	Strategy eleven Carry and trend (adjusted prices)	Strategy seventeen Carry and trend (normalised prices)	Strategy seventeen Carry and trend (normalised prices, and adjusted prices)
Mean annual return	26.5%	28.8%	27.5%
Costs	−1.1%	−1.1%	−1.1%
Average drawdown	−8.9%	−8.6%	−8.7%
Standard deviation	20.9%	21.0%	20.9%
Sharpe ratio	1.27	1.32	1.32
Turnover	46.5	48.3	47.6
Skew	0.76	0.76	0.75
Lower tail	1.86	1.90	1.85
Upper tail	1.75	1.79	1.70
Alpha	22.3%	22.8%	22.9%
Beta	0.30	0.34	0.32

Which of these should you trade? There is no slam dunk obvious stand out winning strategy here, and the performance statistics are virtually identical. So it comes down to preferences.

I can understand why you may wish to stick to strategy eleven. You may find the normalisation rather un-intuitive, making it harder to judge what the strategy is doing. Another consideration is the additional work that would be generated by the normalisation procedure. Naturally, there would be even more hard labour if you continued trading the original trend rule as well. In that case this chapter would have been a useful diversion, one that is necessary to understand the next couple of strategies which build on the normalisation methodology to create genuinely innovative trend strategies.

But for an automated trader like myself the additional effort is dealt with by computing power, and the lack of intuition by better diagnostic reports. Although the expected benefit of adding a strategy with a 97% correlation is limited, it is still positive. I also think it's plausible that the backtested correlation is under selling the additional diversification we're getting, since correlation is a linear measure. For me at least, it makes sense to trade both kinds of trend, as well as carry.

What about...

In strategies twelve through sixteen I described a number of ways you could modify the basic trend and carry strategies in Part One. You may well be wondering if any of these also work with normalised trend. Here is a brief summary of my analysis:

- **(Strategy twelve) Adjusting trend according to forecast strength with a non-linear mapping:** No significant improvement. I don't recommend this change.

- **(Strategy thirteen) Modifying trend to reduce the forecast when volatility is particular high:** Similar results when using the normalised synthetic spot price: a modest but significant improvement in the SR.

- **(Strategy fourteen) Using the synthetic spot price rather than the back-adjusted price to calculate trend:** Not applicable.

- **(Strategy fifteen) Accurate carry:** Not applicable.

- **(Strategy sixteen) Modifying the relative allocation to trend and carry based on historic performance:** Similar results when using the normalised synthetic spot price: a small improvement in the SR.

- **(Strategy sixteen) Reducing the allocation to trend just for equities:** An even stronger result than for basic trend: equities with normalised trend have a slightly negative SR, in contrast to every other asset class. This change will improve performance but may not be robust to accusations of over fitting.

As these results are in line with those for the basic EWMAC trading rules, I'd advise adopting the same policies for normalised trend. These also give us some hope that the results from strategies twelve through sixteen are not just a statistical or data mined fluke, as they are robust to changes in our trend following rules.

The results above will also apply to the other trend style strategies that follow in Part Two, unless I note otherwise: strategies eighteen and nineteen.

Strategy seventeen: Trading plan

All other stages are identical to strategy nine (standalone trend) or strategy eleven (combined with carry).

Strategy	Go long or short one or more instruments with variable risk estimate and a combined forecast from multiple trend filters. Modify the trend filters so they use normalised price as an input.
Instrument(s)	Any that meet minimum capital, liquidity and cost thresholds.
Choose trading rules for each instrument	Turnover figures are in table 73.
Trading rule variations	Construct one or more trend filters of the form EWMAC(N, 4N) where N is one of 2,4,8,16,32,64.
Normalised price	Given a back-adjusted price p_t where $P_0^N = 0$: $$P_t^N = (100 \times [p_t - p_{t-1}] \div \sigma_{p,t}) + P_{t-1}^N$$
EWMAC calculations	To calculate the N business day span price exponentially weighted moving average using the normalised price P^N: $$\lambda = 2 \div (N+1)$$ $$EWMA_i(N)_t = \lambda P_{i,t}^N + \lambda(1-\lambda)P_{i,t-1}^N + \lambda(1-\lambda)^2 P_{i,t-2}^N + \ldots$$
Raw forecast for a given EWMAC(N)	Normalise the raw forecast, using a daily standard deviation of price changes for the normalised price, σ_N: $$\text{Raw forecast}_{N,i,t} = (EWMA(N)_{i,t} - EWMA(4N)_{i,t}) \div \sigma_{Nt}$$
Scaled forecast for a given EWMAC	$$\text{Scaled forecast}_{N,i,t}$$ $$= \text{Raw forecast}_{N,i,t} \times \text{forecast scalar}_N$$ Forecast scalars can be found in table 29 on page 177.
Capped forecast for a given EWMAC	$$\text{Capped forecast}_{N,i,t}$$ $$= \text{Max}(\text{Min}(\text{Scaled forecast}_{N,i,t}, +20), -20)$$
Allocating forecast weights	Use table 36 on page 193 for a standalone trend strategy. Use table 51 on page 233 when combined with carry. See page 306 when combined with carry and original trend.
Forecast diversification	FDM values: Use table 36 on page 193 for a standalone trend strategy. Use table 52 on page 234 when combined with carry, or when combined with carry and standard trend.

Trend following asset classes

Market trends tend to be synchronised within asset classes. It's rare that the S&P 500 index falls and the Eurostoxx 50 rises. Generally speaking if Oil is up, Gas will also be in a bull market.

I've spent many years looking at these common trends and thinking deeply. I have asked myself philosophical questions, like: Where do trends come from? Is there one big trend in a given asset class, or are there lots of individual trends that just happen to be happening at the same time? If in reality there is just one underlying trend in say equities, then are the trends we see in individual equity indices just manifestations of that trend?

A more formal way of describing this is that there is a *latent* trend which drives all equity indices, where latent just means hidden. Then any individual equity index whose price we can see consists of that latent trend, plus some idiosyncratic noise. In such a world it would make sense to come up with some way of measuring that latent trend, by looking across many instruments in a given asset class, and then put a position on in multiple instruments to capture the latent trade.

Handily, the price normalisation from the previous chapter gives us a neat way to build a price index for each asset class. We can then trend follow that price index, using all of the instruments that make up the index.

> **Strategy eighteen:** A trend strategy that uses the
> normalised futures price for a given asset class as an
> input into the EWMAC trading rule.

Building an asset class index price

Most asset classes have one or more indices that try to capture the entire universe of investable instruments that fall within them. In equities there are indices like the MSCI World, whilst bonds have the Barclays Global Aggregate Bond Index. There is the DXY – US Dollar Index – in FX, and the S&P GSCI Commodity Index.

Mostly these indices are calculated using the percentage returns of individual instruments, weighted by market capitalisation or similar metrics. Of course it would be straightforward to get these indices and then apply a trend following rule to them. However, there are some problems with this approach. Firstly, it is out of scope for this book – I'm only using strategies that can be traded solely with futures prices. Secondly, these indices give a higher implicit weight to instruments with higher volatility. Also, the universe of instruments in a given index will probably be different from what we're actually trading. Finally, we may feel that the market cap weightings are heavily biased.[194]

I have an alternative proposal, which is to **construct an index from the volatility normalised futures prices of each instrument**. This requires no additional data and accounts for different risk across instruments. Additionally, we can customise the basket of instruments to reflect what we are trading and choose our own weighting scheme.

We begin with the calculation of a normalised price for each instrument i in the asset class from strategy seventeen:

$$P_{i,t}^N = (100 \times [p_{i,t} - p_{i,t-1}] \div \sigma_{p,i,t}) + P_{i,t-1}^N$$

Next we calculate an average daily return for the asset class R, by averaging returns over instruments $i = 0$ to $i = j$, where j is the number of instruments in a given asset class. For simplicity I use equal weights and take a simple average, but it's possible to use other weights if you wish:

$$R_t = ([P_{0,t}^N - P_{0,t-1}^N] + [P_{1,t}^N - P_{1,t-1}^N] + ... [P_{j,t}^N - P_{j,t-1}^N]) \div j$$

Finally, we sum up the R terms to get a normalised price for an asset A:

$$A_t = (R_1 + R_2 + ... R_t)$$

Obviously A_0 will be zero. One interesting thing about this method is that you can include instruments in the calculation that you do not actually trade, either because they are too expensive or illiquid, or because you have insufficient capital. That will give you a more robust measure of asset price trends. The results in this chapter use

---

194　For example, 69% of the MSCI World Developed Equity Index is currently in US stocks.

asset price indices that have been constructed using over 140 instruments, rather than the 102 tradeable instruments I use for the Jumbo portfolio.

Figures 70 and 71 show the normalised price for each asset class. As these are normalised prices, they have consistent volatility over time. You can clearly see significant trends, such as the equity bear markets of the early 2000s and 2008.

FIGURE 70: NORMALISED ASSET CLASS TREND FOR FINANCIALS

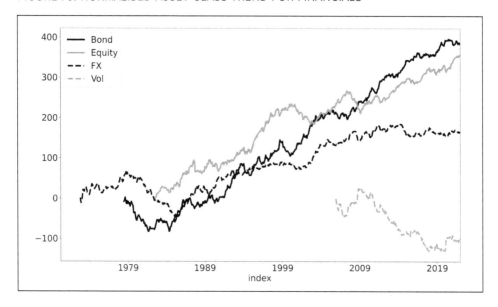

FIGURE 71: NORMALISED ASSET CLASS MOMENTUM FOR COMMODITIES

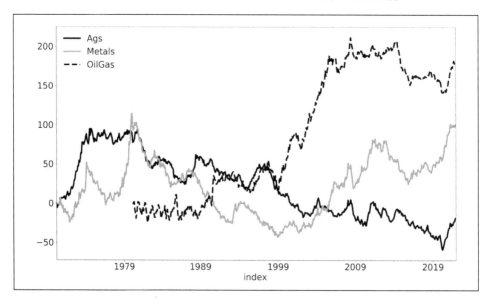

Trend following an asset class

We now have a price, and we already know what we can do with a price: we can apply trend trading rules to it! The strategy will look exactly like strategy nine, with two important differences. Firstly, rather than use the back-adjusted price for a given instrument, we will use the *normalised* price for the relevant *asset class* that a given instrument is in. Secondly, **every instrument in a given asset class will have the same forecast for a given trend speed**.[195]

I will not explain, yet again, the process of how to go from a given price to a trend following strategy. We have seen this twice now, in strategies nine and seventeen. As usual, we use up to six different speeds of EWMAC rules here to create a combined forecast. The forecast scalars are identical to those for strategy nine, and the turnover for each trend speed is roughly the same as for strategy seventeen. You can also use the forecast diversification multipliers that I estimated in strategy nine.

Tables 76 and 77 show the average performance for instruments within a given asset class. You can compare these to tables 37 and 38 on page 195, which show analogous performance figures for the original EWMAC rule in strategy nine. Some uninteresting figures have been removed to save space.

TABLE 76: MEDIAN INSTRUMENT PERFORMANCE FOR ASSET CLASS TREND ACROSS FINANCIAL ASSET CLASSES

	Equity	Vol	FX	Bond
Mean annual return	3.1%	12.5%	4.9%	13.2%
Costs	−0.5%	−1.1%	−0.6%	−0.6%
Standard deviation	25.8%	25.6%	24.0%	26.0%
Sharpe ratio	0.12	0.49	0.19	0.52
Skew	0.28	0.37	0.73	0.77
Lower tail	3.13	3.15	3.07	2.56

---

195   However, they could have different combined forecasts, since not all instruments in a given asset class will be cheap enough to trade every single speed of asset class trend.

TABLE 77: MEDIAN INSTRUMENT PERFORMANCE FOR ASSET CLASS TREND ACROSS COMMODITY ASSET CLASSES

	Metals	Energy	Ags	Median
Mean annual return	11.8%	8.9%	7.7%	7.1%
Costs	−0.5%	−0.5%	−0.4%	−0.5%
Standard deviation	25.4%	25.9%	25.5%	25.5%
Sharpe ratio	0.45	0.36	0.30	0.30
Skew	1.65	0.88	0.90	0.57
Lower tail	3.00	3.24	2.48	2.93

The good news is that the median performance appears to be better, with a Sharpe ratio (SR) of 0.3 versus 0.23 for the original multiple trend portfolio in strategy nine. We seem to get 'cleaner' trend signals by following asset prices rather than individual instruments (do not pop the champagne, as there is disappointment on the way in a page or so).

Looking across individual asset classes, the most significant improvement is in equities,[196] where we've struggled so far to make money with trend. Using the entire asset class to get a signal produces an SR of 0.12, which isn't great, but it's certainly better than the SR of 0.03 for strategy nine (back-adjusted price trend following), and the negative SR for strategy seventeen (normalised trend).

Next let's cue up the Jumbo portfolio to see how the aggregated performance compares to the other two trend strategies we have developed. Table 78 has the results. The outperformance that we got a moment ago for the average instrument has vanished. Instead of an SR improvement, we're now underperforming. What happened?

---

196   One implication of this is that the approach in strategy sixteen of reducing the trend versus carry allocation just for equities does not make as much sense here.

TABLE 78: PERFORMANCE OF DIFFERENT TYPES OF TREND FOLLOWING FOR AGGREGATE JUMBO PORTFOLIO

	Strategy nine Multiple trend (Back-adjusted price)	Strategy seventeen Multiple trend (Normalised price for instrument)	Strategy eighteen Multiple trend (Normalised price for asset class)
Mean annual return	25.2%	28.2%	24.0%
Costs	−1.2%	−1.4%	−1.3%
Average drawdown	−11.2%	−12.9%	−14.6%
Standard deviation	22.2%	24.4%	23.5%
Sharpe ratio	1.14	1.15	0.97
Turnover	62.9	72.1	65.5
Skew	0.98	0.93	0.94
Lower tail	1.99	1.87	1.94
Upper tail	1.81	1.80	1.82
Alpha	18.8%	20.1%	15.9%
Beta	0.43	0.55	0.46

Remember from Part One that we get significant diversification benefits from trading trend across as many different instruments as possible. But the construction of this new trading rule means that we have almost no diversification of forecasts *within* each asset class. Except for some unusual cases, most instruments within a given asset class would have the same sign of position on: all long, or all short. Hence, the only source of diversification is what we obtain by trading *across* asset classes. That reduces our diversification benefit – the improvement in performance between the median instrument and the aggregate results – from a factor of five, to just over three. This is enough of a penalty to negate any improvements we saw at the instrument level.

With all that said, there are certainly situations in which asset class trend would make sense. In particular, if you have limited capital and can only trade one or two instruments in each asset class, then it might be sensible to follow the trend for the entire asset class, using a price index that includes all the instruments you can't actually hold positions in.

Asset class trend with carry

Given the evidence I've presented so far, it probably wouldn't make sense to replace our original trend following rules with asset class trend. Again, this will depend on the capital you can deploy. Someone with a smaller trading account who can only trade a few instruments in each asset class may well be better off using asset class trend. And there might be an argument for using asset class trend in equities, where it is certainly better.

But would it make sense to combine asset class trend with the other trading rules we've seen so far? Then we would have four trading rules: carry, plus three kinds of trend: original, normalised and asset class.

First of all, let's quickly remind ourselves of how to use the top down method to allocate forecast weights.

- Allocate 60% to divergent (trend) rules. Allocate 40% to convergent (carry).

- Within trend: Allocate a third to original trend, a third to normalised trend and a third to asset class trend (20% each).

- Within carry: We only have a single trading rule, which receives 40% of the allocation.

- Within a given trading rule, allocate equally across variations of each given trading rule.

Once again I will use this example: the WTI Crude Oil future, which can trade all four carry rules and the four slowest trend rules for all three types of trend, for a total of 16 rules:

- Allocate 60% to divergent trend and 40% to convergent carry.

- Within trend: Allocate a third to original trend, a third to normalised trend and a third to asset class trend (20% each):

  - Within original trend: Allocate 20% ÷ 4 = 5% to each of EWMAC8, EWMAC16, EWMAC32 and EWMAC64.

  - Within normalised trend: Allocate 20% ÷ 4 = 5% to each of the four trading rule variations.

  - Within asset class trend: Allocate 20% ÷ 4 = 5% to each of the four trading rule variations.

- Within carry: We only have a single trading rule, which receives 40% of the allocation:

  - Allocate 40% ÷ 4 = 10% to each of carry5, carry20, carry60 and carry120.

We also need some forecast diversification multipliers. Multipliers for an appropriate number of trading rule variations can be found in table 52 (page 234).

Table 79 shows what happens to strategy eleven (original trend plus carry) as we add the two new types of trend: normalised and asset class.

TABLE 79: EFFECT OF ADDING DIFFERENT TYPES OF TREND TO CARRY PLUS TREND STRATEGY

	Strategy eleven Carry and trend (adjusted prices)	Strategy seventeen Carry and trend (normalised prices and adjusted prices)	Strategy eighteen Carry and trend (asset class price, normalised prices and adjusted prices)
Mean annual return	26.5%	27.5%	28.3%
Costs	−1.1%	−1.1%	−1.1%
Average drawdown	−8.9%	−8.7%	−9.1%
Standard deviation	20.9%	20.9%	21.7%
Sharpe ratio	1.27	1.32	1.31
Turnover	46.5	47.6	46.1
Skew	0.76	0.75	0.71
Lower tail	1.86	1.85	1.85
Upper tail	1.75	1.70	1.81
Alpha	22.3%	22.9%	24.0%
Beta	0.30	0.32	0.31

The SR falls slightly when we add asset class prices, but due to a slightly lower beta the alpha is higher. Although modest, the increase in alpha is statistically significant.[197]

Again, you may feel that this very modest improvement in performance isn't worth the extra hassle, particularly if you are not running a fully automated trading strategy. Personally, as I said in the last chapter, I am happy to run with as many different kinds of trend as I can get my hands on.

It's also worth noting, again, that traders with limited capital will reap a greater reward from using asset class trend. You could also get an additional benefit from this strategy by increasing the proportion of asset class trend in equities, where it does relatively well, although that could conceivably be over fitting.

---

197   Even small differences in performance can be statistically significant if the relevant returns have very high correlation. The correlation between all three kinds of trend is around 0.96, and the correlation between the strategies shown in this table is even higher: around 0.98.

Strategy eighteen: Trading plan

All other stages are identical to strategy nine (standalone trend) or strategy eleven (combined with carry).

Strategy	Go long or short one or more instruments with variable risk estimate and a combined forecast from multiple trend filters. Modify the trend filters so they use normalised price for the relevant asset class as an input.
Instrument(s)	Any that meet minimum capital, liquidity and cost thresholds.
Choose trading rules for each instrument	Turnover figures are in table 73 on page 304.
Trading rule variations	Construct one or more trend filters of the form EWMAC(N,4N) where N is one of 2,4,8,16,32,64.
Normalised asset class price	We begin with the calculation of a normalised price for each instrument i in the asset class: $$P^N_{i,t} = (100 \times [p_{i,t} - p_{i,t-1}] \div \sigma_{p,i,t}) + P^N_{i,t-1}$$ Next, we calculate an average daily return for the asset class R, by averaging returns over instruments $i = 0$ to $i = j$: $$R_t = ([P^N_{0,t} - P^N_{0,t-1}] + [P^N_{1,t} - P^N_{1,t-1}] + ... [P^N_{j,t} - P^N_{j,t-1}]) \div j$$ We add up the R terms to get a normalised price for an asset A: $$A_t = (R_1 + R_2 + ... R_t)$$
EWMAC calculations	To calculate the N business day span price EWMA using the normalised asset price A: $$\lambda = 2 \div (N + 1)$$ $$EWMA_i(N)_t = \lambda A_t + \lambda(1 - \lambda)A_{t-1} + \lambda(1 - \lambda)^2 A_{t-2} + ...$$
Raw forecast for a given EWMAC N	Normalise the raw forecast, using a daily standard deviation of price changes for the normalised asset price, $\sigma^A_{p,t}$. Every instrument i in a given asset class will have the same forecast: $$\text{Raw forecast}_{N,i,t} = (EWMA(N)_{i,t} - EWMA(4N)_{i,t}) \div \sigma^A_{p,t}$$
Scaled forecast for a given EWMAC	$$\text{Scaled forecast}_{N,i,t} = \text{Raw forecast}_{N,i,t} \times \text{forecast scalar}_N$$ Forecast scalars can be found in table 29 on page 177.

Capped forecast for a given EWMAC	**Capped forecast$_{N,i,t}$** **$= Max(Min(Scaled\ forecast_{N,i,t}, +20), -20)$**
Allocating forecast weights	Use table 36 on page 193 for a standalone trend strategy. Use table 51 on page 233 when combined with carry. See page 316 when combined with carry and other types of trend.
Forecast diversification	FDM values: • Use table 36 on page 193 for a standalone asset class trend strategy. • Use table 52 on page 234 when combined with carry and/or standard trend.

Cross-sectional momentum

Two hedge fund managers walk into a bar (no, this is not the start of a joke). One (Charlotte) works for a futures trader – a commodity trading adviser. The other (Eric) is employed by an equity market neutral hedge fund. A conversation begins:

> Eric: *"Can I buy you a drink?"*
>
> Charlotte: *"Triple Jack Daniels, neat, with a tequila chaser."*
>
> Eric: *"Eh and a rum and coke please."*
>
> Charlotte (slams empty glass on table): *"So what do you do?"*
>
> Eric (sipping quietly): *"We buy stocks that we think are undervalued according to a set of factors, and sell stocks that we think are overvalued. We do this so that we have no exposure to the overall market: we are equity neutral."*
>
> Charlotte: *"Can you give me an example?"*
>
> Eric: *"Well one of our main factors is momentum. So we will buy stocks that have gone up by more than the index, and sell stocks that have gone down."*
>
> Charlotte: (coughing and spluttering) *"That's not momentum! Momentum is when you buy something that has gone up, and sell something that has gone down. Who cares what the index has done?"*
>
> Eric: (shouting) *"Nonsense!"*

A scuffle ensues, in which Eric's HP calculator is badly scratched, and Charlotte's vintage CME trading jacket is ripped...

Who is right? Well both are. To traders from different worlds, momentum is a homonym: the same word but with divergent meanings. Traditionally, futures traders weren't concerned about any fancy academic sounding notion of being 'equity neutral'. But the equity market neutral hedge fund industry was heavily influenced by academic work in the 1990s,[198] which defined trading strategies in terms of baskets of long and short stock positions, matched to ensure there was no net market exposure. To this day, if you talk to academic economists about momentum, they will automatically assume you mean **cross-sectional momentum**.

So far in this book we've focused on **time series momentum** – what a traditional futures trader would call **trend following** – buying and selling with no regard to the relative strength of a particular instrument versus an index, and caring only about the absolute performance of a given instrument.

But there is nothing to stop futures traders from using cross-sectional as well as time series momentum: and the work we've done developing normalised prices for instruments and asset classes will be extremely helpful with this strategy.

Strategy nineteen: A strategy that uses cross-sectional momentum within asset classes.

A cross-sectional momentum trading rule

We begin with the normalised price for a given instrument (strategy seventeen) P^N and the normalised price for the relevant asset class A for that instrument (strategy eighteen). The relative price, R, is just the difference between them:

$$R_{i,t} = P^N_{i,t} - A_{i,t}$$

We can take a difference because both types of normalised price are in the same 'scale-free' volatility normalised units. If R is going up, it means that a given instrument is outperforming its asset class, and vice versa. To get a feel for what R looks like, here is the relative price for S&P 500 micro futures in figure 72.

---

198 The original work was done by Eugene Fama and Ken French ('The cross-section of expected stock returns', *The Journal of Finance* 47, 1992). Subsequently, the momentum factor was added by Mark Carhart ('On persistence in mutual fund performance', *The Journal of Finance* 52, 1997).

FIGURE 72: CONSTRUCTION OF RELATIVE PRICE FOR S&P 500

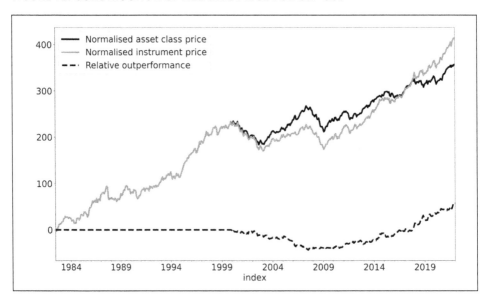

Until the year 2000, the asset class and instrument price are identical. This is because the S&P 500 is the only equity instrument for which I have data up to that point. As a result, the relative price is initially zero. To ensure we don't get a load of zero forecasts, which would mess up the position scaling equations, I remove these zeros from the data before continuing. After 2000 the prices start to deviate, and the relative price line shifts away from zero. There is an underperformance from the 2000 tech crash into the 2008 financial crisis, followed by a long period of outperformance.

An obvious next step would be to apply an exponentially weighted moving average to the relative price. This would certainly work, but for variety I'm going to adopt another approach which is a little simpler, and perhaps more intuitive.

First of all, we measure the average outperformance over some *horizon* of days. For example, for a horizon of H days:

$$\text{Outperformance}_H = (R_{i,t} - R_{i,t-H}) \div H$$

Just as with the span used for moving average crossovers, the longer the horizon, the slower the trend we are looking for. This produces a rather noisy estimate, so we're also going to apply an exponentially weighted moving average smoothing:

$$\text{Forecast} = \text{EWMA}_{\text{span}=H\div4}(\text{Outperformance}_H)$$

Because both prices in the calculation are normalised, we don't need to divide by the volatility of the relative price.[199] The span of the smooth is fixed at a quarter of the horizon length. I chose this ratio arbitrarily to avoid fitting it, but I also did some sensitivity checks and the performance isn't overly sensitive to getting this ratio exactly right.

Is this relative value?

"Hang on," you are probably thinking, "am I still reading Part Two, 'Advanced trend following and carry strategies'? Shouldn't this chapter be in Part Five, 'Relative value strategies?'" On the surface, it does look like this is a relative value strategy: we go long something (e.g. S&P 500) when it has gone up *relative* to something else (e.g. equities generally). But no, you haven't accidentally skipped ahead a few chapters.

For this strategy we construct a trading rule forecast and use that in the same position sizing methodology that I use throughout Parts One, Two and Three. Hence this properly belongs with other strategies that use this methodology. It's also easier to explain it here, having just discussed the mechanics of normalised pricing for instruments and asset classes which we need to calculate the relevant forecast.

In contrast, as you will see in due course, the relative value strategies in Part Five use a very different method for sizing positions and trading them. They are very concerned with ensuring *market neutrality*: the concept that got Eric hot under the collar in the imaginary dialogue at the start of the chapter.

In strategy nineteen we generate a cross-sectional forecast, and then ultimately use that as one of many forecasts to decide what direction we think the S&P 500 will head in next. The fact that the S&P 500 is outperforming means we're more likely to be long S&P, but **there is no guarantee we'd end up with an exactly balanced set of equity positions which had no overall market exposure.**

---

199   A good question is whether we could apply this same simplified approach to the other strategies we've applied to normalised prices: strategies seventeen and eighteen. The short answer is yes, this would work, although obviously we would need to use different forecast scalars. In writing this book I thought it would be easier to use EWMAC as much as possible, but I also feel it's important to show that there are other methods of constructing forecasts that work equally well with normalised prices.

As with EWMAC we need to determine what set of horizons we should trade. I decided to begin with a five business day horizon, with a two-day span for smoothing.[200] This is equivalent to looking at relative outperformance over the last week. For the same reasons that I used a doubling of spans for EWMAC when generating my set of trading rule filter speeds, I also double successive horizons in this strategy. This gives me the following: five days (two-day smoothing span), 10 days (roughly two weeks, with a three-day smoothing span), 20 days (about a month, with a five-day span), 40 days (two months, 10-day span), 80 days (four months, 20-day span) and 160 days (eight months, 40-day span).

Forecast scalars for each horizon are given in table 80. Don't forget to apply a cap of 20 on the absolute forecast value after you've scaled it.

TABLE 80: FORECAST SCALARS FOR DIFFERENT HORIZONS OF CROSS-SECTIONAL MOMENTUM

	Forecast scalars
Horizon5	56.1
Horizon10	79.0
Horizon20	108.5
Horizon40	153.5
Horizon80	217.1
Horizon160	296.8

How do the different horizons perform? The answers are in tables 81 and 82. For comparison with earlier tables, these show the aggregated results across a Jumbo portfolio with all instruments included – even those that are too expensive to trade for a given trading rule.

---

200   As a quarter of the horizon can be a non-integer value, and spans need to be integers in the software I'm using, I actually use the rounded value of a quarter of the horizon. I also apply a minimum span of two days, hence a two-day smoothing span for a horizon of five days.

TABLE 81: CROSS-SECTIONAL MOMENTUM PERFORMANCE FOR SHORTER HORIZONS

	Horizon5	Horizon10	Horizon20
Mean annual return (gross)	−0.9%	5.2%	9.8%
Mean annual return (net)	−13.8%	−4.3%	5.6%
Costs	−12.7%	−9.4%	−4.1%
Standard deviation	21.1%	21.3%	20.3%
Sharpe ratio	−0.65	−0.20	0.28
Turnover	598	407	172
Skew	0.59	0.55	0.35
Lower tail	1.50	1.44	1.54
Annualised alpha (gross)	−3.9%	3.4%	7.1%
Annualised alpha (net)	−16.6%	−6.0%	3.0%
Beta	0.16	0.10	0.18

Aggregated Jumbo portfolio results.

TABLE 82: CROSS-SECTIONAL MOMENTUM PERFORMANCE FOR LONGER HORIZONS

	Horizon40	Horizon80	Horizon160
Mean annual return (gross)	9.6%	5.3%	6.8%
Mean annual return (net)	7.2%	3.7%	5.6%
Costs	−2.3%	−1.5%	−1.2%
Standard deviation	19.8%	18.6%	18.8%
Sharpe ratio	0.36	0.20	0.30
Turnover	85.9	46.2	26.4
Skew	0.20	0.22	0.14
Lower tail	1.44	1.49	1.58
Annualised alpha (gross)	6.5%	2.4%	4.1%
Annualised alpha (net)	4.2%	0.8%	2.9%
Beta	0.20	0.19	0.18

Aggregated Jumbo portfolio results.

Your first instinct is probably that these are disappointing figures, when we compare them to earlier results for individual trend speeds such as those in strategy nine (tables 30 and 31). The Sharpe ratio (SR) is less than a third of what we managed earlier. But this shouldn't really be a shock. In strategy eighteen I demonstrated that quite a large proportion of the trend profits made in a given instrument are coming from following the direction of the relevant asset class. If we strip out the asset class trend and focus purely on the residual cross-sectional effect, then it's not a surprise that there isn't much left over.

Multiple cross-sectional momentum

Let us continue down the well-trodden path and combine different horizons together to make a single strategy that trades multiple variations of the cross-sectional momentum trading rule. This might produce greater benefits than we've seen in the past, since the correlation between these cross-sectional momentum rules is lower than for the EWMAC based rules we've used before.[201]

I'm going to use exactly the same approach as before to select forecast weights. Firstly, I will discard trading rules that are too expensive for a given instrument. Table 83 shows the turnover figures I need for this step.

TABLE 83: TURNOVER PER YEAR FOR EACH HORIZON, AVERAGED ACROSS INSTRUMENTS

	Turnover
Horizon5	120.1
Horizon10	80.6
Horizon20	35.5
Horizon40	17.4
Horizon80	8.5
Horizon160	4.1

Secondly, I will equally weight selected variations of the cross-sectional momentum rule. Thirdly, I apply a forecast diversification multiplier (FDM). Table 84 shows the relevant figures. As you would expect, given that the correlation between different horizons is lower, the FDM figures here are higher than for the various trend rules we've seen so far.

---

201 For example, the correlation between adjacent horizons is around 0.70 versus the 0.87 for adjacent EWMAC filters. Similarly, for horizons that are two apart, the correlation is 0.47 rather than 0.60.

TABLE 84: FORECAST DIVERSIFICATION MULTIPLIER AND FORECAST WEIGHTS GIVEN CHOICE OF HORIZONS FOR AN INSTRUMENT

	Forecast weight, per horizon	FDM
Horizon5, 10, 20, 40, 80, 160	0.1667	1.49
Horizon10, 20, 40, 80, 160	0.20	1.40
Horizon20, 40, 80, 160	0.25	1.30
Horizon40, 80, 160	0.333	1.21
Horizon80, 160	0.5	1.11
Horizon160	1.0	1.0

Finally, we apply a forecast cap of 20 to the combined and scaled forecast. The results are shown in table 85, along with the performance of the other trend strategies we have seen so far. Sadly, this is a relatively poor strategy. It has absolutely no redeeming features except for a slightly better lower tail.[202]

TABLE 85: PERFORMANCE OF AGGREGATE JUMBO PORTFOLIO FOR VARIOUS TREND AND MOMENTUM STRATEGIES

	Strategy nine Multiple trend (Back-adjusted price)	Strategy seventeen Multiple trend (Normalised price for instrument)	Strategy eighteen Multiple trend (Normalised price for asset class)	Strategy nineteen (Multiple cross-sectional momentum)
Mean annual return	25.2%	28.2%	24.0%	6.1%
Costs	−1.2%	−1.4%	−1.3%	−1.4%
Average drawdown	−11.2%	−12.9%	−14.6%	−40.0%
Standard deviation	22.2%	24.4%	23.5%	18.1%
Sharpe ratio	1.14	1.15	0.97	0.34
Turnover	62.9	72.1	65.5	81.4
Skew	0.98	0.93	0.94	0.51
Lower tail	1.99	1.87	1.94	1.49
Upper tail	1.81	1.80	1.82	1.47
Alpha	18.8%	20.1%	15.9%	2.4%
Beta	0.43	0.55	0.46	0.24

---

202   Incidentally, the SR for equities on this strategy isn't especially bad: it's −0.05 versus a median of 0. This isn't great, but is by no means the worse: both bonds and metals have worse performance. You may also be interested to know that the method outlined in strategy thirteen also improves performance here, although not by enough to make it interesting.

Cross-sectional momentum with carry and trend following

I'd be surprised if you looked at the results so far and thought "Yes! Cross-sectional momentum is for me." On its own, this is not an especially profitable strategy. The SR of 0.34 is only barely statistically significant. The annual alpha of 2.4% certainly isn't. Does that mean Charlotte has won the argument over Eric? Possibly. But relative momentum does have one advantage. It's quite different compared to the trend following type of momentum that we've used so far. This isn't a surprise, as going long and short instruments in the same asset class will give it quite different properties.

The correlation of strategy nineteen with carry is just 0, versus around 0.30 for the trend following strategies we have already seen. Similarly, its average correlation with the trend strategies is a mere 0.31, compared to over 0.90 elsewhere. This is good news. In theory a small allocation to a trading rule which is sufficiently diversifying can improve the SR, even if the trading rule has a relatively poor SR.

To test this I will further adapt strategy eighteen, which included carry plus the three types of trend following style momentum I've considered so far: trend based on adjusted prices, normalised prices and asset class prices. Hopefully you are now sufficiently familiar with the top down method for choosing forecast weights that I do not need to explain the procedure again. Forecast diversification multipliers for an appropriate number of trading rule variations can be found in table 52 (page 234).

How does cross-sectional momentum shape up when included with carry and trend following? Table 86 has the results.

TABLE 86: EFFECT OF ADDING VARIOUS TYPES OF MOMENTUM AND TREND FOLLOWING TO CARRY

	Strategy eleven Carry and trend (adjusted prices)	Strategy seventeen Carry and trend (normalised prices and adjusted prices)	Strategy eighteen Carry and trend (asset class price, normalised prices and adjusted prices)	Strategy nineteen Carry and trend (cross-sectional momentum, asset class price, normalised prices and adjusted prices)
Mean annual return	26.5%	27.5%	28.3%	27.0%
Costs	−1.1%	−1.1%	−1.1%	−1.1%
Average drawdown	−8.9%	−8.7%	−9.1%	−8.8%
Standard deviation	20.9%	20.9%	21.7%	20.8%
Sharpe ratio	1.27	1.32	1.31	1.30
Turnover	46.5	47.6	46.1	43.9
Skew	0.76	0.75	0.71	0.70
Lower tail	1.86	1.85	1.85	1.82
Upper tail	1.75	1.70	1.81	1.73
Alpha	22.3%	22.9%	24.0%	23.8%
Beta	0.30	0.32	0.31	0.31

There is no clear improvement here. One reason for this might be that the cross-sectional momentum has been given a 15% allocation.[203] This is a bit larger than the point at which the diversification benefits are overcome by the poorer standalone SR of cross-sectional momentum. With a smaller allocation of say 5%, we'd see a small improvement in backtested performance. I currently use a 12% allocation in my own trading system, since I'd rather have a little more diversification even at the expense of sacrificing some backtested SR.[204]

---

203 Remember that 60% of our total forecast weight is allocated to divergent strategies; this is apportioned between the four kinds of momentum and trend following rules that we trade, leaving 15% for cross-sectional momentum.

204 The logic for this is that correlations are more predictable than SRs. So it's not impossible that relative momentum could perform better than other types of momentum in the future, but it's almost certain that it will continue to have a relatively low correlation.

Strategy nineteen: Trading plan

All other stages are identical to strategy nine (as a standalone strategy) or strategy eleven (when combined with carry).

Strategy	Go long or short one or more instruments with variable risk estimate and a combined forecast from multiple look back horizons of cross-sectional momentum.
Instrument(s)	Any that meet minimum capital, liquidity and cost thresholds.
Choose trading rules for each instrument	Turnover figures are in table 83.
Normalised asset class price	We begin with the normalised price for a given instrument (strategy seventeen) P^N and the normalised price for the relevant asset class A for that instrument (strategy eighteen). The relative price, R is:

$$R_{i,t} = P^N_{i,t} - A_{i,t}$$

We now calculate the average outperformance over some *horizon* of H days:

$$\text{Outperformance}_H = (R_{i,t} - R_{i,t-H}) \div H$$

Finally, we apply a smooth to it to get our forecast:

$$\text{Forecast} = \text{EWMA}_{\text{span}=H \div 4}(\text{Outperformance}_H)$$ |
| **Scaled forecast for a given horizon** | $$\text{Scaled forecast}_{N,I,t}$$ $$= \text{Raw forecast}_{N,i,t} \times \text{forecast scalar}_N$$

Forecast scalars can be found in table 80. |
| **Capped forecast for a given horizon** | $$\text{Capped forecast}_{N,i,t}$$ $$= \text{Max(Min(Scaled forecast}_{N,i,t}, +20), -20)$$ |
| **Allocating forecast weights** | Use handcrafting method discussed in strategy nine. |
| **Forecast diversification multiplier (FDM)** | FDM values:

Use table 84 for a standalone relative momentum strategy.

Use table 52 (page 234) when combined with carry and or trend following strategies. |

Cross-sectional carry

I've spent a lot of time in the last few chapters coming up with new and exciting ways to measure trends across and within asset classes. No doubt the carry strategy is feeling neglected, so let's turn our attention to that. Carry on normalised prices does not make any sense. But we could, for example, construct an 'asset class carry' strategy that blends together carry forecasts from different instruments. That would be an obvious counterpart to the asset class trend I developed in strategy eighteen. However, carry is quite different from trend, and this does not produce a worthwhile strategy.

A more promising idea is to use the idea of cross-sectional forecasts within asset classes, but for carry rather than momentum.[205] We know that carry is profitable, but unless you have a diversified portfolio of instruments, it has relatively unpleasant skew and other risk properties. Perhaps we can benefit from hedging out our carry bets with other instruments in a given asset class.

> **Strategy twenty:** A strategy that uses cross-sectional carry within asset classes.

Constructing a cross-sectional carry forecast

We begin with the raw carry forecast from strategy ten, for some instrument:

$$\text{Carry forecast} = \text{Annualised raw carry} \div (\sigma_p \times 16)$$

Next, we take a smooth of this carry forecast. In principle we could use a number of different smooths, as I did in strategy ten. We know from strategy ten that carry

---

205   As with relative momentum, there is a fair amount of attention on relative carry in the academic research, for example in the canonical paper 'Carry' by Ralph S.J. Koijen, Tobias J. Moskowitz, Lasse Heje Pedersen, and Evert B. Vrugt. *Journal of Financial Economics*, 127, no. 2 (2018).

forecasts with different smooths are highly correlated. In this strategy, for simplicity, I will use a single 90-day smooth:

$$\textbf{Smoothed carry forecast} = \textbf{EWMA}_{\text{span=90}}(\textbf{Carry forecast})$$

For each time period we now calculate a median[206] carry forecast, averaging across the current carry forecast for all instruments in a given asset class, and we subtract the median forecast from the forecast for a given instrument to get the cross-sectional carry forecast. For smoothed forecasts F, across instruments i, with j instruments in a given asset class:

$$\textbf{Cross-sectional carry forecast}_{i,t} = \textbf{F}_{i,t} - \textbf{Median}(\textbf{F}_{1,t} \ldots \textbf{F}_{j,t})$$

We need an example. Figure 73 shows the carry calculation for the US 2-year bond future. The solid black line is the median carry for all the bond futures in my data set. Carry in bonds depends on the slope of the yield curve, and you can see it falling when the yield curve flattens across most countries in 2007 and 2019. US 2-year bond carry is marked with the grey line, and this follows the same cycle but with more exaggerated movements. The dotted black line shows the difference between these lines, which is the cross-sectional carry.

FIGURE 73: RELATIVE CARRY FOR US 2-YEAR BOND FUTURES

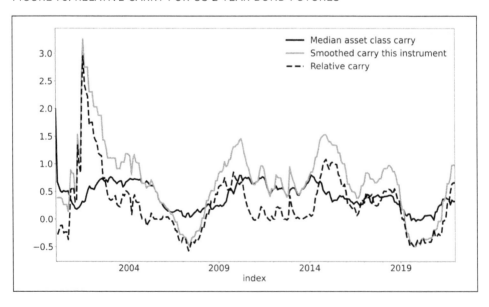

---

206   I use the median rather than the mean as it is more robust to outlier values. This means that we are guaranteed to have an equal number of long and short positions, but it also implies that the average mean forecast for this strategy won't necessarily be zero.

The forecast scalar for cross-sectional carry with a smoothing span of 90 days is 50. Our scalar is a little higher than the value of 30 we used for normal carry, since calculating a relative value reduces the magnitude of our raw forecasts. Naturally, we'd apply the normal cap of 20 to the absolute size of the scaled forecast.

Standalone performance of cross-sectional carry

Let's first consider the standalone performance of cross-sectional carry. Since outright carry varies across asset classes, it would be interesting to see what it looks like for the cross-sectional variety. In tables 87 and 88 I analyse the median performance of each instrument within a given asset class. As usual, I've dropped any instruments which are too expensive to trade. To do this I needed the turnover figure, which comes out at a measly 2.9. These results can be directly compared with tables 46 and 47 on page 222, which have the figures for directional carry, strategy ten.

TABLE 87: MEDIAN INSTRUMENT PERFORMANCE FOR CROSS-SECTIONAL CARRY STRATEGY ACROSS FINANCIAL ASSET CLASSES

	Equity	Vol	FX	Bond
Mean annual return	0.2%	3.1%	1.8%	1.8%
Standard deviation	10.4%	16.8%	21.8%	25.2%
Sharpe ratio	0.03	0.19	0.10	0.09
Skew	0.00	−2.22	−0.72	−0.16

TABLE 88: MEDIAN INSTRUMENT PERFORMANCE FOR CROSS-SECTIONAL CARRY STRATEGY ACROSS COMMODITY ASSET CLASSES

	Metals	Energy	Ags	Median
Mean annual return	5.4%	5.4%	0.5%	1.3%
Standard deviation	17.3%	27.1%	32.1%	17.6%
Sharpe ratio	0.26	0.22	0.01	0.11
Skew	0.72	0.29	−0.10	−0.12

As with cross-sectional momentum, these results are not especially good. The Sharpe ratio (SR) is about half what we saw for directional carry, with only a modest improvement in skew. As we saw in strategy ten, there is a fair amount of variation in standard deviation, as we don't see the same strength of forecasts in every asset class. Here standard deviations are higher in asset classes where there is more dispersion in carry. Interestingly, whilst the performance of directional carry was significantly better in the financial markets (equities, bonds, FX and volatility), there is no such clear distinction here.

Now let's consider the aggregate performance of the Jumbo portfolio for cross-sectional carry. The results are in table 89.

TABLE 89: PERFORMANCE OF ORIGINAL AND CROSS-SECTIONAL CARRY

	Strategy ten Carry	Strategy twenty Cross-sectional carry	Strategy ten & twenty Carry (70%) plus cross-sectional carry (30%)
Mean annual return	19.7%	5.7%	16.1%
Costs	−0.8%	−0.7%	−0.7%
Average drawdown	−18.6%	−37.7%	−15.0%
Standard deviation	20.8%	16.1%	18.0%
Sharpe ratio	0.94	0.31	0.89
Turnover	19.2	17.6	17.3
Skew	0.41	0.21	0.09
Lower tail	1.57	1.58	1.60
Upper tail	1.49	1.45	1.42
Alpha	19.1%	2.5%	14.3%
Beta	0.06	0.17	0.13

Aggregated Jumbo portfolio.

The aggregate SR for strategy twenty is about three times higher than the median for individual instruments, but that's actually a little disappointing – we got a fourfold boost in the original carry strategy when moving from the average instrument up to the Jumbo portfolio. Apart from slightly lower turnover, there is nothing about cross-sectional carry that improves upon the original carry in strategy ten.

The correlation of original and cross-sectional carry is around 0.31, which is similar to the correlation between original and cross-sectional momentum. Despite the lower SR, there is some potential diversification benefit to be gained from combining the two carry strategies. The third column of the table shows one possibility, with 70% of the forecast weights allocated to original carry, and the remaining 30% to the cross-sectional variety. Reducing the cross-sectional weight further would improve the backtested SR, but – as I have said before – we do not want to rely too much on the backtested SR when deciding our forecast weights.

Cross-sectional carry with trend and directional carry

Let's see what happens if we take strategy nineteen – which includes all the types of momentum we've developed so far, plus directional carry – and add in cross-sectional carry. Using the top down method for allocating forecast weights, we would put half of our 30% carry allocation into directional carry and half into relative carry. The rest of the strategy will remain unchanged. This strategy effectively represents all the standalone trend and carry strategies we've developed so far, although it excludes the optional adjustments I discussed in strategies twelve to sixteen. The results are in table 90.

TABLE 90: EFFECT OF ADDING RELATIVE CARRY TO OTHER STRATEGIES WITH TREND

	Strategy nine Trend (adjusted prices)	Strategy eleven Carry and trend (adjusted prices)	Strategy nineteen (Four types of trend/ momentum, original carry)	Strategy twenty (Four types of trend/ momentum, both types of carry)
Mean annual return	25.2%	26.5%	27.0%	26.8%
Costs	−1.2%	−1.1%	−1.1%	−1.1%
Average drawdown	−11.2%	−8.9%	−8.8%	−8.6%
Standard deviation	22.2%	20.9%	20.8%	20.4%
Sharpe ratio	1.14	1.27	1.30	1.31
Turnover	62.9	46.5	43.9	46.2
Skew	0.98	0.76	0.70	0.60
Lower tail	1.99	1.86	1.82	1.81
Upper tail	1.81	1.75	1.73	1.69
Alpha	18.8%	22.3%	23.8%	23.1%
Beta	0.43	0.30	0.31	0.33

Aggregated Jumbo portfolio.

Again, the decision about adding this strategy depends on your preferences and beliefs. If you would prefer a smaller set of trading rules, or if you believe that backtested statistics are 100% reliable, then cross-sectional carry probably does not deserve a place in your portfolio. Personally, I prefer to have a large number of diversified trading rules, and I'm a little sceptical of any backtested results.

We are now done with carry and trend. Part Three will expand our horizons to other types of trading strategy. However, these will still generate trading rule forecasts, which means we can easily combine them with the strategies we've seen so far.

More trading rules or more instruments?

Here are some interesting observations:

- Consider table 16 (back on page 116). With ten *instruments*, the IDM is 2.2. At the top end of the table, with 30 or more instruments the IDM is 2.5.

- Table 52 (page 234) is the equivalent for forecast diversification multipliers (FDM). With ten trading rule *variations*, the FDM is just 1.35. For 30 trading rule variations, the FDM is 1.81 and never goes above 2.0.

- For strategy nine we saw an almost five-fold increase in SR when moving from a single instrument to the Jumbo portfolio of over 100 instruments. Carry had a smaller improvement, but the SR was still quadrupled for the larger portfolio compared to a single instrument.

- However, in table 90, in going from strategy nine (one type of trading rule), to strategy twenty (six types of trading rule, with 30 different rule variations), the SR only increases modestly, from 1.14 to 1.31. Most of that increase occurs when we add carry to trend, in strategy eleven.

Diversification multipliers are effectively a measure of *expected* diversification – measured as a reduction in expected risk. The improvements in SR are a measure of *realised* diversification, using risk adjusted return as the appropriate metric. In both cases the results are the same: **the potential improvements from adding instruments is significantly higher than what can be achieved by adding trading rule variations.**

Some of this is because many of the trading strategies I've added so far are very similar, with relatively high correlations. This is because we've stuck to two distinct trading styles: carry and trend, and variations on these two themes that are highly correlated with each other. The two relatively uncorrelated strategies, cross-sectional trend and carry, don't perform as well on an outright basis, and so don't produce much of an improvement even when combined with their directional cousins. The trading strategies in Part Three onwards are less correlated with trend and carry, and will add significant value.

Nevertheless, the message is clear: **you will get a larger benefit from adding instruments to your portfolio than from adding new trading rules**. This is probably a difficult pill to swallow. Adding instruments is mostly a mechanical task involving tedious calculations and mechanical back filling of price databases. In contrast, finding a new trading strategy involves the thrill of exciting research. It's also hard to justify writing a book containing several hundred pages of material on novel trading strategies, with just a few devoted to the more important job of selecting new instruments to trade!

However, there are two groups of traders for whom adding strategies is better than adding further instruments. The first group consists of traders with limited capital. Because of the issues with minimum capital I outlined back in Part One, they can't trade the Jumbo portfolio or anything like it. For them the best option is to trade as many instruments as possible, and then add trading rules to eke out better performance.

In the second group we have traders who have plenty of capital but who have already exhausted the potential for including instruments. With over 100 instruments the Jumbo portfolio already has excellent diversification, and there is little value to be had in adding 100 more. You would probably be better off adding trading strategies.

Strategy twenty: Trading plan

All other stages are identical to strategy ten (standalone carry).

Strategy	Go long or short one or more instruments with variable risk estimate and a forecast based on cross-sectional carry.
Instrument(s)	Any that meet minimum capital, liquidity and cost thresholds.
Choose trading rules for each instrument	Use the usual speed limit. This trading rule has a turnover of 2.9.
Forecast calculation	We begin with the raw carry forecast from strategy ten, for some instrument:

Carry forecast

= Annualised raw carry ÷ (σ_p × 16)

Smoothed carry forecast

= EWMA$_{span=90}$(Carry forecast)

For smoothed forecasts F, across instruments i, with j instruments in a given asset class:

Relative carry forecast (i)

= $F_{i,t}$ − Median($F_{1,t}$, $F_{2,t}$ ... $F_{j,t}$)

Scaled forecast	<div align="center">**Scaled forecast$_{i,t}$** **= Raw forecast$_{i,t}$ × forecast scalar**</div>

Forecast scalar = 50.

PART THREE

Advanced Directional Strategies

You must read all of Part One before reading Part Three.

You do not have to read Part Two before reading Part Three.

Strategies in Part Three use the same position management framework described in Part One, which is based on the idea of constructing *forecasts*: quantified predictions of future risk adjusted returns. They can be used individually, combined with each other or with strategies nine, ten and eleven, or with any of the strategies in Part Two. Unlike the strategies in Part Two, they are not restricted to trend and carry, but seek to exploit other sources of returns.

The following standalone strategies can be used *in addition* to carry and trend:

- **Strategy twenty-one:** Breakout.

- **Strategy twenty-two:** Value.

- **Strategy twenty-three:** Acceleration.

- **Strategy twenty-four:** Skew, a case study. (This strategy explains how to adapt any quantifiable value for use as a forecast, using skew as an example.)

The following strategy overlay can be used with *any* trading strategy:

- **Strategy twenty-five:** Dynamic optimisation (for when you can't trade the Jumbo portfolio).

STRATEGY TWENTY-ONE

Breakout

Although I have not done any serious scientific research to corroborate this, I would imagine that breakout style trading rules are amongst the most popular in the trading arena. As a substitute for serious research, I naturally turned to Google. My searches turned up 215,000 hits for 'trend following trading', 550,000 for 'momentum trading' and 434,000 for 'carry trading'. But I got over 600,000 hits[207] for 'breakout trading'.

The intuitive idea behind breakouts is very appealing. Prices wander around within some kind of natural range, until they reach the extremes of that range. There is some 'resistance' at the edge of the range, with 'the market' determined to prevent prices leaving the range. However, once we break out of the range, the sky is the limit and all the pent up demand to sell or buy is unleashed, resulting in the price reaching parabolically for the sky (or the ground, if we have a bearish breakout signal).

At first glance, breakout trading doesn't sit well with the strategies I've described so far in this book. Breakout traders often determine the 'correct' ranges by using decidedly non-scientific concepts like Fibonacci series, and I openly mocked the idea of such 'magic numbers' back in strategy one. It's also not obvious to me why 'the market' would want to keep prices in a certain range, although I suppose there are sometimes plausible reasons relating to option hedging. Finally, it isn't clear how we'd translate a binary signal – have we broken out of the range or not – into a continuous *forecast*: a prediction of risk adjusted returns.

But it turns out that it is quite straightforward to construct a breakout style trading rule which uses forecasts, and which doesn't require any Fibonacci or other such mumbo jumbo.

---

207 To be pedantic, this is the combined number of hits for 'break out trading', 'breakout trading' and 'break-out trading'.

Strategy twenty-one: A strategy that uses a breakout style calculation to provide a forecast.

Constructing a breakout forecast

The first job is to come up with some – properly scientific – method for determining a price range. In fact, we need nothing more complicated than the minimum and maximum price that has been achieved over recent history. Given some horizon in days, h, and back-adjusted series of daily closing prices, p_t:

$$\text{max}_{h,t} = \text{maximum}(p_t,\ p_{t-1},\ p_{t-2} \dots p_{t-h+1})$$

$$\text{min}_{h,t} = \text{minimum}(p_t,\ p_{t-1},\ p_{t-2} \dots p_{t-h+1})$$

We can vary the *horizon* in days, depending on whether we want to capture breakouts from long established price ranges, or if we're concerned with ranges that are only a few days old. This is analogous to varying the span of exponentially weighted moving averages in the various trend filters. A short horizon will be more reactive when prices begin to move, but will also have higher trading costs.

Consider the price chart in figure 74. This shows the back-adjusted price for WTI Crude Oil futures, and also the maximum and minimum ranges over a 320 business day horizon – about 15 months. For the first few years Crude remains mostly inside a range, although it does test the ceiling a couple of times. Then in October 2014 it breaks through the bottom of the range. A bear market begins which lasts for the next 18 months.

FIGURE 74: BACK-ADJUSTED PRICE, ROLLING MINIMUM AND ROLLING MAXIMUM FOR WTI CRUDE OIL

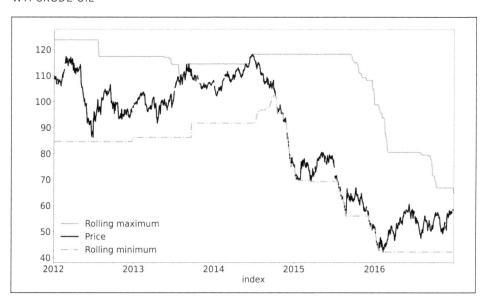

Clearly we will be at our most bearish from October 2014 when the price hits the minimum. But the forecasts we used for trading rules in Parts One and Two don't usually go from a standing start to bearishness or bullishness in a single day. We would want to gradually increase our position *in advance* of the breakout, so when it occurs we already have the maximum forecast on.

There is a straightforward way to achieve this, which is to calculate where the current price is within a recent range[208] of prices:

$$\text{mean}_{h,t} = (\text{max}_{h,t} + \text{min}_{h,t}) \div 2$$

Raw forecast

$$= \text{EWMA}_{\text{span}=h\div4}[40.0 * (p_t - \text{mean}_{h,t}) \div (\text{max}_{h,t} - \text{min}_{h,t})]$$

---

208   Although I independently developed this formulation of the breakout rule, I have subsequently learned that it is very similar to the 'stochastic oscillator' developed by George Lane in the 1950s, although that uses the formulation (price – min) ÷ (max – min). Like many technical analysis indicators, it's unclear exactly how this oscillator should be used. From wikipedia.org: 'According to George Lane, the stochastics indicator is to be used with cycles, Elliott Wave Theory and Fibonacci retracement for timing. In low margin, calendar futures spreads, one might use Wilders parabolic as a trailing stop after a stochastic entry. A centrepiece of his teaching is the divergence and convergence of trendlines drawn on stochastics, as diverging/converging to trendlines drawn on price cycles. Stochastics predicts tops and bottoms.' I hope that clarifies things for you.

Notice that we apply an exponentially weighted moving average (EWMA) to the forecast, with a span that is equal to a quarter of the horizon.[209] As I noted back in strategy eight, this kind of smoothing is an excellent way of reducing the trading costs of a strategy without penalising its performance. If we didn't apply this smooth then the forecast would change sharply every time the price changed.[210]

Now, why do we multiply by 40? Well, with this multiplier when the price is equal to the rolling minimum, the raw forecast will be at its minimum possible value of –20, and when the price hits the rolling maximum the forecast is +20. Handily, 20 is also the absolute maximum forecast value that I permit in my trading strategies. This multiplication will produce a forecast that has roughly the right distribution, although as we shall see in a moment a forecast scalar is still required to get it spot on.

Note also that we don't apply any kind of standard deviation normalisation here. This is because the price range will already reflect the historical volatility of a given instrument. If an instrument has a lower standard deviation, then it is also more likely to have a tighter range. A tighter range will result in a forecast which is more sensitive to smaller price changes.

Of course, it isn't always the case that a lower standard deviation results in a tighter price range. This would only be true if prices followed a random walk.[211] But if there has already been a consistent trend, then the trading range will be quite wide relative to the standard deviation. In this situation we will have lower forecasts for breakout than if we had divided the forecast by volatility instead of, or in addition to, the range normalisation. This is consistent with the idea of breakouts. We don't want a large forecast if a trend has already occurred as we're trying to catch the start of a trend. Excluding volatility normalisation from the forecast calculation also reduces the correlation between the breakout rule and the exponentially weighted moving average crossovers (EWMAC) based trend rules in Parts One and Two, and there isn't much of an effect on outright performance.

Finally, you can see that in the equation above which calculates the raw forecast it's pretty unlikely we would have a zero forecast on, unless the price was currently equal to the centre of the range (*mean*). Hence, this breakout rule is perhaps misnamed. It will have more in common with a trend rule which gradually builds positions, like the EWMAC, than it does with a pure breakout strategy which has no position on

---

209 The choice of span length relative to horizon was made arbitrarily to avoid over fitting; however, as usual I subsequently checked that performance wasn't overly sensitive to the precise choice of parameter value.

210 We could also use an exponentially weighted moving average for the rolling minima and maxima; however, this wouldn't reduce trading costs significantly and makes the rule more complex than it needs to be without any clear performance benefit.

211 A random walk just means that prices don't have any clear trend or auto-correlation in returns.

until the breakout actually occurs. We could address this by introducing a threshold region around the middle part of the range where no position is held, but this will definitely increase transaction costs and will also be a tempting opportunity to over fit the additional parameter that would be required.

Figure 75 shows the raw and smoothed forecast for the price chart in figure 74. Notice how noisy the raw forecast is. Smoothing reduces this considerably, at the cost of a lag to the forecast.

FIGURE 75: RAW AND SMOOTHED FORECAST FOR BREAKOUT WITH 320-DAY HORIZON, WTI CRUDE OIL

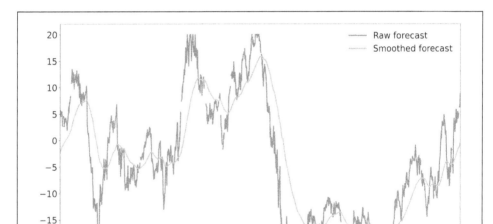

Different speeds of breakout

As we did with trend and carry, we can run the breakout system at different speeds by changing the horizon parameter, h. Breakout look back horizons that are too short will result in penal trading costs, whilst excessively long horizons will produce strategies that trade so infrequently it will be difficult to assess their performance. A 10-day breakout is the fastest I trade. As there are five business days in a week this equates to a two-week horizon.

For trend, in strategy nine I constructed a series of strategy variations by doubling the spans of the moving averages I was using. This approach resulted in adjacent variations which had similar correlations, resulting in a set of trading rule variations that was consistently diversified. Similarly, if I kept doubling the horizon length for the breakout system, then I also found that adjacent breakouts had similar correlations. As a result I trade 10, 20, 40, 80, 160 and 320-day breakouts. This gives me six different variations, the same number of trend trading rule variations that I had in strategy nine.

As I have done with other trading strategies, I multiply the smoothed forecast by a **forecast scalar** to ensure it has the right scaling:[212] an average absolute value of 10. Estimated forecast scalars are shown in table 91. As usual this was calculated by pooling estimates across all the instruments in my data set. In theory, we also need to apply a cap on the absolute forecast value of 20. But as the forecast before scaling cannot be larger than 20, and all the forecast scalars are less than one, this step is actually redundant.

TABLE 91: FORECAST SCALARS FOR DIFFERENT BREAKOUT HORIZONS

	Forecast scalars
Breakout10	0.60
Breakout20	0.67
Breakout40	0.70
Breakout80	0.73
Breakout160	0.74
Breakout320	0.74

First let's check to see if we have a consistent correlation pattern. Table 92 has the results. There is a similar pattern here to table 33 (page 184, strategy nine) which has the equivalent statistics for EWMAC trend. Adjacent variations have higher correlations than those that are further apart. However, the correlations here are a little lower than in strategy nine. There, adjacent variations had a correlation of around 0.87, whilst here adjacent breakout horizons have a correlation of approximately 0.83.

---

212   You might expect that multiplying the raw forecast by 40 would obviate the need to apply a further forecast scalar. In fact this would only be the case if the distribution of the price within its range had a uniform distribution.

TABLE 92: CORRELATION MATRIX OF RETURNS FOR DIFFERENT BREAKOUTS, PLUS AVERAGE CORRELATIONS

	10	20	40	80	160	320
Breakout10	1	0.80	0.55	0.40	0.28	0.26
Breakout20		1	0.83	0.62	0.42	0.33
Breakout40			1	0.83	0.60	0.45
Breakout80				1	0.84	0.64
Breakout160					1	0.86
Breakout320						1
Average versus other horizons	0.55	0.67	0.72	0.72	0.67	0.59

Next, let us examine the performance of the different horizons which are shown in tables 93 and 94. Again these can be compared with tables 30 and 31 (pages 178 and 179), which have the analogous values for the EWMAC trend strategy.[213]

TABLE 93: PERFORMANCE FOR SHORTER BREAKOUT HORIZONS

	Breakout10	Breakout20	Breakout40
Mean annual return (gross)	15.1%	21.6%	21.8%
Mean annual return (net)	6.3%	17.5%	19.6%
Costs	−8.6%	−4.0%	−2.2%
Average drawdown	−120.0%	−14.1%	−11.6%
Standard deviation	21.0%	21.0%	21.1%
Sharpe ratio	0.30	0.83	0.93
Turnover	365.3	170.3	81.4
Skew	0.91	1.29	0.94
Lower tail	1.64	1.71	1.68
Upper tail	1.83	1.76	1.73
Annualised alpha (gross)	12.3%	18.2%	18.0%
Annualised alpha (net)	3.7%	14.2%	15.8%
Beta	0.17	0.23	0.27

Aggregated Jumbo portfolio results with all instruments included regardless of cost.

---

213 The figures here are for the Jumbo portfolio, and so are better than those that would be achievable for a single instrument. They also cover every instrument in my data set, which means that the costs of faster breakout variations will be exaggerated, since they include instruments that are too expensive to trade given the likely turnover.

TABLE 94: PERFORMANCE FOR LONGER BREAKOUT HORIZONS

	Breakout80	Breakout160	Breakout320
Mean annual return (gross)	24.4%	19.9%	20.5%
Mean annual return (net)	23.1%	18.9%	19.7%
Costs	−1.4%	−1.0%	−0.8%
Average drawdown	−10.0%	−13.3%	−14.3%
Standard deviation	20.9%	20.6%	20.6%
Sharpe ratio	1.10	0.92	0.96
Turnover	42.4	23.8	15.2
Skew	0.69	0.34	0.39
Lower tail	1.83	1.80	1.76
Upper tail	1.59	1.52	1.40
Annualised alpha (gross)	19.9%	13.9%	14.2%
Annualised alpha (net)	18.6%	12.9%	13.4%
Beta	0.31	0.40	0.43

Aggregated Jumbo portfolio results with all instruments included regardless of cost.

The general pattern of results here is similar to that for strategy nine. Pre-cost performance is similar across different variations of each rule, with the exception of the very fastest variation (EWMAC2 for strategy nine, breakout10 here). Costs and turnover reduce as we slow down. The skew of monthly returns generally improves as we reduce the horizon length, although as with EWMAC this will be different if we measure skew using daily, weekly, or annual returns. Finally, with longer horizons more of the return is coming from exposure to a long only benchmark, hence beta increases as we slow down.

Trading a combined breakout strategy

If I could only trade one of the breakout variations, I'd probably plump for breakout80. But we don't have to choose a single horizon: we can trade a combination of all six breakout variations. To do this we follow the same procedure that I used for strategy nine, where I combined together six EWMAC variations. If you have read Part Two, then you will have seen this done several times before.

Firstly, for each instrument we select the subset of breakout rules which can be traded given my 'speed limit' on trading costs. Here is the formula to check if a particular trading rule can be used with a given instrument. The annual turnovers you need are in table 95.

Maximum turnover

$$= [0.15 - (\text{Cost per trade} \times \text{Rolls per year})] \div \text{Cost per trade}$$

TABLE 95: FORECAST TURNOVERS FOR BREAKOUT RULES

	Turnover
Breakout10	74.7
Breakout20	35.1
Breakout40	17.4
Breakout80	8.7
Breakout160	4.2
Breakout320	2.0

Next, we need to come up with some forecast weights to decided how to average out the individual forecasts from each variation. As in previous strategies, I opt for a simple equal weighting across all the breakout horizons that I am using for a particular instrument. Because of the diversification across forecasts we now need to apply a forecast diversification multiplier (FDM) to the combined forecast. Appropriate estimates for FDM are shown in table 96. Finally, we cap the combined forecast at a maximum absolute value of 20.

TABLE 96: FORECAST WEIGHTS AND FDM FOR A GIVEN SET OF BREAKOUT RULES

	Forecast weight for each rule variation	FDM
Breakout10, 20, 40, 80, 160, and 320	0.167	1.33
Breakout20, 40, 80, 160, and 320	0.2	1.24
Breakout40, 80, 160, and 320	0.25	1.17
Breakout80, 160, and 320	0.333	1.10
Breakout160, and 320	0.50	1.07
Breakout320	1.0	1.0

Evaluating the performance of the combined breakout strategy

We are now ready to look at the performance of the combined breakout strategy. As I've done numerous times before, I will focus on both (a) the average performance you could expect from trading a single instrument, and (b) the aggregate return statistics for the Jumbo portfolio, with over 100 instruments. Table 97 has both sets of figures.

TABLE 97: PERFORMANCE OF COMBINED BREAKOUT TRADING RULE: MEDIAN INSTRUMENT AND AGGREGATE JUMBO PORTFOLIO

	Median average per instrument	Aggregate Jumbo portfolio
Mean annual return	5.6%	20.3%
Costs	−0.5%	−1.1%
Average drawdown	−22.9%	−8.6%
Standard deviation	18.7%	17.3%
Sharpe ratio	0.30	1.17
Turnover	16.1	55.4
Skew	0.85	0.64
Lower tail	2.88	1.86
Upper tail	2.48	1.68

It's worth briefly comparing these results to strategy nine, multiple trend (equivalent values for strategy nine are in tables 37 and 38 on page 195). The Sharpe Ratio (SR) for the median instrument is higher for breakout, 0.30 versus 0.23 for trend. But the aggregate performance on the Jumbo portfolio is only slightly better: 1.17 for breakout, against 1.14 for trend. We get a more modest 'diversification bonus' with breakout than we did for trend following. Skew is similar for the median instrument on both strategies, but a little worse for breakout on the aggregate portfolio: 0.64 versus 0.98 for trend following.

I haven't included full results for different asset classes here, but as with strategy nine equities are a clear outlier with a median SR across instruments of 0.10, significantly lower than any other asset class. Still, that is an improvement on strategy nine, where the median SR for equities was just 0.03.

Breakout with trend and carry

The joy of using trading rule forecasts is that we aren't limited to just using breakout as a standalone strategy. We can combine it with carry (strategy ten), trend (strategy nine), or any other strategy from Parts Two and Three. This requires the following procedure, which we saw in strategy eleven (trend and carry combined), and also in Part Two:

- We have six EWMAC trading rule variations (strategy nine), four carry variations (strategy ten) and six breakout variations (strategy twenty-one).

- Using the relevant turnover figures for each variation, for each instrument we select a subset of trading rule variations which meet our speed limit.

- Using the top down methodology from strategy eleven (page 230), we allocate a set of forecast weights.

- We calculate a forecast diversification multiplier, depending on how many rule variations we have selected.

- We cap the combined forecast at an absolute value of 20.

Here's a reminder of the 'top down' method for allocating forecast weights:

- Split the list of trading rules by **style**. Allocate between styles according to your preferences.

- Within a given style, allocate equally across **trading rules**.

- Within a given trading rule, allocate equally across **variations** of each given trading rule.

Breakout is clearly in the divergent trading style, along with trend following. Hence we can allocate weights as follows:

- Our two styles are convergent (carry) and divergent (trend and breakout). I allocate 40% to convergent and 60% to trend, for consistency with strategy eleven.

Within trading styles:

- We have one trading rule in carry, which receives 40% of the allocation.

- We have two divergent trading rules: EWMAC and breakout. Each receives half of 60%: 30% each.

Within carry:

- We have up to four variations of carry, which share 40% equally between them.

Within EWMAC:

- We have up to six variations of the EWMAC rule, which share 30% equally.

Within breakout:

- We have up to six variations of the breakout rule, which share 30% equally.

For the forecast diversification multiplier, we can use table 52 on page 234, which is a generic table that applies to any potential set of well-diversified trading rules.

The results from trading this combined strategy are shown in table 98, along with some results we've already seen before for various individual strategies.

TABLE 98: PERFORMANCE OF AGGREGATE JUMBO PORTFOLIO: TREND, BREAKOUT AND COMBINED WITH CARRY

	Strategy nine Multiple trend	Strategy twenty-one Breakout	Strategy eleven Carry and trend	Strategy twenty-one Carry, breakout and trend
Mean annual return	25.2%	20.3%	26.5%	25.7%
Costs	−1.2%	−1.1%	−1.1%	−1.0%
Average drawdown	−11.2%	−8.6%	−8.9%	−8.4%
Standard deviation	22.2%	17.3%	20.9%	19.9%
Sharpe ratio	1.14	1.17	1.27	1.29
Turnover	62.9	55.4	46.5	42.3
Skew	0.98	0.64	0.76	0.68
Lower tail	1.99	1.86	1.86	1.83
Upper tail	1.81	1.68	1.75	1.73
Alpha	18.8%	16.1%	22.3%	22.1%
Beta	0.43	0.29	0.30	0.26

The improvement to strategy eleven from adding breakout is modest, with mixed results depending on which statistic you look at. This is to be expected as trend and breakout are fairly similar, with a correlation of 0.97. Breakout and carry have a correlation of 0.31, which is virtually identical to the correlation of trend and carry. Still, as I discussed at length in Part Two, if you do not incur any additional workload then I would advocate adding additional types of trading rule even if they are very similar to what you already have.

Strategy twenty-one: Trading plan

All other stages are identical to strategy nine.

Strategy	Go long or short one or more instruments with variable risk estimate and a combined forecast from multiple breakout variations.
Instrument(s)	Any that meet minimum capital, liquidity and cost thresholds.
Choose trading rules for each instrument	Only choose trading rule variations where: **Turnover < [0.15 – (Cost per trade** **× Rolls per year)] ÷ Cost per trade** Turnover figures are in table 95.
Trading rule variations	Construct one or more trend breakout forecasts with horizon N, where N is one of 10, 20, 40, 80, 160 and 320.
Rolling minimum, maximum, and mean	Given a back-adjusted price p and horizon in days h: $$\text{max}_{h,t} = \text{max}(p_t, p_{t-1}, p_{t-2} \ldots p_{t-h+1})$$ $$\text{min}_{h,t} = \text{min}(p_t, p_{t-1}, p_{t-2} \ldots p_{t-h+1})$$ $$\text{mean}_{h,t} = (\text{max}_{h,t} + \text{min}_{h,t}) \div 2$$
Smoothed forecast for a given horizon h	**Smoothed forecast** $$= \text{EWMA}_{h \div 4}[40.0 * (p_t - \text{mean}_{h,t}) \div (\text{max}_{h,t} - \text{min}_{h,t})]$$
Scaled forecast for a given variation N and instrument i	**Scaled forecast$_{N,i,t}$** $$= \text{Smoothed forecast}_{N,i,t} \times \text{forecast scalar}_N$$ Forecast scalars can be found in table 91 on page 346.
Allocating forecast weights	See table 96.
Forecast diversification multiplier (FDM)	See table 96 for FDM values.

STRATEGY TWENTY-TWO

Value

Value is a very popular trading strategy in equities. We find some stocks that have attractive accounting ratios: low price-earnings (P/E) or high dividend yields for example. Those cheap shares are purchased, and for extra returns we can sell short expensive stocks with high P/E ratios or low yields. Running a value strategy is particularly satisfying as it means we 'buy low and sell high'. In contrast when trend following we 'buy high and sell higher', which somehow feels wrong.

But you have to be patient to be a value trader. Unlike trend, which tends to play out over several weeks or months, stocks can remain cheap or expensive for years at a time. Indeed, there are long periods of time when the entire strategy of equity value badly underperforms, such as from January 2017 to October 2020.[214]

How can we apply a value strategy to futures? We could calculate P/E ratios for the S&P 500 by aggregating the P/E ratios for individual firms within the index. From personal experience I can tell you that this is quite a lot of work, and it's difficult to apply this methodology outside of equities. It certainly isn't obvious what the equivalent of a P/E ratio for Corn or Bitcoin is.[215]

Fortunately, there is a simpler way to calculate value. As equity earnings are relatively stable, changes in P/E ratios are mostly driven by prices. So, a simplified value strategy

---

214 During this period the cumulative underperformance of the US value factor was −54.7%. Subsequently, from November 2020 to April 2022, the corresponding figure was +52.5%, effectively reversing almost the entire period of underperformance. All figures from AQR (www.aqr.com/Insights/Datasets/Century-of-Factor-Premia-Monthly).

215 There are well-established value strategies in some other asset classes. For example, in FX, there are a series of models that use economic data to calculate a fair value for exchange rate levels, of which my favourite is BEER ('Behavioural Equilibrium Exchange Rate'). Upon discovering this, my immediate response was to develop a series of trading strategies with internal codenames such as WINE ('World Index for Natural Exchange rates') and CIDER ('Commodity Index Diversified Equilibrium Return strategy'). True story.

for equities is to buy stocks whose prices have fallen, and sell those whose prices have risen. Hence value for any arbitrary asset is roughly equivalent to a very slow mean reversion strategy. With such a strategy, assets that have outperformed over the last few years will be expected to underperform in the future, and vice versa.

> **Strategy twenty-two:** A value type strategy which goes long instruments which have underperformed in the last five years, and goes short instruments which have outperformed.

A forecast for value

How do we measure outperformance or underperformance over a period of time? There are numerous ways of doing this which will give similar results, but I prefer to repurpose a measure that I developed in Part Two for strategy nineteen. If you didn't read that chapter, it may be worth briefly reviewing the first section where I explain how to calculate the relative outperformance of an instrument within an asset class.

To briefly recap, we begin with the volatility normalised price for a given instrument i (from strategy seventeen) P_i^N and the normalised price[216] for the relevant asset class A_i for that instrument (which is derived in strategy eighteen). The relative price, R, is just the difference between them. For some day t the relative price will be:

$$R_{i,t} = P_{i,t}^N - A_{i,t}$$

Next we measure the average daily outperformance over some *horizon*. Until now I have used relatively short horizons, but here we want to capture a very slow mean reversion effect. So we will measure our horizon H in years. Assuming there are around 256 business days in a year:

$$\text{Outperformance}_H = (R_{i,t} - R_{i,t-(256 \times H)}) \div (256 \times H)$$

This produces a rather noisy estimate, so we also apply an exponentially weighted moving average to smooth things out a little. As we are calculating the outperformance over a multi-year horizon, a 30-day span is sufficient here to reduce costs without penalising performance. Finally, because we are expecting mean reversion in returns we apply a minus sign to the outperformance before calculating the forecast.

---

216 Alternatively, you could use the pure spot price calculated in strategy fourteen. This doesn't affect the results very much, but some traders may prefer it.

$$\text{Forecast} = \text{EWMA}_{span=30}(-\text{Outperformance}_H)$$

What sort of look back horizon should we use for value? From previous academic research,[217] value is something that plays out over long, multi-year horizons. One year is undoubtedly too short, since we know from strategy nine that trend is still effective at this trading frequency. But we don't want a horizon that is too long: it will be difficult to assess the performance of a trading strategy that has a 10- or 20-year horizon. I decided to consider value over a five-year[218] horizon. In fact the results are fairly similar for shorter horizons (between two and four years), and there is no benefit in using multiple horizons.

As usual, we multiply the forecast by a forecast scalar, which for five-year value is 7.27, and then apply a cap on the absolute scaled forecast of 20. The forecast turnover for value is 8.7, which we will need when deciding whether a given instrument is cheap enough to trade this strategy.

Assessing the performance of value

Because value reverts over such a long horizon, it is never going to be a trading strategy with amazing performance. The average performance of value across instruments is slightly negative, although interestingly it has a significantly positive Sharpe Ratio (SR) in both equities and bonds. Perhaps this is no coincidence: value does well in individual shares where there is a large universe of assets with relatively high correlations. Equities and bonds are two of the larger asset classes in my data set, and many of the instruments in them are highly correlated.

I would caution against putting too much weight on these findings, as the use of a five-year look back means we really have almost no statistically significant evidence. Perhaps more than anything else, value is a strategy which you have to believe in, rather than test with empirical data.

Can value add value when combined with other trading strategies? The correlation of value with trend is -0.03, and with carry is just 0.16; a fair bit lower than the trend versus carry correlation of 0.31. We know from financial theory that even a money

---

217   Five years is used in the seminal academic work on this strategy by Clifford Asness, Lasse Pedersen and Tobias Moskowitz, 'Value and Momentum Everywhere', *The Journal of Finance* 68, no. 3 (2013). The authors use the ratio of log prices as their value measure, so the results won't be identical to mine.

218   An alternative is to remove the final year, so you are effectively trading four-year mean reversion with a one-year lag. This will remove the strong momentum effect that occurs up to a one-year holding period. Personally I find this to be rather weird, and it seems unnecessary if you are also trading a trend strategy.

losing strategy can improve the SR of a portfolio if it has a negative correlation with the pre-existing assets.

It's trivial to add value to strategy eleven, which currently trades just trend and carry. First we need to calculate some forecast weights. Remember from earlier chapters that we need to first determine which trading style value belongs in. Is it divergent, like trend following and the breakout strategy from the previous chapter, or is it convergent like carry? Convergent strategies make money when markets move towards their equilibrium, and both value and carry would seem to fall into this category.

Hence we can allocate forecast weights as follows:

- Our two styles are convergent and divergent. I allocate 40% to convergent and 60% to divergent, for consistency with strategy eleven.

Within trading styles:

- We have two convergent trading rules. I allocate 35% to carry and 5% to value. I explain the reasons for this weighting below.

- We have one divergent trading rule for trend, which receives 60% of the allocation.

Within carry:

- We have up to four variations of carry, which share 35% equally between them.

Within value:

- We have a single variation, which receives a 5% allocation.

Within EWMAC:

- We have up to six variations of the EWMAC rule, which share 60% equally.

Notice above that I didn't follow my usual practice of splitting the convergent allocation in half between the carry and value strategies, which would have given value a 20% allocation rather than the 5% it receives. The primary reason for this is that value is not a very profitable strategy. I wanted to illustrate in this chapter that a highly diversifying money losing strategy can add additional returns, but only if given a modest allocation. An allocation of 20% to value would be too high to illustrate this, as it would result in poorer performance.

It could be argued that fitting the weights in the way I have done above is in sample fitting, and this argument would be correct. As always these results should be used to give an indication of the potential performance of this strategy in the future, rather than a realistic indication of what we could have achieved in the past.

We also need some forecast diversification multipliers; once again you should use table 52 on page 234 for this purpose.

Table 99 has the standalone aggregate Jumbo portfolio for value, and also shows what happens to strategy eleven when we allocate 5% to value. As I noted earlier, value is pretty mediocre on a standalone basis, as attested by the first column of the table. Perhaps the only light on this particular dark horizon is a modestly positive alpha, thanks to its negative beta.

TABLE 99: PERFORMANCE FOR VALUE, TREND AND CARRY

	Strategy twenty-two Value	Strategy eleven Trend (60%) & carry (40%)	Strategy twenty-two Trend (60%), carry (35%) & value (5%)
Mean annual return (net)	−1.0%	26.5%	27.0%
Costs	−0.8%	−1.1%	−1.1%
Average drawdown	−66.7%	−8.9%	−9.1%
Standard deviation	16.8%	20.9%	21.0%
Sharpe ratio	−0.06	1.27	1.29
Turnover	11.7	46.5	48.5
Skew	0.21	0.76	0.82
Lower tail	1.32	1.86	1.89
Upper tail	1.49	1.75	1.74
Annualised alpha (net)	2.9%	22.3%	22.6%
Beta	−0.25	0.30	0.31

Looking at the final two columns shows a different story. We have indeed achieved financial alchemy: adding a diversifying money losing strategy has actually improved the performance of strategy eleven, although not by much. Because the improvement is entirely down to correlations, which are relatively predictable, you should be fairly confident that the additional returns can be earned in the future.

Value in futures markets is unlikely to be as effective as in equities, and is nowhere near good enough to trade on a standalone basis. Still, there are modest benefits to be earned by including a small allocation to value in your suite of trading strategies.

Strategy twenty-two: Trading plan

All other stages are identical to strategy nine

Strategy	Go long or short one or more instruments with variable risk estimate and a forecast based on mean reversion in outperformance over the last five years.
Instrument(s)	Any that meet minimum capital, liquidity and cost thresholds.
Choose trading rules for each instrument	Only choose trading rule variations where: $$\text{Turnover} < [0.15 - (\text{Cost per trade}$$ $$\times \text{Rolls per year})] \div \text{Cost per trade}$$ Turnover of the value rule with horizon, $H = 5$ years is 8.7.
Outperformance for a given horizon H	We begin with the volatility normalised daily price for a given instrument (strategy seventeen) PN and the normalised price for the relevant asset class A for that instrument (strategy eighteen). The relative price, R, for some instrument i on day t will be: $$R_{i,t} = P^N_{i,t} - A_{i,t}$$ For horizon H in years, assuming there are around 256 business days in a year, the average outperformance will be: $$\text{Outperformance}_H = (R_{i,t} - R_{i,t-(256 \times H)}) \div (256 \times H)$$
Raw forecast for a given horizon H	$$\text{Forecast} = \text{EWMA}_{span=30}(-\text{Outperformance}_H)$$
Forecast scalar	Forecast scalar is 7.27 for horizon, $H = 5$ years.

Acceleration

I occasionally co-host a podcast[219] with some other traders. We share a fondness for trend following, but have different philosophies about many other things. However, there is one thing we can agree on: probably the most difficult time to be a trend follower is when a trend has clearly started, but our lagging entry rules have yet to wake up to this new reality. Stuck with the wrong position we are unable to benefit from the initial stage of the trend. The second most difficult time is when a trend has clearly ended, and we face the ignominy of holding on as the price starts to move against us.

An apparently easy solution to this is to trade variations of these rules which catch up quicker: faster look backs for exponentially weighted moving average crossovers, or shorter horizons for breakout rules. Unfortunately these faster strategies will often be too expensive to trade, and we risk encroaching on a time horizon where trend following no longer works as effectively.[220]

A better solution is to use the approach I introduced in strategy seven: forecasts which adjust their position size according to the strength of the trend, rather than holding a constant position and only closing it once the trend has clearly ended. Some of my fellow podcasters think this approach is heretical, but even if you are not ideologically opposed to it, it can only get you so far. You will still be on the wrong side when a trend reverses, although you will begin to cut your position faster if you are using forecasts.

One way to get round this could be to look at the *rate of change* in a trend following forecast. To borrow a metaphor from physics, a trend following forecast is effectively a measure of the *speed* and *direction* in a price. This implies that the rate of change of such a forecast will be the **acceleration** (or de-acceleration). We can use this acceleration measure as a forecast in its own right.

---

219 www.toptradersunplugged.com/podcasts/systematic-investor
220 Remember from strategy nine that pre-cost performance starts to degrade once we are down to the two fastest variations: EWMAC4 and EWMAC2. After cost returns look even worse.

Strategy twenty-three: A strategy that uses
acceleration: the rate of change in a trend forecast.

Defining acceleration

We start with some trend following forecast. In principle this could be anything, but let's stick to using the familiar exponentially weighted moving average crossover (EWMAC), which I defined in Part One. The forecast will be calculated using one of our six standard EWMAC pairings: EWMAC(2,8), EWMAC(4,16) and so on. Since all the EWMAC rules are in the form (N,4N) I only need to specify the faster moving average: N. Such a forecast will be positive if there is a bullish trend established, and negative in a bearish environment.

$$\text{Raw EWMAC forecast}_{N,t} = (\text{EWMA}_{N,t} - \text{EWMA}_{4N,t}) \div \sigma_{p,t}$$

Forecasts are also scaled to ensure they have an average absolute value of 10:

$$\text{Forecast}_{N,t} = \text{Raw forecast}_{N,t} \times \text{EWMAC forecast scalar}_N$$

We now consider the rate of change in the forecast over some arbitrary number of business days. For simplicity and to avoid fitting any additional parameters, I'm going to look at the change that occurs over the span of the EWMAC faster moving average N.[221] This gives us the following definition:

$$\text{Raw acceleration}_{N,t} = \text{Forecast}_{N,t} - \text{Forecast}_{N,t-N}$$

Because the EWMAC forecast is already divided by the annual standard deviation of returns we don't need to apply another risk adjustment, although for technical reasons the forecast will still need correctly scaling so we apply another forecast scalar:

$$\text{Acceleration}_{N,t}$$
$$= \text{Raw acceleration}_{N,t} \times \text{Acceleration forecast scalar}_N$$

This will be different from the forecast scalar that is used in the original rule. Forecast

---

[221] As usual when I chose an arbitrary parameter I also performed some sensitivity analysis to check that I hadn't just been lucky, and that performance wasn't too dependent on the parameter being exactly the same as the fast moving average span.

scalars[222] for different variations of the acceleration forecast are given in table 100. It turns out that acceleration2 and acceleration4 are prohibitively expensive to trade, with turnovers that are much higher than those for EWMAC2, so I only use four acceleration rule variations.

TABLE 100: FORECAST SCALARS FOR DIFFERENT SPEEDS OF ACCELERATION

	Forecast scalars
Acceleration8	1.87
Acceleration16	1.90
Acceleration32	1.98
Acceleration64	2.05

It is helpful to think about the four possible scenarios we can get with the combination of a trend following and acceleration forecast:

1. Trend negative, Acceleration negative: A bearish trend is getting more bearish.

2. Trend negative, Acceleration positive: The bearish trend becomes less bearish, indicating it could be about to end.

3. Trend positive, Acceleration positive: An established bullish trend is getting more bullish.

4. Trend positive, Acceleration negative: A bullish trend is getting less bullish, indicating it could be near the end.

In scenarios one and three the two forecasts agree with each other, suggesting we should have a larger position on. Scenarios two and four are giving us mixed messages, which would imply a smaller position.

An example will make things clearer. Consider figure 76, which shows the price of Bitcoin futures in late 2020 and early 2021. They were rallying for most of this period, before the trend ended in April 2021.

---

222   Notice the pattern first seen in strategy nine, whereby these scalars change by the square root of two as we double or halve the speed of the rule.

FIGURE 76: BACK-ADJUSTED PRICE OF BITCOIN FUTURES

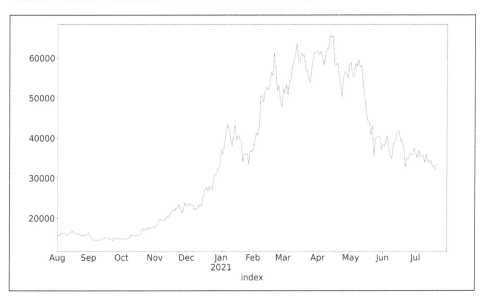

Now look at the raw forecasts shown in figure 77. The dark grey EWMAC64 trend forecast is long throughout this period, remaining bullish even though the market has clearly turned. On the upside we do reduce our forecast as the trend becomes unclear. But we'd still be making losses, even though they are smaller than if our forecast had remained constant. The relevant acceleration64 forecast is also long until June 2021, so we are initially in scenario three: a bullish trend that is getting more bullish. However, once the trend forecast has been slowing for a few weeks it turns negative indicating a shift to scenario four: a weakening bullish trend.

FIGURE 77: RAW FORECASTS OF EWMAC64 AND ACCELERATION64 FOR BITCOIN FUTURES

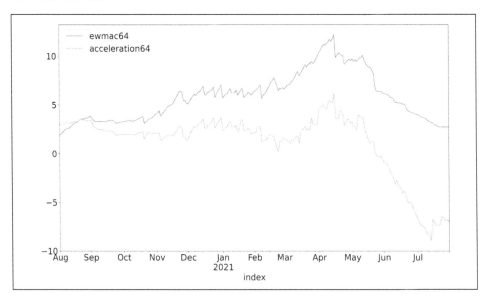

A potential criticism of my formulation for acceleration is that it will be too similar to the EWMAC trading rules from which it is constructed. To address this accusation I calculated the correlation[223] between the returns of the various speeds of EWMAC and acceleration. The results are shown in table 101. They were derived using the aggregate returns of the Jumbo portfolio, but returns for any randomly chosen individual instrument will show a similar pattern.

All the correlations are low enough that we can be confident that these rules are doing fairly different things. As a comparison, if you have read the chapter for the normalised trend strategy seventeen, you will know that it has a correlation with mixed trend (strategy nine) of 0.97; nothing here is over 0.76.

---

223   There is an interesting pattern whereby a given acceleration rule with speed N usually has the highest correlation with the EWMAC rule that has a slow EWMA span of N. So acceleration8 is most similar to EWMAC2,8; acceleration16 has a close cousin in EWMAC4,16, and so on.

TABLE 101: CORRELATION MATRIX OF RETURNS FOR ACCELERATION AND EWMAC FORECASTING RULES

	Acceleration8	Acceleration16	Acceleration32	Acceleration64
EWMAC2,8	0.72	0.56	0.38	0.18
EWMAC4,16	0.69	0.75	0.58	0.31
EWMAC8,32	0.40	0.71	0.76	0.50
EWMAC16,64	0.08	0.38	0.68	0.66
EWMAC32,128	−0.07	0.09	0.39	0.63
EWMAC64,256	−0.07	−0.02	0.09	0.33

The performance of acceleration

Next, let us examine the performance of the different horizons which are shown in table 102 for an aggregate Jumbo portfolio. As in previous chapters I haven't yet excluded any instruments which are too expensive to trade a given variation, so these figures can be compared directly with tables 30 and 31 (pages 178 and 179), which have the analogous statistics for the EWMAC trend strategy. From the previous section, the best comparison for an acceleration variation with speed N is the EWMAC with a slow EWMA span of N. Hence, for example, we should compare acceleration8 with EWMA2,8.

Although profitable, none of these acceleration rules is as good as the EWMAC rule with which they are most closely matched. However, the acceleration rules have a much lower beta than EWMAC, suggesting they might be a useful diversifying strategy.

TABLE 102: PERFORMANCE FOR DIFFERENT ACCELERATION VARIATIONS

	Acceleration8	Acceleration16	Acceleration32	Acceleration64
Mean annual return (gross)	11.1%	17.5%	12.8%	13.1%
Mean annual return (net)	4.8%	14.1%	10.6%	11.2%
Costs	−6.2%	−3.3%	−2.2%	−1.9%
Average drawdown	>100%	−19.9%	−25.9%	−28.7%
Standard deviation	24.7%	24.1%	24.5%	24.4%
Sharpe ratio	0.20	0.59	0.43	0.46
Turnover	258.8	136.2	81.6	57.9
Skew	0.97	1.55	1.11	0.34
Lower tail	1.75	1.72	1.71	1.86
Upper tail	1.99	1.94	1.87	1.72
Annualised alpha (gross)	10.0%	15.6%	11.9%	11.8%
Annualised alpha (net)	3.8%	12.3%	9.7%	9.9%
Beta	0.07	0.13	0.07	0.09

Aggregated Jumbo portfolio results with all instruments included.

Trading a combined acceleration strategy

Next, I will follow my usual approach of combining the acceleration variations into a single strategy. I will not bore you with the details that you will have seen before. Table 103 has the forecast turnovers, which are required to determine which instruments can trade which variations of acceleration.

TABLE 103: FORECAST TURNOVERS FOR ACCELERATION

	Turnover
Acceleration8	64.0
Acceleration16	34.4
Acceleration32	20.9
Acceleration64	14.9

Now, let us look at the correlations between different variations of acceleration, which you can find in table 104. Notice that these are much lower than the correlations we have seen for EWMAC and other trading rules, where adjacent variations typically have correlations over 0.8. This suggests that we will get a decent improvement from trading multiple variations of acceleration, thanks to the availability of plenty of diversification.

TABLE 104: CORRELATIONS OF ACCELERATION VARIATIONS

	Acceleration8	Acceleration16	Acceleration32	Acceleration64
Acceleration8	1	0.53	0.07	−0.07
Acceleration16		1	0.51	0.04
Acceleration32			1	0.50
Acceleration64				1
Average versus other horizons	0.18	0.36	0.36	0.15

Table 105 has the forecast weights for a given set of acceleration forecasts. It also includes the forecast diversification multipliers (FDM). These are somewhat higher than for strategy nine, which uses multiple variations of the EWMAC rule: the highest FDM for strategy nine from table 36 (page 193) is just 1.26 (with six variations of EWMAC). Again, this is because of the relatively low correlations between variations of the acceleration rule.

TABLE 105: FORECAST WEIGHTS AND FORECAST DIVERSIFICATION MULTIPLIERS (FDM) FOR DIFFERENT SETS OF ACCELERATION RULES

	Forecast weight for each rule variation	FDM
Acceleration8, 16, 32, 64	0.25	1.55
Acceleration16, 32, 64	0.333	1.37
Acceleration32, 64	0.50	1.17
Acceleration64	1.0	1.0

We can now consider the performance of this combined acceleration strategy, which is shown in table 106. As usual I show the statistics for both the median individual instrument, and the aggregate figures for the Jumbo portfolio. A useful benchmark would be table 39 on page 196 which has the aggregate results for strategy nine trading a combination of EWMAC forecasts. The combined strategy for acceleration does well enough, but is not quite as good as EWMAC, although the monthly skew is identical.

Perhaps the most striking result here is the improvement from the median instrument, which is barely profitable, to the aggregate portfolio. The Sharpe ratio (SR) increases by a factor of nine! This is certainly the largest diversification benefit we have seen so far: for strategy nine the same increase was just under five. However, the skew does not show a similar improvement, since the median for an individual instrument is already relatively high.

TABLE 106: PERFORMANCE OF COMBINED ACCELERATION TRADING RULE: MEDIAN ACROSS INSTRUMENTS AND AGGREGATE JUMBO PORTFOLIO

	Median average across instruments	Aggregate Jumbo portfolio
Mean annual return	1.4%	16.7%
Costs	−0.7%	−1.9%
Average drawdown	−32.7%	−17.2%
Standard deviation	24.8%	23.2%
Sharpe ratio	0.08	0.72
Turnover	24.9	99
Skew	0.94	0.98
Lower tail	3.05	1.77
Upper tail	3.09	1.91

Acceleration with carry and trend

As I did with breakout and value, I will test the effect of adding acceleration to the carry and trend strategy that I introduced in strategy eleven. I will use the usual top down method for allocating forecast weights:

- Our two styles are convergent and divergent. I allocate 40% to convergent and 60% to divergent, for consistency with strategy eleven.

Within trading styles:

- We have one convergent trading rule. I allocate 40% to carry.

- We have two divergent trading rules: EWMAC, which receives 30% of the allocation, and acceleration, which gets the other 30%.

Within carry:

- We have up to four variations of carry, which share 40% equally between them.

Within acceleration:

- We have up to four variations, which share 30% equally.

Within EWMAC:

- We have up to six variations of the EWMAC rule, which share 60% equally.

With forecast weights in hand I ran the backtest and got the results shown in table 107.

TABLE 107: PERFORMANCE OF AGGREGATE JUMBO PORTFOLIO FOR CARRY, TREND AND ACCELERATION

	Strategy nine Multiple trend	Strategy twenty-one Acceleration	Strategy eleven Carry & trend	Strategy twenty-three Carry, acceleration & trend
Mean annual return	25.2%	16.7%	26.5%	26.9%
Costs	−1.2%	−1.9%	−1.1%	−1.3%
Average drawdown	−11.2%	−17.2%	−8.9%	−8.5%
Standard deviation	22.2%	23.2%	20.9%	20.9%
Sharpe ratio	1.14	0.72	1.27	1.29
Turnover	62.9	99	46.5	59.1
Skew	0.98	0.98	0.76	0.91
Lower tail	1.99	1.77	1.86	1.79
Upper tail	1.81	1.91	1.75	1.80
Alpha	18.8%	15.2%	22.3%	24.0%
Beta	0.43	0.11	0.30	0.22

Although costs are a little higher, thanks to the increased turnover brought in by acceleration, this is a pretty decent improvement on all other measures. It does seem like acceleration gives us an edge when added to the basic carry and trend strategies from Part One.

Strategy twenty-three: Trading plan

All other stages are identical to strategy nine

Strategy	Go long or short one or more instruments with variable risk estimate and a forecast based on the difference between two trend forecasts.
Instrument(s)	Any that meet minimum capital, liquidity and cost thresholds.
Choose trading rules for each instrument	Only choose trading rule variations where: $$\text{Turnover} < [0.15 - (\text{Cost per trade}$$ $$\times \text{ Rolls per year})] \div \text{Cost per trade}$$ Turnover figures are in table 103.
Trading rule variations	Construct one or more acceleration forecasts built from EWMAC(N,4N) pairings where N is 8, 16, 32 or 64.
Raw forecast for a given variation N and instrument i	$$\text{Raw EWMAC forecast}_{N,i,t}$$ $$= (\text{EWMA}(N)_{i,t} - \text{EWMA}(4N)_{i,t}) \div \sigma_{p,i,t}$$ $$\text{EWMAC forecast}_{N,i,t}$$ $$= \text{Raw forecast}_{N,i,t} \times \text{EWMAC forecast scalar}_{N,i,,t}$$ $$\text{Raw forecast}_{N,i,t}$$ $$= \text{EWMAC forecast}_{N,i,t} - \text{EWMAC forecast}_{N,i,t-N}$$
Forecast scalars	Forecast scalars are in table 100.
Allocating forecast weights	See table 105.
Forecast diversification multipliers (FDM)	See table 105 for FDM values.

STRATEGY TWENTY-FOUR

Skew – A case study

I make no attempt in this book to cover every possible futures trading strategy: that would be impossible. So it's unlikely that this book will include every strategy that you might want to trade. If you are reading this book there are chances that you have some potential strategies that you have picked up elsewhere or invented yourself. Wouldn't it be nice to trade them alongside the strategies I've introduced here?

The aim of this chapter is to provide a guide to fitting 'any' trading strategy into the *forecasting* framework I've used in Parts One, Two and Three.[224] I've deliberately put 'any' in quotes because the strategy must conform to certain requirements. Primarily, it must use a quantifiable piece of data that can be transformed into a forecast. In addition to this, there are other desirable attributes that I will discuss throughout the chapter.

Because it's much easier to understand what is going on with an example, I'm going to use *skew* as a case study in this chapter. We already know from earlier chapters in Part One that assets with positive skew like the VIX future are likely to underperform over time, and vice versa. It seems plausible that traders and investors dislike negative skew and are thus willing to pay a risk premium to avoid holding it: a premium that we can earn by holding instruments that have negative skew. In this chapter I will show you how to turn this idea into a trading strategy.

> **Strategy twenty-four:** A strategy that buys assets with more negative skew, and goes short assets with more positive skew.

---

224 Due to space constraints this chapter doesn't go into significant detail on the subject of designing and fitting trading strategies. If you are seriously interested in designing your own strategies, then I would suggest reading my first book, *Systematic Trading*.

Step one: choose a strategy that makes sense

I like to trade strategies which make sense: I need to know *why* I'm making money. Often that involves identifying who is on the other side of my winning trades, and understanding why they are happy to lose – and keep losing. An important concept from Part One of this book was the idea of *risk premia*: being paid by the market for risks that the average investor or trader doesn't want to take. Strategies that deliver risk premia are my bread and butter. Does skew fit neatly into the category of risk premium strategy?

It's a yes from me. Most people *love* positively skewed instruments and are willing to pay over the odds to own them. Consider a lottery ticket, an asset with a very high positive skew. Most of the outcomes will involve a small loss, with a tiny possibility of a massive return. In most lotteries only about half the ticket prize goes into the prize fund, so the expected value of a $1 lottery ticket is only about 50 cents. Similarly, in a horse race the outsiders are normally priced at very poor odds. That 50-1 horse is more likely to be a 250-1 nag that is fit only for giving small children rides at the beach. In the world of finance, far out of the money options are marked up at a premium price, whilst moon-shot meme stocks trade on very high earnings multiples – assuming they have any earnings at all.

All this love for positive skewed assets implies that any negatively skewed asset should attract a risk premium,[225] and we would be paid handsomely to own it.

Step two: choose a robust and quantifiable statistic

We need to be able to calculate a quantifiable forecast to construct a trading strategy of the type used in this book. That rules out subjective chart patterns, unless we can use some kind of pattern recognition algorithm to recognise them. It will make it tricky to trade merger arbitrage: a strategy that requires judging whether a particular merger agreement is likely to pass regulatory hurdles and meet with regulatory approval. You will struggle to measure the mood in the earnings conference call when deciding whether to buy a stock, unless you use some kind of voice analysis software. But

---

225 None of this extensive empirical evidence explains why people love positive skew, but if that is a concern then we can use ideas from behavioural finance like prospect theory that justify this behaviour.

as long as you can come up with a number[226] that is correlated with your future expectation of price movements,[227] then you can construct a forecast.

The forecast should also be *robust*. Robust forecasts should not be too sensitive to small perturbations in the market. For example, using moving averages is more robust than using the underlying price, since a single daily return will only have a limited impact on the moving average. A good test of whether a strategy is robust is to add a small amount of noise to back-adjusted prices, before feeding them into your backtesting software. If the underlying forecast is robust then the resulting positions and performance will be mostly unchanged.

Let's now consider the case study we are using in this chapter: skew. Estimating skew is straightforward. Since we want our forecast to be time varying we will want to update our estimate every day (assuming we are using daily data). Theoretically we would only need a few observations to calculate skew, but to get a more accurate estimate we should probably use a few weeks of data as an absolute minimum. To avoid using information that is out of date, we probably don't want to use more than a year of data. This suggests that we should estimate skew over multiple horizons that will fall in an interval between one month and one year in length.

Now, is skew robust? Not especially. Consider the plot in figure 78. This shows an estimate of skew for the VIX future, estimated over rolling three-month periods. Notice how the skew moves down in late March 2020 when a single large negative daily return occurs on the day when the VIX fell sharply from a historically high level. The skew estimate moves up again in mid-June when that large return drops out of the rolling window. Of course this is an extreme example: not many instruments are as volatile as the VIX, and 2020 was an especially volatile year, but skew is certainly sensitive to the inclusion or exclusion of a few outlier returns.

---

226 This number could even be derived from a subjective opinion, as long as it can be quantified. In my earlier books on trading, *Systematic Trading* and *Leveraged Trading*, I introduced the idea of a *semi-automatic trader*. Such a trader will quantify their gut feeling for a given trade on a scale from –20 to +20, which corresponds to the forecast scaling I use: (a) an average absolute forecast of 10, (b) positive forecasts are bullish and negative are bearish, and (c) absolute forecasts are capped at a maximum of 20.

227 At this stage we aren't concerned about the forecast being proportional to the expected risk adjusted return: that will come later.

FIGURE 78: ROLLING ESTIMATE OF SKEW FOR VIX FUTURES

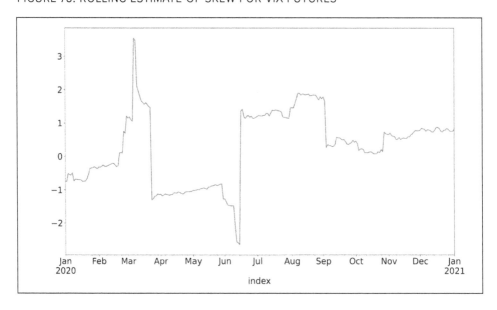

There are several steps we could take to address this. We could, for example, change the estimation of skew from a rolling window to an exponentially weighted window. There would still be a sharp fall in VIX skew in March 2020, but there would be a gradual return to normal over the following months rather than the sharp spike upwards in mid-June. Alternatively, we could use some more robust measure of skew that reduces the effect of outliers, such as the tail measures I introduced in strategy one.

For simplicity I decided to stick with the standard skew formula, but to reduce the impact of noisy returns I will limit myself to estimation windows that are at least three months in length. Following my usual practice of doubling horizons, spans and windows, this gives me a set of three variations for the skew strategy: three, six and 12-month windows. As I am working with data at business day frequency, I decided to use the following neat set of window lengths: 60 days, 120 days and 240 days. Naturally I could do some kind of optimisation to find the best performing estimation window, but that would invite over fitting and is unlikely to make much difference to the final results.

Since high positive skew implies poor expected returns, I just put a minus sign in front of the rolling skew estimate to get a raw forecast. For some series of percentage returns[228] in the back-adjusted price, r_t, with an estimation window, w, the forecast is:

---

228   Remember that in a backtest to calculate percentage returns you should take the difference between two daily back-adjusted prices, and divide by the current futures price at the time, *not* the back-adjusted price.

$$\text{Raw skew forecast}_{w,t} = -\text{Skew}(r_t, r_{t-1}, r_{t-2}, \dots r_{t-w+1})$$

The formula for skew is available in all common spreadsheet packages and most backtesting software.

Risk normalise to get a forecast

Back in strategy seven I defined a forecast as a **prediction for risk adjusted prices**. If we risk adjust by dividing by the standard deviation of returns, then the forecast will be **proportional to a prediction of the Sharpe ratio (SR)**. If done correctly, risk adjustment should result in a dimensionless forecast that can be directly compared across time periods and instruments.

Think back to the strategies introduced in Part One: trend and carry. For trend we took the difference between two moving averages, which are in price units. We then divided these by the standard deviation of changes in price. Since the units match, we end up with a dimensionless risk adjusted forecast. Similarly for carry, we calculated the carry as an expected change in price over a year. Again, dividing this by the standard deviation of daily prices resulted in a forecast that was risk adjusted.

Unusually, skew does not require any explicit risk adjustment. The standard formula for calculating a skew statistic already divides by the standard deviation. Hence we can directly compare estimates of skew for different instruments and across different time periods, and no further risk adjustment is required.

What type of strategy?

It's important to understand exactly how the effect we are hoping to capture with our trading strategy works. For example, consider some arbitrary forecast f which has already been risk adjusted. There are a number of different ways we could trade this forecast:

- Absolute: When f is positive we go long, when f is negative we go short.

- Demeaned: When f is larger than the global historical average (calculated across all assets and over all available history) we go long, when f is below that we go short.

- Relative: When f is larger than its historical average for the relevant instrument (calculated across all available history) we go long, when f is below that we go short.

- Cross-sectional: When f is larger than the current average forecast (calculated for the current time period, across all available assets) then we go long, when f is below that we go short.

- Asset class cross-sectional: When f is larger than the current asset class average forecast (calculated for the current time period, across all assets in the relevant asset class) then we go long, when f is below that we go short.

- Aggregated asset class: When the current asset class average forecast (calculated for the current time period, across all assets in the relevant asset class) is higher than the current average forecast for all instruments, then we go long all instruments in that asset class, otherwise short.

- Static: When the historical average of f for the relevant instrument (calculated across all available history) is larger than the historical average for all instruments, then we go long, otherwise short.

We have already seen examples of some of these strategy types. Both strategy nine (EWMAC trend) and ten (carry) use *absolute* forecasts. But if we wanted to reduce the normal positive beta of EWMAC, then we could use a *demeaned* forecast, so that we would only be long if the current trend was stronger than the average trend had been historically. Strategies nineteen and twenty in Part Two were both *asset class cross-sectional* strategies, for trend and carry respectively. We have also seen an *aggregated asset class* strategy: strategy eighteen.

The choice of strategy is not always straightforward. Obviously outright performance is important. For example, if you read Part Two you will know that most of the performance of trend occurs at the asset class level, so there is less value from using the asset class cross-sectional version of trend. But some traders may deliberately choose weaker strategy variations, if for example they have a lower beta. Lower beta strategies are likely to do better if secular market trends of the past are not repeated and for institutional traders may also be better suited to certain investor style mandates.

Some important words of warning: such a large variety of options is a gold embossed invitation to over fit your trading strategy. To avoid this you should focus only on variations which have sound logic behind them and that suit any preferences you have. Alternatively, if you do consider a large set of alternatives then you need to properly evaluate them without over fitting.[229]

Let's think about how these different strategy types could be used with skew. We know from Part One (tables 3 and 4 on pages 49 and 50) that most asset classes have negative skew, with the obvious exception of volatility instruments like VIX, and the less obvious exceptions of bond and agricultural markets (which on average have modestly positive skew). So if we traded an *absolute* skew measure, then we would have a bias towards long positions, except in those three asset classes. We would have

---

229   For example, in my own backtesting, I fit forecast weights using only backward looking data and a robust process. This means I can consider a very large pool of potential strategies without in sample fitting occurring.

more long positions in equities (median skew –0.78), but seriously short positions in volatility (skew 0.73). Additionally, if the average level of skew becomes more negative than usual, our average position would be longer than usual, and vice versa. Loading up on long positions in the aftermath of a systemic market crash that caused skew to fall across the board is risky but also tends to be profitable. This source of profits is known as **global timing**.

Demeaning would remove the long bias in the backtest, resulting in lower outright performance, but probably producing a lower beta and perhaps a better alpha. But it would do nothing about the biases across different asset classes.

A *relative* skew strategy would expect to have an average position of zero in any given instrument.[230] We would go long instruments that have recently experienced significant negative skew relative to their own history. This would also remove the bias in positions across different asset classes. However, that bias is also a source of value. Apart from bonds, which unusually have positive skew and a high SR, there is an almost perfect negative correlation between skew and performance in tables 3 and 4 (pages 49 and 50) across asset classes.

Cross-sectional skew would always have a zero net forecast across all instruments in our data set at any given moment. Asset class biases would remain, and we would profit from them, but we would not benefit from global timing. If we use *asset class cross-sectional* skew, then we would remove asset class biases but could still have biases on positions within asset classes. For example, we would expect emerging market FX to have lower skew than developed markets, unless we split the FX asset class up for the purposes of this strategy. We'd also still lack the ability to globally time skew.

Aggregated asset class skew implies we would maintain asset class bias and benefit from global timing, but would lose the ability to earn anything from cross-sectional skew within asset classes. But it might make sense to trade this plus asset class cross-sectional skew, since then we can optimise the risk allocation between these two sources of return.

Finally, a *static* strategy might seem an odd choice since we would never change our forecast.[231] The asset class biases for skew would be permanently baked in, and we wouldn't benefit from any timing effects. I suppose such a strategy might be attractive to a risk parity style investor who wishes to earn the risk premium from skew without doing too much trading.

---

230 Note this is only an expectation, and even in a backtest it's unlikely we would hit exactly zero. Consider for example an instrument with a relatively short history during which the level of skew is always rising. Since the average skew to date will always be less than the current estimate of skew, there would be a persistent upward bias in the forecast.

231 Actually, assuming we estimated the average skew for an instrument by looking at all available historical data, we would gradually change our forecasts over time.

You can see from this discussion that strategy selection should mostly involve considering which types of risk you are prepared to take, and be paid for, and which you want to avoid. It is not just about selecting the strategy variant that has the highest backtested SR. To keep things simple, and to avoid over fitting, I will stick to the most basic form of the skew strategy in this chapter: **absolute skew**. This means we will go long if a skew estimate is below zero, and go short if it is above zero.

Slow down the forecast

Every forecast has an optimal trading frequency. This frequency is effectively the point **where if it trades any slower there will be a degradation of after costs performance**. It's unlikely that the raw forecast will already have the optimal turnover, unless it has been designed with smoothing baked in, as we do with EWMAC. For example, the raw carry forecast I developed in strategy ten is extremely noisy and can be slowed down considerably without affecting its performance.

There are many ways to slow down a trading strategy, but I have generally stuck to using an exponentially weighted moving average (EWMA) of the raw forecast. In previous strategies I avoided calibrating the span parameter which dictates the degree of smoothing in an EWMA, and I have no intention of changing my approach here. I arbitrarily set the span at a quarter of the length of the skew estimation horizon. For some window w that is either 60, 120 or 240 days the smoothed forecast will be:

$$\text{Smoothed skew forecast}_{w,t}$$
$$= \text{EWMA}_{\text{span}=w\div4}(\text{Raw skew forecast}_{w,t})$$

Applying the smooth reduces the turnover of skew60 by two-thirds without damaging performance. It has similarly dramatic effects on the other two skew variations.

Check distribution: scale and cap the forecast

We now have a forecast that is robust, doesn't change too quickly and is risk normalised. However, it is unlikely it will meet the requirement to have an average absolute value of 10. We need to estimate the forecast scalar to ensure the forecast is correctly scaled. For some forecasts we can work out roughly what the scalar should be without necessarily estimating it from the data: an example would be the breakout forecast discussed in strategy twenty-one. But usually we will use historical data from a backtest to measure the actual average absolute forecast in our backtest, and from that derive the forecast scalar.

If we have done our job properly, then we can and should pool the history of the forecast estimate over all the instruments with available data, by stacking the forecast history for each instrument so we have a single data series. It is also helpful at this stage to get a feel for the shape of the distribution of forecasts. It's better to have a 'nice' distribution for forecasts: Gaussian normal is ideal, but failing that something without serious kurtosis, skew or biases would be acceptable. I check the distribution at this stage rather than earlier, since smoothing can improve the forecast distribution by reducing the effect of outliers. However, if there are serious problems with the distribution, then they will need to be fixed by modifying the raw forecast.

Figure 79 shows the distribution of the skew60 forecast, pooled across all the instruments in the Jumbo portfolio. It is clearly not Gaussian – but I have seen worse.

FIGURE 79: POOLED DISTRIBUTION OF SMOOTHED SKEW FORECAST BEFORE SCALING

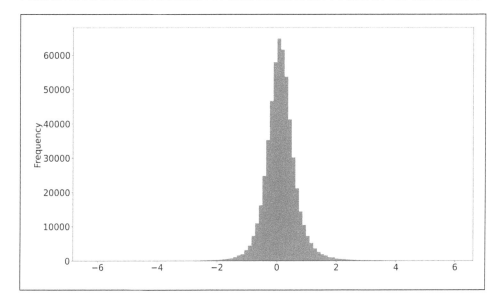

The mean of the forecast is slightly positive, but we knew that would be the case since the average instrument in our data set has slightly negative skew on average. A seriously biased forecast mean would result in a forecast scalar that is potentially wrong.[232]

The distribution does have some seriously fat tails; however, these will be dealt with by forecast capping. Ironically, the distribution of skew forecasts is itself skewed. It has a

---

232 Consider an upwardly biased forecast that had a Gaussian distribution with a mean of +5, and a standard deviation of 5. On the face of it, the forecast scaling should be around 2, since that will produce a forecast distribution with a standard deviation of 10. However, the average absolute value of the original forecast will be around 5.8, resulting in an estimated forecast scalar of around 1.7. If the bias in the backtest is not present in the future, then the scaled forecast will have an average absolute value of around 8.5, less than the intended value of 10.

small amount of positive skew – since the forecast is the skew with a minus sign this suggests that the distribution of skew is slightly negatively skewed. Still, there are no weird lumps in the distribution which would suggest serious problems; for example, a bi-modal distribution with two humps would be difficult to use as a forecast.

From the distribution, the average absolute value of the forecast is 0.30, suggesting we should use a forecast scalar of 10 ÷ 0.3 = 33.3. As I have done previously, we also need to *cap* the scaled forecast at an average absolute value of +20. This implies that any skew with an absolute value larger than 20 ÷ 33.3 = 0.6 will produce a capped forecast.

What about the other skew rules, skew120 and skew240? In fact, they have slightly nicer distributions, since the effect of outliers is dampened by the use of longer estimation windows and higher spans for smoothing. This also reduces the average absolute value of their distributions, which is pushed up by outliers for skew60. As a result the appropriate forecast scalars are a little higher: 37.2 for skew120 and 39.2 for skew240.

Now we have the scaled forecasts, we can estimate the forecast turnovers, which we use to see which instruments are cheap enough to trade a given variation. Again, these figures can be calculated by averaging across multiple instruments to get a more accurate result. The turnovers are quite low: 8.5 for skew60, 4.0 for skew120 and 1.9 for skew240.

Evaluate the strategy: individual variations

At this stage we haven't done any backtesting. This is deliberate. If you use backtests to design your strategy, you will risk over fitting. The only data we have used is the time series of the estimated skew, to get an idea of its properties and to estimate the forecast scalar and turnover. Indeed, if the strategy you are testing is something that you have successfully traded for many years, or which has been researched in an academic paper, you might just get away without doing any backtesting at all.

Usually though we would want to make a final check of the performance and other behaviour of the strategy, to see what we are letting ourselves in for. Table 108 shows the backtested results for the three variations of the skew strategy.

TABLE 108: PERFORMANCE FOR DIFFERENT SPEEDS OF SKEW TRADING RULE

	Skew60	Skew120	Skew240
Mean annual return (gross)	14.4%	17.9%	17.0%
Mean annual return (net)	13.0%	16.9%	16.1%
Costs	−1.4%	−1.1%	−0.9%
Average drawdown	−26.6%	−23.4%	−36.7%
Standard deviation	21.8%	22.6%	22.8%
Sharpe ratio	0.60	0.75	0.71
Turnover	43.6	25.6	18.1
Skew	−0.40	0.01	−0.10
Lower tail	1.71	1.73	1.74
Upper tail	1.61	1.50	1.51
Annualised alpha (gross)	8.8%	9.5%	7.0%
Annualised alpha (net)	7.4%	8.4%	6.1%
Beta	0.38	0.56	0.66

Using aggregate Jumbo portfolio with all instrument included.

You have seen enough of these tables to know what we are looking for:

- Is the strategy profitable before costs? Are there any patterns, such as performance improving as we slow down or speed up?

- Are the costs excessive?

- Is the turnover especially high?

- Is the strategy close to the standard deviation target of 20%?

- What are the other risk statistics like: skew, lower and upper tail?

- Is this just a long only strategy in disguise, with a high beta and low alpha? Or is it doing something quite different?

For the three skew variations we can draw the following conclusions:

- The strategy is profitable, with a reasonable SR. We'd expect a lower SR if we were looking at the average for a single market, rather than the Jumbo portfolio.

- Costs and turnover are reasonable. Turnover will always be higher for the Jumbo portfolio than for individual instruments, because it uses more leverage to take account of diversification across markets (this is achieved by the instrument diversification multiplier).

- Standard deviation is on target.

- Given the strategy deliberately buys assets with negative skew, we might expect to see negative skew here. In fact this is only a serious problem for the variation with the shortest horizon, skew60. This is because skew tends to mean revert after a few months, so we get approximately zero skew for the slower variations.

- Since in the backtest skew has been negative on average, we would expect to see a long bias here, resulting in high betas. As with trend, the long bias is more pronounced for slower variations of the forecast.

It's also useful to check the correlation of the three different skew horizons. That will help us decide whether we have the right number of variations. If correlations are very high, then we could probably simplify the strategy by removing some. If they are too low, then we could perhaps add some additional variations. It will also give us an indication as to whether my preferred option for weighting forecasts would be sensible: an equal weighting across all variations that are cheap enough to trade.

Table 109 has the correlation figures for skew. The values here are lower than for the trend variations in strategy nine, so there is perhaps space for some additional variations such as skew80, skew100, skew200 and so on.

TABLE 109: CORRELATION MATRIX OF RETURNS FOR DIFFERENT SKEW HORIZONS

	Skew60	Skew120	Skew240
Skew60	1	0.68	0.48
Skew120		1	0.76
Skew240			1

Evaluate the strategy: combined variations

Having produced a set of variations, we now need to check how they will perform in combination with each other. The details of this process appear in earlier strategies, so I will not repeat them. To do this we require the appropriate forecast diversification multipliers (FDM). With three variations of skew my estimate of the FDM is 1.18, with two variations 1.10, and with a single variant of any trading rule the FDM will always be equal to 1.

For skew in particular it makes sense to look at the statistics for instruments that live within different asset classes, since we know skew varies so much between them. Tables 110 and 111 have the figures, which as in previous chapters are the median for each statistic taken across instruments within the appropriate asset class, with a global median in the final column of the second table.

TABLE 110: PERFORMANCE FOR COMBINED SKEW: MEDIAN ACROSS INSTRUMENTS IN A GIVEN FINANCIAL ASSET CLASS

	Equity	Vol	FX	Bond
Mean annual return	8.9%	3.3%	4.2%	7.3%
Costs	−0.3%	−1.9%	−0.3%	−0.4%
Average drawdown	−21.7%	−46.6%	−36.1%	−24.3%
Standard deviation	28.7%	32.2%	26.9%	24.6%
Sharpe ratio	0.32	0.09	0.16	0.32
Turnover	7.9	8.3	8.0	7.7
Skew	−0.44	−2.21	−0.25	−0.20
Lower tail	2.81	2.89	2.72	2.56
Upper tail	1.98	1.58	2.26	2.30

TABLE 111: PERFORMANCE FOR COMBINED SKEW: MEDIAN ACROSS INSTRUMENTS IN A GIVEN COMMODITY ASSET CLASS

	Metals	Energy	Ags	Median
Mean annual return	8.4%	11.5%	1.6%	7.1%
Costs	−0.3%	−0.3%	−0.2%	−0.3%
Average drawdown	−70.5%	−33.7%	−58.8%	−28.4%
Standard deviation	29.7%	26.6%	20.0%	27.1%
Sharpe ratio	0.27	0.43	0.08	0.26
Turnover	8.2	6.9	6.6	7.7
Skew	0.37	−0.43	−0.06	−0.20
Lower tail	2.46	2.91	2.82	2.74
Upper tail	2.57	2.81	2.74	2.23

Performance is mixed, although all asset classes are profitable. Perhaps the most interesting figures to look at here are the standard deviation, skew and SR. A higher standard deviation indicates that the absolute size of the forecasts is larger in this asset class than on average. We can see that the volatility asset class has the highest standard deviation, which should not be unsurprising given it contains two instruments (VIX and VSTOXX) with almost permanently high positive skew.

The skew for vol instruments trading this strategy is also extremely negative. Again, this should not be a huge shock since we would have spent most of our time short volatility futures. But this does not produce a meaningfully high SR. From tables

10 and 11 (back on page 92), we could earn a median SR of 0.32 just by having a consistent and fixed short forecast for vol: here we get just 0.09. We must not forget there are only two volatility instruments in the Jumbo portfolio, so it could be difficult to draw meaningful conclusions.

Aside from volatility, however, there is no clear relationship across asset classes between standard deviation, skew and SR.

Once we understand what is going on at the level of an individual instrument, the next step is to look at the aggregate performance of the Jumbo portfolio with over 100 instruments. Table 112 has the statistics, and I have added some figures for previous strategies to provide some benchmarks.

TABLE 112: PERFORMANCE OF AGGREGATE JUMBO PORTFOLIO FOR LONG ONLY, TREND, CARRY AND SKEW STRATEGIES

	Strategy four Long only	Strategy nine Multiple trend	Strategy ten Carry	Strategy twenty-four Skew long/ short
Mean annual return	15.4%	25.2%	19.7%	17.9%
Costs	−0.8%	−1.2%	−0.8%	−0.9%
Average drawdown	−24.7%	−11.2%	−18.6%	−28.4%
Standard deviation	18.2%	22.2%	20.8%	22.4%
Sharpe ratio	0.85	1.14	0.94	0.80
Turnover	20.7	62.9	19.2	23.9
Skew	−0.04	0.98	0.41	0.14
Lower tail	1.44	1.99	1.57	1.72
Upper tail	1.24	1.81	1.49	1.52
Alpha	0	18.8%	19.1%	8.5%
Beta	1.0	0.43	0.06	0.62

Skew is certainly not as good as trend or carry, in fact it doesn't do as well as a dumb long only strategy. This is despite trend and skew having very similar average performance for an individual instrument. Do you remember the magic of diversification? Going from a single instrument to the Jumbo portfolio leads to an almost five-fold improvement in SR for trend in strategy nine. For the skew strategy the improvement is smaller: from 0.26 for the median individual instrument in table 111, to 0.80 for the Jumbo portfolio in table 112. That is a three-fold increase, which isn't bad, but does suggest that there is significantly less diversification benefit available here than in strategy nine.

It's also helpful to plot the performance of a strategy against its peers, which I've done in figure 80. You can see that skew suffers the same drawdown as the long only strategy in the early 1980s. But in the early 2000s it outperforms everything. This was the time of the 'great moderation' when the riskiest financial assets were deemed to be safe: a prime example being debt secured on US mortgages. Of course this ended badly for the US mortgage market, but the skew strategy only suffered a small setback before continuing to make profits until the COVID-19 pandemic hit markets in early 2020.

FIGURE 80: CUMULATIVE PERFORMANCE OF SKEW WITH OTHER TRADING STRATEGIES

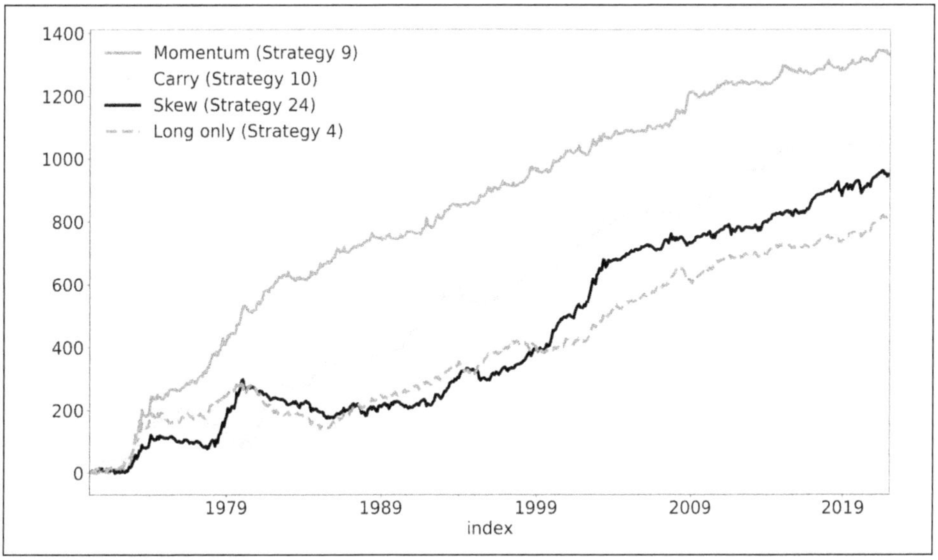

Evaluate the strategy: with other strategies

We are not quite done. Many strategies aren't that great in isolation, but do well when traded together since they add diversification. Take the value strategy in strategy twenty-two. It actually lost money, but still improved upon carry and trend when it was given a modest allocation. Skew is not a money loser, but still offers excellent diversification. The correlation of the combined skew strategy with both strategy nine (trend) and ten (carry) is very low: around 0.14.

I will follow my usual approach of using strategy eleven, which trades both carry and trend, as a benchmark. To add skew to carry and trend we just need to decide whether it is a *convergent* strategy like carry or value; or a *divergent* strategy such as trend, breakout or acceleration. Returns from the skew strategy are equally uncorrelated with trend and value, so there is no clear evidence for this decision. However, given that negative skew assets tend to do badly during market crises, it seems most appropriate to put it into the convergent bucket.

This will produce a forecast weight of 20% for skew, since it will take half of the 40% I usually allocate to convergent strategies, with carry picking up the remainder.

Table 113 has the good news. As we would expect, adding a strategy with low correlation and reasonably good SR like skew, results in a significant improvement to our performance. The improvement isn't as good if we look at alpha, since there is definitely more of a long bias than before. And of course the positive skew of monthly returns that we have come to expect from a strategy dominated by trend has been reduced slightly. But skew is a worthy addition to our list of strategies, as well as being a useful example to use as a case study.

TABLE 113: PERFORMANCE OF AGGREGATE JUMBO PORTFOLIO FOR CARRY, TREND AND ACCELERATION

	Strategy twenty-four Skew	Strategy eleven Carry and trend	Strategy twenty-four Carry, trend and skew
Mean annual return	17.9%	26.5%	28.9%
Costs	−0.9%	−1.1%	−1.2%
Average drawdown	−28.4%	−8.9%	−8.4%
Standard deviation	22.4%	20.9%	21.0%
Sharpe ratio	0.80	1.27	1.38
Turnover	23.9	46.5	56.1
Skew	0.14	0.76	0.62
Lower tail	1.72	1.86	1.85
Upper tail	1.52	1.75	1.67
Alpha	8.5%	22.3%	22.5%
Beta	0.62	0.30	0.44

Some other trading strategies and why I don't trade them

There are many more strategies that I could have discussed which would seem to fall under the remit of Part Three, but which aren't included here. I will highlight two types of strategy which I don't trade myself, but which are quite popular and you might have expected to find in this book.

Firstly, I've excluded any strategies that exploit seasonal and calendar effects. These are popular in the energy and agricultural markets, where different seasons produce different weather patterns which could affect prices. But they are also surprisingly popular in the equity and bond markets, where for many years there was a cottage industry of academic researchers producing papers about the 'January effect' (stocks usually go up in January), the 'Turn of month effect' (stocks inevitably rise in the last few days of the month) and the 'Friday effect' (you can probably guess what happens at the end of the working week).

I have a few issues with these types of strategies. For a start, they are likely to work in different ways on different markets. For example, equity calendar effects seem to be related to tax optimisation, and different countries have different tax year ends. It seems likely that seasonality would affect Corn and Natural Gas markets differently.

I would rather not run a different set of strategies for each instrument without strong evidence that this was the right approach. To do this properly would require a seriously complicated backtest, where each instrument was allowed to choose from a large menu of alternatives based only on historical returns. For example, to test a generic calendar effect we'd need at least 12 different strategies: one for each month. With so many options I would expect to find some strong patterns just through luck, making it difficult to distinguish between these and any real seasonality in the data.

Finally, I am a sceptic that such strategies are likely to work in the future, even if they have worked in the backtest. The day of the week or month of the year is information that everyone knows. Tax effects aside, there is also no obvious reason why people would need a risk premium to hold certain assets at certain times of the year or on some days of the week. These strategies seem to mostly rely on people knowingly doing something dumb. Probably at some point in history large pension funds always reallocated between bonds and equities on a single day, producing a turn of month effect. This might have worked in the past, but nowadays very few large pension funds are consistently stupid.

The second type of strategy I have studiously avoided is any sort of cross market forecasting. An example would be using the returns in the USD/GBP FX rate to predict those in the FTSE 100, perhaps on the grounds that the FX market is more efficient than the UK equity market. (Note: this is quite different from trading two or more instruments in a *relative value* strategy, which I consider in Part Five.) It's easy to think of periods when such a strategy would have succeeded. For example, the 2008 equity market crash was presaged by a severe crisis in the credit markets that occurred almost a year earlier.

My objections here are similar to those for calendar and seasonality. Most of the popular strategies of this type are very specific to certain sets of markets, about which plausible anecdotes can be told. Once again, to properly test all possible alternatives would require a huge amount of effort: with 100 instruments for a single prediction lag I'd need to test $100^2 - 100 = 9,900$ strategies. By pure chance many hundreds of these would look like plausible strategies, regardless of their actual merit.

As with seasonality and calendar effects, I am extremely sceptical about the future performance of cross market strategies. There is no good reason to think why one particular instrument should be *consistently* more efficient than another at digesting market news.

Strategy twenty-four: Trading plan

All other stages are identical to strategy nine

Strategy	Go long or short one or more instruments with variable risk estimate and a forecast based on skew, going long negative skewed and short positive skewed assets.
Instrument(s)	Any that meet minimum capital, liquidity and cost thresholds.
Choose trading rules for each instrument	Turnovers: 8.5 for skew60, 4.0 for skew120 and 1.9 for skew240.
Forecast calculation for skew with window _w_	For some series of daily percentage returns, r_t, (where percentages are calculated by taking the difference in back-adjusted prices, and dividing by the price of the futures contract that was actively traded at that time):

Raw skew forecast$_{w,t}$

$$= -\text{Skew}(r_t, \ r_{t-1}, \ r_{t-2}, \ \dots \ r_{t-w+1})$$

Skew forecast$_{w,t}$

$$= \text{EWMA}_{\text{span}=w \div 4}(\text{Raw skew forecast}_{w,t})$$

Forecast scalars	Forecast scalars, skew60 = 33.3, skew120 = 37.2, skew240 = 39.2
Forecast diversification multipliers	With three skew variations: 1.18.
	With two skew variations: 1.10.
	With one skew variation: 1.00.

STRATEGY TWENTY-FIVE

Dynamic optimisation (for when you can't trade the Jumbo portfolio)

I would imagine that one of the most surprising parts of this book was when I revealed the benefits available from diversifying beyond a single instrument to the Jumbo portfolio, which contains around 100 futures markets. It is not unreasonable to expect your risk adjusted returns to double, triple or even quadruple when you move from one to 100 instruments. Indeed, in strategy nine we see an almost *five-fold* improvement.

There are very few things in finance that will quadruple your expected performance, which is why large hedge funds trading futures make every effort to include as many markets as possible in their portfolios. Indeed, many of them have gone beyond futures to over the counter (OTC) markets such as FX forwards and interest rate swaps.

This is all well and good if you have the minimum account size of $50 million, which I estimate is sufficient to trade the Jumbo portfolio. But almost all retail traders, and quite a few institutions, will fall short of this. I am not giving away much private financial information when I tell you that my own trading account doesn't quite run to the level where I could trade the Jumbo portfolio!

In strategy four I already outlined a process for selecting a *static* set of instruments which would give you the best bang for your limited buck. But there is an alternative. What if it were possible to notionally trade the 100 or so instruments in the Jumbo portfolio, but then *dynamically* select the set of instruments that gave you the best possible portfolio on any given day, given your limited capital? Such a strategy could allow someone with a relatively small account to achieve performance that is almost as good as a large hedge fund.[233]

---

[233] Note that it isn't possible to employ this kind of strategy if you trade in the typical fashion used by most traders, with discrete trades, rather than by continuously calculating optimal positions and then trading to achieve them.

Strategy twenty-five: Dynamically optimise the
positions produced by an underlying trading strategy
to make best use of limited capital.

Health warning: It would be almost impossible to run this strategy without coding it up using a programming language. Sample python code for this strategy is available from the website for this book. This chapter also includes the most sophisticated mathematics in the book: you will need to be familiar with covariance matrices, vectors and dot multiplication.

The problem of small trading accounts

Suppose we are trading the Jumbo portfolio with some arbitrary set of trading rules. Assuming we are trading once a day, we'd get the closing prices for each instrument, and then do all of our calculations to calculate the *optimal position*. The size of these optimal positions will depend on the capital in our account. For example, with $50 million we might be long 14.2 S&P 500 contracts, which we can happily round to 14 futures contracts. But with a $100,000 trading account our optimal position will be just 0.0284 contracts, which rounds to precisely nothing: no position. With the 100+ instruments from the Jumbo portfolio, but only $100,000 to trade them, it is likely that most – if not all – of your positions would be rounded to zero.

Earlier in the book I suggested applying a minimum capital level to ensure you could trade a given instrument. An implication of this is that you have to choose a small subset of the Jumbo portfolio to trade with. This means you will be unable to benefit from all the potential diversification benefits of the Jumbo portfolio, resulting in lower expected returns and poorer Sharpe ratios (SRs).

You are also likely to suffer regret if profits in a given year are confined to one or more instruments that you couldn't manage to squeeze into your portfolio. For example, a small account might only trade one instrument from the FX asset class. But as I write this in the first few months of 2022, the only FX future in the Jumbo portfolio which has done anything interesting is JPY/USD. Imagine how you would feel if you did not select that as your sole representative of the FX asset class!

Optimising for the best portfolio

How does dynamic optimisation solve this problem? It does the following: every day we will calculate the best possible set of positions that can be held, given that positions in futures markets can only be integers. The best set of positions are those that most closely match the optimal, unrounded portfolio of positions.[234]

We need to introduce some formal notation. Suppose that we have a set of optimal unrounded positions in each instrument, where N_i is the unrounded number of contracts of instrument i that we would ideally hold. These will have been calculated using the trading capital that we have available, using combined forecasts, instrument weights and the instrument diversification multiplier (IDM). Importantly, these positions will be *before* buffering has been applied, since buffering requires knowledge of the positions we currently hold. Since we can't hold positions in unrounded amounts, it is nonsensical to consider buffered unrounded positions.

It turns out to be more natural to perform this optimisation using *portfolio weights*, where a portfolio weight is equal to the notional value of a position as a proportion of our trading capital. For example, a portfolio weight of say +0.50 would mean we had a long position whose notional value was equal to half our capital. Recycling some formulae from strategy two, we define a portfolio weight for a given instrument i as:

$$\text{Optimal unrounded portfolio weight, } w_i$$
$$= N_i \times \text{Weight per contract}_i$$

$$\text{Weight per contract}_i$$
$$= \text{Notional exposure per contract}_i \div \text{Capital}$$

$$\text{Notional exposure per contract}_i$$
$$= \text{Multiplier}_i \times \text{Price}_i \times \text{FX rate}_i$$

Our objective is to find the best set of weights, w^*_i, for which we minimise the standard deviation of the **tracking error portfolio**. This standard deviation is calculated using the two sets of weights and the covariance of asset percentage returns. Furthermore, the covariance is calculated from the correlation and annualised standard deviation of percentage returns for the underlying instruments, *not* the trading sub-strategies.

$$\text{Tracking error weight } e_i = w^*_i - w_i$$

---

234   I am very grateful to Doug Hohner who contacted me after reading on my blog about some early research into this problem that had failed miserably. It was his idea to use the objective of minimising the tracking error with the greedy algorithm, and then to apply a cost penalty and use buffering on the final positions to reduce costs further. I have made several modifications to his methodology, so naturally any flaws with this strategy are entirely my responsibility.

Vector of tracking errors e = [e_0, e_1, e_2, ...]

Covariance of asset percentage returns = $\Sigma = \sigma^T . \rho . \sigma$

Standard deviation of tracking error portfolio = $\sqrt{(e^T . \Sigma . e)}$

Note that T is the transposition operator, and the dots (.) in the final formula are matrix dot multiplication.

Because we can only take integer positions, our w^* must be in whole units of weight per contract. So for example if the weight per contract in a given instrument is 0.32, then we can only have a w^* which is one of the following values: ..., –0.96, –0.64, –0.32, 0, +0.32, +0.64, +0.96, ... and so on.

The correlation matrix ρ and the annualised standard deviation σ are both calculated from the percentage returns of all the instruments we are trading. Recall from Part One that we calculate daily percentage returns in the following way: given a back-adjusted price, p, and the price of the traded futures contract on the appropriate day, F:

Percentage return, $r_{\%t} = (p_t - p_{t-1}) \div F_{t-1}$

To find the standard deviation we use the standard method introduced in strategy three: a EWMA with a 32-day span. For correlation a longer look back is appropriate: I use the last six months of weekly returns.[235] You can also use an exponentially weighted correlation, but it doesn't really add any value. More details are given in Appendix B.

The greedy algorithm

There are a number of ways we could solve this optimisation, but I will use the *greedy algorithm*. From the internet (www.maixuanviet.com/greedy-algorithm.vietmx):

> *A greedy algorithm is an approach for solving a problem by selecting the best option available at the moment. It doesn't worry whether the current best result will bring the overall optimal result. The algorithm never reverses the earlier decision even if the choice is wrong.*

---

235   See Appendix B.

To use this method to solve the optimisation, we can use the following approach:

1. Come up with a set of starting weights. This is equal to a zero weight in all instruments. These starting weights become the **current best** solution.

2. Find the **proposed** set of weights that is the best we can do, starting from the **current best** solution.

3. We set the **proposed** solution to be initially equal to the **current best** solution.

4. Loop over all the instruments which we can have weights for. For each instrument calculate an **incremented solution**:

   i. If the optimal unrounded weight for that instrument is positive, then add the weight per contract to the **current best** solution weight for this instrument. This is equivalent to buying an additional contract for that instrument.

   ii. If the optimal weight for that instrument is negative, then subtract the weight per contract from the **current best** solution weight for this instrument. This is equivalent to selling an additional contract for that instrument.

   iii. Evaluate the tracking error for the **incremented solution**. If it is better than the **proposed solution**, then set the **proposed solution** to be equal to the **incremented solution**.

5. After completing the instrument loop you will have the **best proposed solution**. This will be the best solution we can have that involves adding or subtracting one contract for a single instrument.

6. If the **best proposed solution** has a lower tracking error than the **current best** solution, then it becomes the new **current best** solution. Repeat from step 4.

7. If the **best proposed solution** is the same as the **current best** solution, then the current best solution is considered optimal. Stop.

I will now explain this in some detail, using a simple example. I assume a trading capital of $500,000, and the example consists of three instruments: the US 5-year and 10-year bond futures and the S&P 500.

Table 114 has all the numbers we will need, with the exception of the correlation. I assume the correlation between US 5-year and US 10-year bonds is 0.9, and between the two bond markets and the S&P 500 is −0.1. Details of how I calculate these correlations are given in Appendix B.

TABLE 114: ARBITRARY EXAMPLE FOR DYNAMIC OPTIMISATION ASSUMING TRADING CAPITAL OF $500,000

	US 5-year bond	US 10-year bond	S&P 500 (micro)
Optimal position in contracts (a)	0.4	0.9	3.1
Notional exposure per contract (b)	$110,000	$120,000	$20,000
Weight per contract (c = b/capital)	0.22	0.24	0.04
Optimal weight = a × c	0.088	0.216	0.124
Annualised % standard deviation of returns	5.2%	8.2%	17.1%

Standard deviations and weights per contract are correct at the time of writing, however the unrounded optimal positions shown are entirely arbitrary. Together with the annualised standard deviations, this gives the covariance matrix shown in table 115.

TABLE 115: COVARIANCE MATRIX FOR DYNAMIC OPTIMISATION EXAMPLE

	US 5-year bond	US 10-year bond	S&P 500
US 5-year	0.002704	0.003838	−0.000889
US 10-year	0.003838	0.006724	−0.001402
S&P 500	−0.000889	−0.001402	0.029241

Step 1: We set the **starting weights** to be all equal to zero. For convenience, I can write this set of weights as follows: [0.0, 0.0, 0.0].

Step 2: These starting weights are also the initial **current best** solution.

In the final column of table 116 I've added the tracking standard deviation which I get for the weights in a given row. Obviously for the optimal weights (second row) the tracking error is zero, but what about the tracking error for the current best solution, all zero weights [0.0, 0.0, 0.0]? Plugging these into the formulae above with the covariance matrix in table 115 gives a standard deviation of tracking error of 2.67% a year:

$$\text{Tracking error weight } e_i = w_i^* - w_i$$
$$= (0 - 0.088), (0 - 0.216), (0 - 0.124)$$

$$\text{Vector of tracking errors } e = [e_0, e_1, e_2, ...]$$
$$= [-0.088, -0.216, -0.124]$$

$$\text{Covariance of asset percentage returns}$$
$$= \Sigma = \sigma^T.\rho.\sigma \text{ (figures in table 115)}$$

$$\text{Standard deviation of tracking error portfolio}$$
$$= \sqrt{(e^T.\Sigma.e)} = 0.0267$$

TABLE 116: STARTING WEIGHTS AND TRACKING ERROR

	US 5-year bond	US 10-year bond	S&P 500	Standard deviation of tracking error for weights
Weight per contract	0.22	0.24	0.04	N/A
Optimal weight (a)	0.088	0.216	0.124	0%
Current best solution (b)	0	0	0	2.67%

Step 3.1: Next, we set the **proposed solution** to be equal to the **current best** solution: zero weights for all three instruments, with a tracking error of 2.67%.

Step 4: We loop over all three instruments. Let's start with the US 5-year bond future.

Step 4.1: The optimal unrounded weight for this instrument is positive, so we add the weight per contract (0.22) to the **current best** solution weight for this instrument (0). This is equivalent to buying a single US 5-year contract.

Step 4.2: We now evaluate the tracking error for this **incremental solution**.

In table 117 the standard deviation of the tracking error for this incremental solution works out to over 3%. Since this is greater than the 2.67% error for the proposed best solution (which is all zero weights), we do not change the proposed best solution.

TABLE 117: WEIGHTS AND TRACKING ERROR AFTER BUYING ONE US 5-YEAR BOND FUTURE

	US 5-year bond	US 10-year bond	S&P 500	Standard deviation of tracking error
Weight per contract	0.22	0.24	0.04	
Optimal weight (a)	0.088	0.216	0.124	0%
Current best solution (b)	0	0	0	2.67%
Proposed solution (c)	0	0	0	2.67%
Incremental solution (b incremented)	0.22	0	0	3.43%

Step 4.1: Now we consider the US 10-year bond future. The optimal weight here is positive, so again we add the appropriate weight per contract to the **current best** solution, which is equivalent to buying a single contract.

Step 4.2: This stage is shown in table 118.

TABLE 118: WEIGHTS AND TRACKING ERROR AFTER BUYING ONE US 10-YEAR BOND FUTURE

	US 5-year bond	US 10-year bond	S&P 500	Standard deviation of tracking error
Weight per contract	0.22	0.24	0.04	
Optimal weight (a)	0.088	0.216	0.124	0%
Current best solution (b)	0	0	0	2.67%
Proposed solution (c)	0	0	0	2.67%
Incremental solution (b incremented)	0	0.24	0	1.53%

The tracking error of this incremental solution is 1.53%, lower than the 2.67% for the current proposed solution. So this incremental solution [0, 0.24, 0] becomes the new **proposed** solution.

Finally for this loop we consider the S&P 500.

Steps 4.1 and 4.2: The optimal weight is again positive, and the relevant calculations are in table 119.

TABLE 119: WEIGHTS AND TRACKING ERROR AFTER BUYING ONE S&P 500 FUTURE

	US 5-year bond	US 10-year bond	S&P 500	Standard deviation of tracking error
Weight per contract	0.22	0.24	0.04	
Optimal weight (a)	0.088	0.216	0.124	0%
Current best solution (b)	0	0	0	2.67%
Proposed solution (c)	0	0.24	0	1.53%
Incremental solution (b incremented)	0	0	0.04	2.51%

Notice that we don't increment the **proposed solution**; instead we are always starting from the baseline of the **current best** solution. This incremental solution has a tracking error of 2.51%. This is inferior to the proposed solution, so the proposed solution remains unchanged.

Step 5: We have now iterated once through the available instruments. The **best proposed** solution is to have portfolio weights of [0, 0.24, 0]. This is equivalent to just buying a single US 10-year bond future. Notice that the proposed solution after iterating through every instrument *will always be only one contract different from the current best solution*; except in the case where the current best solution can't be improved upon.

Step 6: Is the **proposed** solution better than the **current best** solution? Yes, the tracking error for the latter has a standard deviation of 1.53%, lower than the 2.67% for the current best solution. We now set the current best solution to be equal to the proposed solution: [0, 0.24, 0].

We are now back at step 4. To save time and paper, table 120 shows all the iterations for this stage in one place. You can see that the proposed solution remains unchanged until we buy our first S&P 500 contract. At this point the proposed weights are [0, 0.24, 0.04], so we have purchased one US 10-year, and one S&P 500.

TABLE 120: WEIGHTS AND TRACKING ERRORS IN SECOND PASS THROUGH STAGE 4

	US 5-year bond	US 10-year bond	S&P 500	Standard deviation of tracking error
Weight per contract	0.22	0.24	0.04	
Optimal weight (a)	0.088	0.216	0.124	0%
Current best solution (b)	0	0.24	0	1.53%
Start: Proposed solution	0	0.24	0	1.53%
1st incremental solution	0.22	0.24	0	2.35%
Unchanged proposed solution	0	0.24	0	1.58%
2nd incremental solution	0	0.48	0	2.30%
Unchanged proposed solution	0	0.24	0	1.58%
3rd incremental solution	0	0.24	0.04	1.506%
Updated proposed solution	0	0.24	0.04	1.506%
Best & final proposed solution	0	0.24	0.04	1.506%

Since there has been an improvement on the current best portfolio, we replace this with the proposed solution. Table 121 shows the next set of iterations.

TABLE 121: WEIGHTS AND TRACKING ERROR IN THIRD PASS THROUGH STAGE 4

	US 5-year bond	US 10-year bond	S&P 500	Standard deviation of tracking error
Weight per contract	0.22	0.24	0.04	0%
Optimal weight (a)	0.088	0.216	0.124	2.81%
Current best solution (b)	0	0.24	0.04	1.506%
Start: Proposed solution	0	0.24	0.04	1.506%
1st incremental solution	0.22	0.24	0.04	2.30%
Unchanged proposed solution	0	0.24	0.04	1.506%
2nd incremental solution	0	0.48	0.04	2.44%
Unchanged proposed solution	0	0.24	0.04	1.506%
3rd incremental solution	0	0.24	0.08	1.504%
Updated proposed solution	0	0.24	0.08	1.504%
Best & final proposed solution	0	0.24	0.08	1.504%

Again, we improve upon the proposed solution only when we buy another S&P 500 contract. Our final proposed solution is [0, 0.24, 0.08], equivalent to buying one US 10-year and two S&P 500 contracts. This proposed solution becomes the new current solution, which we use in table 122 for the next iteration.

TABLE 122: WEIGHTS AND TRACKING ERROR IN FOURTH PASS THROUGH STAGE 4

	US 5-year bond	US 10-year bond	S&P 500	Standard deviation of tracking error
Weight per contract	0.22	0.24	0.04	0%
Optimal weight (a)	0.088	0.216	0.124	2.81%
Current best solution (b)	0	0.24	0.08	1.504%
Start: Proposed solution	0	0.24	0.08	1.504%
1st incremental solution	0.22	0.24	0.08	2.26%
Unchanged proposed solution	0	0.24	0.08	1.504%
2nd incremental solution	0	0.48	0.08	2.58%
Unchanged proposed solution	0	0.24	0.08	1.504%
3rd incremental solution	0	0.24	0.12	1.53%
Unchanged & final proposed solution	0	0.24	0.08	1.504%

After the final pass is completed the proposed solution is unchanged. Since we can't improve on the current best solution we do not repeat stage three again. We are at **step seven,** and we halt. Our final job is to convert the optimised weights back into positions. These positions will always be integers, so no rounding is required.

$$\text{Optimised position } N_i$$
$$= \text{Optimised portfolio weight } w_i \div \text{Weight per contract}_i$$

Let us review what the dynamic optimisation has done, by reviewing the results in table 123. Our positions are not that different from what we would get by simply rounding our optimal unrounded positions, but we only have two S&P 500 futures rather than three. My intuition is that we have some unused US interest rate risk that we would like to have, since we don't have a position in the US 5-year bond. Since bonds and equities are slightly negatively correlated, adding an S&P 500 future would effectively remove some interest rate risk from our portfolio, making it inferior to the optimised weights with only two S&P 500 futures.

TABLE 123: FINAL POSITIONS FOR DYNAMIC OPTIMISATION EXAMPLE

	US 5-year bond	US 10-year bond	S&P 500 (micro)
Optimal unrounded position (a)	0.4	0.9	3.1
Weight per contract (b)	0.22	0.24	0.04
Optimal weight = a × b	0.088	0.216	0.124
Optimised weight (d)	0	0.24	0.08
Optimised position = d ÷ b	0	1	2

I have run this optimisation with countless examples, and the results are fascinating and intuitive. For example, if an instrument has a large minimum capital and we can't take a position in it, it will take positions in instruments with smaller weights per contract that are correlated and have the same sign of position on (long or short).

It also has a number of advantages over more complex optimisation methodologies. Firstly, it is very robust and unlikely to generate sparse portfolios consisting of positions in just one or two instruments.[236] Similarly, it won't take potentially dangerous hedged positions since the optimised position will always be in the same direction as the forecast.[237] Finally, it is very fast, even with over 100 instruments.

The main disadvantage is that it may miss a slightly better set of optimal weights that will give a small improvement on the tracking error. But this is a small price to pay, since these optimal weights are often less robust. A less apparent disadvantage of this optimisation is that it is very expensive to trade, but I will deal with this problem in the next section.

Dealing with costs: a cost penalty

It is instructive to compare the *dynamic* optimisation with the *static* optimisation I developed in strategy four (page 112). The former selects the best set of instruments to have positions in every single day, whilst the latter is a one-off exercise to choose which instruments to trade.

---

236 Unless you have an extremely small trading account and the optimal solution is for positions in just one or two instruments.

237 For example, if the correlation between the S&P 500 and bonds was significantly negative, then the globally optimal solution produced by other optimisation methods would involve going short S&P 500 as a proxy for a long position in US 2-year bonds. This is perverse, since we want to be long S&P 500, and also risky, since correlations have a nasty habit of changing when you are most exposed.

Some of the criteria used are effectively the same in both methodologies. For example, both will only hold positions in which we have sufficient capital to trade. This is explicit in the static optimisation, but implicit in the dynamic version. Under dynamic optimisation it is very unlikely we will take a position in an instrument with excessive minimum capital, since this would result in a very large tracking error.

Both algorithms try to maximise diversification. In the case of the static optimisation this is explicit. We achieve diversification in the dynamic optimisation by holding a set of instruments which have the lowest possible tracking error against the maximally diversified Jumbo portfolio.

There is one important difference. The static optimisation assumes that all instruments will have the same pre-cost SR. This makes sense, since there was insufficient evidence that any one instrument will perform better than another in a given strategy, over a sufficiently long backtest.[238] In contrast the dynamic optimisation is using underlying positions that have been scaled for forecast strength. Since we assume that forecast strength is a good predictor of risk adjusted returns in the near future, this means the dynamic optimisation is effectively incorporating different estimates for SRs for each instrument into its calculations.

However, there is an important element of the static optimisation which we haven't yet used: **costs**. The static optimisation seeks to use instruments with lower costs, whilst the dynamic optimisation has no concept of costs. Fortunately, it is possible to modify the tracking error equations to include costs:

$$\text{Optimal unrounded portfolio weight } w_i = N_i \times \text{Weight per contract}_i$$

$$\text{Previous position as number of contracts held} = P_i$$

$$\text{Optimised portfolio weight } w_i^* = N_i^* \times \text{Weight per contract}_i$$

$$\text{Previous (current) weight } w_i^P = P_i \times \text{Weight per contract}_i$$

$$\text{Cost in weight terms } w_i^c = (C_i \div \text{Capital}) \div \text{Weight per contract}_i$$

$$\text{Tracking error weight } e_i = w_i^* - w_i$$

---

238   There are some situations where there might be sufficient evidence to do this. For example, in strategy sixteen I discussed how we might down weight equities in a trend strategy.

$$\text{Vector of tracking errors } e = [e_0, e_1, e_2, ...]$$

$$\text{Trade as a weight } \Delta_i = abs(w_i^P - w_i^*)$$

$$\text{Cost of all trades } \delta = sum(\Delta_0 w_0^c + \Delta_1 w_1^c + \Delta_2 w_2^c + ...)$$

$$\text{Covariance of asset percentage returns} = \Sigma$$

Tracking error, standard deviation and cost penalty
$$= \sqrt{(e^T.\Sigma.e)} + 50\delta$$

New terms introduced in these equations are:

- Currently held, or previous, number of contracts P_i in each instrument i.
- The position weight implied by those previous contracts, w_i^P.
- The estimated cost of trading a single contract of instrument i, C_i, in the same currency as our capital.
- That cost translated into the cost of trading a given weight, as a proportion of capital w_i^c.
- Trades in weight terms, Δ_i.
- The cost of all trading in weight terms, δ.
- The total cost is multiplied by 50 and then added to the tracking error. Since we are trying to minimise the tracking error, this means we will seek out optimised sets of weights which have a lower cost of trading.

No doubt you have a couple of questions about this modification. Firstly, where does the 50 come from? I optimised this to keep the level of costs roughly the same as costs for strategy eleven, but in reality any number between 10 and 100 will give very similar results.

Secondly, how do we calculate the cash cost of trading a single contract, C_i? In fact we already discussed this in Part One:

$$\text{Spread cost, price points} = (\text{Bid} - \text{Offer}) \div 2$$

$$\text{Spread cost, currency} = \text{Multiplier} \times \text{Spread cost price points}$$

Total cost per trade, currency
$$= \text{Spread cost currency} + \text{Commission per contract}$$

This cost would need to be converted into the same currency your trading capital is denominated in, before dividing by the capital to get the cost as a weight.

This is fine if we are doing the dynamic optimisation today, but not if we are backtesting, since today's currency costs are likely to be unrealistic if used in the past. For backtesting we will need to adjust the historical costs in currency terms, using the method I proposed for strategy five (back on page 133).

The current costs per contract for the three assets I used in the earlier example are $0.875 (S&P 500 micro), $11.50 (US 10-year) and $5.50 (US 5-year). These are already in the correct currency, so I just divide by the trading capital I was using ($500,000), and by the weight of each contract (0.04, 0.22 and 0.24 respectively).

$$\text{Cost in weight terms } w_i^c$$
$$= (C_i \div \text{Capital}) \div \text{Weight per contract}_i$$

$$\text{Cost in weight terms, US 5-year } w_0^c$$
$$= (5.50 \div 500000) \div 0.22 = 0.0050\%$$

$$\text{Cost in weight terms, US 10-year } w_1^c$$
$$= (11.50 \div 500000) \div 0.24 = 0.010\%$$

$$\text{Cost in weight terms, S&P 500 } w_2^c$$
$$= (0.875 \div 500000) \div 0.04 = 0.0044\%$$

These are sufficiently low that they would not affect the outcome of our earlier example, but let's recalculate the tracking error for the optimised solution to get a feel for the effect of applying a cost penalty.

The original tracking error of the final set of weights [US 5-year = 0, US 10-year = 0.24, S&P 500 = 0.08] was 1.504%. Let's assume that our starting weights were all zero, because we had no positions. This gives us trades as weights Δ_i equal to the absolute value of the optimised weights: 0, 0.24 and 0.08. Plugging these and the wc calculated above into the appropriate formula, we obtain:

$$\text{Cost of all trades } \delta = \text{sum}(\Delta_0 w_0^c + \Delta_1 w_1^c + \Delta_2 w_2^c + ...)$$

$$= \text{sum}(0 \times 0.005\% + 0.24 \times 0.01\%$$
$$+ 0.08 \times 0.0044\%)$$

$$= 0.00275\%$$

$$\text{Tracking error} = \sqrt{(e^T.\Sigma.e)} + 50\delta$$
$$= 1.504\% + 50 \times 0.00275\% = 2.208\%$$

Dealing with costs: buffering

Using a cost penalty reduces the turnover of the dynamic optimisation by some margin, but it is still higher than you would expect. The main reason for this is that the optimisation only ever puts on a position in the same direction as the underlying forecast, long or short. As a result, whenever a forecast changes sign from long to short, we will *always* close our entire position in that instrument (and possibly open a new position in the opposite direction).

This behaviour is unaffected by the imposition of a cost penalty, and results in a lower bound below which turnover can't be reduced. It turns out this lower bound is actually quite high. Increasing the cost penalty further to try to reduce turnover only results in trading being limited to the very cheapest instruments, and heavily penalises after costs performance.

However, there is a solution at hand. Remember that we inadvertently dropped another element of our original trading system which helps to reduce costs: **buffering**. Back in strategy eight, on page 167, I set the trade buffer at 10% of the average position that we expected to hold. I then constructed a buffer zone around the optimal position that we wanted to hold. If a current position were outside this zone then we would trade to the edge of the buffer. But if the position was inside the buffer zone then no trading was necessary.

It didn't make sense to use buffered positions as an input into the dynamic optimisation, so the unrounded positions we are trying to match are calculated before a buffer is applied. Unfortunately, it isn't practical to do this type of buffering on individual positions in the dynamic optimisation. But we can implement buffering on the *entire portfolio* by using the general idea of buffering, but in tracking error units rather than position units.

To achieve this we first set a tracking error buffer in standard deviation terms, B_σ. The tracking error is always positive, because it is the sum of two positive figures: an annualised standard deviation, and annualised costs. So our modified buffering methodology will look like this:

- Calculate the optimised portfolio of rounded positions using the dynamic optimisation method.

- Check the tracking error of the optimised portfolio versus the positions we already hold.

- If this tracking error is smaller than the buffer, then no trading is required.

- If this tracking error is larger than the buffer, then trade until the tracking error is equal to the buffer.

Let's discuss this in detail, using the earlier example with three futures markets: US 5-year bonds, US 10-year bonds and S&P 500. The first question we need to answer is what the buffer, B_σ, should be. The analogous equivalent to the average position, used in the original buffer, is our average risk target τ. This is measured as an annualised standard deviation of returns. The 10% symmetric buffer we used for position buffering is equivalent to a 5% asymmetric buffer for tracking error. This gives us the following calculation for an equivalent tracking error buffer:

$$B_\sigma = 0.05\tau$$

Since I use a 20% risk target in this book, the optimal buffer B_σ is 1%.

Next, we calculate the tracking error of our **current portfolio** against the dynamically **optimised portfolio**. Note: this is *not* the same as the tracking error of the **optimised portfolio** against the original **optimal unrounded** positions. We are now trying to see if the current portfolio is sufficiently similar to the optimised portfolio that no trading is necessary. This tracking error consists purely of the standard deviation and doesn't include the cost penalty, since we've already used costs in determining what the optimised portfolio will be:

$$\text{Optimised portfolio weight } w^*_i = N^*_i \times \text{Weight per contract}_i$$

$$\text{Previous weight } w^P_i = P_i \times \text{Weight per contract}_i$$

$$\text{Tracking error current weight } e^P_i = w^*_i - w^P_i$$

$$\text{Vector of tracking errors } e_p = [e^P_0, e^P_1, e^P_2, ...]$$

$$\text{Tracking error, } T = \sqrt{(e_p{}^T . \Sigma . e_p)}$$

We already have the optimised portfolio for our earlier example: [US 5-year = 0, US 10-year = 0.24, S&P 500 = 0.08]. I will assume that we do not have a current portfolio: all of our positions are currently zero: [0, 0, 0]. If I plug in the optimised weights from earlier, and current portfolio weights of zero, I get a standard deviation of 2.35%. This is considerably higher than the buffer of 1%, so we will want to do some trading.

If we were to trade all the way to the new optimised weights, we would get a tracking error of zero. But as we did earlier with position buffering, we actually want to trade to the *edge* of the buffer, i.e. trade in such a way that our tracking error is equal to the size of the buffer, 1%. To achieve this we calculate an adjustment factor, which is the distance we need to travel from the current portfolio such that the tracking error is equal to the buffer. If the tracking error of the current versus optimised portfolio is T, then:

$$\text{Adjustment factor, } a = \max([T - B_a] \div T, 0)$$

In the example we are considering, since $T = 2.35\%$ we have:

$$\text{Adjustment factor, } a = \max([2.35\% - 1\%] \div 2.35\%, 0) = 0.57$$

We now need to multiply the trades that would be required to trade all the way to the optimised portfolio by a:

$$\text{Required trade}_i = \text{round}(a \times [N^*_i - P_i])$$

For example, to achieve the optimised portfolio weight for S&P 500 (0.08) without considering buffering, we would need to buy $0.08 - 0 = +0.08$ weight units of S&P 500. This corresponds to two contracts, since the weight per contract is 0.04. If we multiply the required trade of +0.08 by 0.57, then we get a trade of +0.0456. Similarly the required trade in the US 10-year is reduced from +0.24 to +0.138. Since the required trade in US 5-year is zero, this is unchanged.

Next, we convert the required trades into contract units. For S&P 500, $+0.0456 \div 0.04 = +1.14$ and for US 10-year bonds $+0.138 \div 0.24 = +0.57$. Finally, these required trades are rounded to whole contracts to produce the trades we will actually do. We buy one S&P 500 contract, and a single US 10-year bond future, ending up with weights of [0, 0.24, 0.04] instead of the optimised weights of [0, 0.24, 0.08].

Notice that the required trade is virtually identical to what we would do without buffering, except we buy one less S&P 500 future. If you are curious, if we calculate the tracking error of this new set of weights against the optimised portfolio it comes out to almost zero: 0.2%. Although in principal we are trading to the edge of the buffer, because of rounding effects it is very unlikely that the tracking error after buffering will be exactly equal to the buffer width of 1%: it could be more or less.

Testing and understanding dynamic optimisation

Analysing a complex strategy like dynamic optimisation is a serious and lengthy business, and could probably almost fill an entire book by itself. It is useful, for example, to understand the likely range of tracking errors over time, and to see how well the dynamic optimisation tracks the expected risk of the unrounded optimal positions. We should confirm that the calibrated parameters for cost penalty (50) and buffer (1%) produce the results we expect and that the backtest is not too sensitive to small changes in those values.

There is no space[239] for all of that here! But it should be some comfort that I have thoroughly tested this strategy and I am very confident about its properties. In fact, I have been using it to trade my own money on every single day since mid-October 2021.

Rather than force you to read a few hundred pages of detailed analysis, I'm going to do a straightforward three-way test. All three options are trading variations of strategy eleven: a combination of carry and trend, with forecast weights determined by the cost of the relevant instrument.[240]

The three strategies we will consider are:

1. The full Jumbo portfolio: 100 instruments with $50 million of capital.

2. A $500,000 account with a fixed set of 27 instruments[241] selected using the static methodology for instrument selection described back in strategy four (on page 112).

3. A $500,000 account with 100 instruments using dynamic optimisation.

We would expect the first option to perform the best, but the whole point of this chapter is that it is only available to people with $50 million lying around idly. Someone with a $500,000 trading account has the choice between trading either the second or third option, using either static or dynamic optimisation to limit the number of

---

239   Further analysis is available on some blog posts I wrote that are linked to from the website for this book.

240   Although I use strategy eleven as my benchmark here, it's actually possible to run dynamic optimisation on any strategy from Parts One, Two or Three of this book. But it isn't suitable for strategies in Parts Four and Five.

241   For reference, the instruments selected when I did this exercise were; in equities: Kospi, NASDAQ micros, Eurostoxx, Swiss SMI, EU dividend 30; in metals: Gold micro and Bitcoin micro; in bonds: Eurodollar, Korean 3-year and 10-year, US 2-year and 10-year, German Schatz and Bobl, French OAT, Italian BTP; in agricultural markets: Lean hogs, Live cattle, Wheat, Corn; in FX: JPYUSD, MXPUSD, GBPUSD, NZDUSD, EURUSD; and in energies: Henry Hub Natural Gas minis, WTI Crude mini.

instruments they are trading. With a relatively small account the full Jumbo portfolio is not a realistic possibility: chances are that most of the positions will be less than a full contract. The results are in table 124.

TABLE 124: STRATEGY ELEVEN WITH DIFFERENT CAPITAL LEVELS AND TYPES OF OPTIMISATION

	No optimisation 100 instruments $50 million	Static optimisation 27 instruments $500,000	Dynamic optimisation 100 instruments $500,000
Mean annual return	26.5%	25.8%	25.7%
Costs	−1.1%	−1.0%	−1.0%
Average drawdown	−8.9%	−9.5%	−9.4%
Standard deviation	20.9%	21.8%	21.1%
Sharpe ratio	1.27	1.18	1.22
Turnover	46.5	32.1	48.8
Skew	0.76	0.19	0.79
Lower tail	1.86	1.69	1.86
Upper tail	1.75	1.54	1.73
Alpha	22.3%	21.6%	22.9%
Beta	0.30	0.25	0.29

As we would expect, the full Jumbo portfolio with $50 million in the first column is the best. But it is gratifying to see that the dynamically optimised version of this Jumbo portfolio can almost replicate its performance with only 1% of the available capital: $500,000. We lose just a few SR units in risk adjusted returns. The costs and turnover are also very similar, suggesting that we did a good job in calibrating the cost penalty and buffer size.

But what is going on in the middle column? It looks like the static portfolio, consisting of just 27 instruments, is almost as good as the dynamic portfolio – with the possible exception of skew, which looks worse. Given the considerable amount of effort required for dynamic optimisation, is it really worth it?

In fact, the static portfolio has a hidden advantage. Just by luck, the static portfolio consists of instruments that have done better on average in the backtest. This allows it to overcome the disadvantages of being insufficiently diversified compared to the Jumbo portfolio, in both its original and dynamic flavours.

We can see this if we look at the average performance for the median instrument. The results are in table 125. Notice that the 27 instruments in the static portfolio have better performance on average than the 100 instruments in the Jumbo portfolio. If we consider the SR, the average instrument in the static portfolio has a 26% improvement over the average for the full Jumbo portfolio. This is dumb luck, pure and simple. The static portfolio does not consider historical instrument performance, and we know that it's futile to try and select instruments on the basis of such statistics. Costs are slightly lower in the static portfolio, but the reduction in costs only explains a tiny fraction of the higher after cost performance.

TABLE 125: PERFORMANCE OF MEDIAN INSTRUMENT FOR JUMBO AND $500,000 STATIC PORTFOLIOS

	Median instrument Jumbo portfolio 100 instruments	Median instrument $500k static portfolio 27 instruments
Mean annual return	5.7%	8.2%
Costs	−0.4%	−0.34%
Average drawdown	−24.9%	−30.1%
Standard deviation	21.7%	22.5%
Sharpe ratio	0.27	0.34
Turnover	11.8	11.7
Skew	0.63	0.70
Lower tail	3.11	2.71
Upper tail	2.67	2.39

It's possible to do a crude adjustment for this outperformance by appropriately adjusting certain statistics for the static portfolio in table 124 by the relative performance ratio 1 + 26% = 1.26. The results are in table 126. For the static portfolio, they now reflect what we expect on average from the static selection process, assuming it had neither good nor bad luck.[242] You can see that the dynamic optimisation now has a more significant advantage over the static optimisation.

---

242   This assumes that the amount of diversification available across the 27 instruments I happened to select is about what you would expect for a portfolio of this size. I confirmed this crude result with a more thorough exercise using a Monte Carlo methodology to run multiple tests of instruments selected using sub-sets of the available backtested data.

TABLE 126: SELECTED PERFORMANCE STATISTICS FOR DIFFERENT TYPES OF OPTIMISATION, WITH ADJUSTMENTS MADE TO STATIC PORTFOLIO

	Jumbo portfolio 100 instruments $50 million	Adjusted static portfolio 27 instruments $500,000	Dynamic optimisation 100 instruments $500,000
Mean annual return	26.5%	20.5%	25.7%
Average drawdown	−8.9%	−14.8%	−9.4%
Standard deviation	20.9%	21.8%	21.1%
Sharpe ratio	1.27	0.94	1.22
Alpha	22.3%	16.2%	22.9%

To summarise, if we can only trade 27 instruments we can expect an SR of 0.94 for strategy eleven. If we could trade 100 instruments with no issues with minimum capital, then this would be pushed up to an SR of 1.27. But using dynamic optimisation with less capital allows us to capture almost all of this diversification benefit, with an SR of 1.22.

Putting aside outright performance, how closely does the optimised dynamic portfolio match the performance of the Jumbo portfolio with $50 million? Very closely indeed. The correlation between the two strategies is 0.99: they are virtually identical. This is staggeringly good given we only have 1/100 of the capital available to the full Jumbo portfolio. In contrast, the static portfolio manages a correlation of just 0.78 with the full Jumbo portfolio.

It is also interesting to see how dynamic optimisation performs with different levels of capital. With more trading capital we would expect a closer match to the unrounded portfolio: it would be even more highly correlated, and the tracking error would typically be very low. But with only a few thousand dollars we would be reduced to trading a very small number of futures that had very low minimum capital requirements. The performance of this emasculated portfolio would be quite different from that achieved by the unrounded positions, and tracking errors would be substantially higher.

Let's do one more comparison to get a feel for how capital will affect our results. In the introduction I said that this book was suitable for traders with at least $100,000 in their trading accounts. Can a trader with the absolute minimum capital available get much of the benefit of strategy eleven with just a tiny fraction of the $50 million needed to trade the full Jumbo portfolio?

I re-ran the static selection methodology with $100,000 in capital, and this time it selected 16 instruments.[243] The median SR for this set of instruments was even higher, 0.41. So to adjust the performance of the static portfolio I used a factor of 1.52: the ratio between the median SR of the average instrument I selected, and the average across the entire Jumbo portfolio. The results are in table 127.

TABLE 127: SELECTED PERFORMANCE STATISTICS FOR DIFFERENT TYPES OF OPTIMISATION, WITH AND WITHOUT ADJUSTMENTS MADE TO STATIC PORTFOLIO

	Jumbo portfolio 100 instruments $50 million	Static portfolio 16 instruments $100,000	Adjusted static portfolio 16 instruments $100,000	Dynamic optimisation 100 instruments $100,000
Mean annual return	26.5%	23.6%	15.5%	20.0%
Costs	−1.1%	−0.9%	−0.9%	−0.5%
Average drawdown	−8.9%	−7.9%	−12.0%	−9.6%
Standard deviation	20.9%	21.3%	21.3%	18.8%
Sharpe ratio	1.27	1.11	0.73	1.06
Alpha	22.3%	20.2%	13.3%	17.8%

Once adjusted for dumb luck in instrument selection, the performance of the static portfolio looks even worse than before. The dynamic strategy has also slipped slightly because it has less capital, but its relative outperformance versus the static strategy has improved markedly. Interestingly, the costs of the dynamic optimisation are about half the level of the other strategies. This is because the dynamic optimisation achieves its excellent performance without holding many positions. In contrast to the 16 instruments in the $100,000 static portfolio, the dynamic variant holds an average of just seven instruments, and never has more than 15. The difference of course is that the 15 positions held by the static strategy remain unchanged, whilst the dynamic strategy can choose the positions that best represent the Jumbo portfolio whilst minimising trading costs.

---

243   For reference they were, in equities: Kospi, NASDAQ micros; in metals: Gold micro; in bonds: Eurodollar, Korean 3-year and 10-year, US 2-year, German Schatz, Italian BTP; in agricultural markets: Lean hogs; in FX: JPYUSD, MXPUSD, GBPUSD, NZDUSD; and in energies: Henry Hub Natural Gas minis, WTI Crude mini.

What about the correlation of the $100,000 portfolios with the full $50 million Jumbo strategy? The correlation of monthly returns for the dynamic and Jumbo portfolios is a very impressive 0.91. To reiterate, we are now trading just 0.2% of the $50 million in the full Jumbo portfolio in the dynamically optimised strategy, with just seven positions on average. This is a remarkable performance! In contrast, for the static optimisation the correlation has fallen to just 0.50.

In conclusion, the less capital we have, the fewer instruments we can trade with the traditional version of strategy eleven and the poorer our expected performance will be – unless we are very lucky and happen to pick instruments that do particularly well in the backtest. We will also have a lower correlation with the performance we could generate with unrounded positions, or equivalently with tens of millions of dollars in capital.

In contrast, with less capital the dynamic optimisation also loses performance, but the reduction is relatively modest. It also maintains a higher correlation with the performance we could achieve with unrounded positions. Table 128 lays out the figures clearly.

TABLE 128: SHARPE RATIO AND CORRELATIONS FOR DIFFERENT TYPES OF OPTIMISATION WITH VARYING CAPITAL LEVELS

	$100,000	$500,000	$50 million
Sharpe ratio:			
Static (adjusted)	0.73	0.94	1.27
Dynamic	1.06	1.22	Not required
Correlation with $50 million static strategy:			
Static	0.50	0.78	1.0
Dynamic	0.91	0.99	Not required

Other benefits of dynamic optimisation

There are many other benefits of using the dynamic optimisation strategy, apart from using it to trade a much wider variety of futures than would otherwise be possible with a small account.

For example, you could include additional futures in the set of instruments which you generate potential optimal positions for, but then not actually allow yourself to hold optimised positions in those instruments. These could be instruments which are too costly to trade, have insufficient liquidity, or for which there are trading restrictions. In my own portfolio I generate positions for approximately 150 futures, but I only allow myself to trade around 100.

The advantage of this is that we will effectively get a better forecast by combining information from more instruments. For example, if you have read Part Two, then you will know from strategy eighteen that most trends happen across an asset class. It might be that there is a decent trend in a particular group of assets, but there is a much stronger trend in instruments which we can't trade. By using dynamic optimisation we can transfer risk to correlated markets which we can trade, even if they don't have strong forecasts in their own right.

You can also set position limits in the dynamic optimisation. For example, you might not want to hold more than 10 VIX contracts. I explain the use of position limits more in Part Six, when I discuss risk management.

There might be a situation where you are temporarily unable to trade a given instrument, for example because it has an idiosyncratic market holiday, but where you wanted to reduce risk and cut an existing long position. Again, this can be dealt with by setting a minimum and maximum position limit for a given instrument, equal to its current position. The optimisation will do a proxy trade in instruments whose markets are currently open, either selling a positively correlated instrument or buying a negatively correlated instrument if one is available, and has the appropriate sign on its forecast.

Another advantage comes when you come to roll your futures contracts. In the traditional strategy, we assume that we want to hold the same positions after the roll. But in a dynamic strategy, it might sometimes make sense to force an instrument that is about to roll to close. Then the optimisation will subsequently decide if opening the same position again in that instrument makes sense, or if it would be optimal to trade something else. This is particularly useful if you find a given instrument is very expensive to roll. I discuss rolling tactics more in Part Six.

All of the above requires the dynamic optimisation to work with constraints. This makes the method a little more complicated, and I discuss the required modifications on the web page for this book.

Strategy twenty-five: Trading plan

Strategy	Dynamically optimise the positions held for a given strategy to make.
Optimal unrounded positions	Begin with the optimal unbuffered positions generated by the underlying strategy, in numbers of contracts: $$N_{i,t} = \text{Capped combined forecast}$$ $$\times \text{ Capital} \times \text{IDM} \times \text{Weight}_i \times \tau$$ $$\div (10 \times \text{Multiplier}_i \times \text{Price}_{i,t} \times \text{FX}_{i,t} \times \sigma_{\%,i,t})$$
Current positions	$$\text{Current position held in a given instrument} = P_i$$
Notional exposure per contract	$$\text{Notional exposure per contract}_i$$ $$= \text{Multiplier}_i \times \text{Price}_i \times \text{FX rate}_i$$
Weight per contract	$$\text{Weight per contract}_i$$ $$= \text{Notional exposure per contract}_i \div \text{Capital}$$
Optimal unrounded portfolio weight	$$w_i = N_i \times \text{Weight per contract}_i$$
Previous portfolio weight	$$w_i^P = P_i \times \text{Weight per contract}_i$$
Currency cost per contract traded, C_i	$$\text{Spread cost, price points} = (\text{Bid} - \text{Offer}) \div 2$$ $$\text{Spread cost, currency}$$ $$= \text{Futures multiplier} \times \text{Spread cost price points}$$ $$\text{Total cost per trade, currency}$$ $$= \text{Spread cost currency} + \text{Commission per contract}$$ Costs need to be converted to the account base currency, and for backtests adjusted using the method outlined in strategy five (page 133).
Optimised weights	$$w_i^*$$
Tracking error weights	$$\text{Tracking error weight } e_i = w_i^* - w_i$$ $$\text{Vector of tracking errors } \underline{e} = [e_0, e_1, e_2, \ldots]$$

Instrument daily percentage returns for a given instrument	Given a back-adjusted price, p, and the price of the traded futures on the appropriate day, F: $$\textbf{Percentage return} = (p_t - p_{t-1}) \div F_{t-1}$$
Covariance of instrument percentage returns	Calculated from instrument percentage returns. Given a standard deviation, σ (calculated from daily returns using an EWMA with a span of 32 business days, and multiplied by 16 to annualise) and correlation of daily instrument percentage returns, ρ (calculated using the last 6 months of weekly returns): $$\Sigma = \sigma^T . \rho . \sigma$$
Cost of trading	$$\textbf{Cost in weight terms } w_i^c$$ $$= (C_i \div \textbf{Capital}) \div \textbf{Weight per contract}_i$$ $$\Delta_i = abs(w_i^p - w_i^*)$$ $$\textbf{Cost of all trades } \delta$$ $$= sum(\Delta_0 w_0^c + \Delta_1 w_1^c + \Delta_2 w_2^c + ...)$$
Tracking error with cost penalty	$$\textbf{Tracking error} = \sqrt{(\underline{e}^T . \Sigma . \underline{e})} + 50\delta$$
Greedy algorithm	Use the greedy algorithm to find the optimised weights w^* which minimise the tracking error with cost penalty.
Optimised position	$$N_i^*$$ $$= \textbf{Optimised portfolio } w_i^* \div \textbf{Weight per contract}_i$$
Tracking error of previous versus optimised weights	$$\textbf{Tracking error current weight } e_i^p = w_i^* - w_i^p$$ $$\textbf{Vector of tracking errors } \underline{e_p} = [e_0^p , e_1^p, e_2^p, ...]$$ $$T = \sqrt{(\underline{e_p}^T . \Sigma . \underline{e_p})}$$
Buffering	$$B_\sigma = 0.05\tau$$ $$\textbf{Adjustment factor, } \alpha = max([T - B_\sigma] \div T, 0)$$ $$\textbf{Required trade}_i = round(\alpha(N_i^* - P_i))$$

PART FOUR

Fast Directional Strategies

You must read all of Part One before reading Part Four.

You do not have to read Parts Two or Three before reading Part Four.

Strategies in Part Four use a modified version of the same position management framework described in Part One. Until now I have exclusively used daily data, but these strategies will generate their forecasts more frequently: I backtest them on hourly data, but in principle they could trade virtually continuously.

For this reason, these strategies can't be combined with strategies from Parts One, Two and Three, but have to be traded independently (though I will discuss methods for trading them in parallel in the most efficient manner).

The following fast directional strategies are included in Part Four:

- **Strategy twenty-six:** Fast mean reversion.
- **Strategy twenty-seven:** Safer fast mean reversion.

Fast mean reversion

How can I describe the strategies introduced so far in this book? A polite description would be *sedate*. They trade once a day using daily data, and not especially quickly. The average holding period for many instruments runs into several weeks: a consequence of avoiding a heavy penalty in trading costs. Yes, they are profitable. But they don't exactly make the heart race. They are certainly a far cry from the frantic activity that most people picture when they think of trading.

In this part of the book I'm going to move away from strategies that trade daily, and turn up the speed dial a few notches. But I won't be diving into the intricacies of high frequency trading (HFT): I lack both the expertise and the resources to venture into this area. Instead I will be focusing on strategies that we can test reasonably accurately using hourly data. Their holding periods are typically one or two days – well above the sub-second realm where HFT funds practice their craft.

This first strategy seeks to capture the *mean reversion* in prices that is prevalent at this time scale.

Strategy twenty-six: Trade a fast mean reverting forecast.

The non-fractal nature of markets

Many traders are convinced that markets are *fractal*[244] in nature. It's difficult to define a fractal, so let's consider the most famous example: the Mandelbrot set. You can download software that will display this on your computer monitor in glorious

---

244 Mostly this is a vague belief that the same strategies can be used regardless of time scale, but some are explicit in this belief, for example Edgar Peters in his 1994 book, *Fractal Market Analysis: Applying Chaos Theory to Investment and Economics*.

technicolour. At first glance the set looks like a funny shaped blob, with a smaller blob on one side. However, the edges of the blob are not smooth.

Because of how the set is defined, you can use the software to zoom in further. At a higher magnification you will notice something weird: the fuzzy edges of the blob look eerily similar to parts of the starting set. Zooming in even further you will see further repetitions, including perfect copies of the original set.

What does this have to do with trading? Well, let's suppose you are the sort of trader who uses chart patterns to trade, and that there is a particular pattern which you are convinced is extremely bullish. It won't matter if you see the pattern on a chart with monthly price data, or with weekly, daily, or even minute by minute bars. The idea is that the price series is fractal: patterns that appear at coarse frequencies will also be apparent when you zoom in by using more frequent price data.

I've noted before that I'm not the sort of trader who believes in chart patterns. As it happens, I also don't believe that markets are fractal. In support of this assertion, consider the following selection of strategies:

- Strategy twenty-two: Value – a **mean reversion strategy** with a multi-year horizon.

- Strategy six: Slow **trend** – using an exponentially weighted moving average EWMAC64.

- Strategy nine, intermediate speeds of **trend** – EWMAC8, EWMAC16 and EWMAC32.

- Strategy nine, fastest variations of **trend** – EWMAC2 and EWMAC4.

- High frequency trading (not included in this book). At its core this is a **mean reversion** strategy which aims to buy at the bid and sell at the ask.

Perusing this list, and thinking about the performance of each strategy, a pattern becomes clear. We can't just use the same type of strategy regardless of holding period and price data frequency – **markets are not fractal**. Instead, it looks like there are holding periods when trend works well, and others where the opposite strategy – mean reversion – is better. If we speculatively fill in some gaps, we get the following:[245]

---

[245] It seems likely that there are further switches in optimal strategy between the hourly frequency, and the sub-second realm of high frequency trading. There are a number of systematic traders exploiting *relative value* mean reversion in the minute by minute region, but I am not aware of any evidence that we could profitably trade *directionally* either with trend or mean reversion at this speed.

Multi-year horizons	**Mean reversion** works (although because of the slow timescale the results are not statistically significant, as the value strategy in Part Three attests).
Several months to one year horizon	**Trend following** works, but is not at its best (consider the slightly poorer results we get for EWMAC64 versus faster trend variations).
Several weeks to several months horizon	**Trend** works extremely well (consider the excellent performance of EWMAC8, EWMAC16 and EWMAC32).
Several days to one week	**Trend** is starting to work less well (EWMAC4 and especially EWMAC2 perform somewhat worse than slower variations, even before costs are deducted).
A few days	We might expect **mean reversion** to work?
A few hours	We might expect **trend** to work?
Less than a second	**Mean reversion** works well (high frequency trading is very profitable).

Ignoring the high frequency region, it is clear there might be scope for additional trading strategies which trade faster than the quickest I have considered so far. But, there are a couple of hefty metaphorical elephants in this particular room. The first is that I have no evidence that I can casually interpolate the neat pattern whereby different frequencies of price data alternate between trend and mean reversion. The other problem is trading costs. These are already a serious problem for the fastest trading rule variation in Part One (EWMAC2). Am I seriously suggesting we can trade even quicker?

It turns out that there is some truth in my theory – mean reversion does become apparent at holding periods of a few days. And with some careful thought we can reduce costs to the level where at least one of the effects above can be exploited. This chapter will cover a strategy that trades **mean reversion** with a holding period of **a few days**.

What about fast trend following?

When I planned this book it had originally been my intention to include a trend strategy with a holding period of less than a day. If my thesis above is correct, then there should be profitable *trend* strategies in this region.

Unfortunately I was unable to find any strategies that fitted the bill. All the strategies I tested had very low or negative returns, even before costs. This remained true even if I dropped my usual assumption of conservatively lagging fills by a single time interval, one hour in this case. It is possible that the trend effect I am looking for does not become clear until the holding period is significantly shorter than what I can accurately test using hourly data.[246]

Even if I had found such a strategy, it is unlikely I could have traded it as the costs would have been horrific. The cost reduction execution tactics I use in this chapter are no use with trend type strategies that have to pay the full execution spread when trading.

A fast mean reversion forecast

Earlier in the book I rather blithely defined mean reversion as 'what goes up, must come down'. A more formal definition is that we expect a price to return to its **equilibrium** value. A price that is higher than the equilibrium is a bearish signal, whilst a price that is below where it ought to be is an indication that you should go long. A straightforward way of measuring an equilibrium is to return to our favourite smoothing tool, the exponentially weighted moving average (EWMA).

We calculate the equilibrium from a series of daily back-adjusted futures prices p_t, indexed to weekdays.[247] It seems reasonable to use a span of five days for the EWMA, since that will be approximately one week worth of week days:

$$\text{Equilibrium}_t = \text{EWMA}_{\text{span=5}} \ (p_{t-1}, \ p_{t-2}, \ p_{t-3}, \ ...)$$

Here p_{t-1} is the last available daily closing price. As I have done several times before the choice of a five-day span was arbitrary and done without backtesting to avoid over fitting, although I also tested other spans to check that it was a robust option. In principle you could use a slightly shorter or longer span and it would not significantly

---

246   A promising strategy I was unable to replicate the results for involves using the return from the last 24 hours (Sandrine Ungari, Gilles Drigout, 'Short term trend following', Unpublished presentation by Société Générale 2019). Another approach that I was unable to test for lack of data involves predicting the last hour of returns based on the returns since last night's close until one hour before closing (Guido Baltussen, Zhi Da, Sten Lammers, Martin Martens, 'Hedging demand and market intraday momentum', *Journal of Financial Economics* 2021). Both papers speculate that their strategies' profits can be explained by the predictable behaviour of gamma hedging options market markers. I also tried novel strategies using moving averages on hourly prices, but to no avail.

247   In principle we could calculate this equilibrium from hourly price data, but it is more straightforward to use daily prices for this purpose when it comes to testing and implementing the strategy. Firstly, we don't have to deal with the overnight gaps of varying length that would appear in some but not all markets. Secondly, a daily calculation allows the production code implementation to be split into an overnight calculation plus a very lightweight process which checks the current price against the pre-calculated equilibrium.

affect the performance. I do not test multiple spans for this strategy as I have done elsewhere, as the resulting variations are highly correlated. It is also much harder to trade multiple variations of this strategy than it was for the strategies in Parts One, Two and Three.

The raw forecast will be equal to the equilibrium *minus* the price:

$$\text{Raw forecast}_t = \text{Equilibrium}_t - p_t$$

Thus we will have a positive forecast – a long position – when the current price is below the equilibrium; and we go short if the price is higher than the equilibrium. In principle the price could be checked at any frequency, although as I have already mentioned I am using hourly data[248] in this part of the book for backtesting.

As this is a forecast, we need to convert it into a risk adjusted value. As we have done before, we achieve this by dividing the raw forecast by the daily standard deviation[249] of price returns. This can be calculated directly or derived from the annual standard deviation of *percentage* returns, $\sigma_\%$, which I used throughout Part One, by multiplying by the price[250] and dividing by 16 (to convert from annual to daily volatility):

$$\text{Risk adjusted forecast}_t = \text{Raw forecast}_t \div \sigma_{p,t}$$

$$\sigma_{p,t} = (p_t \times \sigma_{\%,t} \div 16)$$

From there we proceed as normal: multiplying by the forecast scalar (which I estimate at 9.3), capping the absolute forecast size and calculating the optimal position size. However, there is one important difference between this and previous strategies: **we do not use buffering**. The nature of this strategy is that we will always want to have the rounded optimal position on. Applying buffering would decimate the profitability of mean reversion.

Figure 81 shows an example, for the US 10-year bond future during the 2020 COVID-19 market panic. The grey line is the hourly price. The black line is the

---

248   An important caveat is that my hourly data history only goes back to 2013, just under ten years, rather than the maximum of 50 years for daily data.

249   I could use a standard deviation calculated using hourly prices, but again it is simpler to calculate this on a daily basis and use the resulting estimate throughout the following day. In any case, updating standard deviation estimates on an hourly basis would not result in any significant difference, given we are using a one month half life.

250   Remember we calculate standard deviation using daily returns, so this should be calculated using the previous day's closing price for the currently traded futures contract.

equilibrium price, which updates every day. As we would expect for a moving average, it is smoother than the grey line but also lags.

FIGURE 81: EQUILIBRIUM AND HOURLY PRICE FOR US 10-YEAR FUTURE

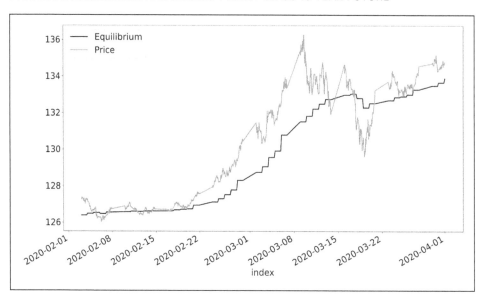

If the price (grey line) is higher than the equilibrium (black line), then we go short. We would be persistently short from late February onwards, which as it turns out was a money losing trade. However, once the market settles at a higher level we would buy the dip on 13th March when the black line goes below the grey. A few days later we sell the rally going short again, and then buy the dip again around 19th March.

Smarter execution of a mean reversion strategy

Before I continue with my usual analysis, I have an admission to make. This strategy has one huge disadvantage. It trades insanely quickly, with a turnover of around 140 times a year – a holding period of less than two weekdays. This is partly by design and also because it does not use buffering. Using my usual 'speed limit' rule, there are only a handful of instruments[251] where we can trade it. For everything else it would just be too expensive. It seems futile to continue with this strategy unless we can do something to push those trading costs down to a reasonable level. We can't slow the

---

251 For reference these are mostly equities: CAC40, Dow Jones, NASDAQ micro, Russell 2000, S&P 500 micro; plus a single metal future - Gold micro.

strategy down without significantly affecting its performance, but we can improve our execution.

I haven't worried too much about how trades are executed in this book so far. For backtesting purposes I have previously assumed that strategies generate positions daily using closing prices, and that the resulting trades are executed at the close of the following day. I also calculate costs and fill prices assuming that a strategy always submits a market order: buy at the bid and sell at the offer. The difference between where we are filled and the mid-market price, halfway between the bid and the offer, is the spread cost. For each instrument I use estimated bid-ask spreads from my own trading system, which checks and records spreads throughout the day. Finally, I also include the cost of paying brokerage commission on each contract traded.

All this made sense for the types of strategies I was analysing. A day or so of delay made no difference to performance. Always paying for a market order is also fine, given I have already ensured that any given strategy and instrument combination could afford to cover the resulting trading costs. The resulting execution costs would be reasonably accurate, except for larger traders who would be unable to execute at the top of the order book. They would need to estimate their expected slippage from the mid price, using level 2 historical data or costs from live trades done in bigger size.

However, this fast mean reversion strategy is quite different. It has some interesting characteristics which make it possible to use some funkier execution tactics. In particular, it's possible to use *limit* rather than market orders.

It's much easier to explain how with an example. Let's stick with the US 10-year bond future. As you can see from figure 81, at one point in early March 2020 we had an equilibrium price of 132.5 and an hourly price of 133. The annual percentage standard deviation of returns, $\sigma_\%$, was around 6%:

$$\text{Raw forecast}_t = \text{Equilibrium}_t - p_t = 132.5 - 133 = -0.5$$

$$\sigma_p = (p_t \times \sigma_\% \div 16) = 133 \times 0.06 \div 16 = 0.4987$$

$$\text{Risk adjusted forecast}_t = \text{Raw forecast}_t \div \sigma_p$$
$$= -0.5 \div 0.4987 = -1.0025$$

$$\text{Scaled forecast}_t = \text{Risk adjusted forecast}_t \times \text{forecast scalar}$$
$$= -1.0025 \times 9.3 = -9.32$$

This forecast doesn't require capping or combining with any other forecasts, so we can plug it straight into the standard position sizing formula:

$$N_t = \text{Capped forecast} \times \text{Capital} \times \text{IDM} \times \text{Weight}_i$$
$$\times\, \tau \div (10 \times \text{Multiplier} \times p_t \times FX_t \times \sigma_{\%,t})$$

It will make our life easier if we split this into the *average position*, which is what we obtain with a forecast of +10, and a forecast scaling component:

$$N_t = (\text{Capped forecast} \div 10) \times \text{Average position}$$

Average position
$$= \text{Capital} \times \text{IDM} \times \text{Weight}_i \times \tau \div (\text{Multiplier} \times p_t \times FX_t \times \sigma_{\%,t})$$

What does this look like for US 10-year bonds? For simplicity, let's assume we are trading only this single instrument, so our weight and IDM will both be 1. Suppose we have an arbitrary $500,000 of capital. As US 10-year bonds are valued in US dollars our FX rate is also 1. The futures multiplier for US 10-year bonds is 1,000. Finally, I use the usual risk target τ = 20%.

Our average position will be:

Average position
$$= 500000 \times 1 \times 1 \times 0.2 \div (1000 \times 133 \times 1 \times 0.06) = 12.53$$

A scaled forecast of –9.32 gives us an unrounded optimal short position of just over 11 contracts:

$$N_t = (\text{Capped forecast} \div 10) \times \text{Average position}$$
$$= (-9.32 \div 10) \times 12.53 = -11.68$$

Since we cannot trade fractional contracts we round this, to acquire a short position of 12 contracts in US 10-year bonds.

So, I hear you ask, where do limit orders come in? What we can do with the mean reversion strategy, which would be much harder for any other strategy, is to **calculate the current price that would be required to produce a given position**. That then allows us to place limit orders at the appropriate level.

Because this is a mean reversion strategy, the price at which we would want to sell will be higher than the initial price, and the buying price would be lower. Hence we put on two limit orders which bracket the initial price. We need a buy limit order below the current price, to purchase a single contract at the price implied by an optimal position of short 11 contracts. Then, above the current price, we would have another limit order. This would be a sell order for a single contract, with whatever price is required to achieve an optimal position of short 13 contracts.

What happens next? The most likely outcome is that the price will eventually rise or fall until one or the other limit orders is touched and executed. And there is good news. Because these are limit orders **we are not paying any spread costs**. Given certain assumptions, which I will discuss in a moment, our order will be filled at our limit price with only a brokerage commission payable.

How can we calculate the limit prices? Firstly, I substitute the forecast formula into the position sizing equation:

$$N_t = \{[\text{Scalar} \times (\text{Equilibrium}_t - p_t) \div \sigma_p] \div 10\} \times \text{Average position}$$

I can rearrange this to solve for the price which would imply a given position N_t:

$$p = \text{Equilibrium}_t - [N_t \times 10 \times \sigma_p \div (\text{Scalar} \times \text{Average position})]$$

First of all, the buy order. If we buy one contract then we will have a position of –11. If we substitute a position of N = –11 into the formula to get the limit price we get:

$$p = \text{Equilibrium}_t - [N_t \times 10 \times \sigma_p \div (\text{Scalar} \times \text{Average position})]$$
$$= 132.5 - [-11 \times 10 \times 0.4987 \div (9.3 \times 12.53)] = 132.97$$

We create a limit order to buy a single contract if the price falls from 133 to 132.97. In fact, since the tick size for US 10-year bonds is 1/64 = 0.015625, the actual limit price would be 132.96875.

Similarly, for the sell order, our short position will increase to –13 for which the price would need to be:

$p = 132.5 - [-13 \times 10 \times 0.4987 \div (9.3 \times 12.53)] = 133.05$

Hence we will have a limit order to sell one contract if the price rises from 133 to 133.05; again in practice this would be at 133.046875. After we've put in those orders we have the following setup:

Sell limit order	133.046875 (Sell 1, to go short 13 contracts)
Current price and position	133.00 (Short 12 contracts)
Buy limit order	132.96875 (Buy 1, to go short 11 contracts)

As it happens the price rises to 133.078125 in the following hour, so our sell order would have been executed. Our position is now short 13 contracts. We now create a new sell limit order whose price is implied from a position of –14:

$$p = 132.5 - [-12 \times 10 \times 0.4987 \div (9.3 \times 12.53)]$$
$$= 133.099 \sim 133.09375$$

Obviously, we also have a new buy limit order for a position of –12, which comes in with a limit price of 133.015625. We modify the price of the existing unfilled buy order from 132.96875 to 133.015625, and we end up with:

New sell limit order	133.09375 (Sell 1, to go short 14 contracts)
Current price and position	133.078125 (Short 13 contracts)
Modified buy limit order	133.015625 (Buy 1, to go short 12 contracts)

We would continue executing the strategy in this manner as prices changed throughout the day. Now let us consider the impact of the forecast cap, where absolute forecasts cannot be larger than 20. Returning to the original example, suppose that the current price was a little higher, but all other values remain unchanged:

$$\text{Raw forecast}_t = \text{Equilibrium}_t - p_t = 132.5 - 134.5 = -2.0$$

$$\text{Risk adjusted forecast}_t = \text{Raw forecast}_t \div \sigma_p$$
$$= -2 \div 0.4987 = -4.01$$

$$\text{Scaled forecast}_t = \text{Risk adjusted forecast}_t \times \text{forecast scalar}$$
$$= -4.01 \times 9.3 = -37.3$$

We cap this at –20, giving an unrounded optimal short position of just over 25 contracts:

$$N_t = (\text{Capped combined forecast} \div 10) \times \text{Average position}$$
$$= (-20 \div 10) \times 12.53 = -25.06$$

Now the buy limit order price will be set where we would be short 24 contracts:

$$p = 132.5 - [-24 \times 10 \times 0.4987 \div (9.3 \times 12.53)]$$
$$= 133.5271 \sim 133.53125$$

What about the sell limit order? There isn't one. We don't want to go any shorter than 25 contracts, regardless of what happens to the price, since the scaled forecast is already beyond its maximum. Hence we use the following rules:

If scaled forecast <= −20: No sell limit order

If scaled forecast >= +20: No buy limit order

All of this assumes that the markets are open 24 hours a day, and that prices don't suddenly jump to a new level which may be beyond our limits. In practice life is never that simple. Returning to our original example, imagine that we reach the end of the day with our original set of orders intact:

Sell limit order	133.046875 (Sell 1, to go short 13 contracts)
Current price and position	133.00 (Short 12 contracts)
Buy limit order	132.96875 (Buy 1, to go short 11 contracts)

It is unwise to leave limit orders on the book overnight, for reasons that will become apparent in a moment. By default, limit orders will usually be automatically cancelled at the end of the day, but if not you should cancel them yourself. Let's assume that we cancel all our orders at the end of the day with a clean slate.

Now imagine that the following day the price opens sharply up, at 134.5, but with an unchanged equilibrium price and standard deviation estimate. We have already calculated the optimal position for a current price of 134.5: it is to go short 25 contracts, some distance from our current position, short 12. We should immediately sell 25 − 12 = 13 contracts to get ourselves back to the optimal position. This should be done as a standard *market* order. This will probably fill at a tick or two below 134.5. We would probably need to do occasional market orders during the day as well, in the event of the price gapping up or down.

The additional rule to implement this behaviour is: If the rounded optimal position is more than one contract away from the current position, then immediately trade a market order in a size that gets you to the rounded optimal position.

Assumptions when backtesting a limit order strategy

As I've noted already, when backtesting a strategy with market orders we can either (a) assume that we pay half the bid-ask spread when executing, which is fine for smaller traders, or (b) model the likely slippage from larger orders using level 2 order book data and empirical data.

A market order doesn't affect the likely behaviour of other market participants, at least in the short term, since it will be executed before anyone in the market can modify their own orders. Of course if you repeatedly place sell orders then the price will go downwards from where it would have been without your intervention. This would be true even if on paper the orders could have been filled at the quantity that is usually available at the best bid. That is why it is better to use empirical data from actual orders when estimating the effect of trading a sizable proportion of the daily volume in a market.

But a limit order can affect other people's behaviour. To take an extreme example, suppose we place a very large limit buy order one tick below the current best bid. That order will signal to other market participants that there is a big buyer in the market and they will almost certainly react by raising their bids and offers, making it very unlikely the large limit order will be hit. Indeed, this is one of the tactics used by so-called market 'spoofers' to drive up prices (placing large orders that you don't intend to get filled is against market regulations, so don't do it!).

One nice feature of the mean reversion strategy is that it will always place orders for one lot, as long as your capital isn't too large. Again, unless you are trading in significant size, these orders will also be spaced out in the order book. Limit orders of a single contract that are spaced out in the order book are unlikely to affect market behaviour significantly, assuming the market is sufficiently liquid. So it's probably reasonable for small traders to assume in a backtest that they would have been filled if the historical price series went through their limit price.

However, this isn't true for larger traders. As we allocate more capital to this strategy, we'd find that our single lot limit orders got bunched tighter and tighter together. Subsequently, with even more capital allocated, they would no longer be single lot orders.

For example, with $50 million in capital, the original position from the example above would be short 1,168 contracts. The limit price for the buy order that would be placed around the original position, calculating from a position of $1168 - 1 = 1,167$ contracts is 132.999. But this is less than one tick away from the starting price of 133. In fact to get a limit price of 132.984375, one tick below the starting price, we would need to create a limit order derived from an optimal position of 1,132 contracts. We would need to place a buy limit order of $1168 - 1132 = 36$

contracts, one tick below the current price, and also a sell order for 32 contracts one tick above it.

Would limit orders of 32 and 36 contracts respectively change the behaviour of the market? Perhaps not in the highly liquid US 10-year bond future, but at some point we would be placing orders that were sufficiently large to cause other market participants to start reacting, and making it less likely that our backtested assumptions would be correct. Effectively, this imposes a capacity constraint for strategies like these.

The capacity constraint isn't so much because this is a mean reversion strategy, or because it is using limit orders, but because it is a strategy which is trading quickly. Any strategy which trades quickly in large size is going to end up with lower performance than what can be achieved with less capital. Just because we are using limit orders doesn't mean we can escape this effect.

Of course the strategies in Parts One, Two and Three also have a capacity constraint, but because they trade relatively slowly their capacity is likely to be significantly higher.

Which instruments can we trade?

Using the smart limit order execution tactic reduces costs considerably.[252] However, not all instruments will have costs that are low enough to trade this strategy. Technically, we can't use the usual speed limit test to check this, because the normal risk adjusted cost methodology won't apply for a strategy which uses a mixture of limit and market orders. However, as an approximation, you can assume a turnover of 45 for this strategy, which you can check using the usual speed limit formula and the standard risk adjusted cost per trade:

Maximum turnover
= [0.15 – (Cost per trade × Rolls per year)] ÷ Cost per trade

---

252 To backtest this strategy with hourly data I assumed that limit orders were executed one hour after submission at the limit price if the next price was lower than the limit for a buy order, or higher for a sell order. I assumed that market orders were also executed with a one-hour lag, with my normal assumptions for bid-ask spreads. All types of orders still incur commissions. Commissions and spreads are deflated in the historical backtest in accordance with my normal methodology.

This implies that there are 18 instruments in the Jumbo portfolio which are too expensive to trade, since their maximum turnover calculated with the appropriate costs per trade figures is less than 45. But this still leaves 84 instruments to play with.

Performance of fast mean reversion

How well does the mean reversion strategy perform with smarter execution tactics? Let's first consider the median performance across instruments, and within different asset classes. This will give you some idea of what you could achieve if you traded a single instrument. The results are in tables 129 and 130. They **cannot** be directly compared with previous tables of the same type. This is because I only have hourly data from 2013 onwards. Also, the costs figures shown are only for commissions and do not include spread costs. This is because I am using a mixture of limit orders and market orders, and only market orders are subject to spread costs. However the mean returns shown are still accurate post cost returns, which include the spread cost on market orders.

TABLE 129: MEDIAN INSTRUMENT PERFORMANCE SINCE 2013 ACROSS FINANCIAL ASSET CLASSES FOR FAST MEAN REVERSION

	Equity	Vol	FX	Bond
Mean annual return	15.0%	23.5%	17.1%	11.4%
Costs (commission)	−1.0%	−2.3%	−1.2%	−1.3%
Average drawdown	−9.9%	−16.0%	−7.6%	−8.9%
Standard deviation	27.4%	31.3%	23.5%	26.1%
Sharpe ratio	0.54	0.75	0.73	0.44
Turnover	57.4	49.1	63.9	53.0
Skew	−0.96	−2.31	−0.34	−0.65
Lower tail	3.35	4.20	2.95	3.38
Upper tail	1.78	2.17	1.79	1.86

Hourly data since January 2013.

TABLE 130: MEDIAN INSTRUMENT PERFORMANCE SINCE 2013 ACROSS COMMODITY ASSET CLASSES FOR FAST MEAN REVERSION

	Metals	Energy	Ags	Median
Mean annual return	6.1%	0.6%	−1.6%	10.7%
Costs (commission)	−1.0%	−0.3%	−1.8%	−1.0%
Average drawdown	−13.6%	−15.8%	−36.1%	−11.0%
Standard deviation	26.2%	28.1%	26.1%	26.4%
Sharpe ratio	0.19	0.04	−0.06	0.41
Turnover	59.4	57.1	59.4	57.4
Skew	−0.74	−1.00	−0.92	−0.82
Lower tail	4.30	3.29	3.21	3.35
Upper tail	1.68	1.93	1.99	1.86

Hourly data since January 2013.

Even with the caveat that we only have eight years of data, these results look pretty good. The average Sharpe ratio (SR) of 0.41 is extremely good for an individual instrument, despite higher than usual turnover and costs. There is also an interesting pattern across asset classes. The financial instruments in table 129 are consistently better than the commodities in table 130.

On the downside, the skew and lower tail are pretty horrendous. This should not be surprising. Mean reversion strategies have a well-deserved reputation for horrible skew, since they usually make steady profits, but then hang on to losing positions rather than closing them as a trend strategy would do. The persistent short in US 10-year from February 2020 that I discussed earlier is a classic example. But there is some good news: negatively skewed strategies tend to have better drawdowns than their positively skewed cousins, and this is clearly the case here.

As is my usual practice I also analysed the aggregate performance of the Jumbo portfolio. In table 131 I also include the performance of the trend and carry strategies from Part One, but only since 2013 for consistency with the faster mean reversion strategy.

TABLE 131: PERFORMANCE OF AGGREGATE JUMBO PORTFOLIO SINCE 2013: TREND, CARRY AND MEAN REVERSION

	Strategy nine Multiple trend	Strategy ten Carry	Strategy twenty-six Fast mean reversion
Mean annual return	13.8%	8.7%	17.6%
Costs	−1.1%	−0.7%	−3.1%
Average drawdown	−15.0%	−10.2%	−7.3%
Standard deviation	17.5%	15.3%	22.0%
Sharpe ratio	0.79	0.56	0.80
Turnover	40.6	10.5	39.2
Skew	0.20	−0.31	−1.46
Lower tail	2.96	2.06	2.74
Upper tail	2.01	1.33	1.98

Costs for fast mean reversion are commissions only. For trend and carry they include both spread costs and commissions.

The higher costs of the fast trading strategy twenty-six are no surprise, even though they include only commissions. Even with this handicap the fast mean reversion strategy is comparable with trend on an SR basis, and is a little better than carry. However, the skew is worse than it is for the Part One strategies, although the lower tail doesn't look too bad.

The correlation of mean reversion is around −0.28 with trend and +0.15 with carry. This suggests there would be considerable benefits from trading fast mean reversion alongside these other strategies. However, this can't be done just by combining forecasts together, because of the different execution tactics required. They would need to be traded separately.

Trading multiple strategies without forecast combination

In the first three Parts of this book I have used forecast combination to blend different strategies together. This is extremely useful: it reduces costs and makes life much simpler as we don't need to calculate optimal positions and trades for many different types of trading rules.

However, it won't always be appropriate to mix and match different strategies in this way. A strategy like fast mean reversion doesn't play well with the daily strategies from Parts One, Two and Three. The latter are all designed to trade on daily data, with buffering, and the use of market orders. In contrast, fast mean reversion can trade on continuous prices, does not use buffering, and tries to use limit orders where possible.

To use some jargon, the daily strategies have relatively slow 'alpha decay'. We can take our sweet time about executing their orders, since we know we will be holding our positions for weeks or months. But this clearly isn't true for the fast mean reversion strategy.

How can you trade a daily strategy alongside fast mean reversion? A simple option is to let both strategies generate their own optimal positions and orders, and **trade them in separate accounts**. This makes the attribution of profits very straightforward, but has several potential downsides. It is rather inefficient when it comes to margin usage and costs.

If their positions are uncorrelated to some degree, then you could save on margin requirements by **allowing both strategies to trade in the same account**. This could also reduce per account costs, such as data fees, and make it easier to meet minimum trading requirements. There would be a little more work in performance attribution, but it wouldn't be impossible since each trade is allocated to a given strategy.

With some effort you can also save on transaction costs, **by netting trades from the two strategies against each other before execution**. Try this: every morning first generate the orders required by your daily trading strategy, but do not execute them. Then turn on your mean reversion strategy. This will generate orders throughout the day. If any of these orders can be partially or fully netted off against an existing daily order, then that will reduce transaction costs for both strategies. Towards the end of the day you should execute any outstanding daily orders that have not been netted out.

This is very efficient, but also pretty complicated, and makes it much harder to work out which of your strategies is currently profitable. A simpler alternative is to **only trade mean reversion on a selected group of instruments, and keep other instruments purely for daily trading systems**. It would be sensible to select instruments for fast mean reversion that have the lowest risk adjusted commission costs and acceptable levels of minimum capital. It would be less sensible to risk over fitting and only trade financial assets with the mean reversion strategy. These do better in tables 129 and 130, but as I have explained at length in earlier chapters, these differences in instrument performance are rarely statistically significant.

If you are using the dynamic optimisation technique from Part Three (strategy twenty-five) for your daily trading, then you can achieve this very neatly by setting zero position constraints on the instruments you have reserved for mean reversion trading. The dynamic optimisation method will also allow you to make best use of the capital you have reserved for daily trading.

Figure 82 shows the cumulative account curves for the strategies in table 131 in the period when I have hourly data. Ignoring the underwhelming performance of carry, it is useful to focus on the different characters of trend and mean reversion. They have similar overall performance but take very different paths to get there. Mean reversion shows a classic negative skew pattern of a long period of steady returns, followed by a crash when the COVID-19 panic hits in 2020. It also begins underperforming in early 2022, when the invasion of Ukraine leads to elevated levels of risk.

FIGURE 82: ACCOUNT CURVES FOR MEAN REVERSION AND OTHER STRATEGIES USING HOURLY DATA SET

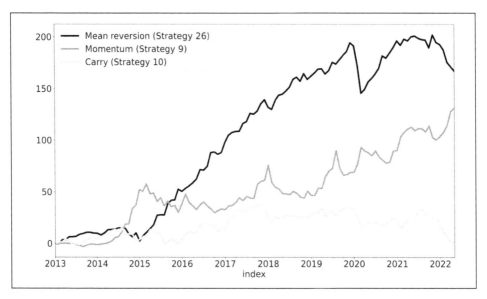

In contrast, trend has a very typical positive skew experience: short periods of strong performance, followed by slow downtrends. It tends to do better when mean reversion is suffering: notably in March 2020 and the first quarter of 2022, but also in late 2014 and the second half of 2017.

Summary

I'd be extremely cautious about trading this mean reversion strategy. Its tendency to hang on to losing positions, and to 'catch falling knives' when prices continue to move against it, make it very dangerous indeed. However, there is an easy way to make this strategy safer: improving its performance, whilst preserving most of its diversifying qualities. All will be revealed in the next chapter.

Strategy twenty-six: Trading plan

All other stages are identical to strategy nine.

Strategy	Go long or short one or more instruments with variable risk estimate and a mean reverting forecast based on a fast updating equilibrium price.
Instrument(s)	Any that meet minimum capital, liquidity and cost thresholds. Costs should be below 3% per year, assuming a risk target $\tau = 20\%$.
Forecast calculation	For some back-adjusted price p_t: $$\text{Equilibrium}_t = \text{EWMA}_{\text{span}=5}\,(p_t,\ p_{t-1},\ p_{t-2},\ ...)$$ $$\text{Raw forecast}_t = \text{Equilibrium}_t - p_t$$ $$\text{Risk adjusted forecast}_t = \text{Raw forecast}_t \div \sigma_p$$ $$\sigma_p = (p_t \times \sigma_\% \div 16)$$
Scaled forecast	$$\text{Scaled forecast}_t$$ $$= \text{Risk adjusted forecast}_t \times \text{Forecast scalar}$$ Forecast scalar = 9.3.
Capped forecast	$$\text{Capped forecast}_t$$ $$=\text{Max}(\text{Min}(\text{Scaled forecast}_t, +20), -20)$$
Optimal unrounded position	$$N_t = (\text{Capped forecast} \div 10) \times \text{Average position}$$ $$\text{Average position} = \text{Capital} \times \text{IDM} \times \text{Weight}_i$$ $$\times\ \tau \div (\text{Multiplier} \times p_t \times \text{FX}_t \times \sigma_{\%,t})$$
Market order	If the rounded optimal position is more than one contract away from the current position, then immediately trade a market order in a size that gets you to the rounded optimal position.
Buy limit order	If scaled forecast >= +20: No buy limit order. Otherwise: Buy one contract with limit price, for current position in contracts C: $$p = \text{Equilibrium}_t - [(C + 1) \times 10 \times \sigma_p$$ $$\div (\text{Scalar} \times \text{Average position})]$$

Sell limit order	If scaled forecast <= −20: No sell limit order.
	Otherwise: Sell one contract with limit price, for current position in contracts C:
	$$p = \text{Equilibrium}_t - [(C - 1) \times 10 \times \sigma_p$$ $$\div (\text{Scalar} \times \text{Average position})]$$
Limit order management	If a buy limit order is executed, create a new buy limit order and modify the existing sell limit order so it has the correct price.
	If a sell limit order is executed, create a new sell limit order and modify the existing buy limit order so it has the correct price.
	Cancel all limit orders at the end of the day.

STRATEGY TWENTY-SEVEN

Safer fast mean reversion

The pure mean reversion strategy I described in strategy twenty-six works well but is not without problems. In particular, it has viciously negative skew and suffers badly when risk levels are elevated. In theory, this makes it a good diversifier for trend style strategies, but you would have to be a very brave person to trade it on an outright basis.

This next fast strategy combines the two pure price effects that most strategies seek to capture: mean reversion, but also trend. Strategy twenty-seven is profitable because these two effects work at different time scales. By combining them we can create a strategy that trades quickly but also benefits from slow moving trends. Introducing an element of trend following to the mean reversion strategy makes it more profitable, but also safer.

Additionally, I bring in a concept from Part Two: **reducing forecasts when volatility is high**. Mean reversion is a classic convergent strategy. It does well when markets are stable, but loses badly when the excrement hits the rotating blade. Reducing position size when things get heavy prevents it getting run over by a volatility spike.

Together these two changes turn fast mean reversion into a highly profitable and ultimately safer strategy.

> **Strategy twenty-seven:** Trade a mean reverting forecast which does not oppose a trend forecast, and reduces positions when volatility is high.

Fast mean reversion plus 'slow' trend following

The basic mean reversion strategy has some interesting properties. Notably, it is trading directly against the current trend, which makes it a very nice diversifier when traded alongside the strategies in Part One. But this also brings dangers. Suppose a price is on a sharp down trend. We will keep buying, as the market looks cheaper and cheaper relative to its equilibrium. This 'catching a falling knife' behaviour can lead to ugly losses. As a result, the skew on mean reversion strategies is usually heavily negative.

One solution is to apply a stop loss to the strategy. We keep buying as the price falls, but if the price falls too far we immediately close our position. I'm not keen on this idea. How far is 'too far' – where should we set the stop loss? Once we've closed our positions, when should we reopen them? Using stop losses also leads to path dependence,[253] which makes the strategy harder to backtest.

There is a simpler way, which is to **only trade the mean reversion when it is in the same direction as the current trend**. Effectively this means we buy on dips under the prevailing trend, and sell on rallies above the trend. To do this we first calculate a mean reversion forecast using the approach from the previous chapter:

$$\text{Equilibrium}_t = \text{EWMA}_{span=5} (p_t, p_{t-1}, p_{t-2}, ...)$$

$$\text{Raw forecast}_t = \text{Equilibrium}_t - p_t$$

$$\sigma_p = (p_t \times \sigma_\% \div 16)$$

$$\text{Risk adjusted forecast}_t = \text{Raw forecast}_t \div \sigma_p$$

We now apply a *forecast overlay*: if the forecast from a trend trading rule has a different sign to the mean reversion forecast, then we set the risk adjusted mean reversion forecast to zero. In principle we could use any trading rule or combination of rules for the trend following overlay, but to keep things simple I will just use a single rule from Part One: the EWMAC rule with spans of 16 and 64 days, EWMAC16 for short.

How does the overlay affect the behaviour of the mean reversion rule? Consider a market in an uptrend, with EWMAC16 calculating a positive forecast. If the current price falls below the equilibrium, then we will go long. When the current price is equal to the equilibrium, we would close our long position at a profit. But if the price subsequently rises above the equilibrium *we do not go short*, since this would be the opposite of the prevailing trend. As a result we end up tactically 'buying the dip' and trading the mean reversion below the current trend line.

If the market starts to sell off, then we will initially be long, since the current price is likely to be persistently below the equilibrium and the EWMAC forecast is also still long. But after a week or so of losing money, depending on the precise nature

---

253 Path dependence in this context means our forecast on any given day will depend on what our forecast was yesterday, and makes backtesting more complex and less intuitive.

of the underlying price changes, the EWMAC forecast will turn negative. Now there is a conflict between the signs of the two forecasts, so we close our long mean reversion position. We would not reopen any trades until the current price is above the equilibrium, at which point we would go short.

This modification removes the need for an explicit stop loss. Instead, the trend overlay gets us out of losing positions. It also increases the correlation between the mean reversion and trend strategies, from fairly negative to modestly positive. But on the upside it improves the outright performance of mean reversion, as well as making it much safer.

Less mean reversion when risk rises

Mean reversion also does badly when volatility rises. We can see this in figure 82 on page 436. The COVID-19 pandemic and the invasion of Ukraine are both painful periods for the pure mean reversion strategy. If you read Part Two, you will know that trend and carry also suffer when risk levels rise. I explored this phenomenon in strategy thirteen. At the same time I also introduced a technique for modifying forecasts so that they are lower when volatility is higher. We can use exactly the same method here to make mean reversion a little safer.

It is probably worth reading that earlier chapter if you haven't done so already, but here is a brief summary of the methodology. Let $\sigma_{i,t}$ be the current estimated level of percentage standard deviation of returns for a given market i, measured using the method developed in strategy three. Then the *relative* level of volatility $V_{i,t}$ is the current estimate divided by the ten-year rolling average. Assuming 256 business days in a year, that would be:

$$V_{i,t} = \sigma_{i,t} \div \text{mean}(\sigma_{i,t-2560}, \sigma_{i,t-2559}, \dots \sigma_{i,t})$$

Given the relative level of volatility, V, we take the quantile point Q based on historical data for a given instrument:

$$Q_{i,t} = \text{Quantile of } V_{i,t} \text{ in distribution}(V_{0,t} \dots V_{i,t})$$

The quantile point will vary between 0 (if this is the lowest value we've seen so far) and 1 (for the highest). A value of 0.5 would indicate this is the median point in the historical distribution. We then calculate a vol multiplier, M:

$$M_{i,t} = \text{EWMA}_{10}(2 - 1.5 \times Q_{i,t})$$

Adjusted risk adjusted forecast
= Risk adjusted forecast$_{i,t}$ × M$_{i,t}$

Once we have applied the *volatility forecast multiplier* and the *trend forecast overlay*, we proceed with the usual calculations. Firstly, we apply a forecast scalar. The effect of the forecast overlay is to turn off the mean reversion strategy about half the time, so a higher forecast scalar is required: I estimate it to be around 20. We then cap the forecast, calculate the optimal position and use the execution methodology described in strategy twenty-six to keep costs low.

However, we need to modify the relevant equations to account for the effect of the vol multiplier, *M*. Firstly, the formula for optimal position, giving the forecast *scalar* and equilibrium price, is:

$$N_t = \{[M_t \times Scalar \times (Equilibrium_t - p_t) \div \sigma_p] \div 10\} \times Average\ position_t$$

Average position
= Capital × IDM × Weight$_i$ × τ ÷ (Multiplier × p$_t$ × FX$_t$ × σ$_{\%,t}$)

Then, as before, I rearrange that to get the buy and sell limit prices, given the current position *C*:

Buy limit price, p$_t$
= Equilibrium$_t$ − [(C+1) × 10 × σ$_p$ ÷ (Scalar × M$_t$ × Average position$_t$)]

Sell limit price, p$_t$
= Equilibrium$_t$ − [(C−1) × 10 × σ$_p$ ÷ (Scalar × M$_t$ × Average position$_t$)]

Performance of safer mean reversion

What effect does the application of these two changes have on the mean reversion strategy? Tables 132 and 133 have the median performance across instruments. These can be directly compared with tables 129 and 130 on pages 432 and 433, which cover the original mean reversion strategy.

TABLE 132: MEDIAN INSTRUMENT PERFORMANCE ACROSS FINANCIAL ASSET CLASSES FOR SAFER FAST MEAN REVERSION

	Equity	Vol	FX	Bond
Mean annual return	9.8%	16.3%	10.0%	18.3%
Costs (commission)	−0.6%	−1.2%	−0.7%	−0.7%
Average drawdown	−8.4%	−11.4%	−7.8%	−3.9%
Standard deviation	21.5%	27.1%	18.3%	18.4%
Sharpe ratio	0.43	0.60	0.54	1.00
Turnover	81.3	68.4	92.1	77.6
Skew	−0.77	−2.41	−0.27	−0.11
Lower tail	5.77	10.85	4.52	4.10
Upper tail	1.92	2.83	2.22	2.32

Hourly data since January 2013.

TABLE 133: MEDIAN INSTRUMENT PERFORMANCE ACROSS COMMODITY ASSET CLASSES FOR SAFER FAST MEAN REVERSION

	Metals	Energy	Ags	Median
Mean annual return	8.7%	9.2%	8.5%	10.2%
Costs (commission)	−0.6%	−0.2%	−1.0%	−0.6%
Average drawdown	−11.5%	−9.1%	−12.5%	−8.1%
Standard deviation	18.7%	19.7%	18.7%	19.5%
Sharpe ratio	0.43	0.47	0.46	0.54
Turnover	83.0	83.6	83.9	81.9
Skew	−0.74	−0.65	−0.94	−0.57
Lower tail	5.42	4.91	5.12	5.08
Upper tail	1.98	2.64	2.35	2.12

Hourly data since January 2013.

These are *very* good results. Firstly, let's examine the skew. We were deliberately trying to engineer out some of the negative skew associated with mean reversion, so it's satisfying to see that we have achieved this: the median monthly skew across all instruments goes from –0.82 to –0.57. Both tails have got worse, but this is not surprising. Remember, we applied a forecast overlay which turns the strategy off about half the time, and then roughly doubled the forecast scalar to compensate. This will have the effect of making the returns more extreme.

It isn't often that we achieve the holy grail of improving both skew and Sharpe ratio (SR), but this is one occasion. All asset classes now have a decent average SR, and the overall median has improved from 0.41 to 0.54.

What about the aggregate performance across the Jumbo portfolio? The numbers are in table 134. For your convenience, I have also included statistics for the original mean reversion strategy.

TABLE 134: PERFORMANCE OF AGGREGATE JUMBO PORTFOLIO SINCE 2013 FOR ORIGINAL AND SAFER FAST MEAN REVERSION

	Strategy nine Multiple trend	Strategy ten Carry	Strategy twenty-six Fast mean reversion	Strategy twenty-seven Safer, fast mean reversion
Mean annual return	13.8%	8.7%	17.6%	31.6%
Costs	–1.1%	–0.7%	–3.1%*	–1.9%*
Average drawdown	–15.0%	–10.2%	–7.3%	–2.0%
Standard deviation	17.5%	15.3%	22.0%	14.8%
Sharpe ratio	0.79	0.56	0.80	2.14
Turnover	40.6	10.5	39.2	65.7
Skew	0.20	–0.31	–1.46	1.36
Lower tail	2.96	2.06	2.74	2.29
Upper tail	2.01	1.33	1.98	2.13

* Costs for fast strategies are commission only and do not include spread costs on market orders.

Curiously, the monthly skew is significantly positive for this aggregate portfolio: we get a significant skew benefit from diversification, as we have seen for other strategies. It looks like the negative skew events in individual assets aren't significantly correlated, or at least weren't in the ten years or so covered by this backtest. This might be a little misleading, as the skew for other time periods is quite different: it's 0.25 for daily returns, –0.36 for weekly and –0.06 for annual returns. On balance I would be surprised if the skew of this strategy were actually significantly more positive than for trend, but we've certainly eradicated the worst of the negative skew in strategy twenty-six.

Also surprisingly, turnover has increased, but costs are lower. Again, this is a consequence of using a forecast overlay to turn the strategy off periodically. This brings the average position down, and hence increases turnover – which is a multiple of the average position. But as we are trading only about half the time, our costs are reduced. They do not quite halve, since we have the additional costs from closing positions when the trend forecast flips to an opposing sign.

But what jumps out from this table is the SR. It is impressively large, and the first we have seen in this book that is over two. In my career as a quantitative trader I have always had a long standing policy: **I do not trust a backtested Sharpe ratio over two**. There are certainly plenty of reasons not to trust this one.

Firstly, the historical backtest period, just under ten years, is shorter than I would like. There are good reasons to suppose that the last ten years included unusual market conditions that might just have favoured this strategy. Secondly, it is hard to backtest a strategy deploying limit orders that effectively trades continuously using hourly data. There may well be assumptions or errors in my code that make the results look better than they really would have been.

Finally, I can easily be accused of the sin of in sample fitting. From reading this book you will probably conclude that I added two modifications to the original mean reversion strategy after examining its performance. In reality, I actually began testing with a more complex version that included the trend forecast overlay, and then decided it would be easier to explain if I began with a simple pure mean reversion strategy. The choice of EWMAC16 as the overlay was purely arbitrary and not fitted, although of course I already knew that this was a profitable trend strategy in its own right.

But it is true that the volatility multiplier feature was added later. In my defence, it would have been fairly obvious that a mean reversion strategy would have done badly when volatility is higher without looking at the backtest. Also, I took the volatility scaling feature 'off the shelf' from strategy thirteen without making any further changes to it.

With that all in mind, figure 83 shows the cumulated account curve for both the original mean reversion strategy and the strategy with the two modifications I made in this chapter. There is a clear improvement during high volatility periods such as early 2020 and the first quarter of 2022.

FIGURE 83: EFFECT OF ADDING SAFETY CHANGES TO MEAN REVERSION STRATEGY

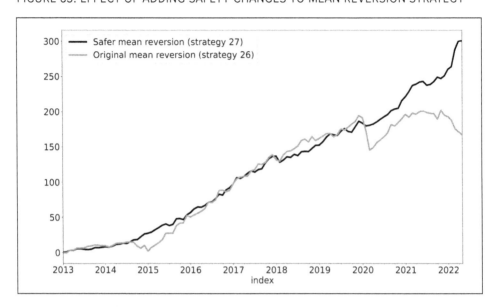

Would I trade this strategy with my own money? Yes, absolutely, but with a number of caveats. Firstly, it would require a significant amount of capital[254] to trade the aggregate Jumbo portfolio and realise the full possible benefits on display in table 134. As I do not have the necessary $50 million or so, I would have to trade a smaller sample of instruments. Although the single instrument SRs in tables 132 and 133 are impressive, the skews are pretty ugly, and I would not be able to diversify them away with just a few instruments.

Secondly, I would not want to put all my money in this strategy. I would trade it alongside a daily strategy, incorporating carry and trend, plus other strategies I explored in Parts Two and Three. As table 135 clearly shows, the correlation of the safer strategy with carry and trend is still relatively low, although higher than for original mean reversion.[255]

---

254 Note that it's not possible to use the dynamic optimisation methodology introduced in strategy twenty-four to trade this strategy, so we'll need the full minimum capital in every instrument we trade.

255 However, the additional performance and better skew of safer mean reversion overcome this higher correlation at a portfolio level when combined with carry and trend. We get a higher SR and better skew using safer mean reversion for any combination of strategy eleven and mean reversion. For example, for a 50% allocation to strategy eleven (trend and carry), plus 50% in fast mean reversion, the SR with safer mean reversion is higher: 1.89 rather than 1.65 for the original mean reversion strategy. As you would expect the skew is also better for a 50/50 portfolio with safer mean reversion, with monthly skew of 0.59 rather than –0.29.

TABLE 135: CORRELATION MATRIX OF RETURNS FOR VARIOUS STRATEGIES SINCE 2013

	Trend	Carry	Trend and Carry	Mean reversion	Safer mean reversion
Trend (Strategy 9)	1	0.15	0.88	−0.24	0.34
Carry (Strategy 10)		1	0.50	0.08	0.01
Trend and carry (Strategy 11)			1	−0.15	0.33
Mean reversion (Strategy 26)				1	0.43
Safer mean reversion (Strategy 27)					1

Sadly, putting less money into the strategy would further reduce the number of instruments I could trade it with. If I stick to the tradition of putting 40% of my capital allocation into convergent strategies, then the maximum I would like to allocate to a mean reversion strategy would be half of that: 20%. If you are feeling extremely brave, then the optimal allocation to safe mean reversion to maximize SR and alpha is around 85% (assuming the other 15% is in strategy eleven, so the allocation to convergent strategies is effectively 91%[256]). Even a relatively modest 50% allocation to strategy twenty-seven still has an excellent Sharpe, but improves the skew to levels that are no longer scary, though that particular blend is still 70% convergent.

Finally, this strategy is significantly more complicated to run than a daily trading strategy. It is almost inconceivable that it could be implemented without the use of a fully automated trading system. Additionally, because of the large number of intra-day orders that it places, there is scope for the strategy to lose significant amounts of money in a very short period of time. Hence, I would advise very careful testing and monitoring for this strategy.

This strategy probably does have a very high expected SR, even if it is not really over two. But achieving it will require significant levels of capital,[257] experience and technical skill. It will not be easy.

---

256   60% of strategy eleven is in divergent strategies (trend), and that is 15% of the overall allocation, so we only have 0.6 × 0.15 = 0.09 in the divergent bucket, leaving the rest (mean reversion and carry) in convergent strategies.

257   But not too much capital! As I already discussed in the previous chapter, unlike the slower strategies discussed in this book this strategy will also have relatively limited capacity, suggesting that this strategy will also be problematic for multi-billion dollar funds.

Strategy twenty-seven: Trading plan

All other stages are identical to strategy twenty-six.

Strategy	Go long or short one or more instruments with variable risk estimate and a forecast based on fast mean reversion, plus a trend overlay and volatility level multiplier.
Risk adjusted forecast calculation	We begin with the mean reversion forecast from strategy twenty-six: $$\text{Equilibrium}_t = \text{EWMA}_{\text{span}=5}\ (p_t, p_{t-1}, p_{t-2}, ...)$$ $$\text{Raw forecast}_t = \text{Equilibrium}_t - p_t$$ $$\text{Risk adjusted forecast}_t = \text{Raw forecast}_t \div \sigma_p$$ $$\sigma_p = (p_t \times \sigma_\% \div 16)$$
Trend overlay	Calculate an EWMAC16,64 forecast using daily data. If this has a different sign from the risk adjusted mean reversion forecast, then set the mean reversion forecast to zero.
Volatility multiplier	Let $\sigma_{i,t}$ be the current estimated level of percentage standard deviation of returns for a given market i, measured using the method developed in strategy three. The *relative* level of volatility $V_{i,t}$ is the current estimate divided by the ten-year rolling average: $$V_{i,t} = \sigma_{i,t} \div \text{mean}(\sigma_{i,t-2560},\ \sigma_{i,t-2559},\ ...\ \sigma_{i,t})$$ We take the quantile point Q based on historical data for a given instrument: $$Q_{i,t} = \text{Quantile of } V_{i,t} \text{ in distribution}(V_{i,t}\ ...\ V_{i,t})$$ We then calculate a vol multiplier, M: $$M_{i,t} = \text{EWMA}_{10}(2 - 1.5 \times Q_{i,t})$$ $$\textbf{Modified risk adjusted forecast}$$ $$= \textbf{Raw risk adjusted forecast}_{N,i,t} \times M_{it}$$
Scaled forecast	$$\textbf{Scaled forecast}_{i,t}$$ $$= \textbf{Modified risk adjusted forecast}_{i,t} \times \textbf{forecast scalar}$$ Forecast scalar = 20.

PART FIVE

Relative Value Strategies

You must read all of Part One before reading Part Five.

You do not have to read Parts Two, Three or Four before reading Part Five.

This part of the book is about relative value (RV) strategies. Rather than predicting the direction of individual asset prices, we are trying to forecast the direction of one asset relative to another.

We can categorise RV strategies in the following ways:

- By the type of assets: (a) **across instruments**, (b) For different expiries of the same instrument – **calendar trades**.

- By the number of markets included: (a) two markets – **spread trades**, and (b) three markets – **triplet trades.**

The following RV strategies are included in Part Five:

- **Strategy twenty-eight:** Cross instrument spreads.

- **Strategy twenty-nine:** Cross instrument triplets.

- **Strategy thirty:** Calendar trading strategies (both spreads and triplets).

Cross instrument spreads

Futures trading is risky. We are at the whims of the markets. If we are long S&P 500, and global equities crash, then we are toast. A short German bond position can be very profitable, until the day the ECB decides to initiate a surprise new round of QE and the resulting price spike empties our trading account. It is all very well being long Corn on a nice bullish trend, but what if unusually good weather in the USA increases supply and kills the price? Fortunately, it is possible to trade without being exposed to market movements – at least in theory.

The answer is to trade **relative value (RV)**. Instead of an outright long on the S&P 500, we could hold a long hedged with a short on the Eurostoxx. As long as US equities outperform Europe, then we are in the money. Short German bonds can still be profitable, if they are paired with a long Italian BTP position that doesn't do quite as well in a rally. Long Corn and short Wheat may well be a good trade, even when the sun shines more than is expected.

RV is not easy. It requires higher leverage than the directional trading strategies we have seen so far in this book. There are hidden risks and dangers inherent in this style of trading, and the costs can wipe you out. But it is still a useful weapon to have in your trading strategy armoury.

> **Strategy twenty-eight:** Trade pairs of instruments as relative value spreads.

What is a spread instrument?

A **spread** is where we trade two related instruments together, with a long position in one hedged with a short in another, effectively creating a new **synthetic instrument**. To create this new instrument we need some instrument **weights** as, in one sense, a spread instrument is like a mini hedged portfolio. As this is a spread strategy, these weights will be long on one instrument and short on the other. These weights determine the relative size of positions we would put on to express a trade in a given spread, and are also used to calculate the price of the synthetic instrument. Formally:

A spread instrument Ra/b is long instrument a and short instrument b in a ratio of R:1 (and if R=1 then we write a/b).

Let's take an example. Suppose we want to trade (a) the US 5-year bond and (b) US 10-year bond in a spread strategy. These instruments are clearly related; they are both US bond futures with nominal maturities that are only a few years apart. Initially let's assume that we wish to have the following relative weights, 1.5:1 on the 5-year and 10-year bond respectively, implying R = 1.5 and we can use the shortened form: **1.5US5/US10**.

A ratio of 1.5:1 means that our mini-portfolio consists of a long position in US 5-year bonds that is 1.5 times the value of a short position in US 10-year bonds. I will discuss the calculation of an appropriate value for the relative weight R later in the chapter.

How do we find the price of our synthetic instrument? That's easy, given prices in each instrument of p_a and p_b:

$$p^\Delta = Rp_a - p_b$$

Clearly this price could easily be zero or negative, but this doesn't matter as long as we are careful to handle prices with this in mind. For our example, right now the prices of US 5-year and 10-year bonds are around 112 and 119 respectively. Therefore the spread price is:

$$p^\Delta = Rp_a - p_b = 1.5 \times 112 - 119 = 49$$

A useful question to ask at this point is the following: How much profit will we make if the price of this spread goes from 49 to 50? We need to revisit some of the equations from Part One. Firstly, the value of a futures position holding N contracts is equal to:

$$\text{Notional exposure (Base currency)}$$
$$= N \times \text{Notional exposure per contract (Base currency)}$$

$$\text{Notional exposure per contract (Base currency)}$$
$$= \text{Multiplier} \times \text{Price} \times \text{FX rate}$$

Suppose we hold N_a contracts of instrument a, and are short $-N_b$ of instrument b. The value of our short position in instrument b is:

Notional exposure$_b$ (Base currency)

= N$_b$ × Multiplier$_b$ × Price$_b$ × FX rate$_b$

For instrument a we will have some number of contracts N_a:

Notional exposure$_a$ (Base currency)

= N$_a$ × Multiplier$_a$ × Price$_a$ × FX rate$_a$

The net exposure of our mini-portfolio will be equal to:

Net notional exposure (Base currency)

= (N$_a$ × Multiplier$_a$ × Price$_a$ × FX rate$_a$)

− (N$_b$ × Multiplier$_b$ × Price$_b$ × FX rate$_b$)

To simplify this I will need to specify how many contracts of N_a I need for each short contract of N_b:

N$_a$ ÷ N$_b$ = (R × Multiplier$_b$ × FX rate$_b$) ÷ (Multiplier$_a$ × FX rate$_a$)

If I substitute that into the net exposure formula, and do some rearranging:

Net notional exposure (Base currency)

= N$_b$ × (Rp$_a$ − p$_b$) × (Futures multiplier$_b$ × FX rate$_b$)

= N$_b$ × p$^\Delta$ × (Futures multiplier$_b$ × FX rate$_b$)

If I say that a short position of one contract in instrument b is equivalent to one unit of the synthetic instrument, then the net notional exposure per unit of the synthetic instrument will be:

Notional exposure per synthetic contract (Base currency)

= p$^\Delta$ × (Futures multiplier$_b$ × FX rate$_b$)

This is analogous to the usual formula for net exposure per contract, except that we have replaced the price with p^Δ and are using the multiplier and FX rate for instrument b. This makes sense, since everything has been normalised to be relative to a single contract of b.

Let us return to our example. Our choice of instruments makes our calculations easier, as they are both denominated in US dollars, and also have the same futures multiplier (1000). Since we are short US 10-year bonds, that is asset b and we will always short a single contract for each one unit long in the synthetic spread instrument. But how many long US 5-year bond futures should we own? Remember that $R = 1.5$, so for every short US 10-year bond future contract, we will hold this many 5-year bond futures:

$$N_a = (R \times Multiplier_b \times FX\ rate_b) \div (Multiplier_a \times FX\ rate_a)$$
$$= (1.5 \times 1000 \times 1) \div (1000 \times 1) = 1.5$$

For this simple case, everything cancels except R. Of course we can't buy fractional contracts, but I will deal with that problem later. The net notional exposure per unit of the synthetic contract is:

$$\text{Notional exposure per synthetic contract (Base currency)}$$
$$= p^\Delta \times (Futures\ multiplier_b \times FX\ rate_b) = 49 \times (1000 \times 1) = \$49,000$$

If the spread price goes to $50, then the exposure value will increase to $50,000 and we will have made $1,000. More generally, every unit of price will increase the value of what we hold by the futures multiplier for instrument b multiplied by the FX rate.

The implications of this analysis are important: **we can treat these synthetic spread instruments like standard futures instruments.** We can calculate profits, and also back-adjusted prices, by plugging the back-adjusted price of the underlying futures into the equation for p^Δ. In principle, we can also use our standard position sizing equations and trading strategies to trade them. The only difference is that when a buy (or sell) of X contracts is called for, we would actually buy (or sell) $X(N_a \div N_b)$ contracts of instrument a, and sell (or buy) X contracts of instrument b.

It isn't *quite* that simple, which is why this chapter runs to a few more pages, but that is the basic idea behind synthetic spread instruments.

What is the risk of a spread instrument?

A spread instrument has a back-adjusted price, and we can measure the standard deviation of that price. It won't make much sense to measure it as a percentage, $\sigma_\%$, since there is a chance the spread price will be close to zero or negative. But we can measure it from daily price returns σ_p, as we did when using standard deviations for the purpose of risk adjusting forecasts. Remember that:

$$\sigma_p^\Delta = \text{Standard deviation}(p_t^\Delta - p_{t-1}^\Delta, p_{t-1}^\Delta - p_{t-2}^\Delta, \ldots)$$

As I write this chapter the standard deviation of the spread 1.5US5/US10 has a standard deviation of 0.159. This is lower than the standard deviations for each of the US 5-year (currently 0.379) and US 10-year (0.568) bond futures.

That shouldn't be surprising. We have effectively hedged out some of the risk inherent in holding US bonds. In fact, as the synthetic spread instrument is effectively a mini-portfolio, we can calculate precisely what we expect the standard deviation of the spread price to be. We just need the correlation between the daily returns of the two assets as price differences, ρ. Using the standard formula from financial economics 101 for portfolio risk with two assets:

$$\sigma_{\text{portfolio}} = \sqrt{(w_a{}^2 \sigma_{p,a}{}^2 + w_b{}^2 \sigma_{p,b}{}^2 + 2\rho w_a w_b \sigma_{p,a} \sigma_{p,b})}$$

$$\rho = \text{Correlation}([p_{a,t} - p_{a,t-1}], [p_{b,t} - p_{b,t-1}] \text{ over t})$$

For spread instruments where the weights are $w_a = +R$ and $w_b = -1$, we obtain:

$$\sigma_p^\Delta = \sqrt{(R^2 \sigma_a{}^2 + \sigma_b{}^2 - 2\rho R \sigma_a \sigma_b)}$$

We can check this makes sense for 1.5US5/US10, given the correlation is currently 0.961:

$$\sigma_p^\Delta = \sqrt{(R^2 \sigma_a{}^2 + \sigma_b{}^2 - 2\rho R \sigma_a \sigma_b)}$$
$$= \sqrt{(1.5^2 0.379^2 + 0.568^2 - 2 \times 0.961 \times 1.5 \times 0.379 \times 0.568)} = 0.159$$

I don't intend to use this more complex method to derive the standard deviation of the price, but it is very useful for the intuition it provides. Notice that the standard deviation of the spread will be smaller if the correlation ρ is closer to 1. That makes sense: the more closely related the two instruments are, the better the hedge will be, and the smaller the resulting risk.

As a result the main danger with spread trading is **correlation risk**.[258] If correlations fall, then our trades will get riskier. As an example, imagine that the correlation of US

---

258 Note for risk managers: you can use this formula if you wish to calculate the standard deviation of the spread from its components, the standard deviations for each leg, and the correlation. That will allow you to make assumptions about the likelihood of correlations falling or risk rising. The risk figures derived with this method can either be used for position sizing, or to assess the risk of the portfolio.

5-year and 10-year fell from its current level of 0.961, down to 0.86. A pretty modest reduction in correlation, but it would translate to a near doubling in risk from 0.159 to around 0.30!

Position sizing for spread instruments

Now would be a good point to revisit the position sizing formulae from Part One. The optimal number of contracts for some instruments is:

$$N_t = \text{Scaled forecast}_t \times \text{Capital} \times \text{Weight}$$
$$\times \text{IDM} \times \tau \div (10 \times \text{Multiplier} \times p_t \times \text{FX rate}_t \times \sigma_{\%,t})$$

We need to modify this, by substituting $\sigma\%$ with our alternative measure of standard deviation, σ_p^Δ for daily price returns in the spread price p^Δ:

$$\sigma_{\%,t}^\Delta = (\sigma_p^\Delta \times 16) \div p_t^\Delta$$

Alternatively we can measure σ_p^Δ directly from the difference of daily spread prices. For measuring standard deviations for the purpose of position sizing we can use the tricks we learned in strategy three: use an exponentially weighted standard deviation with a 32-day span and a blended span of past and future volatility.

The *weight* in the formula above will be the proportion of our capital which we have allocated to this particular spread instrument, and the instrument diversification multiplier (IDM) will be calculated using the method in strategy four or using the approximations from table 16 in that chapter.

We also need to replace N with N_b, since we are trying to work out the number of units for the synthetic instrument, and each of those consists of a single short contract position in instrument b. Similarly, the futures multiplier and FX rate will also be for instrument b (the price will cancel). After doing all that, we obtain:

$$N_{b,t} = \text{Scaled forecast}_t \times \text{Capital} \times \text{Weight} \times \text{IDM}$$
$$\times \tau \div (10 \times \text{Multiplier}_b \times \text{FX rate}_b \times \sigma_p^\Delta \times 16)$$

Consider once again the example of the spread 1.5US5/US10. We assume that we have $500,000 in capital, and that we are only trading a single spread instrument, so *weight* = *IDM* = 1. I use a risk target τ of 10%. This is lower than usual, for reasons I will explain shortly. Finally, suppose we currently have an average sized scaled forecast of +10. With the current daily standard deviation of 0.159 that I calculated earlier that gives us the following position in instrument b, the US 10-year bond:

$$N_{b,t} = (+10) \times 500000 \times 1 \times 0.1 \div (10 \times 1000 \times 1 \times 0.159 \times 16)$$

$$= 19.7 \text{ contracts}$$

Hence we will be short 19.7 contracts of US 10-year futures. From previous calculations we know that $N_a \div N_b = 1.5$, so we will be long 1.5 times as many US 5-year bond futures for each US 10-year short, hence we will have an optimal position that is long 29.5 contracts of US 5-year.

For comparison, if we had the same figures as in the example, but were trading US 10-year bonds individually with a directional trading strategy, then using the standard deviations I disclosed earlier in the chapter we would have a position of around 5.5 contracts, and for US 5-year bonds it would be approximately 8.2 contracts.

This should not be a surprise. RV trades require bigger positions and more leverage[259] than directional trades, because the underlying price is less volatile, and we have to scale up more to achieve a given risk target. At current prices, the total absolute notional exposure of this spread trade is nearly $5.6 million:[260] over 11 times our capital. Some comparable figures are just under $1 million for the US 5-year as an individual directional trade with the same capital, and $650,000 for the US 10-year on the same basis.

Hence the real danger in an RV trade is that you set it up when correlations are very high, leading to a low estimated standard deviation, and hence a high leverage. If correlations subsequently fall, then the trade will become very risky overnight. If many people have the same trade on, then you will be caught in a 'death spiral' as traders with too much leverage receive margin demands and will be forced to liquidate. It's for this reason that many of the largest trading blow ups in history[261] have been caused by RV or other hedging trades that suddenly stopped hedging.

For this reason I advocate **using a lower risk target for spread trades**. An annualised

---

259 Does this also mean they will use more margin? Not necessarily. It depends on the broker, the exchange and the precise mixture of products.

260 This is made up of a long position in US 5-year bonds worth $3.3 million, and a US 10-year short of around $2.3 million.

261 As I write this the most unsuccessful RV traders in history are: with the second biggest trading disaster of all time, a loss of around $9 billion in 2022 values, by Bruno Iksil, 'The London Whale' of JPMorgan in credit default swaps (CDS); at #3 in the all time list with $9bn is Howie Hubler of Morgan Stanley also in CDS; at #6 we have $6.5bn Brian Hunter of Amaranth in Natural Gas futures; and finally #7 $4.6bn John Meriwether and Long Term Capital Management in fixed income, plus a few other things.

percentage standard deviation of τ = 10% is reasonably conservative. But please bear in mind that the inherent risk in trading with such large amounts of leverage implies that even 10% might be too aggressive.

What are the appropriate weighting for a spread instrument?

What are the best weights for a spread trade: the best value of R? There is actually no easy answer to this question. A naive response is to look for the optimal set of weights that will give us the most profitable trading strategy. But that is almost certainly a path to over fitting. Much better to set the weights, and then see how well a given strategy does trading the resulting synthetic instrument.

Alternatively, perhaps we are looking for the purest synthetic instrument: an instrument which does the best job of hedging? Have we hedged out the risk of the 'the market' – are we market neutral? That will depend partly on our weights, and partly on how we define 'the market'. We could, for example, adopt a technique from the equity market and construct the spread such that it is beta neutral, where beta is the coefficient of risk against 'the market'. There are other asset class specific techniques: in fixed income, for example, we could use duration neutral weightings.

I am going to choose an easier route, and focus on outright rather than market related risk. To measure outright risk we can look at the standard deviation of the spread price which I defined above:

$$\sigma_p^\Delta = \sqrt{(R^2\sigma_a^2 + \sigma_b^2 - 2\rho R\sigma_a\sigma_b)}$$

What ratio R will give us the least volatile spread price, and hence the lowest risk? With a little mathematics[262] we can show that the standard deviation will be minimised when:

$$R^* = \rho\sigma_b \div \sigma_a$$

This neat little equation has some important implications. Firstly, for R > 1 instrument a must have a lower standard deviation than instrument b. Strictly speaking R could take any value but I find R > 1 more intuitive, so this implies we should always put the instrument with the lower risk in position a.

However, this ordering is just a convention. To see why, let's consider a simplified case where the daily standard deviations for price returns are the same for a and b:

---

262 Differentiate with respect to R and set to zero to find the minimum.

$$R^* = \rho\sigma_b \div \sigma_a = \rho$$

Now, what happens to the optimal value of R if we switch instruments a and b?

$$R^* = \rho\sigma_a \div \sigma_b = \rho$$

The implication of this is that for correlations below 1 we would have the same R < 1 regardless of the ordering of instruments. But that doesn't make sense! If the correlation were say 0.5, then the theoretically optimal hedge for one contract of a would be 0.5 contracts of b, whilst simultaneously the best hedge for one contract of b would 0.5 contracts of a!

Because the ordering is irrelevant for the calculation of the optimal R, the best value of R that will minimise spread price risk is just **the ratio of the standard deviations for each individual instrument, measured over daily price changes**:

$$R = \sigma_b \div \sigma_a$$

For example, for the spread US5/US10 the daily price return standard deviation for US 5-years is currently 0.379, and for US 10-years is 0.568. The best R will be the ratio of these:

$$R = \sigma_b \div \sigma_a = 0.568 \div 0.379 = 1.499 \sim 1.5$$

A familiar number.

The use of this formula also implies that the optimal ratio would usually not be close to being an integer, or even a 'nice' figure like 1.5. Also, optimal ratios will vary over time, as relative standard deviations change. For example, the optimal ratio of R for US5/US10 has varied between 1 and 2.75 over the last 30 years. Non-integer ratios make it operationally difficult and unintuitive to run a trading strategy, unless the ratio is something like 1.5 or 2.5. Varying ratios also reduce intuition, as well as making the backtesting process very complicated.

In some cases there are certain ratios which are standardised in the market. This might be an advantage for very large institutions who wish to trade their spreads as off-exchange block trades. It could also be an advantage if you believe that a trading strategy is self-fulfilling, and you want to be looking at the same price as the rest of the market. Using market conventions also means that you can directly download the price, or read discussions about the spread without having to recalculate any figures that are quoted.

Later in this chapter I will specify some R for each spread I look at. These will mostly be calculated using the optimal R^* method above, averaged over the last ten years,[263] and then rounded to the nearest 'nice' figure. But in some cases where market conventions exist I will use those as an alternative.

Although this approach has some clear advantages, there are also disadvantages. Using fixed ratios implies that we will not be using the optimal hedge ratio, and we will have a higher correlation with outright prices.

Choice of spread instruments

What is the minimum capital for a spread instrument?

We can easily adapt the minimum capital formula from Part One:

Minimum capital 4 contracts

$$= (4 \times \text{Multiplier}_i \times \text{Price}_{i,t} \times \text{FX rate}_{i,t} \times \sigma_{\%,i}) \div (\text{IDM} \times \text{Weight}_i \times \tau)$$

With the same substitutions that I have made before, we get the following for spread instruments, indexed i:

Minimum capital 4 contracts

$$= (4 \times \text{Multiplier}_b \times \text{FX rate}_{b,t} \times \sigma^\Delta_{p,i} \times 16) \div (\text{IDM} \times \text{Weight}_i \times \tau)$$

Remember that the risk target, τ, should be lower for spread instruments – I suggested 10%. That implies a higher level of minimum capital, but this will be offset by the lower standard deviation inherent in spread prices.

All of the above assumes that the number of contracts required in instrument a for each single contract of instrument b ($N_a \div N_b$) is an integer. If this is not the case, you will need to multiply the minimum capital by the ratio required to achieve integer contracts for both a and b.

For example, if with a single contract of b ($N_b = 1$) the position in instrument a $N_a = 0.5$, the minimum capital required would be doubled, resulting in an effective minimum position of $N_a = 1$ and $N_b = 2$ holding two units of the synthetic instrument. Our actual minimum would be twice that calculated using the minimum capital formula above. For $N_a \div N_b = 0.4$, we would need minimum capital that was five times higher, resulting in minimum positions with one unit of $N_a = 2$ and $N_b = 5$.

---

263   Averaged over all the data where less than ten years is available.

If the minimum capital becomes excessive as a result of this, you may want to make a small adjustment to R. Take an extreme example, if $N_a \div N_b = 0.95$, then you would need to multiply the minimum capital by 20 to achieve integer contracts. It would make much more sense to tweak the value of R, such that the optimal value for N_a was 1.

What is the minimum capital for 1.5US5/US10 if we assume it is the only spread we are trading? First of all, let's ignore the issue of non-integer contracts:

$$\text{Minimum capital 4 contracts}$$
$$= (4 \times \text{Multiplier}_b \times \text{FX rate}_{b,t} \times \sigma^\Delta_{p,i} \times 16) \div (\text{IDM} \times \text{Weight}_i \times \tau)$$

$$= (4 \times 1000 \times 1 \times 0.159 \times 16) \div (1 \times 1 \times 0.10) = \$101{,}760$$

But we need to multiply the RV minimum figure by two, since $N_a \div N_b = 1.5$, and so the effective minimum position is two units of the synthetic instrument with $N_a = 3$ and $N_b = 2$. This gives us minimum capital for the spread trade of just over \$200,000.

Again, it is useful to compare this to the minimum capital for standalone directional trades in US 5-year and US 10-year. With a matching 10% risk these figures would be \$242,000 for US 5-year and \$363,500 for 10-year. Of course we would be happy to trade those with a higher risk target ($\tau = 20\%$), so more realistic values are half of those shown: \$121,000 for 5-year and \$181,000 for 10-year bond futures.

What does it cost to trade spread instruments?

We also need to adapt the cost calculations from Part One to cover spread instruments. It's almost always the case that we will need to execute a spread trade across instruments as two separate trades,[264] so this is just a matter of adding together the costs from each instrument.

Firstly, let's bring in the basic cost equations. Remember that the spread here refers to the bid-ask execution spread, not to spread trading!

$$\text{Spread cost, price points} = (\text{Bid} - \text{Offer}) \div 2$$

$$\text{Spread cost, currency}$$
$$= \text{Futures multiplier} \times \text{Spread cost price points}$$

---

264 Obviously you would want to do these trades simultaneously to reduce the risk of having a temporarily unhedged position.

Cost per contract

= Spread cost currency + Commission per contract

We need to add up the costs, first ensuring they are both in the same currency. As usual, we normalise against currency b. Also recall that we trade $N_a \div N_b$ units of instrument a for each one of instrument b:

Cost instrument a

= ($N_a \div N_b$) × Cost per contract(a) × FX rate$_b$ ÷ FX rate$_a$

Cost instrument b = Cost per contract(b)

Total cost = Cost instrument a + Cost instrument b

Finally, it is useful to calculate costs on a risk adjusted basis, so that we can see if something is cheap enough to trade. In Part One I did this by dividing by the price multiplied by the futures multiplier, and then the standard deviation of the price. However, as we are not using percentage standard deviations in this part of the book, we can replace this with the daily standard deviation of price returns (σ_p^Δ). We also need to substitute in the futures multiplier for instrument b as everything is standardised to that:

Risk adjusted cost per trade

= Total cost ÷ (σ_p^Δ × 16 × Multiplier$_b$)

Let's return to our example, 1.5US5/US10. For US 5-year bonds:

Spread cost, price points = 0.004

Spread cost, currency

= Multiplier × Spread cost price points = 1000 × 0.004 = $4

Cost per contract

= Spread cost currency + Commission per contract

= $4 + $1.50 = $5.50

And for US 10-year bonds:

$$\text{Spread cost, price points} = 0.01$$

$$\text{Spread cost, currency} = 1000 \times 0.01 = \$10.00$$

$$\text{Cost per contract} = \$10.00 + \$1.50 = \$11.50$$

We can now work out the cost of trading each unit of the spread:

$$\text{Cost instrument a (US 5-year)}$$
$$= (N_a \div N_b) \times \text{Cost per contract(a)} \times \text{FX rate}_b \div \text{FX rate}_a$$

$$= 1.5 \times \$5.50 \times 1 \div 1 = \$8.25$$

$$\text{Cost instrument b} = \$11.50$$

$$\text{Total cost} = \$8.25 + \$11.50 = \$19.75$$

$$\text{Risk adjusted cost per trade}$$
$$= \text{Total cost} \div (\sigma_p^\Delta \times 16 \times \text{Multiplier}_b)$$
$$= 19.75 \div (0.159 \times 16 \times 1000) = 0.00776$$

As a comparison, for an outright trade in US 5-year the risk adjusted cost per trade comes out at 0.00091, and for US 10-year it is very similar: 0.001. The cost of trading the spread is almost eight times the cost of trading each of the legs! This is partly because we are trading $R + 1 = 2.5$ contracts rather than just one, and also because the standard deviation of the spread price is considerably lower than on the individual legs of the trade.

One final point, if you are in the unusual situation of having two instruments with different rolling schedules, then to calculate rolling costs you should use the number of rolls for the instrument with the most rolls per year.

Examples of spread instruments

With over 100 instruments in my data set, there are nearly 5,000 possible spread instruments. Clearly, I'm not going to analyse them all. Indeed, many of these would have correlations that are too low to make them sensible choices for spread instruments. Others might have high correlations, but for no good reason. Using them as spread instruments smacks of *data mining*, a close cousin to the sin of over fitting.

As an example of such data mining, I remember a long discussion whilst I was working in the hedge fund industry, when a couple of researchers tried to justify the New Zealand dollar / US dollar FX versus Live Cattle spread trade they wanted to investigate, after a thorough search of every possible spread had thrown it up as a promising candidate. Perhaps, one of them mused, it was related to New Zealand's sizeable lamb exports, and surely lamb and beef were economic substitutes? Fortunately good sense prevailed that day, and we did not pursue that particular strategy.

To further minimise the number of possibilities, I will only consider spreads that occur within asset classes. There are more likely to be high correlations with good justifications for instruments that share an asset class.

Finally, I will not include here every possible spread instrument, even of plausible highly correlated assets. This is for space reasons, because there are often a number of possible spreads which would be very similar. For example, we could trade US 2-year bonds versus US 5-year, as well as US 5-year against US 10-year. It is difficult to say which of these is a better option, and inclusion of only one of them in this list does not indicate any preference on my part, or any expectation of superior performance. Naturally, if you have the necessary capital, you could trade both of them.[265]

Fixed income spreads (bonds and STIR)

I used 1.5US5/US10 as an example in this chapter for a couple of reasons. As I noted at the very start of this book, my first finance job was on an investment bank desk, where I worked as a fixed income trader. Later in my career as a hedge fund manager I managed a large portfolio of fixed income trading strategies, which included several that traded spreads. But irrespective of my personal experience, in many ways fixed income is the spiritual home of spread trading. This is mainly because the correlations between many bond and short-term interest rate (STIR) futures are extremely high.

Table 136 shows a selection of some of the vast number of possible fixed income spreads. All of the tables in this section have the same format, regardless of asset class, so it is worth explaining them in some detail. In each row I include the two instruments in the relevant spread, the correlation of daily price returns ρ, my suggested ratio R, and the number of long contracts for instrument a required to hedge one short contract of instrument b ($N_a \div N_b$), calculated with the formula:

---

265 It is also possible to trade a *triplet* instrument of US 2-year, 5-year and 10-year. I explore this possibility in the next chapter.

$$N_a \div N_b$$

$$= (R \times \text{Futures multiplier}_b \times \text{FX rate}_b) \div (\text{Futures multiplier}_a \times \text{FX rate}_a)$$

With the exception of cross currency instruments, $N_a \div N_b$ will remain constant. I have also put in the minimum capital assuming $\tau = 10\%$, and the risk adjusted cost to help you choose suitable spreads.

TABLE 136: SOME EXAMPLES OF FIXED INCOME SPREADS

Instrument a	Instrument b	ρ	R	$N_a \div N_b$	Minimum capital	Risk adjusted cost
US 5-year	US 10-year	0.96	1.5	1.5	$200,000	0.0078
German Schatz (2-year)	German Buxl (20-year)	0.57	10	10	$1,000,000	0.0024
Korean 3-year	Korean 10-year	0.85	3	3	$200,000	0.0058
US 10-year	Ultra US 10-year	0.97	1	1	$200,000	0.0040
US 10-year	US 10-year swap	0.93	1	1	$200,000	0.0071
Eurodollar	US 2-year	0.82	1.25	1	$100,000	0.0051
German Bund (10-year)	US 10-year	0.79	1.1	1	$400,000	0.0018

A word of warning for wannabe fixed income spread traders: I note above that I prefer to use ratios calculated using the optimal R method above to give the lowest standard deviation, using data averaged over the last ten years:

$$R^* = \sigma_b \div \sigma_a$$

But the last ten years, from 2012 to early 2022, have been pretty unusual in the fixed income markets, with suppressed volatility in yields for much of that period, especially at the front of the yield curve. That distorts the value of R calculated using relative standard deviations over that period.

To take an extreme example, the relative duration weight of the German 2-year Schatz to 20-year Buxl spread would be around 7, but the ratio value I have calculated from the data would be significantly higher. I have made some attempt to correct for this problem: the ratios shown here are an average of the calculated empirical values combined with my best guess of what the ratios would be in a 'normal' interest rate environment.

Equity spreads

Correlations in equities aren't as high as they are for bonds. Of course, they are usually higher within countries than across countries. Within countries we can do spreads such as a sector versus an index, large cap versus small cap, or tech versus index. Table 137 shows some examples of equity spreads.

TABLE 137: SOME EXAMPLES OF EQUITY SPREADS

Instrument a	Instrument b	ρ	R	$N_a \div N_b$	Minimum capital	Risk adjusted cost
Nikkei	S&P 500	0.67	3	0.05	$2,400,000	0.00074
EU Auto	Eurostoxx 50	0.73	2.5	0.5	$440,000	0.0024
Russell 2000 (small cap US)	S&P 500 (large cap)	0.66	1	10	$1,200,000	0.00052
S&P 500	Dow Jones	0.93	5	0.05	$880,000	0.00094
S&P 500	NASDAQ	0.93	1.25	0.5	$3,600,000	0.00033

Volatility spreads

There are only three volatility instruments in my data set, and only two are liquid enough to be included in the Jumbo portfolio: the US VIX and the European VSTOXX. This leaves us with only one possible spread strategy, as shown in table 138.

TABLE 138: THE ATLANTIC VOLATILITY SPREAD

Instrument a	Instrument b	ρ	R	$N_a \div N_b$	Minimum capital	Risk adjusted cost
V2X (VSTOXX)	VIX	0.83	1	9	$350,000	0.011

FX spreads

The FX asset class is unusual, because all the instruments within it are pairs of currencies. Most of the liquid futures in the Jumbo portfolio are paired against the US dollar, but there are also a few cross rates like EUR/GBP. So you might think it would make sense to use spreads in the FX markets as a way of creating additional cross rates. You could, for example, trade AUD/USD as a spread with JPY/USD, to create AUD/JPY. There is in fact an AUD/JPY future, but it is not especially liquid.

However, this misses a crucial point: I define spreads as the **difference** between two prices, but the correct way to calculate a cross rate from two individual FX rates is to use the **ratio**. Hence, it would not be theoretically correct to use synthetic spread instruments as a proxy for cross rates.

For this reason I decided against including FX spread instruments in this book.

Agricultural spreads

The agricultural asset class is very diverse, and effectively consists of several sub classes: grains, softs, meats and indices. Within those we have further divisions, for example within the grains there are Corn, Oats, Rice, Wheat and the Soy complex. We would expect the highest correlation within the most granular groups, but we can also compare instruments across sub-classes.

TABLE 139: EXAMPLES OF SOME AGRICULTURAL SPREADS

Instrument a	Instrument b	ρ	R	$N_a \div N_b$	Minimum capital	Risk adjusted cost
Soy oil	Soybeans	0.65	6	0.5	$880,000	0.0020
Wheat	Red Wheat	0.85	1	1	$210,000	0.0054
Live cattle	Feeder cattle	0.71	1	1.25	$2,000,000	0.0035
Oats	Corn	0.42	1	1	$450,000	0.0076

Metals spreads

Like agricultural markets, we can separate metals out into three main groups: precious, non-precious and the new-fangled crypto markets which appear to be most highly correlated with the metals asset class. Again, we can do spreads within, or across, these groups. Incidentally, you may have been expecting to see Gold/Bitcoin in this list: the ancient safe haven in times of crisis, and the more modern equivalent. But their correlation is slightly negative, suggesting that the so-called 'digital Gold' a.k.a. Bitcoin isn't as shiny as you might have thought.

TABLE 140: EXAMPLES OF SOME METALS SPREADS

Instrument a	Instrument b	ρ	R	$N_a \div N_b$	Minimum capital	Risk adjusted cost
Ethereum	Bitcoin (micro)	0.53	5	0.01	$7,500,000	0.0048
Silver	Gold (micro)	0.79	20	0.2	$375,000	0.0013
Gold (micro)	Platinum	0.56	1	5	$500,000	0.0019
Copper	Iron	0.22	10	0.04	$6,000,000	0.0026

Energy spreads

The energy group is the most interesting, because many of the instruments are products which are created by refining Crude Oil. Hence, there are strong logical reasons[266] for any empirical relationship between different instruments. This can lead to issues for traders who use quantitative methods for calculating spreads, as we do here. There might be a good fundamental reason why the relative production cost of a product like Heating Oil has changed, which will impact on the spread between Crude and the relevant product. A purely backward looking calculation for the appropriate ratio will miss this.

Some energy futures also have 'last-day' variations, which are highly correlated with their vanilla cousins. Finally, we can consider different grades or locations for the same product, such as the two key benchmarks for Crude: Brent and WTI.

There is an obvious spread missing from this list. You might expect that, although the production of Natural Gas and Oil is only indirectly related, to some degree they act as substitutes so there ought to be a reasonably stable relationship. But their correlation is actually very low, making them unsuitable for a spread market.

---

266   This is also true of the Soy complex, and to an extent with Grains and Meat.

TABLE 141: SELECTED ENERGY SPREADS

Instrument a	Instrument b	ρ	R	$N_a \div N_b$	Minimum capital	Risk adjusted cost
Heating oil	WTI Crude (mini)	0.90	16.66	0.2	$3,600,000	0.00098
Gasoline	Heating oil	0.93	1	1	$840,000	0.0020
Henry Hub Gas (mini)	HH Gas last-day	0.97	1	4	$600,000	0.0064
WTI Crude (mini)	Brent last-day	0.98	1	2	$370,000	0.0045

Trading strategies for spread instruments

Forecasting and position sizing for spread instruments

To reiterate: the significant advantage of trading spreads as *synthetic* instruments is that we can treat them like any individual instrument. This means we can use the standard position sizing formula, but with a few tweaks:

$$N_{b,t} = (\text{Capped combined forecast}_{i,t} \times \text{Capital} \times \text{IDM} \times \text{Weight}_i \times \tau)$$
$$\div (10 \times \text{Multiplier}_i \times \text{FX rate}_{i,t} \times \sigma_p^\Delta \times 16)$$

Number of contracts (N)	This is the reverse of the position required in instrument *b* (substitute longs for shorts, shorts for longs). For instrument *a* we would hold the reverse of that position in relative size $N_a \div N_b$, using the formula calculated earlier in the chapter.
	For example, if $N_b = 2$, and $N_a \div N_b = 1.5$, then we would be short 2 contracts of instrument *b*, and long 3 contracts of instrument *a*.
Instrument weight and instrument diversification multiplier (IDM)	The instrument weight, *weight$_i$*, will be the weight given to the synthetic instrument. You can still use the handcrafting approach from strategy four to set these.
	The calculation of the IDM would be the same, but using the returns of trading a sub-strategy for each synthetic spread instrument to estimate the correlation matrix. Alternatively you can still use the approximate values in table 16 back on page 116.
Risk target	The risk target, τ, should be set more conservatively than the 20% I recommended earlier in the book: I suggest 10%.

Futures multiplier and FX rate	These are for instrument b.
Standard deviation of returns	This is the daily standard deviation of price returns for the synthetic instrument price, which will be equal to: $$p_t^\Delta = Rp_a - p_b$$ $$\sigma_p^\Delta = \text{Standard deviation}(p_t^\Delta - p_{t-1}^\Delta,\ p_{t-1}^\Delta - p_{t-2}^\Delta,\ ...)$$

Buffering for spread instruments

Although most of the strategy engineering from Part One works seamlessly with spread instruments, this is not quite true of *buffering*. Remember that for buffering we established a no trading buffer zone around the optimal position, and then checked to see if the current position was outside the zone. If it was, then we traded to the edge of the buffer.

How do we do that for spreads? Do we buffer each leg of the strategy separately? That wouldn't make sense, as our position will frequently be temporarily unhedged. Instead, I suggest[267] buffering the position for instrument b, and then if a trade is required we will execute a matching trade for instrument a.

Let's begin by updating our calculation for the width of the buffer zone for a spread instrument i:

$$B_{i,t} = 0.1 \times \text{Capital} \times \text{IDM} \times \text{Weight}_i \times \tau$$
$$\div\ (\text{Multiplier}_b \times \sigma_{p,i,t}^\Delta \times 16 \times \text{FX rate}_{b,t})$$

The key changes I have made here are to replace the annualised percentage standard deviation with its daily equivalent for price differences, and to make it clear that the multiplier and FX rates refer to instrument b. Now we define the buffer zone. Given an optimal position of $-N_b$ for instrument b:

$$\text{Lower buffer, } B_{i,t}^L = \text{round}(-N_{b,t} - B_{i,t})$$

$$\text{Upper buffer, } B_{i,t}^U = \text{round}(-N_{b,t} + B_{i,t})$$

---

267   A more complex alternative is to buffer the instrument that has the highest outright trading costs.

We now compare our current position C_b in instrument b to the buffer:

$$B^U_{i,t} \leq C_{b,t} \leq B^L_{i,t} : \text{No trading required}$$

$$C_{b,t} < B^L_{i,t} : \text{Buy } (B^U_{i,t} - C_{i,t}) \text{ contracts}$$

$$C_{b,t} > B^U_{i,t} : \text{Sell } (C_{i,t} - B^U_{i,t}) \text{ contracts}$$

Importantly at this point we don't actually do any trading, because we now need to see what this implies for instrument a. Firstly, if we don't trade instrument b, then we wouldn't trade instrument a either. If we do trade instrument b then we will need to do a matching trade for instrument a. To do this, we set $-N^*_b$ to be equal to the rounded position we would have after doing the buffering trade, and then calculate the optimal position that is implied for instrument a:

$$-N^*_{b,t} = B^L_{i,t} \text{ or } -N^*_{b,t} = B^U_{i,t}$$

$$N_{a,t} = N^*_{b,t} \times (R \times \text{Futures multiplier}_b \times \text{FX rate}_{b,t})$$
$$\div (\text{Futures multiplier}_a \times \text{FX rate}_{a,t})$$

We may need to round this to get a whole number of contracts. Then we compare our current position in instrument a and see what trade is required. Finally, we can do both of the trades, for instrument a and also b. We should do them as close to simultaneously as possible, to avoid the risk of temporarily owning a partially unhedged position.

Trend trading of spread instruments

Since the vast majority of my trading rules are based on the back-adjusted price of an instrument, it is possible in theory to use almost any of them for synthetic instruments (an obvious exception are the carry strategies, but I will come to those in a moment).

I have insufficient space to perform a full analysis of all possible trading strategies across all possible instruments. Instead I am going to focus on trading a single trading rule, EWMAC16, with a subset of assets that are all US bond futures. This might seem like a perverse choice, since all the spread instruments are likely to be highly correlated. However, this will allow us to get some intuition into how different spreads trade more easily than if we considered a more heterogeneous set of instruments. Of course if you are cynical, you would suspect I am covering US bond futures because of my fixed income background.

To begin with, let us consider the raw materials that we have – the instruments from which we will construct our spreads. I will ignore the ultra US 10-year treasury note, since it is very similar to the classic US 10-year note and has much less history. I will also drop the US 3-year bond; again this is in the Jumbo portfolio but has very limited history. This leaves us with the five futures in table 142.

TABLE 142: SELECTED US BOND FUTURES

	Market code	Annual standard deviation, σ%	Multiplier	Minimum capital (τ = 20%, 4 contracts)	Risk adjusted cost per trade
US 2-year	ZT	1.8%	2000	$74,000	0.0031
US 5-year	ZF	4.7%	1000	$108,000	0.00091
US 10-year	ZN	6.8%	1000	$160,000	0.0010
US 20-year	ZB	13.1%	1000	$370,000	0.0017
US 30-year	UB	19.9%	1000	$610,000	0.00091

If you are a bond aficionado you will have spotted that my labelling does not correspond exactly to the official name of each bond future. Instead I am using names that reflect the current deliverable bonds for each future. For example, the future with the market code ZB is ambiguously labelled 'US Treasury bond future' on the CME website. But the current deliverable basket includes any bonds with a remaining maturity between 15 and 25 years, so I label this as the 20-year bond.[268]

Notice also from table 142 that the standard deviation increases with maturity. In fact, if interest rates had the same volatility at every maturity, then the standard deviations for each bond future would be in the ratio of their duration (duration, a measure of bond risk, increases with maturity). This is also reflected in the minimum capital figures in the table, which are proportional to standard deviation. The only discontinuity is caused by the change in futures multiplier from $2,000 to $1,000. Risk adjusted costs also tend to fall as standard deviation rises; again there is a discontinuity, this time caused by the doubling in tick size between 5 and 10-year bonds.

Now let us consider the current correlation matrix of these six instruments, in table 143.

---

268   In fact there is a product with code TWE which is explicitly labelled as a 20-year bond future, but this does not meet my liquidity requirements and hence does not appear in my data set.

TABLE 143: CORRELATION MATRIX OF RETURNS FOR US BOND FUTURES

	2-year	5-year	10-year	20-year	30-year
2-year	1	0.92	0.82	0.62	0.50
5-year		1	0.96	0.81	0.70
10-year			1	0.92	0.83
20-year				1	0.96
30-year					1

Instrument a in rows, instrument b in columns.

As we might expect, the closer together two bond maturities are, the higher their correlations will be. Bond futures with similar maturities have very high correlations, some of the highest you will see between any instruments in my data set. Distant maturities have relatively low correlations. Indeed, the US 2-year bond has a far higher correlation with German 2-year Schatz bond futures (around 0.64) than it does with US 30-years (0.50).

This information will feed into our decision about which spreads to trade. There are ten possible combinations available here. Let's begin by examining the values of the price ratio R in table 144 estimated using historical data for correlations and standard deviations, with the formula:

$$R = \sigma_b \div \sigma_a$$

TABLE 144: ESTIMATED VALUES OF PRICE RATIO R FOR DIFFERENT US BOND FUTURE SPREADS

	5-year	10-year	20-year	30-year
2-year	2.5	4	7	10
5-year		1.5	3	4
10-year			2	3
20-year				1.5

Instrument a in rows, instrument b in columns.

As we would expect, distant maturities have a higher R because the ratio between the standard deviations is usually larger, although not always.

Tables 145 and 146 have the minimum capital and the risk adjusted cost of trading. Spreads with adjacent maturities have lower risk, so higher costs, but lower minimum capital. Similarly, costs reduce and required capital rises as the average maturity of the spread increases.

TABLE 145: MINIMUM CAPITAL FOR DIFFERENT US BOND FUTURE SPREADS, $\tau = 10\%$, HOLDING FOUR CONTRACTS

	5-year	10-year	20-year	30-year
2-year	$83,000	$200,000	$600,000	$1,000,000
5-year		$100,000	$470,000	$900,000
10-year			$600,000	$1,500,000
20-year				$470,000

Instrument a in rows, instrument b in columns.

TABLE 146: RISK ADJUSTED COST FOR DIFFERENT US BOND FUTURE SPREADS

	5-year	10-year	20-year	30-year
2-year	0.0063	0.0044	0.0022	0.0012
5-year		0.0078	0.0024	0.0012
10-year			0.0043	0.0015
20-year				0.0030

Instrument a in rows, instrument b in columns.

Broadly speaking, we can trade spreads that are close together such as 2.5US2/US5, or further apart like 10US2/US30. Intuitively, closer spreads such as 2.5US2/US5 are akin to forward interest rates. They are going to be closely related to the slope in the yield curve between the two maturities. We might expect them to be fairly idiosyncratic and not closely related to the interest rate level or the economic cycle, potentially making them good diversifying instruments.

Conversely, something like 10US2/US30 is effectively a bet on the slope of the entire yield curve. Short rates are controlled by central banks whilst long rates reflect expectations. As a result, upward sloping yield curves are associated with a low point in the interest rate cycle, whilst a flat yield curve usually means rates are about to be cut and tend to presage economic recessions.

Let's focus on two spreads that typify these possibilities: 7US2/US20 and 1.5US5/US10. I've chosen these to maximise the available data history. The price of each spread is shown in figures 84 and 85.

FIGURE 84: SYNTHETIC INSTRUMENT PRICE FOR 7US2/US20

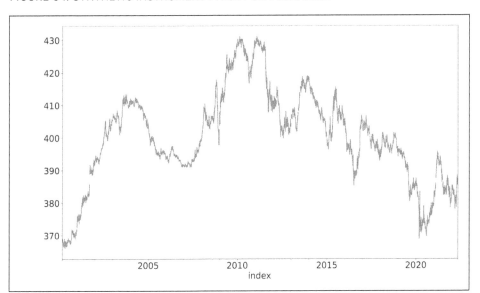

FIGURE 85: SYNTHETIC INSTRUMENT PRICE FOR 1.5US5/US10

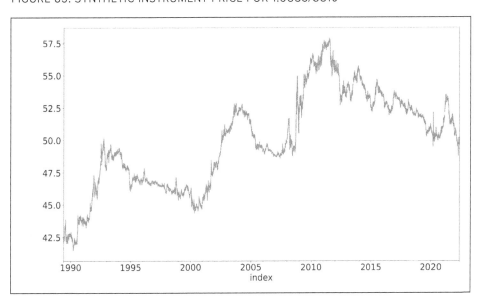

The wider spread, 7US2/US20, certainly tracks the interest rate cycle. It is rising until 2004 as rates are cut and the yield curve steepens, then falls when interest rates start to rise. Then it rallies when the cycle begins again, with interest rates slashed during the market crash of 2008. Thereafter the relationship is less clear, but the rate cuts during the COVID-19 related panic of 2020 are clear to see. Perhaps surprisingly, the 1.5US5/

US10 price also follows interest rates, although again this becomes muddier when we enter a period of very low rates following the 2008 crash.

Most importantly, it looks like there are some nice trends in the back-adjusted price, so let's see what happens if we test the EWMAC16,64 trading strategy with the ten different spread instruments we have available. As a benchmark, I will also consider the performance of the individual instruments using the same trading rule. All the results are in tables 147 to 150, with one type of statistic shown in each table.

TABLE 147: SHARPE RATIO FOR DIFFERENT US BOND FUTURE SPREADS TRADING EWMAC16 RULE

	2-year	5-year	10-year	20-year	30-year
2-year		0.17	0.18	0.40	0.20
5-year			−0.12	0.14	0.11
10-year				0.20	0.10
20-year					0.06
Outright	0.64	0.54	0.43	0.30	0.43

Instrument a in rows, instrument b in columns. Final row is outright directional instrument trading rule performance.

TABLE 148: SKEW FOR DIFFERENT US BOND FUTURE SPREADS TRADING EWMAC16 RULE

	2-year	5-year	10-year	20-year	30-year
2-year		1.0	0.90	1.31	2.52
5-year			1.18	1.36	3.47
10-year				1.39	3.67
20-year					6.40
Outright	1.32	0.95	1.03	1.25	1.74

Instrument a in rows, instrument b in columns. Final row is outright directional instrument trading rule performance.

TABLE 149: LOWER TAIL RATIO FOR DIFFERENT US BOND FUTURE SPREADS TRADING EWMAC16 RULE

	2-year	5-year	10-year	20-year	30-year
2-year		3.42	3.19	3.01	3.02
5-year			3.75	3.67	3.02
10-year				3.38	3.12
20-year					3.31
Outright	3.38	2.94	2.98	2.93	2.84

Instrument a in rows, instrument b in columns. Final row is outright directional instrument trading rule performance.

TABLE 150: CORRELATION AGAINST US 10-YEAR INSTRUMENT PERFORMANCE FOR DIFFERENT US BOND FUTURE SPREADS TRADING EWMAC16 RULE

	2-year	5-year	10-year	20-year	30-year
2-year		0.37	0.39	0.36	0.27
5-year			0.14	0.23	0.20
10-year				0.28	0.21
20-year					0.18
Outright	0.71	0.94	1.0	0.90	0.40

Instrument a in rows, instrument b in columns. Final row is correlation against returns from outright directional instrument trading rule.

All the figures should be familiar, with the exception of table 150. This shows the correlation of the returns[269] obtained by trading EWMAC16 on a given spread or outright directional instrument, against the returns generated from trading the same trend strategy on the outright US 10-year bond futures. I'm using this as a crude measure of the diversification available from a given synthetic instrument.

The top section of each table shows the figures for spreads, and the bottom rows are the result of trading individual instruments. A word of warning: there are different lengths of data available for each instrument, and hence for each spread that involves that instrument. This might distort the data. In particular there are only 12 years of history for US 30-year bonds and this particular bond seems to have some slightly unusual characteristics which could be real or due to the unusual nature of the

---

269   As I noted earlier, we could reduce these correlations by using hedge ratios that were regularly re-estimated rather than fixed.

available history. In particular, US 30-years have a lower correlation with the US 10-year, and an unusually high positive skew.

With that in mind, let me summarise the results:

- In terms of SR, none of the spreads is as good as any individual instrument with the possible exception of US2/US20. There is some weak evidence that spreads consisting of adjacent maturities have worse performance.

- Perhaps surprisingly, the positive skew is very good. This goes against the traditional idea that there is more tail risk in RV strategies. But then we are trend following the spreads, which makes it less likely we will remain in a losing position if a spread price moves sharply against us.

- However, the lower tail – a more robust measure of downside risk than skew – is significantly higher. It looks like it is highest for spreads that are more highly correlated. This suggests the excellent skew estimates are driven by a few positive outliers, which have greater impact when we use more leverage.

- Generally spreads are more diversifying than the outright instruments, which have correlations with the US 10-year of over 0.90. The exception is the outright US 30-year bond.

Broadly speaking, there is something of value here. Intuitively there will be times when outright fixed income trend following does not work on a directional basis, and then we can get some benefit if we also have spreads in our portfolio.

Carry trading for spread instruments

Unlike most trading rules which only use back-adjusted price, the carry rule is going to require some additional modifications before we can use it with synthetic spread instruments. Let's go back to basics and begin with the carry calculations from strategy ten. The raw carry will be calculated using one of the following formulae:

$$\text{Raw carry} = \text{Price of currently held contract}$$
$$- \text{price of further out contract}$$

or

$$\text{Raw carry} = \text{Price of nearer futures contract}$$
$$- \text{price of currently held contract}$$

How can we use this with a spread strategy? Firstly, we replace the prices in the above equations with spread prices, assuming that both instruments are using the same type of raw carry calculation:

Raw carry = Spread price of currently held contract – Spread price of further out contract

or

Raw carry = Spread price of nearer futures contract – Spread price of currently held contract

Now given:

$$p^\Delta = Rp_a - p_b$$

We obtain:

$$\text{Raw carry} = (Rp_a{}^{current} - p_b{}^{current}) - (Rp_a{}^{further} - p_b{}^{further})$$

or

$$\text{Raw carry} = (Rp_a{}^{nearer} - p_b{}^{nearer}) - (Rp_a{}^{current} - p_b{}^{current})$$

Next we have to make some assumptions:

- Both instruments have the same number of rolls per year.
- Both instruments always roll on the same day.

If these rules are broken, it is not the end of the world. But it will mean that carry estimates will be distorted during periods when the rolls are not synchronised. To take an extreme example, if you have an instrument that rolls monthly, and another that rolls every three months, then the carry estimate will be wrong around two-thirds of the time. But since I use a smoothed estimate of carry this will mostly come out in the wash. You might remember from strategy ten that we faced far worse problems when trying to estimate carry on certain outright instruments.

With those assumptions we can use the months between contracts (current vs further, or nearer vs current) for instrument *b* in the following formula:

$$\text{Expiry difference in years}$$
$$= \text{abs(Months between contracts)} \div 12$$

$$\text{Annualised raw carry} = \text{Raw carry} \div \text{Expiry difference in years}$$

Finally, we replace the annualised percentage standard deviation with the daily returns standard deviation, σ_p of the spread price:

$$\text{Carry} = \text{Annualised raw carry} \div (\sigma_p^\Delta \times 16)$$

$$\text{Smoothed carry forecast} = \text{EWMA}_{span}(\text{Carry forecast})$$

We would then proceed to cap the forecast and apply the usual position sizing and buffering methods. Let's see how carry performs on spread instruments. Tables 151 to 154 are in the same format that I used for EWMAC16, but now the statistics are for carry. To be precise they are for carry60, which I arbitrarily chose. However, the results will be very similar for other carry smooths.

TABLE 151: SHARPE RATIO FOR DIFFERENT US BOND FUTURE SPREADS TRADING CARRY60 RULE

	2-year	5-year	10-year	20-year	30-year
2-year		−0.07	−0.06	0.06	−0.13
5-year			−0.07	0.00	−0.11
10-year				0.25	−0.08
20-year					−0.05
Outright	0.25	0.47	0.48	0.57	0.20

Instrument a in rows, instrument b in columns. Final row is correlation against returns from outright directional instrument trading rule.

TABLE 152: SKEW FOR DIFFERENT US BOND FUTURE SPREADS TRADING CARRY60 RULE

	2-year	5-year	10-year	20-year	30-year
2-year		0.37	0.57	0.68	−0.53
5-year			−0.03	0.25	−0.85
10-year				−0.09	−0.93
20-year					1.04
Outright	−0.09	0.04	−0.07	0.25	0.11

Instrument a in rows, instrument b in columns. Final row is correlation against returns from outright directional instrument trading rule.

TABLE 153: LOWER TAIL RATIO FOR DIFFERENT US BOND FUTURE SPREADS TRADING CARRY60 RULE

	2-year	5-year	10-year	20-year	30-year
2-year		1.41	1.53	1.90	2.67
5-year			1.45	1.84	3.20
10-year				1.56	2.81
20-year					2.14
Outright	1.85	2.31	2.19	2.03	2.70

Instrument a in rows, instrument b in columns. Final row is correlation against returns from outright directional instrument trading rule.

TABLE 154: CORRELATION AGAINST US 10-YEAR INSTRUMENT PERFORMANCE FOR DIFFERENT US BOND FUTURE SPREADS TRADING CARRY60 RULE

	2-year	5-year	10-year	20-year	30-year
2-year		−0.47	−0.5	−0.41	−0.16
5-year			−0.22	−0.3	−0.01
10-year				0.01	−0.02
20-year					0.07
Outright	0.72	0.93	1.0	0.8	0.22

Instrument a in rows, instrument b in columns. Final row is correlation against returns from outright directional instrument trading rule.

Let's start with the good news: the spread carry strategies are highly diversifying, with zero or negative correlation with returns from trading carry on the outright directional instruments. But this is 'diworsification': SRs are basically zero, and the tail risk measures are nothing to write home about. At least in US fixed income, carry on spreads doesn't seem to work that well.

Conclusion

Spread trading is not straightforward and has inherently more risk than directional trading. It requires higher leverage and its returns have ominous looking return distribution lower tails. You may need more capital and it certainly has higher costs. Plus, at least for the tiny sub-set of spread instruments I examined in this chapter, it doesn't look as though spreads perform as well as directional trades. By hedging out much of our risk, we appear to be losing out on earning risk premia. This is especially true of carry.

But it is not all bad news. Spread trading strategies will almost certainly have lower correlation than directional strategies traded on outright instruments. Hence, they are highly diversifying. For a large institutional fund that already trades all the available liquid futures, there could be some mileage in adding spread strategies to their portfolio.

Strategy twenty-eight: Trading plan

All other stages are identical to strategies nine and ten.

Strategy	Go long or short one or more synthetic spread instruments. A long position in a synthetic spread instrument index i consists of a long position in instrument a and a short in instrument b.
Back-adjusted price calculation	Given back-adjusted prices for instruments a and b, and a ratio R with by convention $R > 1$: $$p^\Delta = Rp_a - p_b$$
Standard deviation of daily price returns	$$\sigma^\Delta_p = \text{Standard deviation}(p^\Delta_t - p^\Delta_{t-1}, p^\Delta_{t-1} - p^\Delta_{t-2}, \ldots)$$ You can estimate this using the techniques in Part One: exponential weighting and averaging with a long run estimate.
Recommended ratio, R	Given the daily standard deviation of price returns σ_p in instruments a and b: $$R = \sigma_{p,b} \div \sigma_{p,a}$$
Number of contracts to hold per long one unit of synthetic instrument	$$\text{Instrument } b = -1$$ $$\text{Instrument } a = (R \times \text{Multiplier}_b \times \text{FX rate}_b)$$ $$\div (\text{Multiplier}_a \times \text{FX rate}_a)$$
Minimum capital	$$\text{Minimum capital 4 contracts} =$$ $$(4 \times \text{Multiplier}_b \times \text{FX rate}_{b,t} \times \sigma^\Delta_p \times 16)$$ $$\div (\text{IDM} \times \text{Weight} \times \tau)$$ This assumes that $N_a \div N_b$, the number of contracts required for each single contract of N_b, is an integer. If this is not the case, you will need to multiply the minimum capital by the ratio required to achieve integer contracts for both N_a and N_b.

Cost calculation	**Spread cost, price points = (Bid – Offer) ÷ 2** **Spread cost, currency** **= Futures multiplier × Spread cost price points** **Cost per contract** **= Spread cost currency + Commission per contract** **Cost instrument a** **= (N$_a$ ÷ N$_b$) × Cost per contract(a) × FX rate$_b$ ÷ FX rate$_a$** **Total cost** **= Cost instrument(a) + Cost instrument (b)** **Risk adjusted cost per trade** **= Total cost ÷ (σ_p^Δ × 16 × Multiplier$_b$)**
EWMAC and similar trading rules	Use the back-adjusted price for the synthetic spread instrument as an input.
Carry calculation	**Raw carry = (Rp$_a$^{current} – p$_b$^{current}) – (Rp$_a$^{further} – p$_b$^{further})** or **Raw carry = (Rp$_a$^{nearer} – p$_b$^{nearer}) – (Rp$_a$^{current} – p$_b$^{current})** Use the months between contracts (current vs further, or nearer vs current) for instrument *b* in the following formula: **Expiry difference in years** **= abs(Months between contracts) ÷ 12** **Annualised raw carry** **= Raw carry ÷ Expiry difference in years** **Carry = Annualised raw carry ÷ (σ_p^Δ × 16)** **Smoothed carry forecast** **= EWMA$_{span}$(Carry forecast)**

Instrument weight and IDM	The instrument weight, *weight$_i$*, is the weight given to the synthetic instrument. Use the handcrafting approach from strategy four to set these.
	To calculate IDM use the returns of trading a sub-strategy for each synthetic spread instrument to estimate the correlation matrix. Alternatively, use the approximate values in table 16 back on page 116.
Risk target, τ	I recommend 10%.
Optimal position size to hold in instrument b	$-N_{b,t} = -$**Scaled forecast$_t$ × Capital × Weight × IDM** $$\times\ \tau \div (10 \times \textbf{Multiplier}_b \times \textbf{FX rate}_{b,t} \times \sigma^{A}_{t} \times \textbf{16})$$
Buffer width	$$B_{i,t} = 0.1 \times \textbf{Capital} \times \textbf{IDM} \times \textbf{Weight}_i \times \tau$$ $$\div\ (\textbf{Multiplier}_b \times \sigma^{A}_{p} \times 16 \times \textbf{FX rate}_{b,t})$$
Buffer zone	Given the optimal position of $-N_b$ in instrument *b*: $$\textbf{Lower buffer, } B^{L}_{i,t} = \textbf{round}(-N_{b,t} - B_{i,t})$$ $$\textbf{Upper buffer, } B^{U}_{i,t} = \textbf{round}(-N_{b,t} + B_{i,t})$$
Trading decision (instrument b)	Calculate the optimal position as above, updating values of forecasts, capital, price, FX and standard deviation estimate ($\sigma_\%$). Calculate the buffer zone around the optimal position. Then given a current position in round contracts for instrument *b* of *C*: $$B^{U}_{i,t} \leq C_{b,t} \leq B^{L}_{i,t} : \textbf{No trading required}$$ $$C_{b,t} < B^{L}_{i,t} : \textbf{Buy } (B^{U}_{i,t} - C_{i,t}) \textbf{ contracts}$$ $$C_{b,t} > B^{U}_{i,t} : \textbf{Sell } (C_{i,t} - B^{U}_{i,t}) \textbf{ contracts}$$
Trading decision (instrument a)	If no trades are required for instrument *b*, then do not trade instrument *a*.
	Otherwise, calculate the buffered position in instrument *b* from the current position adjusted for any required trades. $$-N^{*}_{b,t} = B^{L}_{i,t} \text{ or } -N^{*}_{b,t} = B^{U}_{i,t}$$
	Calculate the optimal position that would be implied by that buffered position: $$N_{a,t} = N^{*}_{b,t} \times (R \times \textbf{Multiplier}_b \times \textbf{FX rate}_{b,t})$$ $$\div\ (\textbf{Futures multiplier}_a \times \textbf{FX rate}_{a,t})$$
	Round that optimal position, then from the current position in instrument *a* calculate the trades required to achieve it.
	Execute the trades for instrument *a* and instrument *b* as close together as possible.

Cross instrument triplets

In the previous chapter I introduced the idea of spread trading: offsetting the risk of owning one instrument by shorting another correlated asset. But why stop there? Why shouldn't we offset the risk with two instruments? This strategy introduces the idea of trading **triplets**: synthetic instruments containing *three* underlying instruments.

Before you read this chapter, consider everything that is dangerous and toxic about spread trading: higher leverage, costs and minimum capital requirements. It's even worse for triplets! If you don't have the cash, skills and the stomach to cope, save yourself the hassle and skip this chapter.

> **Strategy twenty-nine**: Trade triplets of one instrument against two others as a relative value strategy.

Defining a triplet

In this chapter I will mostly be extending what we have already used in creating spread strategies from two to three instruments. Let's begin with a definition:

A triplet instrument $Xa/b/Yc$ is short instrument b and long instruments a and c in the ratios X:1:Y

Notice that we are defining everything here against a **base** instrument consisting of a short position in the middle instrument b, and long positions in the other two instruments a and c. In contrast, for strategy twenty-eight, the base was the second instrument b and we had a long position in only one other instrument. Triplets like this are often known as **butterflies**. Instrument b is the body of the butterfly, and instruments a and c are the wings.

Effectively in strategy twenty-eight, being 'long the spread' means an expectation that the spread would widen. Here being 'long the butterfly' means we expect the price spread between the middle instrument and the other two instruments will widen.

Now for the price. For spreads we had:

$$p^\Delta = Rp_a - p_b$$

Hence, to calculate the price of our synthetic triplet instrument, given prices in each instrument of p_a, p_b and p_c:

$$p^\Omega = Xp_a + Yp_c - p_b$$

As in the previous chapter I'm going to use a concrete example throughout for my explanation. Previously this was the 5-year and 10-year US bond future. To these, let's add the 2-year bond future. It is most appropriate to set instrument a as the 2-year, b as the 5-year and c as the 10-year. This will maximise the correlations between a and b, and b and c.[270]

I will explain later how to estimate an appropriate value of X and Y, but for now I will use X = 1.5 and Y = 0.25. The shortened form for the synthetic triplet is **1.5US2/US5/0.25US10**. The price of this triplet is currently:

$$p^\Omega = Xp_a + Yp_c - p_b = (1.5 \times 105) + (0.25 \times 118) - 112 = 75$$

Calculations for triplets

Let's quickly race through all the tedious calculations required to trade triplets, before moving on to some interesting analysis and examples. To begin with, how do we set the weightings X and Y? Recall from strategy twenty-eight that we derived the following formula to set the equivalent ratio R such that it minimised the expected standard deviation of the spread price:

$$R = \rho\sigma_b \div \sigma_a$$

---

270 For fixed income butterflies like this, triplets are effectively a bet on the curvature of the yield curve. Since interest rates and prices are inversely related, being long this butterfly means you expect 5-year US interest rates to rise versus 2-year and 10-year rates, hence the yield curve will get more concave, or in simpler terms the curve will get curvier.

486

Where σ_a and σ_a were the daily standard deviations of price differences for the two instruments, and ρ was the correlation of price differences. How can we extend this to three instruments? In the previous strategy, instrument a was doing the job of hedging instrument b. This time round, it's a and c that are sharing the hedging duties. Let's allocate half the work of hedging to each instrument. Then we can say:

$$X = \rho_{a,b}\sigma_b \div 2\sigma_a$$

$$Y = \rho_{b,c}\sigma_b \div 2\sigma_c$$

In this previous chapter I simplified the formula for R by removing the correlation. We can do a similar thing here, but only if the correlations $\rho_{a,b}$ and $\rho_{b,c}$ are very similar, in which case X and Y are equal to half the ratio of the relevant standard deviations:

$$X = \sigma_b \div 2\sigma_a$$

$$Y = \sigma_b \div 2\sigma_c$$

What about our example, 1.5US2/US5/0.25US10? The correlation between US 2-year and US 5-year is currently around 0.92, whilst for US 5-year and US 10-year it is a little higher: 0.96. The respective standard deviations are 0.14 for US 2-year, 0.38 for 5-year and 0.57 for the 10-year bond future. Hence we have:

$$X = \rho_{a,b}\sigma_b \div 2\sigma_a = (0.92 \times 0.38) \div (2 \times 0.14) = 1.25 \sim 1.50$$

$$Y = \rho_{b,c}\sigma_b \div 2\sigma_c = (0.96 \times 0.38) \div (2 \times 0.57) = 0.32 \sim 0.25$$

As you can see, I have adjusted the value for Y downwards to 0.25 to make it a rounder number, and also pushed X up to 1.5 for reasons that will become apparent shortly. For position sizing we can use exactly the same formula as in strategy twenty-eight, where our position in instrument b will be short N_b contracts calculated as follows:

$$N_{b,t} = \text{Scaled forecast}_t \times \text{Capital} \times \text{Weight} \times \text{IDM}$$
$$\times \tau \div (10 \times \text{Multiplier}_b \times \text{FX rate}_b \times \sigma_p^{\Omega} \times 16)$$

Where σ_p^{Ω} is the standard deviation of daily price returns for the triplet price. As before I would suggest using a lower value of τ for relative value trading: I recommend 10%.

Then it's a matter of calculating the required long positions in instruments a and c:

$$N_{a,t} = N_{b,t} \times (X \times \text{Futures multiplier}_b \times \text{FX rate}_{b,t})$$
$$\div (\text{Multiplier}_a \times \text{FX rate}_{a,t})$$

$$N_{c,t} = N_{b,t} \times (Y \times \text{Futures multiplier}_b \times \text{FX rate}_{b,t})$$
$$\div (\text{Futures multiplier}_c \times \text{FX rate}_{c,t})$$

Remember, we always hold long positions in a and c if we are short b, and vice versa. This gives us the same formula for notional exposure as we had in the previous chapter:

$$\textbf{Notional exposure (Base currency)}$$
$$= p^\Omega \times (\text{Futures multiplier}_b \times \text{FX rate}_b)$$

Back to our example. All of our instruments are denominated in US dollars. US 5-year and 10-year bonds have a multiplier of 1,000, whilst US 2-year has a multiplier of 2,000, and I set $X = 1.5$ and $Y = 0.25$. We are long US 5-year bonds (asset b) in one single contract for each unit of the triplet. For every short 5-year bond futures contract, we will hold this many 2-year bond futures:

$$\textbf{Relative position in } a, \; N_{a,t} \div N_{b,t}$$
$$= (X \times \text{Futures multiplier}_b \times \text{FX rate}_b) \div (\text{Futures multiplier}_a \times \text{FX rate}_a) =$$
$$(1.5 \times 1000 \times 1) \div (2000 \times 1) = 0.75$$

Plus we will have this position in 10-year bond futures:

$$\textbf{Relative position in } c, \; N_{c,t} \div N_{b,t}$$
$$= (Y \times \text{Multiplier}_b \times \text{FX rate}_b) \div (\text{Futures multiplier}_c \times \text{FX rate}_c)$$
$$= (0.25 \times 1000 \times 1) \div (1000 \times 1) = 0.25$$

We need some arbitrary figures to make this concrete. Let's assume that we have $500,000 in capital, a risk target τ of 10%, that we are only trading a single triplet instrument so *weight* = 1, and that we have an average scaled forecast of +10. The standard deviation of the daily returns for the triple price, σ_p^Ω, is 0.089. As you would expect, this is lower than the standard deviations in each of the three legs of the triple.

Firstly, we need to calculate the position we have in instrument b, the US 5-year bond. We will be short N_b contracts:

$$N_{b,t} = \text{Scaled forecast}_t \times \text{Capital} \times \text{Weight} \times \text{IDM} \times \tau$$
$$\div (10 \times \text{Multiplier}_b \times \text{FX rate}_b \times \sigma_p^\Omega \times 16)$$
$$= 10 \times 500000 \times 1 \times 1 \times 0.10 \div (10 \times 1000 \times 1 \times 0.089 \times 16) = 35.1$$

We will be short 35.1 5-year bond futures. From this we can imply the long positions we require in the US 2-year (N_a) and US 10-year (N_c) bonds:

$$N_{a,t} = N_{b,t} \times (N_{a,t} \div N_{b,t}) = 35.1 \times 0.75 = +26.3$$

$$N_{c,t} = N_{b,t} \times (N_{c,t} \div N_{b,t}) = 35.1 \times 0.25 = +8.8$$

To get a feel for the different leverage of outright, spread and triple instruments examine table 155. This shows the average position that would be required if we were trading the legs individually, or trading the 1.5US5/US10 spread example from the previous chapter, or if we were holding the triple. In all cases I am assuming the same capital and risk target, τ. I've also added the sum of the absolute notional exposure summed up across all the legs in each row. You can clearly see how much extra leverage we need for spreads and triplets, due to the lower risk inherent in the hedged price.

TABLE 155: POSITION SIZES FOR OUTRIGHT, SPREAD AND TRIPLE INSTRUMENTS

	Contracts 2-year	Contracts 5-year	Contracts 10-year	Total notional exposure
US 2-year	11.6			$2,300,000
US 5-year		8.2		$920,000
US 10-year			5.5	$650,000
1.5US5/US10		+39.3	−19.7	$6,700,000
1.5US2/ US5/0.25US10	+26.3	−35.1	+8.8	$10,400,000

With $500,000 in capital and a risk target of 10%.

Now let us consider the minimum capital. Again, we can use the same formula as in strategy twenty-eight:

Minimum capital 4 contracts

$$= (4 \times \text{Multiplier}_b \times \text{FX rate}_{b,t} \times \sigma_p^\Omega \times 16) \div (\text{IDM} \times \text{Weight}_t \times \tau)$$

As before, this assumes that $N_a \div N_b$ and $N_c \div N_b$ – the number of contracts we hold for each single contract of instrument b – are both integers. If this is not the case, you will need to multiply the minimum capital by the ratio required to achieve integer contracts in each of N_a, N_b and N_c.

Let's do this calculation for our example. To begin with, we ignore the issue of non-integer contracts:

Minimum capital 4 contracts

$$= (4 \times 1000 \times 1 \times 0.089 \times 16) \div (1 \times 1 \times 0.10) = \$56,960$$

However, because $N_a \div N_b = 0.75$ and $N_c \div N_b = 0.25$ we have to multiply this by four, giving us just over \$200,000 in minimum capital requirements.

The final calculations we need to revisit are those for risk adjusted costs. First of all we need to calculate the cost of trading one contract of each individual instrument:

Spread cost, price points = (Bid − Offer) ÷ 2

Spread cost, currency
= Futures multiplier × Spread cost price points

Cost per contract
= Spread cost currency + Commission per contract

The costs for instruments a and c need to be converted so that they are in the same exchange rate as for instrument b, and to reflect the different number of contracts traded for each single contract of instrument b:

Cost instrument a
$$= (N_a \div N_b) \times \text{Cost per contract(a)} \times \text{FX rate}_b \div \text{FX rate}_a$$

$$\text{Cost instrument b} = \text{Cost per contract(b)}$$

$$\text{Cost instrument c}$$

$$= (N_c \div N_b) \times \text{Cost per contract(c)} \times \text{FX rate}_b \div \text{FX rate}_c$$

Finally, we can add up the costs and risk adjust them:

$$\text{Total cost}$$

$$= \text{Cost instrument a} + \text{Cost instrument b} + \text{Cost instrument c}$$

$$\text{Risk adjusted cost per trade}$$

$$= \text{Total cost} \div (\sigma_p^\omega \times 16 \times \text{Multiplier}_b)$$

Examples of triplets

In strategy twenty-eight I pointed out that there were nearly 5,000 possible spread instruments given the instruments in my data set. The number of possible triplets is even higher! Here are a selection of some plausible triplets that I would consider trading. To reiterate my earlier comments, this selection does not reflect any endorsement on my part. I do not know if these particular triplets have unusually high backtested SRs or other desirable characteristics.

Tables 156 to 158 cover all the asset classes in which triplets are available. There are no spreads for FX instruments – for reasons I explained in the previous chapter – or for volatility where there are only two liquid instruments in my data set. In each case I include the two instruments in the spread, and the two correlations of price returns ρ for the pairs *a,b* and *b,c*. For space reasons I exclude all the additional information I calculated for each spread covered in strategy eight.

TABLE 156: SOME EXAMPLES OF FIXED INCOME TRIPLETS

Instrument *a*	Instrument *b*	Instrument *c*	ρ (a,b)	ρ (b,c)
US 2-year	US 5-year	US 10-year	0.92	0.96
US 10-year	US 20-year	US 30-year	0.92	0.96
German Schatz (2-year)	German Bund (10-year)	German Buxl (30-year)	0.81	0.88
Japanese JGB (10-year)	US 10-year	German Bund (10 year)	0.59	0.79
Italian BTP (10-year)	German Bund (10 year)	French OAT (10-year)	0.79	0.83

TABLE 157: SOME EXAMPLES OF EQUITY TRIPLETS

Instrument *a*	Instrument *b*	Instrument *c*	ρ (a,b)	ρ (b,c)
S&P 400 (mid cap)	S&P 500 (large cap)	Russell 2000 (small cap)	0.89	0.84
EU Auto	Eurostoxx 50	EU Utilities	0.73	0.54
DAX 30	Eurostoxx 50	CAC 40	0.97	0.97

TABLE 158: SOME EXAMPLES OF TRIPLETS IN THE COMMODITY FUTURES MARKETS

Instrument *a*	Instrument *b*	Instrument *c*	ρ (a,b)	ρ (b,c)
Soy Oil	Soybeans	Soy Meal	0.65	0.68
Butter	Milk	Cheese	0.46	0.87
Wheat	Corn	Oats	0.64	0.42
Silver	Gold	Platinum	0.79	0.57
Gasoline	WTI Crude	Heating Oil	0.96	0.90

Trading strategies for triplets

It would be extremely time consuming and tedious to analyse just one trading strategy for the innumerable possible combinations of triplets. Instead I'm going to limit myself to three well known examples:

- **US yield butterfly (triplet):** US 2-year, 5-year and 10-year bond futures. As I've already mentioned, this is effectively a bet on the curvature of the US yield curve.

- **Soy crush spread (triplet):** Soy meal, Soybeans and Soy oil. This is a production 'spread', since Soybeans are used to produce Meal and Oil.

- **Oil crack spread (triplet):** Gasoline, WTI Crude Oil, and Heating Oil. Again Crude Oil is refined to produce Gasoline, Heating Oil and other products.

Note that the latter two are commonly referred to as 'spreads', but I think this is confusing given the nomenclature I am using, so I will refer to them as triplets. For consistency I will also label the US yield butterfly as a triplet. Also note that in the Soy and Oil examples I'm using industry standard ratios to calculate the triplet price, whilst the US yield example has ratios estimated using the same logic as in strategy twenty-eight: a blend of empirical estimates from the last 10 years and duration weights, to account for the unusual interest rate environment over the previous decade.

Tables 159 and 160 show some characteristics of these triplets, whilst in figures 86, 87 and 88 I have plotted the synthetic prices.

TABLE 159: CHARACTERISTICS OF EXAMPLE TRIPLETS (A)

	X	Y	$N_a \div N_b$	$N_c \div N_b$
US yield	1.5	0.25	0.75	0.25
Soy crush	0.5	3.0	0.25	0.25
Oil crack	6	6	0.142857	0.142857

TABLE 160: CHARACTERISTICS OF EXAMPLE TRIPLETS (B)

	Risk adjusted cost	Minimum capital
US yield	0.0118	$172,000
Soy crush	0.00169	$1,900,000
Oil crack	0.000856	$850,000

FIGURE 86: SOY CRUSH TRIPLET, SYNTHETIC PRICE

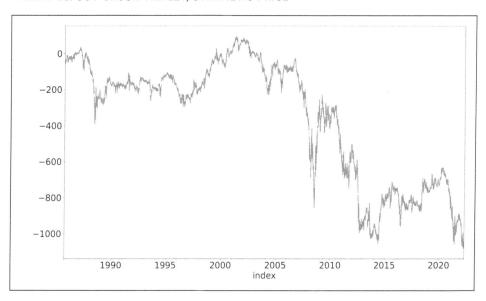

FIGURE 87: US YIELD CURVE TRIPLET, SYNTHETIC PRICE

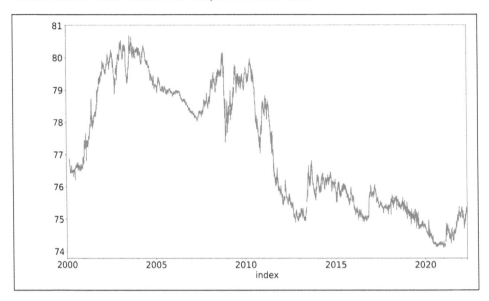

FIGURE 88: OIL CRACK SPREAD, SYNTHETIC PRICE

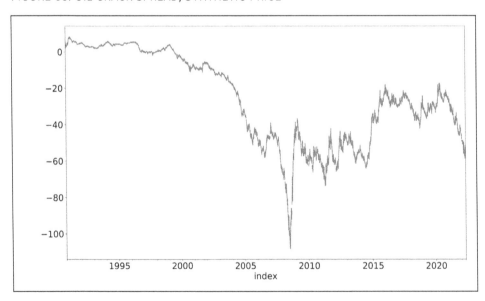

Trend following with triplets

As I did for strategy twenty-eight, I'm going to look at the performance of a single trading rule: EWMAC16. Whilst this is not definitive, it will give some idea of the characteristics we can expect from trading triplets. The results are in table 161 and are quite varied.

TABLE 161: PERFORMANCE FOR EWMAC16 WITH DIFFERENT TRIPLETS

	US yield	Soy crush	Oil crack
Mean annual return	−0.7%	1.6%	5.8%
Costs	−1.13%	−0.3%	−0.1%
Average drawdown	−30.5%	−32.8%	−12.6%
Standard deviation	9.6%	11.6%	12.7%
Sharpe ratio	−0.07	0.14	0.46
Turnover	13.0	14.5	14.7
Skew	1.20	1.26	1.14
Lower tail	4.16	3.97	3.72
Upper tail	4.25	4.01	3.65
Correlation with instrument *b*	0.36	0.96	0.92

The return for trend is slightly positive before costs for two of the triplets, and extremely good for the Oil crack. Of course, we should be extremely cautious about extrapolating these figures given this is just three triplets with a single trend trading rule.

More interesting are the risk statistics. As with spread strategies the skew is positive, but the tail measures are very high. The final row is also illuminating. It shows the correlation of the strategy returns for the triplet instrument against the returns achieved when trading the same strategy directionally with just instrument *b* from the relevant triplet. We get decent diversification in the US yield curve, but in the two commodity triplets we get almost none.

Carry with triplets

We had to modify the calculation of raw carry for spread strategies, and a similar modification is needed for triplets:

$$\text{Raw carry}$$

$$= (Xp_a{}^{current} + Yp_c{}^{current} - p_b{}^{current}) - (Xp_a{}^{further} + Yp_c{}^{further} - p_b{}^{further})$$

or

$$\text{Raw carry}$$

$$= (Xp_a{}^{nearer} + Yp_c{}^{nearer} - p_b{}^{nearer}) - (Xp_a{}^{current} + Yp_c{}^{current} - p_b{}^{current})$$

With that in mind, how well does the carry trading strategy do when applied to the three example triplets? As I did in strategy twenty-eight, I will focus on a single trading rule: carry60.

The statistics in table 162 have much in common with those for trend in the previous table. The Oil crack spread is the standout performer. It even has pleasantly positive skew, unusual for a carry strategy. But it is somewhat correlated with trading carry directionally just on WTI Crude: the correlation of 0.75 is pretty high, although not as high as the correlation of 0.96 between trading the Soy crush and outright Soybeans.

TABLE 162: PERFORMANCE FOR CARRY60 WITH DIFFERENT TRIPLETS

	US yield	Soy crush	Oil crack
Mean annual return	2.8%	1.3%	7.9%
Costs	−0.8%	−0.1%	−0.1%
Average drawdown	−15.3%	−28.9%	−9.4%
Standard deviation	14.5%	15.2%	12.8%
Sharpe ratio	0.19	0.09	0.62
Turnover	10.0	7.3	7.1
Skew	−0.07	0.07	0.85
Lower tail	2.35	2.55	2.61
Upper tail	2.63	2.50	2.92
Correlation with instrument b	0.23	0.96	0.75

Conclusion

Trading triplets is like trading a supercharged version of instrument spreads. Everything that is bad for spreads – high leverage, higher costs, more tail risk – is worse for triplets. With spreads there were some promising results, but the limited evidence we have examined in this chapter leads to somewhat gloomy conclusions. With the possible exception of the crack spread, the performance of both trend and carry is underwhelming, and also highly correlated to the underlying instruments.

We might have expected that mean reversion would be a better trading strategy for triplets than trend. After all, the yield curve cannot hold a weird curve shape forever, neither can the prices of different Soy products be out of line with their relative costs of production, with the same logic applying to the Oil crack triplet. Although there are likely to be systematic shifts in production costs, in the short and medium term relative prices should remain close to an equilibrium.

However, we don't see significantly negative performance for trend, as we would expect to see if mean reversion were the optimal strategy at this time horizon. It might be that a version of strategy twenty-six, fast mean reversion, would be profitable here, but it would be extremely difficult to execute given it would require near simultaneous fills of limit orders across three different markets. Nevertheless, I am sure there are some readers who are up for the challenge.

Strategy twenty-nine: Trading plan

All other stages are identical to strategy twenty-eight.

Strategy	Go long or short one or more synthetic triplet instruments. A long position in a triplet consists of a long position in instruments a and c, a short in instrument b.
Back-adjusted price calculation	Given back-adjusted prices for instruments a, b and c, and ratios X and Y:$$p^\Omega = Xp_a + Yp_c - p_b$$The standard deviation of daily price differences for p^Ω is σ^Ω.
Recommended ratios X and Y	Given the daily standard deviation of price returns in instruments a, b and c, and correlations ρ:$$X = \rho_{a,b}\sigma_b \div 2\sigma_a$$$$Y = \rho_{b,c}\sigma_b \div 2\sigma_c$$
Number of contracts to hold per long one unit of synthetic instrument	Instrument $b = -1$Instrument a $N_a \div N_b = (X \times \text{Multiplier}_b \times \text{FX rate}_b) \div (\text{Multiplier}_a \times \text{FX rate}_a)$Instrument c $N_a \div N_c = (Y \times \text{Multiplier}_b \times \text{FX rate}_b) \div (\text{Multiplier}_c \times \text{FX rate}_c)$

Cost calculation	**Spread cost, price points = (Bid − Offer) ÷ 2**
	Spread cost, currency **= Futures multiplier × Spread cost price points**
	Cost per contract **= Spread cost currency + Commission per contract**
	Cost instrument a **= (Na ÷ Nb) × Cost per contract(a) × FX rateb ÷ FX ratea**
	Cost instrument c **= (Nc ÷ Nb) × Cost per contract(c) × FX rateb ÷ FX ratec**
	Total cost = Cost instrument(a) **+ Cost instrument(b) + Cost instrument(c)**
	Risk adjusted cost per trade **= Total cost ÷ (σ_p^Ω × 16 × Multiplierb)**
EWMAC and similar trading rules	Use the back-adjusted price for the synthetic spread instrument as an input.
Carry calculation	**Raw carry = (Xp_a^{current} + Yp_c^{current} − p_b^{current})** **− (Xp_a^{further} + Yp_c^{further} − p_b^{further})** or **Raw carry = (Xp_a^{nearer} + Yp_c^{nearer} − p_b^{nearer})** **− (Xp_a^{current} + Yp_c^{current} − p_b^{current})**
Risk target, τ	I recommend 10%.
Optimal position size to hold in instrument *b*	**−$N_{b,t}$ = −Scaled forecast$_t$ × Capital × Weight × IDM** **× τ ÷ (10 × Multiplierb × FX rateb,t × $\sigma_{p,t}^\Omega$ × 16)**
Optimal position size to hold in instrument *a*	**$N_{a,t}$ = $N_{b,t}$ × (X × Multiplierb × FX rateb,t)** **÷ (Multipliera × FX ratea,t)**

Optimal position size to hold in instrument c	$$N_{c,t} = N_{b,t} \times (Y \times \text{Multiplier}_b \times \text{FX rate}_{b,t})$$ $$\div (\text{Multiplier}_c \times \text{FX rate}_{c,t})$$
Buffer width	$$B_{i,t} = 0.1 \times \text{Capital} \times \text{IDM} \times \text{Weight}_i \times \tau$$ $$\div (\text{Multiplier}_b \times \sigma_p^\Delta \times 16 \times \text{FX rate}_{b,t})$$
Buffer zone	Given the optimal position of $-N_b$ in instrument b: $$\text{Lower buffer, } B_{i,t}^L = \text{round}(-N_{b,t} - B_{i,t})$$ $$\text{Upper buffer, } B_{i,t}^U = \text{round}(-N_{b,t} + B_{i,t})$$
Trading decision (instrument b)	Calculate the optimal position as above, updating values of forecasts, capital, price, FX and standard deviation estimate ($\sigma_\%$). Calculate the buffer zone around the optimal position. Then given a current position in round contracts for instrument b of C: $$B_{i,t}^U \leq C_{b,t} \leq B_{i,t}^L : \text{No trading required}$$ $$C_{b,t} < B_{i,t}^L : \text{Buy } (B_{i,t}^U - C_{i,t}) \text{ contracts}$$ $$C_{b,t} > B_{i,t}^U : \text{Sell } (C_{i,t} - B_{i,t}^U) \text{ contracts}$$
Trading decision (instruments a and c)	If no trades are required for instrument b, then do not trade instrument a or instrument c. Otherwise, calculate the buffered position in instrument b from the current position adjusted for any required trades. $$-N_{b,t}^* = B_{i,t}^L \text{ or } - N_{b,t}^* = B_{i,t}^U$$ Calculate the optimal positions that are implied by that buffered position: $$N_{a,t} = N_{b,t}^* \times (R \times \text{Multiplier}_b \times \text{FX rate}_{b,t})$$ $$\div (\text{Futures multiplier}_a \times \text{FX rate}_{a,t})$$ $$N_{c,t} = N_{b,t}^* \times (R \times \text{Multiplier}_b \times \text{FX rate}_{b,t})$$ $$\div (\text{Futures multiplier}_c \times \text{FX rate}_{c,t})$$ Round those optimal positions, then from the current positions in instruments a and c calculate the trades required to achieve them. Execute the trades for instruments a, b and c as close together as possible.

Calendar trading strategies

The two cross instrument strategies I've explained so far, for spreads and triplets, have some serious disadvantages. For starters, it's difficult to find sets of instruments which have reasonably stable relationships, with relative constant standard deviations and correlations. Secondly, it isn't that straightforward to execute the trades that come out of these strategies.

A much easier solution is to move away from trading relative value *across* instruments, and instead do it *within* instruments. For example, instead of trading US 5-year bonds against US 10-year bonds, we could trade the Eurodollar future which expires in two years against the contract expiring in three years. This brings some advantages. Firstly, the relationship between these futures will be relatively stable. Secondly, we can usually execute them as a single trade rather than two separate orders. Finally, the equations become simpler and more intuitive.

> **Strategy thirty**: Trade calendar spreads and triplets composed of different expiries for the same instrument.

Where can we trade calendar spreads and triplets?

One of the problems I had when analysing spreads and triplets across instruments was the sheer diversity of options. This is not going to be a problem with calendar spreads! We can only trade these in instruments when we have sufficient liquidity to hold positions in at least two or three contracts at any one time. For example, it isn't really practical to trade the first US 10-year bond expiry against the second. As I write this chapter the next expiry is June 2022, which is massively liquid, but the September 2022 expiry has just 3% of the volume and open interest available in June.

As for December 2022, a princely open interest of just 34 contracts firmly rules out the trading of triplets in US 10-year bonds.

That limitation rules out all the bond futures, equity indices, metals and FX. But we are still left with the short-term interest rate (STIR) futures, the volatility futures, and great swathes of the energy and agricultural sectors including WTI Crude, Corn and Wheat. In particular, there are dozens of liquid expiries available in the key STIR markets like Eurodollar, and in the full size WTI Crude Oil contract.

In this chapter I will focus on the following examples:

- The VIX volatility future.

- Eurodollar STIR futures.

- WTI Crude Oil.

As with the cross instrument strategies I make no claim that there is anything special about these particular markets. However, there is good liquidity in trading spreads across these markets, and they are favoured by many traders. They all exhibit some interesting properties that also apply to other markets: they have an interesting term structure[271] of volatility, and WTI Crude also experiences seasonality effects.

Let's briefly revisit the concept of spread and triplets. In each case we construct a **synthetic instrument**, whose prices are calculated from the back-adjusted prices of two or three real instruments. In both cases instrument b is the **base** instrument. For a long position of one unit in a synthetic **spread** we are always short one contract of instrument b, and long sufficient contracts of a to hedge our exposure in b. In triplets, we are also short one contract of instrument b, hedged by appropriately sized long positions in two other markets: instrument a and instrument c.

For calendar spreads and triplets, we just substitute different instruments for different **expiries** for the same instrument:

- A long calendar **spread** consists of a short position in expiry b, hedged by a long position in expiry a.

- A long calendar **triple** is a short position in expiry b, hedged by long positions in expiries a and c.

By convention, expiry a will expire sooner than expiry b, and if you are using triplets expiry b will have a shorter maturity than expiry c. In principle these expiries can be in adjacent contracts, e.g. monthly for VIX and WTI Crude, and quarterly for Eurodollar. But they can also be spaced further apart, e.g. every six months or annually.

---

271 The *term structure* of volatility just refers to the fact that different expiries of the same instrument will often have different levels of standard deviation of returns.

The shortest expiry *a* could be the front contract, but it may also be one further out on the curve.

I will **reference expiries relative to the front contract**. For my Eurodollar examples expiry *a* will be the eighth quarterly contract which expires in approximately two years' time, with expiry *b* six months afterwards; and for triplets expiry *c* will be a further six months in the future. As I write this chapter those contracts are June 2024, December 2024 and June 2025. But just as for instrument trades we would need to roll these positions at regular intervals to maintain the required distance to expiry. Importantly, for calendar spreads and triplets you must **always** roll the individual legs at the same time.[272] This is especially important for synthetic instruments that cover adjacent expiries. If you roll the first leg of a spread into the contract month of the second leg, without rolling the second leg, then you will no longer have a spread trade!

For WTI Crude[273] for expiry *a* I will use the second monthly contract, for *b* the third, and *c* will be the fourth monthly contract. I use the second contract for the same reasons I do in the directional strategies: so I can calculate carry correctly by comparing the traded contract and a nearer contract. These positions will need to be rolled before the first contract expires. I do something similar for VIX, except that the spread is calculated from the third and fourth contracts. Table 163 shows these examples and currently referenced contracts.

---

272   These rolls will themselves be spread trades.
273   I could also specify the WTI Crude in specific calendar months, as I did for the standalone instrument where I stuck to trading December. This would remove seasonal effects, but I deliberately wanted to include those here.

TABLE 163: EXAMPLE SPREADS AND TRIPLETS, AND CURRENTLY REFERENCED CONTRACTS

	Expiry a	Expiry b	Expiry c	Roll cycle
Eurodollar spread	8th quarterly (June 2024)	10th quarterly (December 2024)		Quarterly
Eurodollar triplet	8th quarterly (June 2024)	10th quarterly (December 2024)	12th quarterly (June 2025)	Quarterly
WTI Crude spread	2nd monthly (June 2022)	8th monthly (December 2022)		Monthly
WTI Crude triplet	2nd monthly (June 2022)	8th monthly (December 2022)	14th monthly (June 2023)	Monthly
VIX spread	3rd monthly (July 2022)	4th monthly (August 2022)		Monthly
VIX triplet	2nd monthly (June 2022)	3rd monthly (July 2022)	4th monthly (August 2022)	Monthly

Example dates correct as of 1st May 2022.

Finally, note that a spread is effectively a bet on the steepness of the futures price curve, whilst a triplet is a bet on its convexity.

Calculations for relative value calendar trades

I can't really put this off any longer – I need to cover the tedious calculations required for relative value (RV) strategies, modifying them for calendar trades. The good news is that these equations can be somewhat simpler. All the futures multipliers are the same across each leg of the trade, as are the FX rates. It also turns out that we don't need to calculate the ratios R (for spread trades) or X and Y (for triplets), since there are market conventions.

Let's begin by revisiting our basic price equations. For spreads, given prices in each instrument of p_a, p_b:

$$p^\Delta = Rp_a - p_b$$

And for triplets, given prices in each instrument of p_a, p_b and p_c:

$$p^\Omega = Xp_a + Yp_c - p_b$$

What values should we use for R, X and Y? Remember that for spreads we used the following equation to estimate the appropriate value of R:

$$R^* = \sigma_b \div \sigma_a$$

Where σ_a and σ_a were the standard deviations of price differences for the two instruments. If we assume that the standard deviations are identical for both legs of the spread then the correct value of R is exactly one.

In fact, **the usual convention in calendar spread trading is to set $R = 1$**. Using a market convention will make it easier and cheaper to trade these instruments, since we can often get quotes to trade the spread rather than having to trade the individual legs, potentially creating risk and also incurring higher trading costs. However, as I discussed in strategy twenty-eight, there are downsides to using fixed weights such as $R = 1$. If standard deviations are not equal[274] across maturities, then the hedge ratio will not be optimal, and we will have a higher correlation to outright trades.

What about triplets? Across instruments we had:

$$X = \rho_{a,b}\sigma_b \div 2\sigma_a$$

$$Y = \rho_{b,c}\sigma_b \div 2\sigma_c$$

It turns out that if both pairwise correlations are equal, and if we also assume identical standard deviations, then we get $X = Y = 0.5$. This is also the market convention.

Hence for calendar trades we always have:

$$p^\Delta = p_a - p_b$$

$$p^\Omega = 0.5p_a + 0.5p_c - p_b$$

What about position sizing? We can use the same formula as for previous RV strategies.

---

274   There is a well-known theoretical result known as the Samuelson effect which assumes that the volatility of futures prices will increase as they get closer to their maturity. This effect can be seen clearly in many instruments, for example in the VIX volatility future, but it is not universal, e.g. during the period of effectively fixed interest rates that characterised much of the 2010s the volatility of the first few expiries in interest rate futures contracts was extremely low. I discuss some other implications of patterns of non-stationary volatility in the first chapter of Part Six, 'Rolling and contract selection'.

If σ_p is the standard deviation of daily price returns for the spread or triplet price, then the position in the base expiry b will be:

$$-N_b = -\text{Scaled forecast}_t \times \text{Capital} \times \text{Weight}$$
$$\times \text{IDM} \times \tau \div (10 \times \text{Multiplier} \times \text{FX} \times \sigma_p \times 16)$$

Notice that I have removed the instrument subscripts for FX and futures multiplier, since these will be the same for all of the legs in the trade. As before I would suggest using a lower value of the annualised risk target τ for RV trading: I recommend 10%.

Now for the positions in the other legs. This is the formula we had for spread trading across instruments:

$$N_{a,t} = N_{b,t} \times (R \times \text{Futures multiplier}_b \times \text{FX rate}_{b,t})$$
$$\div (\text{Multiplier}_a \times \text{FX rate}_{a,t})$$

For calendar spread trading, where the multipliers and FX are identical, and with $R = 1$, we can simplify this considerably to just:

$$N_{a,t} = N_{b,t}$$

We will always have an equal and opposite signed position in the two expiries we are trading. A long position in one unit of the spread will be:

- Short 1 contract of expiry b.
- Long 1 contract of expiry a.

Similarly for calendar triplets, given a position of $N_{b,t}$ in the base expiry b we have:

$$N_{a,t} = 0.5 N_{b,t}$$

$$N_{c,t} = 0.5 N_{b,t}$$

Since we can't hold half a contract, the minimum position we can effectively hold will be two units of the synthetic triplet instrument. A long position in two units of the triplet will consist of:

- Short 2 contracts of expiry b.
- Long 1 contract of expiry a.
- Long 1 contract of expiry c.

I think it is useful at this stage to return to our examples. As I have done in the last two chapters, let us assume that we have $500,000 in capital, a risk target τ of 10%, that we are only trading a single spread or triplet instrument so instrument weights and IDM are both equal to one, and that we currently have a scaled forecast of +10 (an average long position).

Here is the calculation for VIX, with the standard deviation of the daily change in price $\sigma_p = 0.277$, our position in expiry b would be:

$$-N_{b,t} = -\text{Scaled forecast}_t \times \text{Capital} \times \text{Weight} \times \text{IDM}$$

$$\times \tau \div (10 \times \text{Multiplier} \times FX_t \times \sigma_p \times 16)$$

$$= -10 \times 500000 \times 1 \times 1 \times 0.1$$

$$\div (10 \times 1000 \times 1 \times 0.277 \times 16) = -11.2$$

For a spread trade, we would be short 11.2 contracts of expiry b, and long 11.2 contracts of expiry a. What about a triplet trade? The standard deviation for the price of the triplet in VIX is currently 0.0829, so we have:

$$-N_{b,t} = -10 \times 500000 \times 1 \times 1 \times 0.1 \div (10 \times 1000 \times 1 \times 0.0829 \times 16)$$

$$= -37.7$$

So we are short 37.7 contracts of expiry b. For expiry a and c, the optimal triplet position will be exactly half that: long 18.9 contracts in each.

As I did for cross instrument trades, I think it is interesting to compare the current positions in the RV trades to corresponding positions in a directional trade. So, for example, with an outright directional trade in expiry b on VIX, which is the third contract, the current standard deviation of price returns is 0.86, and the optimal position would be 3.63 contracts. I have put all the figures for VIX and the other two example instruments in table 164.

TABLE 164: EXAMPLE POSITION SIZES FOR OUTRIGHT, SPREAD AND TRIPLE CALENDARS

	Expiry *a*	Expiry *b*	Expiry *c*	Total absolute notional exposure
Eurodollar outright		13		$3.2m
Eurodollar spread	+70	−70		$17.3m
Eurodollar triple	+120	−240	+120	$118m
VIX outright		3.63		$104,000
VIX spread	+11.2	−11.2		$640,000
VIX triple	+18.9	−37.7	+18.9	$2.15m
WTI Crude outright		1		$100,000
WTI Crude outright	+2.23	−2.23		$446,000
WTI Crude outright	+2.16	−4.33	+2.16	$866,000

With $500,000 in capital and a risk target of 10%.

The leverage numbers vary somewhat across instruments, and are especially scary for the low standard deviation Eurodollar, but it's probably better to focus on the relative changes in leverage for different types of trading within each instrument. Moving from an outright to a spread increases leverage by around five times for each instrument. Going from a spread to a triple multiplies the leverage required for the same target risk by seven times for Eurodollar and three for VIX, but by less than twice for Crude.

What lies behind this disparity? The correlations are different. Correlations between expiries *a* and *b* are all relatively high: 0.94 for Crude, 0.98 for Eurodollar and for VIX 0.99. The correlation of *b* and *c* is similar for VIX and Eurodollar, but for Crude it is much lower: 0.88. Hence the Crude triplet price is riskier and requires less leverage. Incidentally, if I had chosen adjacent quarterly expiries for Eurodollar, and adjacent monthlies for Crude Oil, the leverage required for both spreads and triplets would be significantly higher as the correlations would be much closer to 1.

Now let us consider minimum capital. Again, we can use the same formula as in strategy twenty-eight:

Minimum capital 4 contracts

$$= (4 \times \text{Multiplier} \times \text{FX} \times \sigma_p \times 16) \div (\text{IDM} \times \text{Weight} \times \tau)$$

This will work fine for calendar **spreads**, but since we cannot hold half contracts we will have to double this for calendar **triplet** trading (where we hold half the required position in *b* for expiries *a* and *c*). Let's do this calculation for Eurodollars. First for spreads, where the standard deviation of daily returns is 0.018 and the futures multiplier is 2,500:

Minimum capital 4 contracts
$$= (4 \times 2500 \times 1 \times 0.018 \times 16) \div (1 \times 1 \times 0.10) = \$28,800$$

Now for triplets: the multiplier is the same but naturally the standard deviation is lower:

Minimum capital 4 contracts
$$= (4 \times 2500 \times 1 \times 0.0052 \times 16) \div (1 \times 1 \times 0.10) = \$8,320$$

As I noted above, we have to double this giving us a minimum capital of $16,640 for Eurodollar triplets.

The final calculations we need to revisit are those for risk adjusted costs. In the two previous strategies I did this by adding up the costs for each leg of the spread or triplet. But calendar trades can usually be executed as a combination trade rather than separately, and in most cases this will be cheaper than trading each leg.

Let's first remind ourselves how to calculate the cost of trading one contract of an outright instrument:

Spread cost, price points = (Bid − Offer) ÷ 2

Spread cost, currency
= Futures multiplier × Spread cost price points

Cost per contract
= Spread cost currency + Commission per contract

For a spread trade, the cost of trading one synthetic unit of the spread (one contract of expiry *a*, and another of *b*) will be:

Spread cost for combination, price points
= (Bid − Offer) ÷ 2

Spread cost, currency

= 2 × Futures multiplier × Spread cost price points

Cost per contract

= Spread cost currency + 2 × Commission per contract

Similarly, for a triple it will be:

Spread cost for combination, price points

= (Bid − Offer) ÷ 2

Spread cost, currency

= 3 × Futures multiplier × Spread cost price points

Cost per contract

= Spread cost currency + 3 × Commission per contract

Then in both cases to calculate the risk adjusted cost, where σ_p is the daily standard deviation of the spread or triplet price:

Risk adjusted cost per trade

= Cost per contract ÷ (σ_p × 16 × Multiplier)

Again, this will probably make more sense with an example. Consider VIX futures. The minimum tick for an outright trade in VIX is 0.05; but for spread trades in VIX it is 0.01. If the bid and offer are 0.01 apart then:

Spread cost for combination, price points

= (Bid − Offer) ÷ 2 = 0.01 ÷ 2 = 0.005

Spread cost, currency

= 2 × Futures multiplier × Spread cost price points

= 2 × 1000 × 0.005 = $10

$$\text{Cost per contract}$$
$$= \text{Spread cost currency} + 2 \times \text{Commission per contract}$$

$$= 10 + (2 \times 2.2) = \$14.40$$

$$\text{Risk adjusted cost per trade}$$
$$= \text{Cost per contract} \div (\sigma_p \times 16 \times \text{Multiplier})$$

$$= 14.40 \div (0.277 \times 16 \times 1000) = 0.0032$$

Finally let's consider the carry calculations for spreads and triplets. We can use the same formula as we did for cross instrument RV trading, except that the values of R, X and Y are now fixed at 1, 0.5 and 0.5 respectively. Hence for spreads we have:

$$\text{Raw carry} = (p_a{}^{current} - p_b{}^{current}) - (p_a{}^{further} - p_b{}^{further})$$

Or

$$\text{Raw carry} = (p_a{}^{nearer} - p_b{}^{nearer}) - (p_a{}^{current} - p_b{}^{current})$$

For all three of our example instruments in this chapter, we would use the second of these equations since we never trade the front contract. Notice that for VIX, where we trade adjacent monthly expiries, the nearer contract for expiry b will actually be the current contract for expiry a. In this case, the carry calculation ends up looking like a triplet price:

$$\text{Raw carry (adjacent)} = p_a{}^{nearer} - p_b{}^{nearer} - p_a{}^{current} + p_b{}^{current}$$
$$= p_a{}^{nearer} + p_b{}^{current} - 2p_a{}^{current}$$

Putting that irrelevant but fun diversion to one side, let's see how to calculate carry for actual triplets:

$$\text{Raw carry}$$
$$= (0.5p_a{}^{current} + 0.5p_c{}^{current} - p_b{}^{current}) - (0.5p_a{}^{further} + 0.5p_c{}^{further} - p_b{}^{further})$$

or

$$\text{Raw carry}$$
$$= (0.5p_a{}^{nearer} + 0.5p_c{}^{nearer} - p_b{}^{nearer}) - (0.5p_a{}^{current} + 0.5p_c{}^{current} - 0.5_b{}^{current})$$

Again we would only use the second of these for VIX, WTI Crude and Eurodollars, and the formula would be somewhat simplified in the case of adjacent expiries as we have for VIX.

Choice of instruments and expiries for calendar trades

To some extent the appropriate choice of instruments and expiries for calendar spread and triplet trading is not dissimilar from the approach you would take when selecting instruments for outright directional trading. You should consider minimum capital and trading costs, and not pay too much attention – if any – to outright performance.

However, the additional dimension of deciding on which expiries to trade makes things a little more complex. We can break this down into two separate decisions:

- How far along the curve to trade the first expiry, a.

- What distance to place between expiry a, and expiries b and c.

Placing the first expiry is actually no different from deciding where on the futures curve to trade an outright directional strategy. You will need to consider liquidity, but also certain other factors. I discuss this topic in more detail in Part Six.

In terms of distance between expiries, the key factor is the *correlation* between the different legs of a spread or triple. The closer together each expiry is, the higher the resulting correlation between their price returns. Higher correlations will make for lower standard deviation and thus lower minimum capital, but will result in significantly higher risk adjusted costs and leverage. RV trades constructed from highly correlated expiries also tend to have somewhat hideous tail ratios.

For the three examples I am using in this chapter, I chose to trade the second, third and fourth contracts of VIX because liquidity starts to run dry if we go any further out on the curve. I avoid the first contract because I can't calculate carry on it, and specifically for VIX the returns of the front contract tend to have unattractive tail properties.

For Eurodollar and Crude I had more options available since the available liquidity on both instruments goes out for several years. I decided to spread the expiries out a little, to reduce the correlation between them. This decision has a significant effect: if I had selected adjacent quarterly expiries for Eurodollar then the notional exposure for a triplet position with just $500,000 of capital would have run into billions of dollars!

The nature and character of spreads and triplets

Before we consider how to trade these synthetic calendar instruments, it is worth examining some to get an intuition of how they behave. Check out figures 89, 90 and 91, which show the prices for the three spreads that we are using as examples.

FIGURE 89: VIX CALENDAR SPREAD PRICE

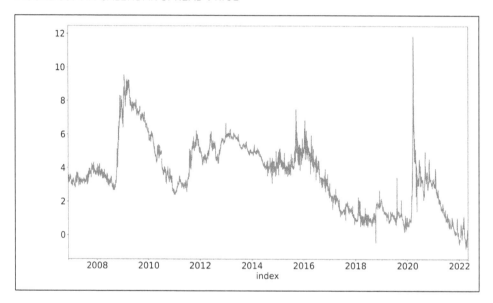

FIGURE 90: WTI CRUDE CALENDAR SPREAD PRICE

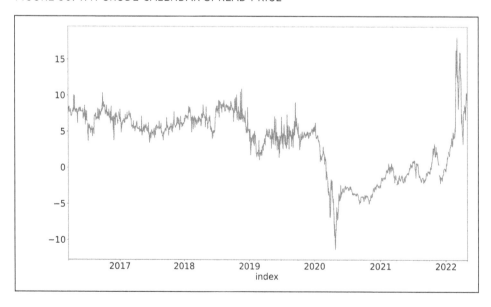

FIGURE 91: EURODOLLAR CALENDAR SPREAD PRICE

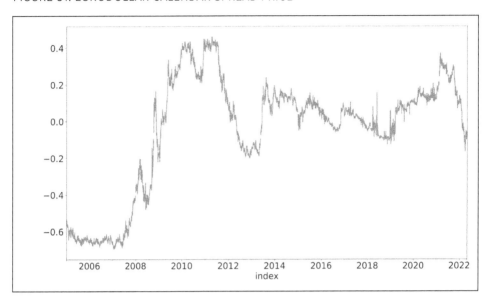

Each spread goes through long periods where it trades around some equilibrium, but then in periods of crisis it is shocked to a new level. After each shock the equilibrium has usually shifted. For example, consider WTI Crude. For several years the spread closely hugs the $6 level, but then it becomes sharply negative during the 2020 COVID-19 market panic which saw a massive bear market in outright Crude prices. The spread then slowly returns to around $6, but there is more volatility during the invasion of Ukraine in early 2022.

We see similar behaviour for triplets. For reasons of space, I will plot just one triplet, VIX, which is shown in figure 92.

FIGURE 92: VIX CALENDAR TRIPLET PRICE

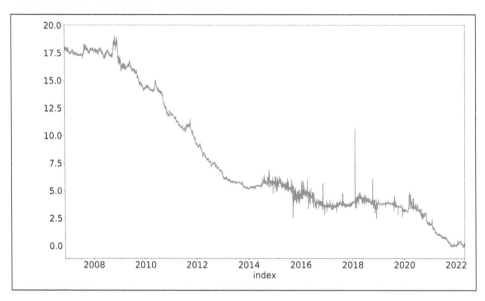

Note that the triplet price gets spikier once we have hourly data after 2013. Again, there is a period of relative stability when the triplet price mostly mean reverts around an equilibrium price of around $4, but this is preceded and followed by periods of adjustment.

Trading calendar spreads

Let's wheel out our favoured trading strategies from Part One, which we also used to analyse cross instrument spreads in strategy twenty-eight. Firstly, consider the results of applying the EWMAC trend rule to the three example spreads we're using. The statistics are in table 165.

TABLE 165: PERFORMANCE FOR EWMAC16 WITH DIFFERENT CALENDAR SPREADS

	VIX	WTI Crude	Eurodollar
Mean annual return	−1.0%	1.1%	1.2%
Costs	−1.6%	−0.1%	−2.2%
Average drawdown	−12.9%	−4.6%	−14.7%
Standard deviation	7.2%	7.1%	9.1%
Sharpe ratio	−0.14	0.15	0.13
Turnover	9.9	9.6	11.7
Skew	4.29	2.32	2.59
Lower tail	5.8	6.7	3.60
Upper tail	5.1	9.5	4.79
Correlation with expiry *b*	0.24	0.26	0.27

Final row shows correlation of returns for EWMAC16 spread strategy versus outright EWMAC16 strategy on expiry b.

The results are not especially impressive, but these bare numbers do not really reflect what is going on. Figure 93 is more illuminating. It shows the cumulative performance from trading the WTI Crude spread, the price of which can be found in figure 90. As we might expect, during the long periods of time when the spread is mean reverting, the trend rule does badly. But then there are short crisis periods when we make large profits very quickly.

Although the resulting returns have some correlation with a directional trade on WTI Crude, as the figure on the final row of table 165 attests, they are much less like normally distributed Gaussian returns. This non-normality is evidenced by the very high tails, high positive skew and undershooting of risk target, at least when measured using an inappropriate standard deviation statistic, which assumes that returns are vaguely Gaussian in nature.

FIGURE 93: CUMULATIVE PERCENTAGE RETURNS FOR WTI CRUDE CALENDAR SPREAD

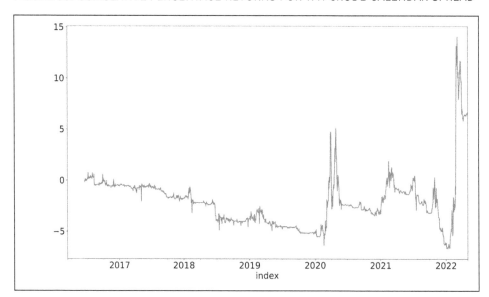

Now let's turn to carry, in particular the carry60 trading rule I also used in strategy twenty-eight. This was not a particularly profitable rule when applied to cross instrument trades, but how does it do here? Table 166 has the numbers, which are singularly unimpressive.

TABLE 166: PERFORMANCE FOR CARRY60 WITH DIFFERENT CALENDAR SPREADS

	VIX	WTI Crude	Eurodollar
Mean annual return	−2.4%	4.0%	−1.2%
Costs	−4.3%	−0.1%	−2.4%
Average drawdown	−34.3%	−7.4%	−38.4%
Standard deviation	20.8%	14.9%	18.6%
Sharpe ratio	−0.12	0.27	−0.06
Turnover	12.4	7.82	9.3
Skew	0	0.84	0.73
Lower tail	1.93	3.68	1.28
Upper tail	1.81	5.52	1.43
Correlation with expiry *b*	0.21	0.13	−0.39

Final row shows correlation of returns for carry60 spread strategy versus outright carry60 strategy on expiry b.

Trading calendar triplets

For consistency and completeness I will now repeat the same tests on the calendar triplets, firstly with the EWMAC16 trend rule, the results for which can be found in table 167.

TABLE 167: PERFORMANCE FOR EWMAC16 WITH DIFFERENT CALENDAR TRIPLETS

	VIX	WTI Crude	Eurodollar
Mean annual return	1.0%	−1.6%	−4.2%
Costs	−2.9%	−0.1%	−3.9%
Average drawdown	−9.3%	−5.5%	−37.0%
Standard deviation	8.4%	4.3%	4.8%
Sharpe ratio	0.12	−0.37	−0.87
Turnover	8.6	7.9	8.1
Skew	1.49	−2.53	0.47
Lower tail	5.89	7.80	5.67
Upper tail	6.94	4.79	4.67
Correlation with expiry *b*	0.06	0.12	0.18

Final row shows correlation of returns for EWMAC16 triplet strategy versus outright EWMAC16 strategy on expiry b.

Once again, a picture is worth a thousand words, or at least can be more informative than a dull table full of numbers. Figure 94 shows the cumulated account curve for EWMAC16 trading the VIX future. There is a clear striking pattern, which should be no surprise if you look again at figure 92, which shows the price of the VIX triplet. We have decent returns until 2013, after which the price enters a period of stable mean reversion, and so we would expect to gradually lose money with a trend strategy.

FIGURE 94: CUMULATIVE PERCENTAGE RETURNS FOR VIX CALENDAR TRIPLE

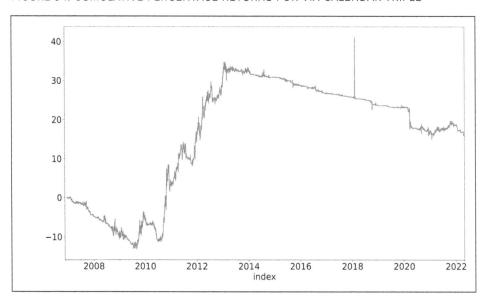

Finally, let's consider the carry strategy for calendar triplets, which can be found in table 168. As it was for cross instrument triplets, this is not a particularly profitable strategy.

TABLE 168: PERFORMANCE FOR CARRY60 WITH DIFFERENT CALENDAR TRIPLETS

	VIX	WTI Crude	Eurodollar
Mean annual return	−2.4%	−0.2%	−0.7%
Costs	−7.0%	0.1%	−4.6%
Average drawdown	−23.4%	−3.4%	−22.3%
Standard deviation	14.8%	8.3%	14.5%
Sharpe ratio	−0.16	−0.02	−0.04
Turnover	15.1	8.1	7.4
Skew	−0.54	−0.15	5.28
Lower tail	2.95	3.76	3.66
Upper tail	3.08	3.40	4.63
Correlation with expiry b	0.01	0.19	0.12

Final row shows correlation of returns for carry60 triplet strategy versus outright carry60 strategy on expiry b.

Conclusion

It seems more natural to construct calendar spreads and triplets from expiries of the same contract, rather than across instruments. It is certainly easier to do the required calculations and trade the resulting synthetic instruments. However, expiries of the same instrument tend to have very high correlations, resulting in high leverage and some very fat tails in the return distribution.

It is difficult to trade RV calendar strategies, since they switch between very consistent mean reversion and episodic sharp movements to new equilibrium. This produces trend returns that have the character of strongly positively skewed strategies like option buying: long periods of steady losses, followed by strong returns when the equilibrium shifts. Such strategies are always unlikely to be wildly profitable if returns are measured using a symmetric statistic like SR. It might be that something like strategy twenty-seven, which combines mean reversion and trend, would work well on calendar spreads and triplets.

But you will have to conduct that analysis yourself, as this is the final trading strategy in this book.

Beyond triplets

There is clearly scope for many additional RV strategies that I have not included in this book, by going beyond three expiries or instruments, and to four, five, six or more different legs.

For example, in the STIR futures complex, there are *pack spreads*. A pack is a series of four consecutive expiries, such as the 2023 pack – all the Eurodollars expiring in 2023. A pack spread would be something like long the 2023 pack, and short the 2024 Eurodollar pack; a triplet could be 2023/2024/2025. A *bundle* is a series of packs, such as the 2023/2024 bundle. Bundles can also be traded as spreads or triplets.

We can also imagine creating a pack of US bond futures (2-year, 3-year, 5-year, 10-year, 20-year and 30-year) and trading it against a pack of German bonds (Schatz, Bobl, Bund and Buxl).

More generally, a *condor* is a four legged equivalent of the butterfly calendar triplet which involves hedging a short exposure in the middle two contract expiries, with long exposures in the outer two expiries.

Generalised to any number of instruments or expiries, RV strategies effectively become a form of *statistical arbitrage ('stat arb')*. Stat arb traders will often use statistical techniques such as regression or vector auto-regression to find the appropriate pairs, triplets, or larger sets of legs that form co-integrated assets. Such traders will easily have the mathematical sophistication required to extend the simple equations in this part of the book to four or more assets.

Strategy thirty: Trading plan

All other stages are identical to strategies twenty-eight and twenty-nine.

Strategy	Go long or short one or more synthetic spread instruments, formed of expiries from the same instrument. A long position in a synthetic spread instrument consists of a long position in expiry a and a short in expiry b.
	Or
	Go long or short one or more synthetic triplet instruments. A long position in a triplet consists of a long position in expiries a and c, and a short in expiry b.
Back-adjusted price calculation	Given back-adjusted prices for expiries a, b and c: $$p^{\Delta} = p_a - p_b$$ $$p^{\Omega} = 0.5p_a - p_b + 0.5p_c$$
Standard deviation of daily price returns	Where p is either a spread or triplet price: $$\sigma_p = \text{Standard deviation}(p_t - p_{t-1}, p_{t-1} - p_{t-2}, ...)$$ You can estimate this using the techniques in Part One: exponential weighting and averaging with a long run estimate. Note that: $$\sigma_p = (p_t \times \sigma_{\%}) \div 16$$
Minimum capital	$$\text{Minimum capital 4 contracts}$$ $$= (4 \times \text{Multiplier} \times FX_t \times \sigma_p \times 16) \div (\text{IDM} \times \text{Weight} \times \tau)$$ Use the above equation for spreads. For triplets, double the minimum capital shown here.

Cost calculation	For spreads:

$$\text{Spread cost for combination, price points}$$
$$= (\text{Bid} - \text{Offer}) \div 2$$

$$\text{Spread cost, currency}$$
$$= 2 \times \text{Futures multiplier} \times \text{Spread cost price points}$$

$$\text{Cost per contract}$$
$$= \text{Spread cost currency} + 2 \times \text{Commission per contract}$$

For triplets:

$$\text{Spread cost for combination, price points}$$
$$= (\text{Bid} - \text{Offer}) \div 2$$

$$\text{Spread cost, currency}$$
$$= 3 \times \text{Futures multiplier} \times \text{Spread cost price points}$$

$$\text{Cost per contract}$$
$$= \text{Spread cost currency} + 3 \times \text{Commission per contract}$$

In both cases:

$$\text{Risk adjusted cost per trade}$$
$$= \text{Cost per contract} \div (\sigma_p \times 16 \times \text{Multiplier})$$

EWMAC and similar trading rules	Use the back-adjusted price for the synthetic spread instrument as an input.

Carry calculation	Spreads:

$$\text{Raw carry} = (p_a{}^{current} - p_b{}^{current}) - (p_a{}^{further} - p_b{}^{further})$$

Or:

$$\text{Raw carry} = (p_a{}^{nearer} - p_b{}^{nearer}) - (p_a{}^{current} - p_b{}^{current})$$

Triplets:

$$\text{Raw carry} = (0.5p_a{}^{current} + 0.5p_c{}^{current} - p_b{}^{current})$$
$$- (0.5p_a{}^{further} + 0.5p_c{}^{further} - p_b{}^{further})$$

Or:

$$\text{Raw carry} = (0.5p_a{}^{nearer} + 0.5p_c{}^{nearer} - p_b{}^{nearer})$$
$$- (0.5p_a{}^{current} + 0.5p_c{}^{current} - 0.5_b{}^{current})$$

Risk target, τ	I recommend 10%.

Optimal position size to hold (spreads)	$N_{b,t} = -\text{Scaled forecast}_t \times \text{Capital} \times \text{Weight} \times \text{IDM}$ $\times \tau \div (10 \times \text{Futures multiplier} \times \text{FX rate}_t \times \sigma_{p,t}^{D} \times 16)$

$$N_{a,t} = -N_{b,t}$$

Optimal position size to hold (triplets)	$N_{b,t} = -\text{Scaled forecast}_t \times \text{Capital} \times \text{Weight} \times \text{IDM}$ $\times \tau \div (10 \times \text{Futures multiplier} \times \text{FX rate}_t \times \sigma_{p,t}^{D} \times 16)$

$$N_{a,t} = -0.5N_{b,t}$$

$$N_{c,t} = -0.5N_{b,t}$$

PART SIX
Tactics

You must read all of Part One before reading Part Six.

You do not have to read Parts Two, Three, Four or Five before reading Part Six.

This part of the book is about *tactics*. We are not concerned here with predicting the movement of the markets, which was covered by the 30 chapters that made up Parts One to Five, but rather with the efficient and safe management of our trading strategies.

The following tactics are included in Part Six:

Tactic one: Contract selection and rolling

Tactic two: Execution

Tactic three: Cash and compounding

Tactic four: Risk management

Contract selection and rolling

There is no such thing as a VIX US volatility future.

Of course I'm being pedantic. There's actually several such futures, expiring on different dates. Right now, as I type this paragraph, there are actually nine different monthly expiries quoted on the CME website, although only the first few of these have any meaningful volume. But there is no *perpetual* future.

The fact there is no single VIX future, which I can hold for as long as I desire, means we need to make some decisions. To replicate a position in a perpetual future I would need to decide which of the available expiries to buy, then decide how long to hold on to that particular expiry, before acquiring a position in a new expiry by **rolling** my position.

This chapter concerns itself with three interrelated questions:

Which expiry date to hold.

When to roll to a new expiry date.

How to roll to a new expiry.

Which expiry date to hold

You might think it is straightforward to decide which expiry date to hold, and in many cases it is. With the exception of the volatility futures, in most of the financial asset classes only the front contract is liquid. This is true of almost all equity, bond and FX futures, as well as the metals.

However, in the short-term interest rate (STIR), volatility, energy and agricultural sectors things are different. There are often many different expiries which are sufficiently liquid to trade. Deciding which to hold is a question of balancing out several different factors.

To make things more concrete in this section, I'm going to consider an example: the VIX future. Table 169 has a list of all the current expiries, with their price, volume and open interest.

TABLE 169: KEY CHARACTERISTICS OF VIX EXPIRIES AS OF MAY 2022

	Price	Volume	Open interest
Spot price	28.48		
June 2022	29.45	67,000	123,000
July 2022	30.13	33,200	59,000
August 2022	30.11	10,400	48,000
September 2022	30.15	7,000	21,000
October 2022	30.10	5,500	13,400
November 2022	29.55	3,000	9,500
December 2022	28.60	1,100	4,900
January 2023	28.95	30	217
February 2023	29.125	0	0

Liquidity

It is dangerous to own an expiry which isn't very liquid, even if it has other advantages. Chances are it will also be more expensive to trade, since with fewer market participants the spreads in that market will be wider. Before doing anything else you should apply a minimum liquidity threshold to all the potential expiries in a given instrument. Anything falling below that threshold should be excluded.

Back in strategy three I outlined some criteria to determine which instruments are liquid enough to trade. Firstly, they should have a volume of at least **100 contracts a day**. Secondly, they should have at least **$1.25 million of volume in USD risk terms**. To calculate the volume in risk terms, we use the following:

$$\text{Average daily volume in USD risk}$$
$$= \text{FX rate} \times \text{Average daily volume} \times \sigma_\% \times \text{Price} \times \text{Futures multiplier}$$

where $\sigma_\%$ is the annualised standard deviation of percentage returns. You should apply these filters to all expiries, and only those that pass should be considered.[275]

---

275   I use volumes averaged over the last 30 days for these calculations.

Let's see how these filters apply to the VIX. In table 170 I have estimated $\sigma_\%$ and used that to calculate the USD risk volume, using the futures multiplier for VIX, which is $1,000. You can see that January and February 2023 do not meet the 100 contracts per day minimum, neither do they meet the requirement for at least $1.25 million of daily volume in risk terms.

TABLE 170: CURRENT VOLUME FOR VIX EXPIRIES

	Price	$\sigma_\%$	Daily volume in contracts	USD risk volume
June 2022	29.45	66.8%	67,000	$1,320 million
July 2022	30.13	51.5%	33,200	$510 million
August 2022	30.11	43.9%	10,400	$140 million
September 2022	30.15	36.1%	7,000	$75 million
October 2022	30.10	31.7%	5,500	$52 million
November 2022	29.55	30.5%	3,000	$27.1 million
December 2022	28.60	30.0%	1,100	$9.4 million
January 2023	28.95	29.6%	30	$270,000
February 2023	29.125	29.3%	0	$0

Incidentally, it isn't always the case that liquidity falls away gradually as it does here for VIX. In certain other futures there are more interesting patterns. For example, in full sized WTI Crude Oil we see the same general pattern of reducing liquidity into the future, but the June and December contracts in successive years have better volume and open interest than other months. Another unusual instrument is Gold, which lists additional contracts so that you can always trade the nearest three months, but these extra expiries are not very liquid, so in practice you have to choose from the core contracts: February, April, June, August, October and December.

Risk

Once you have filtered instruments for liquidity, the next step is to consider the risk of different expiries. This might seem a strange step – surely all contracts trading for a given instrument are likely to have similar risk? In fact this is rarely the case. Look back at table 170. You can see that the annualised standard deviation for different VIX expiries has a clear pattern: high for the front contract, and then gradually reducing.

This **volatility term structure** is fairly typical of the VIX, and is known as the

'Samuelson[276] effect'. Other patterns appear elsewhere. For example, in the Eurodollar interest rate future, the current term structure shows standard deviation sharply increasing with contract maturity for the first four quarterly futures. Thereafter the volatility gradually declines.

Term structure in Eurodollars changes over time, depending on the current phase of interest rate policy. During the very low interest rates prevalent for most of the 2010s, volatility of Eurodollar futures was extremely low for the first few contracts and then monotonically increased well into the future. But if the next Fed decision is expected shortly and will be very close, then the front Eurodollar contract may have the highest volatility of all. In general, known events in the future like crop reports, elections or economic announcements can also distort the volatility level for specific expiries in different instruments.

Thinking about contract selection, should we prefer high or low volatility? High volatility will mean lower leverage and reduced risk adjusted trading costs. Low volatility implies lower minimum capital. On balance, **I prefer high volatility**. This means staying away from the front end of the Eurodollar futures curve, but it would also imply a preference for the front of the VIX curve.

However, there are other measures of risk we need to consider. Prices for certain expiries can be somewhat jumpy with tail risk or skew which is not adequately captured when using just a standard deviation estimate to measure risk. You can use measures like kurtosis or my own tail ratio statistics to quantify these risks. Again, this is true for the front end of most interest rate futures markets. As interest rates are traditionally set in increments of 25 basis points, a change in expectation about next week's rate change will usually cause a relatively large jump in price.

But jumpiness is also a feature of the front VIX contract. Spot VIX is extremely jumpy, and this infects the front of the futures curve more than subsequent expiries. Hence, despite its high standard deviation, I generally avoid trading the first VIX expiry.

Seasonality

Many futures are seasonal. This clearly applies to agricultural futures, but also to energy markets. We saw back in strategy ten that this will affect the carry that a given instrument experiences, if you consistently hold the first or second contract throughout the year.

It's for this reason that I advocate holding a fixed calendar month expiry where

---

276 Paul Samuelson 'Proof that properly anticipated prices fluctuate randomly', *Industrial Management Review*, 1965.

possible. I implement this strategy in full size WTI Crude where I only ever hold the next December contract, and in many agricultural instruments such as Corn and Wheat. It's not possible to do this everywhere, however. For example in Henry Hub Natural Gas there isn't sufficient liquidity far enough into the future to stick to a fixed calendar month.

Carry calculation

Back in strategy ten I discussed two possible methods to calculate raw carry. The more precise option involves comparing the price of the currently held futures contract to a nearer contract. Clearly this will not work if we hold the front contract, so you should avoid it if you can. If you are forced to hold the first expiry, then you will have to use the less precise method for carry calculation that compares the current contract to the price of a further out expiry.

Physical delivery and cash settled

VIX contracts are cash settled. On expiry you will receive the difference in cash between the final settlement price and the price you initially paid (in practice most of this sum will already have been credited or debited from your account in the form of variation margin). Cash settlement is de rigueur in equity indices, short-term interest rate futures like Eurodollar and volatility futures like the VIX.

But most futures are actually physically settled, including most bond and foreign exchange futures, and virtually all physical commodities including Gold and Wheat. If you're still long on the expiry date then you will be expected to take actual delivery of a bond, some foreign currency, a few bars of Gold, or bushels of Wheat. Allegedly, this happened to the legendary economist John Maynard Keynes, who had to store his unexpected Wheat delivery in the chapel crypt of the Cambridge University college whose endowment he was managing. If you're short, then you'll be legally required to transfer a bond or currency, or worst still arrange to take some Gold or Wheat to a specific warehouse.

This is fine for commodity houses that have access to warehouses and supplies of Wheat, but not at all fine for everyone else. As a result futures brokers will forcibly close your position if it's still open when a contract expiry is looming. **This is another reason to avoid the front contract**. You do not want to risk physical delivery of a future, or more likely have your broker closing out the position if you get too close to the expiry date.

Does this mean we don't need to worry about expiry in cash settled contracts, like the VIX? In fact, there is a potential risk from holding these right up to the last possible moment. Cash settlements occur against a price that is measured over a relatively short window of time. These prices are open to manipulation. This is unlikely to be a serious issue in the VIX, but could easily be a problem in more thinly traded instruments.[277]

Reducing roll frequency

Like all trading, rolling from one futures contract to the next costs money in spreads and commissions. So ideally we would roll as little as possible. With some instruments it's possible to **reduce rolling frequency by holding a contract that is further out into the future**. A classic example of this is Eurodollar. This has high risk adjusted costs, since the standard deviation is pretty low, so it is quite expensive to hold if we roll it every three months.

Which Eurodollar contracts can we hold? There are liquid quarterly expiries for the next six years or so. For the reasons I've already touched upon, I would strongly advise avoiding the first year of expiries, due to their lower volatility and ugly tail risk. Any expiry that is more than three years in the future currently has a standard deviation that is a little too low. However, that leaves a large window of possible contract dates that you can trade, between one year and three years.

In theory you could adopt the following strategy:

- Initially buy or sell a future that is three years out, which as I write is June 2025.

- After three months start **passively rolling** the future (I explain what this is in a few pages' time) into a new contract: June 2027. I explain why you should use June 2027 in a moment.

- After a couple of years it will be May 2024. June 2025 now has about a year of maturity left and is in danger of its expiry falling below the required minimum of one year. If you still hold any June 2025, then roll it all into the contract which now has three years left before expiry: June 2027.

This means that in the worst case scenario, where you do not naturally close your position through passive rolling, you will be rolling every two years rather than every quarter. It will probably be slightly more expensive to do each roll trade, since these

---

277 Even highly liquid futures can be manipulated. Consider the Eurodollar interest rate futures, which originally settled against the LIBOR interest rate. This was not calculated from actual trades but instead based on a survey of a relatively small pool of banks, which made it straightforward to influence the rate by submitting quotations that were biased upwards or downwards. There have been several prosecutions of traders implicated in this activity, including several ex Barclays colleagues of mine, and many have spent significant time in jail. In my opinion this is all rather unfair given it was a widespread practice in financial markets, and allegations of more serious manipulation by senior bank officials at the behest of governments and central bankers have gone unpunished.

will consist of a spread trade for contracts that are two years apart rather than three months apart, and the former will probably have a wider bid-ask spread. But reducing the number of rolls by a factor of eight will save a lot more money in the long run.[278]

Holding multiple months

There is no law saying that you have to hold your entire futures position in a single contract month. There can be advantages to holding positions in two, three, or more expiries at a time. Doing this allows you to do your rolling more gradually. Also, if you are a large fund with significant positions, then you can avoid being too large a part of the market in one delivery month. Indeed, there are often regulatory limits on the size of positions that can be taken by a single entity in one expiry.

This will make your trading process a little more operationally complex. But it can make sense.

Summary

It is difficult to summarise the factors above into a single cohesive rule that will apply to all futures contracts. But here are some rules of thumb:

- Only trade liquid expiries. For many financial futures and metals, this means you can only trade the front contract.

- Where you do have a choice, avoid the front contract if at all possible. Otherwise you won't be able to calculate carry accurately, and the price is often jumpy. You could also run into problems with physical delivery, or suffer from the manipulation of settlement prices for cash settled contracts.

- It is usually better to be further out on the curve if possible: the second, third, fourth or later expiries. This often has better risk properties, and you will be able to roll less frequently.

- Where relevant, consider trading a fixed calendar month expiry so your back-adjusted price does not have seasonality.

- You may want to hold your position in more than one month at a time, especially if you have large positions.

---

278   One criticism of this technique is that the character of the new contract will be quite different from the previous expiry. For example, the standard deviation will change rather abruptly if there is a particularly steep volatility term structure.

Choosing contracts with the best forecasts

For instruments with a wide choice of expiries we might be tempted to try to pick the expiries on which we have the highest chance of making profitable returns. In the context of the trading strategies in this book, that means picking the expiry with the largest combined forecast.

It is a bit weird to think of choosing the expiry with the highest *trend* forecast, since trend is based on the back-adjusted price, which itself is made up of prices from contracts with consecutive expiry dates. If instead we measured the trend on a contract by contract basis, and then picked the best one, we'd face a number of issues. Primarily we'd struggle to measure anything but the very shortest trends, unless the relevant contract had already been liquid for at least a year and ideally longer.

But it could make some sense to choose the expiry with the best *carry* forecast, which will be the month with the highest or lowest risk adjusted roll yield.

From table 170 a quick back of the envelope calculation reveals that the risk adjusted carry varies considerably over the current VIX futures curve. It's high and positive for the front contract, a little lower for the second, and then goes negative over the next few expiries. Interesting patterns like this are common in VIX futures.

This suggests that if we were only trading carry then we should probably hold the December 2022 contract, which has the largest absolute value for the carry forecast. In that case we would be short, since the carry forecast is negative.

But we can't ignore trend entirely. Assuming we are trading some variation of strategy eleven, carry and trend, it's no good having a high carry forecast if trend gives us the opposite signal. This implies that if the trend forecast requires a short position, then we should indeed trade December 2022. But if trend were long, then the front contract would be best since it has the highest positive carry. Of course, if we did trade the front contract, then we wouldn't be able to measure the carry of the front contract accurately unless we used the spot price, so the second contract would be a good compromise.

These sorts of calculations get quite complicated rather quickly. Personally, I like to keep things simple and ignore this factor when deciding which contract to hold.

When to roll to a new expiry date

Once you have established a position in a specific expiry date, when should you roll it to a new date? Indeed, what should that new date be? To an extent, this decision will be made using similar criteria to those we used above to select the starting contract month.

If you have to hold the front contract because the second contract is not liquid, then you will obviously want to roll into the second contract once it is liquid enough to trade. This logic will apply to most financial futures, FX and metals. This will usually be a few days before the expiry of the front month, although for some instruments like Korean bonds you won't be able to roll until the expiry is imminent.

Importantly, for certain physically settled futures you will have to close your position several days *before* the actual expiry date. This could be because your broker doesn't want the slightest risk of physical delivery, but there is another possible reason: certain futures have a **first notice date (FND)**. This is the earliest date on which the holder of a long position can be notified that they will be expected to take physical delivery, and is usually a few days before the expiry date. If you're still holding a long position on the FND then you are potentially at risk of receiving physical delivery. You should close your position a few days before the FND, or risk pre-emptive action from your broker.

Similarly, **if you have decided to hold the second contract**, then you will probably want to roll into the following contract once it is liquid enough to trade, and certainly before the first contract expires. For example, I'm currently holding the second contract of VIX (July 2022). I could probably roll into August 2022 now, since from table 170 it is sufficiently liquid, although the standard deviation is a little lower so I might want to wait. But I definitely want to roll before the June 2022 VIX expires; if I don't then my July 2022 position will become the front month, and I certainly don't want that for the reasons I've already explained.

If you are **trading even further out on the curve**, then you have some flexibility. I am currently trading Eurodollar June 2025, about three years into the future. I could systematically roll my position every quarter to ensure it is always around three years away. Alternatively, I could follow the strategy discussed above and wait for up to a couple of years before rolling to reduce the frequency of my rolls. Or I could do something in between, rolling every six months or every year.

Finally, if you are holding a **fixed calendar month**, then you should roll before that becomes the first contract, if not sooner. That is so you can continue to measure carry accurately. For example, if you're consistently holding December WTI Crude, then you would want to roll out of December 2022 at least a few days before November 2022 expires.

Does it matter when you roll?

One day, when I was still working in hedge funds, I was approached by a couple of researchers from another team. They had discovered something that was rather interesting.

We'd recently launched an initiative to clean up the disparate data sets of price history that we had lying around, and consolidate them into a single 'golden source' that we could use for future research. These guys had been given this tedious but important assignment. One of the issues they had discovered was that our back-adjusted prices for US bond futures assumed we could roll just before the expiry. In reality, we would have rolled before the first notice day, rather than risk having the physical bonds delivered to us.

To fix this they went back and modified the roll calendar in our database, and then regenerated the back-adjusted price. To make sure they hadn't done something stupid, they then plotted the old and new prices on the same chart. Naturally, they had expected to see an almost perfect match.

To everyone's surprise, the curves didn't match up. The new curve was almost identical to the old one, with one important difference. It had a lower upward gradient, translating to a slightly lower return. Effectively the market was willing to pay a small additional premium to people who had the capacity to hold a long position in the bond future past the point when they might have to receive a physical delivery.

Although this didn't have a significant effect on our trading strategies, it was a timely lesson in ensuring that our backtests were as realistic and as accurate as possible.

How to roll to a new expiry date

This might seem like a trivial matter: a roll is a roll, right? But there are actually a few different alternative methods to consider.

Roll with individual legs

The simplest way to roll a position is with two separate trades: a closing trade in the currently held expiry month, and an equally sized opening trade in the new expiry. However, this has two key disadvantages. Firstly, it's expensive. You will pay two separate sets of costs related to bid-ask spreads. Secondly, it's potentially dangerous.

There is no guarantee that the pair of trades will execute simultaneously, leaving you open to the chance that you will either have twice the risk you want (if the closing trade does not execute), or none at all (if the opening trade fails).

Where possible you should avoid this option. If you have no choice, then do the trade gradually in tranches, and avoid trading just before the close.

Roll with a spread trade

Rather than using two separate trades, it is much better to use a spread trade. This is a spread that will be executed in the market as one order. It has two key advantages. Firstly, there is no chance of one leg being executed and not the other. Also, it is usually much cheaper to trade. Broadly speaking, you would expect to pay half the spread cost from doing one rather than two trades. In some markets, such as the S&P 500 future, the spread markets have a smaller tick size than the outright, resulting in even tighter spread costs.

All this assumes that there is a liquid spread market in the relevant future. This is usually the case, and indeed in instruments like Eurodollar the spreads are more liquid than the outrights. But it is not always true.

Passive rolling

Rolling with a spread trade is cheaper than trading separate legs, but it is not the cheapest method of all. Even cheaper is to roll **passively**. With passive rolling, you do your roll as part of your normal trading activity. To achieve this:

- If you are doing a trade that **reduces** your position, then you close or partially close your position in the **current** month.

- But if you are doing a trade that **increases** your position, then you do that in the **next** contract month.

Over time your position will shift naturally from the current to the next month. Because we aren't doing any additional trading just for the purpose of rolling, the roll trades are costing us nothing.[279]

This option is available for a given instrument once the next contract month is liquid. In many cases this won't leave a window of opportunity that is long enough to complete

---

279   Since we are still calculating our forecasts using the price of the current month, whilst holding position in a blend of the current and next month, you could argue that there is some basis risk in our trading strategy; but it should be minimal.

all the rolling that is needed. At some point you will have to use a spread trade, or a pair of individual trades, to roll the residual contracts you still hold in the current expiry. But for an instrument that trades relatively quickly, or rolls infrequently, it might be possible to completely avoid doing any explicit roll trading.

As I noted above, you may want to hold positions in more than one delivery month. If you are passively rolling, you will naturally have positions in both the current and next contract expiry. But you can extend this further. Suppose you are holding positions in three months; for the sake of argument June, July and August 2022. You would do any closing trades in June 2022 and any opening trades in August 2022, with no trades at all in July 2022.

Then once you have closed all your June 2022 positions, you would start doing any opening trades in September 2022 and any closing trades in July 2022. It's easy to see how this procedure can be generalised for any number of months.

Natural close

A special case of passive rolling is when your strategy naturally wants to close its entire position in a particular instrument. At that point, if you are ready to roll, you would immediately switch to trading the next contract date, so that when a new position was opened it would already be in the correct expiry. This avoids the complexity of holding positions in multiple expiries. Achieving this requires some luck and a daily review of all of your currently closed positions.

Allow expiry and then reopen

The two basic problems with roll trading through separate trades are the cost and the risk of having a doubled up or zero position. But what if we are relaxed about having a zero position for a short period of time? If it is very expensive to trade a given instrument, and the spread market is not very liquid, then it might make sense to let the future expire. Then on the following day you can reopen a position in the new contract month. That way you only pay trading costs on the opening trade. Naturally, this would only make sense for cash settled futures.

Using this method assumes that the gains from halving the trading cost outweigh the risk of having no position on in the time period between the future settling and when you are able to open a position in the new expiry.

Incidentally, foreign currency futures are a possible exception to the rule of never letting physically settled contracts expire. Assuming you have a multi-currency trading account, it's usually straightforward to deliver or take delivery of different currencies when the relevant future expires. The delivery process will usually involve a credit to your account in one currency, plus a loan in another. You can then do a spot FX trade to remove the credit and loan from your account. This will incur transaction costs, and possibly some interest charges during the period before the spot trade is settled, so it is unlikely to be cheaper than rolling, but could make sense in some circumstances.

Risk, position sizing and rolls

Cast your eye back to table 170, which showed that the standard deviation of VIX futures is currently higher for earlier deliveries than for those that mature later.

Let's pretend that you currently have a position in July 2022, which currently has an annualised standard deviation of just over 51%. Now suppose this translates to a position of 100 contracts for a particular trading strategy with some arbitrary account size and forecast. Next you roll into August 2022, where the risk is somewhat lower: 44% per year.

Theoretically, your position is now too small. All other things being equal, we scale positions inversely with standard deviation. The correct position will now be:

$$100 \times 0.51 \div 0.44 = 115.9 \sim 116$$

We appear to be light 16 contracts. Okay, this looks like a problem, but what will actually happen in practice?

On the day you roll the back-adjusted price series for the last month or so it will probably consist entirely of July 2022 prices. Assuming the term structure of volatility is linear, then as July 2022 ages, its standard deviation would have risen from the start of the month to the end. When we roll into August 2022, the standard deviation drops back down as we push out a month into the future and move out along the term structure of volatility. As the August contract ages, its standard deviation would rise until the next roll date, when the cycle would repeat.

If we were to plot the current standard deviation over time, then we'd see a sawtooth type graph with abrupt drops on roll dates, interspersed with gradual rises. If we sized our positions based on the current level of standard deviation, then these would also show a sawtooth shape, with positions increasing dramatically when we roll, then reducing gradually.

However, we don't measure the *current* level of standard deviation, because that's very hard to do with daily data, and it would give us a prediction of future volatility that is too noisy. Instead, we use an exponentially weighted rolling window to calculate our estimate. If we were to plot this estimate, it would still show the sawtooth type shape, but the peaks and troughs would be much shallower.

(In fact, if we were to use a simple rolling window that had a span of longer than a month, then the sawtooth would completely disappear.)

The sawtooth effect is further ameliorated by using a weighted average of recent standard deviation and a long run estimate. Ultimately, the effect is reduced to a few contracts on an arbitrary 100 contract sized position. In reality, even this small change in position size will be indiscernible once all the other factors that can cause optimal positions to change are taken into account.

It's also worth pointing out that this is only a problem in certain instruments and for traders with large positions. Someone holding fewer than eight contracts of VIX wouldn't see any discernible sawtooth effect at all, as their rounded optimal position would remain constant.

Still, this is yet another reason for staying away from the front end of the curve in instruments like VIX and Eurodollar. Changes in standard deviation tend to be larger at the front of the curve, making this problem potentially more serious.

Special cases

The tactics above are generally applicable to most trading strategies in this book, but there are some special cases where you may need to apply slightly different methods.

Dynamic optimisation (strategy twenty-five)

If you are using the dynamic optimisation strategy from Part Three, then it's possible to set constraints on position sizes and trades. That gives you a neat way to implement the rolling technique where we allow positions to expire before reopening them.

To do this, we set a constraint such that no trade will be generated for the relevant instrument. Then when the expiry has occurred, we update our current positions to reflect the fact we no longer have a position. The optimiser may then reopen a position in the new contract month. But it may also decide that it is cheaper or better to put the risk elsewhere.

Another option is to use constraints to avoid taking on new positions in contract dates which will be expiring soon, but where the next contract date is not yet sufficiently liquid. Thus you can avoid the expense of opening a new position and then having to roll it shortly afterwards. The optimiser will transfer risk to other instruments so you don't miss out.

Fast directional strategies (Part Four)

By their nature fast strategies will trade much more frequently than slow ones. This makes it more likely that passive rolling will work effectively. However, you need to be careful about holding positions in multiple months, since it can make it more complex to calculate prices for limit orders. These would need to be adjusted so they are appropriate for different contract months.

Personally, I'd advocate the simplest method, which is to wait until the strategy closes its current position and then switch to trading the next contract date before a new position is opened. Since these strategies trade quickly, you won't have to wait very long.

Relative value (Part Five strategies)

Relative value (RV) strategies bring some complexity. For cross instrument RV, rolls should ideally be co-ordinated to happen at the same time, which may not be easy. However, the real challenges arise when we trade calendar spreads and triplets within the same instrument.

Rolling an RV calendar position is a little tricker than just rolling an outright. Imagine we are trading a Eurodollar RV spread, with equal and opposite positions in June 2023 and December 2023. To roll this requires doing two separate spread trades simultaneously: June to July 2023, and December 2023 to March 2024. It could be possible to execute these as a single four leg order with the resulting benefits that would bring, but it might be tricky to find liquidity for that specific spread.

There are particular issues when the RV legs are in adjacent expiries. Consider the VIX spread I used as an example in Part Five, which right now would be between July 2022 and August 2022, and which I will roll into the August 2022 and September 2022 spread. The fact that August is both the current and the next contract for different legs of the spread makes for significant operational complexity.

TACTIC TWO

Execution

I am often invited to give guest lectures at various universities. It can sometimes be a challenge to get the bored students to engage with my tedious slides mostly filled with ugly equations, so I use a few tricks. One of these is to put up a blank slide, and then say: "I am going to let you into a secret. There are only two ways to make money in trading or indeed in any business. Two ways which I am now going to exclusively reveal to you. Two things that are the secret of my success."

After a few more minutes of this motivational speaker style build up, when the tension in the room has reached unbearable levels, I reveal the next slide, which is also blank apart from two bullet points:

- Make more money before costs.

- Pay less in trading costs.

Most of the attendees are completely underwhelmed by this, but usually enough of them laugh to justify me repeating this shtick in the following year.

For most of this book we have focused on the first of the two bullet points: making more money before costs. That is not to say that trading costs have been ignored. I have been very careful to repeatedly point out that you must ensure that any given instrument can be traded with a specific strategy without incurring excessive annual costs, using my concept of a speed limit on trading frequency. I have also used techniques like forecast smoothing and position buffering to reduce unnecessary trading to an absolute minimum.

But I have treated the cost of each trade as an external factor which we can measure, but have no control over. I have always assumed that we place market orders,[280] which get filled at the best bid or ask, and therefore pay half the bid-ask spread as a **spread**

---

280   An exception to this were the fast directional strategies in Part Four, which used limit orders for execution. I will discuss those in more detail later in this chapter.

cost, as well as having to fork out brokerage commissions. Can we do better? In this chapter I discuss ways to reduce costs by using smarter execution tactics.

Advanced cost measuring and modelling

If you can't measure it, you can't manage it.

Attributed variously to W. Edwards Deming and Peter Drucker

To do any serious work on improving execution costs, we need to be able to measure them. I use three different sources to measure my expected and actual spread costs:

1. Regularly sampled bid-ask spreads which I capture throughout the day, even for instruments I am not currently trading. The expected cost will be half the spread: the difference between the mid and the bid or ask.

2. Half the bid-ask spread that is present in the market when I submit an order. I also store the size of the order being placed at that time.

3. The actual difference between the mid price and where I am actually executed. I also store the size of the order.

To an extent sources 1 and 2 are equivalent, though perhaps you could argue that the spreads I measure for trades (2) could be biased towards certain times of the day when I tend to do my execution; this is not true of regularly sampled spreads (1). Arguably it is more realistic to use actual trade data (3), especially for larger funds that will not always be able to trade at the top of the order book. I use these figures for several different purposes:

- I use regular samples (1) to calculate an expected bid-ask spread for instruments which I have not yet begun trading. This allows me to calculate an expected risk adjusted cost, determine if a given instrument is cheap enough to trade, and decide which trading rule variations meet my *speed limit* given the risk adjusted cost of trading.

- For instruments I am trading, I calculate the expected bid-ask spread on an ongoing basis, combining data from all three sources to come up with a single figure. This allows me to check it is appropriate to continue trading[281] a given instrument, and to periodically check I have the correct set of trading rules, given current cost levels. To calculate the expected spread I use an average of the sampled spreads from source 1, plus the higher of the figures from expected and realised spreads when

---

281 Expected trading cost is also used as a direct input into my version of strategy twenty-five, dynamic optimisation.

trading (2 and 3). I use the higher figure from sources 2 and 3 to reflect the fact I use an execution algorithm, which means I will sometimes do a little better than the bid-ask spread.

- I use the difference between expected and actual fill spread costs at the point of trading (2 versus 3) to measure the efficacy of my execution algorithms, which I will discuss in a few pages.

- Using actual fill spreads (3) I can see the effect of trading frequency and size on costs. This is not so important for a retail trader like me, but vital for a large institutional trader. I will discuss this later in the chapter.

- By analysing spreads by time of day and week day, I can determine if there are times when a given instrument will be cheaper or more expensive to trade. Again, I will discuss this in more detail shortly.

- In principle, I could use historical data on actual traded spreads and commissions to calculate expected costs in backtests, rather than using the methods I explained in Part One, which rely on extrapolating and adjusting the current level of trading costs into the past. Of course this is only an option if you have been trading for a long period of time.

When to trade

Liquidity, and therefore trading costs, have changed considerably over time. Back in the 1980s, when traders in the City of London used to go to the pub every lunchtime, you probably wouldn't want to try executing anything after 12 pm. Even now, Friday afternoons are a relatively quiet time except when nonfarm payrolls are coming out, or major options expirations are happening. In the summer many hedge fund manager types go to their estates in the Hamptons or the Dordogne, whilst great chunks of the winter are spent in Aspen or Verbier. As a junior trader I was left in sole charge of the trading book in the dark miserable days between Christmas and New Year.

There are well-known patterns in spreads and liquidity. Whilst you are unlikely to reduce costs significantly through careful optimisation of trading times, you can certainly avoid doing something stupid, and unnecessarily increasing your costs by trading when the market is bound to be thin. Here are some key trading periods to avoid:

- In US equities opening and closing times are when much of the trading happens. However, in many futures markets the opposite is true. The open and close are thinly traded, with wide spreads set to catch the desperate or unwary trader. It is often better to wait until the market has been open for 30 minutes, and stop trading 30 minutes before the close.

- Some futures markets effectively trade around the clock, such as those listed on the CME Globex platform. However a US future is unlikely to be as liquid during the overnight session as it is during the day. Refer to figure 95 for an example. This shows the 90th percentile of the bid-ask spread for Eurodollar futures by hour of the day, calculated from my own regular price sampling process. Notice the higher spreads during the overnight period.

- Avoid trading shortly before or after major economic news releases like nonfarm payroll or crop reports, or when election results are being released. The market is likely to be thin, and there will be sharp movements in prices.

- Be careful trading during holiday periods when the exchange is open but many people are likely to be away. You can't really turn off your strategy for a whole day or week, but you may want to limit your trading to smaller maximum order sizes (see the next section). Also be aware that exchange holidays in the USA will reduce liquidity in other countries where markets remain open. The reverse is true for specific products; for example, a Japanese holiday would result in less trading of the JPY/USD FX future.

- Large institutional funds should avoid trading at set times during the day, or they risk being picked off if fleeter footed traders can spot the pattern and front run them.

FIGURE 95: 90% PERCENTILE OF SAMPLED BID-ASK SPREAD FOR EURODOLLAR FUTURES BY HOUR OF DAY (UTC TIME ZONE)

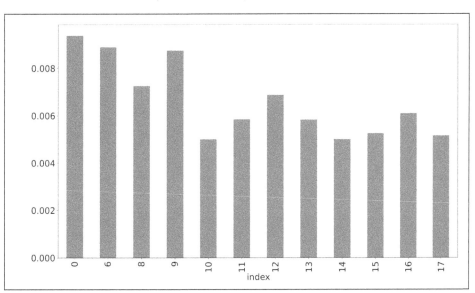

How often to trade and in what size

Let's assume that you are a large institutional trader who is running a daily trading strategy. You have to buy 1,000 contracts of VIX in the next 24 hours: roughly 1.5% of the daily volume. How are you going to do it? There are roughly 28,000 seconds in an eight-hour trading day, so should you submit a one contract buy order every 28 seconds? Or submit a single 1,000 lot order in one go and see what happens? Both of these extreme options sound crazy, and we probably want to do something in the middle, but what would be best? Ten contracts every 280 seconds? A hundred contracts every 2,800 seconds – about 45 minutes – has passed?

A related question: what costs can you expect from doing this kind of volume? It hopefully goes without saying that you won't pay half the bid-ask spread on a single 1,000 contract market buy order! As I write this there are only 100 contracts at the best ask price in the VIX.

But it's also unlikely we will be paying only half the bid-ask spread doing 1.5% of daily volume, even if we do single contract trades. The market might not initially react, but a constant stream of one lot orders will soon cause the price to move up from where it would have been without our participation – an example of so-called 'permanent' price impact.

If you can no longer assume that the spread cost will be invariant to the size of your trades, or that the price won't be impacted by your trading, everything gets a little more complicated. Consider these decisions:

- The decision about what instruments are cheap enough to trade.

- Whether a given instrument is liquid enough to trade.

- What trading rule variations you can use for a given instrument.

- What instrument weight you should allocate.

In Part One I assumed these decisions could be made independently, but now they will have to be made jointly considering feedback effects. For example, a higher instrument weight will mean you are a larger proportion of the volume, and hence you might want to remove trading rules that have a higher turnover.

Of course, these are all problems that only large institutional traders need to concern themselves with, and the solution is to experiment with different order sizes and collect data. Ultimately you need to be able to produce a function that will calculate the expected bid-ask spread for a given size of trade and proportion of daily volume. You can then use this to make well-informed decisions about appropriate trade size and likely costs.

If you don't want to actually trade in large size just to gather data – a potentially expensive exercise – a proxy is to collect level two data from further down the order book and use this to model the likely costs of large orders. But bear in mind this will only be an estimate. In particular you should be very wary of extrapolating cost figures for larger volumes than you are actually trading, since costs do not increase in a linear or predictable way once you are a significant proportion of the traded volume in a given instrument.

Using an algo for execution

Everything in this chapter so far has assumed that we use **market orders** and pay half the bid-ask spread every time we trade. However, it is possible to do a little better, by using **execution algorithms ('algos')**.

To see how this might work, let's consider the two main types of order that can be used for trading, and their advantages and disadvantages:

Market order	**Advantages**: Cost is known (half the bid-ask spread for small orders). Will almost always execute.
	Disadvantage: Will always pay half the bid-ask spread.
Limit order	**Advantage**: Can be cheaper than a market order. If we get filled at the best bid for a buy, or best offer for a sell, we effectively get paid to trade with a negative spread cost.
	Disadvantages: Cost is unknown, as is time to execution. Could end up being significantly more expensive than a market order, if the market moves away from its initial level before we get filled.

In its most basic form an execution algo works by switching between (a) executing **passively** using limit orders, in the hope of getting a better fill, and (b) **aggressive** execution where we submit a market order and so have to pay the spread, getting the best bid for a sell, and paying the best offer on a buy. Clearly the decision about whether to be executing passively or aggressively at any given moment could depend on many factors, and some execution algos are quite complex.

If you want to utilise the power of algos, then you have a few options. One is to build your own, assuming you have the skills and infrastructure to do so. A second is to utilise the third-party algos offered by brokers, banks and third-party providers like Quantitative Brokers. A third is to use the old fashioned method of manual execution, by employing a human execution trader. This might seem like a step backwards, but an experienced ex-floor trader can still be superior to an automated algo in many instruments, especially for larger orders, and for a large enough account will usually be cheaper than submitting market orders.

You also have the option of using more than one of these routes to market. An advantage of this is that you can run natural experiments, randomly allocating orders to different routes and measuring the costs of execution for each route. With enough data you can generate quite sophisticated rules such as: 'For a VIX order of more than 100 contracts traded between 10 am and 12 pm, we have a 74% chance of getting the best fill from algo ZZZ.'

As you would probably expect given my background in systematic futures trading, I have built my own simple execution algo which I have used in one form or another since I began trading my own capital over eight years ago. The algo begins passively by placing a limit order on the appropriate size of the current bid-ask. If I am buying, I will place an order with a limit price equal to the current best bid, and if selling at the current best ask. Then the algo waits for one of three things to happen.

Firstly, an **adverse price movement**. For example, if I am buying and the current mid price moves upwards, or when selling the mid price falls.

Secondly, an **imbalance in the size of the bid-ask spread**. How do I define an imbalance? Suppose we are buying and trying to buy at the ask. An imbalance would occur if the size on the bid side was more than five times greater than that on the ask side. Such an imbalance suggests a lot of buying pressure, most likely to lead to an adverse price movement in the very near future.

Thirdly, a **timeout**: more than five minutes has elapsed since the initial order was placed.

If any of these events occurs, then I switch from passive to aggressive execution. In the aggressive execution mode I will set my limit price at the current best bid if I am selling, or the current best offer if I am buying. I will remain in the aggressive mode until I am filled.

In practice then, if there has been an **imbalance** or **timeout** then as long as I am quick enough, I should be able to get filled at the best bid if I am buying and offer if I am selling; the same price I would have received had I issued a market order to begin with. In this case I get no cost or benefit from using the algo. If I am not quick enough, or if there has already been an **adverse price movement**, then I will end up chasing the price away from where it initially began. In this situation the algo will do worse than a market order.

For example, suppose as I come to trade that an imaginary market, with a 0.01 tick size, has a spread of 100.01 to 100.02. A market buy order would have cost me 100.02, but instead using my algo I initially placed a limit buy order of 100.01. Subsequently, an imbalance develops on the order book, so I switch to aggressive mode, and move my buy limit price higher to the best offer price: 100.02.

However, before I get filled the inside spread moves to 100.02 to 100.03. As I am in aggressive mode I immediately move my buy limit price up to the new best offer:

100.03. At this point the best outcome is that I get filled at 100.03, which is 1 tick worse than I would have paid for a market order (100.02). But it's also possible that the market keeps moving away from me faster than I can update my limit orders, or that it gaps upwards by several ticks before I am filled.

Hence the return profile of an execution algo is very much like a negatively skewed trading strategy. We make steady profits from being paid to trade if the initial limit order gets filled, but big losses when passive mode fails and our fill price is significantly worse.

How effective is this relatively simple algo? Figure 96 has the evidence, with figures from my actual trading system. The light grey line shows the cumulative spread costs I would have paid if I had always submitted market orders and paid the bid-ask spread. Over the 20 months shown in the graph this would have amounted to a cost of just over 3.6% of my capital. The dark grey line is what I actually incurred in spread costs and amounts to around 3%. The difference between these is the contribution of my execution algo, which has saved me around 0.6%. The cumulative profits from my algo are shown in the black line.

I have reduced my costs by around one sixth – not bad for a few lines of code, and with no need for a sophisticated, low latency, high frequency trading fund style infrastructure.

FIGURE 96: CUMULATIVE COSTS AS A PERCENTAGE OF CAPITAL FOR AUTHOR'S TRADING SYSTEM FROM SEPTEMBER 2020 TO APRIL 2022. THE *X*-AXIS IS THE INTERNAL ORDER ID

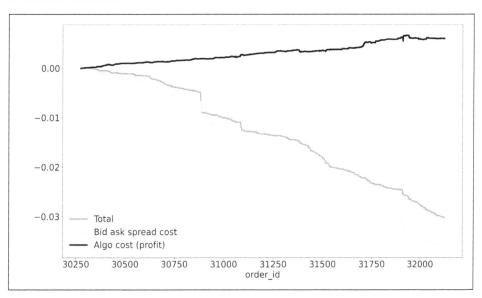

Special case: fast directional strategies (Part Four) – trading with ladders

We can't use an execution algo for the fast directional strategies of Part Four, because they mostly use limit orders. However, there is scope for making some tweaks to the process I discussed in Part Four. Let's remind ourselves of the initial situation in the example I set up for strategy twenty-six, when I was explaining how we set limit orders:

Sell limit order	133.046875 (Sell 1, to go short 13 contracts)
Current price and position	133.00 (Short 12 contracts)
Buy limit order	132.96875 (Buy 1, to go short 11 contracts)

As you may remember, the price rose to 133.078125 in the following hour, so the sell order above would have been executed. Our position is now short 13 contracts. We now create a new sell limit order whose price is implied from a position of –14 and that has a limit price of 133.09375. Additionally, we also require a new buy limit order for a position of –12, which needs a limit of 133.015625.

In the original example, I said we should modify the price of the existing unfilled buy order from 132.96875 to 133.015625:

New sell limit order	133.09375 (Sell 1, to go short 14 contracts)
Current price and position	133.078125 (Short 13 contracts)
Modified buy limit order	133.015625 (Buy 1, to go short 12 contracts)

Now let's consider an alternative method. Rather than modifying the limit price, you could **leave the existing buy limit order on the order book** for the original price and **create a new buy order**. This leaves us with a short *ladder*[282] of limit orders, covering a wider range in the market:

New sell limit order	133.09375 (Sell 1, to go short 14 contracts)
Current price and position	133.078125 (Short 13 contracts)
New buy limit order	133.015625 (Buy 1, to go short 12 contracts)
Existing buy limit order	132.96875 (Buy 1, to go short 11 contracts)

---

282   A **ladder** of orders is just a series of orders left in the order book at different prices. For the mean reversion strategy, a ladder consists of sell limit orders above the current price, plus buy limit orders below it.

Then if the market trades down to 133 again, resulting in the position reverting to –12, you would already have your buy limit order in place. You just need to create a new sell order, with your original order remaining in place:

Existing sell limit order	133.09375 (Sell 1, to go short 14 contracts)
New sell limit order	133.046875 (Sell 1, to go short 13 contracts)
Current price and position	133.00 (Short 12 contracts)
Existing buy limit order	132.96875 (Buy 1, to go short 11 contracts)

In a fast moving market this method reduces the need to have an execution algorithm reacting quickly to fills arriving. In fact, since you can pre-calculate all the limit orders you will need on a given day, you can set up an entire ladder of orders when the market opens, covering all possible positions that could be achieved. To maintain the ladder you only need to replace orders above or below the point when existing orders get filled.

However, since modifying and cancelling orders often attract different fees you would need to think carefully about what the optimal strategy would be. Also bear in mind that leaving orders on the books gives high frequency traders (HFT) information that they can use against you. This may not be problematic for retail traders, but one consequence of this strategy is that people with more capital will have limit orders that are closer together in price. Hence if you leave unfilled orders on the book, rather than modifying them, you may end up with dozens or even hundreds of orders.

For example, with $50 million in capital, the original position would be short 1,168 contracts. The limit price for the buy order that would be placed around the original position, calculating from a position of 1168 − 1 = 1167 contracts is 132.999. But this is less than one tick away from the starting price of 133. In fact to get a limit price of 132.984375, one tick below the starting price, we would need to create a limit order derived from an optimal position of 1,132 contracts.

We would need to place a buy limit order of 1168 − 1132 = 36 contracts, one tick below the current price, and also a sell order for 32 contracts one tick above it. This isn't too bad,[283] but you could imagine the excitement of the HFT community if you carelessly left dozens of orders for 30 plus contracts one tick apart strewn all over the order book. In practice this means there is an upper limit on the capital that can be deployed in this particular strategy. If you have to place limit orders for more than a

---

283   Rather than an explicit buy order, someone who is buying more or selling several contracts per tick might want to consider order types that are not visible in the order book.

few contracts, then you should think carefully about limiting the instrument weight you have allocated.

Another question to consider is whether the ladder of orders should be left on the books overnight, or cancelled. By default, limit orders will usually be automatically cancelled at the end of the day, but you can create orders that will remain active for longer.

From the earlier example in strategy twenty-seven:

> *Now imagine that the following day the price opens sharply up, at 134.5 ... the optimal position here would be to go short 25 contracts: some way from our current position of short 12. We should immediately sell 13 contracts ... This should be done as a standard market order. This will probably trade at a tick below 134.5.*

Notice that the price of just under 134.5 is much better than we would have achieved if we had left a ladder of limit orders on the book between 133.00 and 134.50. This is an argument for not leaving a limit order on the book overnight. Had we done so, we would have been filled at an average price of around 133.75. The only circumstance when it would have made sense to leave limit orders would be if prices jumped up suddenly to 134.5 on the open, and then dropped back to 133 before we had a chance to submit our market order.

On balance then I would avoid leaving limit orders active overnight.

Cash and compounding

A futures trading account effectively consists of a big pile of cash, with various derivative futures contracts sitting on top of it. So far in this book we have concerned ourselves exclusively with the futures contracts, but it would be dangerous to ignore the cash. Whilst competent cash management won't make us billionaires, a little astute tinkering can squeeze a little bit of extra performance out of our accounts. We also want to avoid doing something stupid with our cash that will result in eventual bankruptcy, no matter how good we are at predicting the direction of futures prices.

In this chapter I will also consider the question of *compounding*, which relates to cash management, since different compounding methods will require different tactics for cash withdrawal.

Futures and margin

Let's consider what happens to our futures account as we trade. Imagine that we begin on day one with a fresh account, consisting only of cash in US dollars:

Free cash	$500,000

Now suppose we decide to buy one contract of the S&P 500 micro future. That currently requires $1,150 of initial margin. The margin doesn't leave our account, but it is moved to a new segregated area. The clearing house that is responsible for ensuring we honour our trades now has a legal claim on the margin.

Free cash	$498,850
Initial margin	$1,150
Total	$500,000

Notice that this also puts an absolute limit on the number of S&P 500 futures we could buy in one go: we only have enough cash for 434 contracts. However, as I discussed back in Part One, we'd be completely insane to do that. The notional exposure of that position would be around $8.7 million, and the annualised standard deviation as a proportion of our account value would come in at over 250% per year – over 12 times my suggested risk target, τ = 20%.

Back to the example, where we've sensibly only bought one contract. What happens if we are unlucky, and the price of S&P 500 moves against us by 40 points? With a futures multiplier of $5, that will cost us $200. Where does that $200 come from? It can't come from the initial margin, since as we still hold our futures position we need to keep posting that. Instead this **variation margin** comes out of our free cash:

Free cash	$498,850 – $200 = $498,650
Initial margin	$1,150
Total	$499,800

Now let's assume we go completely crazy at this point, driven insane by the thought of losing $200, and decide to load up with as many S&P 500 futures as we can get away with: another 433 contracts.

Free cash	$700
Initial margin	$1,150 * 434 = $499,100
Total	$499,800

It turns out this was a bad move, as the S&P 500 drops by a further point just after we do this trade. This costs us $5 for each of our 434 contracts, or $2,170. But we don't have $2,170 in spare cash! If we're lucky the broker will make a margin call: an email or phone call to demand we pay up the missing money. If we are unlucky – or slow to respond to the call – then the broker will liquidate all or part of our position to release initial margin which can cover the shortfall in free cash.

How serious a problem is this likely to be? After all, you are sensible traders who have read the 400 or so pages in this book so far, and are unlikely to do something as crazy as put on an $8 million S&P 500 position, in a $500,000 trading account. In fact, with my suggested risk target of τ = 20% you are unlikely to run into frequent margin problems. In my own account I run a slightly higher risk target (τ = 25%), and I average around 30% margin usage, typically leaving 70% of my account value as free cash.

Under capitalising and over capitalising an account

Bearing in mind that you are unlikely to use more than 50% of your account for margin, why not deliberately **under capitalise** your account and only deposit half of your designated trading capital? So we would have something like this:

Spare cash (elsewhere)	$250,000
Free cash (account)	$248,850
Initial margin	$1,150
Total	$500,000

There are two potential advantages to doing this:

1. The spare cash can be invested elsewhere to achieve a higher return than the interest paid on cash by the broker.

2. It reduces the exposure in the event that your broker goes bust.

Personally, I am against this. Remember that the free cash in your account is not really free or spare; it is there to cover potential calls for variation margin, and hence any likely losses from your trading strategies. If you have a severe loss then you will need to immediately top up your trading account from your spare cash stored elsewhere. If that cash has been invested, and the investment has temporarily or permanently fallen in value, then you have a problem.

There is also a good chance that you will get into the habit of feeding your trading account with additional capital when you lose money. Whilst not a problem for institutional traders, this sort of behaviour can quickly turn a retail trader into an addict, feeding metaphorical coins into the allegorical slot machine of the market.

What about the risk of broker bankruptcy? If you are genuinely worried about being exposed to your broker going bust, then you should probably find a new broker, or use multiple brokers[284] to limit your exposure to a single counterparty. Under capitalising your account also makes life complicated. When sizing your positions you will have to add together your account balance and the spare cash elsewhere to calculate notional capital.

---

284 This makes particular sense if you would be the beneficiary of a government-backed insurance scheme if the broker goes bust. These schemes usually have a maximum limit on the loss that is covered.

What about doing the opposite: over capitalising your account? That is certainly safer, but it has the obvious disadvantage that you are increasing your exposure to the broker, and you are effectively reducing the return you will get on your capital since the excess cash could have been invested elsewhere.

I generally advise **full capitalisation**: putting all your notional trading capital into your account, no more and no less.

What to do with free cash?

Right at the start of this book, I said that all my backtest accounting is done on the basis of excess returns, excluding any interest paid on margin. I also noted that it was an irrelevant assumption at the time of writing, since interest rates were close to zero. Although benchmark interest rates have been rising as I write this book, they are still not that great. My broker is currently paying 0.33% on USD balances above a certain level, 0.41% on GBP, and still charging interest on EUR deposits (e.g. effectively a negative interest rate).

Can we do better? After all, with 70% on average of our account value as free cash, then earning a modest extra 3% on that would add up to 2.1% a year. That doesn't sound much, but it's just over 0.10 Sharpe ratio (SR) units on a τ = 20% trading strategy. That's not a bad improvement, and it doesn't require much extra effort.

The problem is that to get more return, you will have to take more risk. A globally diversified exchange traded fund (ETF) of government bonds currently yields about 2.5%. Government bonds sound safe, but whilst I have been writing this book that particular ETF has fallen in price by over 12%. To get over 3% in yield, we would currently need to cast our net wider, into even riskier territory: emerging markets, junk corporate bonds or equities. Adopting this tactic means we are effectively increasing our risk target, except in the unlikely event that the new investment is negatively correlated to our trading strategy.

What about hedging our exposure? For example, we could sell bond futures to hedge the interest rate risk of a bond fund.

As you might expect, there is no free lunch on offer here. Either our hedge will be perfect, in which case we would earn a net zero return minus transaction costs, or it would be imperfect and we would have created a leveraged position with exposures we probably don't understand. After all, if we were experts in trading leveraged debt then we would be doing that, not trading futures. The hedge itself will also consume free cash, unless it coincidentally netted off against an existing futures position.

My recommendation is to put up with low returns and keep your net account balance in cash. If you disagree with me and decide to go down this route, then it goes without saying that anything you invest in has to be extremely liquid. You might have to sell it quickly to meet margin demands.

Margin and FX

Let's return to our original example:

Free cash	$500,000

Instead of trading S&P 500, suppose we decide instead to purchase 50 contracts of German Bund 10-year bond futures. The initial margin required is €235,000, or about $250,000. No problem, we have plenty of cash. But it's in the wrong currency: we want euros but we have US dollars.

There are two possible options here. Firstly, we could do an FX trade to get the required margin, selling USD and buying EUR. I call this the **FX trade option**, and I'm using the word 'option' here to mean *choice*, not a financial derivative. After buying the Bund and doing the forex trade, our account would look like this:

Free cash	$250,000
Initial margin	€235,000 [worth $250,000]
Total	$500,000

Alternatively there is the **FX borrow option**: we could borrow euros to make the initial margin payment:

$ Free cash	$500,000
€ Loan	(€235,000)
Initial margin	€235,000
Total	$500,000

With many brokers, unless you do the explicit FX trade, you will end up automatically borrowing. Now suppose that you are a little unlucky with your bet on German interest rates and you lose €20,000, about $21,270. If you are pursuing the **FX trade option**, then you will sell dollars and buy more euros to cover this loss:

Free cash	$228,730
Initial margin	€235,000 [worth $250,000]
Total	$478,730

Alternatively if you are an **FX borrower**, then you would borrow more euros to cover the loss:

$ Free cash	$500,000
€ Loan	(€255,000) [worth $271,270]
Initial margin	€235,000 [worth $250,000]
Total	$478,730

Now imagine that we get lucky and the market moves in our favour, so that we can close our bund trade without a gain or loss. If we are **FX borrowers** then we would repay our euro loan from the initial margin that was released. However, if we had opted for the **FX trading** choice, then we would be left with surplus euros in our account:

Free cash	$228,730
Free cash	€255,000 [worth $271,270]
Total	$500,000

At this stage we could either hold on to our euros ready for the next trade, or convert some or all of them back into dollars.

Which of these methods is best: FX trading or FX borrowing? There are quite a few factors to consider.

Firstly, it costs money to do FX trades. However, this is likely to be a relatively small amount. Secondly, we usually earn interest on cash that is deposited but have to pay interest on cash we have borrowed. Currently I can earn 0.33% on USD balances, but to borrow in EUR costs me around 1%. This is quite a large difference, because the broker makes a spread between borrowing and lending rates.

Thirdly, we are exposed to FX rates changing. With the **FX trading option**, we do not want EUR to become less valuable relative to USD, because after buying our bunds we have a net balance of €235,000. A 2% depreciation in the euro will cost us €4,700, which is equivalent to $5,000: 1% of our account value. However, if we are **FX borrowers**, things are different. Our net FX exposure after the initial trade is zero, but once we start losing money we have a negative net balance of €20,000. We would be worried about the euro *appreciating* relative to the dollar, although our exposure is much smaller – a 2% depreciation would cost us only €400. Generally speaking, the FX trading approach results in greater exposure to currency rate changes than FX borrowing does.

We can reduce our FX exposure by hedging. It is quite straightforward to hedge FX exposures – there are these things called currency futures that you may have heard about! We can easily hedge €250,000 since each USD/EUR contract is worth precisely €125,000. However, most of the time we won't be able to execute a perfectly matched hedge because we can't trade fractional contracts, although large institutional traders with many millions in FX exposure can get pretty close. Hedges also cost money in transaction costs. You may also face operational difficulties in separating out positions related to your main trading strategy and any hedges.

Is it worth hedging? For most retail traders I would argue it is not. If exchange rates are a random walk over time, then any gains or losses from changes in FX rates would end up netting out to zero and will just add random 'noise' to our returns. Of course, as futures traders we probably believe we can predict the price of FX futures to some degree. You may want to selectively hedge, buying or selling futures that hedge your cash exposure only if the relevant carry and/or trend forecast is in your favour. Just bear in mind that this will effectively increase the implicit instrument weight on the FX asset class, and you may wish to reduce it in your core trading strategy to compensate.

Institutional traders will probably feel differently about hedging, as any noise from FX rate changes will make them less correlated to benchmarks and irritate their investors. Many products are sold as funds hedged into different currencies, so traders working in funds may already be doing plenty of hedging. They can also hedge their large balances more accurately, and they should have the bandwidth to cover the extra work required.

On balance then, I would advocate using the **FX trading** approach to avoid paying interest charges, and living with the noise that comes from having unhedged FX balances. You can minimise this noise by regularly exchanging any excess foreign currency balances that are not required for initial margin or to cover likely variation margin needs, back into your domestic currency.

How significant is the noise from unhedged balances likely to be? As a UK trader who exclusively trades foreign currency denominated futures, in a bad year I might see a 10% appreciation of GBP versus the other currencies I use, resulting in a 10% loss on the margin I am holding. Assuming FX prices are random, a 10% gain is equally likely. Since margin averages around 30% of my account size, that translates to a 3% loss or gain on my notional capital.

Looking back at my trading history since 2014, annual gains and losses of that size due to FX movements are fairly typical. Of course I am up on average, as mostly thanks to Brexit the GBP has depreciated over that period. But that is just luck – over time

I expect these FX movements to have no effect. But if you can't cope with that level of noise, then you should consider partially hedging your exposures if that is possible.

Dealing with margin problems

I noted above that margin problems are rare if you are a sensible trader, but even I have had them occasionally. Because potential margin shortages are effectively a failure of risk management, I will discuss this as part of the next chapter.

Compounding tactics

Back in Part One I had a few things to say about compounding:

> *From this point onwards, all the strategies in this book will show performance statistics and graphs for* **non-compounded percentage returns***...*
>
> *Now for a very important warning: it would be extremely dangerous to actually run your strategy with real money and fixed capital! An important consequence of Kelly risk targeting is that you should reduce your position size when you lose money. A simple way to achieve this is to use the current value of your trading account as the notional capital when calculating your required position. Then any losses you make will result in your positions being automatically reduced, and vice versa for profits.*

In reality there are a few different ways you can go about compounding, or not, the returns in your account:

- Fixed capital with no compounding (don't do this).
- Full compounding.
- Half compounding.

Fixed capital with no compounding (don't do this!)

Let's first consider what happens if we do no compounding at all, as I have assumed in all the backtests we have run so far. First of all let's set up a simple example. I assume we begin with $500,000 in capital. For the sake of this example I am also going to pretend that:

- We are running a variation of strategy three: long only with a fixed amount of target risk.

- We hold a single imaginary instrument in our account.

- This hypothetical market has a tiny futures multiplier such that with $500,000 in capital we currently hold a position of 500,000 contracts.

- The estimated standard deviation of the instrument remains constant and there are no FX translation issues. This means the only factor that will affect our optimal position is the amount of trading capital we have at risk.

- The instrument starts off with a price of $1 and experiences the following sequence of returns: +10%, +10%, –10%, and +10%.

- We recalculate our capital, sample prices and adjust our optimal positions on a daily basis.

All of the above implies we can calculate our optimal position with the simplified formula:

Optimal position = notional capital ÷ price

Let's see what happens:

Start	Notional trading capital = $500,000
	Account value = $500,000
	Position held = 500,000
	Price = $1
	Value of position = 500000 × $1 = $500,000
After day 1: +10%	Profit: 10% on $500,000 = $50,000
	Account value = $550,000
	Notional trading capital = $500,000 (fixed)
	Price: $1.10
	New position = 500000 ÷ 1.10 = 454,454
	Value of position = 454454 × $1.10 = $500,000

After day 2: +10%	Profit: 10% on $500,000 = $50,000
	Account value = $600,000
	Notional trading capital = $500,000 (fixed)
	Price: $1.21
	New position = 500000 ÷ 1.21 = 413,223
	Value of position = 413223 × $1.21 = $500,000
After day 3: −10%	Profit: −10% on $500,000 = −$50,000
	Account value = $550,000
	Notional trading capital = $500,000 (fixed)
	Price: $1.089
	New position = 500000 ÷ 1.089 = 459,137
	Value of position = 459137 × $1.089 = $500,000
After day 4: +10%	Profit: +10% on $500,000 = +$50,000
	Account value = $600,000
	Notional trading capital = $500,000 (fixed)

There are a few interesting things going on here:

- Our notional trading capital is fixed, and because this is the only factor affecting our target notional exposure, the value of our optimal position also remains fixed.

- If we add up the percentage gains and losses, they sum to +20%. Because our capital has remained fixed, we end up with exactly 20% more than we started with. It is this property that makes it easier to interpret account curves with fixed capital.

- After day one our position is too small relative to our account size. If we had made losses, it would have been too big.

- Our account starts off **fully capitalised**, and then becomes **over capitalised** with an account value greater than the notional capital. If we had made losses, then it would become **under capitalised**.

Using fixed capital violates all the key principles of risk targeting – in particular that you should **always adjust your bet size according to how large your stake is**. To see why, consider this: what would happen if instead of experiencing the above sequence of returns, we actually lost 5% a day for the next 20 days? That would be $25,000 per day and would completely clean out our account. Given the choice, you should **never** use fixed capital in a live trading account.

Full compounding

Now what happens if we use **full compounding**? The difference here is that all gains or losses will be added or subtracted from our notional trading capital. Since the account is fully capitalised with exactly enough cash, the trading capital will be equal to our current account value. Assuming we have the same setup as before, with the same sequence of returns, what happens?

Start	Notional trading capital = $500,000
	Account value = $500,000
	Position held = 500,000
	Price = $1
	Value of position = 500000 × $1 = $500,000
After day 1: +10%	Profit: 10% on $500,000 = $50,000
	Account value = $550,000
	Notional trading capital = Account value = $550,000
	Price: $1.10
	New position = 550000 ÷ 1.10 = 500,000
	Value of position = 500000 × $1.10 = $550,000

After day 2: +10%	Profit: +10% on $550,000 = $55,000
	Account value = $605,000
	Notional trading capital = Account value = $605,000
	Price: $1.21
	New position = 605000 ÷ 1.21 = 500,000
	Value of position = 500000 × $1.21 = $605,000
After day 3: −10%	Profit: −10% on $605,000 = −$60,500
	Account value = $544,500
	Notional trading capital = Account value = $544,500
	Price: $1.089
	New position = 544500 ÷ 1.089 = 500,000
	Value of position = 500000 × $1.089 = $561,000
After day 4: +10%	Profit: 10% on $544,500 = $54,450
	Account value = $598,950
	Notional trading capital = $598,950

Notice that:

- Our notional trading capital changes as we make or lose money. In this simple case we maintain a fixed position, holding the same number of contracts every day, but whose value fluctuates as we set it equal to the current account value.

- If we add up the percentage gains and losses we get +20%, but we actually end up with a return that is a little under 20%, equivalent to earning around 4.6% each day.[285]

---

285 This is because with compounding we need to calculate the **geometric mean** of returns rather than the usual arithmetic mean. The geometric mean of the series of returns shown is $\sqrt[4]{[(1 + 10\%) \times (1 + 10\%) \times (1 - 10\%) \times (1 + 10\%)]} - 1 = 4.6\%$.

- Our position is always correctly scaled to our account size.

- We end up with more capital at the end of the four days than we did with fixed capital, but that does not prove anything definitively.

Let us consider again what would happen if instead of experiencing the above sequence of returns, we actually lost 5% a day for the next 20 days? Every day our account size would shrink by 5%, but so would our notional capital and our position. We'd lose $25,000 on day one, but only $23,750 on day two, $22,562.50 on day three and so on. After 20 days we would still have just over $179,000 left in our account. Not great, but an awful lot better than losing all our money, as we would with fixed capital. In fact, **if our risk target is equal to the level obtained with the Kelly criterion, then full compounding will maximise the expected geometric mean of our returns and also the expected final value of our trading account**.

Full compounding should be used by institutions whose clients will expect compounded returns, and by retail traders who are not relying on their accounts for income. Of course, clients occasionally redeem or inject funds, and retail traders may want to go out and buy a sports car. In this case you should just adjust your notional capital by the value of the funds that have been added or withdrawn. This will be automatic if your account is fully capitalised and you have set your notional capital to be equal to your account value, but if not you will have some calculations to do.

Half compounding

When I started trading my own money I was a little nervous about using full compounding. I didn't need to keep growing the size of my trading account, and I wanted to withdraw any profits I made to invest in more benign investments. On the other hand, I knew that using fixed capital was extremely dangerous.

The solution I came up with was to copy the sort of structure used by hedge funds. When you invest in a hedge fund you normally pay a modest management fee, but also a relatively high performance fee, typically 10% or 20% of any profits made. However, you only have to pay the performance fee when the profits are above a **high watermark**. If the fund value is currently in a drawdown then you are only liable for management fees.

I decided to run my trading account like a hedge fund with a 0% management fee and a 100% performance fee. Effectively, any time my notional capital goes above my starting value, I will cap it at a maximum of the starting value, taking all the profits as a 'performance fee' rather than adding them to my notional capital. However, if I subsequently make losses, then these are taken off the notional capital to ensure my risk targeting is correct.

Let's see what that looks like for the simple example:

Start	Notional trading capital = $500,000
	Account value = $500,000
	Position held = 500,000
	Price = $1
	Value of position = 500000 × $1 = $500,000
After day 1: +10%	Profit: 10% on $500,000 = $50,000
	Account value = $550,000
	Notional trading capital = $500,000 (maximum)
	Price: $1.10
	New position = 500000 ÷ 1.10 = 454,545
	Value of position = 454545 × $1.10 = $500,000
After day 2: +10%	Profit: +10% on $500,000 = $50,000
	Account value = $600,000
	Notional trading capital = $500,000 (maximum)
	Price: $1.21
	New position = 500000 ÷ 1.21 = 413,223
	Value of position = 413223 × $1.21 = $500,000

After day 3: –10%	Profit: –10% on $500,000 = –$50,000

Account value = $550,000

Notional trading capital = $500,000 – $50,000
= $450,000

Price: $1.089

New position = 450000 ÷ 1.089 = 413,223

Value of position = 413223 × $1.089 = $450,000

After day 4: +10%	Profit: 10% on $450,000 = $45,000

Account value = $595,000

Notional trading capital = $450,000 + $45,000
= $495,000

Observe that:

- We behave like a fixed capital trader when we are making profits, but when losses occur we act like we are fully compounding, reducing our notional capital and position accordingly.

- We don't compound our gains when we are at or above the high watermark, when our notional capital is equal to the maximum.

- We will always either be fully capitalised (if we made losses from day one onwards), or over capitalised.

Again, think about the Armageddon scenario where we lose 5% a day for the next 20 days. Since we are always under the high watermark of maximum capital, we would behave as if we were fully compounded. As with full compounding, after 20 days we would have just over $179,000 left in our account.

Assuming you are profitable, when half compounding you always will end up with additional cash in your account, over and above what is required to cover your notional capital. In the example above, this is $100,000 after day two; and it remains at this level since we don't exceed the high watermark in the period shown. If you want to avoid becoming substantially over capitalised, then you should withdraw this excess cash regularly.

The half compounding method isn't ideal for extracting a steady monthly income from your trading account, unless your trading strategy is consistently profitable, but then I think it is very risk to rely on your brokerage account to replace your monthly pay cheque. Psychologically, I think of my account as an ATM that spits out money randomly. Any money that is still inside is effectively locked away and can't be touched, but I can do whatever I like with the accumulated profits that it spits out. This also makes for a pleasant feeling when or if your account reaches a 100% profit on your notional capital after taxes, since after that you are effectively playing with 'house money'.

Finally, note that it's possible to run a version of this with a 50% performance fee, or indeed any figure you like.

TACTIC FOUR

Risk management

I started the first chapter of this book with a quote from the film *Margin Call*, so it seems appropriate to end the final chapter with this:

> *Look I run risk management... I don't really see how that's a natural place to start cutting jobs.*

Eric Dale, the risk manager played by Stanley Tucci in the film *Margin Call*, reacting to being fired.

Being a risk manager for a bank or hedge fund is a tough job. You are probably underpaid relative to the more glamorous traders and portfolio managers, and your job has no upside: only the downside of something going wrong. As Eric found out, you are treated as a cost centre and an obvious place to start making redundancies in a crisis. But risk managers are often the unsung heroes[286] of many financial businesses, and risk management is a vital discipline that is often overlooked.

Did I write this chapter just for institutional risk managers? Absolutely not. Risk management is everyone's job and should form a key component of any trading strategy. The strategies in this book already have risk management baked into them, because they automatically resize positions according to the expected risk of a given position. But there are other things we can do to allow ourselves to sleep a little better at night.

---

286 Spoiler alert: Eric Dale ends up effectively saving the firm – that just fired him – from bankruptcy.

Dealing with margin problems

The most obvious and immediate danger to a futures trader, or anyone using any type of leveraged derivatives, is a margin call. If you receive a margin call, then your risk management process has already gone badly wrong!

I noted in the previous chapter that margin problems are rare if you are a sensible trader, but even I have had them occasionally. Sometimes the margin on certain futures is temporarily increased to excessive levels due to market events. For me personally, the most recent episode was in February 2018, when the level of the VIX doubled in a single day on the back of a sharp drop in US equities. Unsurprisingly, the margin on VIX and European VSTOXX futures was dramatically increased. I had to act fast to prevent a margin call and having some of my positions involuntarily liquidated.

To ensure you never get a margin call you need to put in place a **risk management process**. All such processes should include the following steps:

- Something you can measure and quantify on a regular basis.

- A level at which you will take action.

- The action you will take.

- When to reverse the action you have taken.

The first thing you need to do is **measure**: have a good handle on your margin usage. I check mine every day. Next is to decide what maximum **level** of margin you would be comfortable using. In the previous chapter I said margin usage for directional futures traders with risk targets of $\tau = 20\%$ should average around 30% of account value.[287] Let's say we will get concerned when our margin usage is over 50% and take action when it hits twice our average: 60%. Now you need to decide what **action** you will take when your margin goes over the required level.

All risk management actions are of two types: **specific** and **generic**. A *specific* response would be to start cutting or closing positions that had the largest margin requirements, until we get our margin down to an acceptable level, like 50%. Superficially that seems the most logical move, but this will effectively introduce a tracking error versus the positions we would have had on without any margin issues.[288] It might be better to take *generic* action and temporarily reduce *all* of our positions by the same ratio. For

---

287   I am assuming that your trading account is fully capitalised. If it is under capitalised, then clearly your first move if margin is tight should be to transfer some or all of your spare capital into the account.

288   If you are using strategy twenty-five 'Dynamic optimisation', then you can do this by setting position limits on the instruments with margin issues and allow the optimiser to redistribute capital to less margin hungry markets.

example, if our margin usage is currently 75% then we would reduce all our optimal positions by a third, bringing initial margin down to 50% of our account value.

Finally, we need to decide when to **reverse** our action. In this case, we can return to trading as normal once our margin usage is back below 50%.

An exogenous risk overlay

The method I have used for building up portfolios of futures contracts since strategy four may seem quite complicated, but from a risk management perspective it is actually rather simplistic and potentially dangerous. Although it does a good job of hitting its expected risk target, τ, on average over long periods of time, there are many days when it is taking excessive and potentially dangerous positions.

To deal with this I use a **risk overlay**. The overlay is exogenous (outside) the trading strategy, but it can still be implemented systematically. It takes the positions the trading strategy would want to take as its input and then calculates a **position multiplier**. A multiplier of one means we make no change to our optimal positions. A multiplier that is less than one means we multiply all optimal positions by the multiplier. The multiplier can't be greater than one – we never take more risk than the original strategy would want to.

As you can see, this is a more complex example of the risk management process I outlined above:

- Something you can measure and quantify: A position multiplier.

- *A level at which you will take action*: When the required multiplier is less than one.

- *The action you will take*: Multiply all positions by the multiplier.

- *When to reverse any action taken*: When the multiplier is equal to one.

The position multiplier will be equal to the lowest of the following values, each a multiplier designed to deal with a specific type of risk:

- Estimated portfolio risk multiplier.

- Non-stationary risk multiplier.

- Correlation risk multiplier.

- Leverage risk multiplier.

Estimated portfolio risk multiplier

With the exception of strategy twenty-five, none of the strategies in this book care about *portfolio level* risk. We are very careful to target risk on positions in individual instruments, depending on the strength of our forecasts. We also take into account the *average* level of diversification across different instruments, when we multiply everything by the instrument diversification multiplier (IDM). If we have done all of that correctly, then at least in the backtest we should hit our expected average risk target, τ.

But we take no account of what our expected risk will be on a day to day basis. Let's think about the circumstances in which expected risk will be significantly higher than average:

- Our forecasts are unusually strong.

- Two instruments where we have the same sign of position on, whose returns have historically been uncorrelated, currently have temporarily highly correlated returns.

- Two instruments where we have the opposite sign of position on, whose returns have historically been highly correlated, have temporarily anti-correlated returns.

- Two instruments with highly correlated returns, but which normally have positions of opposite signs, have temporarily got positions with the same sign.

- Two instruments with highly anti-correlated returns, but which normally have positions of the same sign, have temporarily got positions with different signs.

Trading is all about taking risks – but taking the right ones. Of these factors, only the first is a legitimate reason to have higher expected risk. The rest are an annoying side effect of the process we use to target long run strategy risk, rather than trying to achieve the same expected risk on a daily basis. If there is a perfect storm of weirdly signed positions and unusually sized correlations, then our expected risk could be much higher than average, without the justification of higher conviction reflected in forecasts with large magnitudes.

What we require is a multiplier that is less than one when our expected risk goes above some level. Sometimes this will be overly conservative, as the increase in risk will have been driven by high forecast conviction, but more often than not we do not really want the additional volatility.

I am going to use the same process for all four of these multipliers, starting with this first example, the portfolio risk multiplier:

- Measure something (X), in this case the expected portfolio risk.

- From the historical distribution of X in my backtest, find the 99% quantile point. This is the **maximum X**.

- If at any point X is above the maximum, then apply a multiplier to all positions such that X is equal to maximum X.

This will apply to any X as long as it is something which scales linearly, if we multiply all our positions by some constant. If we halve our positions, then X should also be cut in half. Obviously this applies to estimated portfolio risk.

Why have I chosen the 99% percentile point, implying the multiplier will be working 1% of the time? To an extent this is arbitrary. I do not want the multiplier to be engaged at all times, or it will badly distort the performance of the underlying trading strategy. But if the multiplier hardly kicks in at all, then it won't be much use. If I have four of these multipliers, each of which is active 1% of the time, then if they are uncorrelated my total position multiplier will be active around 4% of the time: about two weeks out of every year. That seems about right.

Let's begin by measuring our first X: the expected annualised percentage standard deviation of our portfolio returns.

We calculate the expected portfolio standard deviation:

$$\text{Portfolio } \sigma = \sqrt{(w\ \Sigma\ w')}$$

Here w is the vector of position weights and Σ is the covariance matrix[289] of percentage instrument returns, not sub-strategy returns (see Appendix B). We are performing matrix multiplication inside the brackets. A **position weight** is equal to the notional exposure value of our position in a given instrument, divided by the capital, and with an appropriate sign (positive if long, negative if short). Given a position of N contracts in instrument i the instrument weight is:

$$w_{i,t} = N_{i,t} \times \text{Multiplier}_i \times \text{Price}_{i,t} \times \text{FX rate}_{i,t} \div \text{Capital}$$

For my benchmark I'm going to use the final strategy from Part One: strategy eleven with carry and trend, over the entire Jumbo portfolio. The results will be similar for

---

289   The method isn't too sensitive to how the covariance matrix is estimated. You can use a simple or exponentially weighted covariance estimate: about a six month span will give you a good forecast. Or you can do what I do, which is to use my existing estimates for the annualised standard deviation $\sigma_\%$ combined with a separate estimate of correlations. My correlation estimate is based on weekly returns, which reduces bias caused by markets closing at different times, and uses an exponentially weighted estimate with a six-month span. See Appendix B for more information.

other trading strategies in this book. Figure 97 shows the historical time series of expected risk for strategy eleven.

FIGURE 97: EXPECTED ANNUALISED PERCENTAGE STANDARD DEVIATION OF RETURNS FOR STRATEGY ELEVEN

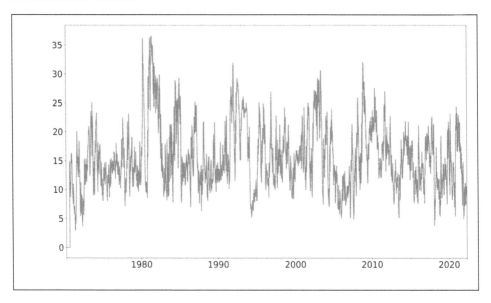

It's worth noting that the more diversified your portfolio, the more stable your risk properties will be, and the lower the value of your maximum risk. That is why the maximum risk gradually comes down over time, since there are fewer instruments in the earlier part of the backtest.

To reflect this, I decided to measure the maximum standard deviation at the 99% percentile point from the last 20 years of data. For strategy eleven this came in at 28%, but I decided to use 30% as this is exactly 1.5 times the target risk τ = 20%. This might seem very conservative. However, you should bear in mind that, due to the non-Gaussian nature of financial asset returns, expected risk generally undershoots the target whilst realised risk comes in very close. Traders with less diversified strategies might want to use a higher limit for standard deviation.

We can now calculate the estimated portfolio risk multiplier, assuming we want expected portfolio risk to be no higher than 30%:

$$M_t(\text{portfolio risk}) = \text{Min}(1, 0.30 \div \text{portfolio } \sigma_t)$$

Here are a couple of examples with current expected standard deviations of 15% and 45% respectively:

$$M(\text{portfolio risk}) = \text{Min}(1, 0.30 \div 0.15)$$
$$= 1.0 \text{ (no change to positions)}$$

$$M(\text{portfolio risk}) = \text{Min}(1, 0.30 \div 0.45)$$
$$= 0.6666 \text{ (cut positions by two-thirds)}$$

Jump risk multiplier

I pointed out above – not for the first time – that financial assets have non-Gaussian risk. As a consequence, estimated standard deviations have a nasty habit of changing rapidly.[290] I get very nervous when the market is quiet, since I know from experience that there is likely to be a storm of volatility that will arrive when it is least expected, with prices jumping out of control.

To some extent I dealt with this in strategy three by promoting the use of a risk estimate which blended long and short run estimates of standard deviation, so that when risk is currently very low, we will ensure our current estimate doesn't drop too far below the long run average. But this is a rather blunt tool, which doesn't help us with instruments with especially nasty tail properties, whose worst days are much, much, much worse than their average days.

To deal with this problem, I use the following method:

- Measure the annualised standard deviation of each instrument from percentage returns.

- Calculate the 99% percentile[291] from the distribution of standard deviations for each instrument. This will be extremely high.

- Estimate the expected portfolio risk using a new covariance matrix Σ^{jump} constructed from these new standard deviation values, plus the original estimates for the correlation of percentage returns.

$$\text{Jump portfolio } \sigma = \sqrt{(w \, \Sigma^{jump} \, w')}$$

---

290 There is an interesting, but ultimately futile, philosophical debate we can have about whether financial asset returns are non-Gaussian with fixed parameters, or Gaussian with varying parameters. But this footnote is too small to contain it.
291 Ideally in a backtest this should be done on a backward looking basis.

What does this new measure of risk look like for strategy eleven? Figure 98 has the results. As you would expect, the risk here is much higher than in figure 97. As a result, the 99% percentile point measured from the last 20 years is also higher, at just over 76%. Again, I decided to make this a round number: 75%, 3.75 times the risk target τ.

FIGURE 98: EXPECTED PORTFOLIO RISK WITH ALL STANDARD DEVIATIONS AT 99% POINT

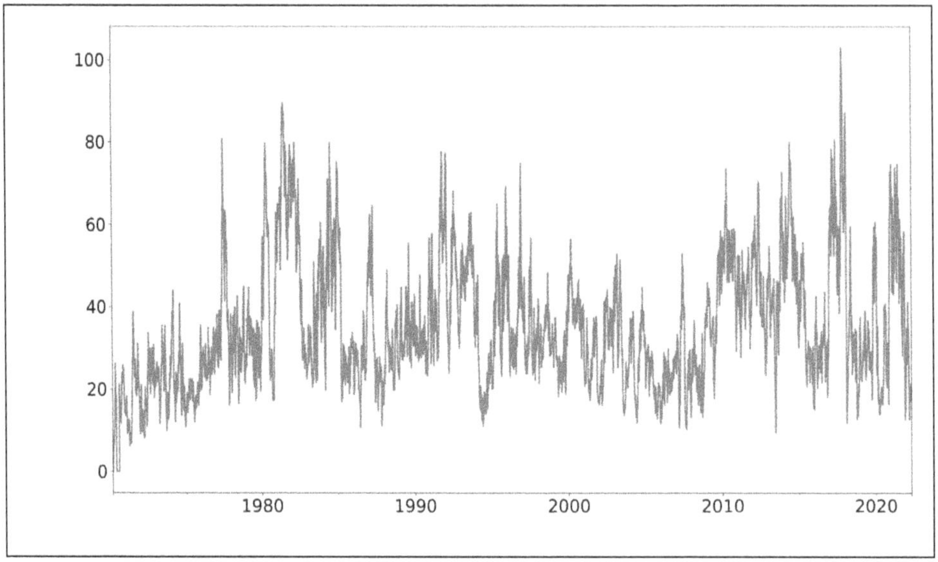

What does the jump risk multiplier look like?

$$M_t \text{ (jump risk) = Min (1, 0.75 ÷ jump portfolio } \sigma_\tau)$$

Correlation risk multiplier

I noted above that one reason for risk increasing is due to an atypical pattern of correlations and positions. Suppose for example that you had just two instruments in your portfolio, US 10-year bonds and S&P 500 equities. In recent history these instruments have had near zero correlation of returns, so it's likely the IDM would have been very high.

Now imagine that you just happened to have large long positions on in both S&P 500 and US 10-year bonds. What will happen if there is a co-ordinated selloff in both equities and bonds, i.e. an upward spike in correlation? By the way, this isn't a made up example, but accurately reflects events in both the summer of 2021 and spring 2022, to name just two occasions when this actually happened.

What measure should we use to construct a risk multiplier to guard us against the risk of correlations ganging up with positions in this way? Consider the expected standard deviation at the portfolio level of a position in instrument i given an estimate of annualised percentage standard deviation $\sigma_\%$ and weight w:

$$\text{Risk}_i = w_i \times \sigma_{\%i}$$

If all the correlations of the instruments we were holding in our portfolio went to 1 or −1, whatever is currently worse for us, then our expected total portfolio risk would be equal to the sum of the absolute value of risk for each instrument:

Correlation shock portfolio σ
= sum(abs(Risk₀), abs(Risk₁), abs(Risk₂), ...)

To get some intuition, let's plot that for strategy eleven: refer to figure 99.

FIGURE 99: STRATEGY ELEVEN PORTFOLIO RISK ESTIMATED WITH SHOCKED CORRELATIONS

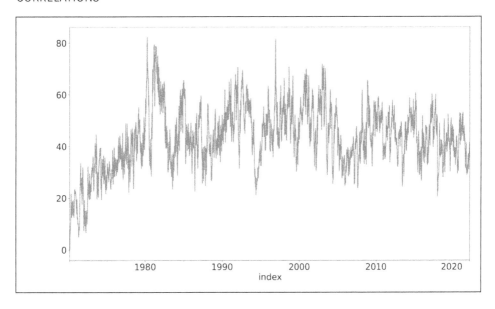

As with the jump risk, this should be much higher than the portfolio risk estimated with the normal correlation matrix. Effectively for jump risk we are taking a worst case scenario for standard deviations, whereas here we are using a worst case scenario for correlations. The 99% percentile of historical correlation shock risk comes in at just over 67%; again to make things neat I will set the maximum to exactly 65%, 3.25 times the risk target of 20%. This gives us the following multiplier:

$$M_t \text{ (correlation shock risk)}$$
$$= \text{Min } (1, 0.65 \div \text{correlation shock portfolio } \sigma_t)$$

Leverage risk multiplier

In many ways leverage is the crudest measure of risk that exists. It's easy to calculate: just add up the absolute value of the notional exposures for each position, and divide by capital. Plus it has a very clear interpretation: if your leverage is 100% and you are long everything, then if the prices for all of your instruments go to zero overnight, you will lose precisely 100% of your capital.

But leverage varies radically by instrument. Someone who was only trading Eurodollars should have a much higher tolerance for large positions than Bitcoin or Ethereum. Eurodollars – arguably the premier pretend money of the past – have very low risk, whilst the cryptocurrency futures – perhaps the pretend money of the future – have extremely high standard deviation. To achieve a 20% risk target with Eurodollars currently requires leveraging your capital about 18 times, whilst in Bitcoin you would use leverage that is considerably less than one.

So it's hard to compare leverage across instruments. Still, putting that issue to one side, let's use the same process as before to calculate a portfolio level leverage risk multiplier. Given portfolio weights w in each instrument i the total portfolio leverage is:

$$\text{Leverage} = \text{sum}(\text{abs}(w_0), \text{abs}(w_1), \text{abs}(w_2), ...)$$

Figure 100 has the leverage for strategy eleven.

FIGURE 100: LEVERAGE AS MULTIPLE OF CAPITAL FOR STRATEGY ELEVEN

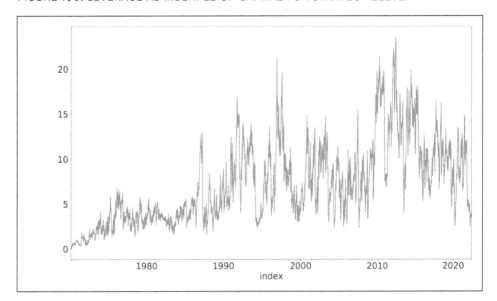

As you can see, it has increased over time. This is partly due to the addition of more instruments and a growing IDM, but also because many of the instruments added have lower standard deviation than the original markets, which were predominately high risk commodities.[292]

For consistency with previous multipliers, I took the 99% percentile of this since 2000, and this gave me a maximum leverage of just over 20, resulting in the following formula for the multiplier:

$$M_t \text{ (leverage)} = \text{Min}(1, 20 \div \text{leverage}_t)$$

A maximum leverage of 20 still seems scarily high, but we do not want this to apply too often and distort the natural positions held by our trading strategies. In fact there are probably better ways to control leverage at the level of an individual instrument, and I will discuss these later in the chapter.

Finally, I should reiterate that your leverage will very much depend on the combination of instruments you are trading, and you should bear this in mind when setting any leverage limits.

---

292   A more complex way of applying this methodology would be to measure, and limit, the leverage by asset class.

Final risk multiplier

As a reminder, here is how we calculate the final risk multiplier. On any given day, it will be equal to the lowest of the following values, each a multiplier designed to deal with a specific type of risk:

- Estimated portfolio risk multiplier.

- Jump risk multiplier.

- Correlation shock risk multiplier.

- Leverage risk multiplier.

The final risk multiplier will either be equal to, or less than, one. We then multiply[293] all our unrounded optimal positions by the multiplier, and then apply buffering in the normal way.

The final risk multiplier for strategy eleven is shown in figure 101.

FIGURE 101: RISK SCALAR FOR STRATEGY ELEVEN

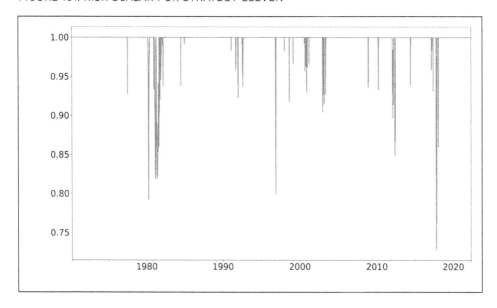

---

293   If you are using strategy twenty-five, 'dynamic optimisation', you should implement this multiplier so it is applied to optimal unrounded positions *before* the dynamic optimisation takes place. With strategies in Part Four application of the multiplier should be done before the start of the trading day to avoid causing unusual behaviour with limit orders. It may be suitable for strategies in Part Five, 'Relative Value Strategies', but you will need to be careful about calibrating the leverage risk multiplier.

The multiplier kicks in just under 5% of the time. This is roughly what we would expect, given each of the four multipliers is calibrated to activate when the relevant risk measure reaches its 99% percentile. It might be interesting to understand when the different multipliers kick in. Here are some of the time periods when the relevant multiplier has had the largest effect:

- In late 2017 and early 2018, it is the jump risk multiplier. At these times volatility dropped very low in many markets, with the VIX approaching single digits.

- In 2012, it is the leverage risk multiplier. This was a period of very low volatility in the interest rate and bond markets, which significantly pushed up leverage.

- In late 2008, it was the estimated portfolio risk multiplier. This was the period of the sub-prime mortgage related financial crisis.

- For many earlier periods it was the correlation risk multiplier. This was particularly active around 1980 when many commodity markets became highly correlated.

Notice that the multiplier has no effect during either the COVID-19 equity market crash of 2020, or the invasion of Ukraine in early 2022.

Table 171 shows the effect of applying the risk multiplier on strategy eleven. As we would expect given we will always have the same or smaller positions, it slightly reduces standard deviation and mean, although the SR is effectively unchanged. But the reduction is extremely small – as we would expect given that 95% of the time the multiplier has no effect. Skew is slightly worse, but the tails are a little better. It's also good to see that the additional trading from winding our positions down, and then back up again, hasn't added to turnover or trading costs.

TABLE 171: PERFORMANCE STATISTICS FOR STRATEGY ELEVEN USING EXTENDED DATA, BEFORE AND AFTER RISK MULTIPLIER

	No risk multiplier	After risk multiplier
Mean annual return	27.3%	27.2%
Costs	−0.9%	−0.9%
Average drawdown	−8.7%	−8.6%
Standard deviation	20.7%	20.5%
Sharpe ratio	1.32	1.33
Turnover	50.3	50.0
Skew	0.59	0.55
Lower tail	1.88	1.84
Upper tail	1.75	1.71
Alpha	22.7%	22.6%
Beta	0.33	0.33

Instruments that are too safe to trade

In the standard position sizing formula we increase our leverage when we see a fall in the standard deviation of the instrument returns. That has some benefits, such as lower minimum capital requirements, but it's also potentially dangerous.

Consider for example the Eurodollar short-term interest rate future. The March 2022 contract, which was the front month when I wrote the first draft of this chapter, had barely moved since April 2020 when the Fed cut interest rates to the bone in the midst of the COVID-19 pandemic. At the time of writing the standard deviation was around 0.0153% a day, or 0.245% a year.

From strategy two we know that the required leverage ratio is equal to the volatility ratio: the ratio of τ and $\sigma_{\%}$, which for front Eurodollar will be 20% ÷ 0.245% = 81.6. So for example, with $100,000 of capital we'd need to hold Eurodollar contracts with a notional exposure of over $8 million – over 30 contracts.

I wish this example were purely arbitrary, but it is not. When I took over the fixed income portfolio at AHL, our Eurodollars were indeed concentrated in the first few expiry dates. The position ran into hundreds of thousands of contracts with a notional exposure of tens of billions of dollars, several times the size of our entire fund. Needless to say, I had difficulty sleeping when I acquired that portfolio. Even counting sheep didn't work: each ram or ewe seemed to represent yet another contract that we owned!

Why was I losing sleep? What can go wrong with this trade? Well, quite a lot. With 80 times leverage a 1.25% movement in the price of Eurodollars would completely wipe out our capital. Of course the extremely low standard deviation implies this is extremely unlikely. But that does not mean such a loss is impossible. Remember, the standard deviation risk measure is imperfect and does not account for the non-Gaussian risk which is common in financial markets. Higher leverage also means higher risk adjusted costs, and the costs for front Eurodollar were very high indeed.

Now, in theory this will be dealt with by the setting of the risk target as I discussed in strategy two – specifically the maximum risk implied by a worst case loss. But since strategy four we have combined different instruments together into a portfolio, and it does not make sense to set different risk targets for different instruments.

A possible answer, which I discussed in strategy three, is to blend your volatility estimate with a long-term average. This will help you with instruments that have temporarily low volatility, as it ensures you don't scale up too much in these regimes. However, it isn't much help for instruments which have permanently low volatility.

Fortunately, there are a number of other possible solutions to this conundrum. Best of all is to **completely avoid instruments with very low volatility**. How do we calculate the minimum level of volatility we're happy with? Firstly, note that the leverage ratio for a given position, as a proportion of your entire capital, using a maximum forecast with an absolute value of 20 will be:

$$\text{Leverage ratio} = (2 \times \text{IDM} \times \text{Weight}_i \times \tau) \div \sigma_{\%,i}$$

Now suppose you want to limit your leverage ratio. If we rearrange the above formula, then this implies that there is a lower limit on the instrument risk ($\sigma_{\%,i}$):

$$\text{Minimum } \sigma_{\%i} = (2 \times \text{IDM} \times \text{Weight}_i \times \tau) \div \text{Maximum leverage ratio}$$

Suppose for example that an average instrument would have a 10% instrument weight, and also that your IDM is 1.5. We assume a 20% risk target and that we don't want a leverage ratio above four at the maximum forecast. The minimum acceptable risk is:

$$\text{Minimum } \sigma_{\%} = (2 \times 1.5 \times 0.10 \times 20\%) \div 4.0 = 1.5\%$$

Hence any instrument with an instrument risk that is currently less than 1.5% a year should be excluded. That will certainly rule out front Eurodollar! Of course, leaving out an instrument is an implicit bet that it will underperform the instruments we keep without any clear evidence, but we don't have much choice. Such an instrument will likely have high risk adjusted costs, so it may well be too expensive to trade in any case.

What happens if an instrument has an acceptable level of risk, but then subsequently sees a fall in volatility? We'd end up with an unreasonably large position. One solution to this is to **set position limits**: basically a maximum number of contracts we will hold, regardless of what the optimal position is. I discuss this later in the chapter. However, if an instrument keeps hitting its position limit for extended periods, then you should probably consider removing it permanently.

A less satisfactory solution is to **adjust your instrument weights**, giving low volatility instruments a lower weight, reducing their impact on your account if they go wrong. Once again, this is effectively a bet that some instrument sub-strategies will do better than others, when you don't have any evidence this is the case.

Finally, for Eurodollar specifically, you can **trade further out on the curve**, where the volatility is currently higher. I discussed this option, which is also valid for certain other futures, in the chapter on rolling and contract selection tactics. This is what we opted for when I was at AHL. You will be pleased to know that after we implemented this plan I was able to sleep like a baby.

Setting position limits

When I first joined AHL they were running their trading strategies in a mixture of different programming languages. There was even a proprietary language which they had developed themselves, in the early 1990s: 'Strategy Design' (SD). SD had a very efficient way of storing time series data like prices, but it couldn't handle more than a few decimal places. For something like the KRWUSD FX rate, which is currently at around 0.0008, you couldn't store prices accurately. To get around this, all the prices were first multiplied by a constant before saving them. As far as I can remember, for KRWUSD the relevant constant was 100,000.

A few months after joining I got approval to run my first trading strategy. I was given permission to trade a few million dollars of the firm's own capital to test that it worked properly, before it was allowed access to client money. A software developer rewrote my rather poor prototype implementation into production quality computer code, and after a few final checks the strategy was set to start running at midnight when the Asian markets opened. I left work with a sense of satisfaction.

I got a phone call at 1 am. It was one of the traders working on the night shift. He was brief and to the point: "Mate. Did you really mean to buy one third of the entire outstanding national debt of Korea?" This wasn't a video call, but I knew he was grinning – the 'salt of the earth' traders loved embarrassing the 'ivory tower' researchers. "Er... no?" I replied, still half asleep and wondering if this was actually a nightmare. "I didn't think so! OK, I will kill this order for 10-year Korean bond futures then. See you tomorrow."

Of course what had happened was the developer (who was also relatively inexperienced) hadn't known about the magic number, and the strategy code had very helpfully multiplied everything by 100,000. Instead of the ten contracts I was supposed to buy, it had decided to buy a million of them. The notional value of this trade was around $100 billion, which as the trader had helpfully pointed out was a sizeable chunk of the Korean government's debt obligations.

The trading strategies I run nowadays are fully automated, with no human trader to sanity check them. So I am extremely careful to make sure nothing remotely like that can ever happen to me. I do this by setting **position limits**. Given that I cap my forecasts at an absolute value of 20, it's possible to calculate the maximum position a strategy should take, and set that as a hard limit which my trading system code will not exceed.

The position limits I use have other purposes, which are relevant even if you are not running an automated system:

- They prevent strategies from building up too much leverage in a more targeted way than the portfolio level leverage risk multiplier.

- For large institutional traders, they ensure you are not too large a part of the market and risk being unable to liquidate your position quickly.

As I did with the risk multiplier earlier in the chapter, I separately calculate position limits for each of the purposes above, and then take the most conservative.

Position limit at maximum forecast

These are the maximum positions we should ever have on normally, with the maximum absolute forecast value of 20:

$$N_i = \text{Scaled forecast}_{i,t} \times \text{Capital} \times \text{IDM} \times \text{Weight}_i$$
$$\times \tau \div (10 \times \text{Multiplier}_i \times \text{Price}_{i,t} \times \text{Fx}_{i,t} \times \sigma_{\%,i,t})$$

$$N_i^{max\_forecast} = (2 \times \text{Capital} \times \text{IDM} \times \text{Weight}_i \times \tau)$$
$$\div (\text{Multiplier}_i \times \text{Price}_{i,t} \times \text{Fx}_{i,t} \times \sigma_{\%,i,t})$$

For this section on position limits I will use a common example to illustrate what is going on. Let's assume that we are interested in the position limit for Eurodollar interest rate futures, that we have \$500,000 in capital, with an IDM of 2.0 and an instrument weight of 10%, plus the usual risk target τ = 20%. The current price is 97, the futures multiplier is \$2,500, and the percentage standard deviation is around 1.1% a year:

$$N_i^{max\_forecast} = (2 \times 500000 \times 2 \times 0.1 \times 0.2) \div (2500 \times 97 \times 1 \times 0.011)$$
$$= 15 \text{ contracts}$$

Mathematically, with the current parameter estimates, our optimal position in Eurodollar futures can never be more than 15 contracts. In practice, the standard deviation and price will change from day to day, so unless you are reviewing these limits on a daily basis it is better to set them with some room for positions to increase should market conditions change. As a rule of thumb I add 50% to the maximum position obtained with the formula above, which translates to a position limit of 22.5, or 23 contracts.

Position limit for maximum leverage

Let's begin with the definition of the leverage ratio for some instrument i:

Leverage ratio = N_i × Notional exposure per contract$_i$ ÷ Capital

To limit the leverage ratio on any given instrument to some specific level, we set a position limit as follows:

$$N^{max\_leverage}$$

= Maximum leverage ratio × Capital ÷ Notional exposure per contract

= Maximum leverage ratio × Capital ÷ (Multiplier$_i$ × Price$_i$ × FX$_i$)

Consider again the Eurodollar futures which I used as an example a moment ago. Assuming we don't want a leverage ratio above two for any single instrument, the maximum position we can hold is:

$$N^{max\_leverage} = 2 \times 500000 \div (2500 \times 97 \times 1) = 4.1$$

This is much lower than what we obtained with the maximum forecast: 15 contracts. The consequence of this is that if the forecast for Eurodollar goes above $20 \times 4 \div 15 = 5.333$, then we will not increase our position any more. This should not be a surprise; the standard deviation of Eurodollar is very low, so the problem we have here is an instrument that is 'too safe to trade'. In this situation we should seriously consider reducing the instrument weight of Eurodollar, or stop trading it altogether.

Position limit as a proportion of open interest

When selecting instruments back in strategy three, I explained that I liked to see a certain minimum volume before trading a given instrument. But I did not set a minimum level for the available open interest in a given market. This could be problematic in an instrument that trades significant volume, but does not have sizeable open interest, due to a large community of scalpers or day traders.

Traders with large account sizes might consider imposing an additional rule, such as for example that they are no more than 1% of the available open interest in a given instrument for the expiry date that they have chosen to trade.

In our example it's very unlikely that the size of the Eurodollar market will be a constraint for a trader with a $500,000 account. Open interest in the June 2025 contract I am currently trading is around 160,000 contracts, which means that with the 1% rule I would be limited to a position of 1,600 contracts.

The very lucky traders who find this is lower than the position limit implied by their maximum forecast should seriously consider reducing their instrument weight.

Final position limit and implementation

The position limit for a given instrument should be set at the minimum of:

- The position limit at the maximum forecast.

- The position limit at maximum desired leverage.

- The position limit as a proportion of open interest.

For our simple Eurodollar example, these figures were 23, 4 and 1,600 respectively. I would use the lowest of these: four contacts.

There are a few ways you can use these limits. Firstly, as I have already mentioned, they make useful guard rails for fully automated trading systems. They can also be used in a more discretionary fashion by traders or risk managers, to alert them to positions of some concern.

Finally, and this is most relevant for larger institutional traders who are considering trading less liquid markets, they should be taken into account when setting instrument weights. If a particular instrument is regularly exceeding its position limit[294] in a backtest, then its instrument weight will need to be reduced.

Position limits and dynamic optimisation

Traders using strategy twenty-five, dynamic optimisation, will have to make a couple of changes to the methodology I've explained above.

Firstly, when calculating the **position limit at maximum forecast**, they should not use the actual instrument weights. This is because when given a set of say 100 instruments and a $500,000 retail sized account, the optimisation will typically select positions in around 10 to 20 instruments. If we used the actual instrument weights, averaging 1%, then the resulting position limits would be far too small.

However, it's important that you should still apply *some* position limits. In

---

294   If you are going to backtest the effect of setting position limits, then you should not use fixed limits, but recalculate them according to historic levels of price, risk, FX rates and so on.

particular, if you have a small set of instruments, it's likely that there will be times when most of your risk is concentrated in just one or two positions. To an extent this is unavoidable, as the nature of trend type strategies in particular is that there are often only a few markets with strong trends at any given time. But it does open you up to idiosyncratic risk if you happen to have all your eggs in the basket of an instrument which is hit with a sudden adverse price movement.

I would advise replacing the actual instrument weight in the position limit calculations with a nominal figure like 10% or 20%. The effect of that would be to limit the possible concentration of risk in any individual instrument to 10% or 20% of your average total risk budget.

Secondly, it's possible to implement the position limits as constraints within the dynamic optimisation itself. This will make the best use of your limited capital, whilst avoiding excessive leverage or too much risk concentration in a single position.

Setting trade limits

As well as position limits, I set limits on the number of trades I can do in a particular instrument. Unlike the other measures in this chapter, this is less about market risk and more about operational risk. Because I run my trading strategies on a fully automated basis, there is a remote chance that it may start over trading: buying and selling many more contracts than I had anticipated. This could be caused by some unusual combination of price movements, some bad data, a flaw in my strategy, or a bug in my code.

To prevent this, I use hard trade limits. For example, I might limit myself to trading four S&P 500 micro futures a day, or 20 a week. Once I have reached those levels then my system will no longer allow any further trades in that instrument, unless I manually override it.[295] Even if you are trading manually, it is still worth calculating these limits. They may not be hard limits as I use in my system, but going over them will give you a clue that something may be going wrong that is worth investigating.

It's straightforward to calculate the trade limits from position limits. First of all we consider what proportion of our maximum position we are likely to trade on a daily

---

[295] In theory it would be possible to incorporate trade limits into the dynamic optimisation used by strategy twenty-five, but personally I do not bother. If there are instruments I do not want to trade for other reasons, then I can apply a hard 'don't trade at all' constraint. Instead, I apply the trade limits in the trading code that runs after the dynamic optimisation has determined the trades it would like to make.

basis. To some extent this will be a property of our underlying strategy and the speed of its trading rule variations, but a rule of thumb will suffice. For strategies in Parts One to Three, it is unlikely that we will want to trade more than a third of our maximum position in a single day.[296]

As an example, in the previous section I worked out that the maximum position given some assumptions for Eurodollar futures would be four contracts. A third of this is just over one contract, which I would round up to two futures. Once I have traded two Eurodollar futures in a given day I would prevent my system from trading any more.

A useful exercise for large institutional traders is to calculate what the maximum trade per day is as a proportion of the typical daily volume. If this is too high then you may want to think about dropping the instrument, reducing your instrument weight, or removing trading rule variations that have high turnover.[297]

---

296   For fast trading strategies in Part Four a much higher figure should be used – around twice the maximum position could be traded daily.

297   You can work out how long it will take to liquidate your position in a given instrument, by dividing the position limit by the trade limit. For example, if your Eurodollar daily trade limit is four contracts, and the position limit is twelve contracts, then you will be able to close out your position within three days.

Glossary

Words **in bold** refer to other entries in the glossary.

Back-adjustment **Back-adjusted price**	Joining together the prices of futures contracts with different expiry dates to make a single price series. See page 19 and Appendix B.
Backtesting	Simulating the performance of a trading strategy using historical data to check its performance and other characteristics. See page 26.
Base currency	The currency your trading account is denominated in.
Buffering	A way to avoid doing small trades which cost money but don't generate value. See page 166.
Calendar spread	A **relative value** trade between two expiries of the same instrument. See strategy thirty. Can also be an order used to execute a **rolling** trade. See page 500.
Capital **Capital, trading**	The amount of money that is at risk when you are trading.
Carry	A type of **trading rule** which calculates the likely return if market conditions remain stable. See strategy ten, page 201.
Contract date **Contract expiry** **Contract month**	Different terms for futures contracts expiring on different dates.
Contract leverage ratio	The contract leverage ratio is the ratio of the notional exposure per contract to our trading capital. The smaller this number is, the more contracts we need to hold for a given amount of capital. See **leverage ratio, volatility ratio** and page 57.
Correlation **Correlation matrix**	A figure which measures the linear relationship between the return of two **instruments, sub-strategies** or trading strategies. A correlation of zero means there is no relationship, and a correlation of one means the two instruments or strategies always move exactly together. A correlation matrix includes all the correlations for a given set of assets. See Appendix B for details on correlation estimation.

Covariance matrix	The product of a vector of **standard deviations** and a **correlation matrix**. Used for risk estimation. See Appendix B for details on covariance estimation.
Directional trading	A style of trading where we bet on the outright direction of a particular instrument, in contrast to **relative value** trading. All strategies in Parts One to Four of this book are directional.
Drawdown **Drawdown, maximum** **Drawdown, average**	The *drawdown* is the cumulative loss incurred by a trading strategy or fund since the most recent high watermark (the highest cumulative gain achieved to date). The *maximum drawdown* is the largest drawdown suffered during some historical period, e.g. live trading history or backtest. The *average drawdown* is the mean value of D_t, where D_t is the current drawdown on any given day t (if at the high water mark, $D_t = 0$).
Excess return	The **total return** from a given asset, less any funding costs. As funding costs are built into futures prices, all futures returns are excess returns.
Exponentially weighted moving average (EWMA)	Given a series of returns $r_0 \dots r_t$ the EWMA(N) with span N can be defined as: $$\lambda = 2 \div (N + 1)$$ $$r^*(\lambda)_t = \lambda r_t + \lambda(1 - \lambda)r_{t-1} + \lambda(1 - \lambda)^2 r_{t-2} + \dots$$
Exponentially weighted moving average crossover (EWMAC)	Given two **exponentially weighted moving averages**, EWMA(X) and EWMA(Y), the EWMAC(X,Y) is equal to EWMA(X) – EWMA(Y). If X<Y then the EWMAC rule will be positive when uptrends have recently occurred, and negative if a downtrend has happened. The EWMAC **trading rule** is used to identify trends. See strategy five.
Forecast **Forecast, combined**	A forecast is a measure of how confident a **trading rule** is; an expectation of future risk adjusted prices. In this book forecasts are scaled to have an expected average absolute value of 10. A positive forecast implies a long position and a negative forecast is short. See page 154. A *combined* forecast is the weighted average of forecasts from different **trading rule variations**, weighted with **forecast weights**. See page 181.
Forecast diversification multiplier (FDM)	A multiplying factor used to compensate for the fact that **forecasts** from different **trading rule variations** are not perfectly correlated, and therefore the scaling of a **combined forecast** will be biased downwards. See page 193.
Forecast scalar	A scaling factor used to ensure that a given **trading rule variation** will produce **forecasts** with an expected average absolute value of 10. See page 157.
Forecast weights	The weights allocated to **trading rule variations** used in combining **forecasts** to produce a **combined forecast**. See page 181.

Front month	The **contract month** which currently has the earliest delivery. Also known as the first expiry or first month.
Gaussian distribution, Gaussian normal distribution	A type of statistical distribution characterised by a 'bell curve'.
Handcrafting	A heuristic hierarchical method for allocating **instrument weights** and **forecast weights**. See page 112.
Instrument	Any future that you can trade, for example S&P 500 micro futures, made up of a series of **contract dates**.
Instrument currency	The currency that the **multiplier** of a particular **instrument** is denominated in.
Instrument diversification multiplier (IDM)	A multiplying factor used to compensate for the fact that returns from different **sub-strategies** are not perfectly correlated, and therefore the standard deviation of their aggregated returns will be below the **target** risk. See page 104.
Instrument weights	The weights used to allocate a proportion of your capital to different trading **sub-strategies**, each trading a different instrument. See page 101.
Jumbo portfolio	The main set of instruments I use in this book to backtest trading strategies. See page 121 and Appendix C.
Kelly criterion Kelly, optimal	A formula which calculates your **target risk** based on your expected **Sharpe ratio**. See page 62.
Leverage ratio	The **leverage ratio** is equal to the absolute value of the **notional exposure** of your position divided by your **capital**. If you have multiple positions for different instruments, then it refers to the total absolute value of your notional exposures, divided by your total capital. See **contract leverage ratio**, **volatility ratio** and page 57.
Margin Margin, initial Margin, variation	The minimum cash down payment you have to make to your broker when making a **leveraged** trade. See page 551.
Mean reversion trading	A style of trading where you expect prices to return to some fair or equilibrium value. Opposite of **trend following**.
Minimum capital	The smallest possible amount of **capital** you need to trade a particular **instrument**. See page 70.
Momentum Momentum, cross-sectional	Sometimes used as a synonym for **trend following**, although I don't use it in this book to avoid confusion. **Cross-sectional momentum** involves buying assets which have gone up in price relative to others, and selling those which have gone down.

Multiplier	The value of a single price point for a given **instrument**. See page 13.
Notional exposure	The cash value of a **position**, such that if the futures price changes by 1% then you will make a profit or loss equal to 1% of the notional exposure. See page 14.
Open interest	Current outstanding number of futures contracts for a given **contract month** in a particular **instrument**.
Order book	An order book shows all the prices at which people are willing to buy (bid) and sell (offer) the relevant future, and the quantities in which they will trade. See page 15.
Over fitting	A trading strategy is over fitted if it has been tweaked to perform incredibly well when **backtested** with historical data. Sadly such strategies won't do so well when traded with real money in the future. See page 27.
Relative value	Style of trading where we bet on the relative price of one asset against each other. Opposite of **directional**. Can be either across instruments, or within instruments (calendar trading, including **calendar spreads**). Strategies in Part Five are relative value.
Rolling	The process of moving our position in a given **instrument** from one **contract month** to the next. See page 533.
Sharpe ratio	A calculation for measuring the risk adjusted performance of a trading strategy. For futures the annualised SR is equal to the annual mean of backtested returns, divided by the annual **standard deviation** of returns. See page 36.
Skew	The asymmetry in a return distribution. The returns from a positively skewed asset will contain more losing days than for those that are negatively skewed. But the losing days will be relatively small in magnitude. A negatively skewed asset will have fewer down days, but the losses on those days will be larger. A **Gaussian normal** distribution has zero skew. See page 37.
Speed limit	Recommended limit on trading speed given cost levels; equal to spending a third of expected pre-cost **Sharpe ratio** on costs. See page 95.
Spread cost	Part of the **trading cost** that arises because, at best, with a market order you will buy at the offer and sell at the bid. Equal to the difference between the mid price (the average of bid and offer), and the price you are filled at. For small traders, equal to half the difference between bid and offer. Larger traders will pay more than this. See page 16.

Standard deviation	A measure of risk. The standard deviation is the typical variation in performance around the average for a given time period, usually one year.
	I measure standard deviation in two ways for this book: $\sigma_\%$, which is the annualised standard deviation in percentage points, and σ_p, which is the daily standard deviation in price points.
	The daily risk in price points (σ_P) is just equal to the current price multiplied by the annual percentage risk, divided by 16:

$$\sigma_P = (Price \times \sigma_\%) \div 16$$

We can also calculate σ_p directly by taking the standard deviation of a series of differences in daily back-adjusted prices:

$$\sigma_P = \text{Standard deviation}(P_t - P_{t-1},\ P_{t-1} - P_{t-2},\ ...)$$

	See Appendix B.
Sub-strategy	A strategy which is trading a single instrument as part of a portfolio, with an allocation of the total available capital equal to the **instrument weight**. See page 100.
Target risk (τ)	The amount of risk you expect to see when trading. I calculate target risk using the annual **standard deviation** of returns. See page 58.
Tick **Tick size**	The smallest possible change in price for a given **instrument**. See page 15.
Tick value	The value of a single **tick** for a given **instrument**. See page 15.
Total return	All the returns earned for a given asset, not just those from the spot price changing, including any dividends, bond coupons, and less any storage or insurance costs. See **excess return**.
Trading cost	The cost paid for trading a given future, equal to the commission paid plus the **spread cost**.
Trading rule **Trading rule variation**	A rule that produces a **forecast**. Examples of trading rules used in Part One are **EWMAC** and **carry**. Trading rules often have parameters that govern their behaviour, allowing us to create multiple **trading rule variations** for a given trading rule.
Trend following	A style of trading which assumes that trends in prices will continue; can be implemented using trading rules like **EWMAC**.
Turnover	The number of times we turn over our average position in a year. See page 85.
Volatility ratio	The volatility ratio is the ratio of our **target risk** to the instrument risk – the current annualised percentage standard deviation of a particular instrument.
	See **leverage ratio**, **contract leverage ratio** and page 57.

Appendices

Appendix A: Resources

Further reading

Leveraged Trading: Robert Carver; 2019, Harriman House

> My third book. Essential reading for traders who wish to learn the basics of futures trading, but then you would expect me to say that.

Options, Futures, and Other Derivatives: John Hull; 2017, Pearson

> Fairly technical introduction to futures and other derivatives.

Fortune's Formula: The Untold Story of the Scientific Betting System That Beat the Casinos and Wall Street: William Poundstone; 2006, Hill and Wang

> Non-technical and enjoyable introduction to the Kelly criterion.

Following the Trend: Andreas F. Clenow; 2012, Wiley

> More detail specifically about trend following.

Expected Returns: An Investor's Guide to Harvesting Market Rewards: Antti Ilmanen; 2011, Wiley

> Great introduction to the concept of risk premia, plus a shopping list of premia to use in trading strategies.

Efficiently Inefficient: How Smart Money Invests and Market Prices Are Determined: Lasse H. Pedersen; 2015, Princeton University Press

> Goes into more detail about several of the strategies in this book, plus excellent sections on execution, backtesting, performance measurement and risk premium.

The Rise of Carry: The Dangerous Consequences of Volatility Suppression and the New Financial Order of Decaying Growth and Recurring Crisis: Tim Lee, Jamie Lee and Kevin Coldiron; 2019, McGraw Hill

> Very interesting book about carry, but more of a philosophical inquiry than a trading manual.

Algorithmic Trading: Winning Strategies and Their Rationale: Ernie Chan; 2013, Wiley

> Goes into some detail about certain key strategies: especially good on mean reversion.

STIR Futures: Trading Euribor and Eurodollar Futures, Stephen Aikin; 2012, Harriman House

> Very strong on relative value calendar trades in short-term interest rate futures (STIR).

Systematic Trading: Robert Carver; 2015, Harriman House

> My first book. Essential reading for traders who wish to develop their own trading systems, but then I am biased.

Useful websites

Links to external websites are accurate at the time of writing, but may break without warning. These links do not constitute recommendations or endorsements. Prices and charges may vary.

Brokers	www.interactivebrokers.com
	www.tradestation.com
	www.ninjatrader.com
	www.ampfutures.com
	www.home.saxo
Execution algos	www.quantitativebrokers.com
Financial data	algoseek.com
	barchart.com
	csidata.com
	eoddata.com
	iqfeed.net
	investing.com/commodities/futures-specifications
	kinetick.com
	data.nasdaq.com
	norgatedata.com
	pinnacledata.com
	portaracqg.com
	tickdata.com
My websites	www.systematicmoney.org/futures-strategies-21-resources
	Resources for this book; contains many useful resources including links to spreadsheets and python code.
	www.systematicmoney.org
	My main website.
	https://github.com/robcarver17/pysystemtrade
	My open source python futures backtesting and trading platform.
	qoppac.blogspot.com
	My blog, with many articles on trading systematically.

Appendix B: Calculations

Back-adjusting a futures price series

Creating an initial back-adjusted price series

We begin with a series of prices for different expiry dates. Let's keep things simple and just use three dated contracts (A, B and C), with a highly unrealistic example in which we only have a few days of prices for each contract. Here is the history of prices so far:

	A	B	C
2nd January 2022	100		
3rd January 2022	100.2		
6th January 2022	100.3		
7th January 2022	99.9	100.2	
8th January 2022		99.9	
9th January 2022		98.7	99.1
10th January 2022		99.0	99.5
13th January 2022			99.9
14th January 2022			100.1

Now to decide when we would have switched from one expiry to the next. For the switch from A to B we don't have any choice; there is only a single date when we have a price for both contracts (7th January). For the switch from B to C we have two options. Let's suppose we always pick the latest date (10th January). Of course this is different from the situation with many futures, where we have prices that overlap for several weeks or months, but in reality there are some futures where switching is only possible on a single day.

We now need to create a new column for the back-adjusted price. This is populated in reverse, starting with the last day with data and going backwards. We begin by copying across the prices for the final contract, C, until we get to the first expiry date (expiry dates are shown in bold):

	A	B	C	Back-adjusted price
2nd January 2022	100			
3rd January 2022	100.2			
6th January 2022	100.3			
7th January 2022	99.9	100.2		
8th January 2022		99.9		
9th January 2022		98.7	99.1	
10th January 2022		99.0	**99.5 ->**	**99.5**
13th January 2022			**99.9 ->**	**99.9**
14th January 2022			**100.1 ->**	**100.1**

We now take the difference in closing price between the current contract C and the previous contract B on the roll date: 99.5 – 99.0 = 0.5. This difference has to be added to all the B prices to make them consistent with C on the roll date:

	A	B	B adjusted	C	Back-adjusted price
2nd January 2022	100.0				
3rd January 2022	100.2				
6th January 2022	100.3				
7th January 2022	99.9	100.2	100.2 + 0.5 = **100.7**		
8th January 2022		99.9	99.9 + 0.5 = **100.4**		
9th January 2022		98.7	98.7 + 0.5 = **99.2**	99.1	
10th January 2022		99.0	99.0 + 0.5 = **99.5**	99.5	99.5
13th January 2022				99.9	99.9
14th January 2022				100.1	100.1

The B adjusted prices are then copied across to become the final adjusted prices for the relevant dates:

	A	B	B adjusted	C	Back-adjusted price
2nd January 2022	100.0				
3rd January 2022	100.2				
6th January 2022	100.3				
7th January 2022	99.9	100.2	**100.7->**		**100.7**
8th January 2022		99.9	**100.4->**		**100.4**
9th January 2022		98.7	**99.2->**	99.1	**99.2**
10th January 2022		99.0	99.5	99.5	99.5
13th January 2022				99.9	99.9
14th January 2022				100.1	100.1

We now create adjusted prices for A: on the expiry date of 7th January the difference between the back-adjusted price and the price of A is 100.7 – 99.9 = 0.8; this is added to the prices for A:

	A	A adjusted	B	B adjusted	Back-adjusted price
2nd January 2022	100.0	100 + 0.8 = **100.8**			
3rd January 2022	100.2	100.2 + 0.8 = **101.0**			
6th January 2022	100.3	100.3 + 0.8 = **101.1**			
7th January 2022	99.9	99.9 + 0.8 = **100.7**	100.2	100.7	100.7
8th January 2022			99.9	100.4	100.4
9th January 2022			98.7	99.2	99.2
10th January 2022			99.0	99.5	99.5
13th January 2022					99.9
14th January 2022					100.1

Finally, we copy across the adjusted prices for A to become the back-adjusted price:

	A	A adjusted	B	B adjusted	Back-adjusted price
2nd January 2022	100.0	**100.8 ->**			**100.8**
3rd January 2022	100.2	**101.0 ->**			**101.0**
6th January 2022	100.3	**101.1 ->**			**101.1**
7th January 2022	99.9	100.7	100.2	100.7	100.7
8th January 2022			99.9	100.4	100.4
9th January 2022			98.7	99.2	99.2
10th January 2022			99.0	99.5	99.5
13th January 2022					99.9
14th January 2022					100.1

We'd continue this process until we had adjusted the oldest contract in our data history.

Keeping the price series up to date

A useful property of back-adjustment is that the current back-adjusted price is equal to the price of the dated product we're currently trading. So ordinarily we can just add new rows as follows:

	C	Back-adjusted price
2nd January 2022		100.8
3rd January 2022		101.0
6th January 2022		101.1
7th January 2022		100.7
8th January 2022		100.4
9th January 2022	99.1	99.2
10th January 2022	99.5	99.5
13th January 2022	99.9	99.9
14th January 2022	100.1	100.1
15th January 2022	101.6	101.6

This would continue until we were ready to roll on to a new contract (D). On the roll date (16th January) we get a price for both contracts:

	C	D	Back-adjusted price
2nd January 2022			100.8
3rd January 2022			101.0
6th January 2022			101.1
7th January 2022			100.7
8th January 2022			100.4
9th January 2022	99.1		99.2
10th January 2022	99.5		99.5
13th January 2022	99.9		99.9
14th January 2022	100.1		100.1
15th January 2022	101.6		101.6
16th January 2022	101.0	101.5	101.0

We take the difference in price between the new contract D and the existing contract C on the expiry date: 101.5 − 101.0 = 0.5. We now add this difference **to the entire back-adjusted price series**:

	C	D	Old back-adjusted price	New back-adjusted price
2nd January 2022			100.8	100.8 + 0.5 = **101.3**
3rd January 2022			101.0	101 + 0.5 = **101.5**
6th January 2022			101.1	100.1 + 0.5 = **101.6**
7th January 2022			100.7	100.7 + 0.5 = **101.2**
8th January 2022			100.4	100.4 + 0.5 = **100.9**
9th January 2022	99.1		99.2	99.2 + 0.5 = **99.7**
10th January 2022	99.5		99.5	99.5 + 0.5 = **100.0**
13th January 2022	99.9		99.9	99.9 + 0.5 = **100.4**
14th January 2022	100.1		100.1	100.1 + 0.5 = **100.5**
15th January 2022	101.6		101.6	101.6 + 0.5 = **102.1**
16th January 2022	101.0	101.5	101.0	101 + 0.5 = **101.5**

We can now discard the original back-adjusted price series, and on subsequent days add additional prices for contract D to the new back-adjusted price series.

Standard deviation estimation

A few different standard deviation estimates are used throughout the book for several different purposes. The following list shows the various purposes for which an estimate is required, and explains which returns and calculation method should be used. Afterwards, I outline details of how to do each type of calculation.

Trading strategy performance analysis	**Returns:** Use daily percentage returns, where the percentage return is just the daily profit or loss of the strategy, divided by the trading capital held at the beginning of the day. In my backtests I normally use non-compounded returns, so the trading capital is fixed.
	Calculation: Use the simple standard deviation formula. Annualise the daily figure, multiplying by 16.
Strategy two position sizing $(\sigma_\%)$	**Returns:** Using daily back-adjusted prices, p_t, and the price of the currently held futures contract p^*_t: $$r_t = (p_t - p_{t-1}) \div p^*_{t-1}$$ The currently held contract will be the same as the back-adjusted price in live trading, but will represent the contract you historically held in a backtest.
	Calculation: Use the simple standard deviation formula over all the returns you have available in the backtest. Annualise the daily figure, multiplying by 16.
	Alternatively: Use the same estimate for position sizing used in other strategies, and take the last value.
All other directional strategies position sizing $(\sigma_\%)$	**Returns:** Using daily back-adjusted prices, p_t, and the price of the currently held futures contract p^*_t: $$r_t = (p_t - p_{t-1}) \div p^*_{t-1}$$ The currently held price will be the same as the back-adjusted price in live trading, but will represent the contract you historically held in a backtest.
	Calculation: Use the exponentially weighted standard deviation formula with a span of 32 days. Blend this with a slower estimate of standard deviation. Annualise the daily figure, multiplying by 16.

Risk adjusted costs per trade	Use: All other directional strategies position sizing ($\sigma_\%$).
Minimum capital	Use: All other directional strategies position sizing ($\sigma_\%$).
Risk adjusting forecasts, daily price standard deviation (σ_p)	**Returns:** Using daily back-adjusted prices, p_t: $$r_t = (p_t - p_{t-1})$$ **Calculation:** Use the exponentially weighted standard deviation formula with a span of 32 days. Blend this with a slower estimate of standard deviation. **Do not annualise.**
Historical cost adjustment (σ_p)	Use: Risk adjusting forecasts, daily price standard deviation (σ_p).
Relative value strategies (σ_p)	**Returns:** Using daily back-adjusted prices, p_t where these are synthetic prices constructed using weights and the back-adjusted prices of individual instruments: $$r_t = (p_t - p_{t-1})$$ **Calculation:** Use the exponentially weighted standard deviation formula with a span of 32 days. Blend this with a slower estimate of standard deviation. **Do not annualise.**

Negative prices

When calculating percentage returns we divide by the currently held contract price, since back-adjusted prices may be close to zero or negative. But it is still possible for current prices to become negative, as occurred in WTI Crude Oil futures in March 2020. In these circumstances I recommend instead estimating σ^p, which does not require dividing by the current price, and deriving $\sigma^\%$ by using some arbitrary positive price $P^\&$.

$$\sigma^\% = 16 \times \sigma^p \div P^\&$$

For $P^\&$ I would use the most recent 'normal' positive price, or perhaps the average price over the last couple of years. We usually multiply the standard deviation estimate by a price, for example when calculating the appropriate position size, so as long as you use the same value in both places the $P^\&$ term will cancel.

Simple standard deviation

To calculate the standard deviation of a series of returns $r_1 \ldots r_T$ we'd first find the mean r^*:

$$r^* = [1 \div T]r_t + [1 \div T]r_{t-1} + [1 \div T]r_{t-2} \ldots +[1 \div T]r_0$$

We can then calculate a standard deviation:

$$\sigma = \sqrt{\{[1 \div T](r_T - r^*)^2 + [1 \div T](r_{T-1} - r^*)^2}$$
$$+ [1 \div T](r_{T-2} - r^*)^2 + \ldots [1 \div T](r_1 - r^*)^2\}$$

This is a daily standard deviation. If we need to annualise it then, under certain assumptions which I discussed earlier in the book, this is done by multiplying by 16.

Exponentially weighted standard deviation

Given a series of daily returns $r_0 \ldots r_t$ the mean will be an *exponentially weighted moving average (EWMA)*:

$$r^*(\lambda)_t = \lambda r_t + \lambda(1 - \lambda)r_{t-1} + \lambda(1 - \lambda)^2 r_{t-2} + \ldots$$

And the corresponding exponentially weighted standard deviation will be equal to:

$$\sigma_{exp}(\alpha)_t = \sqrt{[\lambda(r_t - r^*_t)^2 + \lambda(1 - \lambda)(r_{t-1} - r^*_t)^2 + \lambda(1 - \lambda)^2(r_{t-2} - r^*_t)^2 + \ldots]}$$

It's more intuitive to define our EWMA in terms of their **span**. For a given span in days N, we can calculate the λ as:

$$\lambda = 2 \div (N + 1)$$

Blend of fast and slow estimates

Given some current estimate of σ_t the blended estimate I use is:

$$\sigma_{blend,t} = 0.3(\text{Ten year average of } \sigma_t) + 0.7\sigma_t$$

Correlation estimation

If you want to estimate your own IDM or FDM, or use a method other than handcrafting to calculate forecast or instrument weights, then you will need to estimate correlations.

I use all available data to estimate correlations for these purposes, since I am using trading strategies whose behaviour should remain relatively stable over time. When considering the correlation of instruments, I use weekly data to avoid issues with matching daily returns for markets that close at different times.

Instrument weights and IDM calculation (fixed)	Use weekly returns for the instrument sub-strategy, assuming that the given instrument has all the capital available, i.e. an instrument weight and IDM of 1. Use all the available data for the correlation estimate. Floor negative correlations at zero.
Instrument weights and IDM calculation (variable in back-test)	Use weekly returns for the instrument sub-strategy, assuming that the given instrument has all the capital available, i.e. an instrument weight and IDM of 1. Recalculate the correlation matrix every year, using all available historical data up to that point. Floor negative correlations at zero.
Forecast weights and forecast diversification multiplier (FDM)	Use forecast *values* for each trading rule variation (not the returns). Use all available historical data for the correlation estimate. Floor negative correlations at zero.
	Pooling: You can estimate a different correlation matrix for each instrument, but it's better to use pooled data for this purpose. Create a single correlation matrix estimate by 'stacking' the $T_j \times N$ matrix of forecast values on top of each other, where T_j is the number of observations for instrument i.

Covariance estimation

I use the covariance of instrument returns to estimate portfolio risk, which is required for strategy twenty-five and tactic four. Although these can be estimated directly from the data, because the predictability of correlations and standard deviations is different, it's better to calculate the two components directly and then find the covariance. The estimation window for predicting correlations that works best is an exponential weighting with a six-month span, whilst for standard deviations it's the 32-day span I've used already.

Dynamic optimisation (strategy twenty-five)	**Percentage returns:** Use daily back-adjusted prices, p_t, and the price of the currently held futures contract p^*_t: $$r_t = (p_t - p_{t-1}) \div p^*_{t-1}$$ The currently held price will be the same as the back-adjusted price in live trading, but will represent the contract you historically held in a backtest. **Standard deviation:** Use the annualised estimates of $\sigma_\%$ calculated earlier in Appendix B. **Correlation:** Convert daily percentage returns into weekly returns (it's okay to just add up the percentage returns over a week to do this, or you can estimate them directly from weekly closing prices). Use an exponentially weighted correlation estimate with a span of 25 weeks, or an equally weighted rolling window of 52 weeks. **Covariance:** Given a vector of standard deviations $\underline{\sigma}$ and a correlation matrix ρ, the covariance is: $$\Sigma = \sigma.\rho.\sigma^T$$ Where '.' is dot multiplication, and T is the transposition operator.
Risk management (tactic four): Portfolio risk estimate	Use the same method as for **dynamic optimisation**.
Risk management (tactic four): Portfolio risk jump estimate	Use the same method as for **dynamic optimisation**, but replace the standard deviation estimate with the 99% percentile estimate of standard deviation from historical data.

Backtest turnover calculation

Turnover is a useful diagnostic which I use for crude cost calculations, as well as allowing us to make decisions about whether a particular instrument can be used with a given trading rule variation.

Forecast turnover

For a given scaled backtested forecast f_t calculated daily for each business day, the annualised turnover is equal to:

$$256 \times \text{Mean}(\text{abs}(f_t - f_{t-1}) \div 10, \text{abs}(f_{t-1} - f_{t-2}) \div 10, ...)$$

Notice that we are using scaled forecasts here, and hence we divide by 10, which is the target average absolute value for scaled forecasts. I take an average of forecast turnover estimates across instruments.

Position turnover

For a given backtested position in contracts p_t calculated daily for each business day, the annualised turnover is equal to:

$$256 \times \text{Mean}(\text{abs}(p_t - p_{t-1}) \div p_{t-1}^*, \text{abs}(p_{t-1} - p_{t-2}) \div p_{t-2}^*, ...)$$

where p_t^* is the average position, e.g. the position we would have on that instrument with a forecast of +10.

Forecast diversification multiplier (FDM)

Given N trading rule variations with an $N \times N$ correlation matrix of forecast values ρ, and a vector of forecast weights w with length N and summing to 1, the diversification multiplier will be:

$$\text{FDM} = 1 \div \sqrt{(w.\rho.w^T)}$$

where '.' is dot multiplication and 'T' is the transposition operator. Any negative correlations should be floored at zero before the calculation is done, to avoid dangerously inflating the multiplier. I recommend capping the value of the FDM at 2. Note that the correlations are of forecast values, not the returns from trading an individual forecast.

When backtesting, I recommend estimating the correlation matrix on a rolling basis annually using all historical data available up to that point. You should also use an exponentially weighted moving average of your FDM, to prevent sharp changes in position every new year: something like a 30-day span will suffice.

If you have multiple instruments in your trading strategy, then you can calculate a common FDM for all instruments that share the same set of trading rules with the same forecast weights. To achieve this, I recommend pooling your data to create a single correlation matrix estimate. You can do this by 'stacking' the $T_j \times N$ matrix of forecast values on top of each other, where T_j is the number of observations for instrument i.

Instrument diversification multiplier (IDM)

Given N instruments with an $N \times N$ correlation matrix of instrument sub-strategy returns ρ, and a vector of instrument weights w with length N and summing to 1, the diversification multiplier will be:

$$\text{IDM} = 1 \div \sqrt{(w.\rho.w^{T})}$$

where '.' is dot multiplication and 'T' is the transposition operator. Any negative correlations should be floored at zero before the calculation is done, to avoid dangerously inflating the multiplier. I recommend capping the value of the IDM at 2.5 to avoid excessive leverage on highly diversified portfolios; however, if you do this you will undershoot your expected risk target.

When backtesting, I recommend estimating the correlation matrix on a rolling basis annually using all historical data available up to that point. The process for calculating this correlation matrix is discussed earlier in this appendix. You should also use an exponentially weighted moving average of your IDM, to prevent sharp changes in position every new year: something like a 30-day span will suffice.

Appendix C: The Jumbo portfolio

Tables 172 to 183 are a complete list of all 102 instruments in the Jumbo portfolio, broken down by each asset class. Each table contains:

- A descriptive name for the instrument.

- The market code used by my futures broker for the relevant instrument. Market codes may vary across brokers, and these codes may be different from the official exchange code.

- The exchange where I trade the instrument. There could be other exchanges it is available on.

- The futures multiplier that I use. There may be other instruments with different multipliers available.

- The first year when the instrument appears in my data set, *not* when the instrument began trading, which may be much earlier, or later (some micro or mini futures have had their data backfilled with prices from larger contracts).

I use the following abbreviations for exchanges:

CFE: CBOE futures exchange

CME: Chicago Mercantile Exchange

DTB: Deutsch Borse

ECBOT: Electronic Chicago Board of Trade

GLOBEX: CME Global exchange

MONEP: Marché des Options Négociables de Paris

NYMEX: New York Mercantile Exchange

SGX: Singapore exchange

SOFFEX: Swiss Options and Financial Futures Exchange

Bonds and interest rates

TABLE 172: US BOND AND INTEREST RATE FUTURES IN THE JUMBO PORTFOLIO

	Market code	Exchange	Currency	Multiplier	First year with data
2-year US	ZT	ECBOT	USD	2000	2000
3-year US	Z3N	ECBOT	USD	2000	2020
5-year US	ZF	ECBOT	USD	1000	1989
10-year US	ZN	ECBOT	USD	1000	1982
10-year Ultra US	TN	ECBOT	USD	1000	2016
20-year US	ZB	ECBOT	USD	1000	1978
30-year US	UB	ECBOT	USD	1000	2010
5-year US ERIS Swap	LIW	ECBOT	USD	1000	2020
10-year US Swap	N1U	ECBOT	USD	1000	2013
Eurodollar	GE	GLOBEX	USD	2500	1984

TABLE 173: OTHER BOND AND INTEREST RATE FUTURES IN THE JUMBO PORTFOLIO

	Market code	Exchange	Currency	Multiplier	First year with data
10-year French (OAT)	OAT	DTB	EUR	1000	2012
2-year German (Schatz)	GBS	DTB	EUR	1000	2007
5-year German (Bobl)	GBM	DTB	EUR	1000	2008
10-year German (Bund)	GBL	DTB	EUR	1000	2006
20-year German (Buxl)	GBX	DTB	EUR	1000	2015
3-year Italian (BTP)	BTS	DTB	EUR	1000	2011
10-year Italian (BTP)	BTP	DTB	EUR	1000	2010
10-year Japanese (JGB)	JGB	Osaka	JPY	1000000	2001
3-year Korea	3KTB	Korea	KRW	1000000	2014
10-year Korea	FLKTB	Korea	KRW	1000000	2014
10-year Spanish (Bono)	FBON	DTB	EUR	1000	2016

Equities

TABLE 174: US EQUITY INDEX FUTURES IN THE JUMBO PORTFOLIO

	Market code	Exchange	Currency	Multiplier	First year with data
Dow Jones industrial (micro)	MYM	ECBOT	USD	0.5	2002
Nasdaq (micro)	MNQ	GLOBEX	USD	2	1999
Russell 1000 Value	RSV	GLOBEX	USD	50	2015
Russell 2000 smallcap (micro)	M2K	GLOBEX	USD	5	2015
S&P 400 midcap (e-mini)	EMD	GLOBEX	USD	100	2002
S&P 500 (micro)	MES	GLOBEX	USD	5	1982

TABLE 175: EUROPEAN EQUITY INDEX FUTURES IN THE JUMBO PORTFOLIO

	Market code	Exchange	Currency	Multiplier	First year with data
Dutch AEX	EOE	Euronext	EUR	200	2009
French CAC 40	CAC40	MONEP	EUR	10	2009
German DAX 30	DAX	DTB	EUR	1	2000
Swiss SMI	SMI	SOFFEX	EUR	10	2014
EU DJ Small cap 200	DJ200S	DTB	EUR	50	2013
EU STOXX select dividend 30	DJSD	DTB	EUR	10	2009
EU STOXX 600	DJ600	DTB	EUR	50	2005
EUROSTOXX 50	ESTX50	DTB	EUR	10	2014

TABLE 176: EUROPEAN STOCK SECTOR FUTURES IN THE JUMBO PORTFOLIO

	Market code	Exchange	Currency	Multiplier	First year with data
EU Auto	SXAP	DTB	EUR	50	2015
EU Basic materials	SXPP	DTB	EUR	50	2018
EU Health	SXDP	DTB	EUR	50	2016
EU Insurance	SXIP	DTB	EUR	50	2020
EU Oil	SXEP	DTB	EUR	50	2018
EU Technology	SX8P	DTB	EUR	50	2018
EU Travel	SXTP	DTB	EUR	50	2014
EU Utilities	SX6P	DTB	EUR	50	2014

TABLE 177: ASIAN EQUITY INDEX FUTURES IN THE JUMBO PORTFOLIO

	Market code	Exchange	Currency	Multiplier	First year with data
MSCI Asia	M1MS	DTB	USD	100	2021
FTSE China A	XINA50	SGX	USD	1	2011
FTSE China H	XIN01	SGX	USD	2	2020
Indian NIFTY	NIFTY	SGX	USD	2	2002
Japan NIKKEI	N225M	Osaka	JPY	100	2011
Japan NIKKEI 400	JPNK400	Osaka	JPY	100	2015
Japan Mothers index	TSEMOTHR	Osaka	JPY	1000	2018
Japan TOPIX	MNTPX	Osaka	JPY	1000	2010
Korea KOSDAQ	KOSDQ150	Korea	KRW	10000	2020
Korea KOSPI	K200	Korea	KRW	250000	2014
MSCI Singapore	SSG	SGX	SGD	100	2001
FTSE Taiwan	TWN	SGX	USD	40	2020

Volatility

TABLE 178: VOLATILITY FUTURES IN THE JUMBO PORTFOLIO

	Market code	Exchange	Currency	Multiplier	First year with data
VIX	VIX	CFE	USD	1000	2006
VSTOXX	V2TX	DTB	EUR	100	2013

FX

TABLE 179: MAJOR FX FUTURES IN THE JUMBO PORTFOLIO

	Market code	Exchange	Currency	Multiplier	First year with data
AUD/USD	AUD	GLOBEX	USD	100000	1987
CAD/USD	CAD	GLOBEX	USD	100000	1972
CHF/USD	CHF	GLOBEX	USD	125000	1972
EUR/USD	EUR	GLOBEX	USD	125000	1999
GBP/USD	GBP	GLOBEX	USD	62500	1975
JPY/USD	JPY	GLOBEX	USD	12500000	1977
NOK/USD	NOK	GLOBEX	USD	2000000	2002
NZD/USD	NZD	GLOBEX	USD	100000	2003
SEK/USD	SEK	GLOBEX	USD	2000000	2002

TABLE 180: CROSS AND EM FX FUTURES IN THE JUMBO PORTFOLIO

	Market code	Exchange	Currency	Multiplier	First year with data
EUR/GBP	RP	GLOBEX	GBP	125000	1999
EUR/JPY	RY	GLOBEX	JPY	125000	1999
BRE/USD	BRE	GLOBEX	USD	100000	1995
USD/Offshore CNH	UC	SGX	CNH	100000	2013
INR/USD	SIR	GLOBEX	USD	5000000	2015
MXP/USD	MXP	GLOBEX	USD	500000	1995
RUR/USD	RUR	GLOBEX	USD	2500000	2003
USD/SGD	SND	SGX	SGD	100000	2020

Metals and crypto

TABLE 181: METAL AND CRYPTO FUTURES IN THE JUMBO PORTFOLIO

	Market code	Exchange	Currency	Multiplier	First year with data
Aluminium	ALI	NYMEX	USD	25	2019
Copper	HG	NYMEX	USD	25000	1995
Gold (micro)	MGC	NYMEX	USD	10	1975
Iron	SCI	SGX	USD	100	2014
Palladium	PA	NYMEX	USD	100	1977
Platinum	PL	NYMEX	USD	50	1970
Silver	SI	NYMEX	USD	1000	1970
Bitcoin (micro)	MBT	CME	USD	0.1	2017
Ethereum	ETHUSDRR	CME	USD	50	2012

Energies

TABLE 182: ENERGY FUTURES IN THE JUMBO PORTFOLIO

	Market code	Exchange	Currency	Multiplier	First year with data
Brent Crude last day	BZ	NYMEX	USD	1000	2020
WTI Crude (mini)	QM	NYMEX	USD	500	1988
Gas last day	HH	NYMEX	USD	10000	2006
Gasoline	RB	NYMEX	USD	42000	1985
Henry Hub Gas (mini)	QG	NYMEX	USD	2500	1990
Heating Oil	HO	NYMEX	USD	42000	1980

Agricultural

TABLE 183: AGRICULTURAL FUTURES IN THE JUMBO PORTFOLIO

	Market code	Exchange	Currency	Multiplier	First year with data
Bloomberg Commodity	AIGCI	ECBOT	USD	100	2006
Cheese	CSC	GLOBEX	USD	20000	2010
Corn	ZC	ECBOT	USD	5000	1972
Feeder Cattle	GF	GLOBEX	USD	50000	1977
Lean Hogs	HE	GLOBEX	USD	40000	1974
Live Cattle	LE	GLOBEX	USD	40000	1971
Oats	ZO	ECBOT	USD	5000	1970
Red Wheat	KE	ECBOT	USD	5000	1995
Rice	ZR	ECBOT	USD	2000	1988
Soybeans	ZS	ECBOT	USD	5000	1985
Soybean Meal	ZM	ECBOT	USD	100	1970
Soybean Oil	ZL	ECBOT	USD	60000	1970
Wheat	ZW	ECBOT	USD	5000	1973

Acknowledgements

This is my fourth book. My first three books were released at neat two year intervals, in October 2015, 2017 and 2019. Arguably then, this book is roughly 18 months overdue. Partly this is because I didn't start writing it until late 2021, but this has also been a rather lengthy and complicated project to complete. I would imagine it has not been an easy read, and it was certainly difficult to write.

But this book would have been impossible – rather than just difficult – without the inspiration, help and support of a large number of other people, only some of whom I will name here. As I said in the introduction, my professional trading experience began at Barclays Capital in the early 2000s. My boss, Richard Gladwin, took a chance on hiring me into the graduate scheme despite me not fitting the usual profile. He was also very understanding when I left less than two years later, having decided that the cut and thrust of a trading floor was not for me.

My subsequent futures trading with other people's money was done at Man AHL. I was initially hired there as an intern, despite not conforming to their usual graduate hire stereotype (yes, there is a theme here…), and subsequently spent seven very happy years there as a full-time employee. I could try and list everyone I worked with at AHL who has had something to do with directly or indirectly inspiring the material in this book, but that list would run into dozens of people and I would inevitably forget someone. If you think you would be on such a list, give yourself a pat on the back.

Since leaving AHL I've had the opportunity to further discuss the theory and practice of futures trading with a wide variety of people, just some of whom I will name here: Saeed Amen, Paul Bilokon, Adam Butler, Andreas Clenow, Kevin Coldiron, Arvind Damarla, Jonty Field, Yoav Git, Cam Harvey, Corey Hoffstein, Trevor Neil, Michael Newton, Matt Stevenson, Burak Yenigun, and Sandrine Ungari. In particular, I'd like to thank Doug Hohner, without whom I would not have been able to write the chapter on strategy twenty-six, dynamic optimization.

I am grateful to my followers on elitetrader.com and the collaborators on my open source python trading system, pysystemtrade. My dialogue with them has forced me to continuously explain and review my assumptions about the nuts and bolts of futures trading, which has been excellent practice for writing this book. In most cases I don't know your real names, but I think you will all know who you are. In a similar spirit, I'd also like to thank everyone who leaves insightful questions on my blog, whilst consigning into the innermost circle of hell the much larger number of spammers whose comments I have to regularly weed out.

For the last couple of years I've had a semi regular gig as a guest co-host on the Top Traders Unplugged Systematic Investor podcast. I would like to thank Niels Kaastrup-Larsen for providing me with opportunities to regularly plug this project, and also the listeners who write in with questions. Many of these questions are thought provoking, and have inspired some of the ideas that appear in these pages. It would also be remiss of me not to thank my co-hosts, in particular: Jerry Parker, Richard Brennan, and Moritz Seibert. We don't always agree on everything, but the rigour of having to regularly defend myself against such an illustrious crowd is one of the reasons why this book has been so carefully researched.

For my previous books I pulled together a group of experts to review early drafts; hunting down errors, omissions, confusion, and outright nonsense. This time the crack team of volunteers consisted of Thomas Smith, Helder Palaro, Tansu Demirbilek, and Riccardo Ronco. This job involves many hours of work, for which they get a few measly lines in the back of the book and a signed copy, whilst I get to have my name on the cover and all the royalties. Why anyone would want to volunteer for this I don't know, but hopefully none of them will realise what a poor trade this is. In particular, Riccardo deserves special credit for continuing to hunt down errors and mistakes long after he had completed his official duties.

I've had the same publisher since I began my writing career, which must mean I'm either too lazy to find a new one, or that they are extremely good at what they do. In reality both of these statements are true, but the second is especially so. I'm obliged to Stephen Eckett who originally signed me up, and Chris Parker who produces the covers, but fulsome thanks are also due to Myles, Tracy, Harriet, Lucy, Charlotte, Sally, and Suzanne. Especially Suzanne – she writes the royalty cheques!

A very special thank you goes to Craig Pearce who has been involved in commissioning and/or editing all of my previous books; and who performed both jobs on this occasion. Occasionally I pull one of my old books from the shelf to check something, and I inevitably end up sidetracked by the sheer quality of the product; marvelling at the flowing structure, the beautiful layout, and the wonderful prose. Without Craig the structure would be a mess, the presentation ugly, and the prose would be – at best – buried inside a page of impenetrable nonsense.

Last, and certainly not least, I would like to thank my family. Whilst writing these pages, I looked back at the acknowledgments section of my previous books. In those I've previously thanked my family for their love, support and understanding. Putting up with a fourth book means I should certainly add *patience* to that list!

Index

www.ingramcontent.com/pod-product-compliance
Ingram Content Group UK Ltd.
Pitfield, Milton Keynes, MK11 3LW, UK
UKHW050227140225
455028UK00002B/27